Community and identity

MANCHESTER
1824

Manchester University Press

Community and identity

The making of modern Gibraltar since 1704

STEPHEN CONSTANTINE

Manchester
University Press

Manchester and New York

distributed in the United States exclusively by Palgrave Macmillan

The right of Stephen Constantine to be identified as the author of this work has been asserted by him in accordance with the Copyright, Designs and Patents Act 1988.

Published by Manchester University Press
Oxford Road, Manchester M13 9NR, UK
and Room 400, 175 Fifth Avenue, New York, NY 10010, USA
www.manchesteruniversitypress.co.uk

Distributed in the United States exclusively by
Palgrave Macmillan, 175 Fifth Avenue, New York,
NY 10010, USA

Distributed in Canada exclusively by
UBC Press, University of British Columbia, 2029 West Mall,
Vancouver, BC, Canada V6T 1Z2

British Library Cataloguing-in-Publication Data
A catalogue record for this book is available from the British Library

Library of Congress Cataloging-in-Publication Data applied for

ISBN   978 0 7190 7635 0   *hardback*

ISBN   978 0 7190 8054 8   *paperback*

First published 2009

18 17 16 15 14 13 12 11 10 09   10 9 8 7 6 5 4 3 2 1

The publisher has no responsibility for the persistence or accuracy of URLs for external or any third-party internet websites referred to in this book, and does not guarantee that any content on such websites is, or will remain, accurate or appropriate.

Typeset in Adobe Garamond
by Servis Filmsetting Ltd, Stockport, Cheshire
Printed in Great Britain
by CPI Antony Rowe, Chippenham, Wiltshire

For June

Contents

List of tables

List of abbreviations

AACR	Association for the Advancement of Civil Rights
BL	British Library
CD&W	Colonial Development and Welfare Fund
DG	Deputy Governor
EEC	European Economic Community
GCL	Gibraltar Confederation of Labour
GGA	Gibraltar Government Archives
GL	Garrison Library
GRDA	Gibraltar Ratepayers' Defence Association
GSLP	Gibraltar Socialist Labour Party
HCPP	House of Commons Parliamentary Papers
IFS	Irish Free State
MP	Minute Paper
NS	New Style
ODNB	*Oxford Dictionary of National Biography*
OS	Old Style
TNA	The National Archives, Public Record Office, Kew

Gibraltar in 1952

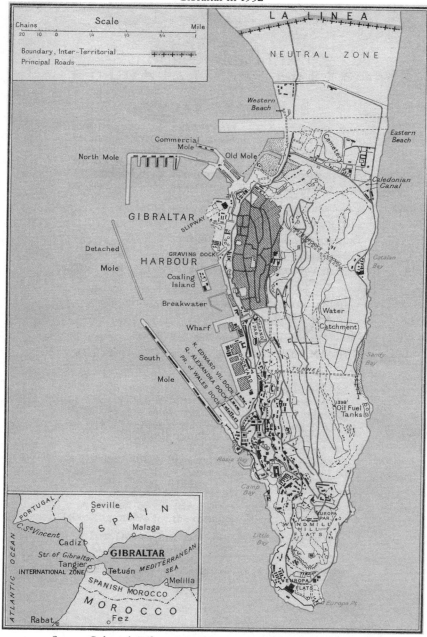

Source: Colonial Office, *Colonial Reports, Gibraltar 1950 and 1951*
(London: HMSO, 1952)

Foreword

Professor Martin Blinkhorn

I am grateful to Stephen Constantine and to Manchester University Press for giving me the opportunity to provide a brief Foreword to *Community and Identity: the Making of Modern Gibraltar since 1704*. To do so is an enormous pleasure, both personally and professionally.

Attentive readers of Stephen Constantine's Introduction will learn what our shared colleagues and friends, both in Britain and in Gibraltar, already know: that the research project of which this book is a major outcome was jointly directed by the two of us. If, as Stephen observes, I can claim credit for the original idea and its early development, it was Stephen who, as the project ended and the time came for us to write 'the Gibraltar book', found himself bearing unforeseen weight due to an untimely acceleration in my loss of sight. What had been conceived as a co-authored book soon became Stephen Constantine's book. Even if, while reading it (or, to be accurate, listening to it), I may have experienced, in much diluted form, the mixed feelings of a natural mother reunited with a child surrendered for adoption and raised by another, any pangs of loss have been comprehensively extinguished by this fine achievement.

It was back in February 1999 that, sitting on a balcony of Gibraltar's Rock Hotel, I began to sketch out the first ideas for a large-scale research project on the history of Gibraltar. Inspiring what eventually became a team-based research project funded by the Arts and Humanities Research Council was the conviction that the history of Gibraltar as a unique, developing and changing *community* had been largely neglected by academic scholars, in Britain and elsewhere. Rather as British governments, from the early eighteenth century down into the second half of the twentieth, had viewed Gibraltar first and foremost as a 'fortress', so historians from outside Gibraltar itself had discussed 'the Rock' chiefly in military, naval and overall strategic terms, paying little heed to the story or analysis of the place itself and its extraordinary population. To do something to rectify this imbalance, via the production of doctoral theses and publications, was the goal of our research group.

While academic historians may previously have given Gibraltar's domestic history less than its due, this does not mean that locally based, Gibraltarian scholars have been equally guilty. Far from it; our work was from the outset greatly nourished by that already carried out by Gibraltarian historians, much of it published by Gibraltar Books or the *Gibraltar Heritage Journal*. Our debt to them all is great. And, while not wishing to turn this Foreword into a full set of acknowledgements, I hope I may be forgiven for extending personal thanks and professional tributes to three people without whose help and labours our project could never even have begun, let alone have progressed and borne fruit; they are Lorna Swift, Librarian of the Gibraltar Garrison Library, and successive Gibraltar Government Archivists, Tommy Finlayson and Dennis Beiso.

Some time in the prehistory of our research project I made what was without question my soundest single move, by asking Stephen Constantine to join me. The reason, aside from personal regard and general intellectual respect, lay in what Stephen could bring to the prospective team as a distinguished historian of the British Empire, with particular expertise in the study of population movements, colonial policy, urban history and public administration. It is upon this experi-ence and expertise that this ground-breaking and consistently illuminating book is firmly founded. As a result, *Community and Identity: the Making of Modern Gibraltar since 1704* is, quite simply, not only the most seriously researched but also the most intellectually rigorous *longue durée* account yet written of Gibraltar's demography, economy, society, political development, and emerging sense of shared identity. From its first section, which offers a fascinating and (as far as the sources allow) complete picture of eighteenth-century Gibraltar, down to a final chapter of wide-ranging reflection on the transformation that has overtaken Gibraltar since 1969, this is an eye-opening and thought-provoking study of the never straightforward route by which a small garrison town became an overpopulated, multi-ethnic colony and this, in turn, a self-governing British Overseas Territory with a strong sense of, and serious claim to, nationhood. Stephen Constantine's conclusions may not all please all Gibraltarians (what set of conclusions could?) but they will need to be taken seriously.

Caton Green
Lancaster

Introduction

Gibraltar has, of course, a very long history. There is archaeological evidence of human settlement on the peninsula stretching back several thousand years. Moreover, in historic times the Rock of Gibraltar was joined by its isthmus politically as well as geographically to a much larger territory. This was the case, for example, following the first Moorish conquest of southern Spain beginning in 711. The connection was sustained after the region was conquered from the north for the Christian kings of Castile, Gibraltar being captured in 1309, lost in 1333, and retaken in 1462. The immediate hinterland, now conventionally called the Campo de Gibraltar, was and is part of the province of Cádiz, itself part of Andalusía. This intimate, frontierless relationship between a rock and a hard place was expressed in the boundaries of administrative units, with the town of Gibraltar under Spanish rule providing an ecclesiastical as well as political centre for an extensive province. Economically the port at the neck of the peninsula was used by traders taking goods out of the region by sea as well as for bringing stuff in, and of course the urban settlement at the end of the sandy isthmus was dependent on supplies from outside. Militarily, the fortress in the town was to guard that point of entry and exit, its walls extending down to the waterfront to protect the dock. Conceptually, it looked defensively south to the straits and Africa, not north to the Campo whose interests it was there to protect. Culturally too, the settlement on the peninsula was for centuries indistinguishable from its hinterland, whether Moorish and Muslim or Spanish and Christian.

The events of 1704 were not intended to disrupt this intimate relationship. In that year, defence as well as offence failed. The defenders failed to exclude another set of external invaders coming, like many of their predecessors, from the south by sea. However, the invaders also failed in their plan to progress beyond the peninsula across the isthmus and conquer mainland Spain. The stalemate and its consequences have determined the three principal themes which I have chosen to address in this book and which therefore have determined its structure.

As will be shown, one result of the Anglo-Dutch capture of only the peninsula of Gibraltar was the virtual depopulation of the site when almost all the former Spanish inhabitants left and trekked north. This was followed by its repopulation, slowly at first but in due course very substantially, by people from many places. Hence the origins of the new settlers and their descendants need to be explored. However, this is not merely a story of inward migration into a vacated space. The conceptual orientation of the town captured by the allies in 1704 was reconfigured following the failure of the invaders to move onwards into southern Spain. Over the next three hundred years, the defensive mindset of the new government of Gibraltar looked north, guarding against a recapture which was expected to be launched down the isthmus and from across the bay. Hence British authorities locally and in London continued to regard 'their' Gibraltar as principally a fortress. Accordingly, attempts were made, for security reasons, to regulate entry into the fortress-town and, certainly, residence within it or anywhere else on the peninsula. Moreover, the terms of the Treaty of Utrecht in 1713, which formally transferred sovereignty, albeit conditionally, to the British crown supposedly denied settlement there of Jews who in fact were among the earliest new arrivals. But they were not the only people who over the years avoided the restrictions which authorities attempted to enforce. Gibraltar's demographic history is indeed a splendid example of the capacity of ordinary folk to defy the rules. Thus, while in the chapters which follow I will trace the policing of entry and the regulations which the British colonial authorities put in place, it is of principal importance to analyse the origins of those who did secure settlement in Gibraltar.

This exercise is particularly necessary because the ethnicity of people in other places has been translated by them into a sense of national identity, and this has carried political implications. It is not giving too much of the story away to note here that the number of British (and Protestant) permanent immigrants settling in 'British' Gibraltar was smaller than the British authorities had initially intended, and that most of those who did take up residence did not even come from other parts of the British Empire. Mainly they came from the littorals and islands of the Mediterranean, and were predominantly Roman Catholics. Eventually they included many from Spain. It is quite conceivable that the cultural consequences of such immigration could have orientated Gibraltar towards Spain, with political consequences which for most (though not all) of the years with which this book is concerned would have been unwelcome to the British imperial government. And yet, for reasons which I will also address, the outcome became a population of multiple ethnic origins which insisted upon its 'Britishness' and seemingly remained committed to the British connection in a post-colonial age. However, at the same time I hope to explain how regulations over settlement which were eventually insisted upon by those speaking on behalf of the civilian community were also instrumental in creating what has in effect become a new ethnicity, of people tracing a common though plural ancestry and describing themselves as 'Gibraltarian'.

The second major theme of the book is to consider why settlers came and stayed. After all, the peninsula was remarkably devoid of natural resources. Geology had provided a bay but that was contested space, and the Rock produced rock. There was little that could be otherwise hunted, reared, harvested or extracted. Before 1704 this had not been a problem, because, as indicated already, the population of the town was supplied by its hinterland, which also provided the exports which passed out via the port and the market for goods brought in. The partition and the political frontier initially closed and thereafter always threatened and sometimes broke that economic relationship. Accordingly, several chapters explore aspects of the economic history of Gibraltar.

On the one hand, it seems, civilian settlers became 'camp followers', dependent substantially for their livelihood on the economic opportunities presented by the British garrison. Political and military calculations by the British government and the support or tolerance or indifference or ignorance of British taxpayers accounted in Gibraltar until quite recently for the presence and pay of several thousand troops, major capital investments in military facilities and eventually for economic aid in various forms. Civilian suppliers of goods and services happily responded to the market demand thereby pumped in. To that extent, political separation from Spain was offset, more than adequately, by a new connection with the British government.

However, on the other hand that link, coupled with the British government's initial policy of making Gibraltar a 'free port', opened to the enterprising some potentially profitable business relations with the British world and international commerce. In addition, in denial of the political partition of 1704, and in defiance of political authorities on both sides of the new frontier, business and labour also found a way of effecting money-making relationships with suppliers and especially with consumers over the border in Spain. Further, and with fluctuations that also need to be considered, the economy of Gibraltar attracted migrant workers who entered daily from across the usually porous frontier. The implications of this for the economy of La Línea, the near neighbour at the other end of the isthmus, and of the wider region of the Campo deserve an extended treatment, but in this book the consequences for Gibraltar of its apparent magnetism are the principal concern. This has to include the impact of the (on average) higher material living standards in Gibraltar, compared with those living 'over the border', upon the self-perception and constructed identity of the civilian population.

But the consequences for the well-being of a rising population squashed not just on to a small peninsula but crammed into a tiny but not tidy town also need to be considered. This connects with the third principal line of inquiry. Although until recently all governors of the British colony were military men and commanders-in-chief of the garrison, they found themselves acquiring responsibility for the urban conditions of the civilian population, especially with respect to public health, because of its bearing on the well-being of the garrison. Hence this study needs to consider the extension of civil administration beyond controls over immigration and residence into coping with such issues as sanitation. Moreover, this task widened to include responsibilities for housing, public utilities, policing, education, social welfare and economic infrastructures. These were matters with which municipal and national governments elsewhere were having to deal, including of course in Britain. There are issues here concerning rising public expectations common to urbanising and modernising societies. However, in the case of a British colony, there arose as elsewhere in the British Empire a tension between good government and self-government, between authoritative and paternalistic administration according to the standards, expectations and goals of those in imperial authority on the one hand and the perceptions, interests and indeed self-interests of the civilian population on the other – and these of course were not necessarily uniform in a society divided by income, status and social class.

The incorporation of members of the civilian moneyed class into administration – as 'collaborators' with the colonial government in the terminology of some imperial history – did not guarantee their agreement with government. More government was more expensive government, and British imperial practice normally required running expenses, except on the military, to be met from local revenues. Hence colonial administration raised issues concerning taxation, which inevitably, among a population becoming soaked in a British culture, generated objections based on the principle of no taxation without representation. Hence a considerable proportion of this book maps out the route whereby a civilian population descended from immigrants mainly of non-British stock managed to secure internal self-government and ultimately a system of parliamentary government and popular democracy modelled on British laws and institutions – while still remaining today a British Overseas Territory, and the only one in mainland Europe. Gibraltarians now constitute a nation, properly defined, and evidently many share an aspiration to become a state. Whether that could or should be their destiny is not on the agenda of this historical work. Indeed, Anglo-Spanish relations past and present, thoroughly treated by other scholars, are not my principal concern, but consideration of them is factored in where appropriate to explain the degree of internal change, and non-change, over three hundred years, and the current circumstances in which Gibraltarians find themselves politically, as well as demographically, economically and culturally.

All history is contemporary history, and all history is autobiography. These clichéd and rather pretentious assertions still contain some truths. The topics chosen for historical inquiry, the questions asked, the form in which findings are presented are conditioned, if not exactly determined, by circumstances in the present. Moreover, all history is autobiographical in the sense that it is hard for historians not to be affected in their choice of topics, in the forms of their research, in their interpretations of events and in the manner of their writing by their own past, their present circumstances and their ideas on the value of historical writing.

Certainly, in contemplating and then in the researching and writing of this book, I have been aware of the 'Gibraltar problem' in international politics today. Had I not been so initially, then I would have been rapidly put right during research trips to Gibraltar. The period of my active research in Gibraltar archives followed shortly after a locally conducted referendum in 2002 on whether Gibraltarians would accept joint British and Spanish sovereignty over their homeland; I was present during two highly political National Days in 2002 and 2005; my writing about cross-border relations, administrative developments and internal constitutional developments in the past was shadowed by contemporary debates on what became the Cordóba Agreement with Spain in 2006 and a new Gibraltar constitution operative from January 2007. With all this going on around me, it was impossible not to be sensitised by some aspects of the present in identifying and interpreting issues in the past for historical study. These recent events (at the time of writing) are also incorporated in the later pages of this book in a manner I hope appropriate to the themes I have judged important.

In order to avoid a potentially distorting concern with current circumstances, I have attempted to place the story I am telling within three wider contexts, sufficiently but discretely I hope, since I have no aspiration to turn a history of Gibraltar merely into a case study of some wider issues of historical change. That said, it was impossible as a British national (or am I English?) not to have been sensitised to current concerns with national identity in the United Kingdom, and elsewhere, and to the considerable academic literature they have generated, and I was aware of such matters when trying to understand the origins and substance of a Gibraltarian national identity. Many of us, including residents in Gibraltar, live in a world of identity politics, and it is proper to acknowledge that such debates have affected, but I hope not distorted, my treatment of the past.

Many people, myself included (born 1947), have also grown up in a decolonising and now (mainly) post-colonial world. Much of my academic career has been concerned professionally with British imperial history, especially with migration, settlement and development policy and with teaching wider thematic matters relating to imperialism. Recently I have benefited from participation in a number of international conferences dedicated to the examination of the 'British World' – most useful, I have found, when considering the transfer and adaptation in a variety of contexts overseas of British institutions and supposed British values. My approach to the study of British Gibraltar has therefore been influenced by the understanding of empire that I have been able to secure from such wider reading, writing and discussions. I also bring to my chosen topics what I think are useful insights into the economic, social and political history of Gibraltar derived from researching and teaching British domestic and urban history, for I do not think it is misleading to see similarities between urbanisation and its consequences in both locations. The smell of sanitation problems, for instance, is much the same everywhere.

One result of the context at the time of writing and of my particular interests is that the book has come out differently from most of those histories of Gibraltar which the reading public can also (and should also) pick up and read. The closest, and for similar reasons, is Edward Archer's *Gibraltar, Identity and Empire*, 2006, which is also prompted by current Gibraltarian aspirations and which also offers a thematic and analytical treatment, with an emphasis particularly on recent times. By way of contrast are two narratives which concentrate, like this one, on the entire period of British control, Allen Andrews's *Proud Fortress: the Fighting Story of Gibraltar*, 1959, and Ernle Bradford's *Gibraltar: the History of the Fortress*, 1971. As their titles suggest, they are principally, though not exclusively, concerned with the British garrison and the military history of the place. This reflects their times and the interests of the writers. Hence the considerable space given to such moments as the capture in 1704, the subsequent Spanish attempts at recapture in 1727 and especially in the 'Great Siege' of 1779–83, and Gibraltar's role in two world wars. This is also true of a more recent study, Maurice Harvey's *Gibraltar: a History*, 1996, brought up to date with the political history of the closed frontier of 1969–85. It is argued elsewhere in this book that the identity of Gibraltarians today is much bound up with memories of the past, and particularly with the British presence. All histories, as cultural products, have the potential to construct popular understandings of the past which can influence the present and the future. Memory matters. Along with much else these texts may have influenced to an indeterminate degree the self-perception of Gibraltarians as much-besieged British subjects, and therefore their current national identities.

Two books, one certainly based on a serious amount of primary research, show the hand of one of Gibraltar's more interesting governors, Sir William Jackson, in charge at a critical time from May 1978 to October 1982. They feed Gibraltarian aspirations to statehood. Jackson insisted to British governments that the interests of Gibraltarians should be protected: his correspondence with the Foreign Office, when it becomes available for inquisitive researchers, will provide interesting reading. In the meantime, one can sample his tone and his agenda in his ambitious and successful 1987 text, *The Rock of the Gibraltarians: a History of Gibraltar*. Courageously, this opens with a substantial treatment of the centuries prior to 1704. His thesis is made explicit in the title of the book and in his preface: 'I hope I have not been too pro-British or too anti-Spanish, just pro-Gibraltarian because I am unashamedly attached to the thesis that Gibraltar is the *Rock of the Gibraltarians*'. If the point has not been made sufficiently clear at the beginning, the epilogue is explicit with reference to Spanish demands: 'the people's right to their home must surely outweigh the territorial claim, based upon events that took place almost three hundred years ago'. Noticeably, however, much of the text follows the familiar structure, with its emphasis, even when addressing the period of British administration, on siege, capture and military and political defence. The title of Jackson's later book of 1995, written with Francis Cantos, the then managing editor of the *Gibraltar Chronicle*, is also revealingly titled, *From Fortress to Democracy*. This is the political biography of Sir Joshua Hassan, the man who did indeed play a remarkable role over some forty years in the advance of self-government inside Gibraltar. He was, in the resounding last words of the text, printed in capital letters, 'FATHER OF THE GIBRALTARIANS'. Among the merits of this book is that it investigates the recent politics of Gibraltar at length and provides, through Hassan's political life, an insight into local politics and administration from the perspective of a Gibraltarian.

Far less likely then or since to win the approval of Gibraltarians (or Jackson) is *Gibraltar the Keystone*, 1967, written by John Stewart, an Ulsterman who had been from 1952 to 1961 the chief engineer and deputy commissioner of works in Gibraltar's colonial administration. His book, part history, part reminiscences, contains a number of amused but critical observations on Gibraltarian civilian behaviour. The author concluded by proposing that Gibraltar's future lay within Spain, where, he opined, it might do some good in promoting democracy in what was still then Franco's Spain. As such, but with a very different style and from a different opening perspective, his conclusions resemble those of George Hills. Hills's book, published in 1974, is a scholarly study based on many archival sources of the long period from prehistory to his present of the place he accurately described in his title as *Rock of Contention: a History of Gibraltar*. From time to time and especially in the last part of the book, Hills, of Anglo-Spanish parentage and a biographer of Franco, indicated that his sympathies lay with Spain. This political concern plus the then restricted availability of primary sources probably explain the limited treatment in his book of the internal economic and social history of Gibraltar.

It will be deduced that all the books reviewed so far were principally written by outsiders. It is therefore important to note that perspectives on the past, and therefore contributions to the formation of a Gibraltarian identity in the present, have also been offered by some of the native born. Some of these have been brief chronicles, like Dorothy Ellicott's *Our Gibraltar*, 1975, though in addition there are more useful, archive-based monographs and articles in the *Gibraltar Heritage Journal* (volume one published in 1993). Many of these are used, with gratitude, in this book. However, two particular works deserve further reference because of their documentary strengths and the way in which they too seem to capture the moment of their creation. They have probably had a formative effect upon the making of a modern Gibraltarian identity. Tommy Finlayson's *The Fortress Came First*, 1990, provides a detailed account based on archival research of the evacuation of most of the civilian population of Gibraltar during the Second World

War. The principal argument of the book is that, after their bruising encounter with British bureaucracy and the experiences of living in the UK, Gibraltarians were determined that the fortress should no longer 'come first'. Hence a post-war determination to secure 'a greater say in the running of their own affairs'. The book is in itself an expression of an independent Gibraltarian identity and no doubt instrumental in encouraging such projections. This is also probably true of Joseph Garcia's *Gibraltar: the Making of a People*, 1994 (second edition 2002). This began life as a University of Hull doctoral thesis and, when published, it won 'The 1994 Heritage Trust Award for the Contribution to Gibraltar's Historic and Literary Heritage'. The book, opening like Finlayson's with the wartime evacuation, tells how the Gibraltarian people 'made themselves' by insisting on their rights to internal self-government and independence from Spain. Still in 1960 'happy colonials' (the author's words), Gibraltarians came to 'see themselves increasingly on the threshold of nationhood'. Garcia, currently leader of the Gibraltar Liberal Party, leaves readers in no doubt that he believes this is a legitimate aspiration. Both these books, strong in archival documentation, reflect the life and times of their authors, like the others mentioned – and like this one.

All the works mentioned, and many others of similar value cited in references and bibliography, have provided me with information and ideas, and I am pleased here to acknowledge their importance in the writing of this book. However, it will be seen that much in all chapters is derived from primary sources, very few of which on the matters I have chosen to address have been used before. There is a daunting amount of untapped material available, and hence my concentration on sources in the Gibraltar Government Archives, the Gibraltar Garrison Library and the National Archives (Public Record Office) at Kew. The first two contain far more than just official documents. Beyond these collections, much use has also been made of British parliamentary papers, some material in the British Library in London, and a fair amount of recently digitised texts which can be found via the internet. There is much more out there, for example, in the UK, among the private papers especially of British personnel who served in Gibraltar, though sampling suggests they are mainly informative on service rather than civilian life. Some collections in Gibraltar remain in private hands, and it is hoped that in due course they will be safely archived and accessible. There is much yet to be explored, including of course Spanish sources. Most in Madrid deal with the higher politics of Gibraltar's history, but a proper investigation of potentially more pertinent local Spanish sources across the frontier was prevented by limitations of time and my ability.

Considerable debts in the preparation of this book are owed to Lorna Swift, who has made the Garrison Library such a remarkably congenial as well as rich treasure house in which to work. All who carry out research in the Gibraltar Government Archives and all who ever read books derived from that research are immensely indebted to Tommy Finlayson and Dennis Beiso, the past and present archivists, for having in the first place rescued and sorted an enormous amount of irreplaceable documentation and for then having made it so accessible to scholars. They deserve to be honoured with properly supportive public record legislation and appropriate funding. It is a quite different experience, though equally enjoyable, to carry out research in the British Library, and especially in the National Archives, where the production of documents ordered by readers in such a miraculously short time deserves applause from all who use the place. It is not merely duty which here insists that acknowledgements for help received should also be made to several Gibraltarians who gave generously of their time and their knowledge, among whom are numbered Joe Ballantine, Sergio Ballantine, Sam Benady, Tito Benady, Clive Beltran, Marilou Guerrero, Bernard Linares, Charlie Rosado and Pepe Rosado.

The passive voice which has crept into the preceding paragraph indicates that the debts acquired and the research compressed into this volume are not only mine. This book is one outcome of a project generously funded by the Arts and Humanities Research Council (AHRC, formerly Board), here formally acknowledged. I was fortunate to be one of the team engaged in the project, and I know my colleagues share my gratitude for the support received, without which archival research on this scale would be difficult to begin and much more difficult to complete. I am also personally indebted to the AHRC for in addition granting me a Research Leave award during which period much of the writing was completed. As for the rest, I am grateful to Lancaster University for matching months of sabbatical leave, and for a great deal more. Lancaster and its History Department – staff and students – have provided me for many years with congenial company, intellectual stimulation and generous support, and this I am here delighted to acknowledge publicly. Publication of this book has also been made possible by a grant from the Scouloudi Foundation in association with the Institute of Historical Research, University of London.

There remains in this introduction just the happy opportunity of expressing my gratitude to the colleagues who worked with me on this project. Historical research has traditionally been an individual enterprise. For me it has been a novel experience, richly rewarding, to operate as part of a team. The original idea was floated by Professor Martin Blinkhorn. The project was formulated as a conjunction between his Hispanic and my British Empire interests, and it would not have been funded and driven forward without his inspiration and hard work. While the usual admissions are made, that errors of fact and faults of interpretation are mine, it is difficult now to be sure quite whose are the original ideas developed in this book and who first located particular items of inform-ation. This is also true of the contributions made by Dr Chris Grocott and Dr Gareth Stockey, the two AHRC-funded doctoral students who were attached to the project. Their earlier Lancaster MA dissertations awakened my own interest in and extended my knowledge of Gibraltar's history, and the influence of their PhD theses on this book is evident to me, and I hope to them. The project and this book also owe much to two research associates, in the initial stages to Dr Bella D'Abrera and subsequently and ever since to Dr Jennifer Ballantine Perera, herself a Gibraltarian. Jennifer's own writings on Gibraltar are in themselves indicative of her scholarly credentials and the contribution she too is making to an understanding of Gibraltar's past. Like my other colleagues, she has been hard-working in the location of historical material and generous in sharing it. Truly, this book is the product of a team effort. I cannot, however, conclude without proper acknowledgement of the contribution made by an unofficial member of the research team, my wife June. Voluntarily she 'signed up'. My gratitude for this, and much else, is indicated in the dedication.

1

The demographic roots of Gibraltarian identity, 1704–1819

The majority of those currently living in Gibraltar, and many of the Gibraltar-born who live outside, regard themselves as Gibraltarians, with a culture and identity sufficiently distinctive in their eyes to qualify Gibraltar as a nation. This is today repeatedly asserted, and it is a main aim of this book to explore and explain the origins of this self-perception. Undoubtedly its roots and nature are plural, but among its most important origins and character lies the ethnic make-up of the population. It is a convention among Gibraltarians and many outside commentators to stress the multiple origins of the population, and to indicate that one distinguishing characteristic is therefore its mix of ethnicities. Gibraltarians, it is said, are or were by origins, among others, British, Spanish, Genoese, Minorcan, Maltese, Portuguese, Jewish and more recently Indian and Moroccan, and they are distinguished either by the blend consequent on inter-marriage or at least by mutual respect and toleration.

It is not the intention of the demographic chapters of this book to dispute this outcome. Rather, they seek to question the assumption implicit in some explanations that this result has just been the happy result of the propinquity in a confined space of a population of immigrants over the past three centuries. The argument will be advanced that much which explains the demographic roots of Gibraltarian identity has been a consequence, until lately largely unintended, of managerial practices by governments.

The analysis offered is divided into three chronological chapters, 1704–1819, 1815–1890s, and from the 1890s to the present.[1] It will be argued, perhaps

---

1 For previous analyses of long-term demographic developments and their conse-quences see H.W. Howes, *The Gibraltarian: the Origin and Development of the Population of Gibraltar from 1704* (Gibraltar: Medsun, 3rd edn 1991); T. Finlayson, 'The Gibraltarian since 1704', *Gibraltar Heritage Journal*, 9 (2002), 23–41; and M. Blinkhorn, 'A question of identity: how the people of Gibraltar became Gibraltarians', in D. Killingray and D. Taylor (eds), *The United Kingdom Overseas Territories, Past, Present and Future* (London: Institute of Commonwealth Studies, 2005).

unexpectedly, that the most important phase for the emergence of the distinctive contribution of demography to Gibraltarian identity was the first century or so of British political control. It was then that the transfer of territorial sovereignty to Britain was secured and, just as important, confirmed, and in the same period substantial numbers of people from several places of origin sought to enter and settle. As a consequence, the first fumbling attempts were made by government to control entry into Gibraltar and to determine and manage rights of permanent and temporary residence. The discriminatory practices then figured out were to be reviewed and revised, very importantly, in subsequent stages, but it was during this first phase of British political control that actions were taken to address the issues which were to determine all subsequent amendments. In sum, it was in this period that the basic demographic prompts for a Gibraltar identity were largely laid down – a population of multiple origins coping with government policies which distinguished between ethnicities and yet treated more or less all civilians as subordinates under military and colonial surveillance.

War and the partition of Gibraltar, 1704–5

The first prompt to a distinctive Gibraltar identity was the failure – not success – of the military expedition of 1704. It needs to be remembered that the European war which broke out in 1702 was a war to determine the succession to the Spanish throne following the death without direct heir of King Charles II. The Bourbon domination of Western Europe and of the Mediterranean seemed to other European nations the likely outcome if Louis XIV of France secured the succession for his grandson, Philip, Duke of Anjou. Hence the traditional enemies of the Bourbons formed an alliance in support of the alternative claimant, the Habsburg Archduke Charles. In August 1704 and as part of a strategy to rouse Spanish backing for the Habsburg succession, an allied army, mainly Dutch and English troops led by Prince George of Hesse-Darmstadt as the Archduke's representative, in conjunction with an Anglo-Dutch fleet under the command of Admiral Sir George Rooke, laid siege to the Spanish fortress on the north-west corner of the Spanish peninsula of Gibraltar. Once the fort and harbour were secured in the name of 'King Charles III' of Spain, the intention was to leave Gibraltar behind and move inland from that base into Andalusía, obtain Spanish popular backing and place Charles on the Spanish throne.[2]

---

2 D. Francis, *The First Peninsular War 1702–1713* (London: Benn, 1975); G. Hills, *Rock of Contention: a History of Gibraltar* (London: Hale, 1974), pp. 164–78. Hills's emphasis on English support for the Habsburg cause is endorsed by W.G.F. Jackson, *The Rock of the Gibraltarians* (Gibraltar: Gibraltar Books, 4th edn 2001), pp. 93–4, 98–9, and M. Harvey, *Gibraltar, a History* (Staplehurst: Spellmount, 1996), pp. 65, 68, 75. The landing took place on 1 Aug 1704 New Style [henceforth NS] and the

However, many Spaniards were alienated from the Habsburgs and sided with the Bourbons, not least because their Catholic sentiments were offended by the strong Protestant element in the allied forces and by news from Gibraltar (and earlier from Cádiz) of their disorderly behaviour and degradation of Catholic shrines.[3] Moreover, reinforced Bourbon forces were robust enough to counter-attack and threaten allied control of Gibraltar. While not strong enough to recapture the fortress in the winter and spring of 1704–5, they were sufficiently powerful to confine allied forces to the peninsula. In these circumstances, making the best of a bad job, the British (no longer just the English after the political union with Scotland took effect on 1 May 1707) revived an old ambition and began to reconceive of Gibraltar not as the launch pad for the allied 'liberation' of Spain but as a more particular British base for controlling the western end of the Mediterranean. Whereas the first governors of the fortress were Habsburg appointments chosen by Hesse, those from 1707 were selected by the British to serve their interests. Moreover, the allies became more ambivalent about the Habsburg cause in Spain when, in April 1711, the Habsburg Emperor Joseph died and his brother the Archduke Charles inherited his vast central European empire as Charles VI.[4]

The transfer of management to Great Britain was then confirmed at the peace negotiations in 1713 when the British insisted that sovereignty over the Gibraltar peninsula must pass from Spain to Britain.[5] This was not a loss which the Bourbon kings of Spain, nor seemingly many Spanish people, were then or later willing to tolerate. Although the counter-attacks in 1704–5 had failed, the siege attempted in 1727 confirmed Spanish indignation at the loss. It is true that British ministers on several subsequent occasions seriously contemplated withdrawing from Gibraltar in return for territorial compensation elsewhere, but this, always difficult enough in terms of domestic and international politics, became even less likely when British political sentiment more generally became attached to retaining 'British' Gibraltar. By the end of the century, the boost to British national pride generated by General Eliott's impressively successful defence of Gibraltar in the 'Great Siege' of 1779–83, in the otherwise dismal War of American Independence, made it even less likely that any British government could abandon the 'Rock'. Later, British support for Spanish resistance

articles of surrender were signed on 5 Aug NS, that is 21 and 25 July 1704 Old Style [henceforth OS]. Whereas most of continental Europe had adopted the Gregorian calendar, the English until after 2 Sept 1752 stuck with the Julian calendar, which both was 11 days behind and began the new year on 25 March.

3 C. Caruana, *The Rock under a Cloud* (Cambridge: Silent Books, 1989), p. 3.
4 Hills, *Rock*, pp. 201–13; Jackson, *Rock*, pp. 89, 113.
5 Exceptionally rare copies of the original printed texts of the 1713 Treaty of Utrecht, in English and in Spanish, are kept in the Gibraltar Garrison Library [henceforth GL].

to Napoleonic France from 1808 was real enough and helped to secure Spanish independence, but at the Congress of Vienna in 1815 the triumphant British were never likely to hand back to Spain a fortress and naval base which during twenty-odd years of warfare had proved strategically useful. As a result, in the post-war years the British government confirmed its control over little more than two square miles of territory connected by a sandy isthmus to mainland Spain.[6]

The peninsula and the Campo de Gibraltar had of course been fought over several times in previous centuries. Conventionally, the attack in 1704 is described as the eleventh siege. But the unprecedented consequence in 1704 was the partition of Gibraltar. At no other time had the peninsula of Gibraltar been separated from its extensive hinterland. Gibraltar the fort and town, limited in territory, small in population and lacking resources, had in the past been serviced economically by its intimate connection with a much more extensive province, an agricultural area replete with livestock and vineyards, and by the same source it had been supplied demographically.[7] Population movement into and out of the town, like the sale of goods and services, had been affected only by market conditions; and the cultural identity of civilians resident at either end of the isthmus had been indistinguishable. But the allied occupation in 1704 and the transfer of sovereignty over the peninsula to Great Britain introduced a political frontier. It severed conventional ties, complicated exchanges, and generated for the new British military owners of the amputated peninsula immense managerial problems. However, new ownership also presented opportunities for mobile or ambitious or displaced civilians, and their arrival was a prerequisite – over the long term – for the formation of a distinctive Gibraltarian identity.

Opportunities for immigrants

Military garrisons, wherever located, normally need and usually attract a civilian population, to provide supplies, labour and other 'personal' services. This

---

6 Hills, *Rock*, pp. 237–58, 278–83, 297, 301–2, 346–57; Jackson, *Rock*, pp. 115–22, 135, 141, 145, 177; G.J. Gilbard, *The Gibraltar Directory* (Gibraltar: Garrison Library, 1877), p. 2, describes Gibraltar at that time as 'about three miles in length, greatest breadth three-quarters of a mile, and circumference about seven miles'. Because of recent land reclamation it is now larger, but still only about 2¼ square miles.

7 Hills, *Rock*, pp. 25, 48, 53, 97, 99, 114; Caruana, *Cloud*, p. 8; I. Lopez de Ayala, *The History of Gibraltar*, [1782], translated and continued by J. Bell (London: Pickering, 1845), pp. 2–3, 25–8, 94–5, 101–4, 132, Appendix I; A.P. Paredes (ed.), *Documentos del Archivo Municipal de San Roque (1502–1704)* (Algeciras: Ilustre Ayuntamiento de San Roque, Delegación de Archivos, 2006).

had been true of Gibraltar under Moor and Spaniard. However, as noted, a consequence of the allied occupation of the peninsula in 1704 was to break the established connections with the people and resources of the mainland. Compounding this difficulty, the allied occupation in 1704 prompted the exodus from Gibraltar of virtually all the resident civilian population. True, such departures had happened on previous occasions in Gibraltar's history when new regimes took over after successful sieges, as in 1309 and 1333.[8] But this time the civilian population's concerns for their safety under British control were compounded by not unreasonable fears of mistreatment by Protestant troops. Most Catholics, perhaps 1,500 families, maybe 5,000–6,000 people, transported themselves and their movables across the new frontier to the Campo de Gibraltar, and especially to San Roque.[9] A British officer listed the names of those few Spanish who remained and were still resident in 1712. There were twenty-five family groups and sixteen individuals, including a couple of friars and two Catholic priests, possibly as few as 70 people, or 120 at most, such as Francisco de Tapia and Mariana de Mendoza and the families of Gonzalo Romero and Diego Lorenzo, plus Father Juan Romero de Figueroa, born in Gibraltar in 1646, who recorded the events of the siege and of the counter-attack in the church registers.[10]

British Gibraltar needed repopulating. In the eighteenth century, the peace-time military garrison fluctuated in numbers from a minimum of just over 1,100 to a maximum of around 5,000, stabilising at about 3,000 in the early

8 Hills, *Rock*, pp. 48, 60.
9 J.I. de Vicente Lara, 'Gibraltar bajo las Casa de Austria (1502–1704) según las reliquias documentales', in Paredes (ed.), *Documentos del Archivo Municipal de San Roque*. Caruana, *Cloud*, p. 6, suggests a total population before the siege of about 6,000, whereas Hills, *Rock*, pp. 176–7, estimates a civilian population of 4,000–5,000. On the behaviour of troops and the exodus see Ayala, *Gibraltar*, pp. 142–3, 156, and GL, *Antecedentes y Notas Puestas en los Libros de Bautismo y Matrimonios de Gibraltar el año 1707 . . . Don Juan Romero de Figueroa*.
10 National Archives [henceforth TNA], CO91/1, and British Library [henceforth BL], Add Mss 10034, 'Some Remarks Concerning Gibraltar, humbly offered by Colonel Joseph Bennett', 22 Nov 1712, and 'Names of Old Inhabitants who remained in Towne on the Capitulation made by the Prince of Hesse'. There are minor variations in the spelling of the names between the two versions, and between transcriptions, such as a copy of the BL text in GL, www.gibconnect.com/~loonylenny/Oldinhabitants/oldinhabitants.htm, T. Benady, 'The depositions of the Spanish inhabitants of Gibraltar to the inspectors of the army in 1712', *Gibraltar Heritage Journal*, 6 (1999), 101–2, and Caruana, *Cloud*, pp. 8–9. See also D. Ellicott, *Our Gibraltar* (Gibraltar: Gibraltar Museum Committee, 1975), p. 19. Those who remained were almost certainly all Spanish, though Howes, *The Gibraltarian*, p. 1, suggests a few may have been Genoese. Others between August 1704 and Bennett's survey in 1712 may have left or died.

nineteenth century (plus wives and children), but boosted according to the needs of war.[11] This may not appear a large force, but it was then among the most substantial of Britain's overseas military establishments. While soldiers were their own labour force, civilian labourers and skilled craftsmen were also required, and officers with families certainly needed servants. Recreational needs generated other demands – the thirst of soldiers for liquor and other comforts being notorious compensations for military life in barracks. Supplies of food and indeed of water were also needed and, since insufficient could be squeezed out of the peninsula's rocky terrain, civilian traders had to be persuaded to ship in stuff or somehow to bring it in overland. There was also the opportunity for settlers to occupy vacated property which had fallen to the crown on annexation and was now available for lease and perhaps for purchase. Wealthy residents attracted more immigrants as servants, labourers and other employees. The military administration also benefited from civilians who might provide revenue, for example from licences, leases and ground rents, to offset the costs of rule. Some governors, especially in the early decades, had an additional interest in allowing almost anyone to take up residence who would buy leases and pay fees, legitimate or otherwise, from which those in authority enhanced their rewards of office.

Accordingly, inducements were offered to persuade merchants and workers to sell their goods and services in Gibraltar and even to take up residence in the town. This had been done before in Gibraltar's history, for example in 1310 when the Spanish government sought to populate the place by providing liberty for convicted criminals and other ne'er-do-wells. The allies opted instead for another precedent, also in the Spanish charter of 1310 and confirmed in that of 1469. In July 1705 the Prince of Hesse-Darmstadt, on behalf of 'King Charles III', had declared Gibraltar to be a 'free port', and this status was confirmed by Queen Anne's government in a proclamation published in Gibraltar in April 1706.[12] Because thereafter most goods could be shipped in and out of Gibraltar

11 Hills, *Rock*, p. 229, proposes 1,100–1,300 in 1715–20; BL, Add Mss 10034, W. Skinner, 'A Short Account of Gibraltar . . . 1704 to 1745', reports 4,730 privates in 1727, at the time of the siege; T. Benady, 'The governors of Gibraltar 2 (1730–1749)', *Gibraltar Heritage Journal*, 10 (2003), 47, cites 2,164 in 1738; T. James, *The History of the Herculanean Straits* (London: Rivington, Cadell and Dodsley, 1771), vol. 2, p. 320, records a military population in 1754 of 3,026, plus 1,426 women and children; Hills, *Rock*, p. 293, reckons 4,000 in 1776; Bell in Ayala, *Gibraltar*, p. 180, reports 5,382 soldiers just before the siege began in 1779; House of Commons Paper 49, 9 Nov 1814 (for 1788–92) and Paper 140, 1 March 1843 (for 1792–1842) give effective figures of around 3,000; Hills, *Rock*, p. 360 offers 7,000 in 1797; Howes, *Gibraltarian*, p. 44, cites 5,139 in 1814, plus 1,615 women and children.

12 TNA, PC1/16/13, copy of proclamation. The order-in-council was 7 Feb 1705 OS, 18 Feb 1706 NS. See also Ayala, *Gibraltar*, pp. 56–8, Appendices I and IV; Hills,

without the payment of duties (though port dues and other service charges might be levied), it was hoped that entrepreneurs would be attracted to settle on the Rock by the prospects of supplying the garrison and of trading across and into the Mediterranean and with Britain, or even into Spain, though normally the last, by land, was supposedly banned by the Treaty of Utrecht.[13]

In sum, for their own needs, British authorities needed to attract civilians to Gibraltar either on a daily basis or as permanent residents. Even before the Treaty of Utrecht and increasingly thereafter, civilians began to reoccupy the town. However, there is good evidence to show that for those in charge the preferred immigrants, residents, merchants and property owners were ideally Protestants and British.

Military security, controls and surveillance

It was not to be expected that entry would be free and easy for all. The British had only recently taken control of a fortress liable to face siege, as had been demonstrated by their own attack and by subsequent Spanish challenges. Moreover, what might be defended from outside assault had also to be protected from inside subversion. Military security was and therefore remained for the British authorities a pressing managerial issue. For civilians seeking entry, and especially residence, the physical and bureaucratic barriers they encountered would repeatedly confirm their subordination to British military control and surveillance. There would also be discrimination by the British in how components of the civilian community were treated. Such fragmentation would handicap the development of a community and therefore delay the evolution of a distinctive sense of a collective self.

The British took over a town largely squeezed within the walls of a fortress. The allies had succeeded in breaching the walls in 1704, but subsequently the fortifications had been extended and made more formidable. Nature had provided security on the unassailable eastern face and north-eastern corner of the Rock.[14] Additional investment turned the north front, facing mainland Spain, into a formidable sequence of walls, towers, a ditch and a glacis, running down from Rock to sea. From there along the west at the water's edge ran a wall, punctuated with bastions and towers. Further walls bisected the peninsula to the south

---

Rock, pp. 53, 99–100, 216; Jackson, *Rock*, pp. 40–1, 114; Benady, 'Depositions', p. 103.

13 See text of Article X in, for example, Hills, *Rock*, pp. 222–3, Jackson, *Rock*, pp. 333–4, and, in English and Spanish, www.gibconnect.com/~loonylenny/utrecht/utrecht.htm.

14 One perilous path up the scarp was obliterated by the English after the siege of 1704–5: Jackson, *Rock*, p. 107.

of the main settlement, running inland from the sea to the crest of the Rock. Approaches to this protective circuit around the town were guarded by fortifications above the beaches to the south, while on the isthmus to the north only two routes led to the walls of the fortress, one from Eastern Bay, over which towered the walls, and the other to the west, going past a fortified outpost and along a narrow causeway hemmed between the sea and an artificially deepened lagoon. Entrances through the walls and into the fortress and town were restricted to three fortified gates, Landport, Waterport and Southport.[15] The governors of British Gibraltar were always military men (until recently) and commanders-in-chief of the garrison, and accordingly in the interests of military security the gates were controlled by soldiers and locked at night.

The necessary corollary – regulating and monitoring entry and settlement – fell to the military and became especially, under the governor, the responsibility of the town major (whose other duties were the maintenance of order among the soldiers). Garrison orders from soon after the British occupation (the first extant dates to 1720) therefore strictly stipulated that all 'strangers' wishing to enter Gibraltar (presumably those not already known as residents, and whether British or not) were expected to state their names, their 'nation' and their business to the officers at the gates and to produce papers to be inspected on behalf of the governor by the town major, or in some circumstances the judge advocate, the legal officer attached to the garrison. Moreover, no resident was to accommodate visitors without reporting their names, their business and their origins to the authorities, on pain of their own expulsion. Exclusion and expulsion orders were sometimes issued.[16] A police officer and clerk were attached to the town major's office in 1803 precisely in order 'to prevent the introduction of improper persons into the Garrison'.[17] By implication, no one in this period, not even a British native or anyone born in Gibraltar, had an absolute right to reside in the town, and therefore a permit also came to be required to authorise longer-term residence. Gibraltar was evidently regarded primarily as a fortress. Anxieties about security also explain why the opening and closing of the gates were signalled by gunfire, why an overnight curfew

15 For a history see D. Fa and C. Finlayson, *The Fortifications of Gibraltar 1068–1945* (Oxford: Osprey, 2006), and A.J. Sáez Rodríguez, *La Montaña Inexpugnable: Seis Siglos de Fortificaciones en Gibraltar (XII–XVIII)* (Algeciras: Instituto de Estudios Campogibraltareños, 2006); and for contemporary descriptions see Ayala, *Gibraltar*, pp. 28–9, 34–5, and J. Drinkwater, *A History of the Late Siege of Gibraltar* (London: Spilsbury, 1785), pp. 26–31.

16 Gibraltar Government Archives [henceforth GGA], Box: Alien Question, 'The History of the Permit System presented by F.S. Flood, 12 May 1871', Appendix A, No 1, Garrison Orders, 27 July 1720–30 July 1730, No 2, 6 Sept 1755.

17 TNA, CO91/43, Duke of Kent to Pelham, 30 April 1803, and see Trigge to Yorke, 17 Sept 1803.

was enforced, and why, reputedly, the governor of Gibraltar slept with the keys under his pillow.[18]

Those tempted to exploit the garrison's demand for trade and labour and who gained temporary or permanent residence would also have been made aware that, once inside, they remained under surveillance. Regular enumeration and report, for example of military personnel and supplies, are characteristic of a military culture, and civilians in Gibraltar could not always evade such inspection. On thirteen occasions between the British occupation and 1816 the government of Gibraltar conducted some kind of whole population census and made other attempts to estimate the size and make-up of the civilian population.[19] Civilians, household by household, were expected to provide the authorities with information about themselves, their families, their servants and their lodgers, and to give details on origins, religion, ages, marital status, eventually their occupations and years of residence. In addition, separate cohorts were also counted, including Colonel Bennett's listing of the population who remained in the garrison after the conquest in 1704, the drawing up of a 'List of the Residents of Gibraltar in the year 1736', and audits of British inhabitants in 1781, of Roman Catholics in 1782, of Jews in 1784 and of Genoese sometime between 1804 and 1815.[20] On three occasions in this period the titles by which civilians held property were also subject to official inquiries, in 1749, in 1770 and in 1817–19. The public were informed of such investigations and of their obligations to cooperate by public proclamations posted in public places, in English and also often in Spanish and Italian. This was how notice of the 1749 inquiry into land titles was given,[21] and also how instructions for the 1791 census (and probably others) were delivered.[22] The *Gibraltar Chronicle*, first published in 1801 and used as the mouthpiece of government, was an additional vehicle for the distribution of orders to civilians.

18 GGA, Box: Despatches from Gibraltar 1815, Don to consuls and responses, 12–16 March 1815, plus copies of Garrison Orders on the night-time curfew 1741–1815.

19 There are reports of censuses in 1725, 1753, 1754, 1767, 1777, 1787, 1791, 1801, 1807, 1811, 1813, 1814 and 1816. In the UK, the first official census was not attempted until 1801, and only each decade thereafter.

20 GGA, Box: Demography, 'List of Residents in Gibraltar 1736', 'List of British Inhabitants 5 August 1781', 'List of the Roman Catholic Inhabitants 1782' (or this may be 1784), 'List of Jews in Town 1784', 'List of Genoese', undated but a comparison of contents with other sources, especially the census of 1791 and references to the Garrison Library built in 1804 and to the Blue Barracks suggest a date between 1804 and 1815.

21 GGA, Box: Crown Lands Series A, 'The Proceedings of a Court of Inquiry', 1 Aug 1749, p. 4.

22 Dated 8 Feb 1791, and quoted in Gibraltar Government, *Census of Gibraltar 2001*, pp. viii–ix.

It should not be expected that the rules and regulations of an eighteenth-century British garrison town were always tightly drawn up, meticulously imposed or scrupulously obeyed. For example, some civilian residents reacted to the land titles investigation in 1749 by pulling down the notice which ordered them to lodge their claims with the court of inquiry.[23] In 1757 the governor had to reissue garrison orders when he discovered that somehow 'several strangers and foreigners of different nations' had gained entry without permits, some even after permits had been refused them. Again, in 1761 residents were once more told that they must report their lodgers or employees to the town major on pain of their own expulsion.[24] The temptation for civilians to ignore demands must have been considerable when the official instructions for the 1791 census rather weakly required returns 'to be dropt into the letter Box address'd to the Secretary, and the Governor hopes there will be no omission'.[25]

British Protestants and the others: censuses, 1725–1816

Demographic quantification always has a managerial purpose. It would have been peculiar if the civilian population of Gibraltar had not deduced the motives and preferences of the British authorities from the questions asked of them, even if the reports themselves were not widely circulated. Most obviously, the census questions were concerned with ethnicity and religion. Implicit in both were British concerns about security, and sensitivity to the composition of the population.

The census of August 1725 revealed a total civilian population of 1,113. Civilian neighbours in these early decades would certainly have been aware of the filling up of Gibraltar's empty houses, albeit slowly, from the nadir of 1704. However, when the collected data were tabulated, it revealed a composition which worried British authorities (Table 1.1).[26]

The proportionately small number of British civilians, only 10 per cent, and

23 GGA, Box: Crown Lands Series A, 'The Proceedings of a Court of Inquiry', 1 Aug 1749, p. 4.
24 GGA, Box: Alien Question, Flood, 'History', Appendix A, No 3, 25 June 1757, 24 Nov 1761.
25 Quoted in *Census of Gibraltar 2001*, pp. viii–ix. A few surviving returns dated 1787 suggest a similar system was employed for that previous census: GGA, Box: Demography, Census Notes 1787–1791.
26 TNA, CO91/1, Kane to Townshend, Sept 1725, review of state of the garrison and enclosing census of civil population, 20 Aug 1725, OS. There is no copy of the census in GGA, but an order requiring 'a list of inhabitants to be made out', dated 2 June 1724, perhaps a preliminary, is included in Flood, 'History', Appendix A, No 1. A similar order was issued 13 Jan 1730, but no evidence of a consequent census seems to have survived.

Table 1.1 *Census of civilian population, 1725*

'Nations'	Males	Females	Totals
British	57	56	113
Genoese	301	113	414
Spaniards	233	167	400
Jews	111	26	137
French	17	6	23
Dutch	8	13	21
Algerines and Moors	5	0	5
Totals	*732*	*381*	*1,113*

Source: TNA, CO91/1, Kane to Townshend, Sept 1725.

especially of so few males, was very apparent, and disconcerting, since the new rulers would have liked more British merchants and other British settlers to boost the British – and Protestant – complexion of the town. Some who came and stayed may have been time-expired soldiers,[27] though there is a surprising gender balance. Attempts had also been made to persuade British Protestant merchants established in Cádiz and Malaga to transfer to Gibraltar, but with limited success.[28] Gibraltar stripped of most of its indigenous population should have been principally replanted as a British military and commercial settlement, but this was not happening.

Article X of the Treaty of Utrecht had particularly required the exclusion of Jews from Gibraltar, and yet this census showed that this had not been effected. British ministers in London repeatedly pressed British governors of the fortress to honour the Utrecht clause and expel the Jews; British governors of the fortress repeatedly assured British ministers in London that they would comply in due course. True, corrupt local officials profited from the deals struck instead with Jews, but the men-on-the-spot also knew that Jews were valuable because their trading contacts, especially with Morocco across the straits, initially provided many of the food supplies which could no longer be obtained so easily from Spain across the isthmus.[29] The Jewish population which had entered shortly after the Spanish exodus, rising perhaps to 200, was only temporarily reduced. In 1725 they were still 12 per cent of the civilian population. Their presence illuminates

27 Howes, *Gibraltarian*, pp. 6–7.
28 Hills, *Rock*, p. 228.
29 See for example BL, Lexington Papers, Add. Mss 46551, vol. XXXII, Thomas Stanwix to Lexington, ambassador at Madrid, 11 April 1713, and TNA, CO91/1, Newcastle to Jasper Clayton, lieutenant-governor, 16 April 1725; and BL, Copies of Letters and Papers relating to Gibraltar, 1727–31, Add Mss 23643, Clayton to minister at Madrid, 24 April and 1 July 1728.

the difficulties caused to British managers by the partition of 'greater' Gibraltar. Of the 111 Jewish males, 86 were reckoned to be from 'Barbary' (Morocco), 17 from Leghorn, 4 from England, 3 from Holland and 1 from Turkey.[30]

One virtue of the Jews in the eyes of British governors was that their religious faith made them no more likely to prefer a Catholic regime than a Protestant one. True, Utrecht had also bound the British authorities to tolerate and protect locally the practice of the Catholic faith, and formally this obligation was honoured. However, in the very early days the military in Gibraltar and government ministers in London were unlikely to forget the Catholic Jacobite rebellion of 1715 back home.[31] In any event, British governors could not ignore, even between sieges, that Catholic Spain wanted to expel the British and reunite Gibraltar with its hinterland.

The large number of Spaniards recorded in this early count, 36 per cent, all of course Roman Catholics, included some of the 200 or so, mainly Catalans, who arrived among Prince George's troops in 1704 and who stayed, plus later adherents of the defeated 'King Charles III' seeking refuge. Many, perhaps all, were ordered to leave in 1727, when a Spanish attack was imminent, but after the war a few returned and others were attracted by the magnet market of the fortress. Some of the men were even formed up as volunteers in a 'Spanish Guard' to supplement British troops as frontier guards under a 'Spanish Sergeant', who also exercised some internal policing duties and provided liaison between civilians and the military.[32] This may be seen as a pragmatic response by the British, not unlike the employment of 'native troops' in other colonies. Genoese families, among the most mobile of Mediterranean people, were attracted early by opportunities in Gibraltar. By 1725 they formed 37 per cent

30 TNA, CO91/1, Kane to Townshend, Sept 1725, census report. The man from Turkey may have been from Algiers, and two of the total were actually from Portugal: T. Benady, 'The Jewish community of Gibraltar', in R.D. Barnett and W.M. Schwab (eds), *The Sephardi Heritage, Vol. 2, The Western Sephardim* (Grendon: Gibraltar Books, 1989), pp. 145–52. See also Sir Joshua Hassan, 'The Treaty of Utrecht 1713 and the Jews of Gibraltar', reprinted in Caruana, *Cloud*, pp. 160–79; M. Benady, 'The settlement of Jews in Gibraltar, 1704–1783', *Transactions of the Jewish Historical Society of England*, 26 (1979), 87–110; T.M. Benady, 'The role of Jews in the British colonies of the Western Mediterranean', *Jewish Historical Studies*, 33 (1995), esp. 47–52; Hills, *Rock*, pp. 227–8.

31 For anti-Catholicism in eighteenth- and nineteenth-century Britain see, for example, L. Colley, 'Britishness and otherness: an argument', *Journal of British Studies*, 31:4 (1992), 316–21.

32 T. Benady, 'Spaniards in Gibraltar after the Treaty of Utrecht', *Gibraltar Heritage Journal*, 7 (2000), 125–6, and see p. 128 for names of fifteen settlers from Spain between 1737 and 1772, and of thirteen men from Gibraltar marrying women from Spain between 1750 and 1771.

of the civilian population, and they remained throughout the eighteenth century a substantial section of the community. They probably found a less suspicious reception than that accorded to the Spanish and were allowed, along with the Jews, to remain during the 1727 siege.[33] Nevertheless, some British observers saw all Roman Catholic settlers as a danger. The reasoning was starkly put by Lieutenant-Governor Kane in 1725: '[T]he greater number of British protestants shall be here and the fewer foreign papists, the greater security it would be to the garrison and the greater would be the traffic for English goods.'[34] All Roman Catholics were entering an ostensibly Protestant fortress. In the 1720s the Spanish needed special permits to gain entry, and Spanish, Genoese and Portuguese arriving by sea only to trade were obliged to do their deals outside the walls, at Waterport.[35]

Contemporary reports are deficient, but later records provide the names, place of origin and dates of arrival of some of those who had settled early and would be counted in this first census of 1725. They included ideal colonists such as the British merchant Edward Pearson, who arrived in 1719, aged 23. But there was also Ana Phelipes, originally from Spain, who entered in 1717, aged 27. The Genoese among the early arrivals included some young members of families, such as Batholome Dagnaino, entering in 1709, aged 9, and Bartolome Bresciano in 1715, aged 7. Many of the Jewish immigrants were from North Africa, such as David Abudarham from Barbary, who arrived as a young man in 1722, aged 25, plus others particularly from Tetuan, including Sénor Simah, who was 29 when he settled in Gibraltar in 1716, and Haim Anahovy, who entered in 1722, aged 17. Other Jews who came and stayed were only children when they entered, including Jacob Cardozo from Portugal in 1719, aged 10, and Joseph Conquy from Holland in 1723, aged 14.[36] At least Jacob Diaz Arias, another Jew, who arrived to set up business in 1713, apparently with the encouragement of the governor, the Earl of Portmore, had been born in London.[37]

Undoubtedly the attempt by Spanish forces to recover Gibraltar in the siege

33 T. Benady, 'Genoese in Gibraltar', *Gibraltar Heritage Journal*, 8 (2001), 85–107; Hills, *Rock*, p. 273.

34 Hills, *Rock*, quoting Kane, p. 234, and see pp. 264, 292; see also in TNA, CO91/1, and BL, Add Mss 10034, 'Some Remarks Concerning Gibraltar, humbly offered by Colonel Joseph Bennett', 22 Nov 1712, on his concerns about the Spanish presence. James, *Herculanean Straits*, p. 295, still refers in 1771 to the Spanish in Gibraltar as 'greatly addicted to gross idolatry and rank superstition'.

35 GGA, Box: Alien Question, Flood, 'History', Appendix A, No 1, orders of 13 Nov and 19 Dec 1720, 30 Aug 1727.

36 Data extracted from GGA, Box: Demography, 'List of Inhabitants 1777'.

37 Benady, 'Jewish community', pp. 147–8, also lists the names of important Jewish merchants in 1717 and refers to other early Jewish settlers from London, Portugal and Leghorn, though mainly from Morocco.

of 1727 was a setback to the development of the civilian community, causing the expulsion of Gibraltar's Spanish population and much destruction of property. Nevertheless, the garrison thereafter was still there to be serviced and other trading opportunities lured in more immigrants. The authorities soon felt the need to know just who had got in. We cannot tell for sure to what extent residents and newcomers were aware of the managerial purpose which lay behind the censuses of 1753 and 1754, though the news in 1745 of a second Jacobite rebellion may have made some of them sensitive when confronted by the census questions. The civilian population, from a low during the 1727 siege of maybe only 500, had recovered to 1,793 by 1753 (1,810 in 1754). Nevertheless, the information gathered would not encourage British authorities to relax. There had been an increase to 414 in 'those of Britain', but they still made up only 24 per cent of this growing settlement. The Jews now totalled 572 or 32 per cent (604 in 1754). True, the number from Spain was substantially lower than before, just 185, only 10 per cent, and the Portuguese were only an additional 25, but since the Genoese had now increased to 597 or 33 per cent, Roman Catholics amounted to 807, 44 per cent of the total population (792 in 1754). The British included some like Henry Murray, who arrived in 1735, aged 23 and became a merchant, William Healey, 1738, aged 27, a wharf keeper, and Richard Catton, 1742, aged 25, who became port sergeant; but there were more like the two young men from Genoa who arrived in 1737, Ambrosio Arecio, aged 34 and Giacomo Morello, aged 19, and two Jews from Tetuan, David Azulay, who settled in Gibraltar in 1727, aged 30 and Isaac Almosini, who followed in 1737, aged 22.[38]

Another check on demographic developments was undertaken in 1767. The order for this census made even more explicit to civilians its purpose and the underlying concern of the authorities, since the data collected were to enable permits of residence to be issued then and thereafter only to 'such Genoese, Jews, etc as may be thought worthy the indulgence of living under the protection of this Garrison'. The Spanish were not mentioned. Only British subjects, 'among which are esteemed the natives of this Garrison of whatever religion', would thereafter be allowed to reside without a permit. Those not complying with the regulations were to be expelled.[39] The results showed what the civilian population in an increasingly busy town would already know, that their numbers had risen substantially, to 2,710. They may have been aware, even from the voices heard on the streets, that the absolute number of 'British' had barely changed,

---

38 James, *Herculanean Straits*, p. 320, and individual data extracted from GGA, Box: Demography, 'List of Inhabitants 1777'. The census reports themselves do not seem to have survived. See also Howes, *Gibraltarian*, pp. 9–10, who uses the 1791 list of residents and cites names with some dates of arrival (but not ages) of those who were adult males in 1759.

39 GGA, Box: Alien Question, Flood, 'History', Appendix A, No 4, 17 Jan 1767.

at 467 a proportionate reduction to 17 per cent, and that there were many Jews, 783, making up 29 per cent. However, overwhelmingly, as Sunday masses would have regularly demonstrated, Gibraltar's population contained mostly Roman Catholics, numbering 1,460 or 54 per cent.[40]

Ten years later, in 1777, civilians were obliged to respond to another census. The questions now being asked exposed another official anxiety. Law and custom throughout the British Empire determined that anyone born within the territories of the crown was a British subject, under the ancient ruling of *jus soli*. Such a person normally inherited the obligations of being a British subject, which included legal, fiscal and possibly military obligations, but also acquired rights to legal, diplomatic and perhaps military protection. Moreover, and in this context more importantly, such a person had theoretically a right to 'belong', a right of residence anywhere in the realms of the crown. Most importantly, this meant in the place of birth, which in this case was Gibraltar. Whereas foreign immigrants, not being British subjects, could quite readily be expelled, those born in Gibraltar, whatever their parentage, had a right to remain. True, in this garrison-colony such rights might be overridden in exceptional circumstances, but otherwise a Gibraltar-born Roman Catholic child of, say, Spanish or Genoese parentage had a legal right of residence. For authorities nervous about garrison security, suspicious of Roman Catholics and worried about the lack of British settlers in Gibraltar, the answers recorded for the questions asked in the 1777 census did not make for pretty reading. This was a population also growing by family formation and natural increase, and no longer only by immigration.

The detailed results were locked up in unpublished reports, but the overall dynamics, as shown in Table 1.2, would have been widely known. The town was more crowded, and by now over half, 1,661, of the civilian population of 3,201 had been born in Gibraltar. But of those 'native born', only 220 were British. To them might be added 286 British non-natives who were also British subjects of British origin. Even so, all 506 of them (or 519 if you add in English and Irish Catholics) amounted to only 16 per cent of the civilian population. The Jewish group, now grown to 863 or 27 per cent of the total, was mainly made up of the 'native born'. Clearly, however, the population was overwhelmingly composed of Roman Catholics, a total of 1,832 or 57 per cent, including still a lot of Genoese immigrants, as an analysis of the names of those born in Gibraltar about this time confirms – Ansaldo, Bonfante, Cepriano and so on. And nearly half of Roman Catholics, 46 per cent, were 'native born'.[41]

---

40 GGA, Box: Alien Question, 'General Abstract of the Number of Inhabitants', probably composed in 1871; reproduced in Howes, *Gibraltarian*, p. 12.

41 GGA, Box: Demography, 'List of Inhabitants 1777', Abstract. Individual entries on the list itself give slightly and inexplicably different totals, aggregating to 517, 1,754 and 860 for the three main headings and 3,131 as the grand total. Howes,

Table 1.2 *Census of civilian population, 1777*

Religion	Nationality	Totals
British or Protestant inhabitants	Natives	220
	Non-Natives	286
Total		*506*
Roman Catholic inhabitants	Natives	845
	Genoese and Savoyards	672
	Spaniards	134
	Portuguese	93
	Minorcans	62
	French	13
	English and Irish	13
Total		*1,832*
Jews	Natives	596
	'Strangers'[a]	267
Total		*863*
Grand total		*3,201*

Note: [a] This title, used instead of 'Non-Natives' in the Abstract, is unique to the Jews.

Source: GGA, Box: Demography, 'List of Inhabitants, 1777'.

Quite where all civilians stood in the military scheme of things was then revealed during the 'Great Siege' of 1779–83, when many of the civilian population were encouraged to leave, perhaps for their own safety but also to eliminate 'useless mouths'.[42] Many, it is true, probably returned afterwards, to a badly damaged town where labour was certainly in demand,[43] but the authorities needed to check who was now in the fortress, so inhabitants were again subjected to official review, in the census of 1787. The total of 3,386 showed little advance in aggregate from a decade earlier. More seriously for the military government, the proportions had not improved, the 512 British forming only 15 per cent and

Footnote 41 (*cont.*)

 Gibraltarian, pp. 12–13, reproduces the data as reconfigured by Flood in his report 1871 and uses, anachronistically, Flood's 'British Blood' and 'Alien Blood' terms; on pp. 18–22 he analyses those born in Gibraltar with Latin and Jewish names and resident in Gibraltar c.1779.

42 Howes, *Gibraltarian*, pp. 15–16, citing garrison orders; Hills, *Rock*, pp. 316, 318; B.H.T. Frere (ed.), *Captain John Spilsbury's A Journal of the Blockade and Siege of Gibraltar 1779–1783* (Gibraltar: Gibraltar Garrison Printing Works, 1908), entries for 21 June and 27 Oct 1779, 20 Feb 1780, 26 Feb and 7 May 1781. Civilians, especially women, had also been encouraged to leave in the 1727 siege: Hills, *Rock*, p. 73.

43 Howes, *Gibraltarian*, pp. 17–18.

still being exceeded even by a reduced number of Jews, 776 or 23 per cent and, as the civilians would also know, by a large increase in the number of Roman Catholics, to 2,098, amounting to 62 per cent.[44]

The holding of yet another census in 1791 was indicative of continuing official anxiety and a further reminder to the civilians that they were being surveyed. Perhaps those civilians born in Gibraltar, whatever their parental origins, were aware of their status, as natives of one of His Majesty's dominions, as British subjects, but their parents and others may have been unsettled when the authorities, via the census, wanted to know 'by what Governor or Commander in Chief's permission each foreigner came here'.[45] Those feeling insecure were most likely to cover their tracks. This perhaps accounts for some (though not all) of the recorded reduction in the total civilian population to 2,948 (down from 3,386 in 1787) (Table 1.3).[46]

Fewer than 14 per cent could be classed as British, a mere 416 even including British-born Jews and a couple of Roman Catholics, a loss in absolute terms of one-fifth since the previous two censuses. There had been a marked decline in the number of British immigrants into Gibraltar, and a comparison between the number of locally born British in Gibraltar in 1777 and in 1791 shows that even those British born in Gibraltar were not staying. If Gibraltar were to remain a British stronghold at the toe of Spain, then the British government could not rely comfortably for security on the ethnically British (and Protestant), whether born in Britain or in Gibraltar. True, the number of Jews, though still more numerous, had also gone down and for similar reasons, but they still accounted for over 23 per cent, overwhelmingly locally born. On the other hand, even though

44 GGA, Box: Alien Question, 'General Abstract', reproduced in Howes, *Gibraltarian*, p. 12. It has to be said that the original data for 1787 have not survived, and the figure in the surviving abstract written up much later looks suspiciously high in comparison with the 1791 data. If correct, the number of Jews had increased by over a hundred in three years from the 655 counted shortly after the siege in 1784: GGA, Box: Demography, 'List of Jews in Town Gibraltar 16 Jan 1784'.

45 Dated 8 Feb 1791, and quoted in *Census of Gibraltar 2001*, pp. viii–ix. See GGA, Box: Alien Question, Flood, 'History', Appendix A, No 5, for extract of a return showing which governor had given permission to enter.

46 Totals calculated from GGA, Box: Demography, 'List of Inhabitants 1791'. These figures, based on the census manuscripts, differ from those in GGA, Box: Alien Question, 'General Abstract', probably compiled in 1870, which first give a total of 2,874 made up of 372 British, 666 Jews and 1,836 Roman Catholics and also revised figures of 2,890, 395, 680 and 1,815 respectively. The latter were used by Flood in his 1871 'History', by Howes, *Gibraltarian*, p. 27, and, for the total, in *Census of Gibraltar 2001*, Table 1. Finlayson, 'Gibraltarian', offers a total of 2,989, made up of 409 'Protestants', 697 'Jews and Moors' and 1,883 'Catholics'. Jackson, *Rock*, p. 224 has a minor variant, leading to a total of 2,900. The discrepancies are not sufficient to affect the argument.

Table 1.3 *Census of civilian population, 1791, with 1777 and 1787 figures for comparison*

Nationality/Religion	Place of birth	Totals		
		1791	1777	1787
British	Gibraltar	211	220	
	Britain	182	286	
	Other	10		
	Total	*403*	*506*	*512*
Roman Catholics	Gibraltar	892	845	
	Genoa	450		
	Savoy	73		
	Genoa and Savoy		672	
	Portuguese	163	93	
	Minorcans	173	62	
	Spaniards	56	134	
	French	13	13	
	British	2		
	Other	30		
	Total	*1,852*	*1,832*	*2,098*
Jews	Gibraltar	467	596	
	'Barbary'/Tetuan	184	267	
	Minorca	17		
	Britain	11		
	Other	14		
	Total	*693*	*863*	*776*
Grand total		*2,948*	*3,201*	*3,386*

Source: GGA, Box: Demography: List of Inhabitants, 1791.

the Roman Catholic population had also recently declined, its total pretty much matched that of 1777, and its proportion had increased by a further notch to 63 per cent. The number of immigrants from Catholic Portugal and Minorca had risen to offset the decline in the numbers arriving from Genoa and the further steep drop in those born in Spain – though so soon after the Siege, the latter might have felt more reason to hide their presence from the authorities. Most importantly, however, births in Gibraltar showed that the Roman Catholic character of Gibraltar was becoming increasingly so, since, alone among the ethnic and religious cohorts, the number of Roman Catholics born in Gibraltar had grown since 1777, making up nearly half of the Roman Catholic population by 1791, 48 per cent. If Gibraltar's civilian population were to develop a communal identity, its core was in the cradle and its religious orientation was clear. However, a public declaration at the time of the 1791 census confirmed the unsteady basis for anyone entering or resident on the Rock, whether foreigner, British subject or even native born: '[N]o person can possess a right to enter and reside in Gibraltar, even though a natural born subject of the Crown, without permission of the Governor of the Fortress and no general right of way to this end has ever been granted.'[47] This was no hollow claim. A substantial number of civilians were expelled following the discovery in 1798 of a conspiracy during the Napoleonic Wars to hand Gibraltar over to Spain.[48]

One calculation based on the census returns from 1753 to 1791 reckons that on average only 16 per cent of the civilian population in the second half of the eighteenth century were British. They were far exceeded by the Jews, 26 per cent, and Roman Catholics, 58 per cent (44 per cent Genoese, 12 per cent Spanish, 2 per cent Portuguese).[49] The subsequent censuses of the early nineteenth century certainly show a rapid increase in civilian numbers, prompted by a prosperity induced by war, by refugees from Genoa escaping conscription into Napoleon's army and latterly by a far more open access during the war between Gibraltar and the Campo. Numbers rose to 5,339 in 1801, to over 6,000 by 1804, and reached 7,501 by 1807, in spite of well over 2,000 deaths due to yellow fever in 1804–5.[50] Growth thereafter was even more rapid: 11,173 by 1811 and a remarkable 12,423 by 1813. But the British share of the civilian population actually fell further, to an average of only 13 per cent between 1801 and 1813. Jews then numbered 15.5 per cent. Gibraltar by this period had become what it remained, overwhelmingly a society of Roman Catholics. Already they formed 71.5 per cent of the total (4 per cent Minorcans, 16.5 per cent Spanish, 20 per cent Portuguese and 31 per cent Genoese and other Italians).[51] This truly cosmopolitan community also included a minor scattering of Austrians, Danes, Dutch, French, Germans, Greeks, Latin Americans, Majorcans, Maltese, Sicilians, Sardinians and even Swiss, and most of these would also be Roman Catholics. An alternative analysis in 1814 of the places of origin of employed adult males (17 years and over) confirms this impression, while again highlighting the Roman Catholic predominance. They included 886 Genoese men, 650 Portuguese, 527 Spanish, 138 Minorcans and 104 Italians – a total of 2,305. There were 489 Jewish men in this community, and even though 145 of them were said to be 'British Jews' that is not many to add to the 403 British men.[52]

The first post-war census, conducted in 1816, only served further to show how successfully civilians had exploited the opportunities which Gibraltar presented, rules and regulations notwithstanding (Table 1.4).

47 GGA, Box: Alien Question, quoted in Attorney-General, 'Memorandum on the Right of Residence in Gibraltar', 6 Jan 1937.
48 TNA, CO91/40, O'Hara to Portland, 29 Dec 1798; Hills, *Rock*, p. 361.
49 Jackson, *Rock*, p. 225.
50 Howes, *Gibraltarian*, pp. 39, 43; Benady, 'Jewish community', p. 162; Finlayson, 'Gibraltarian'.
51 Jackson, *Rock*, p. 225.
52 Howes, *Gibraltarian*, p. 46.

Table 1.4 *Census of civilian population, 1816*

	Males	Females	Totals
British	633	484	1,117
Natives	1,159	1,089	2,248
British and Native Jews	392	378	770
Total	*2,184*	*1,951*	*4,135*
Foreign Jews	169	129	298
Spaniards	1,237	1,505	2,742
Genoese	1,172	646	1,818
Portuguese	839	473	1,312
Minorcans	231	179	410
French	100	48	148
Germans	74	59	133
Italians	99	32	131
Sicilians	56	35	91
Sardinians	56	31	87
Others	89	30	119
Total	*4,122*	*3,167*	*7,289*
Grand total	*6,306*	*5,118*	*11,424*

Source: TNA, CO91/67, Don to Bathurst, 6 July 1816.

The rapid transformative effect of the Napoleonic wars is apparent in the huge increase in the size of the population, mainly accounted for by masses of immigrants crossing a much more open land frontier to capitalise on Gibraltar's war-induced prosperity. Their arrival exceeded considerably the contribution made by natural increase to the number of the native born. The gender balance also suggested how many of those who had recently arrived might stay and breed. What did not change were the categorisation employed by the colonial authorities in analysing this population, and the anxieties those categories reflected and reinforced. In his report, Lieutenant-Governor Sir George Don pointed to the limited number of British subjects, fewer than 10 per cent. Even, optimistically, adding in the 'Natives', whom he referred to as Roman Catholics, and 'British and Native Jews', he could find 'only 4,135 Inhabitants who may be considered as belonging to and attracted by interest to the British Government' – just 36 per cent. On the other hand he noted the very considerable increase in the number of Spanish who had gained entry, along with more from Genoa and Portugal, 'making a total of 7,289 Foreigners who have no interest in our welfare and consequently cannot be depended upon'.[53] The Protestant British settlement at Gibraltar had become in its first century decreasingly so, and now the very security of the garrison seemed much at risk.

53 TNA, CO91/67, Don to Bathurst, 6 July 1816.

People and property ownership, 1712–1819

Audits of property ownership over the century pointed in the same direction. A government report of 1712 lists those who were renting shops and houses. The dark presence of the non-British population is indicated by the imprecise official descriptions of many of these tenants. They include 'The Genoeze Baker', 'A Turk near the Lieut Governors', 'A Genoeze who marryed a black', 'A Spaniard in the House next Lieut. Burdeaux', '2 young Merchant Jews in the Great Street', 'The Jews Taylor at the Corner of the Parade'.[54] A 1736 survey of 300 houses within the fortress shows that 114 of the civilian householders (as tenants or owners) had robustly British (or possibly Irish) names, including 25 who owned more than one property. These were men like Thomas Walters, Archibald Agnew and Robert Hastings, and there were women too, like Mary Roberts, Elizabeth Smith and the Widow Wilson. Even so, judging by names, a substantial number, 71, were probably of 'non-British' origin, like Pedro Solas, Gaspar Lucar, Maria Tanges and Juan de la Rosa, several of whom were also multiple owners.[55]

Roman Catholics and Jews would therefore have had further cause for concern when news broke that the military government was going to investigate property ownership, particularly when they discovered that the members of the Court of Inquiry were British military officers plus prominent British Protestant civilians.[56] As already observed, early governors had not been routinely scrupulous in selling leases (and pocketing rents), and by mid century ministers in London were worried about how much property was now owned by non-British residents (and how little income from rents was accruing to the crown).[57] General

54 TNA, CO91/1 and copies in BL, Add Mss 10034, and GL, Gq314.4689, 'The Names of those who Pay Rent for Shops & Houses . . .', 22 Nov 1712.

55 GGA, Box: Demography, 'List of Residents in Gibraltar 1736', composed by Major F. Montresor, Society of Genealogists, in 1920; copy also in GL. The list is derived from annotations to a plan of the fortress. Identifying nationality, especially of widows, from names alone is admittedly an inexact procedure. The remaining houses were occupied by garrison officers or were in institutional ownership. Property grants to Jews in 1721–23 are reported in Benady, 'Jewish community', p. 151.

56 For names see GGA, Box: Crown Lands Series A, General Bland's Court of Enquiry 1749, 'The Proceedings . . .', p. 1.

57 See, for example, report attached to TNA, CO91/67, Don to Bathurst, 13 Sept 1816. For an example of ministerial concerns see BL, Add Mss 23643, Clayton to Pelham, 11 April, 10 Oct, 10 Nov 1728, and Hardwicke Papers, Add Mss 36137, Pelham to Attorney-General, 27 Jan 1728/9. For examples of 'misbehaviour' by governors and lieutenant-governors see Jackson, *Rock*, pp. 114, 125, Ellicott, *Our Gibraltar*, p. 21, T. Benady, 'The governors of Gibraltar 1 (1704–1730)', *Gibraltar Heritage Journal*, 9 (2002), 43–60, and Benady, 'The governors of Gibraltar 2 (1730–1749)', pp. 49–54.

Sir Humphrey Bland, governor from 1749 to 1754, was instructed in May 1749 to carry out an inquiry. He was first to assert that all the annexed territory was crown property and that ground rents must therefore be paid by all property owners or users, and paid to the crown and not to the governor. He was also to assess the legitimacy of claims and adjudicate in cases of dispute. There followed the instruction most indicative of the official mind and most likely to alarm many Gibraltar residents. The governor was to ensure that in the letting out of property he was to favour 'His Majesty's Protestant Subjects' since at present 'Houses are chiefly inhabited by Jews, Moors and Papists of different Nations, which may prove of dangerous consequence to the Town'.[58]

The inquiry was pursued during August and September 1749, and it confirmed (or rejected) existing claims and formally recorded true titles.[59] Even after this scrutiny, an analysis of the comprehensive list of the properties (dwellings and business premises) upon which ground rent was henceforth to be paid to the crown reveals that civilian proprietors with British (and a few Irish) names numbered only 111 and accounted for only 173 of the 290 properties. To set against Joseph Ashton, Ursula Bradford, William Davis, John Fleming, Richard Holroide, Mary Smith, Benjamin Roberts, Elizabeth Sutherland, Martin Wilson and so on were 94 other proprietors holding 117 properties who had names like Margarita Andola, Jacomo Casanova, Pedro Martinez, Ignacio Patron, Giacomo Rombado, Magdalena de Sala and Abraham Vouga.[60] These returns prompted the governor to try and shore up the British settlement by revised property laws. An addition to the terms of deeds disallowed the inheritance of landed property by persons other than Protestant subjects, unless the heirs 'shall be natives and inhabitants of this town and garrison'. In addition, on pain of forfeiture, property might otherwise only be disposed of (by sale or gift) to 'a Protestant, being one of His Majesty's natural born subjects, and not a foreigner or of any other Religion'.[61] Nine of the fifteen property grants Governor Bland subsequently awarded in the next ten months were to persons with British names, and the rest (certainly four of them) were existing property holders – though there are

---

58 TNA, T1/335/33, and BL, Add Mss 10034, copy of Bland order, 12 May 1749, and report; GGA, Bland's Court of Enquiry 1749, 'The Proceedings . . .', p. 1.

59 A proclamation of 18 May 1751 required proprietors to collect confirmed awards, on pain of forfeiture: TNA, CO91/67, report with Don to Bathurst, 13 Sept 1816. As an example of the Court's proceedings and of subsequent deeds of sale see A. Lombard, 'Fives Courts', *Gibraltar Heritage Journal*, 7 (2000), 49–73.

60 GGA, Bland's Court of Enquiry 1749, pp. 210–13, 'List of the Proprietors of Houses in Gibraltar with the monthly Ground Rents payable for the same to the King'. Benady, 'Jewish community', p. 154, reckons that twenty Jewish property holders had their holdings confirmed.

61 GGA, Bland's Court of Enquiry 1749, p. 208, 'The Confirmation given by Lieut-Governor Bland to the Proprietors of Houses . . .'.

grounds for thinking that some ineligible civilians subverted the restrictions by using frontmen and legal fictions.[62]

The importance for security of this inquiry was subsequently underlined by Bland in the guidelines he saw fit to leave behind for his successors. He criticised his predecessors for not having previously made such a restriction and therefore for

> not encouraging His Majesty's Natural Born Protestant Subjects to get the Property of the Houses, by laying Proper Restrictions against Papists and Foreigners purchasing them, as I have now done: Had this been attended to the whole property of the Houses would have come into the Possession of Protestants by this time, which might have induced many of them to remain here, and have proved a great strengthening to the Garrison, since they are much more to be relied on than the Papists, tho' Born here.[63]

In endeavouring to pass on to future governors his suspicions of Roman Catholics and other 'foreigners', whether immigrant or native born, Bland was of course imposing on all but a handful of civilians resident in Gibraltar an identity which distinguished them from British Protestants – as did the census inquiries – and also denigrated their status. In such circumstances the sense of solidarity and common identity among all civilians which might have been engendered by authoritarian military rule and surveillance would be dissipated by the fragmentation caused by categorisation and discrimination.

A generation on, by the end of the eighteenth century, census returns, as noted, were exposing the failure to establish Gibraltar as primarily a British Protestant community. Moreover, by then even Bland's rule that British Protestants, in their absolutely as well as relatively diminishing numbers, were alone able to acquire property (except by inheritance) was also being undermined. The rule was too much of a constraint on the market for houses and land, and hence subsequent governors, perhaps faced with pragmatic difficulties, 'modified' them, and civilians in any case evaded them. Such goings-on were exposed in another inquiry in 1770, which showed that more property had indeed 'come in the possession of Jews and Catholics', but nothing seems to have been done to prevent the practice.[64] True, a 'List of Inhabitants Houses' in 1778 shows that Bland's deeds, street by street, still largely defined property ownership, but by then fewer than half of the properties included (mainly houses but also a few business

---

62 GGA, Bland's Court of Enquiry 1749, p. 214, 'List of the Proprietors of Houses in Gibraltar with the monthly Ground Rents payable for the same to the King'; Benady, 'Jews in Gibraltar', p. 98.

63 GGA, Bland's Court of Inquiry 1749, 'Extract: An Account of Lieutenant-General Bland's conduct . . .'; TNA, CO91/62, 'An Account of Lieutenant-General Bland's conduct . . .', pp. 3–7, 95–7.

64 TNA, CO91/67, report with Don to Bathurst, 13 Sept 1816.

premises and sheds – and even some ruins) were owned or leased by persons with British (or Irish) names, only 204 of the 449. There were more people with names like Isola, Stella, Salas, Martinez, Corrado, Porral, Aboab and Abudarham in the list than with names like Robertson, Pitman, Chapman, Davies, Ashton, Terry, Boyd and Wood.[65] True, transfer of property to non-Protestants was still being denied as late as 1802.[66] However, in February 1804 Lieutenant-Governor Trigge, particularly supportive of the rights of Jews to secure property as 'useful and good subjects' and even, to a lesser extent, of Roman Catholics, was authorised by the secretary of state to confirm sales of property to Jews and indeed to Catholics who had been resident for at least five years.[67]

Such had been the past breaches in the regulations, so obvious had been the sale of property to other than 'natural born Protestant subjects of His Majesty', and so apparent was it that governors had connived at methods of getting round the strict requirements of the law, that a further inquiry and new rules for property ownership were authorised by orders-in-council (issued by the Privy Council in London) in August 1817 and March 1819.[68] There was also obviously official concern that the concession recently made might be a step too far and that the length of some leases was too long and the ground rents charged were too low. Governor Don was therefore required to appoint 'Commissioners for Settling the Titles to Lands in Gibraltar'. They were to carry out surveys of properties and their values, investigate encroachments and the line of possession since 1749, and determine current ownership and entitlements. Such an inquiry, announced by proclamation, was bound to prompt anxiety among those in possession of houses and other property in the town, not least because the legitimacy of their holdings might be in jeopardy and the threat of forfeiture hung over them.[69] But

---

65 GGA, Box: Demography, List of Inhabitants Houses 1778. For Samuel Abudarham, a Jewish merchant who came from Tetuan in 1742 and became a substantial property owner in Gibraltar, see A. Lombard, 'The Roman Catholic Abudarham family', *Gibraltar Heritage Journal*, 4 (1997), 75–90. For a late example of a governor confirming illegitimately the sale of property to a Jewish family see Lombard, 'Fives Courts', p. 59.

66 Hills, *Rock*, p. 362; TNA, CO91/62, Perceval and Manners Sutton to Sir George Shee, 28 Oct. 1802, concerning an attempted sale to a Jew.

67 TNA, CO91/43, Trigge to Pelham, 21 June 1803, and CO91/62, Hobart to Trigge, 30 Nov 1803 and 6 Jan 1804.

68 See TNA, CO91/67, Don to Bathurst, 13 Sept 1816, sending draft order-in-council and report on past practice and its consequences.

69 GGA, Documents connected with the Commission to Settle Land Titles in 1826, 'Landed Property in Gibraltar', especially 'Appendix (L)' proclamations 4 Dec 1817 and 23 Jan 1818, and 'Appendix (D), The Memorial of the Undersigned Proprietors of Houses and Lands being Inhabitants of Gibraltar', dated 27 Jan 1818, to be sent to Governor Don, signed by 53 'Catholics' and 46 'Hebrews', but just 18 'Protestants'.

it was also to be ascertained through inquiry whether claims had been disallowed because of the conditions which Governor Bland (and some of his successors) had imposed. In fact, and capitulating to demographic trends, the market and public protests, the British government conceded that, provided that claimants were registered as inhabitants, there was no longer to be a requirement that property could only be acquired by 'natural born Subjects' (to inherit) or 'natural born Protestant Subjects' (to buy). Henceforth no distinctions were to be drawn by religion between British subjects, wherever born. By the order-in-council of 1819, even the foreign born would be eligible to acquire property. However, they had to have been registered as inhabitants for fifteen years and not just five, and they had thus to have demonstrated their residential commitment. With this safeguard in place, over the next several years the Commission investigated and determined property ownership without regard to ethnicity or religion.[70] The next step, for examination in a later chapter, was an attempt to tighten up controls over entry and residence. Horses and stable doors come to mind.

Conclusion

Demography reveals the failure of an imperial project to establish at Gibraltar a substantial and principally British Protestant civilian settlement to support the British fortress. For one thing, not until 1801, when the total civilian population topped 5,300, did it equal the 5,000 or so civilian Spanish who, after the occupation in 1704 a century earlier, went into exile. That represents a remarkably slow rate of recovery, confirmatory of the deleterious consequences for civilian life on the Rock of separation from the mainland. Moreover, of the replacements, British settlers were slow to arrive and reluctant to stay. They amounted at most to about one quarter by mid century, and then declined to less than one seventh by the end. Only for a short period were they disproportionately weighty as property owners. Instead, a wide variety of what may be called Mediterranean peoples became absolutely and proportionately more numerous, as merchants, tradespeople, craftsmen, labourers and servants.

That the civilian population grew at all indicates that those gates around the town and fortress were not firmly locked and the walls not impenetrable. Initially, in 1704, only a small population of survivors remained from the previous regime.

The memorial quotes Lieut-Governor Trigge's Proclamation, dated 5 March 1804. A second copy of 6 Feb 1818, to be sent to the Prince Regent, contains some changes in names but similar numbers, 65, 28 and 21 respectively.

70 GGA, *Orders in Council, etc,* 'Titles to Lands, etc . . .', 13th August 1817' and 'Titles to Lands, etc . . . 19th March, 1819'; TNA, CO91/85, 'Final Report of the Commissioners for Settling Titles to Land, 1825'; Benady, 'Jewish community', pp. 166–7.

Only later in the century are there signs that births in Gibraltar were making a noticeable contribution to population growth, although *jus soli* was giving such residents a greater degree of security. Even so, natural increase was limited by deaths, which were particularly savage during outbreaks of yellow fever after the turn of the century, in 1804 and 1814, and by emigration, demographically the equivalent of death, which was carrying off many residents, including an unknown proportion of the native born. It follows that Gibraltar's population grew in the first half of the century primarily by immigration, in the second half still substantially so, and in the early nineteenth century once more especially so. The changing ethnic and religious composition of the civilian population provides confirmation.

That this occurred is also a commentary on British management of the rules of entry and settlement. The garrison regulations suggest that paper documents were required for entry (and indeed exit) and also for residence. Documentary evidence of how, and how rigorously, the rules were applied is largely absent during this period. Governor O'Hara, writing in 1796 to a Baron Cholet, purported to be 'mortified' that the 'King's Commands' prevented him from admitting to the garrison even such a distinguished person. He claimed that Gibraltar was 'the most unfit and inconvenient situation for the residence of Persons of any description except the Troops who compose the Garrison and a few Inconsiderable Traders settled here for lucrative purposes, and to profit of the Money that our Army has to spend'.[71] But he must have known well, as did other more humble folk, that entry was either properly allowed to qualified persons with a contribution to make or could be secured by more devious means. Otherwise Gibraltar's population would scarcely have grown at all.

All civilians in this first century were pretty securely subordinated to British authority, but the military's practices of surveillance and control identified and publicised divisions by ethnicity and religion. A small, largely immigrant, multicultural and often transient group of families and individuals, divided also by wealth and status, was not likely instinctively to bond into a single or singular community. True, the increasing volume of Roman Catholics and then the qualified concessions in 1817–19 on property ownership eased some distinctions between civilians in Gibraltar. By that token the creation of a unifying identity was made more likely, in the long run. That outcome, however, was to be further delayed by how the British government attempted to manage the territory in the nineteenth century. Paradoxically, they obstructed such a development by distinguishing harshly between British subjects in Gibraltar and alien others from outside, a distinction which the civilian community with external connections was unwilling to accept.

---

71 GGA, Letters to Madrid, O'Hara to Marquis of Bute, British Ambassador in Madrid, 25 July 1796.

2

A fortress economy, 1704–1815

The previous chapter noted the modest growth of the civilian population of Gibraltar until early in the nineteenth century and how its ethnic and religious composition did not conform to official British wishes. This chapter will add a further layer of explanation for those developments by exploring the economic history of Gibraltar in the century or so after the allied occupation. Gibraltar was, of course, sufficiently attractive economically after 1704 to induce civilians to enter and settle, and eventually to bring up families there, but conditioning their experiences, positively and negatively, was the partition of Gibraltar, upon which stress has already been placed for its demographic consequences.

Prior to 1704, the comings and goings of a Spanish garrison in the fortress had generated some civilian employment and a market for suppliers of goods and services. However, the number of troops stationed in Gibraltar in the seventeenth century, except during periods of active international hostilities, was not large, too small alone to create a thriving urban economy. Indeed at the time of the allied attack in August 1704 the garrison seems to have been fewer than one hundred.[1] Rather, a civilian population of 5,000–6,000 had settled on the peninsula prior to 1704 because, as noted earlier, Gibraltar had been intimately connected by land to an extensive hinterland. The city council was effectively administering a province; some civilians were substantial landowners with properties across the isthmus to manage and with products to sell; the town was also an ecclesiastical centre. Moreover, ever since the Moorish settlement, the attached port had connected Gibraltar with other parts of Spain and with the littorals of the Mediterranean. The Spanish town of Gibraltar had therefore been sustained primarily as an administrative and market centre, with some geographical advantages.[2] Those assets were less easy to exploit after the British occupation.

---

1 G. Hills, *Rock of Contention: a History of Gibraltar* (London: Hale, 1974), p. 172.
2 For information on the geographical extent, resources and economy of 'greater' Gibraltar before 1704 see Hills, *Rock*, pp. 25, 48, 53, 97, 99, 114; W.G.F. Jackson, *The Rock of the Gibraltarians: a History of Gibraltar* (Gibraltar: Gibraltar Books, 4th edn, 2001), pp. 64–5; C. Caruana, *The Rock under a Cloud* (Cambridge: Silent

It is difficult to trace precisely how, after 1704, the economy of Gibraltar developed and to say much that is exact about living standards during the first century or so of British rule, given the paucity of statistical data. Because the town of Gibraltar became a 'free port', there are not even sound figures for external trade. However, much can be said about some determining factors. It will be shown especially that the partition of the region of Gibraltar had very important consequences for the economy, occupations and living standards, and by implication for a common sense of identity among civilians.

Supplying the garrison and the town

The principal determining factor was obviously the Treaty of Utrecht, which confirmed the transfer to Great Britain of sovereignty over the peninsula (only). British governments in Gibraltar and in London were always aware that the Spanish government deplored the loss. Although, as noted in the previous chapter, British ministers were willing at various times during the eighteenth century to negotiate a withdrawal, they would not allow Gibraltar to be lost in the same fashion as they had gained it. Hence, British Gibraltar was robustly garrisoned to withstand siege. The military presence offered economic opportunities for civilians.

Captain Drinkwater conveniently provides information on soldiers' pay at the time of the 'Great Siege', 1779–83, when the garrison, he says, was nearly 4,000 men. Troops were paid in Spanish currency, but he also gives the sterling equivalent: nine pence a day for a sergeant, six pence for a corporal, four and a half pence for a private. Officers, of course, were paid substantially more. Assuming that the garrison was made up *only* of privates, this means that soldiers' pay grossed up to £27,375 a year,[3] of which a high proportion would be spent locally. Moreover, in addition, each soldier in the garrison received weekly rations: 7 lbs of bread, 2½ lbs of beef, 1 lb of pork, 10 oz of butter, half a gallon of 'pease', 3 pints of 'groats'.[4] Officers of different rank were entitled to receive multiples of

Footnote 2 (*cont.*)

> Books, 1989), p. 8; I. Lopez de Ayala, *The History of Gibraltar*, [1782], translated and continued by J. Bell (London: Pickering, 1845), pp. 2–3, 25–8, 94–5, 101–4, 132, Appendix I; A.P. Paredes (ed.), *Documentos del Archivo Municipal de San Roque (1502–1704)* (Algeciras: Ilustre Ayuntamiento de San Roque, Delegación de Archivos, 2006); and F.M. Montero, *Historia de Gibraltar y su Campo* (Cádiz: Imprenta de la Revista Médica, 1860), who draws much from A.H. del Portillo, *Historia de Gibraltar* [1610–1622] (ed.) A. Torremocha Silva (Algeciras: Centro Asociado de la U.N.E.D., c.1995), pp. 42–6, 53–65.

3 4.5 pence a day, times 365 days a year, times 4,000 men, divided by 240 pence in the pound, to give a total in pounds sterling.

4 The hulled and crushed grain of oats, wheat or other cereals, in effect the basics for porridge. Pints and gallons were measures of loose substances as well as of liquids.

these quantities for the expected number of their servants, from two rations up to six, too much at the top end for personal consumption, and hence either they received their monetary equivalents 'or dispose[d] of them to the Jews . . . who are always ready to purchase, or take them in barter'.[5]

Garrison numbers fluctuated but, as noted earlier, they were always substantial, never less than 1,100 and usually 3,000 or more, sometimes much more.[6] In 1754, for example, there were reported to be 3,026 soldiers stationed at Gibraltar. Moreover, convention allowed officers, and by permission other ranks, to have with them their wives and children, a further 1,426. The total of 4,452 considerably exceeded the number of civilians, reckoned at that date to be a mere 1,810.[7] Although Drinkwater refers to a garrison of around 4,000 at the time of the siege, another near-contemporary calculation gives a total for officers and men in June 1779 of 5,382, plus some 1,500 dependants.[8] The civilian population according to the 1777 census was only 3,201. Even in 1814, when civilians totalled 10,136, the garrison population of 6,754, made up of 5,139 officers and men plus 749 women and 866 children, was still proportionately a very substantial presence.[9] Moreover, pay had risen by the end of the century: a private who had been receiving eight pence a day by 1797 was getting one shilling a day thereafter, further boosting garrison-generated demand.[10]

To get a more complete impression of the potential consumer demand of the British settlement, we need also to factor in the resident civilian population. Of course, initially its growth was substantially a consequence of the economic stimulus provided by the military presence. True, as noted in the previous chapter, the number of civilians had only grown back by the end of the century to what it had been before 1704, and, as we shall see, occupations varied and therefore so did purchasing power and consequent prompts to economic activity. However, it needs little imagination to recognise that even the slow expansion in their numbers, from about a hundred still there after the military takeover in

5 J. Drinkwater, *A History of the Late Siege of Gibraltar* (London: Spilsbury, 1785), pp. 39–40. See also House of Commons Parliamentary Paper [henceforth HCPP], *Further Proceedings of the Lords Commissioners of His Majesty's Treasury*, 118, 1801, p. 76, for a rations list, headed by then with twenty-four rations for the governor, and similarly in 1814 according to the enclosure to TNA, CO91/61, Don to Bathurst, 4 Nov 1814.

6 For numbers see references in Chapter 1, note 11.

7 T. James, *The History of the Herculanean Straits* (London: Rivington, Cadell and Dodsley, 1771), vol. 2, p. 320.

8 J. Bell in Ayala, *Gibraltar*, p. 180, and R. Chartrand, *Gibraltar 1779–83 The Great Siege* (Oxford: Osprey, 2006), pp. 32–3.

9 Howes, *Gibraltarian*, p. 44.

10 Hills, *Rock*, p. 360.

1704 to 5,339 in 1801, constituted numerically a growth in potential consumers, as well as in entrepreneurs and labourers. In market terms, the civilian settlers in Gibraltar were additional sources of demand.

In aggregate, in the early decades, say about 1730, there were probably fewer than 3,500 people living on the Rock (2,300 belonging to the garrison and 1,200 civilians). However, by 1779 there were around 10,000 (6,800 garrison, 3,200 civilians), and by 1814 nearly 17,000 (6,800 garrison, 10,100 civilians). By the latter date this was a larger resident population than ever before in the history of the Gibraltar peninsula, and a market of understandable appeal to the enterprising. The income and living standards of a significant proportion of Gibraltar's civilians certainly benefited from, and indeed may have been utterly dependent on, the demand which the military were pumping into the local economy, but there was the additional and growing civilian market.

Fresh food was much in demand by all inhabitants. Drinkwater refers to supplies of fish, including 'John-doree, turbot, soal, salmon, hake, rock-cod, mullet and ranger', plus mackerel in season and shellfish. Also available were 'roots and garden-stuff' from plots tended by civilians on the neutral ground and, during the siege, at the south end of the Rock.[11] Goats and a few cattle and sheep also secured some grazing. There was also originally some wood for fuel and building, before the Rock was denuded of timber during that century's sieges, and there was much stone, though building materials still had to be imported.[12] Although the British garrison inherited wells and an aqueduct supplying water, constructed in 1571, each army company seems to have employed a waterman with a donkey to distribute supplies.[13] Civilians needed water too, and if not from wells or their own roof-top cisterns, then from similar peripatetic suppliers.

However, the town (and garrison) of Gibraltar had never been able to meet its own needs from peninsula resources. The Rock was too small and too barren to supply more than a trickle of necessities, and neither then nor later did Gibraltar develop much of a manufacturing base. Had the population wedged there by the end of the eighteenth century grown up earlier in the seventeenth century, then the route across the isthmus would have daily witnessed long convoys of supply carts, and the port would have been packed with shipping from southern and eastern Spain. The increasing civilian plus garrison population of Gibraltar in the eighteenth century was therefore a demand-led and supply-side challenge,

11 Drinkwater, *Siege*, pp. 38–9.
12 S. Conn, *Gibraltar in British Diplomacy in the Eighteenth Century* (New Haven: Yale University Press, 1942), pp. 23, 26.
13 T.J. Finlayson, 'Gibraltar's water supply', *Gibraltar Heritage Journal*, 2 (1994), 60–2; D. Ellicott, *Our Gibraltar* (Gibraltar: Gibraltar Museum Committee, 1975), p. 102.

and its sustained growth is evidence of a challenge well met, though not without much stress and discomfort.

External trade

The well-being of Gibraltar's garrison and civilian population had been sustained in the past by external trade links, overland with the Campo and other parts of Spain, and with overseas markets. Such connections were prejudiced by the British occupation and the partition of Gibraltar. Understandable Spanish objections to 'business as usual' across a new and contested frontier were coded into the Treaty of Utrecht. Article X severely limited the opportunities for legitimately securing supplies from Spain for the garrison and civilians. Trade by sea between Gibraltar and the coasts of Spain was allowed, except in goods deemed contraband by the Spanish authorities. However, the historically more substantial and convenient overland route for imports and exports was explicitly barred. There was to be no 'open communication by land with the country round about', to avoid (unspecified) 'abuses and frauds'. The isthmus was henceforth supposed to be a barrier and no longer a link. Goods were not to be imported into Gibraltar overland from Spain, on pain of confiscation; and likewise the 'fraudulent importations of goods' into Spain from Gibraltar were to be blocked. However, it was recognised that communications between Gibraltar and the coast of Spain by sea 'may not at all times be safe or open' –either by storms, one must assume, or the danger from such as North African corsairs. Accordingly, the king of Spain in those special circumstances would allow provisions and other necessities to be bought 'in the neighbouring territories of Spain' and brought in overland for the use of the garrison, civilians and those on ships in the harbour, but only in cash and not by barter or exchange.[14] Lieutenant-Governor Irwin employed this concession in 1766 when he requested permission from the governor of the adjacent Spanish territory to buy, for cash and free of duties, 'twenty sheep and an Ox or two . . . for my Table and those of the Officers under my command'.[15]

It is true that an uncertain proportion of the garrison's supplies was also shipped in from Britain. These included, of course, munitions and other bits of military kit, but security in emergencies and especially against siege required the laying down of imported foodstuffs. The garrison received in the eighteenth century such supplies as might travel well in slow-moving sailing ships, even including some livestock, but largely what was stored and served up in times of duress were 'salt provisions'. Irwin dared to describe these in his letter to Spain

14 Text of Article X in Hills, *Rock*, pp. 222–3, Jackson, *Rock*, pp. 333–4, and, in English and Spanish, www.gibconnect.com/~loonylenny/utrecht/utrecht.htm.
15 GGA, Box: Letters to San Roque 1757–69, Irwin to Crillon, 23 January 1766.

as 'very sufficient and wholesome', but he conceded that they were 'by no means so palatable as fresh'.[16] Moreover, the civilian population could have no licit claim on that provided for troops. For them, the private sector must meet their needs.

Irwin's letter also indicates from where some fresh produce would normally be obtained. 'Beef and Mutton for the Troops' should have come from Tetuan in Morocco, but supply had been prevented by the 'badness of the weather'.[17] What might not be herded across the isthmus had to be ferried in from across the Mediterranean. As mentioned in the previous chapter, a very important reaction to the partition of Gibraltar and the (largely) severed supply link to Spain had been the British government's declaration of Gibraltar as a 'free port' in February 1706.[18] This was designed to attract supplies for civilians and for soldiers, to be shipped in by traders based in Gibraltar or overseas. Ships of all nations, including, remarkably, those with which Britain might even be at war, were free to trade with Gibraltar provided that they also brought in supplies. The lure was that while shippers still paid harbour fees, supplies could be (or at least should be) landed without the payment of those import duties which significantly funded government administrations throughout Europe (including Britain) before the days of nineteenth-century free trade. Merchants might therefore increase their profits either by risking a higher mark-up on tax-free items or by extending their market penetration by selling cheaper goods.

As early as 1712 it was reported that boats were arriving from Barbary, Portugal and even clandestinely from Spanish ports like Malaga, Marbella, Estepona and Tarifa, even though these were enemy towns in an ongoing war. The goods included 'wine, bread, fruit and other refreshments'.[19] By the 1770s, supplies of tobacco, sugar, cotton, timber, dried cod, rum, rice and maize were being brought in by North American, Danish and Dutch merchantmen, and also cattle, sheep, fowl, wood, barley, straw, citrus fruits and oil from North Africa (Tetuan, Tangier, Mogador), wine, brandy, macaroni, lemons, oil, candles, salt, soap, muslin and even chestnuts from Italy (Leghorn, Genoa), and wine, sugar, biscuits, oil, fowl, eggs and charcoal from Spain (Cádiz, Estepona).[20] Drinkwater

16 Ibid.
17 Ibid.
18 TNA/PC1/3170, Papers Relating to Establishment of Civil Government 1705–1758, meeting of Privy Council, 17 May 1705 (OS). The order-in-council is dated 7 Feb 1705 (OS), that is, 18 Feb 1706 (NS), premature insofar as Gibraltar was then still a possession of 'King Charles III'. For a copy of Acting Governor Roger Elliott's confirmatory proclamation of April 1706 see TNA, PC1/16/13.
19 BL Add Mss 10034, 'Some Remarks Concerning Gibraltar, humbly offered by Colonel Joseph Bennett', 22 Nov 1712.
20 Conn, *Gibraltar*, pp. 257–8; Hills, *Rock*, pp. 293–4; Howes, *Gibraltarian*, p. 15. For the importance of Morocco as a source of supply see TNA, CO91/62, 'An Account

after the siege, recollecting in tranquillity, provides a mouth-watering litany: 'The Moors, in times of peace, supply the garrison with ox-beef, mutton, veal, and poultry, on moderate terms; and from Spain they procure pork, which is remarkable for its sweetness and flavour. Fruits of all kinds, such as melons, oranges, green figs, grapes, pomegranates, etc. are brought in abundance from Barbary and Portugal: and the best wines are drank at very reasonable prices'.[21]

Of course, these were not charitable handouts. Gibraltar had to turn human want into market demand. The goods being supplied had to be paid for in cash or by exchange. The garrison had a substantial amount of 'unearned' cash to spend, provided by British taxpayers, as soldiers' pay or as credits to the government for military and administrative expenses, and some of it was available to spend on imports. Indirectly, the same financial source was enhancing the purchasing power of civilians. Civilians were earning fees, wages or cash by selling their services, their labour or their home-produced supplies to the garrison (although as noted there was little enough of these last). In addition, there were those civilians who earned an income by servicing the overseas entrepreneurs who needed dockside help in landing supplies, porters to shift stuff and middlemen to help the selling on. Some of Gibraltar's civilian residents also earned a pretty penny for themselves as agents of overseas suppliers or indeed by themselves setting up as shipowners and importers. Finally, of course, other civilians were indirectly acquiring incomes from the same ultimate sources, by selling services, labour and produce to those civilians who were directly involved, with which to buy their own imported supplies.

Nevertheless, it is abundantly clear that additional and substantial sources of income were needed to pay for externally produced supplies. This came from the re-export trade. Because Gibraltar had been declared a 'free port', no duties were to be levied on exports either. Since Gibraltar had no native produce to sell, it was clearly intended that it might develop economically as an entrepot, a market centre, buying in goods as imports and selling them on as re-exports, literally to wherever the wind might blow (or, as we shall see, deviously overland). Gibraltar's location, adjacent to the Atlantic and at the mouth of the Mediterranean, was a marketing advantage (though wind and currents were not reliably accommodating). A substantial amount of what was imported into Gibraltar – and for some commodities a very substantial amount – was consumed by neither civilians nor garrison. For example, those who supplied Gibraltar from North America with large quantities of tobacco were taking away large quantities of manufactured goods which had previously been brought in for transhipment from Britain and also from France and Holland. Other re-exports were exchanged in Gibraltar for

of Lieut-General Bland's Conduct . . .', pp. 53–4, and also T. Benady, 'Jewish community', p. 145.
21 Drinkwater, *Siege*, p. 39.

wines and citrus fruits slipped in by sea from Spanish suppliers. Manufactured goods, like textiles, were likewise getting through Gibraltar even into Spain and France.[22] As Ayala wrote in 1782, 'Its excellent situation makes it an Emporium for Africa, the Mediterranean, and the Ocean.'[23] The profits and wages generated directly by such re-export activities, and indirectly by the services and labour they supported, attracted yet more immigrants and settlers, boosted Gibraltar incomes and helped substantially to pay for imported supplies. Gibraltar's civilian population after 1704 was driven to entrepreneurial achievement because the easy land route option available before 1704 was being obstructed.

This did not mean that some entrepreneurs based in Gibraltar did not seek to reopen old links by dubious means. The Spanish view about the illegitimacy of overland trade, and in addition their opposition to imports by any route into Spain of goods deemed contraband, were made apparent at Utrecht and repetitively in numerous subsequent exchanges with the British government in London, the British ambassador in Madrid and the British governor in Gibraltar. Like other European nation states in the eighteenth century, Spain determined both whether and at what level duties should be imposed on imports. Spanish authorities believed it was in Spanish national interests to protect Spanish producers by levying duties on classes of imported goods, thereby driving up their prices, and also to raise state revenues by collecting such taxes. Violent clashes between excise men and smugglers getting goods untaxed and illegally across the English Channel from France showed that the British government in the eighteenth century also adhered to the conventional practice.[24] English smugglers took the risks because the level of duties imposed generated a ready domestic demand for cheaper, untaxed supplies, and the same was true for those 'businessmen' seeking to transport untaxed contraband into Spain. The difference in the Spanish case was that the British government had signed up at Utrecht to the frontier closure and to the trading restrictions which the Spanish authorities insisted were necessary to prevent such illicit trade.

Entrepreneurs tempted into the smuggling game therefore had to evade the law. It is in the nature of this business that statistical evidence indicative of scale, especially at this place and in this period, is absent. What is known is that smugglers were, in economic terms, 'merely' engaged in a branch of the re-export trade. As in the case of their legitimate colleagues, their success generated

---

22 Hills, *Rock*, pp. 217, 293.
23 Ayala, *Gibraltar*, p. 176.
24 E.V. Hoon, *The Organization of the English Customs System, 1696–1786* (Newton Abbot: David and Charles, 1968, 1st edn 1937); F.F. Nicholls, *Honest Thieves: The Violent Heyday of English Smuggling* (London: Heinemann, 1973); C. Winslow, 'Sussex smugglers' in D. Hay et al, *Albion's Fatal Tree: Crime and Society in Eighteenth-Century England* (London, Penguin, 1975), pp. 119–66.

incomes for themselves and their agents on the Gibraltar side of the frontier (and also for their Spanish distributors across the way). Smuggling therefore helped to pay for other goods legitimately imported and consumed in Gibraltar, and thereby made more secure Gibraltar's economic foundations and the material well-being of the civilian population. The usual practice was for Gibraltar merchants either directly to buy and ship in quantities of goods from overseas, like tobacco, textiles and other manufactured goods, far beyond the requirements of civilian or garrison consumers, or to buy from overseas suppliers similarly excessive volumes, all tax free. These supplies were not always landed, but could be stored in boats in the bay. Usually those carrying the stuff into Spain by sea were Spanish, Portuguese or Genoese, or, if by subterfuge across that supposed closed land frontier, mainly Spanish. They took the personal risk for some of the financial profit.[25]

'Regulating' the economy

Though one can model in descriptive terms how the eighteenth-century Gibraltar economy worked, some further particulars need to be factored in. This was an economy which was managed, after a fashion. State intervention affected in particular how civilians were allowed economically to operate. The definition of Gibraltar as a 'free port' will mislead if it is assumed that, more generally, Gibraltar functioned as a free market. Such a creature barely breathed even in eighteenth-century Britain. For good reason Adam Smith published in London in 1776 his manifesto for a free market economy, *The Wealth of Nations*. State interference, regulation, protection, assistance – the use of negative or positive terms would reflect whether or not one personally benefited from what government did – characterised both Britain and Gibraltar. But one additional feature determined official practice in Gibraltar. The territory occupied by the allies in 1704 and annexed by the British in 1713 was established as a military base to be managed by military governors, not as a trading post managed by a trading company.

There were, consequently, managerial actions which negatively affected economic performance. For example, many of the prime sites in the territorially limited confines of the Rock were occupied by the military. Certain parts of the town were off limits to civilians; gates were locked at night; a curfew was imposed. As noted, permission for entry and residence was required. However, such constraints self-evidently concerned military security, which was (or should have been) the principal concern of the governor as commander-in-chief, and on the whole the imperative seems in this century to have been accepted by civilians.

25　Benady, 'Jewish community', p. 148; Hills, *Rock*, pp. 372–3; T. Benady, 'Smuggling and the law', *Gibraltar Heritage Journal*, 13 (2006), 89–93.

In addition, sometimes in response to 'abuses' and public demand, governors attempted to regulate prices by proclamation, for example of wine in April 1728 and of beef, mutton, hogs, geese, pigeons and so on by a garrison order in May 1741; and there were repeated attempts to regulate currency exchange rates and coinage, for example by an order in November 1741.[26] In a century when magistrates in England were legally expected to fix prices and wages and prevent forestalling there was nothing unexpected about this.[27]

However, civilians (and indeed some in the military) complained that other interventions in the market served not the military needs of the garrison or the civilian needs of consumers but the financial self-interest of the governor. Mention was made in the previous chapter of the monetary gain which some governors plotted to secure from the granting of leases. Back in Britain, and elsewhere in the British world in the eighteenth century, there was nothing exceptional about officeholders lining their already bulging pockets with such supplements to salary. But some of the practices in Gibraltar became notorious, especially in the first half-century of British rule, when they undoubtedly affected how civilians were obliged to conduct their economic activities.

The very first British-appointed governor, Roger Elliott, serving from 1707 to 1711, saw fit to impose licence fees on merchants, calibrated according to ethnicity (Jews paying most). Colonel Ralph Congreve, lieutenant-governor from 1713 to 1716, seems to have been particularly brutal and blatant in his nest-feathering, and indifferent to the notion of a free market. While formerly anyone with a supply could sell beef to the garrison, for a tidy sum Congreve sold the monopoly on slaughtering cattle to just four men (who were also obliged to provide him with choice cuts free of charge); and even that deal was overturned when another aspiring tycoon, and a Spaniard to boot, offered a still larger payment for the sole privilege. Likewise Jasper Clayton, lieutenant-governor 1726–30, more than doubled his official salary by squeezing the economically active, for example by selling monopolies to chosen contractors who wanted to supply the garrison. Francis Columbine, lieutenant-governor 1730–39, also sold permits to those wanting to fish in the bay or to keep a cow, pig or goat. Some governors 'modified' the notion of Gibraltar as a free port by taxing imports of wine, brandy and rum for the benefit of their private purses,

26 BL, Add Mss 23643, Proclamation by Lieutenant-Governor Clayton, 27 April 1728; 'Historical Events', *Gibraltar Directory 1914*, pp. 100–2, 121; R.J.M. Garcia, 'The currency and coinage of Gibraltar in the 18th and 19th centuries', *Gibraltar Heritage Journal*, 2 (1994), esp. 15–17.

27 The classic contextual exposition is E.P. Thompson, 'The moral economy of the English crowd in the eighteenth century', *Past and Present*, 50 (1971), 76–136; see also D. Hay and N. Rogers, *Eighteenth-Century English Society* (Oxford: Oxford University Press, 1997), pp. 84–113.

not of the administration's treasury. Humphrey Bland, governor 1749–54, insisted on more probity than his predecessors, but unsurprisingly the instructions he set down to guide his successors were not followed to the letter by all of them. Moreover, even he privileged 'British merchants' by allowing them to import wine, albeit after payment of a duty, while imposing a duty 50 per cent higher on 'foreigners'. He also required retailers to acquire a licence to sell wine, fixed prices and prohibited the sale of spirits in public houses, and he licensed a distillery for the production of the Moroccan Jewish drink *mahya* ('horrid Stuff', he called it), though all these measures were his (unsuccessful) attempts to reduce the intoxication level among soldiers and not for his personal gain. He also insisted that to benefit British subjects, at the expense of the French and the Dutch, 'no other Linen but that Manufactured in Great Britain' should be imported, whether for use in Gibraltar or for re-export.[28] This was classic mercantilist manipulation of the market by an authoritarian government, and this plus corruption and petty tyranny probably discouraged some British entrepreneurs from setting up and staying.[29] Jewish merchants, arriving from Morocco where business, bribes and brutality were common bedfellows, seem to have shrugged off such indignities and stayed.[30]

Smuggling, as noted, was important for the economic health of the community as well as of individuals, but London ministers and some governors judged that there were sound political and military reasons why a trade which so angered Spanish officials in Madrid and across Gibraltar's frontier should be discouraged.[31] The consequent 'interference' by some Gibraltar governors in the trade constituted another case, to the aspiring free marketeer, of negative economic regulation. Whether smuggling still occurred depended on the vigilance, energy and indeed probity of Gibraltar's governing elite. Some governors, with a nod and a wink, and something in their pockets, turned a blind eye to corsairs shipping contraband goods from Gibraltar's port into Spain.[32] Bland, again, was adamant that this trade must be stopped, and attempted to insist, for

28 Jackson, *Rock*, pp. 114, 125–6, 189; Hills, *Rock*, pp. 229–30, 289–90; Ellicott, *Our Gibraltar*, pp. 21, 26–7; Benady, 'Jewish community', pp. 146, 154–5; TNA, CO91/62, 'An Account of Lieut-General Bland's Conduct . . .', pp. 7–9, 16–17, 31–3, 88–92, and CO91/11, 12 June 1752 contract; GGA, Crown Lands Series A, copies of orders, contracts, etc, 1 July 1749–17 Dec 1753.

29 For example, on such grounds see complaints of British merchants against General Eliott, 1783–84, TNA, PC1/16/13.

30 Benady, 'Jewish community', pp. 146, 148–9, 151.

31 See for example the instructions, including for the suppression of smuggling, given to George Bubb on his appointment as ambassador at Madrid in 1715: Hills, *Rock*, pp. 230–1; and TNA, T1/369/5, Thomas Fowke, governor, to Henry Fox, secretary of state, 6 Feb 1756, requesting authority to take further repressive action.

32 Hills, *Rock*, p. 289.

example, that only enough tobacco for local consumption should be landed.[33] Enterprising operators then got round the rules by using hulks in the bay, over which the governor had no jurisdiction, as floating warehouses from where to run supplies ashore.[34] Some of Bland's successors were equally hostile to the business, and made efforts to inhibit the trade by naval vigilance and frontier patrols. In 1765, for example, Lieutenant-Governor Irwin was obliged to defend his actions against criticisms by Gibraltar merchants, and the following year he attempted to ingratiate himself with his opposite number in Spain by reporting that 'since I last saw you I have made two seizures of Tobacco, one indeed only of fifty pounds going into Spain by land, but the other on board a Vessel in bags containing some thousand weight'.[35] Good for the external political relations of Gibraltar; bad for business.

But there were also positive steps which governors of necessity took to protect and advance economic activity which advantaged civilian merchants. As indicated, the security of the garrison depended on external supplies and, given the Utrecht rules, that usually meant overseas supplies. Securing facilities for troops also opened up supply chains for civilians, and trading opportunities. One positive step by governors, with immense economic consequences as well as the demographic ones noted in the previous chapter, was to disregard the Utrecht stipulation which prohibited the residence of Jews in Gibraltar. Of course it was not the Jews who were desired, but the trade in essential supplies which Jewish merchants brought with them. The urgency of the matter, as perceived locally, prompted some governors (also not unmindful of prospects for personal gain) to ignore orders and obscure from ministers in London what they were about.[36]

Since Morocco was the obvious source for fresh supplies and since Moroccan traders were often Spanish-speaking Jews (whose Sephardic ancestors had, notoriously, been driven out of Spain in 1492), it was, to say the least, convenient to welcome Jews from Morocco as trading partners. This last was explicitly allowed by a treaty signed by Britain with the emperor of Fez and Morocco in 1721 and extended in 1729, although it self-evidently conflicted with obligations under the 1713 Treaty of Utrecht.[37] However diplomatically unsound, the entitlement was acceptable to Gibraltar governors as economically valuable.

33 TNA, CO91/62, 'An Account of Lieut-General Bland's Conduct . . .', pp. 34–9.
34 Jackson, *Rock*, pp. 189–90.
35 TNA, CO91/14, Irwin to Conway, secretary of state, 16 Dec 1765; GGA, Box: Letters to San Roque 1757–69, postscript to Irwin to Crillon, 23 Jan 1766. See also ibid, Governor William Home to Governor of San Roque, 26 July and 16 Sept 1757, Irwin to the Marquis Vanmarche, 20 May 1766, and John Raleigh, secretary to Governor Edward Cornwallis, to Don Phelipe de Pradon, 27 April 1769.
36 Hassan, 'Treaty of Utrecht', pp. 160–79.
37 Hills, *Rock*, pp. 227–8, 233–4, 283–4; Benady, 'Jews in Gibraltar, 1704–1783', pp. 92–7; Benady, 'Jewish community', pp. 149–50.

But nurturing a relationship with Morocco which was profitable to Gibraltar's economy and Gibraltar merchants needed regular Gibraltar government management. For one thing, it required responding firmly but diplomatically whenever Spanish coastguards, searching for tobacco, intercepted vessels flying British colours and trading to and from Morocco. As one example of many, a protest was made in 1752 when goods to the value of two or three thousand dollars, including gunpowder but on this occasion not tobacco, were seized en route from Gibraltar to Morocco. Such confiscations threatened external commercial exchanges, which were recognised as 'the principal means of our being supplied with fresh Provisions'.[38] Similarly, there were official protests in 1796 following the 'very hostile and outrageous' interception of a Gibraltar vessel bringing in supplies from Barbary, but not, it was protested, carrying either tobacco or a Spanish smuggler.[39]

However, good relations with the (somewhat fragmentary) authorities in the empire of Morocco were also required, as Governor Bland stressed, for the supply of 'live Cattle, Sheep, Fowls, etc', as well as for British commerce generally in the Mediterranean. However, 'as they are a Treacherous, Knavish people, little regarding the Faith of Treaties, when they can gain by the Breach of them, the Governor of Gibraltar must have a Watchful Eye over all their actions'.[40] Complaints to Gibraltar from Tetuan in 1752–53 about the illegitimate issue of 'Mediterranean passes' (which allowed vessels flying the British flag to pass unhindered) and about consequent alleged acts of piracy were treated with emollient phrases and conciliatory actions (and some threats), though it was privately asserted that 'the Moors are a most unreasonable and fickle people, capable on the most frivolous pretences to break with any Nation'.[41] It has been suggested that worrying about trade treaties was one of the pressures of office which in 1776 killed Governor Edward Cornwallis.[42] When French and Spanish forces in 1798

38 TNA, CO91/11, Col Lord George Beauclerk, officer temporarily in command, to British ambassador in Madrid, 3 April 1752 (OS), enclosing letter from Governor of San Roque 6 April 1752 (NS).
39 GGA, Letters to Madrid, Governor O'Hara to Earl of Bute, 7 April 1796.
40 TNA, CO91/62, 'An Account of Lieut-General Bland's Conduct . . .', pp. 43–57, and see also CO91/11, Col William Herbert, officer temporarily in command, to Earl of Holdernesse, secretary of state, 2 Feb 1752 (OS), urging diplomatic action to sustain cooperative relations with Tangier.
41 TNA, CO91/11, Herbert to Holdernesse, 27 Jan 1753, and see also correspondence from W. Petticrew, HM Consul in Tetuan, and with the Alcaide of Tetuan, Mohamet Lucas, 1752–53, and, continuing the dispute, a 'Remonstrance of the . . . British Merchants and other Inhabitants of Gibraltar', 26 Feb 1754, and a 'Protest' from the Alcaide, 28 Feb 1754. For some context see T. Benady, 'The settee cut: Mediterranean passes issued at Gibraltar', *The Mariner's Mirror*, 87:3 (2001), 281–96.
42 J. Oliphant, 'Edward Cornwallis, 1713–76', *Oxford Dictionary of National Biography* (Oxford: Oxford University Press, 2004) [henceforth *ODNB*]; on retaliatory action

'persuaded' Morocco to cut off supplies of fresh food to Gibraltar, Governor Charles O'Hara, perhaps of more robust stock, simply insisted that the emperor should be 'aw'd into a Compliance with his Treaty'.[43]

Fluctuations in the economy

What governors of Gibraltar could not manage was to smooth out the economic fluctuations caused by such exogenous factors as war and disease – and what administration anywhere has? Civilians making a living in Gibraltar in the eighteenth century were peculiarly vulnerable to instability by those very circumstances which accounted for their post–1704 immigration and settlement, namely the separation politically of Gibraltar from Spain and the exodus of its former population. Unhappily for quiet progress, Spanish attempts to recover the Rock militarily were frequent in a century notorious for war. That in the circumstances a civilian population arrived, settled, stayed and increased is indicative of attractive opportunities, if only in comparison with available alternatives.

It is not strange that so few civilians strayed into Gibraltar in the first twenty-five years or so after the military takeover. Rather, it is remarkable that any who arrived then remained. Early arrivals entered a post-siege ruin, with 'accommodation' to spare only after investment in reconstruction.[44] Unsurprisingly, the Spanish were initially very reluctant to allow restoration of the cross-border commerce which might have led to an easier living. The counter-attack of 1704–5 hardly invited relaxed relations. While the Treaty of Utrecht ended international war in 1713, Gibraltar's governors in the subsequent cold-war period could do little enough to ease matters for officers in the garrison, let alone for civilians. The land border remained closed. Even a conditional toleration of sea communications in 1717 was revoked when, in 1718, another Anglo-Spanish war broke out over matters not directly concerning Gibraltar but which again closed down that trading option for civilians, though it did revive healthily the Gibraltar opportunities for Moroccan Jews.[45] Even these advantages were jeopardised when Anglo-Spanish relations in 1727 collapsed again into war, and this time Gibraltar residents faced siege. It was preceded by the expulsion of 400 Spanish residents, caused some deaths from military action and more from disease, and pushed up

Footnote 42 (*cont.*)
    against the 'Emperor of Morocco' see his letter to Egremont, secretary of state, 5 Aug 1762, TNA, CO91/14.
43 TNA, CO91/40, O'Hara to Portland, secretary of state, 16 June 1798, and see also letters of 18 Aug and 29 Dec 1798. For British and especially Gibraltar relations with Morocco see also L. Colley, *Captives: Britain, Empire and the World 1600–1850* (London: Cape, 2002), esp. pp. 69–72, 98.
44 Benady, 'Jewish community', p. 147
45 Ellicott, *Our Gibraltar*, pp. 21–2; Benady, 'Jewish community', p. 149.

alarmingly the price of food (in war some traders always benefit from famine prices). The siege spluttered out after four months, but a peace was not signed until 1729. This brought no reconciliation and no opening of the land frontier, but left behind a diminished civilian population and therefore a reduced market. Indeed, new and formidable Spanish fortifications post-war scored the political division of the isthmus into the landscape.[46]

There were to be two more wars in the next half century, the War of Jenkins' Ear merging into the War of Austrian Succession, 1739–48 and the Seven Years' War, 1756–63. Neither originated in the dispute over Gibraltar and conflict took place away from the peninsula, but each threatened to lick around the Rock and neither concluded with a resolution conducive to relaxed relations across the land frontier. Sea communications only were made a little easier after 1748. Governors seem to have endeavoured, post-war, to improve cross-border political relations but, since this was by taking a firm hand against smugglers, their actions were economically not necessarily a good thing for Gibraltar.[47] However, war also brought its opportunities. Characteristic of eighteenth-century wars was the capture of prizes at sea by privateers as well as by warships, and their subsequent sale. The process had to pass through a court of law. The establishment in Gibraltar of a Vice-Admiralty Court in September 1739 probably did not bring financial benefits to Gibraltar operators until the Seven Years' War (when the loss to the British of Minorca removed the rival Mediterranean establishment). The subsequent selling and buying of ships and cargo then generated a lot of commercial activity and proved a nice little earner for some entrepreneurs.[48] Such sparks to enterprise did not ignite the whole business community, but added fuel to an economy which was already beginning to glow. By the 1760s and 1770s the supply problem for Gibraltar seems to have been eased by trading links and re-exports which no longer needed the succour of legitimate overland trade with Spain (when illegitimate would do). Virtually all the maritime powers had by then appointed resident consuls in Gibraltar to look after their interests.[49] Commenting on relations with Spain at this time, Captain Drinkwater, admittedly from the perspective of a garrison officer, later recalled the 'friendly intercourse' of these years, when 'communication was free and unlimited (except in point of introducing a contraband traffic into Spain)'. It was, he concluded, 'as eligible a station as any to which a soldier could be ordered'.[50]

46 Hills, *Rock*, pp. 264, 273–5, 283–4; Jackson, *Rock*, pp. 139–40; Ellicott, *Our Gibraltar*, pp. 24–5; Anon, *An Impartial Account of the Late Famous Siege of Gibraltar* (London: Warner, 1728); GL, Colonel Guise, 'Journal of the Siege of Gibraltar 1727', and W. Smith, 'Account of the Siege of Gibraltar 1727'.
47 Howes, *Gibraltarian*, p. 8; Benady, 'Jewish community', p. 149.
48 Benady, 'Jewish community', p. 155.
49 Ayala, *Gibraltar*, p. 174.
50 Drinkwater, *Siege*, p. 45.

It was therefore unfortunate for Drinkwater, and more so for resident civilian businessmen, their families and their employees, that in April 1775 American colonists rebelled against British imperial rule. This revolution unleashed an international war in June 1778, when France joined in to exploit the embarrassment of the old enemy; a year later, in June 1779, Spain also pitched in; on 21 June all communication between Gibraltar and Spain was cut off. The 'Great Siege' lasted until 5 February 1783, though the Treaty of Versailles which concluded the war was not signed until 3 September 1783. The personal suffering of the besieged soldiers and civilians is vividly recounted in post-war memoirs – injuries, deaths (more from sickness than gunfire), fear, the splitting up of families when women and children were evacuated.

Such accounts also allude to the destructive, disruptive, negative economic effects of the siege. During its nearly forty-three months, Gibraltar's dependence on overseas supplies for economic as well as military survival was exposed. Incoming supplies of food, of course only possible by sea, were for long periods constrained by enemy warships blockading the approaches. Making matters worse was the Spanish success in January 1781 in persuading the Sultan of Morocco to cut off supplies of fresh food. Price rises, profiteering and the rationing of foodstuffs; General Eliott's publicised experiment of living for eight days on a daily allowance of only four ounces of rice; the protests outside the bakers; the brutal treatment by soldiers of traders found to have secret stocks; the consumption of thistles, dandelions and wild leeks – such incidents are indicative of an economy as well as of a people under pressure. Those writing memoirs were aware of the underlying economic realities behind deeds of heroism when they recounted the arrival of relief convoys in February 1780, April 1781 and October 1782 and the penetration of the blockade by private-enterprise skippers, like Captain Fagg of the *Buck*, evading the Spanish fleet by superior seamanship in November 1779 (only to be caught later, and his vessel sunk). This was not even a war which brought much booty from prize money, the blockade being what it was and little enemy shipping being locally available for the taking.[51]

Recognised too was much physical destruction of the town of Gibraltar, partly at General Eliott's orders (the ploughing up of streets to soften the impact of cannon fire; the demolition of the tower of St Mary the Crowned lest it become a range-finding tool for Spanish gunners), but mainly due to the devastating effect

51 In addition to Drinkwater, see S. Ancell, *A Circumstantial Journal of the Long and Tedious Blockade and Siege of Gibraltar* (Liverpool: Wosencroft, 1784); Mrs C. Upton, *The Siege of Gibraltar from 12th April to 27th May 1781* (London: the author, n.d.); B.H.T. Frere (ed.), *Captain J. Spilsbury's A Journal of the Siege of Gibraltar 1779–1783* (Gibraltar: Gibraltar Garrison Library, 1908); GL, Mrs Green, 'A Lady's Experience in the Great Siege of Gibraltar 1779–83' reprinted from *The Royal Engineers Journal*, 1912.

on virtually all buildings of the 258,000 shots fired into Gibraltar by Spanish guns. Drinkwater recollected that the 'buildings in town . . . exhibited a most dreadful picture of the effects of so animated a bombardment. Scarce a house, north of the Grand parade was tenantable; all of them were deserted. Some few, near South-port, continued to be inhabited by soldiers families; but in general the floors and roofs were destroyed, and the bare shell only was left standing'.[52] Post-war reinvestment in property would be an economic diversion, and delayed for civilians because masons, most recruited in Italy and Portugal, were set first to work by General Eliott on garrison needs, including repairing the damaged fortifications. One visitor in 1792 reported that most of the town's houses were still ruins.

Reconstructing the economy was made more difficult because the embittered Spanish kept access from Gibraltar by sea, as by land, strictly controlled, enforcing quarantine rules, for example, on the pretext that Gibraltar's contacts with infectious Morocco made this necessary.[53] All ships which had called at Gibraltar were quarantined on arrival at Spanish ports. But in addition, General Eliott did not help civilians to get back on their feet when he demanded payment of arrears of ground rent. Moreover, he blocked one form of the re-export trade which might have aided economic (if not political) recovery by not allowing tobacco to be landed for smuggling into Spain. 'I suffer no tobacco to be exported from the Garrison', he reported in October 1786. The consequent economic loss is unintentionally revealed in his confident claim that 'Tobacco . . . is become a small proportion of British commerce, and it is foreign, not English tobacco that the Spaniards are disposed to run at all risks.'[54] Although the civilian population of Gibraltar in 1787 was (perhaps) 3,386 and therefore higher than the 3,201 of 1777, some of those post-war inhabitants were labourers temporarily employed in the reconstruction work, and the fall to 2,958 by 1791 is more indicative of the damaging legacy of the war, as is the reduction in the number of British and Jews, who formed the majority of the business community.[55]

But the gods of battle shift their favours. The French revolutionary and Napoleonic wars in which Britain, and therefore unavoidably Gibraltar, were

52 Drinkwater, *Siege*, pp. 161–2. See also Spilsbury, *Journal*, pp. 52, 61, Ancell, *Circumstantial Journal*, p. 124, and reproductions of Captain Thomas Davis's watercolours in the Gibraltar Museum, printed in T. Benady (ed.), *Guide to the Gibraltar Museum* (Grendon: Gibraltar Books, 1988), pp. 32–3.

53 There had been complaints earlier about such Spanish actions: GGA, Letters to Madrid, 'Memorial of the British Merchants and Traders residing in Gibraltar', 4 April 1776.

54 GGA, Letters to Madrid, General Eliott to Robert Liston, minister-plenipotentiary at Madrid, 9 Oct 1786.

55 Benady, 'Jewish community', pp. 156–9, the figure for 1791 adjusted from 2,874, as in Chapter 1, where the possibly inflated figure for 1787 is also noted.

involved ran from February 1793 to March 1802, and then from May 1803 to the signing of the final peace terms at Vienna in June 1815 and Paris in November 1815. The trickiest period was after the Spanish monarchy, with particular designs on Gibraltar, switched sides and joined France in 1796, and then after Napoleon installed his brother as king of Spain in 1808 and supported him with arms. Not even the popular Spanish uprising removed the threat to Gibraltar until French forces retreated from the region in the summer of 1812, by when British naval supremacy in the Mediterranean was also secure.

In the bleaker months, trade with Spain, whether legitimate or not, was damaged, and there were spasms of insecurity for shipping to and from Gibraltar, especially across the strait to Morocco, where, in the early days, French cruisers were intercepting as many as twenty merchantmen a month.[56] But this time the balance of naval power ensured that Gibraltar was never closely invested. The defeat of a Spanish fleet at Cape St Vincent in February 1797, and more definitively of combined French and Spanish forces at Trafalgar in October 1805, plus the acquisition of Malta by the British in 1800, ensured that thereafter the Mediterranean and the Atlantic became much safer zones for the kind of shipping upon which Gibraltar traders had over the previous century become increasingly reliant. The garrison remained substantial, the civilian population expanded considerably – itself a measure of economic activity – and there was the added bonus of the Royal Navy using the port as a service base: hence the development between 1799 and 1804 of the victualling yard at Rosia Bay, including the recently demolished water tanks.[57] The demand thereby generated by such 'mouths' was met by a wide range of imported supplies from Britain, including of course munitions but also potatoes, butter, cheese, sugar, coffee, cocoa, tobacco, cider, porter, barley, coal, bricks, cordage and other merchandise, for civilian as well as military consumption. Goods coming in from Portugal and Spain (more easily early and late in the wars) and other Mediterranean places included the predictable, such as oranges, fowl, eggs, vegetables, olives, vermicelli and onions, but also soap, salt, timber, tiles, charcoal and much else. Such provisions were part paid for by the garrison and the navy from the hugely increased taxes and credits raised in Britain, with income benefits to civilian employees and suppliers. There was also a healthy amount of re-exports, sometimes with no questions asked about ultimate destinations. British merchants, forbidden to trade with the enemy or unable because of Napoleon's continental blockade to get to other partners, were depositing goods in Gibraltar which other, supposedly neutral traders, like the Americans, could carry into mainland Europe. 'Neutrals' and privateers then carried out products from enemy-controlled territories. Anything passing through Gibraltar meant a cut for those locally involved in the exchange.

56 Ellicott, *Our Gibraltar*, p. 40.
57 Jackson, *Rock*, p. 188; 'Save the Rosia Tanks', www.gibconnect.com/~sda/.

In 1779, prior to the Great Siege, British goods deposited in Gibraltar were valued at less than £5,000, but in the years 1808 to 1812 they were reckoned to be worth around £1,000,000 a year. By then the Anglo-Spanish political relationship had become more amiable, and traders working through Gibraltar were even mopping up behind retreating French armies by re-exporting British manufactured goods to a southern Spain starved of products.[58] Indeed, according to one account, the value of cotton goods exported from Great Britain to Gibraltar in 1812–13 was £1,983,294, nearly 12 per cent of total cotton goods exports, making it the nation's fourth-largest overseas market and more valuable than the USA.[59] In 1814 Gibraltar was even the second-largest market for cast iron.[60] However fragile might be the figures, the rise in scale was unmistakable.

Moreover, these wars also provided a plentiful crop of captured shipping to process as prizes through courts of law and businessmen's pockets. Gibraltar's Vice-Admiralty Court handled 320 cases in 1807 alone; by 1812 at least twenty privateers with letters of marque signed by the governor were operating out of Gibraltar, raiding enemy shipping and selling their gains back at base. Judah Benoliel, who was to end his business career as an international banker with clients who included the future Pope Pius IX, advanced marvellously his fortunes as Gibraltar's leading privateer owner.[61] The booty was even a source of cheap imports. Governor O'Hara admitted in 1797 that 'Although I am by no means partial to Privateers, I must acknowledge that the Garrison and Inhabitants have derived great advantage in receiving many necessary comforts of life through their means particularly by Cargoes of Flour, Sugar and Wine.'[62] All of this primary business generated prosperity for those civilians involved in the financing, equipping and manning of vessels and in the receiving, shifting and selling of goods.

Regrettably, among the imports in September 1804 was yellow fever, probably brought to Europe among cargo from the West Indies and into Gibraltar from southern Spain, although the impact was possibly made worse by home-grown typhus or typhoid fever. In the past, quarantine regulations, which disrupted trade, had been imposed to keep out contagion, for example plague

58 Howes, *Gibraltarian*, pp. 41–3; Hills, *Rock*, pp. 371–2.
59 In 1814–15 the figure of £1,024,704 placed Gibraltar seventh, but not much below Italy, Holland and Portugal: HCPP, *An Account Showing the Amount of Cotton Goods Exported from Great Britain . . .*, HC266, 1815.
60 After the British West Indies: HCPP, *An Account of the Quantity of British Iron Exported . . .*, HC265, 1815, p. 5.
61 Ayala, *Gibraltar*, p. 190; Jackson, *Rock*, p. 203; Benady, 'Jewish community', pp. 159–61.
62 O'Hara to Portland, April 1797, quoted in L.A. Sawchuk, *Deadly Visitations in Dark Times: a Social History of Gibraltar* (Gibraltar: Gibraltar Government Heritage Division, 2001), p. 50.

from Barbary.[63] But there was no avoidance on this occasion. By January 1805, when the epidemic faded away, nearly 6,000 people had died, including 4,864 civilians.[64] There was a further outbreak in 1810, when the land frontier with Spain, recently reopened, was of necessity again closed, albeit temporarily, and a further repetition of the horrors occurred in 1813–14, when nearly a thousand more people, including 640 civilians, died of the disease. For individual families and even some sectors, the economic consequences were devastating, specifically when all communications with Spain were cut. Nevertheless, the prolonged benefits of external war exceeded the intense disruption of internal sickness, and the population continued to grow.[65]

Occupations, ethnicity and living standards

In sum, while the economic development of Gibraltar since 1704 had hardly been a smooth passage, the civilians who settled and some who had merely passed through had not made a bad fist of earning a living in a spot devoid of resources, amputated from its natural hinterland and politically exposed. Buffeted by war and disease, over which no one at the Rock had much control, their numbers had risen shakily, to be boosted considerably by the French revolutionary and Napoleonic wars at the turn of the century. The economy was becoming more diversified, and these changes and particular economic roles associated with ethnicity are apparent from analyses of occupations.

It has already been established that the British authorities wished Gibraltar to be primarily a British settlement, but that those of ethnic British roots were always and increasingly outnumbered by those with Mediterranean origins. It was still intended by regulation that at least the business community – predominantly men of course – as well as those directly employed by the garrison should be primarily British, and by the 1760s many still were, as traders and also as innkeepers, with all the rest to play supporting roles. However, such was the economic need for supplying the garrison and earning the wherewithal to pay for such goods that Jews from Morocco and others, often their kin, attracted for example from Portugal and London, had also long since become acceptable as residents, as merchants and shopkeepers, and also in such trades

63 TNA, CO91/62, 'An Account of Lieut-General Bland's Conduct . . .', pp. 57–64, 76–80, and *The Times*, 11 May 1787, p. 3.

64 Benady, 'Jewish community', pp. 161–2 suggests that this figure is an exaggeration, although the alternative contemporary figure he offers is still an appalling 'upwards of 2,200'. See also L.A. Sawchuk and S.D.A. Burke, 'Gibraltar's 1804 yellow fever scourge: the search for scapegoats', *Journal of the History of Medicine*, 53 (1998), 3–42.

65 Sawchuk, *Deadly Visitations*, pp. 59–60; Howes, *Gibraltarian*, pp. 39–40; Ellicott, *Our Gibraltar*, pp. 62–3, 87, 90, 92, 104; Jackson, *Rock*, pp. 196–7.

as baking and butchering, tailoring and shoemaking. Likewise, some at least of the Genoese also proved of superior use in business, because of their mercantile background. However, most from Genoa were taking up more humble roles, as seamen, fishermen and retailers of wines and spirits, and in such service roles as cooks, gardeners and general labourers. Genoese formed one of the two companies of porters licensed to operate in this regulated economy, the other being of Jews.[66]

Much of this is impressionistic, from contemporary observations, for it was not until the census of 1791 that data were collected about occupations, and even so it may be incomplete. Comparisons with the later census of 1814 are also made difficult by the shifts in occupational definitions which fog all such exercises. Nevertheless, certain clear shapes loom in the gloom, and the results are revealing of the nature of Gibraltar's civilian society at the turn of the century and of the changes accelerated by war.[67]

The rapid increase in population around the turn of the century was not actually represented in an equivalent increase in the working population. Indeed, as a proportion of the total population, the adult occupied population, aged 17 years and older, actually declined between 1791 and 1814, from 45 per cent (1,290 of 2,890) to 31 per cent (3,156 of 10,136). This is perhaps indicative of a more settled society with a low rate of participation by women in the paid workforce and containing more families with dependent children. A further initial observation may be ventured. As noted earlier, the civilian population before the Great Siege, 3,201 in 1777, was less than half of the numbers in the garrison, which, including wives and children, amounted to about 6,800 in 1779. By 1814 the situation had been substantially reversed, with the civilian population of 10,136 being 50 per cent more than the garrison total of 6,754. It would be a gross misreading to suggest that civilians no longer needed the employment and economic demand generated by the British garrison, but it is certainly true that it needed them to a lesser extent. A substantial section of the demand which prompted business supply and a significant amount of the work which generated employment were independent of that directly required by the garrison. We are tracking a commerce-led and diversifying economy. Businesses and workers were not quite so preoccupied with serving garrison officers, soldiers and their families. It is perhaps symptomatic that the trade of sutler – one who sold provisions

66 Ayala, *Gibraltar*, pp. 174–5; Howes, *Gibraltarian*, p. 6; Benady, 'Jewish community', pp. 153, 159.
67 The calculations which follow are based on the tables in the pioneering work of Howes, *Gibraltarian*, pp. 31–6, 59–68, using his principal occupational categories and accepting for this exercise his total population of 2,890 in 1791, not the 2,958 suggested by the raw census data. The discrepancy does not affect conclusions. The analysis of the data he offers should be read in conjunction with what follows.

to soldiers – disappeared as a census category between 1791 and 1814: those formerly so active had presumably spread their market activities.

As one would expect, the absolute numbers of those in 'Commerce' had risen considerably from the post-siege, pre-war 1791 figure of 309 to a late-war 1814 figure of 806, though this was only a modest increase, from 24 per cent to 26 per cent as a proportion of the total adult occupied population. However, the number of wholesale dealers or merchants had increased absolutely and proportionately, from only 32 in 1791, when they made up 10 per cent of the total in this 'Commerce' category, to 290 by 1814, a very substantial 36 per cent. The noticeable fall was of retailers or shopkeepers, down from 34 per cent in this category in 1791, when they numbered 106, to 23 per cent in 1814, by when their numbers had grown only to 182 – though the caveat must here be entered that some retailers were being listed separately as, for instance, grocers. Nevertheless, the emergence of a substantial merchant class is apparent.

Meanwhile, also appearing during the late wars was an economy in which proportionately more of the working population were, roughly speaking, unskilled supporters of those in business. The proportion of the adult occupied population in the category 'Miscellaneous including Unskilled' rose from 18 per cent in 1791 to 33 per cent by 1814, an increase from 226 people to 1,055. (Two respondents in this category, but only two, listed their occupation in 1814 as 'smuggler'.) Again, caution is required, particularly at sub-category level. For instance, the number of porters had declined but the number of carters had increased. Together they totalled 29 in 1791 and 123 by 1814, a proportionately fairly stable section in this 'Miscellaneous including Unskilled' category, 13 per cent in 1791 and 12 per cent in 1814. Even so, the increase in the numbers of such 'fetchers and carriers' lifted their share of the total adult occupied population from 2 per cent to 4 per cent, suggestive of more support for increased commercial activity. However, most striking was the rise in the number of servants. The employment of servants was in Gibraltar, as in Britain (and elsewhere), indicative of the affluence of others. In 1791 the census counted only 18 female servants, a mere 8 per cent of workers in the 'Miscellaneous and Unskilled' category, plus 104 male servants, a far more substantial 46 per cent. However, by 1814 the numbers were 256 female servants and 371 males, the women now making up 24 per cent of the category and the men 35 per cent. Together, male and female servants were only 9 per cent of the total adult occupied population in 1791, but 20 per cent by 1814. Nor is it a frivolous indicator of the affluence of some that the 1814 census recorded 56 proprietors of wine and eating houses (only 9 in 1791) and 12 owners of coffee houses (none listed in 1791).

Gibraltar's civilian society, like every other, was certainly divided into a social hierarchy. There are no figures for incomes, and only impressionistic data for expenditure. We know that wealthy merchants were building or acquiring prestigious town houses and furnishing them appropriately, and that some mixed easily with the officer elite of the garrison. They alone had been able to stump up, not without grumbles, the famine prices charged for foodstuffs during the Great Siege and at times in the Napoleonic wars.[68] The affluent shopper was there to be addressed, as in an advertisement in the *Gibraltar Chronicle* in 1802: 'William King respectfully informs the Ladies of Gibraltar, that he has just received from London, a very fashionable assortment of Ladies Dresses, Caps, Handkerchiefs, Fine Lace Veils, Lace for Cloaks, etc.'[69] On the other hand, there was undoubt-edly, as in every town, a category of the poor, and it takes little imagination to see them in the census data, scratching a living as casual workers, lacking proper accommodation, suffering most from price rises and from social disdain. 'On Saturday last, a woman of bad character having drunk herself dead in a shed near the Castle . . . was found shockingly dirty; it was thought advisable to destroy [the shed] immediately, as well as the furniture and clothes in it, in hopes that this would prove a useful lesson to the Lower Classes.'[70]

Nevertheless, this was not a society strongly divided between a small, employ-ing middle class and a large, employed class of manual workers. Looking in the census data for those who seem likely to have been employees, one can add up for 1791 and 1814 all those who worked for 'Government', whatever their skill or level of responsibility (268 in 1791, including a lot of seamen, 203 in 1814), and add in labourers (63 and 143), servants (96 and 587) and clerks, who would rightly deny being manual workers (24 and 155); and one might throw in waiters (none listed in 1791, only three in 1814), but the totals were still only 451 in 1791 and 1,091 in 1814. In both years they amounted to only 35 per cent of the total adult occupied population. True, the remaining 65 per cent should be divided into employers and self-employed, though the data do not allow us to do this. Nevertheless, the impression left is robust enough, that turn-of-the-century Gibraltar offered the inevitable hierarchy of wealth and status, like eighteenth-century British towns, but one in which the large middle ground was made up of clerks, shopkeepers and self-employed tradesmen (like carpenters, masons, fish-ermen, bakers – and a surprisingly large number of barbers), below them a fair number of manual workers, with a substantial group of merchants on top, plus just a few professional people (such as teachers, doctors, nurses and clergy).

In addition to this hierarchy it is also necessary to observe the divisions by ethnicity. Although the distinctions are not absolute, there was a clustering by ethnicities in certain occupations. First, it is important to notice that the number of British in the adult occupied population increased from 111 in 1791 to 379 in 1814, a rise, remarkably, in their share from 7 per cent to 12 per cent. Although declining as a proportion of the total population, the British loomed larger in

68 See sources in note 51 above and Ellicott, *Our Gibraltar*, pp. 47, 48, 76.
69 *Gibraltar Chronicle*, 21 May 1802.
70 *Gibraltar Chronicle*, 13 July 1805.

these war years in the world of work. Moreover, they increased their numbers especially in 'Commerce' from 30 (16 per cent of the British at work in 1791) to 185 (49 per cent of their number), and thereby the British presence among all those engaged in 'Commerce' grew from 10 per cent to 23 per cent. They virtually held their own as wholesale merchants, their numbers growing from 11 to 91 and their share slipping only slightly from 34 per cent of all wholesale merchants to 31 per cent. More humbly, as this society became bureaucratised, British-born clerks grew in numbers from 6 to 72 (19 per cent of the British at work): 46 per cent of all clerks were British-born by 1814. The British in 'Trades' (shipwrights, carpenters, butchers and so on) were still a substantial presence, 47 in 1791 and 75 in 1814, but these folk formed a reduced proportion of the British working population, down from 42 per cent to 20 per cent. Several of the British of course worked for 'Government' in 1791 and 1814, albeit in decline as a proportion of their total, and latterly mainly as tradesmen, but also and inevitably taking up senior official posts, right up to Captain of the Port. True, by the 1814 census there were in absolute terms, and indeed in proportionate terms, more of the British in the 'Miscellaneous including Unskilled' category, but this is almost entirely accounted for by an increase in female British domestic servants and, not unconnected, of British washerwomen. On the whole, therefore, the British at the turn of the century were still substantially to be counted among the economic elite.

But they shared that position. As frequently noted already, Jewish businessmen were very important for the development of the Gibraltar economy. What needs further to be stressed is that, by 1814, those counted as British and Native Jews, which means predominantly the latter, those born in Gibraltar, had become in aggregate more important as economic movers and shakers than foreign-born Jews living in Gibraltar. True, the latter were the more numerous, 138 in 1791 and 178 in 1814, compared to the native-born Jewish population of 82 in 1791 and 156 in 1814, and, true, a high (but declining) proportion of overseas-born Jews were in 'Commerce', 64 per cent of them in 1791, 51 per cent in 1814. But large numbers were in modest roles, as male domestic servants (26 in 1791, 45 in 1814), porters (10, 17) and hawkers (11, 22). Many, it is true, were retailers (46, 42), but strikingly, only 12 were listed as wholesaler dealers in 1791 and 14 in 1814, by this latter date making up only 5 per cent of those in this occupation. By comparison, British or Gibraltar-born Jews had become a major economic presence. They too were substantially in 'Commerce', 71 per cent of their number in 1791, 64 per cent in 1814. There were not many of them in retail, only 20 in 1791, 19 in 1814. Their most important advance was as wholesale merchants, those mainly engaged in international commerce. In this short period their numbers increased from 6 to 64. By 1814, this group alone made up 41 per cent of all adult British and native Jews in work, and indeed accounted for 22 per cent of all wholesale dealers, up there with the British. Here was a highly successful example of the indigenisation of an occupation by a once immigrant community.

They were emulated by many others categorised in the census as Natives. In 1791 only 200 of them were counted as in the adult labour force, only 16 per cent of the total. Numbers having grown to only 279 in 1814, they then formed barely 9 per cent. It is also true that more, in absolute and proportionate terms, were in the 'Miscellaneous and Unskilled' category, though this was largely due to that increase in domestic service. More interesting, fewer were working in 'Trades'. In 1791 there were already only 87 of them, making up 44 per cent of native workers, but by 1814 they were a mere 64, or 23 per cent. Instead, whereas in 1791 only 38 of them, forming just 19 per cent of their total, were working in 'Commerce', by 1814 there were 110 or 39 per cent so engaged – and more remarkably the number involved as wholesale dealers had rocketed from only 1 in 1791 to a remarkable 54 by 1814, by then amounting to 19 per cent of all Native workers. This boosted their proportion of all the wholesale dealers to 17 per cent (31 per cent were British, and 22 per cent British and Native Jews). Here too, the children of immigrants, in this case Roman Catholics, had settled and many of them had advanced in economic terms.

But there were other, more recent immigrant groups, and a glance at them reveals their largely supplementary service roles. The 1791 census shows that the Genoa-born were numerous among the adult occupied population, 480 of the total (37 per cent) in 1791 and 582 (18 per cent) by 1814. These immigrants made a modest advance in the 'Commerce' group, 59 (12 per cent of that set) in 1791, 135 (23 per cent) in 1814, but even by then 50 of them were only retailers, 32 managed wine and eating houses, and 9 ran coffee shops. Only 1 wholesale dealer was Genoese in 1791, and still only 14 by 1814. On the other hand, those in 'Trades' formed a high proportion of their total, 31 per cent in 1791 and 33 per cent in 1814, although, since many in both years were recorded as sailors, boatmen, ferrymen and fishermen, one might add to their numbers the 182 in 1791 who worked for 'Government' as seamen (oddly, only 7 in 1814). A fair number in both years were also listed under 'Professions', but as ship captains (12 in 1791; 22 in 1814). However, many were landlubbers, working, for example, as cooks, carpenters, shoemakers and tailors, plus a substantial number, 45, who were recorded as gardeners in 1791 (only 11 in 1814). These were skilled and well-established artisans. However, a very large number of other Genoese were listed as 'Miscellaneous including Unskilled', 15 per cent of their number (71) in 1791, rising to 35 per cent (201) by 1814. These were at best self-employed or, more often, humble employees of the better-off, even in 1814, when 8 were washerwomen, 15 were porters, 21 were labourers, 42 were carters and 98 were male domestic servants.

This profile is even more apparent among the Portuguese. Only 103 were recorded as present in the adult workforce in 1791, 8 per cent of the total, but there were 476, 15 per cent, in 1814. By the latter date, more of the Portuguese were in 'Commerce', but the increase was only from 3 to 33, a rise from 4 per cent of their number to only 7 per cent. Only 5 by 1814 were retailers, while only 8 were clerks, and just 11 had become warehouse merchants. There had even been a relative fall in the proportion of those in 'Trades', 48 per cent of their total in 1791 down to 28 per cent in 1814, and by then 44 masons and 16 carpenters made up many of the total of 133. The huge increase was in their roles as support workers, in the category 'Miscellaneous including Unskilled'. In 1791, 31 of the 46 recorded in this group were labourers; by 1814 they numbered 78 of the total of 228, and a further 16 were carters, 16 were watermen, 43 were lightermen and 45 were male servants.

However, the most striking transformation of the employment scene at this time concerned the increase of the Spanish in the occupied workforce, from 18 in 1791, just 1 per cent of the total, to 699, a substantial 22 per cent. True, 89 or 13 per cent of their number in 1814 were in 'Commerce', including 17 who had set themselves up as wholesale dealers, but 44 were clerks (probably indicative of the value of Spanish as a language of business). A significant number, 182 (26 per cent of their number), were in 'Trades', especially as tailors and shoemakers, masons and carpenters, plus 18 as cigar makers and 21 as barbers. But the bulk of Spanish immigrant workers were in the 'Miscellaneous including Unskilled' category. They amounted to 359 or 51 per cent of their number in 1814. A few were carters (12), more were labourers (26), very many were male servants (99), and a remarkable 201 were female servants. In 1791 there had been just one. The possible consequences of the hiring of Spanish women as domestic servants upon the culture of Gibraltar will need later consideration.

Conclusion

The economic history considered in this chapter helps to explain further the demographic story previously analysed. That civilians in Gibraltar were, by the end of the century, both more numerous and, on average, more prosperous shows what skills and labour could accomplish in circumstances which were not propitious to economic good fortune. This was a place handicapped by its separation, usually, from its geographical hinterland and confronted economically by such exogenous factors as war, disease and risks to overseas commerce beyond those which nature commonly chucked at seafarers. The economically active also had to cope with a military government which recognised its dependence on civilians to deliver supplies, but which also had from time to time more pressing priorities, some of them personal and dubious, and whose style of regulatory management could be the constraints on free enterprise of which those spotting the main chance always complain. It is also apparent that, as the century progressed, those opportunities were to be found by addressing a civilian market as well as and not only the garrison.

Economic diversification followed, evidenced in the wider range of occupations recorded in the census returns of 1791 and 1814, as well as in the numbers filling each niche. Eighteenth-century England has been described as a consumer society, with a domestic market not just deepened by prosperity but broadened in the number of its consumers and in the range of desirable goods demanded and supplied.[71] Gibraltar was not Bath, not even by the end of the century (or ever), but there were signs of affluence – in the number of shops and range of goods on sale, in the number of tradesmen making and not just importing consumer products, in the number of places for social intercourse (places to wine and dine or take coffee), in the number of service workers, and especially in the number of domestic servants.

Inevitably, there was a hierarchy of wealth and status. Remarkably, the British retained economically a premier place, even though demographically and as property owners they had become outnumbered. In the higher echelons of business, especially in the wholesale trade, they were, however, sharing the slot by the end of the period especially with Gibraltar-born Jews, and, interestingly, with some Gibraltar-born Roman Catholics. It is worth remembering that all these people were, or were descended from, recent immigrants. Many, certainly, had risen from humble origins. Gibraltar was a place where, with luck and good management (and a capacity to tolerate heat, the levanter and the manners of the garrison), one could get on. Hence the attraction of the place for other, later immigrants. For them, like the Genoese or Spanish fleeing Napoleon, Gibraltar might be the least worst option. But the occupational data in the censuses demonstrate a pattern characteristic of all other societies open to immigrants. Unless blessed with scarce skills and/or capital, those arriving last usually start at the bottom.

One final set of data may confirm the claim. In 1814 only 13 per cent of the British were in the 'Miscellaneous including Unskilled' category. The proportion of the British and Native Jews was similar, 11 per cent. For other Natives, born in Gibraltar, the figure was 17 per cent. However, far more of the first-generation immigrants, those born abroad, were in this category: ·35 per cent of the Genoese, 36 per cent of Foreign Jews, 48 per cent of the Portuguese, 51 per cent of the Spanish. Addressing the issue in a different fashion, of the 1,055 adults in this 'Miscellaneous including Unskilled' category, British and Native Jews contributed 2 per cent (17), other Natives 4 per cent (47), the British 5 per cent (51) and Foreign Jews 6 per cent (64). However, the Genoese made up 19 per cent of the total (201), the Portuguese 22 per cent (228) and the Spanish

71 N. McKendrick, et al, *The Birth of a Consumer Society: the Commercialization of Eighteenth-Century England* (London: Europa, 1982).

34 per cent (359).[72] As a concluding observation it might be suggested that a common sense of identity among civilians was not likely to be forged in a society not just hierarchically arranged – all are – but also divided between natives and immigrants of different origins and distinguished, to a marked extent, by their different occupational roles.

72 Small numbers from other places of origin are excluded from this round-up.

3

Government and politics, 1704–1819

It has been established already that the military conquest of 1704 was followed by failure and frustration. The occupation of Gibraltar in the name of 'King Charles III' was not the prelude, as expected, to his triumphant enthronement in Madrid. As a result, and consequent upon partition and the containment of allied troops behind the walls of a fortified town at the south end of an isthmus on the tip of southern Europe, the problem arose as to who would thereafter govern Gibraltar, and how. Those challenging questions were subject to metamorphosis over the subsequent three centuries, but always at their heart have been two issues. First, there was the question whether the separation between Gibraltar and mainland Spain would be reversed and, if so, how and on what terms. The second concerned the political relationship between the civilian population living in the town and the British military establishment governing it. The former in the period under review was largely (but not exclusively) decided by the British government and by international politics and high diplomacy. The latter, with which this chapter is particularly concerned, was principally (but not exclusively) a matter of local politics, and these in turn were affected by the demographic and economic development of Gibraltar, which has already been traced.

Of critical importance to attracting and retaining a civilian population was the extent to which the governor and commander-in-chief would extend the military authority he exercised over the garrison to control also the civilian population; or more particularly, whether he would rule in an arbitrary fashion or by law. The test of this would be whether cases affecting the person and property of civilians – between government and governed or between civilians in dispute – would be dealt with in open court by procedures which respected the basic principles of justice conventional not only in Britain but, indeed, in all the places of origin of the civilian population, though expressed in different forms. Given the development of Gibraltar over the eighteenth century as a commercial settlement, legal actions concerning property, contract and debt were going to be of immediately pressing importance, and it was inevitable that merchants in particular would press for properly appointed law courts. It will also be interesting to note whether the civilian population crammed into this town, or elements within it, aspired to that degree of municipal self-government which had characterised Gibraltar before 1704, was common in mercantile communities elsewhere in the Mediterranean, and had, of course, for centuries been commonplace (in many forms) in towns across Britain. Gibraltar was a British fortress, but it was also a town and its population, it needs to be remembered, had not been conquered and subjugated by a colonial power. They were voluntary immigrants, and mainly Europeans.

Becoming and staying a British fortress

To understand the politics of the place it is first necessary to recall how the British government in London stumbled into annexation of the Rock, and the consequent obligations it took on.[1] Again, it is worth emphasising that annexation had not been the intention of the allies, nor that of the English government (as it then was) in 1704. Coalition forces were left with a political embarrassment, consequent on their failure to advance off the peninsula on behalf of Habsburg Spain and also, paradoxically, by the failure of Bourbon Spain to reconquer Gibraltar by siege in 1704–5. The military government defending Gibraltar at that point was doing so on behalf of a pretender to the Spanish throne whose cause had not yet expired and was not absolutely to do so until 1711. Certainly, until 1707 the military governor was a Habsburg appointment. Only then did the (by now) British government reimagine Gibraltar as a British possession which might advance British strategic and economic interests in the Mediterranean. Only thereafter did the British government insist on appointing the governor and contrive to exclude its former Dutch allies from the running of the place. Moreover, it was only in 1713, with the conclusion of the War of the Spanish Succession, that sovereignty over Gibraltar was formally transferred from the Spanish crown, legally and by conquest according to the British, conditionally according to the Spanish, irreconcilably by any account.[2]

1 For this narrative see G. Hills, *Rock of Contention: a History of Gibraltar* (London: Hale, 1974), pp. 178–213, and D. Francis, *The First Peninsular War 1702–1713* (London: Benn, 1975), pp. 104–51.
2 Hills, *Rock*, pp. 201–25, and, with information corrected on governors, W.G.F. Jackson, *The Rock of the Gibraltarians* (Gibraltar: Gibraltar Books, 4th edn 2001), pp. 89, 112–14, M. Harvey, *Gibraltar, a History* (Staplehurst: Spellmount, 1996), p. 74, and T. Benady, 'The depositions of the Spanish inhabitants of Gibraltar to the inspectors of the army in 1712', *Gibraltar Heritage Journal*, 6 (1999), 99. On conflicting views of how sovereignty was transferred see S. Conn, *Gibraltar in British Diplomacy in the Eighteenth Century* (New Haven: Yale University Press, 1942), p. 19.

It should not be imagined that British ministers or high command were insensitive to the profound consequences of annexation, either in 1713 or thereafter. For one thing, Spanish resentment reduced the flexibility of international diplomacy. It became more difficult to protect or advance British overseas interests by other than expensive military means. Maintaining the balance of power between European nations depended for the British on international relations which were capable of manipulation. However, between Britain and Spain there were henceforth arthritic complications which others, and that meant France, could inflame. Only in exceptional circumstances, as in 1793–96 in the war against Revolutionary France and from 1808 after the Napoleonic coup in Spain, did other considerations allow Spanish authorities to cooperate with the British. Like cortisone injections into painful joints, these brought only temporary relief. No wonder that from time to time debates broke out in Britain as to the wisdom of retaining a property which carried such expensive overheads, political and also financial, and which in any case might not be the best address for the kind of strategic and economic business the British government was expected to advance overseas.[3]

However, the importance of these debates is that they never led to a negotiated withdrawal. Perhaps the nearest came in sporadic attempts between 1717 and 1721 to use Gibraltar as the bait to tempt Spain into joining an alliance with Britain and to back out of adventures in Italy, but party politics and parliamentary opinion made such deals thereafter increasingly unlikely to succeed, however often they were refloated.[4] Moreover, since loss through military defeat would also be regarded as intolerable, retaining Gibraltar meant that British governments were obliged to invest in the security of the fortress, even though it was part of continental Europe (the first crown possession there since the loss of Calais in 1558) and formerly part of what in the eighteenth century was still regarded as a great military power. Gibraltar was geographically vulnerable to siege and, indeed, to conquest. Hence the definition of Gibraltar in the minds of British ministers as a fortress with a town attached, and the placement there of a very substantial garrison even in times of peace or of cold war. Hence also the extraordinary efforts, when shooting

3 Conn, *Gibraltar*, pp. vii–viii and passim. For examples of contemporary British arguments concerning the value of Gibraltar see Anon, *Some Short Reflections on the Situation of Gibraltar and Its Importance to the Trade and Maritime Force of this Kingdom* (London: Warner, 1731); Anon, *Reasons for Giving up Gibraltar* (London: n.p., 1749); Anon, *The Propriety of Retaining Gibraltar Impartially Considered* (London: Stockdale, 1783). This last, published in the year in which the 'Great Siege' was finally ended, described Gibraltar as 'more splendid than useful', claimed that in 1781 the military expense of its retention came to £350,968 0s 3½d (I like the 3½d), and that it should be restored to Spain: pp. 18–19, 32.

4 Hills, *Rock*, pp. 249–58; Conn, *Gibraltar*, pp. 28–111.

wars broke out, to use Gibraltar as a military and naval base and also, when the fortress was besieged, to sustain the garrison by running supplies through blockades. Hence also the placing of the local management of Gibraltar firmly and exclusively in the hands of a governor who was also ex officio the local commander-in-chief.

It would be a mistake to conclude that the opinions and actions of Gibraltar's civilian population had no bearing on diplomatic and military outcomes. This was, of course, formally true in the sense that they were never directly consulted on diplomatic and military matters. It was also inevitable in the very early days between 1704 and 1713, when Gibraltar was either in or adjacent to a war zone. Moreover, in that decade, and indeed for several years thereafter, there was then little civilian presence in Gibraltar. However, as already described, a civilian population not only became established and increased, but its presence provided for the garrison the lifeblood of ancillary labour power and economic sustenance. Without such transfusions the Gibraltar base would have been less easy to sustain using garrison labour alone, economically more difficult to service, financially more expensive to support and politically more vulnerable to critics in Britain carping to offload a burden.

Military rule(s)

Enough has been said already about the destructive demographic and economic impact of the allied conquest of 1704, and about the initially debilitating consequences for Gibraltar of the Utrecht treaty. Also among the casualties was civil government. In 1310 King Ferdinand had confirmed that the boundaries of Gibraltar, following the conquest by Spain, would stretch right across the isthmus, as under the Moors, to include much of the present Campo de Gibraltar; he had also decreed by charter that this region would be governed by a city council similar to those running other municipalities in Castile. This civilian council was given power to raise and spend its own revenue and justices were appointed, while the military governor was left responsible only for the garrison and had no authority over civilians. Lost to the Moors in 1333, recovered by Spain in 1462, Gibraltar, with even more extended frontiers, was then placed under a governor but again managed through a city council, and with its own coat of arms issued by royal charter in 1502. It was the Gibraltar city council which on 1 August 1704 (NS) rejected the Duke of Hesse-Darmstadt's call to surrender; it was the city council which on 4 August accepted the inevitable; it was the city council with almost all the civilian population, and a small garrison, which on 7 August filed out, taking with it the city's standard and records; and it was this city council which in 1706, with royal authority, re-established itself at San Roque in what had once been part of Gibraltar's domains as, according to King Philip, 'My City of Gibraltar resident in its Campo'. A city council including civilians was not to be re-established on the rock of Gibraltar until 1921.[5]

Until that date, Gibraltar was formally entirely under the rule of a British military governor, answerable only to the crown and British ministers in London. Throughout the eighteenth century and even after, the monarch ruled as well as reigned, though long since guided by advisers on his Privy Council, whose instructions, including to governors of Gibraltar, were often expressed as orders-in-council. As we shall see, externally determined steps in Gibraltar's administrative evolution were also introduced by letters patent, nominally issued by the monarch him/herself. From early days, the Privy Council had devolved on subordinate bodies the responsibility for routine administration, for providing informed advice, and for some lower-grade policy making. One of these bodies, by the opening of the eighteenth century, was grandly entitled the Lords of Trade and Plantations but conventionally called the Board of Trade, whose principal concerns by then were with overseas colonies. However, the crown was also advised personally by ministers, and especially by two secretaries of state who shared a curiously divided responsibility: the Secretary of State for the Northern Department to deal with the Protestant states of Northern Europe, and also for northern England and Scotland, and the Secretary of State for the Southern Department to deal with the rest, including the Catholic states of Europe, plus southern England, Wales and Ireland, and also the American colonies. Because of this last responsibility, the Secretary of State for the Southern Department also sat on the Board of Trade. There was also a Secretary at War, a minor office set up under Charles II to head a War Office which merely provided administrative support for the commander-in-chief of the army. Thus matters remained until, in 1768, a third secretary of state was created to take responsibility for colonial affairs and also to preside (until 1779) over the Board of Trade. Then in 1782 came the great administrative shake-up, after inefficiencies – which in retrospect seem so obvious – were exposed by military and political defeat and the loss of the American colonies. The responsibilities of the secretaries of state were transformed. One of the original two became Secretary of State for Foreign Affairs, heading the Foreign Office. The other was changed to the Secretary of State for the Home Department, in charge of the Home Office, which was also to manage the colonies – while at the same time the Board of Trade and the office of Secretary of State for Colonial Affairs were abolished. However, the former

5 I. Lopez de Ayala, *The History of Gibraltar*, [1782], translated and continued by J. Bell (London: Pickering, 1845), pp. 2–3, 36–7, 56–8, 94–5, 99–111, 135–8, 144–5, 156, 159, Appendices I–VIII; Hills, *Rock*, pp. 53–4, 96–7, 99–103, 170, 174–6. For Spanish documents relating to the surrender see A. Pérez Paredes (ed.), *Documentos del Archivo Municipal de San Roque 1502–1704* (Cádiz: Ilustre Ayuntamiento de San Roque, Delegación de Archivos, 2006), pp. 37–40.

was revived in 1784 and from 1786 became responsible for the truncated empire. Then a third appointment was made in 1794 to manage the war against France, the Secretary of State *for* War, providing ministerial leadership to the War Office (and employing the Secretary *at* War as his subordinate). However, in 1801 his title was transformed into Secretary of State for War and the Colonies, when responsibility for the latter was shifted from the Board of Trade. Just to complete this navigation through the bureaucratic maze, the military side of the office's work decreased after the Napoleonic Wars, while colonial business increased and the minister in charge came to be called familiarly but inaccurately just Secretary of State for the Colonies and his ministry the Colonial Department.[6]

Complex as changes in the allocation of responsibilities in London may seem, there would be no doubt in the minds of civilians in Gibraltar as to where authority lay. British-appointed governors certainly knew, by the terms of their appointment and by the origins of the despatches they received, that they were subordinates ultimately answerable to the crown and, in the first instance, to the Secretary of State for the Southern Department, or from 1782 to the Secretary of State for Foreign Affairs. True, the governor as the local commander-in-chief was also expected to report regularly to the Secretary at War, later to the Secretary of State for War, but actual responsibility for the management of Gibraltar did not devolve to the War Office until after 1801. It should also be said that in the eighteenth century governors were obliged to report on particular matters to other Whitehall departments, like the Treasury. They were also more prone to exchange information directly with British ambassadors and consuls in Spain and North Africa than would be allowed later, after administrative procedures had become more tightly centralised on London-based ministers and business had to be routed through them.[7] Moreover, a powerful personality like Admiral St Vincent could still insist on the spot, in times of war, that the governor should provide the services he required, backed as he was by the authority of the Admiralty.[8]

But despatches were, after all, wind-blown (unless forwarded overland to Gibraltar from Madrid) and sea passages, even by the end of the eighteenth century, could take many days or even weeks, and so governors had a liberty to act independently which many exercised and which, as we have seen, some

6 R.B. Pugh, *The Records of the Colonial and Dominions Offices* (London: HMSO, 1964), pp. 3–7; R.B. Pugh, 'Colonial Office', in E.A. Benians et al., *The Cambridge History of the British Empire*, vol.3 (Cambridge: Cambridge University Press, 1967), pp. 711, 714, 729; A. Thurston, *Sources for Colonial Studies in the Public Record Office*, vol. 1 (London: HMSO, 1995), pp. 3–5.

7 A useful mid-century account is in TNA, CO91/62, 'An Account of Lieut-General Bland's Conduct . . .', 1751, pp. 85–6; and see GGA, Box: Letters to Madrid.

8 Jackson, *Rock*, p. 188. The Board of Admiralty, first established in 1628, had an interest in local administration because of Gibraltar's naval facilities.

exploited. If they went too far they could be subject to recall and investigation, as happened to Lieutenant-Governor Congreve in 1716 and Governor Hargrave in 1749. Even the Duke of Kent, fourth son of George III, having arrived in March 1802 to take up the post of governor and having by December provoked a mutiny among troops by his zealous efforts to enforce military discipline, was called home in May 1803 and not allowed to return.[9]

These, though, were exceptional cases. Gibraltar was a military station and the governors and their senior colleagues were all military men, and were expected to behave as such. Of the fifteen British governors who took office between 1707 and 1814, two, when appointed, were brigadier-generals, two were major-generals, nine were lieutenant-generals and two were full generals. Of the twelve whose year of birth can be recovered, the oldest on appointment was 80 and the youngest 35 (the Duke of Kent), and the average age was 56. These were there-fore senior figures and men of experience. In this period, thirteen appointments were also made as lieutenant-governors, to replace governors substantially absent from their posts (especially the Duke of Kent, nominally still governor until his death in 1820). As one would expect, these were not quite so highly ranked when appointed: six were colonels, but one was a brigadier-general, three were major-generals and three were lieutenant-generals. There were also officers placed tem-porarily in charge, in the absence of a senior, but these were by no means lowly soldiers. Twelve served in this capacity, and three were colonels, one was a brig-adier-general, six were major-generals and two were even lieutenant-generals.[10] The point to emphasise is that all these senior officers were used to a culture of respect for orders given. They were also accustomed to being in command. A self-confident belief in the authority invested in them, professionally as soldiers and administratively as crown-appointed rulers, determined their priorities and performance and the politics of the place as experienced by civilians.

The theatre of military authority was acted out in Gibraltar on a daily basis, beginning with the gunfire signalling the opening of the gates which had, over-night, locked up civilian residents and visitors inside the walls, and concluding with a similar performance at the end of the day to announce again their closure and the impending curfew. In between times, the British flag was flying from the Moorish castle and no doubt elsewhere, incorporating into the 'union jack' the

9 Hills, *Rock*, pp. 289, 361–2; Jackson, *Rock*, pp. 126, 193–6. In addition to E. Longford, 'Prince Edward, duke of Kent', *ODNB*, see D. Ellicott, *Gibraltar's Royal Governor* (Gibraltar: Gibraltar Museum Committee, 1981).

10 Analysis based on lists in Jackson, *Rock*, pp. 89, 115, 132, 150, 180, and on information on those who have secured entry into *ODNB*. Three people were appointed more than once to the same post, in which case only the rank at first appointment is used, and two were appointed to one post and then elevated to higher position(s), in which case ranks at the time of both appointments are used.

crosses of St George and St Andrew from 1707 and also the cross of St Patrick
following the union with Ireland in 1801. Civilians would see regimental pres-
ences in Gibraltar's narrow streets and small squares at the changing of the
guards and in formal parades; and the noise of the soldierly presence would be
heard during training exercises in peacetime – hugely amplified in war. Where
the garrison's allegiances naturally lay was trumpeted on such occasions as royal
birthdays and, for example, on 25 October 1809, when the golden jubilee of King
George III was publicised with ten minutes of celebratory gunfire from over five
hundred cannons, a *feu de joie* from troops, a royal salute from battleships in the
bay and, less noisily, a garrison ball in the evening.[11]

Civilian settlers were also pushed aside in the cramped space by the construction within the walls of quarters for officers and the erection, increasingly outside
the walls, of barracks for soldiers. While officers might be a sober presence in
the Garrison Library, established in 1793,[12] they were just as likely as private
soldiers to be a boozy presence before then and even after, in the drinking
houses and brothels of the town, which were awkwardly adjacent to the homes
of civilians. Civilians could not avoid witnessing the military discipline exerted
by the town major over common soldiers, expressed by arrests, floggings and
occasional executions in public spaces, and over civilians by the same agency
and by the so-called Spanish Guard, later the Genoese Guard.[13] Disciplinary
measures employed were like those which characterised policing in British cities
at the time, the whirligig, the pillory, the iron collar, the triangle, deportation,
occasionally incarceration, or worse.[14] In reconstructing the political world in
which civilians lived it is also essential to remember that soldiers (excluding their
wives and children) were, as late as the 1770s, nearly half as numerous again as
civilians. If only adult civilians are counted, then soldiers at that time were at
least twice as many. The imbalance earlier in the century would have been much
more extreme. It would have been difficult for civilians in Gibraltar not to be

---

11 *Gibraltar Chronicle*, 28 Oct 1809, cited in S. Constantine, 'Monarchy and con-
    structing identity in "British" Gibraltar c.1800 to the present', *Journal of Imperial
    and Commonwealth History*, 34 (2006), 24–5. Even the birthday of the absent Duke
    of Kent was celebrated with a royal salute: D. Ellicott, *Our Gibraltar* (Gibraltar:
    Gibraltar Museum Committee, 1975), p. 83.
12 GGL, Gibraltar Garrison Library minute book 1793–1798. For later history see *The
    Gibraltar Garrison Library: a 200th Anniversary Commemorative Booklet* (Gibraltar:
    Garrison Library Committee, [2004]).
13 For the early history of policing see C. Baldachino and T. Benady, *The Royal
    Gibraltar Police 1830–2005* (Gibraltar: Gibraltar Books, 2005), pp. 1–3.
14 Jackson, *Rock*, pp. 136–7; J.J. Tobias, *Crime and Police in England 1700–1900*
    (Dublin: Gill and Macmillan, 1979), pp. 139–66, esp. 150–1. The punishment
    of civilian women in the whirligig and pillory is described in a soldier's diary, 13
    March, 5 Nov, 29 Dec 1727, published in *The Times*, 19–21 Aug 1929.

conscious of their subordinate place, both numerically and in terms of status and power.

The separation between the garrison and most civilians was also driven home on the sabbath. True, because of the terms of the Treaty of Utrecht the Roman Catholics in Gibraltar were allowed 'free exercise of their religion' and priests openly conducted services at the church of St Mary the Crowned, on a 'prime site' on what later became Main Street. This was in a century when Protestant suspicions of Roman Catholics in England generated vociferous political support in 1710 for Henry Sacheverell's 'church in danger' sermons, and when a 'no popery' reaction to the limited terms of the 1778 Roman Catholic Relief Act culminated in the Gordon Riots in 1780 and nearly three hundred deaths. However, the destruction of shrines, which had characterised the allied invasion of Gibraltar in 1704, became a thing of the past, although after St Mary's was virtually destroyed in the 'Great Siege' the government annexed a considerable part of the site before allowing rebuilding to take place.[15] As we have also seen, and this in spite of the terms of the Treaty of Utrecht, the Jews were allowed to take up residence in Gibraltar. Rabbis conducted services in a synagogue built as early as 1724 (rebuilt 1768) and in another opened in 1800 (rebuilt 1812), and space was found early on for a Jewish cemetery and another was established in 1756.[16]

Nevertheless, as in the United Kingdom, a Protestant Christian ascendancy was proclaimed. The higher status of the Church of England as by law established was driven home, for example, by the disrespectful conversions of the nunnery of Santa Clara into barracks and of the convent of San Juan de Dios into a military storehouse,[17] but it was particularly emphasised by the governor's occupation of the former Franciscan convent as his headquarters from 1711 and the renaming of its chapel as the King's Chapel. It was used by the garrison, which at least until about 1770 was expected to be exclusively Protestant in complexion, and by British civilians who, as we have seen, were economically and socially among the elite. The British were served by three chaplains, two for the Church of England and one for the Church of Scotland. Military parades marching through the narrow streets to church services emphasised the political endorsement of Protestant supremacy.[18] Moreover, after 1717 the Bishop of

15 T.J. Finlayson, *Guided Tour of Gibraltar* (Gibraltar: Estoril, n.d.), p. 43, referring to a rebuild in 1810–11, though T. Benady, *The Streets of Gibraltar* (Grendon: Gibraltar Books, 1996), p. 15, refers to the Royal Engineers assisting in reconstruction in 1801.

16 Benady, 'Jews in Gibraltar', pp. 94, 98; T. Benady, 'The Jewish community of Gibraltar', in R.D. Barnett and W.M. Schwab (eds), *The Sephardi Heritage, Vol. 2, The Western Sephardim* (Grendon: Gibraltar Books, 1989), pp. 151, 153, 160.

17 Ayala, *Gibraltar*, pp. 172–3.

18 *The Convent* (Gibraltar: Gibraltar Heritage Trust, 2002); Hills, *Rock*, p. 292.

Cádiz, who continued to claim jurisdiction over Gibraltar, was always refused entry, and indeed in 1773 Governor Cornwallis broke the previous convention and insisted, with the agreement of London, that he and his successors and not the bishop should appoint the parish priests. To that extent, state control over the Roman Catholic community was being exercised by a Church of England governor, albeit with the advice of the Elders of the Catholic community.[19] Moreover, not until February 1807 was it belatedly announced that 'certain branches of commerce' were not to be restricted exclusively to Protestants and that 'the benefit of the protection of His Majesty's Government is to be extended equally to all individuals living under its jurisdiction'.[20]

The not uncommon tension between the cultural values of civilians and military may have been exacerbated in the tight physical environment of the town by the prejudice of garrison officers and soldiers against 'foreigners'. Anti-semitism can be discerned in the garrison orders which, for some of this period, prohibited Jews from wearing their traditional habits in public. During the 'Great Siege', when many garrison officers and men were covering themselves in stoic glory, others, officers included, were breaking the windows and doors of Jewish homes, beating up and abusing Jews, and desecrating the Jewish cemetery.[21] Governor Bland has been admired in the historical literature for his probity and insistence upon regulation and good order, but he was also a bigoted upholder of the Protestant Ascendancy, as indicated by his determined though unsuccessful attempt to exclude Jews and Roman Catholics from property ownership.[22] In 1756 Lord Tyrawley, one of his successors, privately conveyed an attitude towards civilians which at least some of his colleagues shared:

> This town is granted away in property to fellows, perhaps escaped out of Newgate, and their wives whipped out of Bridewell, to the utter impossibility of lodging the King's Troops with tolerable convenience. Gibraltar must be restored to its first

19 GGA, Box: Letters to Madrid, Cornwallis to Lord Grantham, British Ambassador at Madrid, 15 March 1773, and enclosures; Hills, *Rock*, pp. 231–3, 291; Jackson, *Rock*, pp. 126–7; C. Caruana, *The Rock under a Cloud* (Cambridge: Silent Books, 1989), pp. 11–23.
20 'Historical Events', *Gibraltar Directory 1914*, pp. 117–18.
21 Hills, *Rock*, pp. 290, 319; B.H.T. Frere (ed.), *Captain J. Spilsbury's A Journal of the Siege of Gibraltar 1779–83* (Gibraltar: Gibraltar Garrison Library, 1908), pp. 21, 38; GL, Mrs Green, 'A Lady's Experience in the Great Siege of Gibraltar 1779–83', reprinted from *The Royal Engineers Journal*, 1912, pp. 102, 104. Anti-semitism may explain why some civilian (mainly English) businessmen ascribed the outbreak of yellow fever in 1804 to the unclean habits of Barbary Jews, and poor Catholics: L.A. Sawchuk and S.D.A. Burke, 'Gibraltar's 1804 yellow fever scourge: the search for scapegoats', *Journal of the History of Medicine*, 53 (1998), 27–35.
22 See Chapter 1.

intention, *une place de guerre*: whereas it has dwindled into a trading town for Jews, Genoese and pickpockets.[23]

Good government

Once, in 1798, as mentioned briefly in a previous chapter, the behaviour of the garrison may have provoked some residents, including such solid citizens as Jewish, Genoese and Spanish shopkeepers, to seek not just protection or redress but a change of regime and the return of Gibraltar to Spain. Those involved in the conspiracy also included mutinous Irish troops, smugglers, deserters and other 'foreigners'. The plot was leaked and, it is said, 1,100 civilians were expelled.[24] What is remarkable about this attempted coup is not that so many were involved, or that civilians apparently suffered no worse fate than expulsion – this occurred for the British at an anxious time in the war – but that it is the only recorded attempt at serious civilian rebellion in the long history of British Gibraltar.

In understanding further the politics of Gibraltar during this first century or so, it is therefore also important to accept that the perceived advantages and virtues of British rule for civilians, even British military rule, outweighed its limitations. Any calculus which ignores this truth cannot explain why, over time, substantial numbers of immigrants arrived and enough stayed to enable them to outnumber the garrison by the turn of the century. Much has already been said about Gibraltar's economic and social appeal, relative at least to realistic and less desirable options. Here emphasis needs to be placed on the sufficiency of 'good government', which helps explain that appeal.

In 1782 the Spanish historian Ignacio Lopez de Ayala published his *Historia de Gibraltar*, a text hardly likely to express undue sympathy for the British occupiers. Yet he wrote:

> It was apprehended that amid such diversity of persons of different Religions, Customs, and Interests, quarrels and atrocities would prevail in Gibraltar similar to those existing in other cities in Spain. But the severity of a military Government has prevented such disorders; for individuals resorting thither, being aware of the certainty of punishment awaiting offences, and that the magistrates and those in authority cannot be corrupted, find their own security best guaranteed by not disturbing that of others.[25]

23 TNA, T225/3900, Lord Tyrawley to Secretary at War, 1756, attached to Governor Sir Varyl Begg to Foreign Secretary Sir Alec Douglas-Home, 28 Dec 1972.

24 Compare Hills, *Rock*, p. 361, Benady, 'Jewish community', p. 161 and Harvey, *Gibraltar*, p. 105, with the governor's own brief account of his expulsion of those without permits: TNA, CO91/40, O'Hara to Portland, 29 Dec 1798.

25 Ayala, *Gibraltar*, p. 174.

Ayala's view nicely reflects the Enlightenment values affecting later eighteenth-century Spanish culture. He depicts British military rule as enlightened despotism. This generous interpretation portrays the governor operating like Hobbes's 'Leviathan', ensuring that the 'life of man' in Gibraltar was not 'nasty, brutish and short', by exercising absolute but not arbitrary authority. Viewed from the perspective of late eighteenth-century southern Europe and the Mediterranean, rather than from the Whig Club in Pall Mall, this could indeed seem true and attractive.

The essentials would be laws. A well-ordered society needed a legal system, and this by stages was introduced. Consequent on the initial status of Gibraltar as a Spanish Habsburg possession, Prince George of Hesse had appointed a judge in the name of 'King Charles III', but this appointment lapsed after the transfer of sovereignty to Britain by the Treaty of Utrecht and a legal black hole opened up. Criminal cases were tried by courts martial, proof of the military autocracy which ran the place. However, there was no court to try the kinds of civil and commercial cases which new settlers with business interests in a 'free port' with uncertain property titles were likely to face. Consuls for different trading nations seem to have dealt with some disputes as they cropped up. The initiative for proper legal regulation came in July 1720 from William Hayles and others, 'Inhabitants of Gibraltar', but backed by colleagues in London, who presented a petition to the Privy Council 'praying that a Court of Justice might be erected there for deciding Disputes between the Merchants and recovering Just Debts'. This was then considered favourably by the Lords Commissioners for Trade and Plantations in August and by the Attorney and Solicitor General in September. As a result and quite swiftly, by letters patent dated 4 November 1720, sometimes referred to as Gibraltar's First Charter of Justice, a Court of Common Pleas was established for settling civil actions, especially concerning contracts, debts, trespass and personal matters. However, the still ambivalent nature of law in the town and fortress of Gibraltar remained. The court was to be headed by the judge advocate of Gibraltar, a garrison official conventionally associated with military courts and military law, although assisted by at least one of two 'disinterested' merchants as lay assessors. Moreover, the right of appeal was to the governor, thus again weaving military authority into the dispensing of justice, although there was a further right of appeal in the most serious cases to the Privy Council, as was conventional in the British Empire. To add to the remaining confusion, the law to be applied was that inherited from Spain, although in practice imperfectly understood.[26]

26 TNA, PC1/3170, 'Papers Relating to Establishment of Civil Government, 1705–1758', abstract; report from Attorney and Solicitor General, 13 Sept 1720, read and approved by Privy Council 20 Sept 1720; Commission for Determining Mercantile Disputes in Gibraltar, 20 Sept 1720; preamble to 1752 charter; PC1/4/80, petition

This state of affairs explains why a further petition followed in August 1721 from forty-three merchants, probably London based but trading to Gibraltar, 'praying that proper Persons, independent of the Military Government, might be nominated for executing the Judicature already established'.[27] Consideration of this by the Privy Council, the Attorney and Solicitor General, the Lords Commissioners for Trade and Plantations and senior judges in Britain became entangled in and hugely delayed by more ambitious proposals which came to nothing, and of which more later. What did emerge, the Second Charter of Justice, was therefore not issued until letters patent of 10 May 1740. This too was an imperfect product with a lame outcome. True, it replaced the law of Spain with the law of England, though doubts remained in relation to real property until 1835. The commission authorised the establishment for all civil cases of a Court of Civil Pleas, with right of appeal to a Court of Appeals and from there, if necessary, to the Privy Council. There was also to be a Criminal Court, distinct from a court martial, for 'the Tryal of all Murders, Felonys and Trespasses (Treasons excepted)'. Unfortunately, the Chief Judge appointed in London, one Robert Robinson, bickered over details and delayed indefinitely his departure for Gibraltar, with the result that he did not carry there his commission, the other judges he was responsible for choosing were not appointed and the new courts over which he was to preside were not set up.[28]

Therefore the 1720 Court of Common Pleas headed by the judge advocate alone continued to function, except for criminal court martial cases.[29] It was later said of this time how damaging it was for the well-governing of Gibraltar that, as a result, even 'the greatest and most enormous Crimes, committed by the Civil Inhabitants', went unpunished except by 'turning the Delinquents out

by Hayles and others, 12 July 1720 (misdated 1728 in catalogue); PC1/3/82, Board of Trade report on petition for setting up a civil court of justice; T. Benady, 'The complaint of the Chief Justice of Gibraltar', *Gibraltar Heritage Journal*, 4 (1997), 18–19.

27 TNA, PC1/3170, abstract; PC1/4/109, abstract; PC1/3/96, petition.

28 TNA, PC1/3170, abstract, minutes 21 June 1722–22 Nov 1739, reports and memorials 7 Dec 1722–10 March 1740; PC1/4/109, abstract; PC1/5/51, report to Privy Council, 2 Aug 1739, and accompanying papers; BL, Hardwicke Papers, Add Mss 36137, report of law officers, 16 July 1739; Benady, 'Chief Justice of Gibraltar', pp. 19–20. Richard Jephson (see below) in his dispatch to the Secretary of State, 16 Dec 1812, TNA, CO91/62, indicates that the new courts were not set up. For Robinson's fabulously unconvincing special pleading see his *The Case of the Chief Justice of Gibraltar* (London: Owen, 1749).

29 GGA, Civil Court, Register of Protests 1743–47, confirms some of the Judge Advocate's continuing roles in hearing cases and receiving affidavits concerning, for example, bankruptcies, wills and losses of property to corsairs, and see also the breach of contract case described in Benady, 'Jews in Gibraltar', p. 97.

of Town'.[30] Governor Bland, taking office in March 1749, strongly lamented the absence of civil magistrates and the legally doubtful judicial responsibilities therefore falling on overworked and untrained governors.[31] Accordingly, in August 1749 he proposed to the Duke of Bedford, Secretary of State for the Southern Department, that the authority of the court should be extended so as to allow it to try by summary justice cases which involved 'Frauds, Pilfering, Personal Assaults and Abuses and other Breaches of the Peace, not extending to life and member'. This proposal too was then debated, again at length, by a committee of the Privy Council and by the Attorney and Solicitor General, who concluded that adding to the existing court the power to try such matters by summary justice was unacceptable. Instead a more radical change should be put into effect, and so it came about that a so-called Third Charter of Justice was granted by letters patent dated 1 August 1752 and delivered to Gibraltar in February 1753.

This confirmed and extended the jurisdiction of the existing Court of Common Pleas (revealingly referred to as the Court Merchant) to embrace, for example, probate matters, although it was still presided over by the judge advocate and with two merchants as lay assessors. However (and at last), a Court of Criminal Jurisdiction was created to try 'Murders, Felonies and all other Crimes (Treasons excepted)'. In these cases a Grand Jury system was used at the committal stage (as in England until 1933) to determine whether there was a case to answer, and a Petty Jury was called to hear evidence and deliver verdict. Jurors selected must all be British subjects. The judges were to be the governor, the judge advocate and 'one British merchant' (though filling this last post seems to have become increasingly problematic). They were also to be ex officio justices of the peace, exercising summary justice, with 'the same Powers to Punish as Justices of Peace in England'. Judges were not only to take the oath of allegiance, but also to make a formal declaration against the doctrine of transubstantiation, thus confirming that they were not Roman Catholics. Care was taken to exclude members of the garrison from the jurisdiction of these courts, although there was still a military involvement in the administration of jurisdiction over civilians, especially in the overlapping roles of the judge advocate and the governor.[32]

Nevertheless, merchants trading to Gibraltar a generation later probably had

30 TNA, CO91/11, Col William Herbert, officer temporarily in command, to Earl of Holdernesse, Secretary of State for the Southern Department, 1 Jan 1753.
31 TNA, CO91/62, 'An Account of Lieut-General Bland's Conduct . . .', 1751, pp. 65–8.
32 TNA, PC1/3710, date list, 1752 charter; PC1/6/28, report by attorney and solicitor general on draft charter; CO91/62, D. Ryder and W. Murray to Committee of Privy Council, 22 Jan 1752, copy of charter, report of Attorney and Solicitor General, 9 Aug 1758, and Richard Jephson to Secretary of State, 16 Dec 1812, who provides a useful description of practice. For implementation, including extra pay for the judge

this measure in mind when they reported how a court had been established in Gibraltar to extend 'the blessings of the British Laws to the Inhabitants for the protection of their Persons and Properties'.[33] It is worth noticing that, in spite of the exclusion of Roman Catholics from the office of justice of the peace and the insistence that juries should be made up of British subjects (which would include all those native born), the law would, or at least should, apply equally to all inhabitants. What was true or sufficiently true of England was becoming similarly true in Gibraltar: 'the law . . . was the even-handed guardian of every Englishman's life, liberties, and property. Blindfolded Justice weighed all equitably in her scales. The courts were open, and worked by known and due process.'[34]

In subsequent years, the new judicial system was bedded in and operated. As the workload increased and experience was gained, several issues were raised – the authority of the governor (1757), the constitution of the civil court (1757), the appointment of a deputy judge advocate (1760) and of justices of the peace (1757, 1767), appeals to the governor or to a higher court (1769, 1805), regulations on the expulsion of 'obnoxious persons' (1773), whether the court had power to try cases committed on the so-called Neutral Ground (1774–75, 1803) and so on. But what cropped up with increasing frequency was the independence of the civilian courts from the authority of the military and the governor (1783–84, 1792, 1808), and whether those courts could try members of the garrison for civil offences (1776, 1779, 1805). Related to this was the role, still, of the governor as himself the court of appeal and the role, still, of the judge advocate acting also as a civil judge (1758, 1797, 1799, 1802).[35] Matters reached storm force in an altercation between Lieutenant-Governor Campbell and a civilian judge, Richard Jephson. In 1811–12 Jephson protested against orders received from the governor which, in his opinion, infringed his responsibilities as an impartial judge and required him to accept the governor's overriding executive authority even in judicial cases concerning civilians. He went on to recommend reforms which, among much else, would clarify and determine their respective jurisdictions and obligations.[36]

    advocate, see CO91/11, Herbert to Holdernesse, 1 Jan 1753; copy of proclamation, 18 Feb 1753, 'Historical Events', *Gibraltar Directory 1914*, p. 103.

33 TNA, PC1/16/13, Petition to King in Council, 25 June 1784.

34 R. Porter, *English Society in the Eighteenth Century* (London: Penguin, 1982), p. 149.

35 TNA, CO91/62, 'Heads of Letters to and from Gibraltar on Civil and Criminal Judicature, 1742–1810', and report of Attorney and Solicitor General, 9 Aug 1758, also in PC1/6/69; PRO39/29/3/8/2, Granville Papers, 'Opinion on Administration of Justice at Gibraltar', 1779.

36 TNA, CO91/62, Richard Jephson to Secretary of State, 23 Sept 1811, and attachments, Jephson to Secretary of State, 16 Dec 1812, and see also Jephson to Secretary of State, 23 Feb 1810.

The end result of subsequent and extensive deliberations was the Fourth Charter of Justice, granted by letters patent dated 12 May 1817. This revoked the previous three. It then re-established the Court of Civil Pleas, but with its own civil judge, to be assisted by at least one of two selected lay assessors. The civil judge, judge advocate, governor and one 'natural-born British Subject' remained empowered as justices of the peace to deliver summary justice, following the English model. However, in addition and to expedite business, a small debts court was also set up, to operate one day a week, presided over by either the civil judge or the judge advocate. Moreover, once again to speed up the administration of justice, in this case the application of (English) criminal law, the Court of General Sessions was to be supplemented by a Court of Quarter Sessions presided over by the judge advocate or civil judge, and by a twice-weekly Court of Petty Sessions under the judge advocate. Also established at last was a Court of Appeal, made up of the governor but with the judge advocate present to give legal guidance and retaining the opportunity for further appeal to the Privy Council. Interestingly, juries must be British subjects in cases when the offender was a British subject, but in cases concerning foreigners the jurors need only satisfy a residential qualification of fifteen years.[37] In brief, early in the new century Gibraltar boasted a standard range of English law courts and operated English laws, though it will have been noted that the separation of civilian and military law officers had not been completed.

Mention has already been made of some of the additional weighty legal steps taken to provide an infrastructure to govern economic affairs and encourage Gibraltar merchants, such as the order-in-council of 1706 which declared Gibraltar to be a free port.[38] Another order-in-council, on 14 June 1722, proclaimed the rules about Mediterranean passes, which were designed to protect the legitimate operations of Gibraltar-based shipping with the authority of the British state. Letters patent dated 27 September 1739 set up the Vice-Admiralty Court, which determined civil cases relating to maritime matters and to legalise the sale of ships and cargoes captured in wartime. Two other orders-in-council, of 13 August 1817 and 19 March 1819, already encountered, authorised the inquiry into titles to lands.[39]

---

37 TNA, CO91/67, Don to Bathurst, 10 Oct 1816, on draft charter; CO91/71, report of law officers, 9 Jan 1817; minute of Privy Council meeting, 27 March 1817; Letters Patent, 12 May 1817, in GGA, *Charter of Justice*, etc, Gibraltar Government, Gibraltar, 1827, and copy in Despatches to Gibraltar, Secretary of State Lord Bathurst to Lieut-Governor Don, 27 Feb 1827. For this and much of the above see J.F. Spry (ed.), *The Gibraltar Law Reports* (Gibraltar: Gibraltar Government, 1979), 'Historical Introduction', and C.C. Ross (ed.), *The Laws of Gibraltar* (Gibraltar: Gibraltar Government, 1950), vol. IV, p. i.

38 See also TNA, PC1/3170, Privy Council meeting 17 May 1705 OS, instructions to Attorney and Solicitor General.

39 Ross, *Laws*, IV, p. i; Spry, *Gibraltar Law Reports*, 'Historical Introduction'.

In addition, governors had the authority to issue regulations locally as garrison orders, which were published as proclamations on posters and in the *Gibraltar Chronicle* (established 1801). Reference has already been made to these in relation to permits for entry, for residence and even for fishing, and there were commands concerning the closing of gates, the curfew, sanitation, vaccination and such matters as the keeping of pigs.[40] Of course, these might feel like irritating restrictions, but they were published and, unless arbitrary in their enforcement, they did set known parameters for civilian public and, to an extent, private life. Governor Bland described civilians as 'Jews, Genoese, Spaniards, Portuguese, Irish Papists, Scotch pedlars and English bankrupts . . . the riff-raff of various nations and religions ready to commit any fraud in their power', but in spite of, or more likely because of, this prejudice he concluded his period in office by codifying his administrative practices into twelve 'articles' or regulations which he intended, with some effect, to guide his successors in the ways of good government. While some rules concerned the conduct of Gibraltar's external relations, others covered matters which would instruct civilians in their economic and domestic activities, such as property ownership, taxes, imports, quarantine, the conduct of bakers and rubbish collection.[41] In brief, and no doubt meriting the approval of Lopez de Ayala, Gibraltar became legally on paper and largely in practice a much regulated polity.

Civilian politics: cooperation and protest

All law-abiding civilians benefited from laws they could respect, though some laws (prohibiting smuggling) were less respected than others. Nevertheless, within the parameters publicly set down, and with the town major's military police to maintain order most of the time, opportunities to prosper were created. Naturally, some civilians prospered more than others and, as was established in a previous chapter, a wealthy elite especially of wholesale merchants and property owners emerged, mainly British plus also several (especially native-born) Jews and Roman Catholics. Gibraltar merchants became wealthy enough, and canny enough, to raise a seriously large interest-free loan in 1808, equivalent to over £12,000, to fund Spanish troops driving Napoleonic forces away from southern Spain, and in addition to help equip them. They also clubbed together in 1813 to present a silver plate (worth 200 guineas, it was said) to Commodore Penrose on his departure from Gibraltar 'in recognition of his attention to the Commercial Interest of Gibraltar'.[42]

---

40 GGA, Despatches from Gibraltar 1815, Don to Bathurst, 13 April 1815, enclosing proclamation on responding to fever, and 26 Nov 1815, enclosing proclamation on vaccination, also in *Gibraltar Chronicle*, 2 Dec 1815; Ellicott, *Our Gibraltar*, pp. 89, 102.
41 TNA, CO91/62, 'An Account of Lieut-General Bland's Conduct . . .'.
42 Ellicott, *Our Gibraltar*, pp. 81, 104.

The way the elite of the politically subordinate were raised above the common herd by those in command has been a phenomenon studied more broadly in the British Empire, and evidence of this in Gibraltar is not, of course, confined to this first century. The rewards to leading civilians included their commercial opportunities, but also their elevation in terms of local social status, exemplified by their mixing socially, even Jews, with the governor and garrison officers.[43] One good example, late in this period, was the formation in 1812 of what came to be called the Royal Calpe Hunt. Fox hunting was the elite sport of the military and of English country gentlemen, and officers and aspiring civilians in Gibraltar evidently bemoaned the lack of local opportunities. A fox hunt needed foxhounds as well as foxes, and a representative of the garrison, in fact the garrison chaplain, and a representative of the British civilian community, a lawyer, imported the necessary beasts. With the thaw in relations with Spain after 1808, garrison officers and the civilian elite, and eventually not just the British, were soon bonding on the hunting field, 'the unspeakable in pursuit of the uneatable'.[44]

It is therefore no surprise that governors began to incorporate this wealthy and socially aspiring elite into their governing practices. It has been observed elsewhere in the non-self-governing parts of the British Empire that British rule commonly required the cooperation – conventionally although mislead-ingly called collaboration – of sections of the indigenous population to assist in administration and control, usually in return for commercial rewards and status. There was, in effect, a negotiated informal contract which ensured that both parties benefited.[45] Although few of the indigenous population of Gibraltar remained after the British takeover, immigrants and their native-born descend-ants did grow in numbers and in importance for sustaining the fortress, and even the most authoritarian of governors opted to negotiate with their elite. After all, while the garrison was made up of a large number of soldiers, those who could be employed in civil administration were few. The governor had little in the way of bureaucratic assistance.[46] As late as 1818, Lieutenant-Governor Don's establishment, paid for out of government revenues, amounted to a mere forty

43 D. Cannadine, *Ornamentalism: How the British saw their Empire* (London: Allen Lane: the Penguin Press, 2001); Benady, 'Jewish community', p. 155.

44 G. Fergusson, *The Hounds are Home* (London: Springwood, 1979), pp. 2–3. For an extended discussion of this theme over a longer period see E.G. Archer, 'Imperial influences: Gibraltarians, cultural bonding and sport', *Culture, Sport, Society*, 6:1 (2003), 43–60.

45 R. Robinson, 'Non-European foundations of European imperialism: sketch for a theory of collaboration', in R. Owen and B. Sutcliffe (eds), *Studies in the Theory of Imperialism* (London: Longman, 1972), pp. 117–42.

46 TNA, CO91/62, 'An Account of Lieut-General Bland's Conduct . . .', pp. 65, 69, emphasises the governor's few assistants.

people. Of these, seventeen in the Revenue Department collected government income, four (plus boat crews) in the Pratique Office dealt with quarantine and eight ran the law courts and gaol. That left just a handful directly working for the governor: chief engineer, judge advocate (principal law officer), town major (as head of police), town adjutant (supervisor of markets), inspector of health (the chief medical officer), commissioner of accounts (the auditor), two interpreters and translators, and the governor's principal prop, the civil secretary, who was himself aided only by two clerks. In that year revenue did not quite match expenditure.[47] Civilian assistance with civil administration was therefore a cost-effective response to expanding government tasks. In effect, the politics of Gibraltar in the first century of British rule (and it did not end there) involved not only the assertion by the governor and the British government of military authority but also the negotiated employment of wealthy British, Jewish and Roman Catholic civilians in the delivery of public services.

So, for instance, following negotiations with Governor Bland in 1750, Jewish leaders were given responsibility for maintaining law and order among their community, particularly among unruly Jewish hawkers and porters, for policing the marketing of foodstuffs by Jewish dealers so as to deter 'forestalling' and thereby inflated prices, and for helping the governor to deport Jews who landed without the governor's permission. The governor later even granted the powers of a police officer to a 'Jews Sergeant' to bolster the authority of the community's leaders.[48]

The increase and concentration of the population, especially within the walls, generated sanitation problems. In 1751 Lieutenant-Governor Bland was still relying only on his town major to ensure that the 'scavenger' and civilian householders obeyed garrison orders and kept the streets clean; and General Irwin in 1765 was doing likewise.[49] However, the yellow fever outbreaks in the new century were a powerful prompt for governors additionally to enlist civilians in public health administration. As the mortality figures showed, disease did not discriminate in the close confines of Gibraltar between civilian and military, nor altogether by wealth. In September 1804 Lieutenant-Governor

---

47 *Accounts Relating to the Offices and Revenues of Gibraltar*, HC 68, 1821, pp. 3–4, which also shows, p. 5, that between 1760 and 1819 annual receipts exceeded expenses, except on seven occasions. See also HC 65 and HC 284, 1822, for accounts for 1820 and 1821. Except for the salary of the governor as commander-in-chief, these figures exclude garrison costs.

48 Benady, 'Jews in Gibraltar', pp. 99–101, includes the agreed regulations of 23 July 1750, confirmed repeatedly by later governors; Benady, 'Jewish community', p. 154; A.B.M. Serfaty, *The Jews of Gibraltar under British Rule* (Gibraltar: Garrison Library, new edn 1958, 1st edn 1933), p. 18.

49 TNA, CO91/62, 'An Account of Lieut-General Bland's Conduct . . .', pp. 28–9; 'Historical Events', *Gibraltar Directory 1914*, pp. 105–6.

Sir Thomas Trigge divided the town into districts and appointed committees of civilians to organise the removal of the sick and the burial of the dead; by October, five leading citizens (Allardyce, Rankin, Ross, Smith and Sweetland) were formed into a Committee of Public Health to investigate, report and advise the governor; by November, the committee was also organising nightly patrols to protect the property of the sick or deceased; by January 1805 Trigge's successor, Lieutenant-Governor Henry Fox, had turned the committee into a Board of Health, chaired by his chief medical officer, by adding three civilian doctors (Bolton, Fellowes, Pym) to four of the original five businessmen. It proposed nineteen measures concerning, for example, sanitation, overcrowding, medical procedures and quarantine.[50] During another scare, in October 1810, Lieutenant-Governor Sir Colin Campbell's response was to include ten leading merchants as well as five officials in a Board of Health which was empowered to order householders to put out their rubbish each day for collection and clean the streets outside their homes at least twice a day, and to impose fines for non-compliance.[51]

Lieutenant-Governor Don was especially vigorous in his engagement with public health matters. His consciousness was raised because his arrival to take command in October 1814 coincided with a yellow fever epidemic. He was convinced that a public hospital for 'the poor' was a necessary investment. It is therefore revealing that his first step was to call a committee of local notables and persuade them that the conversion of a barracks into a civilian hospital, with provision also for an outpatients' dispensary, was a necessary measure. The hospital created was divided into three departments, to match the division of the community into Protestants, Roman Catholics and Jews. Don then recruited leading members of each denomination to manage their portion of the hospital, limiting his direct involvement by enhancing their civic responsibilities. There were financial advantages too. Secretaries of state were always anxious to prevent the costs of colonial administration exceeding local budgets and therefore falling on the British taxpayer. Don secured permission for capital expenditure on the conversion of the barracks by reassuring Lord Bathurst that 'After the . . . building is altered, and repaired, all the expenses of the Establishment will, of course, be borne by the Protestants, Catholics and Jews respectively'.[52] Recurrent costs were therefore to be met from charitable donations, fund-raising stunts and fees

50 T.J. Finlayson, *Stories from the Rock* (Gibraltar: Aquila Services, 1996), pp. 6–13; L.A. Sawchuk, *Deadly Visitations in Dark Times: a Social History of Gibraltar* (Gibraltar: Gibraltar Government Heritage Division, 2001), p. 60.
51 Ellicott, *Our Gibraltar*, pp. 87–8; and see GGA, Box: Alien Question, 'The History of the Permit System presented by F.S. Flood, 12 May 1871', Appendix A, No 9, 'Proclamation . . . Regulations for preserving cleanliness', 22 Feb 1812.
52 GGA, Despatches from Gibraltar 1815: Don to Bathurst, 20 March 1815.

charged to other than 'the poor' (although eventually a revenue for the hospital derived from port dues and a tax on flour were found necessary).[53] Don had beauty as well as public health in mind when, in 1815, he set out to raise money for the laying out of walks and shrubberies in the new Alameda Gardens. The administrative model he had already employed served equally well again: he recruited a dozen leading citizens as commissioners to organise the eight lotteries he authorised to bring in the cash.[54]

Likewise, Don appointed prominent civilians as inspectors to supervise the sanitary arrangements of the twenty-seven districts into which he had divided the town within the walls and the six outside, to the south. His appreciation of the collaboration of these 'gentlemen' was officially proclaimed in the press: '[H]aving expressed their readiness . . . to cooperate in the measures of this government towards the security of the Public Health, their services . . . are most gladly accepted.' Their bestowed authority was also emphasised: 'the Civil Inhabitants of the Garrison are earnestly called upon to comply with such directions as may be given to them through the medium of the Inspectors'.[55] And the secretary of state was also reassured about their cost: they were 'sixty-six Gentlemen of the town who act in this capacity gratuitously'.[56]

Leading citizens were also appointed to a Paving and Scavenging Commission. Its origins appear to have lain in a meeting of the Grand Jury which Don had summoned. This was not the first time that this ostensibly judicial body of respectable citizens had been employed for other purposes: it had been called upon in 1804 to make recommendations concerning public health. This time, in January 1815, it agreed that householders should pay a yearly rate to finance a sewerage system as well as street cleaning. Later that year it recommended that revenue should again be raised for expenditure during 1816 on paving and scavenging, and this was approved on 5 December 1815 by the governor and the judge advocate, acting as JPs at a Court of General Session. But there had been some resistance from civilians to paying such a tax, and so Don had already gone further. At his request he received authority by an order-in-council of 30 December 1815 to set up a commission with unchallengeable power to raise rates. Although this contained two technically qualified military officers,

53 GGA, Civil Hospital Minutes 1815, and Despatches from Gibraltar 1816–17 and TNA, CO91/67, Don to Bathurst, 23 Sept 1816, enclosing proclamation (in English, Spanish and Italian) on port dues; S.G. Benady, *General Sir George Don and the Dawn of Gibraltarian Identity* (Gibraltar: Gibraltar Books, 2006), pp. 54–69; S. Benady, *Civil Hospital and Epidemics in Gibraltar* (Grendon: Gibraltar Books, 1994), pp. 18–24.

54 *Gibraltar Chronicle*, 2 Dec 1815, p. 384; Benady, *Don*, pp. 71–4.

55 *Supplement to the Gibraltar Chronicle*, 19 June 1819, which also lists the names of the 'Civil Inspectors'.

56 GGA, Despatches from Gibraltar 1816–17: Don to Bathurst, 1 Nov 1817.

the rest of the ten or twelve members were well-established civilians, like James Bell, Alexander Farquhar, Aaron Cardozo and Judah Benoliel. They were to act as 'Commissioners and Surveyors of the Highways, Streets and Lanes of this Town'.[57] They spent £10,083 in the first half of 1816, mainly on labourers' pay, leaving them with a healthy balance of £11,819.[58] A second order-in-council, of 1 February 1819, extended their responsibilities, so that they now had the authority to set property rates and to raise revenue to spend on 'Lighting the said Garrison and Town of Gibraltar' as well as on 'Paving, Repairing and Cleansing the Streets . . . and . . . the Making and Repairing of the Sewers and Drains'. This represented a noticeable extension of government services and also of the role of appointed (not elected) civilians in their execution.[59]

It is very important to notice the precedent that had been set. To this point, the colonial government under the direction of the governor ran what in today's parlance would be described as a unitary authority, whose authority over all matters applied throughout the territory. The Paving and Scavenging Commission obviously derived its authority from 'central' government and was subject to audit and account. Nevertheless, a subordinate tier of 'local' government had been established, with a civilian membership, its own source of revenue and authority in specific matters over much of the same territorial space. The division of day-to-day responsibilities between a 'central' military government and, underneath it, a single 'local government' was to be characteristic of Gibraltar until late in the twentieth century, with considerable consequences for Gibraltar's politics and the development of a civilian identity.

Civilians were not altogether passive agents and docile collaborators with a military regime. If they had grievances and were sufficiently provoked, they adopted a political method well recognised in British political culture. As loyal British subjects or foreign but settled immigrants, they appealed by petition to the governor or to the crown in London, even for redress against the errors of the crown's agents in Gibraltar. For example, a remonstrance of 26 February 1754 signed by fourteen 'British merchants and others, Inhabitants of Gibraltar' was delivered to Major-General Braddock, temporarily in command of the garrison,

57 *Gibraltar Chronicle*, 6 Jan 1816; GGA, Despatches from Gibraltar 1815: Don to Bathurst, 14 April 1815, and reference therein to his despatch of 13 Nov 1814, and Don to Bathurst, 21 June and 29 Oct 1815.

58 *Gibraltar Chronicle*, 18 May and 10 Aug 1816, Accounts of Scavenging and Paving Department, and also 2 Nov 1816 when the prospect of a reduced rate for 1817 was floated; GGA, Annual Records of Assessed Rate for Paving, Scavenging and Lighting, 1818–65.

59 GGA, *Charter of Justice . . . and Orders in Council, etc*, Gibraltar Government, 1827; TNA, CO91/71, copy of order-in-council 30 Dec 1815, also in CO91/85; Ross, *Laws*, IV, p. i; Benady, *Don*, p. 67; Ellicott, *Our Gibraltar*, p. 106; Jackson, *Rock*, p. 228; Benady, 'Jewish community', p. 165.

seeking the removal of a recent and to them commercially damaging prohibition on trade with the Moroccan port of Arzila. While most of these merchants were British by origin, others, named De la Rosa, De Lara, Cardozo Nunez and Rocatagliata, were not.[60] Likewise, a memorial of 4 April 1776 was signed by fourteen prominent Gibraltar merchants who insisted that action should be taken against the unjustified quarantine laws imposed by Spain which were restricting trade, and this protest was forwarded by the governor to the British ambassador in Madrid.[61] Another petition, dated 25 June 1784 and presented to the King in Council by business colleagues in London, was a strongly worded attack on General Eliott, hero of the 'Great Siege' but not subsequently of Gibraltar merchants. They objected strongly to the damage he was causing to the 'free port', and therefore to their trade, by his hitherto 'unknown, Regulations, Impositions and Restraints'. They judged them to be 'illegal' as well as 'oppressive and injurious'. He was accused of levying certain import duties and of refusing to allow British subjects automatic free entry to Gibraltar. Most strikingly, they claimed that the 'Rights and Privileges of British Subjects' were being abused and they insisted that 'Civil Rights' should be restored so that the 'Inhabitants of Gibraltar and Traders' could enjoy the 'freedom of trade under the Laws and Regulations heretofore established for the Civil Government of that place'. The agreed laws should be made 'permanent and not liable to change at the will of any individual executive officer'.[62] Here too we can detect the British cultural conceit that citizens had rights and that society was or should be governed by the rule of law, equitably applied. It is fair to say that by the end of the century the most important British export to Gibraltar was British law and the notion that its application should be impartial.

Still more interesting, property owners worried by the order-in-council of August 1817, which authorised the inquiry into land titles in Gibraltar, immediately assembled and chose a committee to draw up a memorial asking Lieutenant-Governor Don to suspend the already publicised investigation. When Don replied that he was bound by his instructions and not able to accede

60 TNA, CO91/11, enclosure in dispatch from Braddock, 28 Feb 1754. British merchants and a Jew had made similar complaints in 1718: M. Benady, 'The settlement of Jews in Gibraltar, 1704–1783', *Transactions of the Jewish Historical Society of England*, 26 (1979), 91–2.

61 GGA, Letters to Madrid, 'The Memorial of the British Merchants and Traders residing in Gibraltar', 4 April 1776.

62 TNA, PC1/16/13, Complaint against General Eliott, 31 Oct 1783; response by General Eliott, 19 April 1784; petition to King in Council, 25 June 1784; Explanation of Petition, 10 Sept 1784. See also Benady, 'Jewish community', p. 158, citing TNA, CO91/30, petition, and CO91/31, letters from Eliott, 10 Jan and 15 Nov 1784, CO91/32 Eliott to Sydney, 7 Aug 1785, CO91/34, letter from Eliott, 5 Feb 1787 and petition.

to their wishes, a second memorial was drawn up and sent to him with the request that it be forwarded to the Prince Regent. In reply to this, Don declared that he would not do so without its amendment or, if it were to be sent unchanged, without adding critical comments in his covering despatch. A delegation then went to London to deliver the memorial themselves and to engage in some lobbying of the Secretary of State for War and the Colonies, Lord Bathurst, and also, via learned counsel, to the Privy Council, '*ex parte* inhabitants of Gibraltar'. The importance of this episode is not just that Gibraltar merchants were able to by-pass the governor and go 'to the top', nor even that reasoned argument seems to have led to a modification of the law and to an amended order-in-council of March 1819. More strikingly, what we also see here is the expression of a collective civilian identity, though only among the merchant elite. The committee which drafted the first memorial was carefully constructed to include three representatives 'for Protestants', three 'for Catholics' and three 'for Hebrews'. Signatures to the memorials were signed in columns headed 'Protestants', 'Catholics' and 'Jews'. Distinctions were acknowledged, but a common interest was recognised, and political pressure was being collectively exerted.[63]

On Main Street in Gibraltar stands one physical representation of the mercantile collective sense of self which had emerged in the first hundred years of British rule. It is today Gibraltar's parliament building. It was originally the Exchange and Commercial Library. The civilian elite had apparently been denied use of the Garrison Library and, indicative of their civic aspirations, they had formed their own library in a back street, but 160 Gibraltar merchants then raised enough money to construct stylish new quarters on a premier site. The foundation stone was laid on 19 April 1817 in the presence of Lieutenant-Governor Don and his senior staff and with a military guard of honour. However, the true honours of the day went to the merchant princes of Gibraltar who had voluntarily paid for the building. Their three-in-one component parts were duly recognised in the press report which noted the presence of the 'Grand Jury and Merchants' Society, representing the Protestant Persuasion', the 'Elders of the Church, representing the Roman Catholic Persuasion', and 'Gentlemen representing the Hebrew Persuasion'. An inscription on a silver plate, subsequently placed as a time capsule in a corner of the building, began: 'This Exchange was Erected by the Voluntary Subscriptions of the Merchants of Gibraltar'. It then referred to the laying of the foundation stone by General Don and gave the names of David Johnston, representing 'the Protestant Persuasion', John Maria Boschetti, for 'the Roman Catholic Persuasion', and Joseph Abuderham, for 'the Hebrew Persuasion'. In reporting the ceremony to the War Office, Don declared that he had warmly approved of this initiative because Gibraltar 'may justly be considered one of our

---

63 GGA, Various Documents Connected with the Commission to Settle Titles to Lands 1826.

Chief Commercial entrepots', and yet the 'Commercial Gentlemen of Gibraltar' had hitherto lacked 'a place of meeting for the purposes of transmitting their business'. It was appropriate that Don should acquire posthumous honour when his bust was placed in a niche in the finished building.[64] However, the Exchange was to become more than simply a place for the congregated business class to do their deals or to improve their minds with good literature. The Exchange and Library Committee, elected by subscribers and later also by any householders wishing to participate, began to speak as Gibraltar's representative political body.

Civic self-government

That was in the future. As yet, aspirations even among the elite went no further than to be recruited by the military government to carry out various designated administrative roles – tempered by spats with British authorities in Gibraltar and elsewhere when business interests were threatened. One aspect of contemporary civic culture common in Britain was therefore still absent from Gibraltar. Several centuries of municipal self-government in Britain, and in Spain, had preceded the British annexation of Gibraltar. The constitutions of British towns varied enormously and proper proceedings to 'modernise' representation and clarify powers and responsibilities were not to be initiated seriously until the 1835 Municipal Corporations Act. Nevertheless, as in Spain, most towns in the United Kingdom were managed under charters by local elites, sometimes led by local gentry, often by urban businessmen.

Carlisle provides an approximate comparison with Gibraltar. It was a walled city; it contained a military garrison; it sat on a frontier of some military significance with another kingdom, even after the union of crowns in 1603 and even after the union of kingdoms in 1707 (as the Jacobite rebellion and Scottish occupation of the city were to confirm in 1715 and 1745). Yet the civilian population of Carlisle, by at least the thirteenth century, had secured by charter a degree of independence from the garrison and some powers of self-government. These were exercised, of course, by wealthy citizens, but their numbers were extended to include members of trade guilds from the sixteenth century.[65] Wealthy urban merchants in eighteenth-century Britain would therefore expect to be running their towns and, if denied by a medieval constitution, would be insisting, increasingly, on change.[66]

---

64 GGA, Despatches from Gibraltar 1816–17: Don to Bathurst, 20 April 1817, enclosing page from *Gibraltar Chronicle*, 19 April 1817; Benady, *Streets of Gibraltar*, pp. 13–14; Benady, *Don*, pp. 82–3. The name 'Abuderham' was usually spelt 'Abudarham'.

65 M. Constantine, *Carlisle* (Salisbury: Frith, 2005), pp. 37–8.

66 Porter, *English Society*, pp. 140–2.

In Gibraltar there was one serious and early initiative to seek powers of civilian self-government. Its frustration is revealing of outside British perceptions
of Gibraltar and also of limited aspirations among the civil community. The
1721 petition of London-based merchants, to which reference was made earlier,
initially triggered only a reconsideration by a committee of the Privy Council
of the recently established Court of Common Pleas. However, in December
1722 William Hayles, a leading merchant, and Peter Godfrey, a City of London
MP, widened the agenda by arguing that more was required than laws and law
courts to give security to property. Gibraltar actually needed and financially
could support a 'Civil Government . . . as in the American Colonies'. This should
consist of a 'Mayor, Aldermen [and] Common Council' to be selected annually out of the 'English residing there'. There was more. Two sheriffs should be
chosen out of the Common Council, and two bailiffs should be appointed by
the sheriffs. There should also be a town clerk, a judge of the admiralty, a chamberlain or treasurer for the colony, and a town hall where courts would sit and
records be kept. There should even be a local militia under a 'Muster Master',
whose duties might include preventing soldiers deserting. Precedents were dug
up, particularly the establishment of civil governments in Tangier, Jamaica and
the Leeward Islands. It was claimed that a thousand civilian families were established in Gibraltar and these included two hundred British or Irish subjects of
the crown, who would presumably be the persons suitable to take on the civil
government roles. This proposal was considered by the Privy Council; but then
the matter 'rested'.[67]

It was revived when the question of good government was again raised,
following complaints from Gibraltar residents against Lieutenant-Governor
Clayton. The proposal to introduce into Gibraltar a proper civil government,
distinct from the military, was reconsidered by the Privy Council in December
1728, and between then and July 1730 much work was put into drafting and
amending a 'Charter of Incorporation for Gibraltar'. This was modelled on that
of Tangier, although 'Freedom of this City' might be confined to 'Protestant
Inhabitants only, whereas that of Tangier was extended to Papists'. However,
another version of the draft charter proposed also to include 'as well our natural
born Subjects as Aliens and Strangers', though this was further modified in a
third version to exclude 'Jews and Moors'. If there was uncertainty about the
identity of civilian members of the incorporated town, there was agreement on
the composition of its leaders: a mayor, six aldermen, twelve councillors and

---

67 TNA, PC1/3170, 'Papers relating to Establishment of Civic Government 1705–
1758', petition by London merchants, Aug 1721; minutes of Privy Council, 21 June
1722, report of attorney and solicitor general, 7 Dec 1722; PC1/4/109, 'Abstracts of
All the Proceedings for Establishing a Form of Civil Government at Gibraltar', 22
Aug 1721–14 Dec 1722.

a legally trained recorder. While the first cohort was to be appointed by the crown, thereafter the mayor was to be chosen by the whole corporation from among the aldermen. Vacancies among the aldermen were to be filled from among the councillors and vacancies among the councillors were to be chosen, according to one version, from 'the men of the City being Protestants'. They were to meet at least once a month to make and administer laws (not repugnant to English law) 'for the Good Government of the City and the Establishment and Encouragement of Trade'. Very strikingly, it was agreed that the independence of the civil government from the authority of the governor and the garrison should be demonstrated and enforced. For example, the mayor, aldermen and recorder, but not the governor, should be justices of the peace with authority to try all criminal cases and the recorder should replace the judge advocate on the Court of Common Pleas (the 'Court Merchant'). Also, crimes by members of the garrison, unless they were offences against military discipline only, should be tried by the civil magistrates according to English common law, while the governor on the other hand was to be specifically instructed not to arrest, imprison or try any inhabitants unless they were members of the garrison. Moreover, he should not have a role in appointing civilian officials.[68]

What slowed and then stopped further progress was doubts that there were in fact sufficient suitable civilian inhabitants to take up the offices, or sufficient revenues to pay for a civil administration unless excise duties were exacted. Probably there were also concerns about the reaction of the governor to proposals which would politically clip his wings and, not incidentally, reduce his capacity to make private gain from his public office. In January 1739[69] General Clayton, who while lieutenant-governor from 1726 to 1730 had made a delicious amount of money in 'extras', appeared before the Privy Council, along with several other military officers and also merchants trading to Gibraltar. Together they persuaded Privy Councillors that 'the number of Protestants, British Subjects, resident there, were so small that it would be impossible to choose Officers out of them sufficient to form a Corporation; whereupon the Council dropt the said Charter'. Instead, attention was limited to devising what became the largely abortive amendments of 1740 to the legal system alone.[70] And so matters remained for almost two more centuries.

68 TNA, PC1/4/109, 'Abstracts of All the Proceedings . . .', 4 Dec 1728–28 July 1730, supplemented by papers in PC1/3170, abstract; PC1/4/94, PC1/4/95 and PC1/4/103, report by Board of Trade, 16 Dec 1728, Privy Council order to attorney and solicitor general, and report; PC1/4/105, report by the Board of Trade, 6 Feb, instructions by Privy Council, 18 Feb 1729/30, response by attorney and solicitor general, and draft charter.
69 Reported as January 1738 in PC1/3170, but this is OS.
70 TNA, PC1/3170, abstract and accompanying papers; PC1/5/51, report of attorney and solicitor general, 16 July 1739, and response of Privy Council, 9 Aug 1739.

Conclusion

This early brave effort to bring Gibraltar constitutionally into line with towns in Britain and indeed in other parts of the eighteenth-century colonial empire was clearly prompted by the imperfect legal system in place in those early days, and also by the arbitrary ways and vulture habits of early governors, which threatened the precarious money making of merchants in Gibraltar and, just as much, in London. Civilian aspirations to civic self-government were at this point only a matter of business protection. The goal was shared by British officials in London who wished to raise up Gibraltar after its conquest as a mercantile plantation. But the incentives for self-government diminished, possibly as the proportion of the Gibraltar community which was British and Protestant declined, probably as the rule of law was factored in, certainly when war and siege repeatedly reinforced military priorities. Such reforms as did take place, especially in legal processes, had also eased the anxieties and diminished the frustrations of the civilian elite. Instead, their politics were safely channelled by allowing them to present memorials and petitions to the crown, by incorporating them as (junior) partners in the management of the place, and by rewarding them with an elevated status in the community. Had a municipal corporation been established alongside the garrison command, it is likely that a rougher relationship between civilians and the military would have followed, and a stronger sense of common and separate identity between all civilians might have been forged. In this first century of British rule it did not happen.

Footnote 71 (*cont.*)

See also BL, Copies of Letters relating to Gibraltar 1727–31, Add Mss 23643, for Clayton's earlier crisp but unflattering judgement on those striving locally for a municipal government: 'most of His Majesty's Subjects who live here, cannot elsewhere': Clayton to Pelham, 9 March 1728 OS, that is, 1729 NS. Papers relating to the establishment of civil government in Gibraltar were presented three times to the House of Commons, April 1729, Feb 1730 and Feb 1747, but were not printed: see references in S. Lambert (ed.), *House of Commons Sessional Papers of the Eighteenth Century* (Delaware: Scholarly Resources Inc, 1975).

4

Demographic management: aliens and us, 1815–1890s

The Congress of Vienna in 1815 did not debate the future of Gibraltar at all, and therefore the retention by Britain of sovereignty over the peninsula was confirmed by default. Ambiguities and rival interpretations remained about the status of the so-called neutral ground, but there was no doubt that a frontier zone, if not an agreed frontier line, existed, separating British territory from mainland Spain. However, the fortifications at the Spanish end of the isthmus, stretching from the Fort of Santa Barbara to the Fort of San Felipe, had been dynamited by the British in February 1810 with the consent of the local Spanish commander, in order to frustrate any French military designs on Gibraltar. That levelling of the walls may be said to symbolise an alteration in the relationship between Gibraltar and Spain.

Of course, Spanish claims were not abandoned, and Spanish irritation with the British did not disappear, especially when British forces, mindful of developments in military technology, began to advance their lines over the neutral ground. Moreover, during the nineteenth century the fortifications of Gibraltar were made still more formidable, with a rebuilt Line Wall, the new defences of Wellington Front and additional forts around Rosia and Camp Bays, while serious bits of artillery were being installed, some high on the Rock and many at sea level. The century concluded with a massive investment in naval dockyards and associated works between 1894 and 1906, indicating the Admiralty's increased commitment to Gibraltar as a strategic base.[1] Muzzles pointing down the length of the isthmus, over the bay to Algeciras, and across the straits were to the Spanish a constant reminder of British intrusion, as were the highly visible redcoats of the substantial British garrison and the flotillas of Royal Navy vessels entering and departing.

However, in marked contrast to earlier circumstances, in the century after 1815 there was no Spanish (or French) naval blockade of Gibraltar, no Spanish army digging assault trenches on the isthmus and, indeed, no political will in

---

1   D. Fa and C. Finlayson, *The Fortifications of Gibraltar 1068–1945* (Oxford: Osprey, 2006), pp. 31–44.

Madrid to put Spanish claims to military test. Spain was handicapped politically in the nineteenth century by loss of empire and domestic turmoil, with
regime changes and spats of civil war, particularly in 1833–39, 1843, 1854–56,
1868 and 1873–74. The Spanish economy was decreasingly able to sustain the
pretensions of a great military power.[2] However reluctantly, Spanish authorities accepted that now, at least, was not the time to challenge the occupation of
Gibraltar by the world's best endowed and most arrogant superpower.

The important consequence of this transition for Gibraltar's development
as a civilian settlement in the nineteenth century was the change of the land
frontier from a barrier to a permeable zone of exchange. In the previous century
the frontier had only from time to time been crossed in peacetime by garrison
officers with permits, by smugglers under cover and by traders legitimately
bringing in supplies with Spanish consent when conditions at sea allowed deviation from the strict terms of the Treaty of Utrecht. Now it was different. The
economic consequences of change will be considered in due course. Here, the
demographic effects will be explored. A porous land frontier with Spain allowed
overland migrants to join those arriving as before by sea, and they mixed with
a civilian population which in any case was growing by natural increase. What
was not increasing was the size of Gibraltar to accommodate them. What was
not decreasing was the concern of Gibraltar's local and London managers about
the composition of visitors and of the resident civilian population. Civilian
experiences and, indeed, their sense of a common identity were therefore to
be seriously affected by how, and how effectively, those in authority operated
immigration controls.

Population growth, 1815–1901

The figures in Table 4.1 represent the demographic challenge to British managers
of Gibraltar, but also the consequences of their efforts at population control and,
above all, the decisions and determination of thousands of civilians to obey, or
not, the rules.

We have already seen how the population of Gibraltar increased rapidly in the
late eighteenth century and during the Napoleonic Wars. True, in 1813–14 a devastating epidemic of yellow fever brought the civilian population down by some
two thousand, but by 1826 the demographic recovery had raised the total by over
five thousand. An increase in the civilian population of 51 per cent between 1814
and 1826 impacted seriously on conditions within Gibraltar, troubled severely
those charged with its management and altered fundamentally the relationship
between civilians and military. The return of yellow fever in 1828 had little lasting
effect on the demographic advance of the population, though it confirmed the

---

2 R. Carr, *Spain 1808–1975* (Oxford: Clarendon Press, 1982).

Table 4.1 *Civilian population, 1791–1901*

Date	Total	Inter-census increase/ decrease	Inter-census increase/ decrease annual average
1791	2,948		
1801	5,339	+80.8%	+8.1%
1807	7,501	+40.5%	+6.7%
1811	11,173	+49.0%	+12.2%
1813	12,423	+11.2%	+5.6%
1814	10,136	−18.4%	−18.4%
1816	11,424	+12.7%	+6.4%
1826	15,303	+34.0%	+3.4%
1829	16,394	+7.1%	+2.4%
1831	17,024	+3.8%	+1.9%
1834	15,002	−11.9%	−4.0%
1840	15,554	+3.7%	+0.6%
1844	15,823	+1.7%	+0.4%
1860	17,647	+11.5%	+0.7%
1871	18,695	+5.9%	+0.5%
1878	18,014	−3.6%	−0.5%
1881	18,381	+2.0%	+0.7%
1891	19,100	+3.9%	+0.4%
1901	20,355	+6.6%	+0.7%

Sources: Figures for 1791 in GGA, 'List of Inhabitants 1791'; for 1801–14 in H.W. Howes, *The Gibraltarian* (Gibraltar: Medsun, 1951), pp. 39, 43–4; for 1816 in TNA, CO91/67, Don to Bathurst, 6 July 1816; for 1826 in GGA, Despatches from Gibraltar 1827: Don to Bathurst, 9 Feb 1827; for 1829 in TNA, CO91/97, and GGA, Despatches from Gibraltar 1829: Don to Murray, 6 March 1829; for 1831 in TNA, CO91/113, and GGA, Despatches from Gibraltar 1831: Don to Murray, 7 April 1831; for 1834 in *Census of Gibraltar 2001*, Table 1, p. 1; for 1840 in TNA, CO91/150, Woodford to Russell, 7 May 1840; for 1844 in *Census 2001*; for 1860 in GGA, Despatches from Gibraltar 1861: Police Office, 8 May 1861 (which distinguishes between a 'fixed population' of 15,462 and the total, cited above, which includes an 'Alien floating population residing on the Rock for periods varying from a day to a year': this record is badly water damaged); for 1871–1901 in *Census of Gibraltar 2001*, checked against *Report on the Blue Book for 1888*, p. 8 (for 1881), *Annual Report for 1891*, p. 8, and *Annual Report for 1901*, p. 17, excluding figures for population living on boats in the harbour, who were only counted in 1891 (759) and 1901 (630).

concerns of management. A still larger population overloaded a territory no greater in size and still much contained within garrison walls. Further growth resulted in a civilian population peak of over 17,000 in 1831, more than three times the number in 1801; and the subsequent reduction in recorded numbers by 1834, of a couple of thousand, was possibly in part due to a different counting system, and in any event it did not last.[3] By the 1870s and 1880s, Gibraltar's civilian population, at over 18,000, well exceeded the previous 1831 maximum, although its stability in those decades, as we shall see, inflamed debates about whether Gibraltar was or was not 'overcrowded'. Be that as it may, between 1791 and 1891 the rise by over 16,000 in Gibraltar's civilian population constituted a more than sixfold increase. The figure for 1901 was not to be exceeded until 1951.

To obtain a true measure of the number of people compressed into the space we also need to factor in the figures for the garrison, ideally including wives and children, who in this period were not included in census totals. In 1814, late in the war, when civilians totalled 10,136, the garrison population numbered 6,754, including not just 5,139 officers and men but also 749 women and 866 children. In peacetime, officers and men alone totalled 3,468 in 1830 and 3,420 in 1842. In 1878, after decades of local peace, the garrison numbered 5,797 men plus 533 wives and 1,231 children, a total with other family members of 7,599. In 1891, service personnel including families still numbered 5,896, to be squeezed into the same two square miles or so, alongside 19,100 civilians.[4] Military barracks were still taking up precious space in the old town, as in Grand Casemates, where bombproof barracks were built in 1817, and later at King's Bastion.[5] Other accommodation was occupied by officers with families.

There were already signs from the later eighteenth century that the civilian population was growing by natural increase, the growth only partially offset by emigration. True, in epidemic years death rates were horrendous, but by the end of the nineteenth century crude death rates were not high by contemporary British standards (20.5 per thousand of the fixed civil population in 1881, 20.7 in 1891, 21.35 in 1901). Meanwhile, birth rates were increasing (27.7 births per thousand of the population in 1881, 28.1 in 1891, 31.31 in 1901).[6] Moreover,

---

3 TNA, CO879/9/16, and GGA, Box: The Alien Question, Confidential Print, Africa No 97, Correspondence respecting the Gibraltar Aliens Order in Council, 1873, Appendix, Flood to Williams, 12 May 1871, p. 47, states that aliens on temporary permits, numbering about 1,000, were not included in the count 'in the census of 1834–5', though they were subsequently (and probably previously).

4 Howes, *Gibraltarian*, p. 44, for 1814; HCPP, *A Return of the Number of . . . Officers and Men*, 140, 1 March 1843, which gives garrison figures for 1792, 1822, 1828, 1830, 1835 and 1842; *Report on the Blue Book for 1888*, p. 8, gives 5,708 for 1881; *Annual Report for 1891*, p. 8, gives 5,896, and *Annual Report for 1901*, p. 17, gives 6,475. See also J. Padiak, 'The "serious evil of marching regiments": the families of the British garrison of Gibraltar', *History of the Family*, 10 (2005), 137–50, who provides the data for 1878.

5 Fa and Finlayson, *Fortifications*, p. 31.

6 *Blue Book for 1888*, p. 8, *Annual Report for 1891*, p. 8, *Annual Report for 1901*, p. 17. The 'fixed civil population' excludes aliens, whose age profile and therefore death rate were lower. See S.D.A. Burke and L.A. Sawchuk, 'Alien encounters: the *jus soli* and

immigrants were still clamouring to enter through that porous land frontier, as well as by sea, whether as permanent settlers or as transients temporarily let in or as day visitors: and how hard it was for the authorities to distinguish between the one and the other. Those characteristics which had allowed British Gibraltar to survive and thrive economically in the eighteenth century now became more problematic. Gibraltar had become a still more attractive location for business and employment during the Napoleonic wars, and its appeal, though variable in intensity, was not lost thereafter. The continuing military presence and the already substantial civilian numbers made the Rock still magnetic to migrant labour seeking employment, and that market's demand, the location of Gibraltar between Atlantic and Mediterranean, a frontier with Spain which could be crossed, and the remaining virtues of Gibraltar's free port status continued to pull in entrepreneurs. The opportunities were further boosted when the opening of the Suez Canal in 1869 placed Gibraltar on a shorter all-water route to India and the Far East. Always influencing the decisions of prospective migrants about whether, when and where to move is knowledge (real or imagined) of comparative opportunities. Gibraltar did not have a government seeking to attract settlers by advertising, quite the reverse, but it contained increasingly a civilian population which retained ancestral connections to places of origin. If the data existed to check, one would probably find in Gibraltar, as elsewhere, the clustering of settlement consequent on so-called chain migration – families and neighbours following pioneers. Comparisons between expectations 'here' and those apparently available 'there' were being made, especially by young adults, whether to stay in Genoa, or Catalonia, or Andalusia, or Portugal, or even Britain, or whether to take the boat into the bay or the walk along the isthmus.

Three factors determined the government's treatment of civilians and the reception of immigrants. The first was strategic. Even in the comparatively long European peace of the nineteenth century, Gibraltar was still regarded principally as a fortress. Its security and efficiency conditioned most responses to demographic developments. Governors of the colony were always senior army officers and their responsibilities included that of commander-in-chief of the army garrison. Their 'line manager' was until 1854 the Secretary of State for War and the Colonies, thereafter the Secretary of State for War; Gibraltar did not become a Colonial Office responsibility until April 1867, and even thereafter the War Office was still a powerful influence on the territory's internal affairs, and the development of the dockyard increased the Admiralty's intervention.

reproductive politics in the 19th-century fortress and colony of Gibraltar', *History of the Family*, 6 (2001), p. 537, for a valuable chart showing numbers of births, marriages and deaths, 1830–1900. The average crude death rate for England and Wales 1876–1900 was 19.26, and the birth rate 32.28: R. Woods, *The Population of Britain in the Nineteenth Century* (London: Macmillan, 1992), p. 29.

The second was space and sanitation. Officials and ministers in Gibraltar and in London became increasingly concerned about overcrowding. The nineteenth century inherited not a planned Georgian town, but a confusion of often ramshackle properties on medieval streets, much more like the Avon Street slum district of Bath than its Royal Crescent. In the first part of the century the precise connection between overcrowding and public health was no better understood in Gibraltar than in Britain, but that there was a connection was widely attested, and better understanding later on did not reduce concern. Water supply and sanitation were initially primitive, even where existent. 'Effluvia' in the early part of the century slurped down to the sea, where they encrusted the walls; the gases they gave off discoloured silverware; and neither curfew nor quarantine could keep disease at bay. Governors were not indifferent to the discomfort of civilians, but they were also responsible for the health and efficiency of the garrison. Troops died in considerable numbers in the yellow fever epidemics and their health was a major cause of concern when cholera broke out later.[7] In the eyes of governors, and of London ministers, overcrowding of the town by civilians was the cause of insanitary conditions and of the epidemics which threatened the security of the military base.

The third prompt to demographic controls was the *jus soli*.[8] As explained in a previous chapter, by ancient legal convention those born in the territories of His or Her Britannic Majesty became automatically his or her subjects. While 'subject' does not appear to contain the positive connotations of 'citizen', nevertheless the status of British subject conventionally carried an entitlement, namely to residence anywhere in His or Her Majesty's realms. The nineteenth and twentieth centuries were to be coloured by efforts in Britain and in British-derived overseas communities to escape those implications. Governors of Gibraltar, surrounded by fecund young immigrants and squalling babies, struggled to cope. In their coping they categorised, discriminated and attempted to deny. In responding, civilians identified their interests, established their allegiances and constructed their identities.

Identifying the alien, 1815–1860s

It is not surprising that in 1814, soon after his arrival in Gibraltar, Lieutenant-Governor Don turned his attention to coping with the rise in population. His landing, after all, had been delayed by that outbreak of yellow fever which had immediately afterwards prompted his civil hospital and sanitation reforms. From time to time, some governors and their advisers questioned the right of entry and

---

7 L.A. Sawchuk, *Deadly Visitations in Dark Times: a Social History of Gibraltar* (Gibraltar: Gibraltar Government Heritage Division, 2001).

8 On this theme see Burke and Sawchuk, 'Alien encounters', pp. 531–61.

of residence of British subjects, even of the Gibraltar born, stressing that their principal obligation to military security overrode their duty to respect *jus soli* rights.[9] But Don largely accepted the right of all those born in Gibraltar to be entitled to residence and also the right of all other British subjects to enter and, if they wished, to reside (subject, of course, to good behaviour). Indeed, in an attempt to clarify a confusion he had inherited, he announced in a proclamation issued in June 1816 that those already resident in Gibraltar for ten years or more did not need a residential permit.[10] This measure, drawing a line under the past, extended to such former immigrants some of the entitlements enjoyed by British subjects, including the Gibraltar born.

But this positive was combined with a negative. Henceforth, from 1816, those who were not British subjects, those not already resident in Gibraltar for ten years, those subsequently seeking entry and residence, and even those intending only brief, even daily visits did need to secure a permit and were deemed 'foreigners', 'strangers' or 'aliens'. Here is the heart of what Don, his successors and London ministries henceforth struggled to manage, and which civilians with multi-ethnic origins often sought to ignore. The aim was, on the one hand, to define and identify those, principally British subjects, entitled to residence and, on the other, to define and detect those aliens not so blessed, who could properly be excluded entirely or allowed in conditionally. Enforcing these distinctions required stricter controls at points of entry through the walls, and closer bureaucratic surveillance of those residing within.

There was of course nothing new about requiring those arriving from outside, whether for temporary or lasting residence, to declare themselves and to persuade the military authorities to issue a permit, but Don re-emphasised that obligation within a month of his arrival, by a public proclamation in November 1814. Its content and tenor can stand for several subsequent iterations.[11]

> Whereas Foreigners of all Nations and Strangers have been indiscriminately permitted to establish themselves in this Garrison and whereas the health of the Troops and Inhabitants has been thereby greatly endangered, the public peace disturbed and good order subverted, it is therefore hereby ordered and directed that no person of any description whatever be in future suffered to establish himself in this Garrison without a permit signed by the Lieutenant Governor and countersigned by the Town Major.

9 TNA, CO879/9/16, and GGA Box: The Alien Question, Confidential Print, Flood to Williams, 12 May 1871, p. 41, and attorney-general, 'Memorandum on the Right of Residence in Gibraltar', 6 Jan 1937.
10 GGA, Box: The Alien Question, Flood to colonial secretary, 13 April 1866, quoting Don Proclamation of 29 June 1816.
11 GGA, Box: The Alien Question, Flood to Williams, 12 May 1871, Appendix A, No 10, 12 Nov 1814, and see No 12 and No 13, extracts from Don's despatches 15 Nov and 16 Dec 1814.

In May 1817, to protect the well-being of local labour and to prevent overcrowding and sickness, Don attempted by further measures to obstruct the immigration of 'indigent Foreigners' into Gibraltar. No 'Labourer, Mechanic, Servant or otherwise' was to be allowed a permit of residence unless 'some respectable Inhabitants' had previously applied for such a permit for a specified period for 'mercantile business', had agreed to accept responsibility for seeing such persons leave the garrison when the permit expired and had put up a financial bond as surety. Employers were obliged to register with the town major the address of such employees and to produce them within twenty-four hours if called to do so, or face fines. Moreover, even those aliens already resident had to be registered.[12]

Indicative of bureaucratic surveillance, from 25 July 1817 all permits issued, and any extensions, were duly recorded in large volumes arranged by district (Town Range, Castle, Blue Barrack . . .). These detailed the date and number of the permit, the permit holder's name (Augustin Coda, Francisco Jose, Catalina del Rios . . .), address (Church Street, Prince Edward Road, Library Ramp . . .), trade (servant, shopkeeper, gardener, mason, washerwoman . . .), family size (one, three, five . . .), and 'nation' (Spain, Portugal, Genoa, Sicily, Minorca, France . . .). There followed the duration of the permit (three months, six months, twelve months, 'until further orders' . . .), the length of residence if already in Gibraltar (three months, seven months, three years, twenty-seven years . . .), and, in the column headed 'Under the Responsibility of', the name of the person who had put up the surety bond (Revd Vicar Padre Zino, Henry Stokes, Nicola Morello . . .).[13] At the same time, new orders were issued to the 'Inspectors of Strangers' stationed at Waterport and at Bayside Barrier (protecting Landport), instructing them to interrogate visitors, to look out for subterfuge and to check that those who were admitted on day permits did actually leave at the end of the day. Their orders additionally expose the level of surveillance intended to be exercised over the civilian population: 'As you are supposed to know every person that is an inhabitant of Gibraltar, you are to cause every person that you may happen not to know to be stopped from coming in or going out until the doubts are removed.'[14]

Moreover, even resident civilians would know that they were under inspection. In November 1826 yet another census was held, the seventh in the century. (In Britain there had so far been only three.) It confirmed what residents knew and the governor feared, that the population was still growing rapidly, at well over 3 per cent a year. Census categories no longer focused primarily on religious groups

---

12 GGA, Box: The Alien Question, Flood to Williams, 12 May 1871, Appendix A, No 15, Proclamation 17 May 1817, including specimens of application form and permit; TNA, CO91/95, and GGA, Despatches from Gibraltar 1828: Don to Murray, 31 Oct and 15 Dec 1828.

13 GGA, Permit Books, 5 volumes, 1817–29.

14 GGA, Box: The Alien Question, Flood to Williams, 12 May 1871, pp. 18–19, Appendix A, No 8.

– the battle for a Protestant Ascendancy was long lost – but the underlying official anxieties remained. The census summary organised the population essentially by nationality, beginning with 'British Subjects' (total 976, only 117 of whom were under 12, fewer than 12 per cent of them), then 'Native Christians' (6,416, including 3,759 under 12, nearly 59 per cent of the total) and 'Native Jews' (1,903, including 444 under 12, nearly 37 per cent), summarising all three as 'Natives or British Subjects'. In truth, all these were being recognised as British subjects having been born in Gibraltar (including those with one or more alien parent), or in another of His Majesty's dominions (mainly Britain), but it is apparent that few of the British born, unlike the other components, were staying to raise families. The rest of the table dealt with 'Strangers' living in Gibraltar at the time of the census (6,908). It listed them by their foreign nationality, thus, among others, 'Spaniards' (3,057), 'Genoese' (1,588), 'Portuguese' (876), 'Minorquins', that is Minorcans (461), 'Barbary Jews' (456), 'Italians' (168), 'French' (91), 'Germans' (84), 'Moors' (69), 'United States of America' (23), 'Turks' (14) and even 'Russians' (1). For the British authorities, the new alarm was that the 8,595 'British or Native Subjects' formed only a little more than half of the total civilian population of 15,503. There were, in brief, still too many 'Strangers'. Noticeably too, a far larger proportion of the population captured by the census count were Spanish: uniquely among foreign nationals, they included more females (1,789) than males (1,268).[15]

The young Benjamin Disraeli, visiting in June 1830, rejoiced in the exotic complexion of Gibraltar, 'a wonderful place with a population infinitely diversified',[16] but government was less exhilarated and responded to this kind of demographic data with increased immigration controls and more internal surveillance. In February 1827, Don again assured the secretary of state that he would follow instructions to restrict the admission of foreigners and would be cautious about renewing permits of residence already issued.[17] He might well have expected his efforts to be having the desired effect upon the civilian numbers and behaviour. The gates were guarded, orders were given and proclamations were published. Permits were issued, inspected and recorded. Defaulters were fined.

It was therefore disconcerting when, in July 1828, it was discovered that a notorious pirate, Benito de Soto, responsible for several atrocities – most recently for plundering a British vessel, the *Morning Star*, and murdering the captain and several of the crew – had taken up residence in a tavern in the middle of town.[18]

15　GGA, Despatches from Gibraltar 1827: Don to Bathurst, 9 Feb 1827, and enclosures.
16　R. Blake, *Disraeli's Grand Tour: Benjamin Disraeli and the Holy Land 1830–31* (London: Weidenfeld and Nicolson, 1982), p. 12.
17　GGA, Despatches to/from Gibraltar 1827: Hay to Don, 31 Jan 1827, Don to Bathurst, 12 Feb 1827.
18　For this episode, its consequences and references to sources see S. Constantine, 'The pirate, the governor, and the secretary of state: aliens, police and surveillance in early nineteenth-century Gibraltar', *English Historical Review*, 123 (2008), 1166–92.

Inquiry revealed that Soto had secured a letter of recommendation to a Gibraltar merchant from a duped British vice-consul in Galicia and a permit from a Spanish official in Algeciras and, in May 1828, armed with these bits of paper, he had obtained initially a one-day permit of entry at Waterport, not in the name of Benito de Soto, pirate, but in masquerade as José Pelegrina Sanchez, dealer. Moreover, he had bamboozled a gullible licensed broker to stand surety for him to allow for a longer stay and he had then been allowed by the town major's office, without further inquiry, to extend his residency for 'business reasons'.

Don's protestations to London that this was but an embarrassing lapse in an otherwise sound system did not deflect the Secretary of State for War and the Colonies, Sir Charles Murray, from using his superior authority to insist on radical change. His temper was not sweetened when disease, another outbreak of yellow fever, also penetrated Gibraltar's quarantine defences in the autumn of 1828 and killed over 1,600 people.[19] Moreover, another census he had immediately ordered revealed that the civilian population had still gone up between November 1826 and March 1829, by another thousand. To set against 9,173 'British Subjects and Natives of the Garrison' was a disturbingly large 7,221 'Resident Foreigners' (of whom 1,928 had been resident for less than five years, and 3,445 for over fifteen years).[20] In Murray's mind the connections were obvious. Public health and garrison security must be protected, first, by strictly applying the 'rules of quarantine', second, by the 'cleansing of the Town' and third, and just as important, by 'diminishing the unnecessary part of [the] population', and by this he meant the 'crowds of low foreigners who infest the place'.[21] To achieve this last, by instructions issued in April 1830, the governor's town major was to hand over responsibility for controlling foreign visitors and foreign residents to a civilian police magistrate, appointed by Murray, who was to head Gibraltar's first civilian police force.[22] Even he was allowed to issue only temporary permits. Anything longer than three days had to be authorised personally by the governor. Moreover, granting to an alien a right to permanent residence was to be reserved to the secretary of state.[23] The secretary of state was also to be sent regular statements

19 Sawchuk, *Deadly Visitations*, p. 60.
20 TNA, CO91/97, and GGA, Despatches to Gibraltar 1829: Don to Murray 6 March 1829.
21 TNA, CO92/8, Murray to Don, 28 July 1829.
22 TNA, CO92/10, and GGA, Despatches to Gibraltar 1830: Murray to Don, 30 April 1830; C. Baldachino and T. Benady, *The Royal Gibraltar Police 1830–2005* (Gibraltar: Gibraltar Books, 2005), pp. 3–7.
23 TNA, CO92/8, and GGA, Despatches to Gibraltar 1829: Murray to Don, 19 Jan, 1 March, 3 May, 16 Nov 1829 and see proclamation in the *Gibraltar Chronicle*, 27 Jan 1831.

explaining the reasons why each temporary permit of residence had been issued or extended.[24]

There were going to be no rapid results. Yet another census was held in January 1831, and the recorded population had gone up yet again, to 17,024. Getting in by being born in Gibraltar accounted for only a proportion of the new arrivals: births of 529 in 1830 were only a couple of hundred more than deaths of 332. Altogether, 'British Subjects and Natives' had risen by nearly a thousand since March 1829, to 10,116 (59 per cent), but in spite of all efforts the 'Resident Foreigners and Aliens' had fallen by only 300, to 6,908.[25] The new secretary of state, Lord Goderich, like his predecessor, deplored the consequences for public health and garrison security caused by such excessive numbers, especially of foreigners, and insisted that far fewer temporary permits of residence should be allowed. Don protested that 'as long as the Garrison continues a place of trade and a Free Port' it would always be difficult to limit numbers. But in June 1831, as another tightening of the screw, Goderich demanded that no permit should be extended beyond a year 'without my express sanction'.[26]

As a result, in part, of such measures the census of 1840 revealed not just a reduction in the total population, to 15,554, but a modest rise in the number of British subjects, to 11,313 and a more impressive increase in their share of the total, to 73 per cent (Table 4.2).

However, the categorisation shows that those in authority were still acutely aware of the diminishing proportion of the total number of British subjects who were actually born in the UK, just 868, fewer than 8 per cent as compared with those born in Gibraltar, the other 92 per cent, who included many with one or more alien parent. The future did not look good either, since fewer than 8 per cent of the UK-born 'British Subjects' were aged under 12, whereas the proportion for 'Native Jews' was 26 per cent and for 'Native Christians' a remarkable 39 per cent. With respect to the 'Aliens', it was also apparent that the Spanish-born component of the whole population was not only very large, 14 per cent, but also disproportionately females, and therefore potentially mothers. Moreover, this had of course long since ceased to be even in pretension a Protestant Christian community, since Protestants numbered only 9 per cent of the population, fewer

---

24 GGA, Box: The Alien Question, Flood to colonial secretary, 13 April 1866; and Flood to Williams, 12 May 1871, Appendix A, No 27, despatches to Don, 8 Dec 1830, No 28, 25 April 1831, No 30, 4 June 1831; Box: Miscellaneous Matters Relating to the Alien Question, Police Office to Houston, 12 March 1832; TNA, CO91/113, Don to Goderich, 21 March 1831.

25 TNA, CO91/113, and GGA, Despatches from Gibraltar 1831: Don to Goderich, 7 April and 13 May 1831.

26 TNA, CO92/10, and GGA, Despatches to Gibraltar 1831: Goderich to Don, 7 May and 4 June 1831, and Goderich to Houston, 21 July and 1 Oct 1831; CO91/114, Don to Houston, 17 June 1831.

Table 4.2 *Census of civilian population, 1840*

'Nations'	'Total of each Nation'			Totals
	Males	Females	Totals	
'British Subjects'	426	442	868	
'Native Christians'	4,397	4,715	9,112	
'Native Jews'	631	702	1,333	
Total British subjects				*11,313*
Barbary Jews	253	21	274	
French	43	22	65	
Genoese	618	345	963	
Italians	95	13	108	
Moors	15	0	15	
Portuguese	369	222	591	
Spaniards	792	1,368	2,160	
Others	47	18	65	
Total aliens				*4,241*
Grand total				*15,554*

Source: CO91/150, Woodford to Russell, 7 May 1840.

even than the Hebrew community, who made up 10 per cent, and way behind the Catholic masses, who formed 81 per cent.[27]

Concern about population growth and the alien presence therefore remained, and successive governors were pressed by London to apply the regulations and make reports.[28] True, some governors, and indeed some secretaries of state, were more zealous than others. For example, secretary of state Lord Stanley decided in April 1833 that he needed to see only a monthly total of numbers admitted on temporary permits and not reports on each case; and in

27 In addition there were 14 'Mahomedans'. See also TNA, CO91/150, reply by Russell, 25 June 1840, to Woodford to Russell, 1 June 1840, expressing concerns about children born to alien parents, alien property ownership, and 'the safety of the Place'.
28 TNA, CO92/10, Goderich to Don, 25 April, 9 May, 30 May, 6 July, 2 Aug 1831, Goderich to Houston, 19 Sept 1831, 5 Feb 1832; CO91/134, 'Lists of Applications for the Renewal of Temporary Permits of Strangers already Admitted into the Garrison, 1831–5'; CO92/16, Stanley to Woodford, 14 May, and Stanley to Wilson, 24 Dec 1842; CO91/162, Wilson to Stanley, 5 Jan 1843; CO91/226, containing twelve reports from Gardiner in 1855 covering Nov 1854 to Oct 1855; GGA, Box: The Alien Question, Flood to Williams, 12 May 1871, Appendix A, despatches to Houston, No 38, 23 March 1834, No 40, 31 Dec 1834; Despatches from Gibraltar 1842: Woodford to Stanley 30 June 1842; Box: Police Register of Permits 1831–1833, Register of Temporary Permits 1842–43.

April 1842 he no longer asked for extensions beyond a year to be automatically referred to him.[29] Sir Robert Wilson, governor 1842–48, was certainly strict and exercised less discretion in applying the rules than did his successor, Sir Robert Gardiner, 1848–55,[30] while Sir William Codrington, governor 1859–65, seems to have decided that new permits of residence lasting more than a year should never be issued to aliens.[31] A right of permanent residence granted to aliens therefore became a rare gift, and even temporary permits were sometimes refused and often not renewed (650 in 1832).[32] A Portuguese merchant was not allowed to join his already resident nephew, and applications were rejected likewise from a Moorish Jew, a merchant from Tangier, a 'foreign' physician and 'two young gentlemen' from Buenos Aires. A 'Barbary Jew' and his family who, ten years earlier, had had a temporary permit were denied a permanent right to enter, 'considering the crowded state of our population', and a permit was denied to an Italian businessman, even though his application was supported by a British MP.[33] In spite of some moral qualms, indigent aliens were usually expelled.[34]

29 GGA, Box: Miscellaneous Matters Relating to the Alien Question, Extract of Despatch from Secretary of State to Houston, 24 April 1833; TNA, CO92/16, Stanley to Woodford, 14 May 1842. According to Flood, this last decision was a bad mistake which allowed slackness to creep into the system, TNA, CO879/9/16, and GGA Box: The Alien Question, Flood to Williams, 12 May 1871, p. 47.

30 TNA, CO879/9/16, and GGA Box: The Alien Question, Flood to Williams, 12 May 1871, p. 47.

31 GGA, Despatches to Secretary of State for War, Airey to Ripon, 17 Feb 1866.

32 CO91/159, Woodford to Stanley, 6 July, and Stanley to Woodford, 22 July 1842; GGA, Despatches from Gibraltar 1827: Don to Huskisson, 31 Oct 1827 (a Frenchman's permit, after a residence of four years, was not renewed); Box: Miscellaneous Matters Relating to the Alien Question, Rowan to Houston, 12 March 1832; Box: The Alien Question, Flood to Williams, 12 May 1871, p. 44, Appendix A, Nos 66–71, Sept 1847–Feb 1849 (expulsion on orders of the governor of a tailor to whom the police magistrate had, on his personal surety, allowed a residential permit).

33 TNA, CO92/10, Goderich to Houston, 27 July and 4 Sept 1831; CO91/115, Houston to Goderich, 12 Oct 1831; CO91/139, Glenelg to Woodford, 25 Oct 1837; CO92/16, Stanley to Wilson, 31 Dec 1842; CO91/289, Airey to Duke of Buckingham and Chandos, 22 May 1867; GGA, Box: The Alien Question, Flood to Williams, 12 May 1871, Appendix A, despatches to Houston, No 36, 12 July 1832, No 39, 29 Nov 1834, despatches to Woodford, No 43, 30 Nov 1835, No 44, 21 Feb 1836; Despatches from Gibraltar 1842: Woodford to Stanley, 16 May 1842.

34 For example, TNA, CO92/10, Goderich to Houston, 1 Oct 1831; CO91/115, Houston to Goderich 12 Oct 1831; CO91/116, Houston to Goderich, 8 Nov 1831; GGA, Box: Miscellaneous Matters Relating to the Alien Question, Rowan to Houston, 12 March 1832.

Gibraltar's management was not alone in feeling the need to control the immigration of foreigners into a British military colony. An influx of political refugees into Malta in 1842 prompted the War Office to draft legislation to strengthen its governor's power to cope, and this was extended to include Gibraltar since it, too, experienced an influx of refugees from time to time. Accordingly, the Aliens Order-in-Council, dated 1 February 1843, confirmed that governors in both places could, on their own authority, legally order the expulsion from their territory of 'any person not being a natural born or a naturalized subject of Her Majesty', and order the arrest, imprisonment and then 'forcible removal' of any person, in effect an undesirable immigrant, not leaving as instructed.[35] This was followed in November 1843 by a Gibraltar ordinance which empowered the police to enter and search premises where the governor had 'reason to believe that any Alien may be harboured or concealed and to search for and take into custody such Alien to be dealt with according to Law'.[36] It was then discovered that there was no law prohibiting anyone, whether native or alien, from assisting the entry into Gibraltar of an undesirable, permit-less foreigner, and there were doubts even about the legality of punishing any resident harbouring such a person. Accordingly, in 1846 a further tightening of legislative controls over the civilian population was enacted, and an Aliens Ordinance was issued by the governor to stamp out such misbehaviour. Offenders could be hauled before the Supreme Court and fined or imprisoned.[37]

But there remained the problem of the *jus soli*, and the entitlement of those born in Gibraltar to enjoy permanent rights of residence as British subjects on their native turf. As noted, census data included figures for children aged under 12, but those counted as 'British Subjects' or 'Native Christians' or 'Native Jews' were not necessarily the children of 'British Subjects' or 'Native Christians' or 'Native Jews'. Many would have an alien mother or alien father or could even be the children of two alien parents, and yet by birth in Gibraltar they qualified as natives. In the early years, when population was increasing especially by immigration, marriage between a couple of whom both had been born in Gibraltar was actually uncommon, accounting for fewer than 7 per cent of the married

35 CO158/122, Stanley to Bouverie, 12 Feb 1843; A.V. Laferla, *British Malta* (Malta: Government Printing Office, vol. 1, 1938), p. 202.
36 GGA, Box: The Alien Question, Flood to Williams, 12 May 1871, Appendix A, No 57, 'An Ordinance for Improving the Gibraltar Police', 4 Nov 1843.
37 For background see correspondence on TNA, CO91/173, CO91/176 and CO92/16, and GGA, Despatches to and from Gibraltar 1846; *Orders in Council, Ordinances and Proclamations Relating to Gibraltar* (Gibraltar: Gibraltar Government, 1839, Part III, 1857), p. 25; GGA, Box: The Alien Question, Flood to Williams, 12 May 1871, p. 47, and Appendix A, No 58.

population in 1834, whereas in 13 per cent of marriages one partner was an alien, and the remaining 80 per cent were between two aliens.[38] In the eyes of civilians the marriage of a 'British Subject' or a 'Native' to an alien or marriage between two aliens was a thing of beauty, or at least of convenience, but to the authorities it threatened to increase Gibraltar's resident population by not just one more alien adult but also children born of that marriage. And, of course, children born in Gibraltar but out of wedlock would also be natives of that place with a permanent right of residence. The response of the authorities was predictable: surveillance, prohibition and, if possible, expulsion.

It was already a requirement that a licence of marriage had to be obtained from the office of the civil secretary (not just from the church). In November 1822 Lord Chatham, during his brief appearance in Gibraltar of which nominally he was governor from 1820 to 1835, decreed that a marriage in Gibraltar involving an alien male was to be followed by the exclusion of the couple from Gibraltar. This was obviously a gendered policy. The ineligibility for residence of native wives was determined by the ineligibility of their alien husbands, as case histories revealed. For example, in April 1823 Father John Baptist Zino, the Vicar-General, asked the governor for permission to marry Joseph Otero, native of Spain, servant, and for fourteen years a resident of Gibraltar, to Elizabeth Barn, native of England. As Zino coyly put it, 'I have found out that the above person has been in the habit of communicating with this same woman and has lately had a child by her' – who would of course have been born a British subject. Chatham's response was crisp: 'On condition that the parties quit the Garrison in 3 months.'[39] In 1835 the secretary of state himself confirmed that a Moorish Jew, and therefore an alien, should not be allowed a permit to enter Gibraltar in order to marry and reside with a 'young woman, a native of the place'. There was also, in December 1842, the hopeless case of Louis Garcia, a native of Spain but a permitted resident of fifteen years who, having been the employee of an apothecary, now planned to set up on his own; he wanted a permit of residence for his wife, also a native of Spain, since he could not manage without her 'permanent and continued domestic assistance': application denied.[40] Later, in September 1850, when Sir Robert Gardiner discovered that Chatham's rule had not been consistently applied, he ordered that alien men already married to British or native women would be allowed to remain in Gibraltar on renewable but temporary permits, but their wives must have their babies outside Gibraltar. Henceforth alien men marrying in Gibraltar would only

38 Burke and Sawchuk. 'Alien encounters', p. 534, based on an analysis of 1,672 married couples.
39 GGA, Box: The Alien Question, Flood to Williams, 12 May 1871, p. 43, Appendix A, Nos 16, 17.
40 GGA, Box: The Alien Question, Flood to Williams, 12 May 1871, p. 43, Appendix A, Nos 41, 49–53, and also see Nos 63 and 65 for other cases.

be allowed briefly to remain residents.[41] In 1863 Dr Hauser, 'a Hebrew Alien', after two years in Gibraltar on a temporary permit, was told that if he married a woman in Paris, as he intended, his wife, also an alien, would be 'obliged to be confined without the City and Territory, so that their children would not become British subjects'; there was an inevitable fuss when, in 1866, it was discovered that she had had a baby in Gibraltar.[42]

On the other hand, but not automatically, native men were granted some tolerance. There seems to have been no automatic right for the alien wife to reside in Gibraltar with her native husband. Cases seem to have been treated at the discretion of the governor.[43] In July 1839 the Spanish wife of Joseph Abrines, native of Gibraltar, was allowed to join her husband. Likewise, in July 1842 Mary Parody, a native of Spain but many years a resident in Gibraltar, was granted a permanent permit of residence at the request of her husband of three years, John Parody, native of Gibraltar, who had already had two children by her, 'both natives of this Garrison', though it required the permission of the secretary of state to secure this concession.[44] Moreover, Sir Robert Wilson was influential in ensuring that British nationality legislation passing through parliament in 1847 did not, in the case of colonies, automatically confer British nationality on the alien wives of British husbands.[45] Thereafter their residence in Gibraltar, or indeed expulsion therefrom, had to be approved by the governor, case by case. But there were tricky situations, which in 1866 exercised Gibraltar's attorney-general. F. Solly Flood was particularly concerned that 'Alien prostitutes', not

---

41 TNA, CO879/9/16, and GGA Box: The Alien Question, Flood to Williams, 12 May 1871, p. 48, and Box: The Alien Question, Correspondence Re the Alien Question 1866–1886, copy of Sir Robert Gardiner, Memorandum, 23 Sept 1850. See also GL, Sir Robert Gardiner, 'Report on Gibraltar Considered as a Fortress and a Colony', 15 Jan 1856, appendix 'Report . . . addressed to Earl Grey, Secretary of State', 11 Oct 1850, p. 161, where the governor refers in alarm to 'the swarms of children born in the city, many of whose fathers are alien residents' and the steps he had taken to 'check the evil'.

42 TNA, CO91/264, Codrington to Earl de Grey and Ripon, 12 May 1863, GGA, Despatches to Gibraltar 1866: Peel to Airey, 30 Nov 1866.

43 TNA, CO91/285, Flood to Freeling, 25 Aug 1866, with Acting Governor to Peel, 4 Sept 1866, reviews cases from 1833 to 1866 and shows that some applications were refused and that a wife could even be expelled.

44 GGA, Box: The Alien Question, Flood to Williams, 12 May 1871, p. 43, Appendix A, No 48; TNA, CO91/159, Woodford to Stanley, 6 July, and Stanley to Woodford, 22 July 1842.

45 'An Act for the Naturalization of Aliens', 10 & 11 Victoria c.83, 22 July 1847, amending 'An Act to Amend the Laws relating to Aliens', 7 & 8 Victoria c.66, 6 Aug 1844; TNA, CO91/285, Acting Governor to Peel, 4 Sept 1866, 'Case' quoting Costello, 15 Sept 1859.

content with doing business in Gibraltar's brothels, were luring British 'tommies' into marriage and then claiming rights of residence as British citizens even after their dear husbands had been posted elsewhere. Following an application to London, a ruling by the Crown's Law Officers determined that an alien wife did not become a naturalised British subject by marriage, could be denied entry and could be expelled, and indeed a husband preventing such an expulsion could be guilty of harbouring an alien.[46]

Concerns about births in Gibraltar also explain the introduction of tighter official recording. The British parliament had legislated in 1835 for the civil registration of births, marriages and deaths, but it was not just to catch up that Governor Wilson also passed an ordinance, to come into effect in October 1848, requiring the registration of all births in Gibraltar, with penalties for non-registration, late registration, false registration or falsifying the registration.[47] Registration was to be essential evidence of belonging.

Civilian responses: subterfuge and denial

British intentions are therefore clear enough: to limit Gibraltar's civilian population by distinguishing between 'British and Native subjects' and 'Aliens', and to tolerate the residence and to accept, though reluctantly, the multiplication of the former, while restricting the rights, discouraging the increase and if possible reducing the presence of the latter. Unintended but implicit may have been the implantation of a distinctive identity in the heads of the native born which would separate them from aliens inside as well as outside the territory of Gibraltar. However, the response of civilians to the rules shows how 'irresponsible' they were, and resistant to official efforts at discrimination. There were frontiers on the ground, but less so in people's minds.

Evidence for this lies, of course, in the regulations and the bureaucracy of inspection and surveillance. Repeatedly, attempts were made to separate those who did not wish to be separated, prising apart those classed as legitimate residents and those who, by accident of birth, were not. There was a moral law which ignored such distinctions. Don's 1817 instructions to the Inspectors of Strangers at Waterport warned them to 'take the utmost care that among the fishermen and boatmen who belong to the town and come in at the opening of the gates no strangers without permits creep in with them as there is great reason to think improper persons avail themselves of such opportunities to get into the Fortress'. It was understood that intruders could only gain access with the connivance of those legitimately entitled to enter, since the fishermen or boatmen

---

46 TNA, CO91/285, Acting Governor to Peel, 4 Sept 1866, and enclosure, minutes, and Peel to Airey 9 Nov 1866.
47 *Orders in Council, etc*, Part III, pp. 57–62.

who 'belong' to Gibraltar were also to be detained with those trying to sneak in. Likewise, at Bayside Barrier the inspectors were to ensure that persons without permits should not manage to gain entry by mingling in the company of those who belonged.[48] And yet, in 1828 it was conceded by the town major that illegal immigrants still sometimes slipped in by joining outside working parties, or even mourners returning from the graveyard beyond the walls at North Front – which, to be a successful ruse, would also seem to require connivance; and there were those who borrowed from 'the lowest class of women' in Gibraltar their distinctive red cloaks and, so disguised, somehow slipped in.[49] Sir Robert Wilson alleged in 1844 that there were constant attempts to smuggle pregnant women and new-born children into Gibraltar in order to secure British status, which traffic also suggests insider cooperation.[50] Even the Aliens Ordinance of 1846 outlawing the aiding and harbouring of illegal immigrants presupposes that there were residents in Gibraltar doing the aiding and harbouring. Indeed the immediate prompt for this additional law was the arrest of a Spaniard who had already been ejected once from Gibraltar but who had re-entered by swimming ashore 'from a boat at the Bathing place'. A wet and naked man may have been observed, even in mid-nineteenth-century Gibraltar, but in fact an 'inhabitant, a native' had 'provided him with clothes'.[51] Regulations were trying to impose distinctions which those separately distinguished did not recognise.

Love knows no boundaries. Chatham's regulations to prevent the unpreventable were being repeatedly reiterated because love (or lust) set them at defiance. In this most intimate of relationships, civilians in Gibraltar were rejecting an apartheid based on territorial sovereignty. The census of 1834 suggests some representative (and some defiant) life choices: John Ghiglizza, by then a 51-year-old 'alien' gardener from Genoa, was married to Ana, a 48-year old 'alien' from Spain, and they had three boys and four girls. John Bosura, 41, a storeman from Genoa, was married to Catalina, 41, a native of Gibraltar, and they had six children. Abraham Cohen, 58, an 'alien' shopkeeper from Morocco, had married Esther, a native from Britain, and they had three children. Nicolas Traverso, 43, a native of Gibraltar and a police sergeant, was married to Gertrudes, from Portugal, also aged 43. Augustin and Maria Parody, he a clerk aged 31 and born in Gibraltar, she aged 19 from Spain, already had two babies aged under 2. John McDonald, shopkeeper, from Britain, had fallen for Juana from Spain and, now aged 50 and 42, they had brought up four children, two born in Spain, two

---

48 GGA, Box: The Alien Question, Flood to Williams, 12 May 1871, p. 48, Appendix A, No 8.
49 TNA, CO91/95, Don to Murray, 15 Dec 1828, enclosing report from town major, 1 Dec 1828.
50 TNA, CO91/167, Wilson to Stanley, 18 March 1844.
51 TNA, CO91/173, Wilson to Stanley, 10 June, 26 July and 31 July 1844.

born in Gibraltar. Rare but more acceptable to the authorities would have been Mr and Mrs Robert and Mary Henderson, he a schoolmaster from England, she from Gibraltar, and both Protestants, and Mr and Mrs Ralph Foreman, both English, both Protestant, three children.[52]

In 1837 Father Zino protested that restrictive regulations designed to discourage marriage between aliens and natives or between aliens and aliens were having unintended moral consequences. His parishioners, undeterred from falling in love with aliens, were choosing to live in sin and rear bastards rather than to enter into holy wedlock and be expelled from the garrison. (Better to go to Hell than go to Spain.) He claimed that he was having to baptise at least forty illegitimate children a year, and that other babies were being abandoned, or worse.[53] An official review in July 1840 concluded that 1,821 'children of Alien blood' (how revealing is the language) had been born in Gibraltar since 1831. Of these, 721 were the children of native women and alien men, 292 of alien women and native men, and 808 of parents both aliens. These were pretty alarming numbers, the proportion of 'births from Alien and mixed blood . . . to those from native parents' being as high as 1 to 2.5.[54]

To the authorities this was politically worrisome, because it left doubts about loyalties and reliability, but these liaisons are also evidence of the intimacy between native-born British subjects, immigrant aliens with legitimate if temporary permits of residence and other aliens, especially (but not only) from Spain, who came knocking on the door. In 1832, for example, the police magistrate, having reviewed extant permits of residence, concluded that Gibraltar was indeed overcrowded but that it was difficult to see how to effect a reduction since 'natives and foreigners are intermixed'.[55] And in 1844 Sir Robert Wilson complained that British interests were being threatened by the growing number of inhabitants who were technically British subjects because born in Gibraltar but who were Spanish by ethnic origin, family connections, language, culture, even residence and, he feared, allegiance.[56] The following year, in a further report, civilian resistance, or at least indifference, to segregation was still more starkly indicated: 'the greater part of the Native Inhabitants of Gibraltar are

52 GGA, 1834 Census Database. This census was the first taken by the police magistrate with the authority of the 'Ordinance for Taking an Account, from Time to Time, of the Civil Population of Gibraltar', 12 March 1834, *Orders in Council etc*, pp. 56–60.

53 C. Caruana, *The Rock under a Cloud* (Cambridge: Silent Books, 1989), pp. 213–14, Zino to Woodford, 6 Feb 1837.

54 GGA, Despatches from Gibraltar 1840: Woodford to Russell, 11 Aug 1840.

55 GGA, Box: Miscellaneous Matters Relating to the Alien Question, Rowan to Houston, 12 March 1832.

56 TNA, CO91/167, Wilson to Stanley, 18 March 1844, and his comments on the census return, 6 June 1844.

Aliens in all respects where their religion, language, and Spanish connections are concerned'.[57]

It has to be said that government regulations had some effect, although shortage of affordable accommodation in Gibraltar is as likely to explain the further slowing down of Gibraltar's annual population growth from 1840 as are stricter border controls. Nevertheless, the police magistrate was evidently pleased to report that his census of the civilian population in May 1844 showed an increase of only 269 since that of 1840. While his report passed over the number of 'native children' born to non-native parents, he was obviously relieved that the 'alien population' had gone down by 600 whereas the 'British and Native population' had increased by 869. Comparing this result with that of the census first conducted by the civil police magistrate in 1831, he was able to claim a reduction by 3,267 in the total size of the 'alien population', although 3,641 remained, to set against an increase of 'British subjects' to 12,182. Nevertheless, those 'British subjects' included only 995 from Britain (only 128 aged under 12), whereas there were 1,385 'Native Jews' (358 under 12) and 9,802 'Native Christians' (3,468 under 12, and this category is where most of the Gibraltar-born children of alien parentage would be lurking). There were still 1,892 Spaniards in the count (including 1,195 females, very important for the domestic transfer of culture and language), and 782 Genoese (293 females), 525 Portuguese (205 females), 240 'Barbary Jews' (a mere 20 females, the women usually at 'home' in Morocco), 90 'Italians' (14 females), 53 French (20 females), plus tiny numbers from elsewhere.[58]

But a later police magistrate, F. Solly Flood, produced a much more pessimistic assessment. He calculated that at the end of 1868 the population of Gibraltar amounted to 17,764. He classed only 582, a little over 3 per cent, as British. He reckoned that the rest were made up, first, of 3,480 aliens, with or without permits; second, of 5,525 descendants (he called them 'children' but they could be adults) of alien fathers born in Gibraltar (who counted as natives only under the *jus soli* rule); third, of 6,777 whom he named as 'children of natives incorporated and forming part of the population of alien character' (in other words corrupted); fourth, of 984 'natives of British origin', of whom a large number had also 'become incorporated in the population of alien character'; plus, fifth, of 416 whom he dismissed as 'Maltese and other strangers'. His calculations betray the prejudices and anxieties of an Anglo-Irish Protestant and a British nationalist, but his data also reveal the degrees of intermarriage (or, as he might say, miscegenation) which set government directives at nought.[59]

57 TNA, CO91/173, Wilson to Stanley, 31 July 1845.
58 TNA, CO91/168, Wilson to Stanley, 6 June 1844, and enclosures.
59 TNA, CO879/9/16, and GGA Box: The Alien Question, Confidential Print, Flood to Williams, 12 May 1871, p. 50. Indicative of Flood's denominational allegiance is his memorial plaque in Gibraltar's Anglican cathedral.

Tightening the rules: the Aliens Order-in-Council, 1873

The slower growth of population in the confined spaces of Gibraltar may have suited the accommodation and (less certainly) the employment prospects of resident civilians, but this alone did not reduce the concerns of those in authority. Gibraltar, they still reckoned, was overcrowded, public health was endangered (there were cholera outbreaks in 1860, 1865 and 1885),[60] and too many aliens were a security risk. On the other hand, many aliens with permits were recognised as pillars of the community, or at least as sturdy (and cheap) workers. What was needed was an official review.[61] The difficulty was that this was a matter upon which local inhabitants had opinions, some articulated by powerful voices representing special interests. There began a highly politicised argument between British authorities and sections of the Gibraltar community which altered the law but did not resolve the issue: who was to be allowed to live in Gibraltar and on what terms? While this debate was going on, most of those living on the Rock did just that: they worked, met, married and had children.

The police magistrate and attorney-general, F. Solly Flood, produced a report in April 1866 which urged the reintroduction of 'inflexible rules'. Otherwise, he reckoned, Gibraltar would become a 'rendezvous for traitors' and a 'hot bed for pestilence'. It would not be 'the right arm of England's commercial, industrial, naval and military strength' but 'her greatest curse'.[62] Encouraged by Sir Richard Airey, the governor, Flood then drew up a scheme: to clarify procedure; to determine who was entitled to request permits of residence for immigrants; to decide once and for all who from outside was entitled to entry and residence and for how long; to insert fierce penalties for infringements; and to add to existing restrictions. Thus, for example, he would have ended the long-standing entitlement of aliens resident for fifteen years to acquire property. He would have denied *jus soli* rights to the British or native-born wife of an alien by insisting that her right of residence depended on her inclusion on her husband's permit. Likewise a British or native-born widow of an alien husband would not be allowed automatic right of residence if she had children. He would also have allowed the Gibraltar-born children of alien fathers and the illegitimate children of alien women to reside only with permits, thus denying them too the *jus soli* rights of the native born. Too often, he claimed, confinements in Gibraltar were only being effected to secure those rights, and such children were 'Alien in heart'. By claiming 'British rights' they were setting 'all British Law and all decency and order at defiance

---

60 Sawchuk, *Deadly Visitations*, pp. 159–209, 239–71.
61 GGA, Despatches to Secretary of State for War, Airey to Ripon, 17 Feb 1866.
62 GGA, Box: The Alien Question, Correspondence Re the Alien Question 1866–1886, Flood to colonial secretary, 13 April 1866.

– the word "Native" has thus become synonimous [*sic*] with incorrigible rogue and vagabond'.[63]

Not all of this went down very well, especially with the governor's right-hand man, the colonial secretary, who warned that Flood did not understand the strength of feeling upon such matters among Gibraltar's business classes.[64] This the administration was shortly to provoke in September 1866, when, by a notification in the *Gibraltar Chronicle*, it invited members of the public to suggest ways of improving the system of issuing permits for aliens in a manner which would benefit the territory and prevent overcrowding.[65]

Among those who laid in first was the Right Reverend Dr John Baptist Scandella, of Genoese origin but Gibraltar born, who had become Vicar Apostolic in 1857.[66] He was at the same time in conflict with Flood over the permits he had secured to allow a (disputed) number of 'alien' boys to attend St Bernard's College, an educational foundation catering not just for local children. Flood was insisting that allowing in non-native boys was a violation of the permit system which, he claimed, with some documentary proof, had once specifically outlawed educational purposes as a justification for issuing a permit to an alien.[67] In his response to the administration's invitation, Scandella felt compelled to deplore, like his predecessors, what he saw as the immoral consequences of existing policies, and he feared that changes in the regulations might further outrage 'the principles of Christianity'. He conceded that, due to 'zealous efforts' begun by Dr Hughes, concubinage was less of a problem than in the past (sinful unions down to 250 by 1857 and 36 by 1865). However, he still objected to rules which deterred aliens from marrying because of fear of expulsion and which separated wives from husbands, even from British husbands, and also children from fathers. He warned that the strict application which characterised recent practice (that is by Flood) would lead to the 'most frightful immorality

63 GGA, Box: The Alien Question, Correspondence, Flood to Airey, 15 May 1866, copy with acting governor to Peel, 7 Sept 1866, in Dispatches from Gibraltar and TNA, CO91/285.

64 GGA, Box: The Alien Question, Correspondence, Freeling to Airey, 31 July 1866.

65 *Gibraltar Chronicle*, 16 Sept 1866, copy in minutes on TNA, CO91/285, acting governor to Peel, 7 Sept 1866.

66 Caruana, *Rock*, pp. 69–81.

67 GGA, Box: The Alien Question, Correspondence, Scandella to Airey, 7 Sept, Flood to Freeling 11 Sept, Flood to Freeling, 28 Oct 1866, and enclosures, esp. Flood to Airey, 3 Feb 1866; Despatches to Gibraltar, War Office to Airey, 3 Aug, 19 Oct, 3 Dec 1866. Flood, with his Anglo-Irish connections, possibly had other motives, but even his successor as police magistrate believed that Scandella was deliberately subverting the permit system as part of a Roman Catholic strategy to marginalise the Protestant community: TNA, CO91/319, Williams to Kimberley, 7 Sept 1872, enclosing police magistrate to colonial secretary, 14 June 1871.

. . . especially among the poor classes'. Flood, of course, rejected the claim that his actions were the cause of immorality, partly because he had not, in any case, created the law but was merely charged with applying it, partly because, to his knowledge, illicit unions now numbered only four, and partly because, as comparative statistics showed, he was in any case an old softy and applied the rules 'with great leniency'.[68] This last was an odd defence from someone lamenting previous lax application of the rules and bent on tightening them up. Scandella's facts had been ropey, but with their aid he had still scaled the moral high ground and had there planted the flag of Christian virtue.

Not so the business community. Flood had particularly requested leading civilians, such as members of the Exchange Committee, Sanitary Commission, and Grand Jury, to offer their views. They did. With the governor's sanction and with a Royal Artillery colonel as chairman (Colonel Maberley), a self-selected cohort (George Alton, Benjamin Carver, Francis Francia, Thomas Mosley, Joseph Shakery and W.H. Smith) bonded together in December 1866 into a Commission on Aliens.[69] Their report in March 1867 embraced not a Christian but a free-market morality. True, they piously asserted, like Scandella, that the regulations encouraged concubinage and were repugnant to humanity, but, more seriously, they were repellent to business. The report referred to the lenient period between 1842 and 1865, which Flood deplored, as the time when the rules had been sensibly relaxed, but since then their rigorous application had been causing 'annoyance and hardship', for no discernible military reason, nor because the population was increasing (it was not), nor because aliens were causing overcrowding (they were not, the overcrowded were 'natives' and houses were standing empty), nor because aliens were spreading disease (doctors said not). Occasionally in the past the laws had been applied to protect native tradesmen from alien competitors, but the Commission argued that the laws of supply and demand would better determine the right number of aliens settling in Gibraltar. Restrictions were prejudicial to commerce and to rate-paying, labour-employing residents (like themselves).[70]

It was difficult for the governor to know how to act. Already General Peel, Secretary of State for War, had indicated that he felt the need for a new order-in-council to tighten up the administration of the rules.[71] Moreover, in August

---

68 GGA, Box: The Alien Question, Correspondence, Scandella to Freeling, 5 Oct 1866, Flood to Freeling, 9 Nov 1866.

69 Alton was a Wesleyan minister; Carver and Francia were to become presidents of the Chamber of Commerce; Mosley was a banking agent; Smith ran a shipping agency; and Shakery in 1844 had had to be rescued from Spanish bandits.

70 GGA, Box: The Alien Question, Alton to Airey, 13 Nov 1866, Report of the Commission on Aliens, 11 March 1867.

71 TNA, CO91/319, Williams to Kimberley, 7 Sept 1872, enclosing attorney-general to colonial secretary, 12 May 1871, quoting Peel to Airey, 26 July 1866.

1867 Dr Sutherland's report on the cholera epidemic of 1865, commissioned earlier by the War Office, was published. Among identified causes was over-crowding; among the recommendations were restrictions on aliens: 'the policy of admitting aliens . . . is one of very considerable importance, and which requires to be dealt with'.[72] Gibraltar by then had become a Colonial Office responsibil-ity, but one set of London bureaucrats was much like another, and by the end of the year the Secretary of State for the Colonies, like all his War Office predeces-sors, was insisting that Governor Airey must tackle the sanitation problems of overcrowded Gibraltar, not just with clean water and better sewers but, in effect, by flushing out the aliens. Echoing Sutherland, he insisted that the popula-tion was too large for the number of houses. He wanted to know why the total population was still increasing, why the number of resident aliens appeared still to be growing and whether the number of applications for permits was also on the rise.[73]

During the spring and summer of 1868 despatches from Gibraltar to London were explaining why the number of aliens admitted to Gibraltar had indeed recently gone up (government work schemes, distress across the frontier), why it was want of accommodation, not excess population, which was the cause of overcrowding (a subtle distinction that puzzled the Colonial Office), and how further restrictions on the entry of aliens would create 'discontent . . . and injury to trade, and inconvenience and hardship to families' (suggesting the influence of the Commission on Aliens). Despatches from London to Gibraltar, following some pretty critical Colonial Office minutes, insisted, however, that allowing 'distressed Spaniards' into overcrowded Gibraltar was a 'misplaced charity', and that the regulations controlling the admission of aliens, copies of which the secretary of state wanted to see, should be reviewed, not in 'the interests of com-merce' or 'the general wants of the community' but to protect the 'healthiness of the Garrison'. It was then admitted by the governor that no consolidated set of regulations governing the admission of aliens actually existed; but then the matter was allowed to lapse.[74]

72 HCPP, Dr Sutherland, *Report on the Sanitary Condition of Gibraltar with reference to the Epidemic Cholera in the Year 1865*, 3921–1, Aug 1867, p. 33.
73 TNA, CO92/30, and GGA, Despatches to Gibraltar 1867: Buckingham to Airey, 12 Dec and 17 Dec 1867, and, for a further Colonial Office prod, 17 Jan 1868. For a useful summary of subsequent steps see TNA, CO91/319, 'Précis of Correspondence which led to a Report being called for on the Gibraltar Alien System', 11 Oct 1872, with Williams to Kimberley, 7 Sept 1872. A rare personal touch appears in a comment on this document, written on 31 Oct by a senior colleague: 'Mr Fanshawe's excellent memorandum is a last proof of the serious loss sustained by the Colonial Office in the death of this very careful & promising clerk.'
74 TNA, CO91/297, Airey to Buckingham, 3 March 1868, enclosing report of 27 Feb from Col Baynes, Police Magistrate (damaged copy in GGA), Buckingham to Airey,

No one was really satisfied, certainly not Dr Scandella. In September 1869 he formed a committee representing all three principal religious faiths and, of course, including prominent figures in the business community. They gathered testimony, including from doctors, on the apparently appalling consequences caused to the health of native mothers married to alien men by the rigorous application of the regulations and the insistence that the birth of their children should take place outside Gibraltar.[75] The secretary of state, Lord Granville, was persuaded by the governor's detailed response that the particular charges of 'inhumanity' were 'without foundation', but he was still persuaded that Gardiner's rule of 1850 requiring, in effect, the exclusion of such wives (and their children) from Gibraltar was arousing 'odium and evil consequences' and should be rescinded.[76]

As it happened, this concern was then overtaken by the passage through the British parliament in 1870 of the Naturalization Act, which determined that wives, on marriage, were to acquire the nationality of their husbands, in all Her Majesty's dominions. It was hardly a blow for gender equality (not a popular issue among male legislators anywhere in Europe), but at least in Gibraltar it clarified the rights of 'British' women marrying aliens (they ceased to be British) and of alien women marrying 'British' men (they became British).[77] Nevertheless, civilian protests followed against attempts to expel 'alien couples' who still defied regulations and allowed their children to be born in the garrison.[78] Complaints from aliens unable to set up businesses in Gibraltar also reminded the Colonial Office that it had not received from the governor a consolidated list of the regulations, without which it felt unable to assess such cases. Moreover, doubts were increasing about the legality of the rules that were being locally applied.[79]

After several reminders, in September 1872 the governor, by this time Sir William Fenwick Williams, forwarded a huge bundle of material to the Colonial

3 April, Airey to Buckingham, 12 June 1868; CO92/30, Buckingham to Airey, 2 July 1868; CO91/319, 'Précis'. The general election of 1868 and the establishment of Gladstone's first Liberal government possibly nudged the matter off the political agenda.

75 TNA, CO91/307 and /308 contain reports and responses, and Burke and Sawchuk, 'Alien encounters', pp. 542–9, provide an account. Committee members were Scandella and his colleague MacAuliffe, plus Solomon Benoliel, Y. Bergel, R. Cowell, William H. Francia, Lewis F. Imossi, Dr Joseph Patron and John H. Recaño.

76 TNA, CO92/30, Granville to Airey, 7 Feb 1870.

77 GGA, Box: The Alien Question, Flood to Baynes, 29 Aug 1870, Flood to Williams, 12 May 1871, p. 48.

78 TNA, CO91/319, Williams to Kimberley, 7 Sept 1872, enclosing Acting Police Magistrate to Acting Colonial Secretary, 31 Aug 1872.

79 TNA, CO92/30, Granville to Airey, 7 Feb 1870; CO91/319, 'Précis'.

Office, including an 84-page history of the permit system composed by Flood as attorney-general, which predictably argued for tightening and not relaxing the rules, plus his draft of an order-in-council designed to put beyond doubt the legality of any restrictive rules issued. Whatever concern might have been shown recently for civilian objections to the operation of the permit system, the purpose of reform, as Governor Williams saw it (following Flood), was to shelter the police magistrate from pressure (or to avoid his deviation from the rules) by enshrining agreed regulations in an order-in-council and by requiring a return to the practice of regular accounting to the secretary of state. The objective was unchanged: 'the necessity of maintaining a permit system under rigid supervision in so peculiarly situated a place as Gibraltar, and so guarding against the rapid and large increase of an alien population which would inevitably ensue through the removal or relaxation of such a system, constituting an element of danger to the Fortress in a military as well as a civil sense'.[80]

Since there was no disagreement between the colonial government and the Colonial Office over the need for an order-in-council, the exchanges between the two, which occupied a full year, concerned only the detailed wording of the order. There were no difficulties on most matters, such as ensuring that aliens to be allowed entry for trade were to be restricted to day or monthly passes; that only temporary permits of residence should be issued to alien resident employees and only then with guarantees from their employers covering good behaviour and term of residence; that the past practice of sending applications for such permits to the secretary of state should be resumed so as to protect governor and police magistrate from local pressure; and that the police magistrate and not just the governor should retain the power to expel undesirable immigrants.

But the *jus soli* rights of children born in Gibraltar continued to cause concern. Again, no difficulty was envisaged concerning the marriage of two alien persons temporarily resident: the wording of their permits was to state that they were void on marriage, and the couple must therefore depart before any child could be born. Nor was there any longer an administrative problem about a female British subject marrying an alien man, since she too had thereby become an alien and could be ordered to leave with her husband; she should not be allowed to

---

80 TNA, CO91/318, Kimberley to Williams, 25 June 1872; CO91/319, 'Précis', Williams to Kimberley, 7 Sept 1872, and enclosures. Flood's dispute with his successor as police magistrate over the regulations, plus his writing of a history of the permit system which went far beyond the demands of the Colonial Office, plus his drafting of the order-in-council and associated papers largely explain the delayed submission to the Colonial Office. For a perceptive analysis of Flood's 'history' and his interpretation of the demographic composition of Gibraltar and wider official anxieties see J. Ballantine Perera, 'The language of exclusion in F. Solly Flood's "History of the Permit System in Gibraltar"', *Journal of Historical Sociology*, 20 (2007), 209–34.

re-enter for residence but only, if at all, on a daily or monthly ticket. More problematic was the alien woman marrying a British subject. The belief remained that Spanish prostitutes were acquiring the status of British subjects and a right of residence by luring British soldiers into misjudged marriage. The Colonial Office rooted around in its locker of past practice elsewhere in the empire and located a law in British Honduras that allowed the governor to expel a naturalised British subject (as well as any alien), but officials were disinclined to press this option until experience demonstrated that it was really needed.[81]

The Aliens Order-in-Council, with its sixty-three clauses, four schedules, and thirteen specimen forms was passed on 30 August 1873. The proclamation published by the governor in the *Gibraltar Chronicle* on 1 December 1873 announced its coming into effect on 1 January 1874. The preamble repeated previous official justifications:

> Whereas it is expedient to make better provision to prevent the entry into and residence in Gibraltar of unauthorized persons not being British subjects, and to prevent the further increase of the overcrowded conditions of Gibraltar, whereby the lives and health of the inhabitants and of Her Majesty's officers and servants, and of all other persons resident or being there or resorting thereto, are greatly endangered . . .

A permit allowing the daily entry of an alien could be by day ticket, issued by inspectors of police at the gates, extendable by higher authority for up to ten days. Entry was also allowed on a monthly ticket, but then only by the police magistrate and only at the request of a garrison officer or an official or a substantial rate-paying resident as a guarantor, and although such tickets of entry could be extended this was never to be beyond one year. Very important, these day and monthly tickets did not automatically allow overnight stays. Aliens could only be allowed to stay overnight by securing a temporary permit of residence, which also had to be vouched for by residents, who thereby became liable to meet any medical expenses of permit holders and who were required to ensure the departure of aliens when permits expired. Extensions of different lengths were permitted, up to 30 days in a year for some categories, up to 270 days in a year for a trader, and never beyond 364 days in a year, even for a servant or other employee. No extensions beyond the permitted maxima were allowed except with the special permission of the governor, who in many circumstances (such as continuing employment) would also need the consent of the secretary of state. Moreover, for temporary permit holders there was also the proviso that 'every

81 TNA, CO91/319, letter from Kendall, Police Magistrate, to Colonial Office, 29 Oct 1872, with Williams to Kimberley, 7 Sept 1872, and Kimberley to Williams, 20 Nov 1872; CO91/325 and GGA, Dispatches to/from Gibraltar 1873: Kimberley to Williams, 6 March, 12 May, 10 June, 20 Aug, 18 Sept 1873, Williams to Kimberley, 12 April, 23 May, 25 July 1873.

alien male must immediately upon marriage leave Gibraltar, together with his wife, whether she be an alien, a native, or of other British nationality'. Moreover, no permit was to be issued to an alien husband whose wife had already had a child in Gibraltar since 1 January 1870 or any alien female (married or not) who since then had had a child. With Dr Scandella in mind, it was particularly stated that an alien child being admitted for education must have resided previously within thirty miles of Gibraltar. Even long-term alien residents were now required to renew their permits annually.[82]

Given the grumbling discontent with previous practice, it was hardly likely that the 1873 order-in-council would be launched without protest.[83] First off, predictably, was Dr Scandella, who had to be assured that the agreements he had previously secured on the education of alien youths at St Bernard's College would not be affected, even though this meant making exceptions to the thirty-mile rule which had formed part of those agreements and which was embedded in the new order-in-council. It seems that neither governor nor secretary of state was ready for a fight over this one, though they did demand that he produce evidence that sufficient spaces remained at the school for local children.[84] Obviously, the Vicar Apostolic was still questioning the distinction that the government was anxious to enforce between British subjects, including native-born, who had extensive rights and those they deemed aliens whose rights were nil or, at best, circumscribed.

This is also evident in the amendments which the Exchange Committee was demanding before the order-in-council should come into force. True, their fears that the rules would make the 'servant problem' even more difficult for the moneyed class smack of class interest, but there was also here a challenge to strict segregation of alien and British subject. So, for example, it was unacceptable to the Exchange Committee that such of their members and their employees who were technically aliens but long resident should have their security destabilised

---

82 GGA, Dispatches to Gibraltar 1873: copy of Aliens Order-in-Council with Kimberley to Williams, 20 Aug 1873; Dispatches from Gibraltar 1873: copy of Proclamation. For reminders of the obligation to renew permits see, for example, *Gibraltar Chronicle*, 17 Jan 1876 and 20 Jan 1882, and for their subsequent annual registration see GGA, Register of Aliens, 1874, two volumes.

83 Many of the consequent documents are summarised in GGA, Box: The Alien Question, Gifford, 'Précis of Correspondence on the Aliens Order', 13 Jan 1885, and are printed in TNA, CO879/9/16, and GGA Box: The Alien Question, Confidential Print, Colonial Office, Africa No 97, 'Correspondence Respecting the Gibraltar Aliens Order in Council, 1873', July 1876.

84 GGA, Despatches from Gibraltar 1873: Williams to Kimberley, 2 Dec 1873; Box: The Alien Question, Gifford, 'Précis'; CO91/330, Williams to Kimberley, 24 Jan 1874; and see his letters in *Gibraltar Chronicle*, 31 Jan and 3 Feb 1874, reprinted in Confidential Print, 1876, No 6.

by the obligation to renew their permits annually. Likewise, they argued that it was unjust discrimination to expel those aliens among them who, since 1 January 1870, had had children born in Gibraltar. It was similarly improper to threaten with expulsion alien males who got married, not least, as Dr Scandella had formerly argued and was to do so again, because it would incite illicit unions and the birth of illegitimate children.[85] By implication, alien males should be allowed to marry and reside in Gibraltar. They even argued that it was illegal, in their judgement, to treat as an alien the alien-born wife of a British subject who had become widowed before the coming into effect of the 1870 Naturalization Act. Finally, they were concerned that the right of aliens resident for fifteen years to hold property in Gibraltar, embedded in law since 1819, was not being explicitly confirmed in this new order-in-council, and it should be. Once again they were indicating that more of the privileges of the British subject should be extended to the so-called alien.[86] And once again British administrators were determined to hold the line. While acknowledging that the immediate implementation of the new rules would generate some hardship ('even cruelty'), these cases, they thought, should be dealt with by exceptional concessions rather than by weakening the regulations.[87]

The Exchange Committee's response was a further memorial to the secretary of state in April 1874, arguing that the implementation of the law was indeed hurting 'old and well-conducted inhabitants' and forcing them out of Gibraltar. Their free-market economic case for muddying the distinction between alien and British subject was also more fully expressed. They complained that the regulations increased their difficulty in securing domestic servants and labourers: they deterred aliens from taking up employment in Gibraltar (if they needed to be residents also) because it involved severance from their families. They also claimed that the distinctions being enforced were 'repugnant to friendly intercourse' with other nations, and especially with the Spanish (with whom, of course, many Exchange Committee members were deeply involved commercially). Moreover, they insisted that the overcrowding of Gibraltar and the public health concerns which the 1873 order-in-council was ostensibly intended to address were not caused by surplus labour, for there was a shortage, but by too few homes, for which the solution was government action to encourage housing construction for the 'labouring classes'. These assertions and arguments were again vigorously rejected by officials, more particularly, of course, by Flood, who concluded his

85 Confidential Print, 1876, No 4; GGA, Despatches from Gibraltar 1874: Williams to Carnarvon, 29 June 1874.
86 Confidential Print, 1876, No 1; GGA, Despatches from Gibraltar 1873: Williams to Kimberley, 29 Dec 1873.
87 Confidential Print, 1876, No 2 and No 3; GGA, Despatches from Gibraltar 1874: Williams to Kimberley, 10 Feb 1874, and enclosures.

advice to the governor by insisting that the regulations must be enforced 'if Gibraltar is to be saved from having all English ideas and English feelings from being stamped out'.[88] Here, starkly presented, was the distinction between an administration's efforts to use demographic controls to maintain Gibraltar as a British cultural as well as military bastion and a civilian community which was, in its politics and in its private life, less fussed. Indeed, the labouring classes, mainly Spanish speaking, may not have recognised a distinction between the cultures either side of the border.

The robust rejection of civilian protests was not followed by official indifference to the actual operations of the new regulations. In June 1874 Governor Williams had alluded to the virtue of a review, and in June 1875 he dispatched to the secretary of state just such a report. The committee he had set up, made up only of the police magistrate and two other officials, addressed in particular the objections of the Exchange Committee and especially its claim that the overcrowding in Gibraltar was due to a shortage of housing. It was agreed that more housing should be constructed to ease the pressure on the already existing resident population. However, additional housing should not be constructed, as had been urged, to provide accommodation for alien workers who, they noted, currently lived conveniently close, across the Spanish frontier, in La Línea. Given the ticket of entry system, residence in Gibraltar was not an obligatory consequence of employment in Gibraltar. Moreover, their objection to allowing in aliens as residents was not because of the consequent risk of the overcrowding of persons or the sanitary risk of a larger population: their concern was cultural (and potentially political). The committee concluded that 'These workmen, if permitted to reside within the territory of Gibraltar, did sufficient accommodation exist for them, would form a large alien population, and quickly produce a large increase to it of an alien character.' Further indicative of the cultural and political undertow in arguments ostensibly concerned with space and health were their critical observations on those who were objecting to demographic management. The objections 'chiefly had their origin among persons of alien character or descent'.[89] Since there were few in Gibraltar, even among native-born British subjects, who did not have aliens somewhere in the family tree, this observation said more about the observer than the observed.

Informed of the secretary of state's endorsement of this report, Dr Scandella

---

88 Confidential Print, 1876, No 5; GGA, Despatches from Gibraltar 1874: Williams to Carnarvon, 27 June 1874, and enclosures; Box: The Alien Question, 'Memorial of the Exchange Committee of Gibraltar', 20 April, Kendall to Baynes, 25 April, Flood to Baynes, 28 April 1874. Letters in the *Gibraltar Chronicle*, 9 and 13 Jan 1874, printed in Confidential Print, No 6, contain much of the substance and language of the 'Memorial'.
89 Confidential Print, 1876, No 9.

responded vigorously, both in a typically long letter to the secretary of state and in his highly critical and public pastoral letter for Lent 1876, addressed 'To the Clergy and Faithful of our Vicarate', of which he pointedly forwarded a copy to London.[90] Moreover, discontented with the outcome of the administration's review, he proceeded to hold his own, summoning to his committee of inquiry eleven senior civilians, including of course, leading businessmen such as Luis Imossi and James Speed.[91] Their objections to the aims and means of the 1873 Order-in-Council were becoming repetitive. Again, there was a refusal to accept that Gibraltar by this period was being swamped by an increase in population. In fact, they concluded, there was room for a larger population, since much ground, especially to the south, was undeveloped, and besides, extra storeys could be added to some houses. It was therefore claimed that the number of aliens seeking admission and needed for the economy could be accommodated. Moreover, it was asserted – contrary to official fears and with just as little evidence – that allowing entry to more aliens would not threaten security. The rules were again said to be discouraging marriage but encouraging concubinage and therefore illegitimacy and, indeed, all-round moral corruption. Remarkably, Scandella in his personal letter to Lord Carnarvon even argued that attempting to control population movements by law was in any case doomed: 'Wherever there is capital and commerce thither people flock, either natives or aliens; and every human endeavour to arrest the movement will be vain and fruitless.' The same assertion in the report of his committee even elevated this free market dogma to 'laws established by Divine Providence'.[92]

Civilian responses: the Aliens Order-in-Council, 1885

Lord Carnarvon, secretary of state, had indicated in April 1876 that he expected the new governor, Lord Napier, to conduct a further investigation on the operation of the 1873 order-in-council.[93] However, neither the governor nor the Colonial Office nor even the protestors took much action over revising the law during the next few years. What did occur was an accumulation of experience in its application. There were cases in which the police magistrate and the governor did as promised and moderated the initial impact of the new regulations, though mainly,

90 Confidential Print, 1876, Nos 11 and 12; GGA, Box: The Alien Question, Somerset to Carnarvon, 16 Feb 1876, and enclosures.
91 The other members of similar caste were Richard Abrines, Peter Amigo, Richard Cowell, Thomas French, Daniel Madden, Bartholomew Mascardi, Joseph Patron, MD, Michael Pitman and Joseph Playa.
92 Confidential Print, 1876, No 11, quotation p. 33; GGA, Box: The Alien Question, Scandella to Baynes, 12 Oct 1876, enclosing 'Report on the Alien Question', quotation p. 2.
93 Confidential Print, 1876, No 12, pp. 39–40.

it seems, to allow those who no longer had rights to stay (because they had evaded earlier rules) more time in which to arrange for their departure.[94] There were also cases in which the letter of the law was pretty firmly enforced, sometimes favourably to the applicant, for example by accepting the British status of a child born in Gibraltar to alien parents; but often not, and particularly by insisting that British women who had lost their status by marrying alien men could not as widows automatically reclaim it, and by preventing the wives of aliens from having children in Gibraltar.[95] Later, there were also complaints that Governor Napier was inconsistent and sometimes wayward in his application of the rules, especially concerning births to alien parents, against which so much official hostility had been expressed.[96] But such moderation might have eased opposition for a while.

The collision between official will and popular opinion is indicated by the case of Dr Fernando Suarez, Spanish by birth and a graduate of Seville University. His application to enter Gibraltar and practise as a doctor had been turned down by the governor in November 1873 on the grounds that he was an alien and that, with the arrival recently of two British doctors, local needs were being met. There was therefore no case for granting him a permit of residence, even though Suarez had the backing of the Spanish minister in London and had already acquired some support from locals in Gibraltar.[97] Then, in September 1874, the acting governor, with the approval of the secretary of state, presumably in changed circumstances, granted a special permit of residence to him, his wife and their two children, as allowed by the 1873 Aliens Order-in-Council.[98] Dr Suarez seems at once to have built up a successful and popular practice. However, in September 1877 he was convicted of smuggling a new-born illegitimate child into Gibraltar from Spain, to be passed off as native born, on behalf of a childless couple, Mr and Mrs John Haynes, desperate for a family. He was therefore in breach of the Aliens Ordinance of March 1846, was tried and was fined. The question followed as to whether his special permit of residence should also be revoked. The governor referred the case papers to the Colonial Office, which in fact was cautious in its judgement, scrutinising depositions from eight witnesses, responding to interventions on behalf of Dr Suarez from the Spanish ambassador, assessing reports

94 Such is the impression left by scrutiny of the cases, admittedly not verified, appended to GGA, Box: The Alien Question, 'Report on the Alien Question', and Despatches from Gibraltar 1877: police magistrate to colonial secretary, 12 Nov 1877.

95 GGA, Despatches from Gibraltar 1874: Somerset to secretary of state, 1 and 27 Aug 1874, Edmonds to secretary of state, 26 Sept 1874; Box: Attorney-General's Legal Opinions, 1877–1881, 23 Nov, 26 Nov 1877, 24 Aug, 19 Sept 1878.

96 GGA, Box: The Alien Question, attorney general to acting colonial secretary, 5 Feb 1883.

97 TNA, CO91/326, Williams to Kimberley, 28 Oct 1873.

98 GGA, Despatches from Gibraltar 1874: Edmunds to Secretary of State, 26 Sept 1874.

from Gibraltar's governor, attorney-general, surgeon-general, medical officer and the British vice-consul in San Roque, and considering two memorials from the doctor himself in which he protested his innocence and complained about a mistrial. Eventually, in April 1878, the secretary of state upheld the court's judgment and also concluded that a serious breach of the regulations had occurred. For his act of charity – or subversion – Dr Suarez lost his permit of residence. With his family, he was expelled. The baby, not registered as a Gibraltar-born British subject, was handed over to a foundling institution in San Roque. The law on aliens had been upheld. It is therefore revealing that a petition delivered to the governor in support of Suarez – the guilty, alien, Spanish doctor – was signed by ninety-three Gibraltar residents, four on behalf of charitable relief societies claiming 404 members. The many surnames, indicative of varied origins, include Armstrong, Ellice, Parker, Stansfield and Whitelock, alongside Cortes, Dotto, Martinez, Montegriffo and Parody.[99]

The arrival of a new governor, Sir John Adye, perhaps prompted a relatively new Vicar Apostolic, Dr Gonzalo Canilla, to re-present in February 1883 those old moral objections to the 1873 Aliens Order-in-Council.[100] His argument was that the law did not have the intended effect of reducing overcrowding because its scandalous consequence was to deflect resident aliens away from marriage and into concubinage, with the inevitable conception of the same number of children but born illegitimate. Adye's initial sympathy with this assessment was not shared by seniors in the Colonial Office, who believed that the restrictions were indeed preventing an influx of more aliens, were necessary for military security and were not in fact generating widespread complaint locally.[101]

This olympian perspective was challenged later in the year when, in November, a meeting of 'ratepayers and inhabitants' was followed by a memorial from the Exchange Committee and the Chamber of Commerce (the latter a recent addition to the political voices in Gibraltar). This complained about the immoral consequences of the regulations, although inevitably, from these sources, stress was laid on the economic damage caused by limiting the supplies of resident aliens needed for trade and labour. There was a further grumble that the rules did not prevent the entry of the Maltese, who were British subjects and, apparently, notorious ne'er-do-wells. (As we shall see in a later chapter, complaints against

99 The voluminous correspondence from Sept 1877 to April 1878 is contained in TNA, CO91/342, 343 and 344; GGA, Attorney-General's Legal Opinions, 1877–81, and Despatches to/from Gibraltar 1877 and 1878. The petition is attached to Napier to Carnarvon, 24 Sept 1877.

100 For Canilla and his initial troubled years see Caruana, *Rock*, pp. 82–116.

101 TNA, CO91/362, and GGA, Box: The Alien Question, Adye to Derby, 20 March 1883, enclosing Canilla to Adye, 7 Feb 1883, and minutes in TNA file. For this and what follows see also GGA, Box: The Alien Question, Gifford, 'Précis of Correspondence on the Aliens Order', 13 Jan 1885.

the Maltese were to grow louder.) Administrators were still not impressed, claiming that the number of bastards born in Gibraltar was actually in decline. Moreover, while Lord Derby as secretary of state echoed some Colonial Office concerns about the political wisdom of trying to restrain population increase by controls on alien marriages, Governor Adye did not want anything more than authority to use his discretion in applying unaltered regulations.[102] Thus, civilian pressure to erode those regulations on marriage which were designed to sustain the official distinction between British subject and alien was having, as yet, no effect on either operation or law.

That is why the Exchange Committee returned to the matter in the autumn of 1884, again niggling away at the rules. This time it proposed that aliens should be allowed to marry and stay in Gibraltar, but that their children should be legally classed as aliens. Actually, legislation to effect this had been suggested earlier by the police magistrate, and even in the Colonial Office, as a way of escaping from so many complaints.[103] Evidently, Exchange Committee members were quite comfortable with a change which would have increased the number of aliens in their midst, and they no doubt anticipated that such a relaxation must inevitably lead to ending the obligation on native women who married alien males to follow their husbands into exile. But such a change to the classification of children would undermine the *jus soli* principle and, as Governor Adye put it in a meeting with the committee's leaders, 'the law of England could not be changed to meet the views of the Gibraltar people'.[104]

Rebuffed again, 'friends resident in Gibraltar' contacted a British MP, who forwarded to the Colonial Office their complaints and what turned out to be seriously misleading horror stories. This was exactly what senior figures had come to fear, that the peculiar demographic controls operating in Gibraltar, especially concerning the marriage of aliens, however appropriate to protect the garrison, would be difficult to defend in parliament.[105] Accordingly, the secretary of state recommended that the governor should take another look at the regulations. For the first time it was even suggested officially that restraining population growth might require rules applicable to British subjects as well as to aliens. It is evident from this that recent Maltese immigration was also troubling the Colonial Office.[106] Adye had no problem refuting the detailed

102 TNA, CO91/366, and GGA, Box: The Alien Question, Adye to Derby, 2 Jan, 22 Feb 1884 and enclosures and replies, plus minutes in TNA files.

103 Confidential Print, 1876, No 10, 23 Sept 1875, No 11, 14 Feb 1876.

104 GGA, Box: The Alien Question, Gifford, 'Précis', 30 Sept and 14 Oct 1884.

105 TNA, CO91/362, Adye to Derby, 20 March 1883, minute 31 March; CO91/366, Adye to Derby, 2 Jan 1884, minute 9 Jan.

106 GGA, Despatches to Gibraltar 1885: Derby to Adye, 2 Jan 1885, enclosing Slagg to Ashley, 18 Dec 1884, and Wingfield to Slagg, 1 Jan 1885. (They worked on New Year's Day in those days.)

accusations,[107] but nevertheless he was willing to hold a review. First he contacted Dr Canilla, and then on 28 January 1885, with senior colleagues, he met other leading civilian figures, principally those in business, representing the Exchange Committee, Chamber of Commerce, Sanitary Commission and the 'Hebrew Community' (and a gentleman from the local Spanish language paper, *El Calpense*). There was at least concurrence that alien regulations of some kind were required to prevent overcrowding, itself quite a concession by critics, but it was more predictable that those being consulted wished to restrict residence 'to those whose services will be useful and convenient to the British population, such as professional men, traders and domestic servants'. It was also agreed that any concessions would not be a right but a privilege, which the governor could rescind. It was also implicitly accepted that the *jus soli* principle would be upheld, since female aliens, except in special cases, should still not be allowed to bear their children in Gibraltar. There was divided opinion, even among the civilians, as to whether a native woman marrying an alien man should be required with her husband to leave the garrison. However, over the previous dozen years the number of such marriages had averaged only nine. It was therefore agreed, on balance, that they might remain, as a privilege and not as a right, subject to the governor's approval, conditional on the husband's continuing employment, and still without entitling the wife to have children in Gibraltar. In closing the meeting, Adye indicated that he would now consider any necessary amendments to the Aliens Order-in-Council.[108]

By April his attorney-general, present at the meeting, had drafted clauses for an amended order in conformity with what he and the governor took to be the conclusions of that meeting. The Colonial Office's suggestion that steps might need to be taken to treat some British subjects as aliens was politely turned down. Yet the 1885 Aliens Order-in-Council was not to be proclaimed in Gibraltar until 30 December. Some important amendments were required by the Colonial Office, one set to deal with the treatment of political refugees,[109] but also, to avoid further controversy, an important clause in the draft was to be omitted.

107 TNA, CO91/369, and GGA, Despatches from Gibraltar 1885: Adye to Derby, 28 Jan 1885, and enclosures.
108 GGA, Despatches from Gibraltar 1885: minutes of 'Discussion re Aliens Order in Council, 28 Jan 1885', published in *Gibraltar Chronicle*, 29 Jan 1885.
109 This relates to the case of three Cuban political refugees from Spain who had secured sanctuary in Gibraltar in 1882 only to be handed back to the Spanish authorities, an action which caused a major diplomatic incident and the dismissal of the colonial secretary and the chief inspector of police: see HCPP, *Correspondence Respecting the Expulsion of Certain Cuban Refugees from Gibraltar*, C.3452, 1882, and additional papers in C.3473, C.3475 and C.3548, 1883, and, in brief, T.J. Finlayson, 'The case of the Cuban refugees', *Gibraltar Heritage Journal*, 6 (1999), 35–9.

Both partners in a marriage between aliens or between aliens and natives would be allowed to stay in Gibraltar, although the alien husband would still have to apply, and reapply, for a permit of residence. This did indeed mark an erosion of a distinction which all previous regulations had attempted to uphold. True, data from the 1878 census show that by then both partners in 55 per cent of marriages were native born or were other British subjects, many more than in 1834. Even so, 29 per cent of couples included an alien partner and over 16 per cent of them united two aliens.[110] People power, love across the divide, had triumphed. However, as agreed in the consultation, only by special permission of the governor would a female alien, or a female native who had become an alien through marriage, be allowed to bear a child in Gibraltar. Otherwise, confinements must take place across the frontier. The dangerous consequences of *jus soli* were to be avoided in this fashion.[111] There was some final tinkering with the wording, quibbles from the Exchange Committee seeking further to press the rights of female natives marrying aliens, and even some anxiety as to whether allowing renewable permits to a category called 'Visitor, public' was not actually officially condoning the traffic in Spanish prostitutes crossing the border to work in Gibraltar. However, the 1885 Aliens Order-in-Council was eventually passed on 12 December and came into effect on 1 January 1886.[112]

It should not be deduced that the concerns of the British authorities had ebbed because of the concessions they had made. Indeed, in May 1887 the worry being expressed by a new governor, Sir Arthur Hardinge, about the need to improve Gibraltar's defences, threatened by advances in naval armaments,

110 Burke and Sawchuk, 'Alien encounters', p. 534.
111 TNA, CO91/370, and GGA, Despatches from Gibraltar, and Box: The Alien Question, Adye to Derby, 2 May 1885, and enclosures, minutes in TNA file, Derby to Adye, 17 June 1885.
112 TNA, CO91/371, and GGA, Despatches to/from Gibraltar 1885: Adye to Stanley, 17 July and 6 Nov 1885, Stanley to Adye, 10 Aug and 23 Nov 1885, plus enclosures and minutes; *Gibraltar Chronicle*, 28 Aug and 30 Dec 1885; *The Consolidated Laws of Gibraltar* (London: Stevens, 1890). The issue of 'visitor' permits to Spanish women working as prostitutes in Gibraltar, many in the dozen or so brothels, became again a problem in 1892 when some protested at the increased competition they were facing: TNA, CO91/400, Nicholson to Ripon, 8 Oct 1892; 'Matters have come to a pretty pass', wrote a Colonial Office official (25 Oct), 'when prostitutes petition the Secretary of State to protect them against the injury to their trade by unlimited admission of "public visitors".' Forty-seven 'native prostitutes' were officially deemed too few to service a garrison of 4,926 males, especially when the fleet was also in port: ibid, Nicholson to Ripon, 21 Nov 1892. For the regulatory regime operated by the colonial state see P. Howell, 'Sexuality, sovereignty and space; government and the geography of prostitution in colonial Gibraltar', *Social History*, 29 (2004), 444–64.

rapidly escalated into a ferocious interdepartmental debate on the extent, not the fact, of Gibraltar's being overcrowded and a sanitary risk, and on how and to what level its civilian population might be reduced.[113]

The rules were indeed still tough and strictly applied. Requests for exemptions, and certainly attempts to evade them, received unsympathetic treatment.[114] Moreover, the Aliens Order Amendment Ordinance, passed in 1889, empowered the police to arrest without warrant any alien unable or unwilling to produce a ticket of entry or permit of residence.[115] Also in 1889, Hardinge felt compelled to pass a so-called Strangers' Ordinance. This was a further measure to prevent fraudulent entry, designed like so much else to separate aliens from British subjects. It empowered the police to demand personal details, including of origin, from all arriving in Gibraltar and from all staying in hotels and lodging houses. In particular it required all those claiming to be Maltese and therefore to be British subjects, who enjoyed automatic rights of entry and of residence, to produce an official certificate from Malta as proof.[116]

Conclusion

These last two measures indicate the continuing attraction of Gibraltar to aliens as a place of residence. Moreover, the need for police interrogation at the gates and for still more police inspection within the walls is suggestive of local complicity in their intrusion and the unwillingness of many legitimate residents to object to the alien presence. To that extent, official attempts to impose in civilian minds a tight distinction between British subject and alien immigrant were

113　TNA, CO883/4/10, Confidential Print, Med No 27, 'Defence and Overcrowding', April 1888, see especially Nos 1, 4 and 5, Hardinge to Holland, 14 May, 29 June 1887 and enclosures. Lord Wolseley, then Adjutant-General, insisted that Gibraltar was not a colony but a fortress and urged a reduction of the civilian population to 3,000: No 6, enclosure, 7 Aug 1887; CO883/4/12, Confidential Print, Med No 28, 'Gibraltar Civil Population'; CO883/4/16 Med No 33, 'Report of a Departmental Committee on the Civil Population and Smuggling in relation to Defence', 23 March 1889.

114　For examples see files on cases 1894–99 in TNA, CO91/407, /409, /422.

115　GGA, Dispatches from/to Gibraltar 1889: Hardinge to Knutsford 18 May and 19 July 1889 and Knutsford to Hardinge 3 June and 1 Aug 1889; *Consolidated Laws*.

116　GGA, Despatches from/to Gibraltar 1889: Hardinge to Knutsford, 6 and 10 March, and Knutsford to Hardinge, 30 March and 4 June 1889; *Consolidated Laws*. This measure did not therefore declare that 'only native-born inhabitants' were entitled to residence in the colony, a confusion probably launched by R.A. Preston, 'Gibraltar, colony and fortress', *Canadian Historical Review*, 27 (1946), 406, and repeated by J. Garcia, *Gibraltar: the Making of a People* (Gibraltar: Panorama, 2nd edn 2002), p. 9.

Table 4.3　*Census of civilian population, 1901*

Birthplaces	Males	Females	Totals
UK	758	551	1,309
Gibraltar	7,025	7,736	14,761
Malta	444	171	615
Other British	103	101	204
Foreign countries	166	732	898
Total British subjects	*8,496*	*9,291*	*17,787*
Spain	654	1,520	2,174
Portugal	82	26	108
Italy	30	15	45
France	9	20	29
Africa	94	33	127
Other countries	38	47	85
Total foreign subjects	*907*	*1,661*	*2,568*
Grand total	*9,403*	*10,952*	*20,355*

Source: *Census of the British Empire*, 1901, Gibraltar, p. 73, excluding military population and 630 living on boats in the port and harbour.

continuing to fail. Of course there were class interests involved, of alien civilians looking for work with better pay and conditions in Gibraltar than across the frontier, and of domiciled (and not only native-born) civilians looking for workers who were cheap, amenable and, as aliens without absolute right of residence, ultimately expendable.

In sum, civilians continued defiantly to evade the two starkly separate social identities demanded of them by the authorities, as set out, for example, in the 1901 census (Table 4.3). Gibraltar's managers might take some comfort from these figures, since they show that the modest annual rate of population growth which had set in from the 1830s (see Table 4.1) had been sustained through to the end of the century. Moreover, British subjects now constituted over 87 per cent of the resident population, up from 73 per cent in 1840. To that extent the Aliens orders-in-council appear to have been working.

Nevertheless, it follows that nearly 13 per cent of the resident population were still foreign-born immigrants, and now overwhelmingly they were coming from Spain. One way or another, legitimately or otherwise, their presence confirmed how porous remained that frontier. These Spanish immigrants were also, obviously, mainly Spanish-speaking, and Roman Catholics. They were also mainly female, and it will be recalled that after 1870 an alien woman became a British subject on marriage to a British subject, and so would be her children. Intermarriage had become less common than before, but was by no means rare. Moreover, official commentaries on previous census reports had expressed doubts about the 'Britishness' even of the local born, knowing that virtually all were the descendants of immigrants and that many indeed were of recent 'alien' parentage.

In sum, natives of Gibraltar had been reluctant in the nineteenth century to accept a divide between themselves as British subjects and the alien 'other'. However, as we shall see in a later chapter, not only did they come to accept that distinction in the twentieth century, but a third demographic social category emerged and was eventually officially recognised, distinct both from 'alien' foreigners and from other British subjects – the Gibraltarian.

5

Economy and living standards in the nineteenth century

The virility of an economy and indeed of a nation has often been equated with the population it has been able to support. Mercantilist doctrine in the eighteenth century had commonly adopted population numbers as an indicator of national strength, and nation states in the nineteenth century, new and old, readily represented either their emergence or their growing status in terms of the volume of people within their borders, or in their empires. To a more dispassionate eye, however, mere population numbers are an insufficient indication of how successfully a national economy is functioning and distributing its rewards, or of how well it is managed (if managed at all).

In the case of Gibraltar in the early nineteenth century, population growth was very rapid, even though punctured by massive drops when epidemics hit. Thereafter it grew significantly, although more slowly. Nevertheless, it would be a mistake to deduce too much about the economy from the number of people living in Gibraltar at any one time, or from the slowing down of population growth from the 1830s. As we have seen, the colony's managers tried to obstruct inward migration and settlement and, as we shall see, many of those whose economic livelihoods depended directly on Gibraltar lived across the border in Spain. Accordingly, a chapter examining the economy of Gibraltar in the nineteenth century also needs to consider its relationship with spaces within its economic orbit though outside its political frontiers. In other respects, because of population growth, civilian families in Gibraltar were also becoming increasingly dependent on outside supplies and on British government support. Moreover, this was an economy which government attempted to control. Fortress priorities and security concerns affected not only policies towards population numbers and composition: they also affected, for good and for ill, how the economy operated. Finally, as an important part of the agenda for this chapter, we need to consider more closely the world of work and civilian standards of living so as to see how the resources and opportunities generated by economic activity were divided.

Demand

In 1814 the total resident population of Gibraltar, civil plus military, was around 16,900. By 1901 it was nearly 27,500. In UK terms, Gibraltar remained a town of modest size. Colchester, another garrison town, had a population in 1811 of just over 12,500, but by 1901 this had risen to over 38,000.[1] By 1901 Gibraltar was, of course, physically no larger than it had been in 1814, or indeed in 1704, and yet by 1814 it was supporting a population over three times larger than before the occupation in 1704 and by 1901 well over five times larger. The size of the population which had increased so rapidly during the first third of the nineteenth century and was then sustained at a more slowly growing but still historically high level thereafter may be advanced as an indicator of economic success. At the same time, it is a measure of the economic challenge always faced by the people living in this small, resource-limited space. By 1901, in comparison with 1814, there were 10,000 additional mouths to feed, thirsts to ease, bodies to clothe and appetites for consumer goods to satisfy. There was a population demand which needed to be met by a market supply, and paid for.

Much of the demand derived from the civilian population. In spite of epidemic catastrophes, this had grown from around 10,000 in 1814 to over 17,000 in 1831. In spite also of the restraints on subsequent immigration and of some emigration, it still grew thereafter, though more slowly, to over 17,600 in 1860 and to nearly 20,400 by 1901.[2] This meant that by the end of the century the civil population was almost four times larger than in 1801, then only a little over 5,300. Moreover, its share of the total population including the military grew from 60 per cent in 1814 to over 76 per cent by 1901. Here was a substantial private sector economic demand.

In addition, there was a public sector demand. Indeed, a feature which distinguished Gibraltar (like Malta) as a colony was the proportion of economic activity directly prompted by government, though it is important to distinguish between the colonial government and the military garrison. Economic demand was generated locally by the wages paid to colonial government employees, including the governor, and by the cost of maintaining government buildings such as the Convent and other offices and of administering such services as the law courts, the hospital, the port and the police.[3] However, following conventional imperial government rules, insisted upon by HM Treasury in London,[4] the government was

---

1 *Census of England and Wales*, 1811 and 1901; see also J. Stone, 'Colchester', in P. Dietz (ed.), *Garrison: Ten British Military Towns* (London: Brassey's, 1986).
2 See Chapter 4, Table 4.1.
3 See, for example, heads of expenditure in HCPP, *Statement of the Local Revenues of Gibraltar for 1869*, HC 208, 1871.
4 For an exposition of the principles and practice see S. Constantine, *The Making of British Colonial Development Policy, 1914–1940* (London: Cass, 1984), pp. 12–16.

supposed to be and usually was financially self-sufficient. That is, its expenditure was paid for out of locally raised revenues. Like taxation everywhere, this reduced the incomes of those civilians who paid out more than they directly received back from the state, while official expenditure had precisely the opposite effect on those receiving more in return than they contributed to revenue, such as those in government employment or benefiting from government contracts. Colonial government demand therefore stimulated some parts of the Gibraltar economy, though possibly at the expense of others. As we shall see in the next chapter, issues concerning the payment of rates and taxes were, inevitably, political hot potatoes.

Another portion of public sector demand in Gibraltar derived from the annual recurrent expenditure on maintaining the garrison, and especially on the wages of military personnel. Of great importance is that these costs were paid by the imperial government and not the colonial government, and therefore not by Gibraltar taxpayers. They were embedded in the annual estimates of the army and the navy, voted by the UK parliament. Between 1853 and 1857 military expenditure in Gibraltar was costing the imperial government and UK taxpayer an average of £371,507 a year, an amount exceeded by only two other British bases overseas, at Malta and at the Cape of Good Hope.[5] Although annual costs were subsequently reduced, they still averaged £315,509 between 1866 and 1891, a grand total expenditure on the Gibraltar garrison of £8,203,230 over twenty-six years.[6] In the nineteenth century the garrison establishment was rarely below 5,000, and the practice of allowing officers and even some 'other ranks' to be accompanied by their families meant that altogether the men, women and children of the garrison amounted to 6,754 in 1814 and 6,475 in 1901.[7] In 1814 the garrison made up 40

5 HCPP, *Return of Average Amount of Military Forces maintained in each Colony at Expense of British Exchequer*, HC 114, 1859, p. 2. Another report for the year 1859/60 records imperial government expenditure in Gibraltar of £372,806 on 'troops', £23,066 on 'transport' and £24,823 on 'fortifications and barracks', a total of £420,695: HCPP, *Return of Area, Population, Revenue . . . of each British Colony, 1860 . . .*, HC 147, 1863, pp. 2–3.

6 HCPP, *Statement of Amounts included in Army Estimates for Military Purposes in Colonies*, 1866/67 to 1891/92: these are all the annual reports published. Calculating equivalents today is a complex business, see 'How Much Is That?', http://eh.net/hmit/. Depending on the conversion system adopted and taking 1880 as the base date, the annual average of £315,509 could equate in 2005 to £21 million, or be as high as £317 million. A calculation based on average earnings in 1880 would suggest an equivalent of £151 million a year in 2005.

7 Figures given in HCPP, *Army: Return to an Order of the Honourable House of Commons, dated 1 March 1843*, HC 140, 1843, pp. 2–3; *Statement of Amounts included in Army Estimates for Military Purposes in Colonies*, 1866/67 to 1891/92; *Gibraltar Report for 1901*, Cd.788, p. 17; H.W. Howes, *The Gibraltarian* (Gibraltar: Medsun, 3rd edn 1991), p. 44; J. Padiak, 'The "serious evil of marching regiments": the families of the British garrison of Gibraltar', *History of the Family*, 10 (2005), 137–50.

per cent of the total population camped on the Rock, and still 24 per cent in 1901. Almost certainly the income of, and therefore the demand generated by, members of the garrison, whether individuals or as families, was higher on average than in the civilian sector. In economic terms, Gibraltar's purchasing power was being increased by 'overseas aid' to the garrison from Britain. Each year, British service personnel, in their considerable numbers, were pumping into the local economy much of the pay they received from the British exchequer, and this was gratefully received by those civilians who took their cash in return for goods and services. This was, for Gibraltar's economy, an unearned and very welcome boost. To that extent civilian employment and living standards were significantly dependent on the military presence.

Capital expenditure in Gibraltar confirms this characteristic and was a further source of public sector demand. Most of this, of course, went on defence infrastructure. Each revolution in military technology required a reinforcement of Gibraltar's defences, paid for as capital investment by the British government, all involving local labour and all pumping additional demand into the economy when works were in progress. A tour around Gibraltar today brings one face to face with large amounts of British-funded nineteenth-century construction, including the bomb-proof barracks at Casemates built in 1817, the rebuilt Line Wall and new Wellington Front erected following a defence review in 1841, and the King's Bastion rebuilt to take bigger guns in the 1870s. In 1904 the army built and paid for a new military hospital.[8] Naval needs account for investment in the water tanks at Rosia Bay, made ready by 1804, the associated victualling yard completed in 1812 (costing £60,000), the extension and widening of the old mole in 1851 (£230,000), further developments of naval facilities in 1860 (£82,000) and a cold meat store and additional accommodation in 1900 (£46,000).[9] However, most spectacular – and expensive – was the construction at the end of the century of three dry docks, vast adjacent naval dockyard facilities, extensions to the southern breakwater, a detached mole, coaling jetties and many ancillary works around (and in) the Rock. The initial plans were presented to the British Parliament in the naval estimates for 1894/95, at an anticipated cost of £801,000, soon rising to £4,613,300, to which the colonial government was only required to contribute a share for the construction of a commercial mole at Waterport. True, not all this expenditure was pumped into Gibraltar, much of it being spent on preparatory work in Britain and on shipped-in equipment. Nevertheless, those employed daily on site, including many from across the frontier, rose from around 2,200 in the early years to as many as 5,000 as the works neared completion in 1906. While pay for labourers was low (initially equivalent to around

8 S. Benady, *Civil Hospital and Epidemics in Gibraltar* (Grendon: Gibraltar Books, 1994), p. 49.
9 HCPP, *Navy Estimates 1860–61*, HC 50, 1860; *Navy Estimates 1900–01*, HC 41, 1900.

11p a day), in aggregate an awful lot of cash was there for the spending in Gibraltar.[10] This example confirms how seriously the standard of living of many civilian families, on both sides of the border, depended in the nineteenth century on Gibraltar's role as a military and naval base. As such, like civilians in Malta and Bermuda, or in Colchester and Chatham, they enjoyed benefits derived from Britain's global role and strategies. They were therefore just as susceptible to the pluses and minuses of revaluations by the imperial authorities in London.

Supply

To a certain extent, the very increase in Gibraltar's population allowed a more diversified economy to develop internally. Incomes could be earned by 'taking in each other's washing'. Hence some Gibraltar-based businesses and workers drew some or even all of their income by selling their labour, their skills or their goods to local civilian employers, clients and customers, as well as or instead of to the garrison. For example, local professional men – doctors, teachers, lawyers, brokers, shipping agents, chandlers and so on – sold their expertise to local people, in precisely the same way as did other and more numerous members of the service sector, like household servants. Likewise, most local shopkeepers made much of their living by selling a range of goods to local customers.

However, while skills and a labour force were domestically generated, this was not true of the material products that were being sold. It was a challenge to match growing demand for them with adequate supply. There was little enough that could be derived locally from Gibraltar's own assets to meet garrison or civilian requirements. By 1901 Gibraltar was, of course, no more endowed with natural resources than it had been in 1801, or indeed in 1704. For instance, the Rock probably yielded no more primary products, particularly of foodstuffs, than it had in previous centuries. If anything, with more building encroaching during the century on Gibraltar's confined spaces, fewer patches of grazing remained upon which livestock, with their owners, could scratch a local living. Vegetable plots provided very little of what was needed. The sea was still a productive resource for local consumers, but not fished just by the villagers of Gibraltar's Catalan Bay.[11]

10 D. Fa and C. Finlayson, *The Fortifications of Gibraltar 1068–1945* (Oxford: Osprey, 2006), pp. 31–44; T. Benady, *The Royal Navy at Gibraltar* (Gibraltar: Gibraltar Books, 3rd edn 2000), pp. 72–3, 107–16. Since from 1898 wages were paid in sterling, workers from Spain had the option of exchanging sterling for pesetas, at unfavourable rates, or of buying goods in sterling and then getting them home over the frontier: C.A. Grocott, 'The Moneyed Class of Gibraltar, c.1880–1939' (PhD thesis, Lancaster University, 2006), p. 81.

11 By 1883 most local fishermen were Portuguese or Italians: HCPP, *Gibraltar Tariff Order in Council, 1884*, C.3992, 1884, p. 10.

Only a little import substitution to meet demand was attempted in Gibraltar, most successfully, though belatedly, in increasing local supplies of water, especially by more and larger cisterns and, at the turn of the century, by the installation of corrugated iron catchments, first on the west and then on the east flank of the Rock, which channelled rainwater into the reservoirs excavated within.[12] And yet a common sight on Gibraltar's streets, even late in the century, captured on picture postcards, remained itinerant water carriers from Spain with their donkeys. It is also true that a commercial gas company was formed in 1857, but this was initially for street lighting rather than for cooking and heating, and in any case it was dependent on imported fuel.[13]

Therefore, as in the past, most of what was needed had to be brought in from abroad. The increase in population and in demand made this an increasingly import-hungry economy. Accordingly, trade, employment, incomes and living standards of most civilian families throughout the century depended largely on open frontiers and access by sea. Fortunately, there were few physical problems over importing primary products. Almost all nations in the nineteenth century were being linked into a global economy, some more willingly than others, and most were keen to export their surpluses into foreign markets. For a society dependent on imports, this was of advantage to Gibraltar. Even the Spanish authorities usually allowed head to rule heart. In the interests of their own producers they relaxed their application of Utrecht rules, and during the governorship of Sir Robert Gardiner (1848–55) even abolished what had been, in effect, an export tax. Thereafter, usually, they allowed Spanish exports to enter Gibraltar freely.[14] Moreover, the post-Trafalgar superiority of the Royal Navy pretty much secured freedom of the seas and guaranteed the supply lines which connected the Mediterranean and both sides of the Atlantic with Gibraltar, although there remained occasional and serious bother with pirates, especially in the South Atlantic and off the coast of North Africa.[15]

12 Construction of water catchments on the western side of the Rock began in 1898 and, more famously, on the eastern side in 1903: GGA, Box: Health, handwritten draft of 'Annual Report on the Public Health of Gibraltar for 1903', p. 10; GGA, Water Supply Box: A. Beeby Thompson & Partners, 'Report on Water Supply of Gibraltar', 1934, p. 3; T.J. Finlayson, 'Gibraltar's water supply', *Gibraltar Heritage Journal*, 2 (1994), 60–72.

13 TNA, CO91/383, memorial from Gibraltar Gas Company, with Hardinge to Colonial Office, 7 July 1887.

14 GL, Sir R. Gardiner, 'Report on Gibraltar considered as a Fortress and a Colony', Jan 1856, p. 12.

15 S. Constantine, 'The pirate, the governor and the secretary of state: aliens, police and surveillance in early nineteenth-century Gibraltar', *English Historical Review*, 123 (2008), 1166–92; Benady, *Royal Navy*, pp. 94–5; A.V. Laferla, *British Malta* (Malta: Government Printing Office, vol.1, 1938), pp. 135–6; Hansard, *Parliamentary Debates*, House of Lords, 12 June 1828, cols 1312–15. *The Times*, 19 Sept 1828, p. 3,

There were sometimes disruptions to the inward flow of imports. Amongst the 'livestock' unwittingly imported into Europe, probably from the West Indies, was the infected mosquito carrier of yellow fever, *Aedes aegypti*. As noted in a previous chapter, this prompted the slapping up of quarantine barriers in vain attempts to isolate Gibraltar from infection. This was Gibraltar under siege by a micro-enemy. Importing of goods was therefore interrupted. Fierce though the outbreaks were in 1804, 1813–14 and 1828–29, they were, at least, mercifully brief.[16] Likewise, political problems sometimes affected import flows, for example when local Spanish authorities closed the frontier with Gibraltar during the first half of 1831 after political refugees had taken sanctuary there, and when the northern states interrupted trade by blockading the south during the American Civil War; but though disruptive in the short term, these were only hiccups in the long term.[17] Competition might also threaten imports. Governor Don reported in 1829 his concern that Cádiz had been declared a free port, like Gibraltar, and that this move would divert imports away from Gibraltar, though this threat was removed in 1830 when the former regime was reintroduced.[18] On the whole, Gibraltar had physically no serious problems about securing imports.

The immediate and obvious needs of civilians, as for the garrison, were imports of food and drink.[19] Daily tickets of entry were readily available, enabling Spanish traders to bring in essential supplies by land. These ranged from the hawker on foot with his bag or tray and the waterman with his donkey to the foreign fisherman with his catch and the man with his cart of fresh fruit and vegetables. Of course, Gibraltar traders also went out to fetch in. Larger operators from Gibraltar as well as from abroad were also serving the Gibraltar population by sea, bringing in great volumes of such supplies and other products,

Footnote 15 (*cont.*)

> lists twenty-six piratical incidents in nine months involving British vessels. An order-in-council and an ordinance in 1838 increased local powers to deal with piracy: *Orders in Council, Ordinances and Proclamations relating to Gibraltar* (Gibraltar: 1839), pp. 19–21, 115. Nevertheless, problems with Riff pirates from Morocco recurred throughout the century.

16 L.A. Sawchuk and S.D.A. Burke, 'Gibraltar's 1804 yellow fever scourge: the search for scapegoats', *Journal of the History of Medicine*, 53 (1998), 4–5; L.A. Sawchuk and S. Benady (eds), *Diary of an Epidemic: Yellow Fever in Gibraltar 1828* (Gibraltar: Gibraltar Government Heritage Publication, 2003).

17 TNA, CO91/119, correspondence from 4 Jan 1831.

18 TNA, CO91/101 Don to Murray, 17 Sept 1829; GL, Gardiner, 'Report on Gibraltar', p. 110.

19 Because of Gibraltar's continuing free port status in the nineteenth century, reliable figures for imports or exports 'cannot be ascertained': HCPP, *Return of Area, Population, Revenue, Debt and Commerce of each British Colony and Possession, 1860*, HC 147, 1863, p. 3.

including timber, charcoal (as fuel for cooking and heating), wine, fruit, citrus goods, milk, vegetables and meat, especially from Spain, Portugal and Morocco. Cattle and sheep slaughtered in Gibraltar, virtually all imported, amounted in 1860 to 8,677 animals, plus poultry literally by the basket load.[20] Much also came from Britain, including considerable quantities of butter, cheese, flour, meat, spices, tea, spirits and beer (23,191 barrels of it in 1899). Some of this was derived from other colonial sources and more was shipped in from the colonies direct to Gibraltar. Also directly imported were supplies of another primary product, tobacco – from Cuba and India and from the slave plantations of the United States before the Civil War and by supposedly free labour production thereafter.

Gibraltar consumers also wanted manufactured goods and, as the process of industrialisation accelerated in the UK, British companies were eager to supply Gibraltar dealers with whatever they would take. Shipped out to Gibraltar in 1828 were metal goods, earthenware, hardware, cutlery, glass, hats (647 dozen), hosiery, leather goods, jewellery, and even books (valued at £1,060), but especially textiles – lace, silk, linen, woollens and cotton goods. The Manchester Chamber of Commerce was particularly keen to ensure that Lancashire textiles were landed in Gibraltar. By the end of the century the list had expanded to include, for example, furniture and telegraphic apparatus.[21] So attractive had the market become that British companies set up agencies in Gibraltar to assist the import of consumer goods, and also to sell financial services.[22]

Payment

Whatever was imported into Gibraltar had to be paid for by the economy overall. To take just one indicator, in 1899 the UK imported goods from Gibraltar to the value of £54,897, mainly fruits, cork, hides, wax and, curiously, lots of eggs. (None of these goods originated from Gibraltar.) On the other hand, British and foreign goods exported from the UK to Gibraltar amounted

20 F.S. Sayer, *The History of Gibraltar* (London: Saunders and Ottley, 1862), pp. 463–4.
21 HCPP, *Statement of Imports and Exports between UK and Foreign and British Possessions abroad in the year 1828*, HC 267, 1830; *Annual Statement of Trade of United Kingdom with Foreign Countries and British Possessions, 1899*, Cd.187, 1900, pp. 939–40, data for 1895–99. See also *Draft of an Ordinance together with Correspondence relating to the Proposed Regulation of the Import and Export Trade of the Port of Gibraltar*, C.1783, 1877, p. 47, for an 1876 list of UK exports to and imports from Gibraltar.
22 See advertisements in the annual editions of the *Gibraltar Directory*, the first in 1873, and in A. Macmillan (ed.) *Malta and Gibraltar Illustrated* (London: Collingridge, 1915; facsimile reprint Malta: Midsea Books, 1985), pp. 465–504.

to £754,789.[23] There was a trade gap. In a phrase from northern England that translates into all languages, 'you don't get owt for nowt'.

Most securely financed, as already indicated, were the provisions and equipment shipped in by the War Office and Admiralty from the UK or elsewhere and paid for, ultimately, by British taxpayers or creditors. Considerable though these handouts were, more was needed to plug the gap. Since Gibraltar had no home-produced goods to sell, it was as well that locals could instead make a living by selling services to external customers. In the nineteenth century many of these were connected to shipping. Gibraltar-based shipping companies earned income by deals with overseas importers. All merchants arriving with goods by sea needed and had to pay for the dockside services of, for example, porters, carters, brokers and chandlers. (These deals included in the 1820s the fitting out of Spanish vessels engaged in the slave trade, in defiance of English law and of a proclamation from Governor Don denouncing the practice.[24]) Gibraltar was also valuably placed geographically on a crossroads between routes to and from Western Europe and the South Atlantic and Africa, and also via the Mediterranean between Europe and the Middle East. The port therefore benefited from the considerable increase in world shipping on those routes over the century, since much of the traffic found Gibraltar a useful port of call. Moreover, after a period in the doldrums, the opening of the Suez Canal in 1869 brought more shipping into the Mediterranean and via the shorter all-water route to and from India, the Far East and Australasia. Thereafter, about a third of British overseas trade went through the straits.[25] Much of it called at Gibraltar. For example, 350 vessels arrived there via the Canal in 1888.[26]

In the first half of the century, most shipping was wind-blown. Wind and waves and long voyages made Gibraltar an attractive service depot for ship repairs and reprovisioning. During the second half of the century steamships came to dominate the long-distance routes. In 1882, 2,483 steamers of more than 800 tons called at Gibraltar.[27] Indeed, by the 1880s it was reckoned that

23 HCPP, *Annual Statement of Trade of United Kingdom . . . 1899*, Cd.187, 1900, pp. 939–40. In 1876, UK exports to Gibraltar were £806,810 and UK imports from Gibraltar £111,965 (raw cotton, wool and seeds then made up the principal imports): *Draft of an Ordinance . . .*, C.1783, 1877, p. 47.

24 GGA, Despatches to Gibraltar 1829: copy of letter from Backhouse in Foreign Office to Colonial Office, 27 Feb 1829, and enclosures.

25 Benady, *Royal Navy*, p. 107. For some indicators suggesting a threefold increase from 1876–80 to 1911–13 in the volume of world trade see W. Woodruff, *Impact of Western Man: a Study of Europe's Role in the World Economy 1750–1960* (London: Macmillan, 1966), p. 272.

26 HCPP, *Gibraltar. Report on the Blue Book for 1888*, C.5620, 1889, p. 13: 199 came from India, 61 from Australia, 19 from China.

27 HCPP, *Gibraltar Tariff*, C.3992, 1884, p. 9.

Table 5.1 *Tonnage of steam vessels entered 1887–1914, and tons of coal taken 1901–1914*

Year	Tonnage	Year	Tonnage	Tons of coal
1887	5,169,981	1901	4,112,558	217,927
1888	5,905,312	1902	4,301,142	165,743
1889	6,162,690	1903	3,843,333	122,259
1890	5,670,475[a]	1904	4,347,098	153,257
1891	5,256,863[a]	1905	4,070,987	95,053
1892	4,316,699[a]	1906	4,641,559	162,837
1893	4,567,898[a]	1907	5,010,265	184,906
1894	4,871,221[a]	1908	4,534,715	134,488
1895	4,478,480[a]	1909	4,854,430	147,980
1896	4,277,345[a]	1910	5,438,396	170,942
1897	4,319,974	1911	5,859,096	231,255
1898	4,521,475	1912	6,020,502	239,051
1899	4,282,963	1913	6,278,616	288,725
1900	4,408,197	1914	6,287,900	276,445

Note: [a] Reports for 1890–96 give aggregate figures of tonnage for vessels entering and clearing, and have been halved to give a close estimate for entering only.

Source: calculated from *Gibraltar Annual Reports*, 1887–1914 (which do not include coaling figures before 1901).

Gibraltar's economic strength owed less to local Mediterranean trade and more to the services provided 'as a calling and coaling station for large steamers entering and leaving the Mediterranean', on average between fifteen and twenty a day, a remarkable tally.[28] As Table 5.1 shows, however, it was not thereafter 'plain sailing'.

Although the tonnage of steamships arriving was huge, there were slumps in business. It is apparent from the figures that the volume of vessels using the port in the late 1880s did not return until twenty years later. Bouts of depression in the Black Sea grain trade explained some difficulties, but there was also competition from rival coaling stations in Malta and in Algiers, which eventually prompted improvements in Gibraltar's facilities. Steamships were initially very fuel hungry and needed frequent stops at strategic points like Gibraltar for supplies.[29] This meant coal, and preferably Cardiff coal, the connoisseur's pick. The quantity provided rose, and fell, only to rise again. Fuel imports to Gibraltar from the UK in 1899 were valued at £191,192.[30] Imported coal was loaded into hulks moored in the bay, from which sweated and sweating labourers heaved

28 GGA, Box: Housing, Adye to Stanley, 30 Jan 1886.
29 Woodruff, *Impact*, pp. 238–9, 256.
30 HCPP, *Annual Statement of Trade of United Kingdom with Foreign Countries and British Possessions, 1899*, Cd.187, 1900, p. 939.

it into ships' bunkers. Serious money could therefore be made by Gibraltar businessmen in selling maritime services and also in the provision of maritime supplies. However, those supplies had first to be imported.

In effect, Cardiff coal was a re-export, and so too were other goods sold on to shipping, even the ropes and planks of wood, and later plates of iron and whatnot with which ship repairers turned damaged ships into seaworthy vessels. In the nineteenth century ship supplies and ship repairs constituted one of the only two seriously impressive sectors engaged in adding value to imports, by processing or at least storing and serving up imported raw materials and selling them on, including to external customers, at a consequently higher price. The other sector turned imported raw tobacco into cigars and cigarettes and other tobacco products, also with a view to selling on a proportion as more expensive re-exports. Otherwise, Gibraltar's re-exports were unaltered imports, bought in a cheaper market with the expectation of selling in a dearer one. In sum, that share of Gibraltar's imports not paid for by British taxpayer subsidies to the garrison, by British capital investments in fortifications or by the sale of services had to be funded by importing as cheaply as possible and by re-exporting as much as possible and as dearly as the market would stand. The process, crucial to the material well-being of civilians, was a necessary consequence of Gibraltar's import-hungry but resource-limited society.

The difficult part was re-exporting. While foreign nations were themselves increasingly geared up to export to places like Gibraltar, they could not be relied upon to accept Gibraltar's re-exports. As a minor point, in times of epidemic, quarantine regulations worked both ways, so that while Gibraltar was desperately trying to prevent penetration inwards of its *cordon sanitaire*, so its neighbours, and especially Spain, were determined to prevent infection from travelling the other way. There was a particularly difficult episode in 1853–54, following an outbreak of cholera in Britain which closed off Spanish trade with this British colony.[31]

More seriously, because more persistent, was the refusal of the more robust nation-states of Europe, plus the United States after the civil war, to allow unqualified free access to their domestic markets. For one thing, their governments had found levying duties on imports across their frontiers a convenient way of raising revenue. It needs to be remembered that it took even the British government nearly half the century to reduce piecemeal and then abandon its tariff barriers. The vestigial Navigation Act, a wreckage of the mercantilist eighteenth century, was not absolutely repealed until 1849. And of course, British business was only ready to adopt free trade for itself and to insist upon it by others when there was confidence that, in the ensuing free competition, the 'first

31 HCPP, *Report made by Doctor Baly to the Secretary of State . . . on Quarantine, 1854*, HC 161, 1854–55.

industrial nation' would do rather well. By precisely the same reckoning, other governments were hesitant about abandoning import duties which also served to protect their embryonic manufacturing interests or simply their workforces from foreign (often British) competition.

And yet Gibraltar in the nineteenth century prospered on an astonishingly successful re-export trade. Gibraltar was a massive recipient of imports not destined for local consumption. In 1828 those two square miles or so were the tenth-largest external market of the United Kingdom, receiving goods with an official value of £2,078,694 (when imports from Gibraltar were valued only at £29,768).[32] The appetite of this tiny colony for UK goods was exceeded only by Germany (£9.5m), the United States (£6.8m), the enormous market of the East Indies and China (£6.4), Brazil (£6.1m), the Netherlands (£5.0), Italy (£4.6m), the British West Indies (£4.0m), the vast acreage and huge population of Russia (£2.8m) and British North America, the future Canada (£2.2m). UK exports direct to Spain were valued only at £613,615.[33]

A large proportion of Gibraltar's imports from the UK were manufactured cotton goods; in 1828 they amounted to £638,965 in value; in quantity they added up to 18,507,940 yards. The Gibraltar census in 1829 recorded a civilian population of 16,394, and it is not likely that on average each single person would be buying 1,129 yards of cotton cloth in a year. Spain imported only 327,662 yards direct from the UK. In addition, Gibraltar was also receiving large quantities of cotton pieces made in India. Business was not quite so remarkable by the end of the century, British-made cotton goods averaging 'only' 6,252,620 yards in the final five years, but even this was equivalent to over 300 yards per person per year.[34] The explanation for these bulk imports is, of course, that Gibraltar's port and geographical location made it a handy centre for businessmen to distribute most of their imports as re-exports to the littorals of West Africa and both coasts of the Mediterranean, and not just of textiles.

As noted in a previous chapter, Gibraltar re-exporters in the eighteenth century had faced a Spain which translated its resentment at the amputation of Gibraltar into frontier obstruction, if not military action. Exporting to Spain had therefore been difficult, but the noble principles of free trade between nations had been asserted – by smugglers. It is true that, in the late stages of the Peninsular War, British manufactured goods, especially textiles, had been welcomed readily by

32 Official values ascribed sterling prices to goods recorded only by volume.
33 HCPP, *Account of Value of British, Irish, Colonial and Foreign Produce and Manufactures Imported and Exported, 1829*, HC 292, 1830, p. 2.
34 HCPP, *Statement of Imports and Exports between UK and Foreign and British Possessions abroad in the year 1828*, HC 267, 1830; *Annual Statement of Trade of United Kingdom with Foreign Countries and British Possessions, 1899*, Cd.187, 1900, pp. 939–40, data for 1895–99.

deprived consumers across the frontier. In fact, the sale of re-exports in Spain then and throughout the nineteenth century (and after) depended on this market and, indeed, on Spanish intermediaries to do most of the delivering. The process of exchange was succinctly described in a report of 1854: 'Many of the aliens entering Gibraltar undoubtedly brought with them supplies of articles of food for the inhabitants, but a very large number, it is equally certain, carried out with them goods purchased in the town, especially cotton goods, haberdashery, and hardware.'[35]

Not all re-exports were smuggled into Spain, but legitimate imports were liable to tax.[36] Much therefore was covertly slipped in, and by such means Lancashire textiles continued to flow over the frontier, even though Madrid governments took a very dim view of the practice and attempted to prevent the trade by periodic clampdowns at points of entry by sea or overland. Governor Wilson reported a diminution in trade in 1845 'from greater vigilance on the part of the Spanish authorities in enforcing their fiscal laws'.[37] Economic success depended on eluding the Spanish customs service on land and its armed cutters at sea. Such actions were bound to have political consequences. How governors responded depended on their assessment of the balance of advantages. Offending the Spanish by robust protests could be counterproductive. Denouncing the smuggling trade as disruptive of good international relations would anger interested parties in Britain as well as in Gibraltar.

Particularly problematical, because so voluminous and blatant, was the smuggling into Spain of tobacco and tobacco products. Precise figures are unavailable now, as then, but the rough volume and value of the re-export trade were known to be huge, not just to those involved in the trade but also to governments in Gibraltar and London, and in Madrid. Tobacco imports to Gibraltar in 1846

35 HCPP, *Report made by Dr Baly . . . upon the subject of Quarantine at Gibraltar, 1854*, HC 161, 1854–55, p. 5.

36 In 1876, duties were reckoned to add from 50 to 70 per cent to the cost in Spain of imported Manchester cottons: HCPP, *Draft of an Ordinance . . .*, C.1783, 1877, p. 38. For changes in Spain's fiscal regimes in relation, especially, to industrialisation see references in R. Carr, *Spain 1808–1975* (Oxford: Clarendon Press, 2nd edn 1982), and for a contemporary account, showing some liberalisation from 1869 and then increased protectionism from 1875, see HCPP, *Correspondence respecting Commercial Relations between Spain and Great Britain*, C.3346, 1882, esp. pp. 4–6.

37 HCPP, *Reports to Secretary of State on Past and Present State of H.M. Colonial Possessions*, HC 728, 1846, p. 117. See also undated cutting from *Journal du Commerce* in GGA, Despatches to Gibraltar 1830, referring to the Spanish government's employment of a company whose cruisers were threatening to deprive Gibraltar 'of all its mercantile importance' by preventing 'any importation of smuggled goods into Spain'.

were reckoned to be just short of 70,000 hundredweight, when the Gibraltar civilian population was around 16,000.[38] If calculated in terms of quantities per head of population, and if domestic consumption were assumed, this represented an early grave. But the Levanter cloud was not tobacco smoke. Most of this stuff was transferred to foreign lungs. In 1900, the amount imported was still reckoned to be only a trifle short of 20,000 hundredweight, and of this around 14,000 hundredweight was re-exported.[39] Instructions to governors were that they could not, legally, prohibit the import into Gibraltar of tobacco from Cuba, the United States and India. Moreover, jurisdictional control was doubtful over ships in the bay from which tobacco was often transhipped and smuggled ashore.[40]

Spanish authorities, not of course acting as health agencies, were especially indignant about tobacco smuggling. They wanted to prevent the loss of revenue which they suffered when untaxed tobacco got into Spain. They also aimed to protect the interests of Spanish tobacco importers who paid import duties, of the state-owned companies who had a monopoly on the processing of the raw product and of Spanish workers in cigarette and cigar factories – like Carmen and her colleagues – whose jobs were on the line.[41] The actual techniques of smuggling had not changed much since the pioneering days. Cargoes of raw tobacco arrived, untaxed, in the free port of Gibraltar. Much remained in this state but, as noted, some was processed in Gibraltar. Those doing the smuggling, as middlemen, were still mainly Spanish, some of them hardened professionals. However, many were ordinary men and women from Spain who entered early morning to work in Gibraltar, looking thin, and, having spent some of their day's pay on cheap tobacco goods, left for Spain in the evening, fat, with bundles stuffed under their clothes to sell on over the border. In addition, 'carriages and beasts, which came light and springy into the place, quit it scarcely able to drag or bear their burdens'.[42] British and Spanish frontier guards did not see or, made compliant, chose not to see. Dogs, as four-footed friends, were also enlisted, brought in from Spain in the morning and kept hungry during the day. Then, in the evening, loaded up with several pounds of tobacco, they were

38 GL, Sir R. Gardiner, 'Report on Gibraltar considered as a Fortress and a Colony', Jan 1856, p. 82. A hundredweight (cwt) is equivalent to 50.9 kilograms (kg), and hence 70,000 cwt is the equivalent of 3,563,000 kg, or the weight of a decent-sized crematorium. Gardiner reckoned that under his regime it was brought down by 1848 to fewer than 42,000 cwt.

39 *Gibraltar Blue Book*, 1900.

40 GL, Gardiner, 'Report on Gibraltar', p. 78.

41 For descriptions of the Spanish tobacco industry and use of smuggled tobacco in 1876 see HCPP, *Draft of an Ordinance . . .*, C.1783, 1877, pp. 34–7.

42 GL, Gardiner, 'Report on Gibraltar', pp. 105–6.

sent scampering home for dinner. The fleet of foot evaded the unfriendly fire of frontier guards.[43]

A case in 1832 provides a vignette of how else it might be done. Denominated a 'shopkeeper' but apparently a 'very wealthy man', Mr Canepa had secured forty-six conditional permits of residence for employees in his 'extensive retail trade'. According to a police report, many of them were in fact 'Spanish *contra-bandistas*' who, on each trip back across the border, carried goods to the value of £10 to £12. Since 'the nature of their trade requires concealment from the Spanish *Guarda Costas*, they usually time their visits for the darkest periods of the moon'.[44] Later in the century, in 1889, Gibraltar's chief of police reckoned that, of the 5,000 aliens entering Gibraltar daily, 2,000 returned to Spain laden with tobacco and about 1,000 entered solely for this purpose and made from two to five trips daily.[45] By such and similar means, most imported tobacco or tobacco products got through to Spain, and the profits to Gibraltar civilians helped to fix the trade gap.

The problem for the authorities was how to prevent smuggling, given the cooperation between dealers in Gibraltar and thousands of small-scale Spanish couriers and some large-scale and pretty ruthless Spanish villains. Governor Sir George Don ascribed much of the investment and enterprise in smuggling out of Gibraltar to the 'eager demand of the Inhabitants of Spain for the prohibited Articles of Tobacco and British Cotton Manufactures'.[46] His less tolerant successor, Sir Robert Gardiner, provided several vivid, cred- ible and indignant accounts of how the trade was conducted, and the offence it caused to Spain. However, his politically clumsy attempts to shut down the business were undermined in 1854 by the Duke of Newcastle, the secretary of state, who publicly agreed that importing into Gibraltar was legal and that the smuggling, effected by Spaniards, was not a British responsibility.[47] Subsequent secretaries of state were more resolute in their opposition, for example, Lord Derby in 1876 and Lord Carnarvon in 1877, but they were no more successful in the face of vigorous protests from Gibraltar businessmen and their British allies and the determination of those doing the importing

43 TNA, CO883/4/16, pp. 10–12, provides an eyewitness account, Jan 1888. One clause of the 1896 Tobacco Ordinance stipulated that 'Dogs used or suspected of being used for smuggling shall not be allowed to enter or leave Gibraltar by land or sea', though we are reassuringly told that it was only their owners who were liable to fines or imprisonment for breaches of the rules.

44 GGA, Box: The Alien Question, Flood to Williams, 12 May 1871, Appendix A, Nos 33–4.

45 TNA, CO883/4/16, pp. 10–11.

46 TNA, CO91/101, and GGA, Don's Despatches from Gibraltar 1829: Don to Murray 17 Sept 1829.

47 GL, Gardiner, 'Report on Gibraltar'.

and the smuggling.[48] So serious did the matter remain that in 1889 an official interdepartmental committee – Colonial Office, War Office, Treasury – drew up a report on 'The Civil Population and Smuggling in relation to Defence'. One main cause of the overcrowding which they reckoned jeopardised fortress security was the lure of making money from smuggling, which had now reached 'gigantic proportions'.[49] Not until 1896, following the passage of the Tobacco Ordinance, was the governor empowered to control the place and manner in which tobacco could be imported into Gibraltar and stored (including on vessels in the bay) and to prohibit re-exports by land and to regulate any dispatch by sea; but smuggling was thereafter restricted but certainly not snuffed out.[50]

Smuggling of all kinds of goods, therefore, in part further explains why some businessmen in Gibraltar were keen to maintain easy access into the colony for Spanish labour and Spanish traders. In September 1830 the leading lights of the Exchange Committee, speaking on behalf of the 'Commercial Body of this Place', insisted quite blatantly to the governor that the huge volume of manufactured goods imported into the free port of Gibraltar depended for their further marketing on allowing alien traders into Gibraltar. However, aliens required permits for entry and for short stays, and permits required respectable Gibraltar merchants to put up bonds as surety, for their good behaviour. It was admitted that this good behaviour could not always be guaranteed, since these traders (in fact smugglers) were not of a 'very distinguished rank in society'. Indeed, they might forget to return, as required, their tickets of admission, with unfortunate financial consequences for those standing surety. A relaxation of the rules was requested (though not given).[51]

Remarkably, and again because of the overriding importance of re-export

48 HCPP, *Draft of an Ordinance . . .*, C.1783, 1877, and continuations C.1894, 1877, and C.2145, 1878; GGA, Dispatches to Gibraltar, Carnarvon to Napier, 20 July 1877, also published in *Gibraltar Chronicle*, 15 Aug 1877. See also some heated defences of the economics and ethics of smuggling by Gibraltar merchants in *The Times*, for example, 20 Nov 1872, p. 6, 31 Aug 1875, p. 9, 29 Sept 1875, p. 5, and 21 April 1877, p. 13.
49 TNA, CO883/4/16, Confidential Print, Mediterranean, No 33.
50 'An Ordinance to Regulate the trade in Tobacco', 1 Sept 1896, in B.H.T. Frere (ed.), *The Consolidated Laws of Gibraltar* (Gibraltar: Gibraltar Government, 1913). On smuggling see also R. Sánchez Mantero, *Estudios sobre Gibraltar: Política, Diplomacia y Contrabando en el Siglo XIX* (Cádiz: Diputación Provincial, 1989), chs 3–5; C. Baldachino, 'Co-operation and conflict at North Front', *Gibraltar Heritage Journal*, 6 (1999), 83–98; T. Benady, 'Smuggling and the law', *Gibraltar Heritage Journal*, 13 (2006), 94–8.
51 GGA, Box: The Alien Question, Flood to Williams, 12 May 1871, Appendix A, No 25, letter to Police Magistrate, 22 Sept 1830.

commerce, the chairman of the Exchange Committee, Marcus Henry Bland, born in Liverpool but in Gibraltar heading a highly successful shipping agency, similarly asked the governor quite candidly in 1845 to allow Spanish smugglers into Gibraltar, on the authority of what were known to be permits and passports forged in Spain, because the uncooperative Spanish authorities would not provide proper ones. Neither the governor nor the Colonial Office was persuaded by Bland's bluster that he was, of course, opposed 'to the introduction of Aliens, either for permanent or temporary residence, save and except for such legitimate objects as should warrant their being admitted'.[52]

Similar presumptuous words were used by Gibraltar merchants in 1853 in their protestations to the secretary of state against Sir Robert Gardiner's actions when he endeavoured to obstruct the smuggling trade: 'We will not affect to conceal the notorious fact that Manchester manufactured goods are extensively smuggled into Spain. But we wholly, unequivocally and most emphatically deny that British merchants and agents at Gibraltar are parties to any contraband commerce . . . The business of a merchant of Gibraltar is completed when he has effected the sale of his goods in the open market.'[53] In truth, not only did the larger economy of Gibraltar depend on the linking of virtuous British merchants with unvirtuous Spanish smugglers. So did the incomes and livelihood of large proportions of the civilian population, on both sides of the border. A report of 1876 reckoned that the tobacco trade gave employment in Gibraltar to 26 importers and wholesale dealers, 76 licensed tobacconists and dealers, and about 1,450 men, women and children (cigar-makers, pickers, cleaners, choppers, packers etc). Many families depended on the business for survival, while fat-cat entrepreneurs prospered on the profits.[54]

Economic management

The command and control culture of Gibraltar's eighteenth-century military government which led to efforts to manage the economy also characterised its nineteenth-century successors. This is not surprising, given the continuing fortress priorities of the administration. However, there were some long-term economic trends over which the colonial government had no control. Some of these relate to the global shifts in international trade, ups and downs which were

---

52 TNA, CO91/173, Wilson to Stanley and enclosures, 19 May, and Stanley to Wilson, 6 June 1845; J. Gaggero, *Running with the Baton: a Gibraltar Family History* (Gibraltar: Gaggero, 2005), pp. 16–17.

53 HCPP, *Copy of the Memorial presented to the Duke of Newcastle by a Deputation from the Merchants of Gibraltar*, HC 130, 1854, p. 6.

54 HCPP, *Gibraltar (Tobacco Trade)*, HC 435, 1876; J. Hennen, *Sketches of the Medical Topography of the Mediterranean* (London: Underwood, 1830), p. 80.

determined by worldwide patterns of investment, increases in primary production, improvements in industrial productivity, revolutions in transportation, relative shifts in prices, population growth, and the rise for many consumers in some parts of the world of their standards of living and purchasing power. 'No man is an island, entire of itself', and nor was the peninsula economy of Gibraltar.

That said, there were matters affecting the economy particular to Gibraltar, though most of these, too, were beyond local control. The demobilisation after the ending of the Napoleonic Wars, which caused an economic depression in Britain, affected Gibraltar less severely because the garrison was not much reduced in size, and therefore that British-prompted and British-paid economic stimulus remained intact. More importantly, southern European and possibly North African markets starved of manufactured goods welcomed British products and, as we have seen, one route of entry, especially into Spain, was via Gibraltar. Ill-manned frontiers in unstable post-war Spain and rebellion among Spain's colonies in South America also boosted Gibraltar's fortunes as a re-export route for rebel products to get into Spain.[55] However, the Congress of Vienna in 1815 confirmed that the sovereignty of Malta had been transferred to Britain, and the construction of a Royal Navy base and later a coaling station in that colony's better natural harbour made Malta economically a rival to Gibraltar, with effects upon the volume of shipping using Gibraltar's port. Moreover, the Latin American republics restored their direct trade links with Spain. Difficult decades followed.[56] A supposedly informed insider even judged in 1862 that 'As a commercial station Gibraltar is rapidly sinking into insignificance', apparently because steam navigation was reducing its value as a redistribution centre and because the Spanish authorities had become more vigilant in intercepting smugglers.[57] However, as we have seen, the 1869 opening of the Suez Canal, over which not even the British government, let alone the Gibraltar government, had had any say, increased the volume of trade flowing past Gibraltar, with much traffic calling in. Moreover, with another turn of the wheel, strategic recalculations by the British cabinet at the end of the century led to an upward revaluation of Gibraltar's importance in the imperial scheme of things and the massive investment in the dockyard complex, whose stimulus to Gibraltar's economy has also been noted.[58]

However, that still left much concerning the economy which nineteenth-century governors, like their predecessors, regarded as their responsibility. For

---

55 GL, Gardiner, 'Report on Gibraltar', pp. 108–9.
56 Grocott, 'Moneyed Class', pp. 29–30.
57 Sayer, *Gibraltar*, pp. 495–7. The author was the colony's police magistrate.
58 For the strategic reassessment which led to the investment in Gibraltar as a naval base see A.J. Marder, *The Anatomy of British Sea Power* (London: Cass, 1964, 1st edn 1940), esp. chs 10–11.

example, most understood that the economic prosperity of Gibraltar underpinned its military security, if only because of the government revenue thereby
earned, and it was also generally recognised that, as in the past, harmonious
relations with the neighbours would help. This was not something to be left
entirely to the Foreign Office. Hence the serious purpose behind the fulsome
exchange of niceties with local representatives of the Spanish crown and with the
emperor of Morocco. For example, in 1821 the Spanish commandant accepted
an invitation from the governor to celebrate the coronation of King George IV
by dining at the Convent and attending a ball. Similarly, among several other
examples, the governor of Algeciras responded to an invitation to dinner on
the occasion of Queen Victoria's Diamond Jubilee in 1897 and turned up with
a troop of Spanish cavalry. And there was traffic the other way when royalty
visited Gibraltar and paid their respects by visiting Spanish dignitaries across the
frontier.[59] In addition, of course, there were some pretty hard-headed negotiations, sometimes also involving London ministers, to cope with the economic
disruption with Spain caused by, for example, regime changes, difficulties over
tariffs and smuggling,[60] Spanish coastguard actions against British shipping and
smugglers,[61] the imposition of quarantine[62] and disputes over territorial waters
in the Bay of Gibraltar.[63] It was also judged important to secure British jurisdiction in Morocco over British subjects, including traders, via a consular court.[64]
Resolving such matters directly assisted civilian enterprise.

Internally, and of similar concern to the civilian sector, government methods
of managing economic activity in place by the later eighteenth century continued. Indeed, they were extended by the colonial authorities, who were driven
to recognise that the commercial economy needed greater legal regulation. Of

59 S. Constantine, 'Monarchy and constructing identity in "British" Gibraltar, c.1800
    to the present', *Journal of Imperial and Commonwealth History*, 34 (2006), 23–44,
    pp. 34–5.
60 See for instance, correspondence with Spanish authorities referred to in HCPP,
    C.1783, 1877, C.1894, 1877, C.2145, 1878; and respecting commercial negotiations
    in C.3346, 1882, C.4416, C.4419 and C.4592, 1884–85.
61 See for instance fourteen volumes of correspondence on cases during 1867–78 in
    TNA, FO72/1528–1541.
62 A cholera outbreak in England in 1853 prompted the Spanish authorities to deny
    land as well as sea access to traffic from Gibraltar: HCPP, *Dr Baly . . . Quarantine*,
    HC 161, 1854–55.
63 See HCPP, *Correspondence respecting Maritime Jurisdiction in Gibraltar Waters*,
    C.3551, 1883, for inconclusive negotiations from Oct 1878 to March 1883.
64 Morocco Order-in-Council, 1889. There was also the remarkable agreement reached
    between the British and Spanish governments in 1865 'for the Abolition of the
    Practice of Firing on Merchant-Vessels from British and Spanish Forts in the Straits
    of Gibraltar': HCPP, 3462, 1865.

course, governors first needed to secure their revenues, so as to match increasing responsibilities and costs, hence the twelve orders-in-council and ordinances between 1833 and 1899 which confirmed and modified their revenue-raising powers. The 'free port' status of Gibraltar inhibited raising cash through customs duties on imports (except on wines and spirits from 1865), but substantial amounts were derived from rents from leased crown properties, from property rates, from wharfage tolls and port dues, latterly from post office services, and from the sale of a whole raft of business and other licences to the managers of market stalls, eating houses, taverns, and beer and wine shops, and to brokers, tobacconists, hawkers, porters, carters and drivers of hackney carriages.[65] At one time, a licence had to be bought to ferret for rabbits (suggesting hunter-gatherer activities by civilian Rock-dwellers).[66] More importantly, there were also in this century nine pieces of legislation concerning currency and coinage,[67] five to govern the operations of the port, five relating to quarantine, six dealing with merchant shipping, four with markets, one with bills of exchange, ten with debtors and bankruptcy and, from 1881, eight concerned with the setting up and operations of the government savings bank and post office. Other pieces of legislative control over business operations, increasing late in the century, dealt with liquor licences, hackney carriages, pawnbrokers, scrap metal dealers, water imports, business partnerships, the sale of goods, food adulteration, petroleum products and merchandise marks.[68] In sum, here was being put in place much of the legal infrastructure one would expect in a western business economy.

65 See for example, HCPP, *Return of Area, Population, Revenue . . . 1860*, HC 147, 1863, which records a total revenue raised of £33,512; HCPP, *Wines &c (Gibraltar)*, HC 11, 1861, for revenue of £3,432 secured from the licensing of sellers of 'wines or ardent spirits'; and see Blue Books and HCPP, *Gibraltar, Annual Report for 1893*, C.7319, 1894, for a range of revenue headings. Dates of the introduction of some taxes on trade are given in HCPP, *Draft of an Ordinance*, C.1783, 1877, p. 67; and see HCPP, *Gibraltar Tariff*, C.3992, 1884, p. 15.

66 TNA, CO91/325, copy of permit with Williams to Kimberley, 25 July 1873.

67 Throughout the century, until 1898, Spanish currency was primarily used in Gibraltar – indicative of the economic intimacy between supposedly separate sovereignties – and therefore exchange rates based on the gold *Doblon d'Isabel* by the order-in-council of 1872 had to be reconfigured by the order-in-council of 1881 following recoinage in Spain and the introduction of the gold *Alfonso*. See also GGA, Despatches to Gibraltar 1868: Colonial Office to Airey, 28 Sept 1868, confirming Treasury agreement that the legal currency of Gibraltar was Spanish; also R.J.M. Garcia, 'The currency and coinage of Gibraltar in the 18th and 19th centuries', *Gibraltar Heritage Journal*, 2 (1994), 15–29.

68 Analysis based on 'Chronological Table of the Ordinances of Gibraltar' in C.C. Ross (ed.), *The Laws of Gibraltar* (Gibraltar: Government of Gibraltar, rev. edn 1950), vol. 4, pp. i–xv.

Civilian economic activity was, of course, also much affected by access to land. This had been a vexed issue in the eighteenth century, as we have seen, although attempts to preserve property ownership principally in the hands of British Protestants had been abandoned early in the nineteenth century. Local proprietors had warded off, by protest to the governor and to the Privy Council, what they saw as the threat to their security of tenure in the 1817 order-in-council. New crown leases were thereafter usually fixed to run for twenty-one years.[69] However, there were sixteen pieces of legislation between 1817 and 1896 which dealt directly, one way or another, with land titles, property rights and inheritance. Contested claims fell to the governor and his colleagues to investigate, most comprehensibly in the review which commissioners finally completed in May 1825. This, to the relief and advantage of most private citizens, identified and confirmed properties privately claimed and those still in government hands.[70] Nevertheless, ownership and use of land continued to be a matter of concern to governors and secretaries of state whenever leases expired and were due for renewal or alternative allocation. The order-in-council of 1848 also strengthened the governor's power to buy back land and property needed for 'public service'.[71] Among other issues raised were the sanitary state of accommodation on some plots,[72] whether the duration of leases was sufficiently attractive to draw investment especially in housing,[73] and, vexatiously, the competition for space between civil society and the military. The former wanted land for residential development and business premises, the latter insisted on defence priorities.[74]

The governor of the civilian colony, who was of course also commander-in-chief, was sometimes stuck between these claims. Businessmen in the ship repair business who had erected sheds on the neutral ground at North Front were ordered in 1830 to remove them.[75] On the other hand, in 1850 Sir Robert Gardiner persuaded the War Office to allow him to lay out a cricket pitch in the same area, to avert 'local evils to which the soldiers are here exposed,

69 GGA, Box: Documents connected with the Commission to settle Land Titles in 1826, 'Landed Property in Gibraltar', 1817–18; GGA, *Orders in Council, etc*, 'Titles to Lands, etc . . .', 13th August 1817' and 'Titles to Lands, etc . . . 19th March 1819'.
70 TNA, CO91/85, Final Report of the Commissioners for Settling Titles to Land 1825; GGA, *Orders in Council, etc*, 1827, pp. 64–74, 'Lands, etc . . .', 20th November 1826'.
71 GGA, *Orders in Council etc*, 1857, pp. 56–7, 'Lands, Houses etc required for Public Service'.
72 See, for example, GGA, Despatches to Gibraltar 1829: Murray to Don, 3 March and 22 Nov 1829.
73 See, for example, GGA, Box: Aliens Question, Report of the Commission on Aliens, 11 March 1867.
74 See for example, GGA, Box: Housing, Adye to Stanley, 30 Jan 1886.
75 Despatches to Gibraltar 1830: Murray to Don, 3 Feb and 25 March 1830.

by encouraging them in healthy exercise and amusement'.[76] Turf war broke out repeatedly in the 1860s between governors and the War Department in Gibraltar, with appeals to London, over who had prior claims over unoccupied land, and this must have worried private speculators anxious to get their share.[77] It was again debated at length in 1887–89 by the governor, Colonial Office, War Office and Admiralty and by an interdepartmental committee in which issues concerning the need for more and better housing to reduce overcrowding and improve public health were set against the need to site appropriately the latest guns and other bits of military kit (including the maintenance of clear lines of fire).[78] These were not theoretical matters. Military arguments could deny construction by civilians even on freehold property,[79] but equally, civilians could strike very hard bargains with the military when leasehold land was demanded back prematurely. Between April 1889 and October 1892 the War Office had a difficult and expensive time when it attempted, via the Colonial Office and governor, to exclude civilians from the upper rock by buying back the leases on three properties known as Bruce's, Ince's and Porral's Farms. The Acquisition of Lands Order-in-Council of 1888, which allowed for a jury of civilians to make an assessment of value, set a figure so high in dealing with the first case that the authorities opted to secure the other two by private (and tough) negotiation.[80]

Governors had just as much trouble at the turn of the century with their 'own side'. A committee appointed by the War Office in 1898 to consider measures to improve the condition of the 'city, garrison and territory' claimed that a 'tendency has grown up to regard Gibraltar too much as a colony, and too little as a fortress and garrison'. It regretted that so much land had been allowed to 'fall into the hands of native proprietors', and it urged changes in the leasing system so as to return *all* property eventually to government hands. The governor, Sir Robert Biddulph, ventured to suggest this was not practicable.[81] Nevertheless, his successor, Sir George White, had an equally

---

76 TNA, WO43/881, Gardiner to War Office 30 Jan 1850. He even persuaded HM Treasury to authorise the expenditure of £50 on levelling the ground, seeding grass and sinking a well to secure water for its irrigation.

77 GGA, Despatches to Gibraltar 1863: War Office to governor, 21 May 1863; Despatches to Gibraltar 1865: War Office to governor, 31 Jan 1865; TNA, WO396/73, Legal Opinion on Crown Lands in Gibraltar; and especially CO91/289, Airey to Colonial Office, 2 July 1867.

78 TNA, CO883/4/10, Mediterranean No 27, April 1888, 'Defence and Overcrowding', CO883/4/16, Mediterranean No 33, 'Report of a Departmental Committee on the Civil Population and Smuggling in relation to Defence', 23 March 1889.

79 GGA, Despatches from Gibraltar 1891: Smyth to Knutsford, 8 Jan 1891.

80 TNA, WO33/56, A379, 'Correspondence relating to the Acquisition of Certain Farms at Gibraltar for Military Purposes, 1895'.

81 TNA, WO33/133, 'Report of a Committee appointed by the Secretary of State for War to consider what Measures should be adopted to improve the General

hard time in 1903 ensuring that government revenue, and therefore the interests of the colony and its civilians, was protected when the War Office insisted on increasing its property stake while at the same time trying to escape paying rent.[82]

Also demanding of the governor's consideration when managing the economy was the available labour force. It follows from the volume of cross-border trade in imports and re-exports that the frontier between Gibraltar and Spain was not tightly closed. Indeed, as all the fuss about aliens in Gibraltar confirmed, workers (and others) regularly crossed over from Spain (and from Morocco), and many stayed, legally as conditional residents or otherwise. The problem, of course, was the cramming of aliens into Gibraltar's confined space, with all the attendant health and security risks. Hence the colonial government's efforts to allow access while denying residence. It was therefore enormously beneficial to the Gibraltar economy that many workers with their labour and skills, and traders with their goods, were 'parked' across the bay in Algeciras and especially across the frontier in La Línea, and were allowed in on day tickets. In the month of October 1853 the number of aliens entering daily to work or trade totalled 22,440, an average of 724 a day, two-thirds by land, one-third by sea.[83] In February 1854 they numbered 18,250, an average of 652, over 80 per cent of them male.[84] Over the next decades numbers increased substantially. In October 1867 the monthly total of daily permits was 50,695. By September 1887 it had risen to 94,060, a daily average including Sundays (when numbers dropped by two-thirds) of 3,135 (with over 4,000 on Mondays).[85] In 1887 it was reckoned that, of the 2,170 men employed in the coaling business, 1,270 lived in La Línea, including 50 Gibraltar-born and 20 Maltese.[86] Most manual workers hired for

Footnote 81 (*cont.*)

>   Condition of the City, Garrison and Territory of Gibraltar, November 1898' (The Fleetwood-Wilson Committee), especially pp. 8, 14; CO91/423, 'Gibraltar. Committee's Report: Observations of His Excellency the Governor of Gibraltar', pp. 6–7, enclosed in Fleetwood-Wilson to Colonial Office, 7 March 1899.

82 TNA, WO33/1601, 'Correspondence relating to the Appropriation of Crown Lands for Military Purposes', 1901–6. See also WO33/55, 'Correspondence relating to the Storage of Petroleum on the North Front, Gibraltar, and to Crown Lands generally in that Fortress', 1892–93, which relates to the same issue.

83 Calculated from figures in HCPP, *Dr Baly . . . Quarantine*, HC 161, 1854–55, p. 13.

84 TNA, CO91/226: this representative volume contains reports on the number of daily permits and temporary permits of residence for each month from Nov 1854 to Oct 1855.

85 TNA, CO91/297, Buckingham to Airey, 3 April 1868; GGA, Box: Miscellaneous Matters Relating to the Alien Question, 'Abstract of the Total Number of Aliens . . . September 1887'. A report of 1889 refers to 5,000 a day: TNA, CO883/4/16, p. 11.

86 TNA, CO883/4/12, Mediterranean No 29, 'Gibraltar Civil Population', March 1888, p. 3.

big public work schemes, like the end-of-the-century naval dockyards, were in fact Spaniards resident in La Línea and Algeciras.[87] These commuters were, in effect, Gibraltar's reserve army of labour.

La Línea became a rapidly growing dormitory suburb of the town of Gibraltar, rising from a small village to a town of about 12,000 people by the mid 1880s. Rents there were by then between 4s and 6s (20p to 30p) a month for single rooms (housing five or six people), whereas the Gibraltar equivalent cost far more, from 10s to 18s (50p to 90p) a month.[88] Indeed, in the second half of the century Gibraltar speculators were investing in housing in La Línea, where, in spite of lower rents, a more attractive return could be secured than in Gibraltar, where building regulations to secure sanitary living conditions were becoming more demanding and compliance more expensive.[89] The location of labour in La Línea therefore eased Gibraltar's overcrowding problems and consequently took some pressure off local rent levels (though landlords might jib at that). Moreover, because wages in that part of Spain were in any case comparatively poor (indeed abject), and rents in La Línea lower, wages in Gibraltar for labour hired in from Spain could also be kept down. This reserve army of cheap Spanish labour also gave competitive advantages to Gibraltar employers when dealing with Gibraltar-based workers.[90]

Such workers were not like Turkish (and other) *Gastarbeiter* working in Germany in the 1960s, since these Spanish workers slept in the sovereign territory of one country and worked in the sovereign territory of another. Progressively, in economic terms, this part of Spain was therefore becoming incorporated into Gibraltar. Indisputably, Gibraltar was a far more magnetic market for Spanish workers from La Línea than were La Línea and the surrounding Campo for Gibraltar workers. Gibraltar did not have much residential space for alien workers, except for domestic servants, but it did offer comparatively more work, more pay, more opportunities for making a 'bit on the side' and, just as important, more goods to buy from among Gibraltar's imports. To this one might add that Gibraltar had an equivalent attraction, as a source of tempting manufactured goods, to other neighbouring consumers in the water-linked region which included Algeciras across the bay, the eastern coast of Spain, and Morocco over the straits.

One peculiar government responsibility in relation to labour supply derived from the location in Gibraltar of a convict prison settlement. This was another occasion when, it seems, the local administration, and certainly the civilian

---

87 Benady, *Royal Navy*, p. 109.
88 TNA, CO883/4/12 Mediterranean No 29, 'Gibraltar Civil Population', March 1888, p. 4.
89 *The Times*, 15 Dec 1885, p. 8; GGA, Box: Housing in Gibraltar, memo by M. Campbell, 20 Jan 1886, and Adye to Stanley, 30 Jan 1886.
90 Grocott, 'Moneyed Class', pp. 62–3.

population, had no say in an imperial government initiative. In the eighteenth century convicted criminals had been transported from Britain to the American colonies, until citizens of the United States gained their independence and, unsurprisingly, were not keen to receive British and Irish cast-offs. As is well known, the alternative was instead to open up labour camps in Australia in which to dump these first European pioneers, until assertive Australian colonies with growing numbers of free labour began to resist the practice. Gibraltar had actually been considered in 1779 as one of several possible sites for those sentenced to transportation, and it had again been earmarked as an option in 1831, but Gibraltar only 'got its chance' when the overstocking of Van Diemen's Land (Tasmania) became a concern. An order-in-council in 1841 authorised the setting up of a convict establishment. The first convicts arrived in October 1842. Numbers rose rapidly and accommodation was eventually available for nine hundred. Initially, convicts were 'housed' in hulks in the bay, but then mainly in wooden huts in the dockyard, some built against the Line Wall. This was indeed a labour camp – reformation and redemption through physical labour – and, as such, the governor had at his disposal a workforce under discipline.

Convicts were employed to hack stone out of the quarries and to do construction works for the army and in the naval dockyards, but some also worked as tailors and boatmen. Since pay was worth less than 1p a day, of which half was set aside until sentences had been served, it might be thought that this was very cheap labour. However, convicts also had to be provided with rations, medical care and accommodation, and other costs included paying for the whole paraphernalia of guards and administrators (including a chaplain). In 1849 the total cost was nearly £15,000, but it rose with the increase in numbers to over £25,300 in 1859. A House of Commons inquiry in 1861 was told that the total gross expenditure, including the cost of sending out prisoners and bringing back those who had served their time, would amount to £35,000 a year if the full complement of convicts were obtained. Nevertheless, the army authorities in Gibraltar and most governors (not so the navy) argued strongly for the maintenance of the establishment because, for all their inefficiency – convicts, it was reckoned, did about two-thirds of the work of a free man – they were still attractively cheaper to employ. They each cost only £28 a year, including 'on-costs'. Civilian labourers in comparison were reckoned to be dear, £44 a year, and there were also concerns about letting yet more 'aliens' into Gibraltar. It was reckoned that in 1863 public works to the value of at least £24,360 had been secured from a convict population averaging 862 and at an establishment cost of £25,082: not a bad return. Besides, from Gibraltar's point of view, this was pretty much a 'free lunch', since the costs fell upon British taxpayers. Only changes in penal policy in Britain explain why the average number of convicts had fallen to 245 in 1868. By then the estimated value of work done, just over £8,200, was barely more than half of the running costs of £15,200, but the station did not finally close until 15

May 1875, when the last 127 convicts were sent home to England. Some useful public works had been completed, including cutting a new road to Europa Point, constructing water tanks at Moorish Castle, and the quarrying of 700,000 tons of rock to make the New Mole four times longer.[91]

However, as indicated in a previous chapter, the major labour management headache for the governor and his colleagues was controlling the entry and residence of aliens in Gibraltar. Many in the civilian community were unwilling to exclude them, and this generated challenges to the administration. In 1832, for example, when arguing for less-rigid rules against the immigration of aliens, employers of labour in Gibraltar protested, as did and do employers in other economies, that local workers were idle, untrustworthy, insubordinate. 'It is a general complaint, and apparently too well-founded, that few Natives of the lower Classes are eligible for confidential or active employment.' They were 'brought up in idleness, or what is perhaps worse, congregated in the sedentary and demoralizing occupation of cigar maker, they arrive at maturity with vitiated habits and without physical capabilities or mental instruction to fit them for more useful occupation'. That explained why the 'better classes' gave a 'preference to foreigners'.[92] Perhaps more cynically, probably more accurately, Governor Sir Robert Wilson reckoned in 1847 that resident employers wanted to bring in alien workers because they would work for less pay and could be more easily dismissed and dumped over the border.[93]

Employers certainly betrayed no great respect for government intentions and

---

91 A.G.L. Shaw, *Convicts and the Colonies* (London: Faber and Faber, 1966), pp. 43, 274, 313, 333, 350; Benady, *Royal Navy*, pp. 99–102; S. McConville, *A History of Prison Administration* (London: Routledge and Kegan Paul, 1981), vol. 1, pp. 201–3, 393–6; HCPP, *Estimates for Civil Services, 1849–50*, III, HC 268, 1849, p. 18; *Select Committee on System of Transportation Report*, HC 286, esp. pp. iii–v, 138, 141–3, 147, 154; *Annual Reports of the Convict Establishment of Gibraltar*, for 1863 see Command Paper 3305, 1864; and for 1864, and a further emphatic statement by the governor of the value of convict labour, 3454, 1865, pp. 3–4; and for 1868, 4129, 1868–9; see also GGA, Despatches from Gibraltar 1863: Royal Engineer's Office to Colonial Secretary, 10 Dec 1863, which stresses the value of keeping convict labour, or the need otherwise to recruit two additional companies of Royal Engineers. Sir Robert Gardiner was (ineffectively) hostile to having a convict establishment in what he regarded as a fortress: TNA, CO91/226, Gardiner to Panmure, 21 Aug 1855, paras 17–21. Even as late as June 1874, an official government inquiry favoured retaining the 'Convict Establishment': see report TNA, WO33/27. By an ordinance of 1846, repealed 1875, criminals convicted in Gibraltar could also be sentenced to 'imprisonment and hard labor in the Convict Establishment', though they would be few.

92 GGA, Box: The Alien Question, Flood to Williams, 12 May 1871, Appendix A, No 35, Rowan to Houston, 12 March 1832.

93 GGA, Box: The Alien Question, Flood to Williams, 12 May 1871, Appendix A, No 62, Wilson to Paget, 4 Sept 1847.

endeavoured to increase their alien labour supply. The secretary of state was not impressed that foreigners were being brought in by employers for jobs which natives should surely be capable of tackling. Why, for instance, in November 1831 had four Genoese and four Spaniards been allowed in as journeymen gardeners, and why had a cattle drover to be fetched in from Algeciras? Why had Mr Parody recruited twenty-five alien workers, mainly Spaniards, in five weeks?[94] How had a wealthy retailer managed to secure permits for no fewer than forty-six alien workers in the month of December 1831 alone? The secretary of state suspected that his personal motives were 'unconnected with the public welfare'. He was indeed the smuggling racketeer identified earlier in this chapter.[95]

Most remarkably, perhaps, in June 1837 Governor Woodford received a memorial for forwarding to the secretary of state requesting a relaxation of the rules on aliens which were 'preventing the admission of Foreigners into Gibraltar as household servants', thereby causing 'extreme inconvenience and distress'. Natives of Great Britain were of 'very bad character – both men and women become soon habituated to drinking'; the natives of Gibraltar were worse, the 'most idle, insolent, drunken and worthless class in the community', having acquired dissipated habits by mixing with soldiers; while the number of foreigners currently resident with permits were too few and were learning bad habits from the rest. Because there was so little competition among the local population for employment as domestic servants, those who applied for posts could 'make their own terms', 'set their employers at defiance', and secure 'higher wages than a good servant could be hired in London'. And yet, there across the frontier, 'many respectable and even valuable household servants might be procured if they were permitted to enter the Garrison'. This splendid piece of pleading was signed by forty-three beacons of the community (British, Catholic and Jewish), including the chief justice, the civil secretary, the civil chaplain, the inspector of revenues, the captain of the port, the admiralty doctor, four barristers, two consuls, one doctor, twenty-one merchants and nine other gentlemen. Governor Woodford, with the backing of the secretary of state, stuck to policy and turned down their request.[96]

Occasionally, it is true, resident civilians in Gibraltar complained to the governor about the alien competitors who had slipped in. Societies made up of immigrant stock, whether large like the USA or small like Gibraltar, are not

94 TNA, CO92/10, Goderich to Houston, 28 Dec 1831.
95 GGA, Box: The Alien Question, Flood to Williams, 12 May 1871, Appendix A, Nos 33, 34, Goderich to Houston, 5 Feb, and Rowan to Houston, 22 Feb 1832, and TNA, CO92/10.
96 TNA, CO91/139, Woodford to Glenelg, 1 Oct, and Glenelg to Woodford, 25 Oct 1837. However, Governor Airey could be just as rude about local workers: 'It is well known that the lower orders of the Native population are idle and worthless': GGA, Despatches to Secretary of State for War 1866–1868, Airey to Ripon, 17 Feb 1866.

uniformly welcoming of those seeking to follow. Locating the voice of unskilled native labour in the records of the time is hard, though Governor Don's concerns in 1817 to exclude alien immigrants in the tricky post-war labour market may have been prompted by expressions of local disquiet.[97] Governor Wilson in 1847 claimed to be responding to 'well grounded complaint' from native workers against the excess of aliens when he ordered the police magistrate to enforce the regulations rigidly.[98]

Objections were not only voiced by manual workers. Sometimes politically savvy businessmen and professional folk tried by appeal to government to lock out competitors. Local surgeon-apothecaries in 1827 urged the secretary of state to exclude foreign practitioners.[99] Likewise, ten 'British Subjects and Master Tailors' complained in 1849 about 'the undue admission of foreigners of their profession into this City and Garrison' who were setting up businesses 'with all the freedom of British born subject[s]'. They claimed, correctly, that such competitors infringed regulations 'framed for the protection of British subjects'; they argued, plausibly, that their presence in an overpopulated territory pushed up rents and prices; and they asserted, with breathtaking audacity, that 'an influx of strangers many of them of unknown character' affected not only the health of the public but 'the purity of morals with which every Christian community should be inspired'.[100] This demand for expulsion does not seem to have been accepted. Similarly in 1867, and again in the face of a memorial of protest, after much deliberation Governor Airey allowed Mr Ratino, a Spanish national who worked for a haberdasher, to remain a conditional resident precisely because 'by his exertions the Establishment has obtained a great deal of custom, and I am not surprized that Memorialists, who are in the same trade, should wish him to be expelled from the Garrison . . . [W]holesome competition is advantageous to the place.'[101] Governors, it seems, placed in the position of economic manager, reacted case by case, insofar as the law and grumbling secretaries of state in London allowed them.

Occupations and living standards

Of course, the important issue arising from all this preliminary analysis of the economy and of the role of government is to consider how such matters impacted

97 GGA, Box: The Alien Question, Flood to Williams, 12 May 1871, Appendix A, No 10, 12 November 1814, No 15, Proclamation, 17 May 1817.
98 GGA, Box: The Alien Question, Flood to Williams, 12 May 1871, Appendix A, No 62, Wilson to Paget, 4 Sept 1847.
99 GGA, Despatches to/from Gibraltar 1827: Bathurst to Don, 25 March, and Don to Goderich, 29 May 1827.
100 GGA, Box: The Alien Question, Flood to Williams, 12 May 1871, Appendix A, Nos 66–71, petition to Sir Robert Wilson, 18 Jan 1849.
101 TNA, CO91/289, Airey to Buckingham, 25 July 1867.

on the lived lives of Gibraltar civilians. One important consequence, determining so much about family incomes and living standards, was the distribution of
jobs. The police surveillance of the population upon which the secretary of state
insisted in the early decades of the century has left us with occupational censuses.
They provide insights, albeit through a glass darkly, into how the economy of
Gibraltar was operating at the time, when the period of most rapid population
growth, through immigration, had slowed down. There are uncertainties in the
data, since the returns to the Colonial Office for 1829, 1831 and 1844 lumped
occupations together in not quite consistent categories devised by the police
magistrate, whereas that for 1860 listed each occupation separately (itself an
uncertain process). Table 5.2 has been calibrated to produce as much standardi-
sation as possible, though a further reservation must be entered concerning some
of the figures for 1860 (see note on Table 5.2).

It should be stressed immediately that these figures count only those who
were resident in Gibraltar, and therefore they exclude the large numbers, already
considered, who entered daily to work or to trade. One further preliminary
observation is that the proportion of the 'fixed population' (that is, excluding
temporary visitors) recorded as in employment varied between about 40 per cent
and 45 per cent, suggesting some moments of unemployment.

It is curious to see a reduction in the number of merchants in this trading
economy, in absolute as well as in proportionate terms, but the concentration of
more business into fewer hands is the likely explanation, as also for the reduced
number of brokers, dealers and perhaps even shopkeepers (though the damaged
1860 report is missing a return for the number of grocers). The increase in the
number of clerks, probably working for the fewer but larger business companies,
supports this contention since there had not yet been much of an increase in the
number of professional men who would otherwise be employing clerical workers. In
the light of what has been said about smuggling, it is not surprising that the number
of tobacconists, and especially cigar makers, was so high (42 of the former, 172 of
the latter in 1860), though the combined total of 825 unequivocally recorded in
1844 almost beggars belief – one for every nineteen members of the fixed population of men, women and children. Indicative of an economy and society with more
varied and sophisticated demands are the numbers of 'tradesmen' and 'mechanics'.
In 1860 they included 45 blacksmiths, 208 carpenters, 133 masons and 51 painters,
plus 39 barbers, 47 milliners, 113 shoemakers and 89 tailors.[102] Lumped in with
'Miscellaneous' in 1860 were even five artists, nine architects, two librarians and
seven musicians. It will also be seen that a substantial number of folk were general
labourers and porters and other 'fetchers and carriers'. These would be overwhelmingly men (and boys), such as the mariners, whereas servants were mainly women

102 Figures for these individual trades are listed, from the 1834 census, in Howes, *The
     Gibraltarian*, pp. 113–16, and 1860 census.

Table 5.2 *Occupations by census, 1829–60*

Occupations	1829 Nos	1829 %	1831 Nos	1831 %	1844 Nos	1844 %	1860 Nos	1860 %
Merchants	278	3.7	158	2.4	178	2.5	133	2.1
Brokers	64	0.9	34	0.5	28	0.4	20	0.3
Shopkeepers	323	4.3	298	4.5	265	3.7	196*	3.1
Hawkers, dealers	350	4.7	314	4.7	275	3.9	247	4.0
Wine and spirit dealers, tavern and winehouse keepers	100	1.3	50	0.7	38	0.5	57	0.9
Gardeners, bakers, butchers, fruit and milk sellers	287	3.8	286	4.3	218	3.1	144	3.8
Clerks	364	4.9	291	4.4	394	5.6	403	6.5
Lawyers, notary publics	7	0.1	6	0.1	15	0.2	8	0.1
Doctors, apothecaries	36	0.5	26	0.4	30	0.4	30	0.5
Government employment	184	2.5	114	1.7	104	1.5	56	0.9
Religious establishments	19	0.3	21	0.3	12	0.2		
Landed proprietors	71	1.0	71	1.1	84	1.2	127	2.0
Tobacconists, cigar makers	282	3.8	313	4.7	825	11.6	214	3.4
Tradesmen, mechanics	1,147	15.4	1,038	15.6	1,146	16.2	1,066*	17.1
Mariners, boatmen, lightermen, fishermen	515	6.9	586	8.8	417	5.9	383	6.1
Porters, labourers, carters, coachmen, watercarriers	618	8.3	730	10.9	722	10.2	517*	8.3
Servants, laundresses, seamstresses	2,065	27.7	1,961	29.4	2,109	29.7	1,964	31.5
Miscellaneous	776	10.4	377	5.7	225	3.2	325*	5.2
Total in occupations	*7,467*		*6,672*		*7,094*		*6,240*	
	45.5% of fixed pop		39.2% of fixed pop		44.9% of fixed pop		40.4% of fixed pop	
Without employment: males over 12	no fig.		883		647		–	
females over 12	3,535		4,337		4,176		9,222 (all)	
Children	5,392		4,938		3,906		–	
Grand total of fixed population	*16,394*		*16,830*		*15,823*		*15,462*	

Note: In these tables, the population is divided into those above and below aged 12. Occupations are grouped as closely as possible under headings based on the 1844 return. The 1829 return, mysteriously, gives no figure for males over 12 without employment. The 1860 return is water damaged: allocated numbers account for only 95% of the 'Total in occupations'; groups combined into asterisked totals amount to only 86% of what in aggregate they ought to be; and therefore uncertain numbers need to be added to each.

Sources: Censuses in TNA, C091/98, Don to Murray, 20 May 1829; TNA, CO91/113, Don to Goderich, 13 May 1831;TNA, CO91/167, Wilson to Stanley, 27 Jan 1844; GGA, Despatches from Gibraltar 1861, loose paper.

(but still 853 men among them in 1829), like the large number of seamstresses (878 in 1860) who also served their 'betters'. This remained, unsurprisingly, a society with inbuilt inequalities.

Some of these had an ethnic dimension. It is not surprising that 132 of the merchants resident in Gibraltar in 1844 were 'British Subjects', 'Native Christians' or 'Native Jews' (74 per cent of the total); as were 303 of the clerks (77 per cent), 65 of the landed proprietors (77 per cent), 21 of the brokers (75 per cent) and, of course, all but one of the lawyers (93 per cent). Even 708 of the tobacconists and cigar makers (86 per cent) were 'locals', as were a large number of the servants, seamstresses and laundresses, totalling 1,416 (67 per cent). But 'aliens' were more involved on other rungs of the economic ladder: 119 hawkers and dealers (43 per cent of the total), 328 porters, labourers and the like (45 per cent), 140 shopkeepers (53 per cent), 228 mariners, lightermen, fishermen etc. (55 per cent) and 228 gardeners, bakers, butchers, etc. (57 per cent).

Table 5.3 indicates the principal employments of the 'British' and of the substantial 'alien' cohorts in the population in 1844. It does not show quite the same hierarchy by ethnicity as was discerned in the census return of 1814 analysed in Chapter 4, probably because thirty years later the earlier immigrant flows had become more securely bedded in and fewer were being allowed subsequently to take up residence. However, distinctive distributions may be discerned among the Portuguese, with a large proportion gravitating towards labouring and carrying jobs. The Maltese, late settlers about whom more in a later chapter, were largely driven into hard labour occupations, especially as coal heavers.[103]

Manual workers in regular employment in 1860 usually put in a 54-hour working week over six days. How much they were paid depended, of course, on regularity of employment. Work relying on ship arrivals and activity in the port would vary by the day as well as by the season and (early in the century especially) by weather conditions. The skilled were being paid between 4s 2d and, at the top, 5s 2½d (about 21p–26p) a day or, say, between 25s and 27s (£1.25–£1.35) a week if they got in six days of labour. This would be worth at most £85 a week at 2005 retail prices (though £788 a week in relation to average earnings in 2005 – indicative, and only indicative, of the elite status of such workers). Those in this tradesmen category in the early 1860s, usually after completing apprenticeships, included engineers and fitters at the top and then blacksmiths and moulders, stonecutters and lime-burners, painters and plumbers, sawyers and turners, carpenters and coopers, shoemakers and tailors: in other words, men with skills and responsibilities, as in the UK. The semi-skilled, including quarry miners, riggers, masons, plasterers and tinmen, earned at best 3s 8d, at worst 3s 1½d, between

---

103 TNA, CO883/4/12, Confidential Print, Med. No 29, Gibraltar Civil Population, March 1888, p. 3.

Table 5.3 *Occupations and percentage of occupied population by 'nationality', 1844*

Occupation	British Subjects, Native Christians and Native Jews	Genoese	Spanish	Portuguese
Merchants	2.8	1.9	1.5	0.2
Clerks	6.5	1.9	3.0	0.0
Shopkeepers	2.6	8.9	3.1	1.9
Hawkers and dealers	3.3	3.3	1.2	0.5
Tobacconists and cigar-makers	15.1	2.1	9.0	1.4
Tradesmen and mechanics	16.1	12.4	19.3	23.1
Gardeners, bakers butchers, etc.	2.0	10.3	4.3	1.9
Mariners, lightermen etc.	4.0	17.0	4.0	10.3
Porters, labourers etc.	8.4	10.0	8.5	38.6
Servants, seamstresses laundresses	30.2	23.3	40.4	19.0

Source: Based on TNA, CO91/167, Wilson to Stanley, 27 Jan 1844, census of 1844.

22s and 19s (around £1.10 to £0.90) for a six-day week, if they were lucky. The supposedly unskilled, like boatmen, gardeners and general labourers, were lucky to get above a basic 2s 1d up to 2s 7d, say about 12s to 15s (£0.60–£0.75, or at most £47 at 2005 prices) a week. Boy workers had to make do with just 1s a day, say 6s (30p) a week.[104] The differentials are actually less extreme than one might find in England at this time, where unionised skilled men in an ironworks might be earning up to 50s (£2.50) a week and a labourer only 10s 6d (£0.53).[105] One mid-century resident expatriate had the temerity to insist that 'the rate of wage is excessive'. We know that earnings were higher in Gibraltar than across the frontier in La Línea, but the latter were dismally poor. However, living standards also relate to the cost of living. The same observer acknowledged that prices were 'exorbitantly dear' (double those in Malta and Corfu), no doubt a consequence of local demand pulling up the prices of imported supplies. He also complained that 'house rent is ruinous', reflecting the imbalance between the demand for

104 Data for 'free' labourers' wages are cited in HCPP, *Annual Report on the Convict Establishment*, 3305, 1864, p. 31; and see also similar data in HCPP, *Select Committee on System of Transportation*, HC 286, pp. 142–3.

105 E.H. Hunt, *British Labour History 1815–1914* (London: Weidenfeld and Nicolson, 1981), p. 99.

accommodation and the supply in Gibraltar's confined space.[106] Twenty-five years later a correspondent from *The Times* similarly concluded: 'Rent is preposterously high.'[107]

As was repeatedly said by those in authority, Gibraltar was small and overcrowded. The problems of urban living were of course not unique to the town of Gibraltar, or indeed to the nineteenth century. Urbanisation everywhere concentrated populations. The police magistrate in 1831 reckoned the area of Gibraltar to be one and two-thirds square miles, and he calculated a population density of 10,214 persons per square mile. The census of 1860 claimed a reduction, but only to 9,278 per square mile.[108] In fact, because the town area of Gibraltar, in which most people lived, was much smaller, about one-sixth of a square mile according to one investigator, the population density there worked out at over 100,000 per square mile. By this reckoning, only seven of the worst wards of inner-city London were more crowded.[109] On another calculation, a police magistrate census in 1898 showed that there were only 1,024 houses in the colony, and that 18,155 people were living in just 10,610 rooms.[110] These figures are not extreme by the lamentable standards of the inner-city wards of British cities in the early (or even late) nineteenth century, where multiple occupancy of cheap houses and tenements was also rife, a consequence of housing similarly supplied by private investors aiming to make a profit from tenants who could afford only low rents.

In Gibraltar, the majority of 'houses' were in fact tenements under one roof, many of three and some of four stories, with a patio or yard in the centre and one common entrance. Communal living, to that extent, was the norm. High density of occupancy, however, only became a public health problem if construction and sanitary services were poor. For much of the century they were. Drainage was often deficient, if present; toilet facilities were grim; rubbish collection was minimal; much was dumped in the sea and subject to the whims of wind, wave and tide; gas from street sewers penetrated and poisoned houses; mules, donkeys and poultry shared space with humans; rooms without windows, and therefore

---

106 Sayer, *Gibraltar*, p. 461. This was also the explanation provided by HCPP, *Report of the Barrack and Hospital Improvement Commission on the Sanitary Condition and Improvement of the Mediterranean Stations*, 7626, 1863, p. 26, on why 'Many of the house rents would be considered most exorbitant in any town in Great Britain'.

107 *The Times*, 15 Dec 1885, p. 8.

108 TNA, CO91/113, Don to Goderich, 13 May 1831, census of 1831; GGA, Despatches from Gibraltar 1861: loose paper.

109 Major H. Tulloch, *Water Supply & Sewerage of Gibraltar* (London, n.p., 1890), p. 12.

110 GGA, 'Census of Civil Residents taken by the Civil Police on 31 December 1894 and 1898'.

without access for light or air, were commonplace; the close proximity of some processing businesses contaminated living accommodation; many streets were narrow and airless.[111] It was reported that in 1828 'The condition of the sewers was such that even rats died in them.'[112]

These things were difficult and therefore expensive to put right, especially because a regular water supply was lacking. As a report of 1870 put it, 'The inhabitants . . . of Gibraltar, ever since the population has been as numerous as it is at present, have always been deficient of one of the principal elements necessary to the health of any people, namely, a sufficient supply of Pure Fresh Water.'[113] For a community dependent on the rainfall which fell on the limited acreage of the Rock, too much sunny weather was a curse. The meteorological data collected and reported in numerous reports on Gibraltar was therefore of far more than scientific interest. In 1842 Governor Woodford reported his fear of a deficiency of water owing to the 'extreme dryness of the Spring'. He recorded the restrictions on use which he had introduced, his concern for the 'poorer classes' and his search for alternative supplies.[114] The concern remained grave even at the beginning of the next century. The colony's health officer, in his report for 1903, analysed rainfall over the previous 114 years, calculated the population's needs and current supply, and lamented the consequences of that year's virtual drought, which had lasted 270 days.[115]

We should not imagine, of course, equal density of occupation or equal quality of accommodation for all the population. The 1860 census numbered 1,014 'houses', for a total population, fixed and floating, of 17,647. The sanitary conditions of 822 were categorised as 'good', but nearly a quarter (23 per cent) fell short: 132 were 'indifferent' and 60 'bad'. A report of 1870 calculated 22 as the average number of occupants per house, but a close study of 74 houses produced an average of 56 occupants and, in some cases, as many as 120, 170

111 For one among many descriptions, and this from late in the century, see Tulloch, *Water Supply*, pp. 6–7. See also on accommodation, health and disease, L.A. Sawchuk, *Deadly Visitations in Dark Times: a Social History of Gibraltar* (Gibraltar: Gibraltar Government Publications, 2001.

112 HCPP, *Report of the Barrack and Hospital Improvement Commission*, p. 26.

113 GGA, Water Supply Box: E. Roberts, *Report of a Proposed Scheme for a Supply of Fresh Water to the Town and Garrison of Gibraltar* (Gibraltar: n.p., 1870), p. 3. For the effects of drought and water deficiency on infant mortality, especially among the poor and ill housed, see L.A. Sawchuk, 'Societal and ecological determinants of urban health: a case study of pre-reproductive mortality in 19th century Gibraltar', *Social Science and Medicine*, 36 (1993), 875–92.

114 TNA, CO91/159, Woodford to Stanley, 4 June 1842. See also comments in HCPP, *Report of the Barrack and Hospital Improvement Commission*, p. 24.

115 GGA, Box: Health, handwritten draft of 'Annual Report on the Public Health of Gibraltar for the Year 1903', pp. 10–12.

and a staggering 220 individuals 'living' in one 'house'.[116] The overall density of occupation in 1898 was 1.7 persons per room or 17.7 persons per house. However, in Catalan Bay there were as many as 3.2 persons per room, although only 13.2 persons per house, whereas in South District the figures were 1.8 per room and 14.7 per house. The range in the four divisions of the town within the walls was from as low as 1.2 persons per room and 14.1 per house (Division 1, mainly Main Street and to the west) up to 2.6 per room and as many as 23.1 per house (Division 3, Upper Town).[117] Unsurprisingly, the larger residences for the richer families were not distributed randomly around the town amongst the slums, but concentrated, for example, on Line Wall Road, Irish Town and Main Street, or a carriage ride away in South District – and some of the better off also had property in Spain by which to escape summer heat (and worse).[118]

Seriously unequal was the availability of water. In 1870 it was recorded that there were 988 houses within the walls and in the South District. Of these, 323 had access neither to a tank nor to a well. Inevitably, 'those Districts inhabited by the poorer classes' were the least well served, and 'as they are situated on the higher levels of the town, their only supply has been such as could be carried by donkey and obtained at considerable cost'.[119] For those living on the margin of subsistence, clean water for drinking, cooking and washing was a scarcely affordable luxury. An analysis of the water drawn from a well in the lower part of town also suggests that some families located there would have been well advised to restrict their use: 'The chemical constitution of these waters is extraordinary, both as regards the amount and character of their impurities, when compared with what are considered waters sufficiently pure for town use'. A gallon of such stuff contained nearly 171 grains of 'solid matter', compared with only 2.35 in a Glasgow sample.[120] By 1890 brackish water for other than drinking purposes had become more widely available, provided under pressure via street mains, but it was paid for according to volume used, and drinking water was still scarce. Insufficient water supply and investment in housing were also still limiting the provision of adequate water closets.[121] Moreover, sanitation drains laid after the epidemic of 1828 relied only on gravity and the liquidity of deposits to effect a

116 Roberts, *Supply of Fresh Water*, pp. 3–4.
117 GGA, 'Census of Civil Residents taken by the Civil Police on 31 December 1894 and 1898', and see also 'Census . . . 1899'. The figures for 1894 show 1,032 'houses' and 18,340 people occupying 10,463 rooms, and for 1899 1,023 houses for 18,550 people occupying 10,438 rooms, with very similar inequalities per area.
118 Grocott, 'Moneyed Class', pp. 46–7, 98–100.
119 Roberts, *Supply of Fresh Water*, pp. 3–4.
120 HCPP, *Report of the Barrack and Hospital Improvement Commission*, pp. 31, 274.
121 Tulloch, *Water Supply*, p. 10. A decade later the colony's health officer was still urging the provision of piped drinking water to all homes: GGA, Box: Health, handwritten draft, dated March 1902, of 'Annual Report on the Public Health of

flow downhill, with a result that they tended to block up in the lower reaches of town before, with occasional rainfalls, flopping their contents into the bay just over Line Wall. Houses nearby were affected by 'the pestilential and poisonous effluvia'.[122] Only when the brackish water supply through the sewers was connected in 1895 to a transverse outlet from the town to Europa Point was sewage through the drains kept flowing into the sea, albeit still untreated, 'where the strong currents of the Straits will carry it clear of the Rock'.[123]

Complaints about the consequences of urban conditions, and especially of bad drains, were repeatedly made by sanitary engineers and public health officers,[124] and also by those least directly affected. 'The memorials I receive on this subject from respectable inhabitants of the town', reported Sir Robert Gardiner in 1850, 'represent the present nuisance of stench and foul air as insupportable.'[125] Many of those directly affected also found bad drains insupportable, and died. The consequences of (at best) modest pay and (at worst) high prices for food and rent, plus the concentration of a large population in a small space, produced sanitary conditions for the majority of civilians which were not conducive to public health. Levels of nutrition left families at the best of times vulnerable to infection, and poor housing and disgusting sanitation were excellent environmental conditions for the multiplication of airborne, waterborne and foodborne diseases. The terminology of mid-nineteenth-century medical science, as practised in Gibraltar before a proper registration system was put in place, makes it difficult to be specific about the causes of the 502 deaths recorded in 1860: 'Suddenly' is rather inexact, and even 'Old age' not very informative. 'Teething' seems insufficient to account for 37 dead babies or 'In infancy from weakness' for a further 18. But one can pick out more than hints that infectious diseases were predictably rampant, especially chest infections (consumption, catarrh), plus dropsy, smallpox, cholera and unidentified 'fever'. On average,

Gibraltar for the Year 1901', p. 16. No earlier annual reports appear to have been archived.

122 Hennen, *Sketches*, pp. 10–12; TNA, CO91/289, Airey to Colonial Office, 16 May 1867.

123 HCPP, *Report of the Barrack and Hospital Improvement Commission*, pp. 12, 28; Tulloch, *Water Supply*, p. 54, Plan No 5; HCPP, *Gibraltar Annual Report for 1895*, C.7944, 1896, p. 7. On the controversy surrounding the southern outlet see HCPP, *Papers relating to an Excess upon the Estimated Cost of the Drainage Works*, C.8668, 1897.

124 In addition to sources already cited see HCPP, *Report of Dr Baly on the Sanitary State of Gibraltar, 1854*, HC 274, 1854–55; TNA, CO91/226, report of Col W. Ward, RE, with Gardiner to Panmure, 28 July 1855; HCPP, *Report on the Sanitary Condition of Gibraltar with reference to the Epidemic Cholera in the year 1865 by Dr Sutherland*, HC 3921, 1867, and many official annual reports.

125 GL, Gardiner, *Report on Gibraltar*, p. 100.

death rates in the 1850s averaged 30.4 per 1,000 of the population, 'which is a very high rate on a small fixed population of 15,562 living in a climate not unfavourable to health'. In England and Wales at that time the rate was around 22 per 1,000.[126] Since sea breezes were reputed to be beneficial to health, a later report compared death rates in Gibraltar in 1889 with those in some English seaside towns: Margate 11.57 per 1,000 of the population, Bournemouth 14.05, Southend 15.70, but in Gibraltar 24.5.[127]

However, as even this last figure shows, when compared with earlier data, improvements were taking place. Indeed, when, in 1885, cholera devastated Spain, including districts just across the frontier, mortality in Gibraltar was much lower than feared, a relief achieved by improvements in sanitation and public health care since the previous terrible outbreak in 1865. Measures taken included closing off the importation of water from Spain and the use of a steam-condensing machine to produce 52,000 gallons of distilled water a week.[128] Nevertheless, epidemics recurred, lives were affected and improvements, according to health records, set back. Because of the modest size of Gibraltar's population, disease killing an additional ten or twenty people showed up starkly in crude death rates, which are conventionally calculated as deaths per 1,000 of the population. The mortality rate among the fixed civil population had been 27.4 per 1,000 in 1885, 21.8 in 1886 and 20.5 in 1888,[129] but outbreaks of measles, diphtheria, smallpox and other nasties increased the rate, lifting it, for example, from 20.64 in 1897, to 22.03 in 1899 and to 25.90 in 1900, only to fall back to 21.35 in 1901.[130]

But these are averages. The mosquito was not particularly fussed about status

---

126 HCPP, *Report of the Barrack and Hospital Improvement Commission*, pp. 25, 265–6; R. Woods, *The Population of Britain in the Nineteenth Century* (London: Macmillan, 1992), p. 29.

127 Tulloch, *Water Supply*, p. 8. See also GGA, Box: Health, 'The Annual Report on the Public Health of Gibraltar for the Year 1903', p. 2, for an unfavourable comparison of crude death rates of Gibraltar with death rates for England and Wales, various English counties, and London.

128 *The Times*, 4 Dec 1885, p. 13.

129 *Gibraltar Chronicle*, 21 Feb 1887; HCPP, *Gibraltar, Report on the Blue Book for 1888*, C.5620, p. 8. Most reports based their figures on the fixed civil population, which excluded aliens resident on permits who were, on average, younger and accordingly had a lower death rate.

130 HCPP, *Gibraltar Report for 1897*, C.9046, 1898, p. 10, and also see figures for diphtheria deaths 1894–98 in *Gibraltar Report for 1898*, C.9498, 1899, p. 24; *Gibraltar Report for 1899*, Cd.3580, 1900, p. 20; *Gibraltar Report for 1900*, Cd.788, 1901, p. 16; *Gibraltar Report for 1901*, Cd.788, 1902, p. 17; GGA, Box: Health, 'Annual Report on the Public Health of Gibraltar for the Year 1901', pp. 2–3. In 1901 there were 'only' 371 deaths among the fixed population of 17,373, producing the rate of 21.35 deaths per 1,000.

and income, and those yellow fever epidemics early in the century plagued all
ranks. But that was less true of other epidemics, like outbreaks of cholera and
scarlet fever in which environmental conditions – which in other societies calibrate
with nutritional standards and income – determined susceptibility. Those assaulted
most severely were those trying to cope with the worst sanitary conditions. The
1860 data showed that the death rate was then over 36 per 1,000 in the densely
populated town within the walls, but 27.5 per 1,000 in the South District.[131]
Analysis of 408 civilian deaths from cholera in the outbreak of 1865 revealed death
rates of less than 12 per 1,000 of the population in some parts of the town, while
other parts suffered rates of 46, 63 and even 78 per 1,000. The worst rates were
in the upper town, 'crowded by a poor population . . . most deficient in sanitary
arrangements'.[132] When cholera returned in 1885, 'most of the cases . . . came from
extremely poor and overcrowded centres'.[133] Similar environmental conditions
produced similar public health results in 1901, when 54 of the 380 deaths that
year were ascribed to tubercular diseases. A concerned medical officer noted that
the most affected, as over the previous ten years, were 'the most populous districts'
of the upper town, containing 'a very large number of one-room tenements and
back-to-back rooms . . . chiefly inhabited by the poorer people'.[134]

Particularly vulnerable were children and infants. In 1888, one-third of all
children born in the town did not reach the age of five.[135] Infant mortality rates
(deaths under one year) were particularly grim, averaging over 161 deaths per
1,000 live births even during the last decade of the century. In 1901 'only' 59
Gibraltar-born babies died under the age of one (17 of diarrhoea, indicative
of infection), a rate of 108.45 deaths per 1,000 live births, but in 1903 deaths
increased to 92, largely because of bronchitis and broncho-pneumonia, pushing
the rate back up to 179.6 per 1,000 live births.[136] Data are not available to prove

131 HCCP, *Report of the Barrack and Hospital Improvement Commission*, p. 25.
132 HCCP, *Report . . . on Cholera . . . by Dr Sutherland*, pp. 10–11, 17–18, and Plan No
   2, which plots cholera deaths by district, and Plans Nos 4 and 5, which provide a
   cross-section plan of housing construction in the worst-affected district and layout
   of sewers and patios.
133 *The Times*, 8 Dec 1885, p. 13.
134 GGA, Box: Health, 'Annual Report on the Public Health of Gibraltar for the Year
   1901', pp. 8–9.
135 HCPP *Gibraltar, Report on the Blue Book for 1888*, C.5620, p. 8.
136 GGA, Box: Health, 'Annual Report on the Public Health of Gibraltar for the Year
   1901', p. 4; 'Annual Report on the Public Health of Gibraltar for the Year 1903', p.
   3; HCPP, *Gibraltar Report for 1903*, Cd.1768, 1904, p. 19. For a detailed analysis
   of the level and causes of infant mortality comparing civilian and military data,
   with much on housing conditions and water supplies, see L.A. Sawchuk, S.D.A.
   Burke and J. Padiak, 'A matter of privilege: infant mortality in the garrison town
   of Gibraltar, 1870–1899', *Journal of Family History*, 27:4 (2002), 399–429.

that the infant mortality rate was worse in the less-favoured parts of the town and among families on low incomes, but that, as in Britain, will have been the case.

Conclusion

Analysis of mortality is a sobering note upon which to end an analysis of the material world of nineteenth-century Gibraltar. It would certainly be misleading to imply that the problems of urban life were qualitatively different for civilians of Gibraltar than for, say, citizens of Bolton in Lancashire or, for that matter, of Valetta in Malta. Urbanisation everywhere threw up similar challenges, cultural as well as physical. While conditions in urban Britain, as measured by income and health statistics, were, on the whole, improving more rapidly than in Gibraltar, by the opening of the twentieth century their future trajectory in the same direction seemed pretty well mapped out.

This, for Gibraltar's civilian community, was a quite remarkable achievement, since, as stressed, they were coping within a peculiarly vulnerable economy. Of course, by the late nineteenth century the interlocking of national economies made virtually all populations vulnerable to forces beyond the control of individuals or even of substantial economic sectors, as arable farmers in Britain and handcraft textile workers in British India were then finding. But Gibraltar's substantial civilian population was clinging to a Rock of small size and with virtually no tradeable natural resources. It was therefore dependent on imports for the very stuff of life and for the other things that made up nineteenth-century civilised living. Payment for these necessities and desirables also depended largely on yet more imports, destined for re-export. This obligation to trade, and also to sell services to outsiders, underlined dependence on external markets. Entry to these was never guaranteed, because of other economic competitors or because of obstacles placed politically in their way. There was one further feature which retrospectively shows Gibraltar's fragility. Civilian well-being was also dependent upon the strategic thinking of imperial paymasters and their willingness and ability to fund this garrison town and naval depot, as well as others in Britain and in the empire. Here at least the early nineteenth-century shift of priorities to Malta as the principal base for Britain's Mediterranean fleet had been reversed by the opening of the twentieth century, benefiting Gibraltar living standards.

In the face of handicaps, comparative success had been achieved. This is to be measured especially by the numbers of civilians packed into the town, including – though the authorities did not see it this way – by the proportion of them who, as we have seen, were of alien origin. Migrants move to where prospects seem brighter. As a correspondent in *The Times* put it in 1885, for Spanish workers 'Gibraltar is a sort of El Dorado'.[137] Moreover, the population attracted

137 *The Times*, 15 Dec 1885, p. 8.

by opportunities in Gibraltar included especially those north of the frontier, in the dormitory suburb of La Línea.

What we should not expect to see, and do not find, is equality of rewards. Of course, there were not the class divisions characteristic, many believe, of an industrial society separated on the one hand by ownership of the means of production and on the other by labour power (and skill). This was not an industrial society and labour forces in each business were small, until the dockyards expanded latterly. But, speaking of the majority civilian sector, the economy was a mercantile capitalist one in which the financial rewards of effort and enterprise were divided unequally. There are some data on wage rates but nothing reliable on labourers' actual earnings, and still less is extant, in a society innocent of direct taxes, on the incomes of those in the professions and in business. What we can discern are some things that money can buy and, if not happiness, they did include the labour of others, as domestic servants and other employees, plus better accommodation and superior sanitation and, we may deduce, better diets, better health and longer life. In Gibraltar, as elsewhere, there was a hierarchy and not just a 'two nations' divide. Workers were split by occupation and level of skill (and by age – earning power often varying over a lifetime and affected by physical strength). The business community contained petty traders and shopkeepers as well as professional men and international entrepreneurs.

It is, however, the upper echelons of the business class upon whom some extra attention needs to be focused, because they were, in truth, the generators of opportunity as well as the exploiters of labour.[138] By mid century, and more certainly after the opening of the Suez Canal lent some security to Gibraltar's economy, a comparatively stable moneyed class emerged. Most of the early firms, especially those established by British businessmen, less so of those of Jewish origin, had faded out, to be replaced by a compact group with mixed ethnic origins. Commanding the economy were a limited number of businesses. Advertisements in local guides and trade directories suggest who were by then the main players and their principal playgrounds, and these firms, through inheritance and mutual support, and business acumen were of remarkable longevity.[139] Only a couple of shipping firms remained by the later nineteenth century, principally one established by Marcus Henry Bland in 1810 and continued by his family, but from 1891 run by the Gaggero brothers, who had formerly been managers,[140] and the other set up by Thomas Haynes in 1840

138 For what follows see the exceptionally important analysis in Grocott, 'Moneyed Class', esp. pp. 65–86.
139 For a statistical analysis of advertisements in Macmillan, *Malta and Gibraltar Illustrated*, see Grocott, 'Moneyed Class', p. 65.
140 Gaggero, *Running with the Baton*, pp. 16–19.

and subsequently developed by his descendants. Other shipping companies had survived by becoming shipping agents, like the business founded by the Smith family in 1837, which became Smith, Imossi and Co., following a deal struck in 1859 between William Henry Smith, son of the founder, and Francis Imossi. This was a company that was to roll on down the generations. Like other prosperous survivors, it did so especially by capturing a large share of the coaling business, a trick managed by another shipping agent business, founded by Joseph Rugeroni in 1862 and continued by his son, which diversified from being an organiser of the emigrant trade into coaling. John Carrara's business, established in the 1850s, made a similar successful move, and John Onetti's family firm, set up in 1844, was another. L.H. Fava and Co., founded in 1867, run by a son and a cousin from 1905, also dabbled a bit in coal, but otherwise continued to flourish as a shipping agent. Other businessmen satisfied consumer demand for imported goods as provision merchants. This was for wine and spirits in the case of James Andrew-Speed's firm, operating from 1839, which merged in 1898 with that set up in 1850 by his competitor Jerome Saccone to create the immensely successful and durable Saccone and Speed, which became a limited liability company in 1908.[141] Others with similar interests in provisions included the firms established by the Levy family as early as 1814, by R. and J. Abrines in the 1850s and maintained subsequently by a nephew as well as a son, by Francis Ballestrino in 1860 and kept going by his son from 1874, and by B. Sacarello in 1889. Benady Brothers began as tea suppliers in 1863, and John Risso as a grocer in 1850. Intimately connected with the success of many firms were the financial services provided by the likes of Galliano, the Rugeroni Brothers, and Thomas Mosley, who began as a banking agent in 1829 and whose family lay behind the Anglo-Egyptian Bank set up in Gibraltar in 1864.[142]

Important to recognise is the intimacy which bound together many of these businesses. Much of this was via mutually supportive business interests. So, members of one family firm frequently served on the boards of others, like Louis Lombard becoming attached to L.H. Fava and Co. in the 1890s. Some of it was secured via social and personal bonds, common membership of prestigious social bodies, like the Mediterranean Rowing Club, the Calpe Yacht Club, freemasons' lodges, and of course the Exchange and Commercial Library or, from 1882, the newly formed Chamber of Commerce. Very noticeably, distinctions by ethnic origin or by religion did not seem to impede such bonding. And there was intermarriage. For example, the Rugeronis became related to the Gaggeros and also thereby to the Galliano family. Such liaisons might also facilitate the shift of businesses from one family to another, explaining, for example, the transfer

---

141 Macmillan, *Malta and Gibraltar Illustrated*, pp. 465–7.
142 See also P. Galliano, *The Smallest Bank in the World* (Gibraltar: Gibraltar Books, 2003).

of the firm of A. Mateos and Sons, founded in 1852, to the Imossi portfolio by the start of the new century.

Emphasis upon this civilian elite sector forms a necessary conclusion to this chapter. The politics of nineteenth-century Gibraltar, as we will next see, would be much affected by the relationship between wealthy colonial civilians and the administrative and military managers of this British fortress.

6

Governors and the governed, 1815–1914

The civilian population of Gibraltar during the nineteenth century came in some respects to resemble other communities of largely European immigrant origins. Within the British Empire by the end of the century the predominantly white settler societies of Canada, Australia and New Zealand certainly contained higher proportions of people of British and Irish origin than did Gibraltar, but they had all been enriched by immigrant families and their descendants from other parts of continental Europe. The independent republics of the United States and of Latin America likewise had received and were still receiving settlers from old Europe, and indeed many from Spain. This was a phenomenon in which Gibraltar, in its distinctive (and smaller) fashion, participated. Gibraltar by the end of the century, like some of the others, was even sharing a stream arriving from Malta. Gibraltar civilians, by aspiration and by necessity, also during the nineteenth century became further integrated into a world economy that was increasingly dominated by powerful commercial, industrial and financial enterprises centred on the advanced economies of Western Europe and North America. Domestically, they absorbed the material values and aspirations of western capitalism and accepted, pretty much, the ethics of free economic enterprise, in which capital purchased goods and services as cheaply as possible and endeavoured to sell them as dearly as possible, and in which a supposedly free market in labour determined its price, otherwise known as wages. Consumption patterns were also similar, the goods and services purchased resembling those in other westernised economies, moderated only by regional rather than specifically Gibraltarian tastes.

This chapter is therefore dedicated especially to examining the extent to which two other common though not invariable features of this western (and westernising) world may also be discerned in Gibraltar – on the one hand, the increased authority and roles of government, and on the other, the election of those who exercised that authority and provided services and their accountability to those who elected them.

In spite of a supposed dedication to free market principles in the more advanced capitalist societies, this was a century in which government authority grew and in which public services expanded. Central governments, generally speaking, increased the legislative management of their domestic populations. The process helped to create a sense of collective identity much focused on the citizen's obligations to the state and the state's responsibilities towards the citizen. The state has been defined as the body which claims the monopoly of the legitimate use of physical force,[1] by which is meant external defence (in many states involving compulsory conscription into the nation's armed forces) and the maintenance of internal order (exercised by police forces and penal policies). In addition, governments were also determining much about the life experiences of 'their' people by providing a range of services, or more commonly by requiring their provision by local authorities. These included, taking Britain as an example (and ignoring actual effectiveness of intervention): the new poor law which from 1834 provided extended 'welfare' services, followed from 1906 to 1911 by a raft of additional social measures designed to support the elderly poor, needy school children, the working-class sick and some of the unemployed; the beginnings of control over working conditions via a batch of laws running from the 1802 Health and Morals of Apprentices Act to the 1901 Factory and Workshop Act; public health acts from 1848 followed by specific housing acts, increasingly demanding of compliance; a sequence of police laws, beginning with the Metropolitan Police Act in 1829, leading to police reforms in towns outside the capital from 1835 and in counties from 1839; and the extension of mass education via state subsidies to church schools from 1833, by imposing obligations on local communities to increase the number of schools from 1870 and by making school attendance compulsory from 1880. To this selected list, though least applicable in the British case where immigration controls were minimal until the Aliens Act of 1905, should be added tighter state controls over entry into and residence in national territory by those not 'belonging' by birth or inheritance, on which topic the Gibraltar story has already been told.

It remains to be seen how far the government of Gibraltar resembled in other respects the practice in the 'mother' country in the services and also controls (for these things are invariably married) provided for or exercised over Gibraltar civilians. Lest it be argued that tiny Gibraltar was not 'really' a state but only a town, it should be remembered that much national legislation in Britain and elsewhere initially merely empowered, though later required, local governments, and especially town governments, to provide such services, if they were not already adequately doing so. Hence the duty of policing in Britain was first imposed on borough councils; and to town councils were also granted public health powers, first by permissive legislation and later by mandatory instruction. Similarly state

---

1 M. Weber, *The Theory of Social and Economic Organization* (New York: Oxford University Press, 1947), p. 154: the idea was launched in his 1919 lecture 'Politics as a vocation': www.ne.jp/asahi/moriyuki/abukuma/weber/lecture/politics_vocation. html.

education and the poor law, following central government direction, were run by local ad hoc bodies. The 'nineteenth-century revolution in government',[2] for such with respect to Britain it has been called, was commonly epitomised by the delivery of services by town governments rather than directly by the centre. Right across Europe and its global extensions stand impressive nineteenth-century monuments to municipal enterprise and civic pride: the town hall.

A developing characteristic of town hall (and county hall) government was the accountability of the executive to local electors. Town governments especially were subject to electoral scrutiny, because urban conditions, of the kind already described in the case of Gibraltar, generated demands for services, like the supply of water, gas and electricity, decent sanitation, proper housing regulations and the provision of public transport. The late nineteenth century has indeed been labelled a period of 'municipal socialism' because of the range of town services provided (many now lost to private enterprise).[3] As an inevitable consequence there were always concerns about cost and 'value for money', and not without just cause when expenditure could be high and charges were locally imposed. Hence, real politics were often local politics. In Britain the 1835 Municipal Corporations Act swept away some remarkable former urban constitutions and required the definition by charter of the composition of town councils, the process by which councillors were elected and by whom, and how often they would be held accountable via further elections. Charges for local services and for interest payments on capital borrowed were levied as rates on property, and the rules turned ratepayers into electors. The same political philosophy under-pinned the important reforms which in 1888 introduced elected county govern-ments in Britain and, in 1894, elected urban and rural district councils. Also at a national level, the election of members to the House of Commons (though not, of course, to the House of Lords) was rationalised and, step by step, extended by the parliamentary reform acts, beginning in 1832, so that to the former elector-ate were added qualified urban ratepayers and then, from 1867, all male heads of households in boroughs, and the same, from 1884, in counties. This process of extending voting rights to qualifying civilians characterised, with variable implications for the actual practice of government, all states of western Europe as well as in the Americas.

It was also true of many British overseas colonies. In 1846 the House of Commons demanded a report from the Colonial Office on those colonies from which demands for representative government had been received from civilian colonists. They included the Cape of Good Hope (Cape Colony), New South

2 O. MacDonagh, 'The nineteenth-century revolution in government: a reappraisal', *Historical Journal*, 1 (1958), 52–67.

3 D. Fraser, *Power and Authority in the Victorian City* (Oxford: Blackwell, 1979), pp. 167–73.

Wales, Van Diemen's Land (Tasmania), Western Australia, South Australia, New Zealand, British Guiana, Trinidad, St Lucia and Malta.[4] Where white European (not only British) colonists had settled, colonies also sought not just 'representative' government, allowing for civilians to be consulted by governors, but 'responsible' government, making colonial ministers answerable to locally elected assemblies (with the franchise, of course, variably and largely locally determined). Responsible government so defined was inaugurated in British North America in Nova Scotia in 1848, in Australia in the colony of Victoria in 1855, in New Zealand in 1856, and in southern Africa in Cape Colony in 1872. In chequered fashion, even the British colony of Malta, with its British garrison and naval base, was granted a partially elected legislative council in 1849, with proportionately more elected members in 1887 (though fewer from 1903).[5]

The question therefore to be considered is whether a civilian population in Gibraltar – also of largely European stock, sharing the same economic culture, and affected by problems characteristic of new towns everywhere – received equivalent public services over the course of the nineteenth century and engaged in similar politics. Concerning the latter, it has been asserted on the one hand, that the civilian population in this British colony was powerless and lacked influence over local government.[6] On the other hand, it has been implied that the roots of Gibraltar's current democratic politics can be traced back to the nineteenth century and the formation of bodies supposedly representing the civilian population, like the Exchange and Commercial Library Committee.[7] In assessing the truth of these contrasting claims, we need to remember, of course, the politics of the previous century and the failure then to introduce an elected representative municipal government, and the practice instead of interest-group pressure on government.

The governors

We need to begin with the obvious, that even at the end of the nineteenth century the principal value of Gibraltar for the imperial government lay in its

4 HCPP, *Copies of all Applications from the Colonists of the Cape of Good Hope made to the Colonial Office for Representative Government . . .*, 400, 1846.
5 C. Cassar, *A Concise History of Malta* (Msida: Mireva, 2000), pp. 163, 186, 198; H. Smith, *Britain in Malta* (Malta: Progress Press, 1953), vol. 1, pp. 35–8, 51–72, 228–36.
6 L.A. Sawchuk, *Deadly Visitations in Dark Times: a Social History of Gibraltar in the Time of Cholera* (Gibraltar: Gibraltar Government Heritage Publications, 2001), p. 23.
7 W.G.F. Jackson and F.J. Cantos, *From Fortress to Democracy: the Political Biography of Sir Joshua Hassan* (Grendon: Gibraltar Books, 1995), pp. 4–5; J. Garcia, *Gibraltar: the Making of a People* (Gibraltar: Panorama, 2nd edn 2002), pp. 8–9.

role as a fortress and naval base. This is evident from repeated statements to that effect by politicians and officials, even when it was being acknowledged that the commerce of the colony was important for offsetting costs and even when obligations for the welfare of civilian settlers were also being acknowledged. Actions speak louder than words, and the large number of troops stationed in Gibraltar is a further indication of fortress priorities. Likewise the huge investment in the Royal Navy dockyard speaks volumes for British perceptions of Gibraltar as principally part of an imperial strategic plan. Moreover, the autocratic authority granted to each governor of Gibraltar on appointment remained formally intact. In Malta there was a phase in the 1850s when duties were divided between a governor, with responsibility for civil administration, and a commander-in-chief, who was charged with the security and operational effectiveness of the garrison and naval base.[8] This not very successful division of powers was not even attempted in Gibraltar. Moreover, Gibraltar governors were still actually selected by the War Office, even in the second half of the century, when appointments were formally made by the crown on the recommendation of the Colonial Office.[9]

Between March 1802 and July 1913 twenty men held the highest office.[10] Two of these, for the following analysis, can be ignored. Prince Edward, Duke of Kent, drew the salary of governor from 1802 to 1820, as did his successor, John Pitt, second Earl of Chatham, from 1820 to 1835. Both held office until their deaths, after which they were little more absent from Gibraltar than they had been before. As noted in an earlier chapter, Kent had departed under a cloud in May 1803, and Chatham seems only to have been present early in the 1820s, before scuttling back to Britain and a more clement and less taxing environment. Appointed with full authority in the absence of these governors were lieutenant-governors, Sir George Don, Sir William Houston and Sir Alexander Woodford, the last until in September 1836 he succeeded Chatham as governor. Thereafter governors only were appointed and, unless on leave, they stayed to do the business. Including Don, Houston and Woodford, they were all men of mature experience prior to taking office, yet even in contemporary terms they were not old (though two died in office, Smyth aged 61 and Nicholson 66). The youngest on appointment was Woodford, 52, and the oldest, Williams, was 69 (and he lived until he was 82). The average age was 61 (median 63). On appointment, two

8 A.V. Laferla, *British Malta* (Malta: Government Printing Office, 1938), vol. 1, pp. 233–4, 278–9.

9 A. Kirk-Greene, *On Crown Service: a History of HM Colonial and Overseas Civil Services 1837–1997* (London: Tauris, 1999), pp. 99–100.

10 For the data which follow see W.G.F. Jackson, *The Rock of the Gibraltarians* (Gibraltar: Gibraltar Books, 4th edn 2001), pp. 180, 223, 255, and entries in *ODNB*.

were already major-generals, five were lieutenant-generals and eleven, remarkably, were full generals. These were more elevated profiles than those of their eighteenth-century predecessors. All had seen active service (Napoleonic Wars, Crimea, Indian 'Mutiny', China, Egypt, South Africa). Several had the scars to prove it. But, pertinent to their competence as governors, at least fifteen of these men also had administrative experience in their records, above and beyond the normal duties of operational command, as staff officers for instance, as quartermasters-general and, indeed, as governors. Don and Nicholson had been lieutenant-governors in Jersey, Woodford in Malta and Corfu; Williams had been governor in Nova Scotia and Hunter in Suakin; Smyth had acted as High Commissioner in South Africa and Biddulph in Cyprus. Napier, a Renaissance man, had been responsible for designing and executing major civil engineering projects in India, as well as waging war, studying geology and being a landscape and portrait painter. Moreover, these men were not necessarily at the end of their careers. Nine of the eighteen received further military promotion during or after their time in Gibraltar, and at least five had subsequent important public careers. In sum, in administering the colony and in handling internal and external politics, all governors were used to command and many had had political experience. This needs to be remembered when thinking about the civilians who had to deal with them.

Whatever their terms of appointment might say about their powers, the reality was that governors were politically answerable to London, and only to London, and this too needs to be kept in mind. As noted in a previous chapter, because after 1815 the military duties of the Secretary of State for War and the Colonies decreased while his colonial responsibilities increased, his ministry came to be called familiarly the Colonial Department, though strictly speaking such an office did not come into being until 1854 and the outbreak of the Crimean War, when a separate Secretary of State for the Colonies was appointed, and duties were formally split between a War Office and a Colonial Office.[11] However, because the fortress remained the principal British concern, Gibraltar remained a War Office responsibility until 1867.[12] Even thereafter, governors, as commanders-in-chief of the garrison, still had to deal with the War Office, and increasingly with the Admiralty. Since the War Office appointed War Department

11 R.B. Pugh, 'Colonial Office', in E.A. Benians et al., *The Cambridge History of the British Empire*, vol. III (Cambridge: Cambridge University Press, 1967), pp. 711, 714, 729; A. Thurston, *Sources for Colonial Studies in the Public Record Office*, vol. 1 (London: HMSO, 1995), pp. 3–6.
12 Upon the problems encountered by the War Office in trying to deal with civil matters in Gibraltar after 1854 see GGA, Despatches to Gibraltar 1867: 'Transfer of Correspondence from War to Colonial Office 1867' and TNA, CO91/289, War Office to governor, 30 April 1867.

staff in Gibraltar and the Admiralty likewise had its own navy people there, the governor's authority was not immune to challenge on defence matters, even locally. Moreover, faster communications by sea, by telegraph and even overland by rail through Spain diminished the autonomy (or sometimes the isolation) of the 'man on the spot' and increased the opportunities for London ministers to advise and/or interfere. Those same improvements in communications likewise enabled Gibraltar civilians and interest groups more rapidly to turn to London if dissatisfied in Gibraltar.

Civilian complaints about the conduct of governors were not rare, but disciplinary action by War Office or Colonial Office was exceptional. Following Sir George Don's uniquely long period in office – sixteen years except for the moments when Chatham was briefly present – governors were replaced usually after four or five years. Excluding the two governors who died in office, those in post between May 1831 and July 1910 served on average nearly five and a half years, the shortest, Fergusson, just short of four years, and the longest, Woodford, a little over eight and a half years. This is important to note, because it is repeatedly stated that Sir Robert Gardiner was prematurely recalled in the summer of 1855.[13] He had certainly upset local business groups in Gibraltar and their allies in Britain, especially the Manchester Chamber of Commerce, by his insistence that civilian interests must be subordinated to those of the garrison; and the War Office, no doubt to their irritation, had been obliged to accede to demands from MPs and publish all the correspondence relating to this episode.[14] But the despatches were published in March 1854, and Gardiner did not leave until August 1855, and neither his final despatch to the secretary of state nor the long report on Gibraltar which he subsequently published implies a dismissal.[15] If there was a trigger it was his passing of an ordinance to prohibit unlicensed printing without first securing War Office approval, for which misdemeanour he was reprimanded in July 1855.[16] He had by this time been in office for six years and eight months, giving him a record of continuous service exceeded by only two other governors in the whole period between 1830 and the present day. The career of only one governor, Sir Archibald Hunter, was terminated

13 G. Hills, *Rock of Contention* (London: Hale, 1974), p. 379; W.G.F. Jackson, *The Rock of the Gibraltarians* (Gibraltar: Gibraltar Books, 2001), p. 240; M. Harvey, *Gibraltar a History* (Staplehurst: Spellmount, 1996), p. 120.

14 HCPP, *Gibraltar: Copy of the Memorial presented to the Duke of Newcastle by a Deputation from the Merchants of Gibraltar . . . 27 March 1854*, HC 130, 1854.

15 TNA, CO91/226, Gardiner to Panmure, 21 Aug 1855; GL, Sir Robert Gardiner, *Report on Gibraltar considered as a Fortress and a Colony*, 15 Jan 1856; T.J. Finlayson, 'The press in Gibraltar in the nineteenth century', *Gibraltar Heritage Journal*, 4 (1997), 95–7.

16 HCPP, *Copy of a Despatch . . . relative to the recent Ordinance to prohibit unlicensed Printing*, HC 395, 1854–5, Panmure to Gardiner, 5 July 1855.

prematurely, in June 1913 after three years in post, after he had caused grievous offence locally by undiplomatic criticism in public of the civilian population. But even in this case he had also managed to annoy personally the secretary of state, and staff in the Colonial Office and the War Office had come (unjustly) to doubt his sanity.[17]

The governor was not, of course, alone in the discharge of his duties. His principal assistant was the colonial secretary, a person who, by long duration in office, often accumulated considerable experience. He served, in effect, like the company secretary of a business, or even as a chief executive, with the governor acting as chairman. The colonial secretary read, advised on and drafted many of the replies to official correspondence, met delegates, official and unofficial, and was usually the governor's local spokesperson and contact with the press. George Alderley served for twenty-eight years from 1831 and his successor, Sanford Freeling, for ten.[18] These gentlemen were always British by birth, and usually on a career ladder that often saw them subsequently promoted elsewhere in the colonial service. For instance, in January 1894 Cavendish Boyle, after five years as colonial secretary in Gibraltar, took up a new post in British Guiana, to be replaced by H.M. Jackson, who arrived from the Bahamas.[19] Jackson stayed seven years and was then replaced by Frederick Evans, who served without a break for fourteen years.[20] The colonial secretary was not, however, immune to criticism, no matter how long he had served, as Major-General Robert Baynes discovered in 1882, in spite of his military rank and the experience and authority he had acquired since his appointment in 1868. It was by his instructions that three political refugees from Spain, José Maceo, José Rodriguez and Rogelio Castillo, who had sought sanctuary in Gibraltar, were, in effect, handed back to the Spanish authorities. The breach of extradition law and the consequent

17 I owe much on Hunter's early resignation to the knowledge and insight of Dr C.A. Grocott; see also D.H. Doolittle, *A Soldier's Hero: General Sir Archibald Hunter* (Narrangansett: Anawan, 1991), pp. 289–303; A. Hunter, *Kitchener's Sword-Arm* (Staplehurst: Spellmount, 1996), pp. 200–18; T.J. Finlayson, *Stories from the Rock* (Gibraltar: Aquila, 1996), pp. 104–9; TNA, CO91/452, Hunter to Harcourt, 4 Feb 1913, minutes and attached correspondence; *Gibraltar Chronicle*, 31 Jan 1913, for the offending speech. Hunter continued to cause trouble. For the further rumpus he caused by his remarks about the citizens of Gibraltar when standing as a parliamentary candidate in 1918 see TNA, CO91/470, Smith-Dorrien to Milner, 13 Feb 1919.

18 For a list of colonial secretaries from 1749 to 1962 (usually called civil secretaries until 1859) see *Gibraltar Directory*, 1962, p. 9. For a job description prepared under 'Colonial Regulations' see GGA, Despatches from Gibraltar 1882: copy attached to Napier to Kimberley, 16 Dec 1882.

19 HCPP, *Gibraltar Annual Report for 1894*, C.7847, 1895, p. 7.

20 Information from *Annual Reports*. Evans came back as acting colonial secretary for two more years during the First World War.

political and diplomatic stink caused by this 'act so contrary to modern laws', as *The Times* correspondent put it, cost Baynes his job.[21]

Also close at hand from 1830 was the attorney-general, the man who drafted local ordinances and provided legal guidance to the governor, and the police magistrate, who was responsible for the operational effectiveness of the police as well as for a wide range of other duties. Early on these two posts were often combined in the one person. Important too for the governor were specialist assistants, some drawn from garrison officers, such as the Commanding Officer Royal Engineers and the Principal Medical Officer (who from 1835 doubled as the Inspector of Health for the civilian community),[22] plus personnel to collect revenue and to audit accounts. Even adding in those responsible for the judiciary, the port, the markets, the hospital and public health, plus inspectors of strangers and policemen, this was a modest civilian administration.

In 1869, total expenditure on colonial administration came to less than £30,000 (equivalent to around £2 million in 2005 using the retail price index or £16 million using average earnings).[23] Between 1887 and 1899, expenditure was generally in the £50,000 to £60,000 a year range; thereafter, up to 1906, it rose into the £60,000 to £70,000 bracket; and from then, to 1913, it went up by one further step, but only to a maximum of £82,000. Meanwhile revenue increased at least in pace, to over £105,000 a year. This was a colonial regime which almost always stayed in the black year on year, and as a result its accumulated net assets, mainly invested, were worth more than a whole year's income by 1903, climbing to more than twice as much over the next decade.[24] Civilian objections to tax levels need to be placed in this context, though we will also need to consider shortly the quite separate accounts (and debts) of the Sanitary Commission.

21 And also that of the police magistrate and the chief inspector of police, the latter, cruelly, with loss of pension, on all of which see GGA, Despatches from Gibraltar 1882: memorial of Captain Blair to Napier, 21 Dec 1882, and Buckle to Blair, 22 Jan 1883. Much of the massive amount of material generated by this episode is collected into HCPP, *Correspondence* and *Further Correspondence respecting the Expulsion of Certain Cuban Refugees from Gibraltar*, C.3452, C.3473, C.3475 and C.3548, 1882 and 1883, TNA, CO883/2/7 'Correspondence . . .', PRO30/29/333, 'Correspondence . . .'; see also *The Times*, 7 Sept 1882, p. 5. For a brief account see T. Finlayson. 'The case of the Cuban refugees', *Gibraltar Heritage Journal*, 6 (1999), 35–9.

22 GGA, Despatches to Secretary of State for War, 1866–68: Airey to Ripon, 23 Feb 1866.

23 Total £29,833, of which £5,000 was the salary of the governor: HCPP, *Statement of the Local Revenues of Gibraltar*, HC 208, 1871.

24 HCPP, *Gibraltar Annual Reports*, 1887–1913.

Law and government

For all the authority wielded by governors, they did not govern autocratically. Government by law, and not arbitrary rule, distinguished British overseas as well as domestic administration. Of course, who determined laws, and how, and how they were enforced were contested matters, in Gibraltar as elsewhere. In the eighteenth and early nineteenth centuries, as discussed in a previous chapter, civilians were initially subjected to military laws by means of garrison orders, as determined by the governor though ultimately subject to War Office approval. These were published by proclamation and enforced by the military. At the same time, substantial legal frameworks were laid down centrally in London, by orders-in-council and letters patent, governing such matters as the free port status of Gibraltar, titles to lands, currency, quarantine, the introduction of the paving and scavenging rate and, very important and as described in a previous chapter, the setting up by charters of the law courts which tempered military justice with the judicial practices conventional in Britain's civilian society.

However, doubts arose in London as to the legal authority of the proclamations by which the governor had instructed, managed and disciplined the civilian population. Hence, the Secretary of State for War, Sir George Murray, arranged for the issue of another Charter of Justice for Gibraltar (the fifth) by letters patent dated 1 September 1830. This established a Supreme Court, to be headed by a judge (with experience in UK courts) appointed by the crown (and in the charter the first such judge, Barron Field, was named).[25] This court was to have jurisdiction over civil and criminal matters. While existing courts were scrapped, the Supreme Court was to act as a court of appeal for cases tried by the inferior courts established to deal with minor criminal offences and the recovery of debts. Members of the garrison were still to be tried only by courts martial, but the charter did create a separate judicature which operated independently of the governor, since even appeals from Supreme Court judgments were henceforth to be routed direct to the Privy Council and not via the governor. To that extent his authority was checked, although Murray went out of his way to reassure Governor Don that relieving governors of judicial duties was a principle being adopted in other 'Dependencies of this Country' and was not founded upon any doubts about the impartiality of his past practice. Gibraltar's Supreme Court of Civil and Criminal Justice in Gibraltar was opened, with the due ceremony demanded by the secretary of state, on 25 January 1831.[26] Equally important, following the issue of the

25 Field had previously been appointed Judge of the Court of Civil Pleas. GGA, Despatches to Gibraltar 1829: Murray to Don, 20 Feb 1829.
26 'Charter of Justice, 1ˢᵗ September 1830' in *Orders in Council, Ordinances and Proclamations, relating to Gibraltar* (Gibraltar: Gibraltar Government, 1839);

charter, instructions to governors specifically gave them authority to legislate locally, although here too their independence was controlled, since the laws they wished to enact, which were called ordinances, had first to be drafted by the attorney-general (itself a new post) and then submitted to the crown – in reality the War Office and subsequently the Colonial Office – for approval and, if necessary, for amendment.

Contrary to repeated claims, this did not transform Gibraltar into a colony.[27] The word 'colony' in British imperial terminology never had any legal significance beyond recognition that territorial sovereignty had been transferred to the crown.[28] Everything of importance thereafter depended on the form of administration locally imposed and its relationship with the crown and the imperial government. Even early settlements, as in the West Indies and in North America, which had forms of internal self-government defined by charter, were referred to as colonies. During the nineteenth century the white settler territories where responsible government had been introduced were still referred to as colonies, until in 1907 they came to be called dominions to distinguish them from the territories, still called colonies, to which internal self-government had not been granted. A distinctive title over Gibraltar (or over other fortress possessions, like Bermuda) had never been declared, other than that of being a part of the sovereign territories of the British crown. In that respect, Gibraltar had long since become a British colony by conquest, as confirmed by treaty in 1713. Neither its constitutional status nor even its official title was altered in 1830, as an examina-

Footnote 26 (*cont.*)

TNA, CO92/10, Murray to Don, 11 Sept 1830; CO91/109, Don to Murray, 30 Oct 1830, and attached proclamation. In 1877 the judge was renamed the Chief Justice; in 1888, by a sixth charter, divorce and matrimonial cases came within the Supreme Court's jurisdiction; in 1890 it absorbed the Vice-Admiralty's Court: Jackson, *Rock of the Gibraltarians*, pp. 229–30; Sir J.F. Spry (ed.), *The Gibraltar Law Reports 1812–1977* (Gibraltar: Gibraltar Government, 1979), pp. v–xiii.

27 Jackson, *Rock of the Gibraltarians*, p. 229 is therefore mistaken; and similarly see Jackson and Cantos, *From Fortress to Democracy*, p. 4; Garcia, *Making of a People*, p. 8; Harvey, *Gibraltar*, p. 116. S.G. Benady, *General Sir George Don and the Dawn of Gibraltarian Identity* (Gibraltar: Gibraltar Books, 2006), p. 86, struggles to resolve a problem which does not exist: 'This Charter marks a decisive point in the transition of Gibraltar from a garrison to a colony, but it is not quite clear when the change of status became official.' For an informed explanation of how the misnomer may have arisen and on its perpetuation see T.J. Finlayson, '1830 and all that! A myth exploded', *Gibraltar Heritage Journal*, 8 (2001), 42–6.

28 Nominally, sovereignty over protectorates and protected states had not been so transferred, and India, initially under East India Company rule and then absorbed under direct imperial government control, was always a special case.

tion of the preambles to previous and subsequent nineteenth-century laws makes clear. The Charter of Justice itself refers to, and only refers to, the 'Garrison and Territory of Gibraltar'.[29]

That said, the judicial innovations after 1830 did establish a prestigious and, very important, a civilian authority in Gibraltar, and they allowed courts more space in which to act independently of government. It was that which prompted some contemporaries and subsequent historians to perceive a distinction between a Gibraltar consisting principally of a military fortress and a Gibraltar containing primarily a civilian colony. It is also probable that the existence of a Supreme Court, whose duties included the enrolment of suitably qualified barristers and solicitors, enhanced the status and authority of the legal profession and its attraction for those with grievances against government. Moreover, eminent civilians achieved additional prestige and political confidence because they were appointed as justices of the peace (in the lower courts). Their like, drawn from the Grand Jury, also served on juries in criminal cases, and as assessors and later on juries in civil cases and, as we shall see, on various official administrative bodies. Sir Robert Gardiner claimed in 1854 that the whole paraphernalia of the Supreme Court was an unnecessary extravagance costing annually over £2,660 in salaries and largely responsible for the expenditure which was upsetting the administration's budget. He regretted that it gave a credibility to the civilian side of the settlement, and he even spat out the word 'colony' to describe what he lamented was being allowed to develop, parasitically, in what he insisted was a fort and garrison.[30] In some respects he was, from his perspective, right to be concerned. Officials complained that civilian juries were biased against members of the garrison and government interests: the valuation of Bruce's farm in 1889, referred to in the previous chapter, was a case in point.

One certain consequence of the new charter was more law, in response to what government believed the civilian community needed.[31] Between 1830 and 1914 a legislative framework within which civilian lives in Gibraltar were to be lived

29 Pre–1830 laws refer to 'His Majesty's Garrison and Town of Gibraltar' (1815), 'Our Town and Garrison of Gibraltar' (1827), and 'the Garrison and Territory of Gibraltar' (1817, 1819, 1827, 1829). Post–1830 laws also refer to 'the Garrison and Territory of Gibraltar' (1838, 1839), and to 'Our Town and Garrison of Gibraltar' (1838), 'the City, Garrison and Territory of Gibraltar' (1843, 1846, 1848, 1873, 1885, 1890), and to just plain 'Gibraltar' (1900).

30 GL, Sir R. Gardiner, *Report on Gibraltar considered as a Fortress and a Colony*, 1856, pp. 9, 10–11, 17–19, 47–8, 153–9; TNA, CO91/226, Gardiner to Panmure, 21 Aug 1855, paras 3, 13.

31 What follows is largely an analysis of 'Chronological Table of the Ordinances of Gibraltar' in C.C. Ross (ed.), *The Laws of Gibraltar* (London: Government of Gibraltar, rev. edn 1950), vol. IV, pp. i–xxi.

was laid down, amended and extended. These still included direction through orders-in-council (and letters patent) – sixty-three of them – passed down from London after consultation with the governor and bearing, via the Privy Council, the overriding authority of the crown. These were employed when it was to be insisted, not always successfully, that the governor's actions should be accepted without demur – for example, with regard to raising revenue, the currency, aliens, land tenure, quarantine and port regulations, and the administration of justice.[32] British Acts of Parliament were also simply adopted in Gibraltar, forty-two of them, especially between 1833 and 1839, indicating the increased anglicisation of Gibraltar's legal culture. They bore especially on such subjects as property, coinage, criminal law, legal administration and penal policy. But overwhelmingly, ordinances specific to Gibraltar, drafted locally and approved centrally, sought to guide and control civilian life: a total of 312 in just over eighty years. Of course, the number of laws, and particularly of amended laws, may indicate only initial bad drafting inappropriate to need, but more likely repeated law making on the same subject was indicative of what has been described as the organic growth of government,[33] that is, the adaptation and extension of legislative powers in the light of experience and also, it should be added, changing circumstances, challenges and ambitions. This is suggested by the increased rate of local law making. In the first half of this period, from 1832 to 1873, 39 locally devised ordinances were passed; in the second half, from 1874 to 1914 there were 273.

A draft of all ordinances was always published in the official gazette, the *Gibraltar Chronicle*, in a consultation exercise which allowed interested civilian parties thirty days in which to respond (and to object). In that fashion, and only to that extent, laws were being sanctioned by 'public opinion'. Certainly the practice encouraged especially the moneyed class and ecclesiastical authorities to claim a right to modify draft legislation, if not actually to initiate the process of law making. Indeed, in 1873 the Exchange Committee even demanded the right to comment on drafts of orders-in-council, hitherto usually regarded as reserved business for officials in Gibraltar and London. In some instances that concession was granted.[34] The language of the Exchange Committee's memorial to the secretary of state is particularly revealing of the politics which lay behind their request, an issue to which we will return:

32 See attorney-general to colonial secretary, 14 March 1884, in HCPP, *Gibraltar: Tariff Order in Council, 1884, and Correspondence Relating Thereto*, C.3992, 1884, p. 23.
33 Associated particularly with the interpretation of MacDonagh, 'Revolution in government'.
34 For example, a draft was published of what became the Aliens Order in Council in 1885: TNA, CO91/371, Adye to Stanley, 6 Nov 1885.

As the inhabitants of Gibraltar have no consultative Council and no recognized legislative power, and as the only means of signifying their opinion on proposed legislative enactments is by being permitted to peruse, consider, and comment thereon, your memorialists trust that Your Lordship will see the justice of the claim which your memorialists proffer on behalf of this community, to be permitted to peruse and consider all contemplated legal enactments before they become law, whether Ordinances or contemplated Orders in Council.[35]

It was indicated in a previous chapter that a large amount of legislation established and extended the legal economic infrastructure within which civilians could do business and secure property, and that regular legislation was necessary to raise government revenue. In addition, and more generally, between 1832 and 1914 at least eighty pieces of legislation (orders-in-council and local ordinances) developed legal procedures and penal policies. As also described in an earlier chapter, six major pieces of legislation were concerned explicitly with controlling the entry and especially the residence of aliens. Of related importance was legislation concerned with policing. Until 1830 the policing of civilians as well as soldiers was the responsibility of a military officer, the town major, at whose disposal in addition to troops was also a small civilian force, many of whom were ex-soldiers – but these arrangements were then swept away by Sir George Murray, horrified to learn that a notorious pirate had evaded detection and had secured entry into the garrison. In reaction, Murray ordered Governor Don to establish a civilian police force modelled on London's Metropolitan Police, at this time just taking up its duties. However, in Gibraltar the civil police magistrate appointed to manage the force was also charged to use it in the collection of census data and in the inspection and enforcement of public health measures and, in practice, also as immigration officers. Three major pieces of legislation (1843, 1846 and 1884) boosted its powers and latterly (in 1864) new headquarters were erected and (in 1909) barracks were built to house it.[36]

The internal surveillance role of the police, indicated by its unusual census duties, connects with the incorporation into Gibraltar of laws on the registration of births and deaths, initiated in Britain in 1835. Strikingly, a requirement to register births came first, in 1848, since birth determined right of residence, while the civil registration of deaths followed only in 1868 (both were amended

35 GGA, Despatches from Gibraltar: 'Memorial of the Exchange Committee of Gibraltar' with Williams to Secretary of State, 17 Dec 1873.

36 S. Constantine, 'The pirate, the governor and the secretary of state: aliens, police and surveillance in early nineteenth-century Gibraltar', *English Historical Review*, 123 (2008) pp. 1166–92; C. Baldachino and T. Benady, *The Royal Gibraltar Police 1830–2005* (Gibraltar: Gibraltar Books, 2005). The 1843 Ordinance was one of those measures which had been partly modified after responses to the published draft: GGA, Despatches from Gibraltar 1843: Wilson to Stanley, 31 Oct 1843.

in 1887 and 1889). Other laws relating to families mainly came later: on marriages (1861, 1902, 1903, 1907, 1908, 1914), married women's property (1895, 1908, 1909), incest (1888, 1909) and custody of children (1895). There were, of course, a number of other special concerns attracting legislation, such as military security – leading to prohibitions on sketching and photographing near military installations (1887, 1895, 1901), defence preparations (1896, 1914) and dealing in arms and munitions (1856, 1878, 1885, 1912). There were also laws on extradition (1877), licensing and controlling the press (1868, 1869), friendly societies (1870, 1888), animals (1836, 1909, 1912, 1914) and coping with modernity: traffic regulation (1885, 1894), electric lighting (1892, 1895), motor cars (1913), aerial navigation (1913).

Because of urban conditions and legislative responses in Britain and elsewhere, it is not surprising that a great deal of legislation concerned public health in Gibraltar. In aggregate, between 1865 and 1914 forty-three enactments dealt with the subject, to which one might add the five pieces of legislation dealing with quarantine (1830, 1858, 1886, 1890, 1912). Also we should not forget the 1815 Paving and Scavenging Order-in-Council by which Governor Don had earlier gained the authority to raise rates on property. As we know from a previous chapter, Don had also engineered the establishment of a civic hospital, as well as one for the garrison. The legislation from 1861 onwards also included specific health, medical and sanitation measures: infected animals and dogs (1866, 1880, 1891), street widening (1868), vaccination (1868, 1887, 1906), hospitals and asylums (1884, 1885, 1889, 1894), doctors and midwives (1886, 1907), importation of water (1894), drainage works (1896) and food inspection (1900). Some enactments were specifically concerned to legalise the borrowing of money for sanitation schemes (1891, 1892, 1895, 1896, 1899, 1902). The rest, including hefty orders-in-council in 1865, 1867, 1868, 1874, 1879, 1880, 1883 and 1891, created, empowered and amended the organisation and activities of the Sanitary Commission. This was the successor to Don's Paving and Scavenging Commission and the equivalent to (and, as we shall see, just as controversial as) the local boards of health set up by municipal governments in Britain after the 1848 Public Health Act.

Much that is similar to national and local legislation elsewhere in the western world, and particularly in Britain, may have been spotted in this tour through Gibraltar's nineteenth-century legislative history. But there were also absences. British legal history contains labour laws galore, initially prohibiting 'combinations' and trade unions (1799) or at least greatly inhibiting their activities (1825), and then granting them legal recognition (1871, 1875) and further protection (1906). Incremental legislation concerned the rights and safety of workers in small workshops (from 1878) and indeed, though weakly, of shop workers (from 1886), as well as workers in factories (especially from 1833) and in mines (from 1842), and also outlawed sweated labour (from 1901). However, before

1914 no trade union legislation had been passed in Gibraltar, either to prohibit or to encourage, although, as we shall see, workers began to form unions and take action late in the century. Nor was there protection for workers in shops or those in tobacco manufactories, let alone for those working in dangerous trades, like coal-heavers and dockyard workers. Neither those in government nor the moneyed class were minded to alter things.[37]

Charities: education and poor relief

There was also no public welfare system, not even a poor law, or legislation to encourage let alone to require educational provision. This, it must be stressed, is not altogether surprising. National governments in Britain stepped in, with reluctance, only when existing provision was felt not to be, or no longer to be, providing that which state managers judged necessary to changing needs. Hence, in Britain in 1834 the new poor law replaced the old poor law when those in power concluded that former provision at local level was expensive and disruptive of market efficiency. Similarly, financial and legislative action to increase elementary education came on stream from 1833 and, especially, from 1870, when it was concluded that the need to train and discipline the rapidly growing urban and industrial population was not being met by current private sector educational providers. Even so, as historians now recognise, most state-directed provision did not, in the years before 1914, supplant philanthropic providers of, especially, elementary education and poor relief but, rather, filled in the gaps and/or subsidised them.[38]

There was a state educational sector in nineteenth-century Gibraltar. A non-denominational school, funded by fees, voluntary subscriptions and, later, with a partial government grant, and free to poor children, was set up by government in 1832,[39] and there were also army schools for garrison members and their families, six of them by 1843, eleven by 1902. A few small, private, fee-paying schools had also made a fleeting appearance in the late eighteenth century, and more appeared later. However, as in Britain, competition for souls between rival churches accounts for most of the popular elementary education that became available for civilian children. The minority Methodist church

37 The Truck Ordinance, No 6 of 1895, is perhaps an exception, requiring payment of wages in cash, not in kind: the first Truck Act in Britain was in 1831. The extension to Gibraltar of Britain's Workmen's Compensation Act was considered in 1904 but rejected by the authorities: TNA, CO91/471, Smith-Dorrien to Milner, 18 Sept 1919.

38 G.B.A.M. Finlayson, *The Citizen, the State and Social Welfare in Britain 1830–1990* (Oxford: Clarendon Press, 1994).

39 For an annual report including information on financing see *Gibraltar Chronicle*, 24 June 1859.

seems to have kick-started the business in 1832, only to face competition after 1839 from Anglicans operating through the Society for the Propagation of Christian Knowledge, while the Jewish community also retained its control over young bodies and minds via synagogue teaching and then, from 1855, in a separate school. But the major player came inevitably to be the Roman Catholic Church, with its larger natural clientele and considerable resources. There was an awkward start in 1836 (the hired-in Irish Christian Brothers spoke no Spanish and their pupils no English), but Loreto nuns from 1845 and the return of better-prepared Christian brothers in 1878 produced a local educational service which almost all the children of Catholic civilians attended, including some in fee-paying establishments. The British model was adopted by government to the extent that financial subsidies first provided to the Methodists were extended from 1839 to other educational providers, conditional, as in Britain, on good reports after a school inspection, an inspector of schools being formally appointed in 1880.[40] Even in 1902, at a cost to colonial revenues of £1,636, there were only two non-denominational government schools, catering for fewer than 300 pupils, plus eleven government-aided voluntary sector schools educating the rest, nearly 1,400 children.[41] This system of provision excused the authorities from doing more or, alternatively, made it unnecessary, but schooling in Gibraltar was still not made compulsory until 1917 (in Britain in 1880).[42]

The absence from Gibraltar of a publicly funded poor law was not unique in the British Empire, but it was very rare, even by mid century. In 1845 the House of Commons requested information on 'the provision, if any, made by Law or otherwise, in Her Majesty's different Colonial Possessions, for Destitute Persons'. Many responses referred to charitable provisions, but virtually all colonial governments also provided some form of publicly funded support

40　TNA, CO91/158, Woodford to Stanley, 20 Jan and 3 Feb 1842, and GGA, Despatches from Gibraltar 1877: Napier to Carnarvon, 21 Dec 1877, provide examples of the subsidy system; and see CO91/326, Williams to Kimberley, 23 Aug and 29 Oct 1873, for data on the size of subsidies 1870–72 and for the decision to increase the grants and bring them into line with parliamentary grants to aided schools in England. TNA, CO91/366, Adye to Derby, 29 March 1884, encloses a copy of new regulations governing payment of grants after satisfactory inspection.

41　HCPP, *Board of Education: Special Reports on Educational Subjects Vol. 12, Educational Systems of the Chief Crown Colonies*, Cd.2377, 1905, pp. 445–64, report by G.F. Cornwell, Colonial Inspector of Schools, Gibraltar, March 1902. When charitable subscriptions declined, the inevitable result was an increase in government grant: TNA, CO91/422, Biddulph to Chamberlain, 28 Jan 1899.

42　E.G. Archer and A.A. Traverso, *Education in Gibraltar 1704–2000* (Gibraltar: Gibraltar Books, 2004); E.G. Archer, *Gibraltar, Identity and Empire* (London: Routledge, 2006), pp. 115–20, 122.

for many categories of the poor, some by regular aid to charities, many by operating variants of the English poor law. Most had state-funded or state-subsidised poorhouses, and many provided 'outdoor relief' to families in their own homes. Some operations were funded out of general government revenue; some by specified taxes on, for instance, shipping; many by local rates at parish level. Those governments raising and spending money on the relief of the poor included large spaces, like Canada and the Cape of Good Hope, and tiny dots, like Bermuda, St Lucia, St Christopher and even Heligoland. The government of Malta included expenditure of £13,000 in its 1845 estimates for the institutional or outdoor care of the old, the infirm, widows, fatherless children, and deserted women and children. Only six territories as yet gave no publicly funded support at all, and legislation was in preparation in Hong Kong, St Vincent and Western Australia, leaving completely without public provision only Gambia, Grenada – and Gibraltar. The response from the governor of Gibraltar was the shortest among the thirty-three replies: 'no provision of any kind is made by Law in Gibraltar'.[43]

In 1883 the idea of levying a poor rate to fund the care of the elderly infirm poor in a special ward of the Civil Hospital was at least floated in an official report, but this suggestion was regarded by the governor as inopportune (rather than unnecessary).[44] Matters had not changed by 1912. At the end of that year an exchange of correspondence took place between Governor Hunter and the Chairman of the Sanitary Commission (of which more shortly) which the governor subsequently arranged to have published in the *Gibraltar Chronicle*. Hunter noted that 'a large number of poor people' were 'dependent for their livelihood upon the charity of their well-disposed and better off neighbours', and he regretted that there was 'no Poor Rate and no system of organised Outdoor Relief'. He did not think it right that 'in a British Colony, such a state of affairs should be longer tolerated'. In other words, he wished to see introduced a publicly funded system of relieving the poor which sixty years earlier had become pretty nearly universal, one way or another, throughout the colonial empire as well as in the United Kingdom (and where, by this time, state old age pensions and state insurance schemes were also in place).

The response from the Sanitary Commissioners was that the four asylums by then operating were 'adequate to meet the needs of this place', with a bit of government money for tuberculosis treatment, and that charities raised annually about £5,500, the equivalent of a rate of 6½d (c.2.5p) in the pound. The implication in this latter claim, that rates would have to go up by so much

43 HCPP, *Return of Provision by Law in H.M. Colonial Possessions for Destitute Persons*, HC 702, 1846.
44 TNA, CO91/365, Adye to Derby, 19 Nov 1883, enclosing 'Report of Committee on future Administration of the Gibraltar Civil Hospital, 19 Sept 1883'.

to fund a poor law, was seriously misleading, since much of what was being spent was derived from charitable bequests which generated an income which would not cease even if poor rates were to be additionally levied. It was further claimed that introducing a poor rate would be resented, on the argument (inapplicable if rates were levied on property according to their value) that, were it to be made universal, it would fall on rich and poor alike. Were it instead to be 'limited to the possessors of a certain income', then, it was said, the taxpayers would probably increase rents to compensate, 'to the detriment of the poor and needy', an argument which smacks of a threat and comes pretty high on the scale of disgraceful (and, one might say, insulting to this ostensibly Christian and Jewish society). It was suggested, however, that if there were a shortfall in the funds of charities, implying that charitable donors might not be charitable enough, then the colonial government might slip them subsidies (presumably for spending at the discretion of the charity managers). The commissioners also warned that 'any extended or unwarranted system of outdoor relief would have a tendency to bring back to the Garrison the large number of families and former local residents who have gone to live at La Línea'; driven there, we know, by the low wages paid by employers in Gibraltar and the high rents charged by property owners. The final comment was that a poor law system of outdoor relief would also 'encourage the deep-rooted aversion which exists among the women of Gibraltar to seek a livelihood as domestic servants' and that they would stop working. Since a system of outdoor relief would almost certainly operate in Gibraltar on the 'less eligibility principle', characteristic of the English poor law (rates of relief being lower than subsistence wages), this implies that women in Gibraltar would 'elect' for a low poor relief income in place of the still lower and therefore less than subsistence wages (or unacceptable working conditions) being offered by the moneyed middle class. And in that moral black hole matters remained.[45] In the event, from 1914 and at the request of the Sanitary Commissioners, the colonial government added to a subsidy of £600 which it had been providing for the treatment of tuberculosis victims a further £620 for the relief of the 'indigent sick' and their families.[46]

The connection in all this between religion, charity and the absence of a public poor law system is apparent. Each of the faith communities catered largely for its own. From the 1850s the Hebrew Community Board, run of course by

45 *Gibraltar Chronicle and Official Gazette*, 31 Jan 1913, prints the letters and further comments made by Hunter in a speech at a public meeting. This source, this speech, its context and its consequences are reported in T.J. Finlayson, *Stories from the Rock* (Gibraltar: Aquila, 1996), though the author's reference to 'mismanaging the Poor Relief Funds', p. 107, is misleading.
46 TNA, CO91/484, Monro to Amery, 24 Nov 1925.

prominent Jewish members of the moneyed class – such as the Levys, Serfatys and Hassans – organised poor relief for its co-religionists, funded in effect by obligatory taxes on Jewish merchants and traders. The entire Jewish community seems to have contributed to the Sick Jewish Poor Relief Society founded in 1866, and a Hebrew Poor Asylum was opened in 1907.[47]

Likewise, on behalf of the Church of England, the Committee of the Protestant Orphan Asylum and British Poor Fund raised its own cash and ran its own operation, and had done so probably since the 1770s. Its trustees and executive committee included, of course, prominent members of the moneyed class, including, in 1890, from the Carver, Smith, Mosley, Boulton and Copeland families. It drew its funds not from rates on property but from rents on property vested in trustees and from donations, and it provided monthly allowances (in effect outdoor relief) to 'the Protestant poor', or more precisely, to the widows and orphans of 'artisans, soldiers, and civil servants', a rather bizarre and select clientele. Late in the century the executive committee wanted to establish an almshouse for widows, orphans and the elderly, because 'the Protestant poor live in garrets and cellars in the cheapest and therefore most objectionable tenements of the city', for reasons it is no longer necessary further to pursue. This Church of England committee also wanted to compete with the two asylums built for Roman Catholics out of the substantial bequests left by the late John Gavino, whose assets had funded 'a handsome and comfortable asylum for orphans and necessitous aged persons'. The committee raised some funds by donations and subscriptions, including $25 from the governor, and by cash-raising events. The archdeacon also asked (unsuccessfully) for a government subsidy.[48]

Gavino's Asylum (opened 1850), plus the St Bernard's Asylum, which John Gavino's bequest also funded, accommodated by 1898 about one hundred orphan girls and aged paupers, plus sixteen 'incurables'. The Little Sisters of

---

47 C.A. Grocott, 'The Moneyed Class of Gibraltar, c.1880–1939' (PhD thesis, Lancaster University, 2006), pp. 40, 111; A.B.M. Serfaty, *The Jews of Gibraltar Under British Rule* (Gibraltar: Garrison Library, new edn 1958), pp. 14, 25, 30; *Gibraltar Directory and Guidebook for 1914* (Gibraltar: Garrison Library, 1914), p. 96.

48 TNA, CO91/391, Newdigate to Knutsford, 9 June 1890 and enclosures including copy of appeal and subscription list; GGA, Despatches to Gibraltar 1890: Knutsford to Officer Administering the Government, 30 June 1890; TNA, CO91/409, Biddulph to Ripon, 12 Jan 1895, which letter also describes the administrative difficulties into which the charity had fallen and which required law to sort them out: Ordinance No 2 of 1895, 'To Provide for the Better Administration of the Charity known as the Protestant Orphan Asylum and British Poor Fund', *Consolidated Laws of Gibraltar* (Gibraltar: Gibraltar Government, 1913), vol. 1, pp. 776–7. The three freehold properties held were on Main Street and Turnbull's Lane.

the Poor also provided a refuge for a further eighty 'aged poor'.[49] There were a number of other Roman Catholic welfare agencies, like the two relief societies, 'Sagrado Corazon de Jesus' ('Sacred Heart of Jesus'), which in 1877 together claimed 164 members, and 'Protectora' ('Protectress'– that is the 'Virgin Mary') with its 60.[50] We may deduce from this that the Roman Catholic Church was able to attract substantial cash from its wealthier adherents. On the other hand, with most of the population, residents and alien incomers being Roman Catholics, the demands on its charities were also greater. The mode of raising money and the intended recipients – the deserving elderly poor, widows and orphans – characterised charitable operations elsewhere, and in normal circumstances probably excluded assistance for adult males struggling on poor wages to support families in lousy and expensive tenements. Much like in Britain. Police census reports counted 280 'paupers' in 1894, 345 in 1898 and 387 in 1899, probably enumerating those living in asylums.[51]

Charity was still largely the response in exceptional times. Dr Baly reported graphically on the social consequences of the quarantine imposed during the cholera outbreak in the winter of 1853–54. He noted the casual and unsystematic system of relief characteristic of nineteenth-century societies which depended on charity to deal with public distress: 'The poor apply for alms every Saturday at a fixed hour, at the homes of such persons of the middle and upper classes as are in the habit of dispensing them . . . [T]he number of these alms-seekers increased in a large ratio during the continuance of the "cordon".' He also noted the degradation which some suffered by resort to such forms of assistance: '[M]any persons just above the lowest class, persons ashamed to beg thus publicly, were driven to ask for help privately, and to pledge their goods for the means of obtaining food.' The governor personally donated £100 to provide relief; 600 persons applied, representing with their families 2,000 people. The solomonic business of identifying the 'most necessitous' was delegated to 'three gentlemen'.[52]

49 C. Boyle and R. Banbury (eds), *Gibraltar Directory and Guidebook 1898* (Gibraltar: Garrison Library, 1898), pp. 80–1.

50 GGA, Despatches from Gibraltar 1877: memorial 15 Sept 1877 with Napier to Carnarvon 29 Sept 1877. Two others called 'Liberal' and 'Amistad y Union' ('Friendship and Union') were probably secular, or at least non-denominational. Records for these societies appear not to have survived.

51 GGA, 'Census of Civil Residents taken by the Civil Police on 31st December 1894 and 1898' and 'Census taken by the Gibraltar Police 1899'. The Freemasons also provided relief for the widows and dependants of deceased members: K. Sheriff, *The Rough Ashlar: the History of English Freemasonry in Gibraltar 1727–2002* (Gibraltar: n.p., 2002[?]), p. 230.

52 HCPP, *Copy of the Report made by Dr Baly . . . upon the Subject of Quarantine at Gibraltar, 6th May 1854*, HC 161, 1854–55, p. 7.

When cholera struck again in 1865 and trade was once more interrupted, the response of community leaders was to form a committee (F. Francia, president, A. Larios, treasurer, J.H. Recaño, secretary) in August to raise funds by subscription. The governor led off with $100, the generosity of others also being advertised in a published list in the press – it was good to give and good to be seen to be giving. The aim was to provide relief for 'the necessitous of all persuasions' via a soup kitchen. By October, 610 families numbering 2,601 persons were consuming 1,398 pints of soup and 1,741 pounds of bread a day, at a daily cost of $109 (£22). Francia, speaking no doubt on behalf of informed employers, explained to the governor that 'the disease found the labouring classes and the poor, from the high price of manufactured goods and the prostration of trade, ill-provided with bedding, wearing apparel and other necessaries, and consequently ill-prepared for this terrible scourge'. Having admitted the lamentable earning power of employees in Gibraltar before the cholera crisis, he asked the governor to provide his committee with £1,000 out of government revenues to pay for the financial shortfall being experienced in charity-funded relief for cholera-stricken families, citing government action in 1834 as a precedent.[53] Charity, like employers, did not meet need.

It was pretty much the same story twenty years later, in 1885, when cholera struck again. The 'wealthy inhabitants of Gibraltar all liberally contributed' and £1,600 was raised; eight camp cooking stoves were erected; a daily ration was devised made up of one pint of soup, ¼ lb of cooked meat, 1lb of bread, and some rice or macaroni in the soup, at an all-in cost of 2½d (1p) each; and thus '1,086 families numbering 4,120 persons, were fed gratuitously'.[54] Exceptional circumstances as well as endemic poverty were therefore being addressed by charitable handouts organised by the community's civilian elite. Nobody among the civilian community and few, like Governor Hunter, in the administration seem to have suggested doing it in any other way. No doubt recipients responded to charity with the usual variable degrees of gratitude.

The moneyed class and public services: the origins of the Sanitary Commission, 1865

What the charitable operations indicate is the prominent public role played by leading citizens from the churches and the moneyed class. Spiritually, they were guided by their religious consciences. Financially, they were averting alternative public provision and holding off increases in taxes and the imposition of rates

53 *Gibraltar Chronicle*, 31 Aug 1865, p. 4; TNA, CO91/278, and GGA, Despatches from Gibraltar 1865: Codrington to War Office, 5 Oct, forwarding memorial from Francia, and 3 Nov 1865.
54 *The Times*, 4 Dec 1885, p. 13.

by government, over whose expenditure they would have had less direct control. Socially, they were demonstrating their status or, if you wish, accepting their obligations, as civil leaders. Politically, they were operating in lieu of public servants and, in effect, as alternatives to government. To that extent they were not 'powerless'. Moreover, similar people were also directly involved in public administration.

It was seen in a previous chapter how, by the beginning of the nineteenth century, members of the moneyed class had cohered and established the Exchange and Commercial Library, and how their sort had already been enlisted by early-century governors into the devising and management of public health services (Committee of Public Health 1804, Board of Health 1805, Paving and Scavenging Commission 1815, Civil Hospital committee 1815). It is now necessary to pursue further the inquiry into the roles and influence (or 'powerlessness') of the moneyed class in a period in which, as we have seen, Gibraltar's social as well as economic infrastructure was being developed by law and by government as well as by private sector practice. We will see that increasingly the committee of the Exchange and Commercial Library, although its electoral basis was in reality limited to property owners, claimed to speak for the entire civilian community of Gibraltar. That monopoly was challenged, however, when, in 1882, a breakaway group of senior business folk formed the Chamber of Commerce. As we will also see, other configurations of the moneyed class appeared, in particular in 1891 a group calling itself the Gibraltar Ratepayers' Defence Association and in 1902 the Gibraltar Employers' Federation.[55] Nor should we forget the continuing role of the Grand Jury, made up entirely of propertied people, from among whom the personnel for public inquiries and public bodies were selected by governors.[56]

The establishment in 1865 of Gibraltar's Sanitary Commission and its subsequent contested development are particularly revealing of the role of civilians in public administration and of the politics of Gibraltar. However, it is first necessary to note how little change there had been in public health measures for half a century before its creation. It is obvious enough that rapid population growth, industrialisation and, particularly, urbanisation in the early and mid nine-

55 Grocott, 'Moneyed Class', pp. 39–40, 118–22, 124, 128, 132; and see p. 64 for names of presidents of the Exchange Committee and Chamber of Commerce from 1882, confirming the business basis of both those bodies. For documents relating to the Exchange Committee and the formation of the Chamber of Commerce, see also GGA, Box: Miscellaneous Papers 1881–1883: correspondence 6 Nov–2 Dec 1882, and TNA, CO91/360, Napier to Kimberley, 26 Dec 1882, from which it appears that the latter consisted of merchants who deplored the involvement of the former in public protests against the appointment of Bishop Canilla, and the Exchange Committee's consequent neglect of commercial concerns.
56 Grocott, 'Moneyed Class', p. 36.

teenth centuries had generated alarm in Britain. Legislative and administrative reactions at central government level, however, were initially slow and partial, and much depended on local town council initiatives. However, a clatter of law making in Britain in the late 1840s culminated in the Public Health Act of 1848, which gave local authorities the power to prosecute those responsible for 'nuisances', to provide such amenities as public washhouses, to borrow money on the security of their rates to invest in water supplies and drainage schemes, to set up local boards of health with extensive responsibilities, and to appoint local medical officers of health. Initially this was largely permissive legislation, but the Public Health Acts of 1866, 1872 and, especially, of 1875 compelled local governments to tackle such problems as insufficient water supplies, inadequate sanitation systems and unacceptable housing conditions and, just as important, provided them with methods of more easily raising the capital needed for investment in improvements.[57]

The authorities in Gibraltar were not exactly public health pioneers, although to be fair they were not peculiarly 'behind the times'. Not even the mass slaughters caused by yellow fever and cholera epidemics in the first half of the century generated dramatic public health measures. As we saw in a previous chapter, the epidemic of 1804 prompted the appointment of a Board of Health with civilian members, but it largely served as an advisory body to the governor and the public. Executive action depended on the governor, the revenues he could divert from other government expenditure, what he could persuade the War Office and the Treasury to spend on the garrison, and other demands on the energies, time and expertise of garrison officers, particularly the Principal Medical Officer and the Commanding Officer Royal Engineers. Don's Paving and Scavenging Commission at least went a step further, since its members did have authority to raise money with which to pay for modest civic improvements. Beyond that, and quarantine measures when needed, Don and his successors largely 'improved' public health by continuing with the modest advisory work of the Board of Health, reconstituted in 1831,[58] and of the inspectors and police officers appointed as, in effect, public health officers in each of the districts of the town and the area to the south.[59] The yellow fever epidemic of 1828–29 mainly prompted only an official inquiry and an inconclusive debate between experts on the

57 A.S. Wohl, *Endangered Lives: Public Health in Victorian Britain* (London: Dent, 1983), esp. pp. 142–65; F.B. Smith, *The People's Health 1830–1914* (London: Croom Helm, 1979), pp. 198–9.

58 TNA, CO91/116, Houston to Goderich, 5 Dec 1831, enclosing proclamation.

59 *Gibraltar Chronicle Supplement*, 19 June 1819, p. 1; GGA, Despatches from Gibraltar 1829: proclamation of 20 June in Don to Murray, June 1829; Despatches from Gibraltar 1830: proclamation 6 July in Don to Murray, 19 July 1830.

causes of the disease.[60] Even Don's construction of more sewers, paid for from government revenue, may have done as much harm as good, given their design and the dumping of their contents into the bay.[61] Even the very serious outbreak of cholera in 1853–54 produced only brief official reports on the effects of quarantine and a few remarks on the sanitary state of Gibraltar. Dr Baly's recommendations for protecting public health by improving sanitation were not novel and led to no revolution in government performance.[62] Military engineers were well aware of what, in principle, was immediately needed: a robust water supply and secure sewers discharging their contents well clear of the Rock (albeit still into the bay). However, governors seem only to have itemised costs to the War Office and Treasury without insisting on assistance and did not propose to raise extra revenue from the civilian community to fund such works.[63] Certainly there was no obvious alert from the moneyed class of Gibraltar that major works should be undertaken and that it would pay for them.

Moreover, the method and level of funding for the Paving and Scavenging Commission did not change over fifty years. Financing public services on the basis of rates, a local property tax, initially intended for the relief of the poor, had been characteristic of local government in England since 1601, and this system also supported wider services concerned with nineteenth-century public health. Don's innovation, startling because it was swallowed after some resistance by a moneyed class notoriously hostile to taxation, was to introduce such a practice into Gibraltar.[64] But although the principle was adopted, the levy was and remained

60 For press commentary see, for instance, *The Times*, 26 Feb 1829, p. 5; 24 April 1829, p. 2; 12 Aug 1829, p. 1, and for the official inquiry see TNA, CO91/101, Don to Murray, 17 Sept 1829, and the mass of 1830 material in TNA, CO91/110.

61 For the 1815 plans and subsequent construction see GGA, Despatches from Gibraltar 1815: Don to Bathurst, 10 Jan 1815; Despatches from Gibraltar 1816–17: Don to Bathurst, 28 Sept 1816 and 8 March 1817. Even the drains Don had had constructed to remove 'offensive smells' from around the fish market merely discharged their content into the sea, Despatches from Gibraltar 1815: Don to Bathurst, 4 Jan 1815; Sawchuk, *Deadly Visitations*, pp. 118–26.

62 HCPP, *Report made by Dr Baly . . . 1854*; HCPP, *Report of Dr Baly on the Sanitary State of Gibraltar, 20 July 1854*, 274, 1854–55. See GGA, Despatches to Gibraltar 1854: Newcastle to Gardiner, 1 Aug 1854, for the secretary of state's request that Dr Baly's 'valuable suggestions' should be given early attention, and Despatches from Gibraltar 1854–55: Gardiner to Newcastle, 11 Oct 1854, for the governor's dismissive judgement that the report contained nothing new.

63 For example, TNA, CO91/226, Gardiner to Panmure, 28 July 1855, and Fergusson to Panmure, 3 Sept 1855.

64 Benady, *Don*, pp. 60, 67. It had taken the order-in-council to snuff out resistance: GGA, Despatches from Gibraltar 1815: Don to Bathurst, 29 Oct 1815.

modest. The rate authorised by the 1815 order-in-council for expenditure on paving and scavenging was not to exceed 3 per cent of the yearly rental value of property, to be levied on government as well as on private property.[65] In 1817 the actual rate charged was 1¾ per cent.[66] When, in 1819, responsibilities were extended to cover half the cost of street lighting (the other half to come from government), an additional rate of at most only ⅓ per cent was sanctioned.[67] No further legislation thereafter either added to the commission's responsibilities or removed the financial ceiling so as to allow for an increase in revenue. In 1828 the rates had risen for 'Paving and Scavenging' to the very precise 'Two Dollars Seven Reals and Twelve Quarts' in every hundred dollars, plus 'Two Reals and Four Quarts' for lighting. By 1838 a full 'Three Dollars' and 'Four Reals' were being respectively charged, but in 1865 the charge for paving and scavenging was reduced, marginally, to 'Two Dollars and Eight Reals'. We should also note movements in the rental valuations of property, since these would affect the revenue from the rates. In 1847 rental values amounted to $27,252 a month, but in the economic doldrums of the 1850s they fell, to as low as $25,101 in 1855; but the ceiling on rates remained. The commission's income rose thereafter only because valuations increased, to $31,870 by 1865.[68] Under these constraints Don's Paving and Scavenging Commission continued to pave, scavenge and illuminate the streets, while the military built a few water tanks and dug some drainage sewers, and large numbers of the civilian population festered in their insanitary dwellings.

It is indicative of the lack of local initiative from the civilian community and from the colonial administration in Gibraltar that the Sanitary Commission originated from the War Office in London, and with the welfare of the garrison principally in mind. Concerns about the health of troops stationed in Malta and the Ionian Islands, as well as in Gibraltar, had prompted Sidney Herbert, secretary of state, to appoint the Barrack and Hospital Improvement Commission in 1861, made up of Captain Douglas Galton, Royal Engineers, and Dr John Sutherland.[69] The most important deduction of the commissioners from their on-site inspections was that 'it has been impossible in this inquiry to separate

65 GGA, Despatches from Gibraltar 1816–17: Don to Bathurst, 25 April 1817.
66 TNA, CO91/71, Office of Ordnance to H. Goulborn, War Office, 4 June 1817.
67 'Paving and Scavenger's Rate and Lighting Rate Orders-in-Council', 30 Dec 1815 and 1 Feb 1819, *Orders in Council, etc* (Gibraltar: Gibraltar Government, 1839).
68 GGA, Box: Assessed Rate for Paving, Scavenging and Lighting, 1818–1865.
69 Herbert had been concerned, with Florence Nightingale, about the health of troops during and after the Crimean War: H.C.G. Matthew, 'Sidney Herbert', *ODNB*. He died on 2 Aug 1861, aged only 50. His successor, Sir George Cornewall Lewis, confirmed the appointment of the commission on 14 Aug. The inquiry was conducted between September and November 1861 and the report signed 12 Jan 1863: HCPP, *Report of the Barrack and Hospital Improvement Commission on the Sanitary Condition and Improvement of the Mediterranean Stations*, 7626, 1863.

the sanitary condition of the troops from that of the civil population' and that 'at all the stations sanitary defects existing among the civil population place [troops] in constant danger of outbreaks of epidemic disease'. Therefore, while they had much to recommend in terms of barrack designs and the health care of soldiers, their report insisted that public health measures to improve the sanitary condition of the surrounding civil population were also essential. Their report provided a devastating summary of the consequences of urbanisation in the three colonies and of the deplorable consequences of lamentable private sector provision and inadequate public services.

> In all the towns the drainage, especially the house drainage, is in a very bad condition; the domestic conveniences connected with it are of a rude and unwholesome description, or there are none; the water supply is either deficient in amount or not of good quality, and in no instance is it properly distributed for domestic purposes, or connected with the drainage . . . The dwellings of the poorer classes are of a very inferior description, badly constructed for health, overcrowded, and deficient in domestic conveniences.

Undoubtedly, the minds of the commissioners were coloured by the 'health of towns' movement in Britain, by advances in medical knowledge and in civil engineering and, indeed, by recent British legislation. 'All defects of this kind which used to exist in the worst districts of unimproved English towns before the days of the Public Health Act exist as the rule in these Mediterranean towns.' The work of Don and his successors in Gibraltar, of their military engineers in the construction of water tanks and drains, of the Paving and Scavenging Commission and, one might add, of private investors and charitable agencies was roughly dismissed: 'Little or nothing as yet has been done in the way of improvement in these matters at Gibraltar.' Even the drainage works carried out since the yellow fever epidemic of 1828 were criticised for their design, for the failure, still, to maintain through them a steady flow of water, and for outlets which dumped contents on to a shallow tidal beach. In the quantity and quality of its water supply Gibraltar was the worst of all the stations. Houses were often overcrowded, design poor, facilities lamentable, rents too high, landlords neglectful. Even the collection of data on sickness and mortality was deficient, but, such as it was, pointed to a 'very high rate'.[70]

The commissioners concluded that the governor of Gibraltar and the existing Paving and Scavenging Commission lacked the authority to deal with the principal defects of the town, including those in private property. Existing powers 'belong to a state of sanitary legislation which has been found altogether insufficient for protecting public health'. Therefore an order-in-council was needed to

70 Evidence specific to the civilian community in Gibraltar is on pp. 12, 14–16, 23–35 of the report, of the sanitary state of the troops on pp. 35–82, and of both in statistical data on pp. 265–84 plus plans; quotations are from pp. 2, 3, 25.

give authority to the colonial government 'similar to those in the Public Health Act' so that deficiencies in private housing, in the town drainage system and in the public water supply could be tackled, so that rates could be levied and so that a medical officer of health for the whole territory could be appointed.[71] Captain Galton and Dr Sutherland subsequently provided a summary of their recommendations for the War Office and for the governor. These, in addition to matters specific to the barracks, stressed the importance of legislation. Legal authority was needed to authorise public works but also to override the rights of private property owners in Gibraltar, as in Britain, so as to ensure the provision of adequate house drainage and water supply, the cleansing of filthy houses and the introduction of water closets or latrines, and to require that all plans for future house building be submitted for approval.[72] These reports were the equivalent for Gibraltar, in their political and public health consequences, of Edwin Chadwick's famous *Report on the Sanitary Condition of the Labouring Population of Great Britain*, published twenty years earlier, in 1842.[73]

The reports, with the War Office's endorsement and a request for immediate action, were despatched to Governor Codrington on 28 February 1863. Further instructions from the War Office followed on 30 June, together with copies for guidance of recent British public health laws (especially a Liverpool Sanitary Act), plus detailed directions from Galton and Sutherland on how Gibraltar's law might be framed, on the works to be done, and on the allocation of costs between those to be funded by local ratepayers (public drains, house drains, improvements to housing), those to be paid for by the War Office (the main sewer) and those for which the costs should be shared (brackish water supply, fresh water supply).[74]

As if to drive home the need, cholera again stuck Gibraltar while legislative and administrative preparations were under way. The disease killed over 100 members of the garrison and about 500 civilians between July and October 1865, and prompted another and impressively thorough investigation by Dr Sutherland, who of course stressed the sanitary causes of the epidemic (rather than person-to-person contagion) and the need for urgent action along the lines already recommended, plus the construction of better houses, controls over alien immigration and a proper system of registering the causes of deaths.[75]

71 Ibid, pp. 34–5.
72 GGA, Despatches to Gibraltar from Secretary of State for War, 1861–63: report dated 12 Feb 1863 with Lewis to Codrington, 28 Feb 1863.
73 For which see M.W. Flinn's edition (Edinburgh: Edinburgh University Press, 1965).
74 GGA, Despatches to Gibraltar from Secretary of State for War, 1861–63: Lewis to Codrington, 30 June 1863, and enclosures.
75 HCPP, *Report on the Sanitary Condition of Gibraltar with reference to the Epidemic Cholera in the Year 1865*, 3921–1, 1867: the last recommendation led to Ordinance No 6 of 1868, Registration of Deaths.

Making those preparations was a prolonged and contested business. Their resolution was to have major implications for the politics and future government of the colony. Matters began smoothly enough, since Governor Codrington accepted the need for a new initiative. In July 1863 he sent to London an analysis of the works required, prepared locally in the Royal Engineers' office, and this was followed in August by a draft ordinance drawn up by his attorney-general to empower a body to deal with 'nuisances' and 'the prevention of disease'.[76] However, Codrington had in mind replacing the Paving and Scavenging Commission with its civilian membership by a Board of Health made up of officials (such as the inspector of health and the police magistrate). He argued that 'it is impossible to expect Mercantile men of business to give up the amount of time which will be required' to tackle the sanitary problems which needed to be addressed.[77] In the heated exchanges which followed with the War Office, he objected to some of the expensive and (in his view) unnecessary tasks being laid upon the new body. More important, he continued to claim that an official body would be better able to take the effective action needed and that Gibraltar's merchant class would, in any case, be unwilling to serve, voluntarily and unpaid, on a body which would have extensive and time-consuming duties to perform. It is also apparent, however, that he was not willing to see his authority diminished by delegating major powers and responsibilities to civilians. He reminded the War Office that Gibraltar 'is not England', 'the inhabitants generally are not English', and 'the language even is not that of England'. He warned the War Office (in what proved to be prescient words) that nevertheless 'they value the rights and privileges they possess by English law'. He was convinced that a corporate body of civilians 'managing the affairs of the inhabitants', and with powers to raise and spend considerable amounts of ratepayers' money, was likely to lead to a municipal form of government and to 'elections by which the management of municipal affairs is arranged in England'. He intimated that such developments might not be compatible with the interests of the garrison or of Gibraltar, 'where the sentries of two different nations are kept loaded within musket shot of each other'. He also feared that necessary tasks would not be undertaken unless the government had a representative on whatever body was put in charge of sanitation matters or had power to insist that they be undertaken.[78]

---

76 GGA, Despatches from Gibraltar 1863: Royal Engineers' Office to colonial secretary, 13 July 1863 (this was sent by Codrington to the War Office on 15 July, but no copy of his despatch survives in GGA or TNA); TNA, CO91/265, Codrington to Earl de Grey and Ripon, 3 Aug 1863, and enclosures.

77 TNA, CO91/265, Codrington to Earl de Grey and Ripon, 9 Oct 1863, endorsing report of 30 Sept 1863 by Costello, attorney-general.

78 TNA, CO91/276, Codrington to Earl de Grey and Ripon, 4 Feb and 21 April 1865; CO91/277, Codrington to Secretary of State for War, 5 July 1865.

However, War Office staff in 1864–65 insisted – and this may seem surprising, as it certainly was to their successors – that authority to raise rates and spend money on sanitary reforms, including on major engineering works, must be left to a Sanitary Commission set up by an order-in-council and made up entirely of leading citizens drawn from the Grand Jury, who would of course represent the ratepayers. They claimed that civilians would surely be committed to these duties because they would have a natural interest in improving public health in Gibraltar, and they claimed (rather disingenuously) that their duties would in any case be little more than those voluntarily fulfilled by their predecessors over the previous half century. In sum, this measure was to be recommended because, as far as possible, it gave 'to the Ratepayers the management of their own affairs' and guarded the commissioners 'against uncalled for interference on the part of the Executive Government'. The unacceptable alternative, which the governor seemed to favour, 'does not give the Ratepayers the slightest power even in the administering their own funds but vests that power in Government officials' and 'makes them subject to the arbitrary will of the Governor'.[79] This extraordinary rebuff, tantamount to a reprimand of the governor, suggests that the War Office, led by a reforming secretary of state, Earl de Grey and Ripon, in a government led by Palmerston, had absorbed the aspirations of the British sanitary reform movement and espoused the Liberal political optimism of their minister.[80]

Not surprisingly, War Office staff were therefore pretty annoyed with Codrington for sending to the grand jurors a highly off-putting description of the substantial duties they would have to undertake if their members were to become responsible for improving sanitation in the colony in the fashion proposed by the War Office. He 'has behaved extremely ill in this matter'.[81] So bitter did relations become that the governor even asked for a postponement of proceedings until his term of office had expired.[82] To pull things around, a considerable consultation exercise was then undertaken, fronted, remarkably as it would turn out, by Frederick Solly Flood, the barrister whom we have met already, who had once been a resident in Gibraltar and who, behind the scenes, had been advising the War Office. In February 1866 he was to become attorney-general, after Codrington's departure, and a corrosive critic of Gibraltar's people, but on this occasion he oozed sweetness and light.

79 TNA, CO91/276, War Office to Codrington, 3 April 1865, with Codrington to War Office, 4 Feb 1865; and similarly see CO91/277, Earl de Grey and Ripon to Codrington, 16 Aug 1865, with Codrington to Earl de Grey and Ripon, 5 July 1865.

80 For the reforming zeal of the minister see A.F. Denholm, 'George Frederick Samuel Robinson, First Marquess of Ripon', *ODNB*.

81 TNA, CO91/276, minutes on Codrington to Earl de Grey and Ripon, 18 March 1865.

82 TNA, CO91/276, Codrington to Earl de Grey and Ripon, 13 April 1865.

The several public meetings which he held underlined the War Office's concern to gain the acquiescence of at least the propertied class in measures for which, through the rates, they must partly pay, and to recruit from among them the leading citizens who would do the business. Certainly, those who attended these gatherings expressed serious concern about Gibraltar's sanitary state,[83] but it is noticeable that Flood was especially pressed to explain the allocation of costs between the 'Inhabitants' and the imperial government and to calculate and publish the anticipated effect on the rates of the expected expenditure on the proposed sewerage works and water supply.[84] Ratepayers' views were focused through a so-called Sanitary Committee, appointed at a public meeting on 16 June.[85] The secretary, George Alton, a Wesleyan minister, even had private meetings with the governor and then, through him, went on to ask the secretary of state to accept further amendments when the draft order was eventually published in the *Gibraltar Chronicle* on 26 August; and indeed, some further alterations were accordingly made.[86] The order-in-council, with its 292 clauses and six schedules, was finally issued on 20 November 1865 and came into effect on 9 December.[87]

It is clear from this narrative that the civilian population, or at least some of it, was not 'powerless'. Government in Gibraltar and in London did consult and did adjust legislation in response to the views expressed by, inevitably, articulate ratepayers. Indeed, it was subsequently claimed that Flood had assured ratepayers that this measure implied a recognition by the colonial authorities of the

83 See especially, GGA, Despatches from Gibraltar 1865: memorial (signed by 265 ratepayers 'and other inhabitants') and other attachments with Codrington to War Office, 18 Aug 1865.

84 GGA, Despatches from Gibraltar 1865: Memorial by Grand Jurors, 8 Feb 1865, with Codrington to War Office, 14 Feb 1865; reports in *Gibraltar Chronicle*, 11 April, 18 and 27 May, 3, 10, 14 and 17 June 1865; TNA, CO91/276, Codrington to Earl de Grey and Ripon, 6 May 1865, enclosing report by Flood; CO91/227, Codrington to Earl de Grey and Ripon, 2 June 1865, enclosing reports; CO91/227 and GGA, Despatches from Gibraltar 1865: Codrington to War Office, 30 June 1865, enclosing report by Flood, and also GGA, Despatches from Gibraltar 1867: Airey to Colonial Office, 31 May 1867, enclosing Flood to Freeling, 11 May 1867, a retrospective account of the dispute over the allocation of costs for drainage works and its resolution.

85 For the names of committee members see *First Supplement to the Gibraltar Chronicle*, 17 June 1865.

86 TNA, CO91/278 and GGA, Despatches from Gibraltar 1865: Codrington to War Office, 7 and 9 Oct 1865, the latter enclosing Alton to Codrington, 6 Oct 1865; TNA, CO91/278, Codrington to War Office, 9 Nov 1865; Despatches to Gibraltar 1865: Earl de Grey and Ripon to Airey, 25 Nov 1865. (Governor Sir Richard Airey took over from Codrington in November.)

87 *Sanitary Order in Council, Gibraltar* (London: HMSO, 1865).

civilian community's proper claim to municipal self-government. This was almost certainly untrue, but history is not only what happened, it is also what people believed had happened.[88] As we shall see, Gibraltar ratepayers regarded the responsibilities granted to their leaders as the bedrock of their liberties.

Those leaders were certainly empowered as 'collaborators' (using the term employed in a previous chapter) by their incorporation into the resulting executive agency set up by the order-in-council. Essentially, it replaced the modest Scavenging and Paving Commission with a Sanitary Commission which was granted the powers and given many of the public health duties of municipal authorities in Britain. Hence the commissioners were to make valuations and levy rates, including on crown property. Importantly, a ceiling on rates was no longer fixed by law, though the rates levied required the governor's approval. They were given wide-ranging responsibilities for sanitation, water supply, public highways, street lighting, improving housing conditions, building controls, food inspection and dealing with a variety of public health 'nuisances'. There were to be twelve commissioners, one-third to retire each year. Very remarkably, they were all to be drawn from the civilian community. There were to be no representatives of the colonial government or of the military, even though government, military and naval buildings paid rates and substantial costs for the expected civil engineering works were expected to fall upon the colonial and imperial governments. Prospective commissioners were restricted to those with property and status, defined as occupiers of premises with a rental value of $100 a year or who were either members of the Grand Jury or freeholders or leaseholders of land valued at $5,000.[89] These were stiff requirements. Property qualifications even for members of parliament had been abolished in Britain in 1858, and yet neither in 1865 nor later were there recorded protests by 'poorer' ratepayers against such discrimination, or by those many others not paying rates.

88 TNA, CO91/363, Memorial from Sanitary Commission, 17 April 1883, with Adye to Derby, 19 April 1883. Even the Colonial Office later blamed Flood: CO91/391, minute 15 Nov 1889, attached to Smyth to Knutsford, 23 Oct 1890. Yet in August 1867, and in no uncertain terms, Flood insisted that Gibraltar was principally a fortress 'held for Military and Imperial purposes only' and that not one tenth of the civil population 'is capable of comprehending the value of the English Constitution': CO91/289, Airey to Colonial Office, 23 Aug 1867, enclosing Flood to colonial secretary, 12 Aug 1867.

89 The sentiments remained the same when the order-in-council of 1883 altered this to those occupying and personally paying rates on property rated at 500 pesetas, or those who were either a member of the Grand Jury or possessed property worth annually at least 25,000 pesetas. In 1907 this was further translated into those paying rates of at least £20 a year or possessing land valued at £1,000. The famous Parliamentary Reform Act of 1832 had set a rental valuation in Britain for borough voters of £10 a year; and all heads of households became borough voters in 1867.

Moreover, the Grand Jury was annually to nominate qualified persons and they, with those retiring, would constitute a panel from which the governor would make his selection. This was therefore hardly a democratic breakthrough. No one seems to have proposed publicly any amendment to the draft law in favour of a more radical innovation – elections to office – by then characteristic of Britain. This was not what the Gibraltar moneyed class were seeking. Several merchant princes and lawyers were among the first twelve appointed.[90]

The authority of the Sanitary Commission, though not its accountability to a wider public, was to grow over the next half century. In the early days the commissioners, at their request, were sent copies of British 'health of towns' legislation for their guidance.[91] Some of Gibraltar's subsequent public health legislation, itemised earlier, may be explained as the 'organic growth of government' after the commissioners had gained experience, pushed up against the limits of their legislative powers and responded to altered expectations and demands. Each step in the civil engineering projects for drainage and water supply upon which the Sanitary Commission embarked required additional legislative authorisation: hence further orders-in-council in, for instance, 1868 and 1874. Moreover, as in Britain so in Gibraltar, additional powers were secured to make by-laws, widen streets, construct bathing establishments and wash-houses, further tighten the law on food quality, control vaccination and, very important, pay for public works by loans raised on the security of the rates. Until 1902, borrowing was allowed up to 25 per cent above total rateable value, then, until 1907, up to 75 per cent, and thereafter up to 100 per cent. By the 1880s, the debt at the end of each year amounted to over £50,000 (upon which, of course, interest was being paid out of the rates), and this rose in 1900 to £143,330 and in 1914 to £232,094.[92] There

90 The first appointed commissioners were Richard Abrines, Emile Bonnet, Benjamin Carver Jnr, Joseph A. Crooks, Francis Francia Jnr (the first chairman), Francis Imossi, Solomon Levy, Richard Parody, Michael A. Pitman, John H. Recaño, Joseph Shakery and Musgrave Watson: GGA, Sanitary Commissioners, Minutes of Proceedings, 1865–70, pp. 1, 4.

91 TNA, CO91/289 Airey to War Office, 7 May 1867; CO 92/30, Colonial Office to Airey, 17 June 1867.

92 *Gibraltar Annual Reports*. On the first laws empowering the Sanitary Commission to borrow money and on other early changes see orders-in-council 18 Nov 1867 and 14 May 1868, and TNA, CO91/289, Airey to Colonial Office, 22 June, 15 July, 19 Aug, 9 Dec 1867, CO92/30, Buckingham to Airey, 12 Dec 1867; GGA, Despatches from Gibraltar 1868: Airey to Colonial Office, 7 May 1868; Despatches to Gibraltar 1867 and 1868: Colonial Office to Airey, 19 July, 6 Aug, 22 and 30 Nov 1867, and 15 May 1868. Early problems borrowing locally the approved capital needed for drainage and water supply works, in addition to the finance being provided by the colonial government and HM Treasury, are revealed (just about: the papers are badly water stained) in GGA, Despatches from Gibraltar 1868: Alton to Colonial Secretary, 3

was even a dash of 'municipal socialism' in Gibraltar when, from 1873, the commissioners became responsible (with the military) for the fire brigade and, from 1902, for electric lighting. In the 1880s they even attempted, unsuccessfully, to take over the private-enterprise gas company, established in 1856.[93] Finally, it should be noted that, like the Paving and Scavenging Commission it replaced, the Sanitary Commission was a tier of government inserted beneath the colonial government, with roughly similar territorial jurisdiction and, of course, subordinate and subject to regulation but with particular and growing responsibilities and its own source of revenue. Potentially, therefore, the Sanitary Commission could be an additional or even alternative location for authority and power.

Gibraltar politics: the Sanitary Commission, 1865–91

By the beginning of the new century, Gibraltar was a much more regulated and 'improved' territory. For all its remaining public health problems, it was a better place in which to be born, at which to be stationed and to which to travel. Now the sea breezes prevailed and there were fewer bad smells. The civilian Sanitary Commissioners were unpaid and devoted time, energy and thought to complex matters,[94] and in the early days their efforts received official recognition and approval.[95] A review in 1877 was generally complimentary about what had so far been achieved, in spite of continuing concerns about water supply and the unresolved problem of 'houses unfit for human habitation'.[96] However, the path to public health reform in Gibraltar, as in Liverpool and Leeds, Birmingham and Bradford, was a political battlefield,[97] although, unlike in those English cities, the

Sept 1868 and attachments. At that time it was envisaged that paying interest on the money borrowed would raise rates from 4½ per cent to, eventually, 5⅙ per cent.

93 Finlayson, *Stories from the Rock*, pp. 64–72, 80–1. On electricity see also ordinances of 28 Oct 1892, 4 Oct 1895 and, in Public Health Ordinance, 23 Sept 1907; and on gas see especially TNA, CO91/383, Hardinge to Knutsford, 7 and 28 July 1888, enclosures and replies, CO91/386, Hardinge to Knutsford, 10 Dec 1888 and enclosures.

94 See GGA, Sanitary Commissioners: Minutes of Proceedings. From 1891 commissioners were paid a fee for the meetings they attended.

95 For example, TNA, CO91/289, Airey to Colonial Office, 18 and 28 May 1867; GGA, Despatches from Gibraltar 1868: Airey to Colonial Office, 7 May 1868; *Gibraltar Chronicle*, 21 Feb 1868, remarks by governor at inauguration of new drainage works.

96 TNA, CO879/12/6, 'Report of an Inquiry into the Working and Administration of the Gibraltar Sanitary Commission', 1877, p. 19. For the appointment see GGA, Despatches to Gibraltar 1877: Carnarvon to Napier, 30 Aug 1877.

97 For case studies of these and other cities see Fraser, *Power and Authority in the Victorian City* and also D. Fraser, *Urban Politics in Victorian Britain* (Leicester: Leicester University Press, 1976).

combatants were not rival political parties accusing each other of neglect or profligacy but the colonial and imperial governments, on the one hand, and prominent ratepayers claiming to represent the civilian community, on the other.

For the British authorities, the Sanitary Commission threw up a recurrent problem in the British Empire, the local demand for 'self-government' versus the imperial desire for 'good government', as they saw it – made more imperative because Gibraltar was, for them, primarily a fortress and inadequate provision for public health was a security risk. In the official mind, the political structure set up by the 1865 order-in-council proved in need of amendment, because of problems Governor Codrington had foreseen. However, civilians and, more precisely, some ratepayers came to regard the Sanitary Commission as a recognition of their role and rights as citizens to exercise self-government, at least in public health matters. Moreover, the defence of 'their' Commission helped to generate among at least some ratepayers a more particular sense of a civilian collective identity. Unlikely though it may seem, the order-in-council of 1865, introduced essentially to deal with bad drains and poor water, was mythologised into Gibraltar's *magna carta*.

In retrospect it was remarkable that British authorities had ever granted such responsibilities solely to civilian commissioners. After all, the colonial government and the military paid rates on their property, and the colonial and imperial governments were also responsible for providing much of the capital for civil engineering works. The British authorities soon became uncomfortable with the beast they had created and into whose decision making thereafter they had no direct input. Governor Napier, in office from 1876 to 1883, became particularly impatient with its operations and current organisation. It needs to be remembered that not only was he used to military command, but also he had had immense experience in directing civil engineering projects. Accordingly, following up a recommendation from the 1877 inquiry, he brushed aside ratepayer protests which asserted 'the rights of the people in the management of their local affairs' and, by an order-in-council in March 1880, reduced the number of civilian commissioners from twelve to eight, in order to make room for four so-called 'representative commissioners', two representing the War Office plus one each to speak for the Admiralty and the colonial government.[98]

But further experience persuaded Napier that this was not enough. He believed the civilian commissioners were incompetent, inclined to jobbery in

---

98 TNA, CO879/12/6, 'Report of an Inquiry into the Working and Administration of the Gibraltar Sanitary Commission', 1877, p. 18; CO91/348, Napier to Hicks Beach, 6 Feb and 3 March 1879; CO91/350, Acting Governor to Colonial Office, 17 Sept 1879, enclosing protest from the Sanitary Commissioners, and Napier to Hicks Beach, 20 and 21 Nov, 1 and 16 Dec 1879, the last enclosing protests from the Exchange Committee.

the allocation of contracts and ill-served by the personnel they hired (perhaps corruptly).[99] He complained, for instance, that the superintendent in charge of public works and hired by the commissioners 'cannot read English intelligently enough to profit from books of instructions', and that the civil engineer they were employing lacked appropriate expertise.[100] He claimed that public health improvements were also being inhibited by the commissioners' desire to keep down the rates which they and their like would have to pay. At a petty level, it was said, this included a reluctance to pay for the removal of 'night soil' or to adopt streets as public highways which they would then be obliged to maintain.[101] More seriously, and much complained of by other official observers, it was said that the charge for the water supplied to customers by the Sanitary Commission was set deliberately high so that the profits made could be used to keep down the rates, and not to lower the price or improve the service, even though the consequence was that poor people put health at risk by limiting their usage. It was calculated in 1877 that this practice enabled rates to be reduced from 2s in the pound (10 per cent) to 1s 3d in the pound (6¼ per cent).[102]

Fired up, Napier persuaded the secretary of state to amend the law so that the governor would have far more control over the commission's operations. He even tried, though unsuccessfully, to reduce to six the civilian membership of the commission and to increase to six the representation of the government and the military, and to give the governor the casting vote.[103] At present, he claimed,

99 TNA, CO91/359, Napier to Kimberley, 24 June 1882; CO91/360, Napier to Kimberley, 7 Dec 1882; GGA, Despatches from Gibraltar 1883: memo by Gifford, 12 April, with Adye to Derby, 19 April 1883. See also CO879/12/6, 'Report of an Inquiry into the Working and Administration of the Gibraltar Sanitary Commission', 1877, for other suggestions of incompetence.

100 TNA, CO91/360, Napier to Kimberley, 16 Oct 1882.

101 TNA, CO91/356, draft clause, Attorney-General to Colonial Secretary, 8 June 1881, with Napier to Kimberley, 27 June 1881; CO91/359, Napier to Kimberley, 24 June 1882, Attorney-General to Colonial Secretary, 17 May 1882, and minute of 7 July 1882; also in GGA: Despatches from Gibraltar 1882.

102 TNA, CO879/12/6, 'Report of an Inquiry into the Working and Administration of the Gibraltar Sanitary Commission', pp. 5–8, 19; CO91/359, Napier to Kimberley, 24 June 1882, and Attorney-General to Colonial Secretary 17 May 1882, minute of 7 July 1882; CO91/360, Napier to Kimberley, 16 Oct 1882; CO91/360, Colonial Secretary to Sanitary Commissioners, 17 Oct 1882, with Napier to Kimberley, 16 Oct 1882. In 1912, by when separate accounts were kept, the rates, by then 2s 6d in the pound (12½ per cent), raised £23,757, whereas the sale of brackish water for sanitary purposes brought in £11,859 and of electricity £16,842 (and a profit of £1,950): see *Gibraltar Annual Reports*, and especially HCPP, *Gibraltar: Report for 1912*, Cd.6667, 1913, p. 6.

103 TNA, CO91/356, Napier to Kimberley, 27 June 1881, enclosing Attorney-General to Colonial Secretary, 8 June 1881; CO91/359, Napier to Kimberley, 24 June 1882.

'the Civil Commissioners can always command a majority and can veto or
delay every public work of necessity or improvement however urgently it may
be required for the public health or convenience'.[104] By December 1882, senior
figures in the Colonial Office had even concluded that the 'original creation
of the Commission was a grave mistake' and that its suppression would allow
necessary work to be done 'without the corrupt and inefficient intervention of
an unprecedented body'.[105]

The order-in-council of July 1883 certainly shifted the balance of power. It
authorised the governor to insist that works he deemed necessary should be put
into effect, entitled him to choose the senior personnel to be employed by the
Sanitary Commission and particularly declared that the army's chief engineer
should also be the Sanitary Commission's engineer. This 'counter-revolution'
led to fierce objections by the civilian commissioners. A petition of protest was
signed by 245 'Inhabitants and Ratepayers' and hostile resolutions were launched
by the Chamber of Commerce, the Exchange Committee and the Grand Jury
– though it should be understood that between these bodies there was a considerable overlap in personnel, and certainly all were drawn from the same propertied
and moneyed section of society and, more specifically, of the ratepayers.[106]

Napier's successor, Sir John Adye, was obviously concerned by the strength
of opposition to the new law,[107] and he was placed in a difficult position when,
in September 1883, all but one of the eight civilian members of the Sanitary
Commission resigned (and the one who remained was driven shortly to follow).
No one else agreed to serve. The Sanitary Commission was, in effect, reduced to
its rump of four officials.[108] Colonial Office staff had earlier expected and even
hoped for this outcome, as a prelude to closing the thing down altogether.[109]
However, Adye confessed to some sympathy for civilian commissioners who had
voluntarily taken on public duties, and he believed that the new law was unneces-
sarily stringent. He argued that the 'Government is really stronger and the people
more likely to be contented by having representatives of their own than if they

---

104 TNA, CO91/359, Napier to Kimberley, 24 June 1882.
105 TNA, CO91/360, minutes on Napier to Kimberley, 5 Dec 1882, telegram
     Kimberley to Napier, 16 Dec 1882. Similarly, GGA, Despatches from Gibraltar
     1883: memo by Lord Gifford, Colonial Secretary, 12 April, with Adye to Derby,
     19 April 1883.
106 TNA, CO91/363, and GGA, Despatches from Gibraltar 1883: Adye to Derby, 19
     April 1883, and enclosures, and Adye to Derby, 7 May 1883, with Memorial from
     Ratepayers, 28 April 1883.
107 TNA, CO91/363, Adye to Derby, 19 April 1883.
108 TNA, CO91/365, Adye to Derby, 2 Oct 1883; and see also GGA, Despatches from
     Gibraltar 1883: memos with Adye to Derby, 30 Oct 1883.
109 TNA, CO91/360, minutes on Napier to Kimberley, 18 Dec 1882, and Derby to
     Adye, 13 Jan 1883.

were taxed by a Commission composed solely of Government officials'.[110] When the possibility of non-payment of rates was raised, Adye was even more inclined to revert to the previous law, arguing, like some latter-day American revolutionary, that 'Representation even at Gibraltar should go with Taxation'.[111] For such sentiments one growling Colonial Office civil servant was later to declare that he was 'not altogether the right man in a Fortress'.[112] Nevertheless, battered by yet more protests from the Exchange Committee, and then by a personal visit by Adye to the secretary of state,[113] the Colonial Office caved in and an ordinance was passed in October 1884 which largely restored the earlier arrangements.[114]

Actually, Adye seems to have later regretted this reversal.[115] Certainly, his successor, Sir Arthur Hardinge, was unimpressed by what he had inherited, and in January 1889 proposed another review.[116] This was then subsumed into a wider investigation by the Colonial Office, War Office and Admiralty which also embraced other equally contentious political issues (addressed in previous chapters), namely, reducing alien numbers and population growth and restricting the tobacco trade and smuggling.[117] A report in March 1889 acknowledged that public health had improved, but claimed that the commissioners had become less, not more, effective in recent years and that, for instance, they had not introduced by-laws as they should to enforce housing improvements. There was therefore a case for altering the composition of the commission so as to give greater weight to crown representatives. However, bruised by past experience, the committee backed off from recommending the sort of change which had caused such recent ructions. 'It would be a mistake to assume', they concluded, 'that the people of Gibraltar, because they have no political institutions, are incapable of combining for political purposes, or ignorant of the methods of conducting

110 TNA, CO91/363, Adye to Derby, 19 April 1883; CO91/365, Adye to Derby, 2 Oct 1883.
111 TNA, CO91/365, Adye to Derby, 30 Oct 1883.
112 TNA, CO91/366, minute of 15 Feb on Adye to Derby, 4 Feb 1884.
113 TNA, CO91/365, and GGA, Despatches to Gibraltar 1883: Adye to Derby, 1 Nov 1883, and resolution passed by a meeting of the Exchange Committee on 9 Nov with Amigo to Gifford, 14 Nov, attached to Adye to Derby, 15 Nov 1883; GGA, Despatches to Gibraltar 1884: Derby to Adye, 27 June 1884.
114 The narrative between Nov 1883 and Nov 1884 can be traced in correspondence and minutes in TNA, CO91/365 and 366 and GGA, Despatches from/to Gibraltar 1883 and 1884.
115 TNA, ADM116/799, Attorney-General to Colonial Secretary, 2 June 1891, with Colonial Office to Admiralty, 1 July 1891.
116 TNA, CO91/386 and GGA, Despatches from Gibraltar 1889: Hardinge to Knutsford, 5 Jan 1889, and report from Colonial Secretary.
117 TNA, CO883/4/10, /12, /14, /16, /17, and /19; and see CO91/391, minute 22 June 1889 attached to Smyth to Knutsford, 23 Oct 1890.

an agitation in Parliament and the English press.' This acknowledgement of the political power of civilians – bearing in mind that those involved were only the ratepayers – was coupled with a recognition that one virtue of a system which gave civilians the majority voice on the Sanitary Commission was that ratepayers submitted 'quietly' to the 'imposition of the heavy municipal rates' (though it was conceded that the burden on the military population was per head almost twice as much as that on civilians).[118]

This was not the view of the then Principal Medical Officer in Gibraltar or of all Colonial Office staff. They favoured additional representation of officials on the commission.[119] Nor was it the view of Major Tulloch, later described as the 'highest sanitary engineering authority' in Britain, who had been brought in by the Colonial Office as consulting engineer for the major drainage and water supply projects, shortly to be undertaken to his specifications. His criticisms, expressed in colourful phrases in a report in May 1890, rehearsed all previous arguments about the composition and members of the commission, the limited expertise of their civil engineer, their inadequate public health measures to date and their preoccupation with keeping down the rates.[120] This report swayed the Colonial Office again in favour of a reconstruction.[121] This was also the view of Sir Leicester Smyth, who took over as governor in August 1890 and who, in October, sent in a devastating review of the commission's mistakes, malpractice and membership. He claimed that it was no longer a body which attracted adequate people and therefore the civilian membership should be reduced.[122]

Smyth's illness and premature death interrupted matters, but his successor, Sir Lothian Nicholson, pressed on, with Colonial Office support.[123] A new order-

118 TNA, CO883/4/16, 'Report of a Departmental Committee on the Civil Population and Smuggling in Relation to Defence, 23 March 1889'.
119 TNA, CO91/391, 'Notes relative to Sanitary Arrangements at Gibraltar' and minutes, attached to Smyth to Knutsford, 23 Oct 1890.
120 TNA, ADM116/799, Tulloch to Sir Montagu Ommanney, Crown Agent, 5 May 1890. He even accused commissioners of operating inefficient, coal-guzzling pumping engines because they had a vested interest in coal sales. This report, though edited to remove some of the more provocative and insulting paragraphs, was published as HCPP, *Correspondence respecting the Amendment to the Gibraltar Sanitary Order in Council*, C.6690, 1892. This report is not to be confused with Tulloch's 'Water Supply and Sewerage of Gibraltar', dated 30 April 1890, in which he set out his civil engineering proposals: GGA, Water Supply Box. See also TNA, CO91/411, Ommanney to Colonial Office, 16 March 1895.
121 TNA, CO91/391, draft despatch Knutsford to Smyth, 6 May 1890, with Smyth to Knutsford, 23 Oct 1890; copy also on ADM116/779.
122 TNA, CO91/391, and GGA, Despatches from Gibraltar 1890: Smyth to Knutsford, 23 Oct 1890.
123 TNA, CO91/395, and GGA, Despatches from Gibraltar 1891: Nicholson to Knutsford, 10 June and 24 July 1891; HCPP, *Gibraltar Sanitary Order in Council*, 1892.

in-council, drafted by July 1891, was passed on 26 September. This amendment to the law extended the range of public health matters upon which the commission could (and should) make by-laws, but increased the governor's control over construction work, gave him and not the commission itself the authority to choose its chairman and, most important, altered once more the composition of the commission and gave to the governor greater powers to select even its civilian members. There were henceforth to be five officials, namely the Commanding Officer Royal Engineers, the Principal Medical Officer for the garrison, someone to represent the Admiralty and two representatives of the colonial government; but civilian numbers were reduced to a minority, down from eight to a mere four, including one from the list of common jurors, who were thought to be closer to ordinary folk.[124]

The first meeting of the new commission took place on 30 October 1891. Governor Nicholson was initially pleased to report that he had been able to appoint the necessary four civilian commissioners, including Arthur Rugeroni, chairman of the previous board, and William J.S. Smith, a former member.[125] But the Colonial Office had not expected the shift in the balance of authority to be passively received,[126] so it should not have been surprised when the civilian members almost immediately resigned, when a former civilian chairman, M.A. Serfaty, objected in the press at the implied criticism of previous commissioners, and when harsh words were said the following week at a protest meeting called by the Exchange Committee and attended by a claimed 600 to 700 people. Opened by Lewis F. Imossi, chairman of the Exchange Committee, and chaired by Serfaty, the meeting concluded by forming The Gibraltar Ratepayers' Defence Association (GRDA), a title both revealing of its concern and explanatory of the composition of its committee: Francis Francia, F. Imossi, M.A. Serfaty, John P. Onetti, W. James Smith, Pablo Larios and Alexander Mosley.[127] These gentlemen knew how to exert political pressure, first by a letter of protest to the colonial government, second by complaining to the secretary of state, third by lobbying MPs and finally by despatching two delegations to London. The Grand Jury, or at least some of its members, also registered their objections in a memorial to the governor that went on to the secretary of state. [128]

124 TNA, CO91/395, Nicholson to Knutsford, 10 June 1891, minutes and reply; order-in-council proclamation, *Gibraltar Chronicle*, 28 Oct 1891.

125 TNA, CO91/396, and GGA, Despatches from Gibraltar 1891: Nicholson to Knutsford, 4 Nov 1891; *Gibraltar Chronicle*, 31 Oct 1891.

126 GGA, Despatches to Gibraltar 1891: Knutsford to Nicholson, 27 July 1891.

127 *Gibraltar Chronicle*, 13 and 18 Nov 1891.

128 See Hansard, *Parliamentary Debates*, 1892, vols 2–4, for hostile questions in the Commons about the reduction in the numbers of ratepayer representatives, 18 and 28 March, 4, 7 and 11 April, 5 and 9 May, and especially the debate in the Lords, 16 June 1892; the White Paper containing 73 pages of correspondence and reports

This combination of local and, especially, London pressure seems once again to have been effective, at least to the extent of persuading the secretary of state and the governor that some concession was needed. The former method by which the Grand Jury presented the names of those civilians from whom the governor was to make his selection was to be restored, and the authority of the governor to intervene when major projects were being debated was to be removed. The GRDA did not, of course, regard these concessions as sufficient and more followed, including allowing the commission to choose its own chairman and not making the much-criticised Commanding Officer Royal Engineers an ex officio member. But the amending ordinance passed on 10 March 1893 left the balance of the commission unchanged, whereby the official representatives had a majority of five to the civilians' four.[129] Four prominent figures on the GRDA accepted office – Francia, Larios, Mosley and Smith – but they were obviously discontented with their minority position.[130] After a year's further experience they pressed for increased civilian representation, and when this was denied they resigned. The new governor, Sir Robert Biddulph, detected no substantial public sympathy with this move, and by January 1895 he was reporting that he had appointed in their place Arthur

Footnote 128 (*cont.*)

> which the Colonial Office was obliged to publish: HCPP, *Gibraltar Sanitary Order in Council*, 1892; TNA, CO91/396 and /399, Nicholson to Knutsford, 30 Nov 1891 and 11 April 1892, forwarding protests; GGA, Dispatches from Gibraltar 1892: Nicholson to Knutsford, 27 Feb 1892, and Dispatches to Gibraltar 1892: Knutsford to Nicholson, 2 April, 13 and 30 June 1892, and Ripon to Nicholson, 30 Nov 1892, forwarding protests from GRDA to Colonial Office, and copies of 'Facts about Gibraltar', 23 March 1892, and 'Further Facts about Gibraltar', 7 April 1892, which were also circulated to MPs, the press and others; articles in *The Times* and *Daily News*. Particular animosity was directed against Tulloch and, at the public meeting and in a letter from the committee to the secretary of state, against Captain Buckle, Commanding Officer Royal Engineers, now placed on the commission by the new order-in-council. Indeed, the governor felt compelled to conduct an official inquiry into Buckle's conduct, which exonerated him: GGA, Despatches from Gibraltar 1891: Buckle to colonial secretary, 31 Dec 1891, 'Report of the Commissioners appointed . . . 30 Nov 1891', 18 Dec 1891; Despatches to Gibraltar 1892: Knutsford to Nicholson, 4 Aug 1892.

129 TNA, CO91/399 and 400, and GGA, Despatches from/to Gibraltar 1892: Nicholson to Knutsford and later Ripon, 30 April, 2 May, 9 July, 11, 20 and 30 Aug, and 1 and 8 Sept, 17 and 24 Dec 1892, and attachments and replies; CO91/402, and Despatches from/to Gibraltar 1893: Nicholson to Ripon, 11, 13, 24 Feb 1893, and attachments and replies; Ordinance to Amend the Sanitary Order Amendment Order, Gibraltar, 1891, 10 March 1893. Ripon succeeded Knutsford as secretary of state when Gladstone's fourth Liberal government was formed.

130 GGA, Despatches to Gibraltar 1893: Ripon to Nicholson, 20 April 1893.

Rugeroni and Moses Bergel, former commission members, plus Isaac Levy and Joseph Patron. They were 'men of position and influence [who] represent large interests in Gibraltar'. In other words, some members of Gibraltar's moneyed class settled down to work within the parameters of power laid down by the colonial and imperial governments.[131]

One might reasonably interpret this thirty-year political history of the Sanitary Commission as one in which the British authorities lost a few battles but won the war, in the sense that the commission which they eventually secured had a composition, powers and agenda more aligned to imperial priorities than did that of 1865. Moreover, good works were being done, improvements achieved in civilian health put the garrison less at risk, and ratepayers were being taxed at levels beyond anything they would earlier have tolerated: 2s 6d in the pound (12.5 per cent) by 1913.[132] The public health ordinance of 1907 consolidated the law and left unchanged the composition of the commission and the respective authority of commissioners and governors.[133]

One might also deduce from the ending of the story that only a minority of self-interested personnel cared anyway. Certainly this is not evidence of the onward march of popular democracy. The actual management of the Sanitary Commission was only ever a business which directly concerned ratepayers, and they, as property owners, were only ever a minority: 2,047 out of a civil population of 19,859 in 1891.[134] Even the largest public meeting claimed attendance by only one-third of the ratepayers. Certainly some of those concerned were not well off: those living on the margins had most reason to be concerned by rising rates. But some of those among the better-off lacked moral credibility, since their self-interest could be nakedly revealed. The Exchange Committee complained to the governor in 1884 that the building restrictions imposed by the Sanitary Commission, the rates it levied and the cost of the water it supplied meant that investment in housing had become 'unremunerative'. Apparently, 'poor people' could not pay the rents which, of course, were set by many of their members, who also decided on the wages they would pay for labour.[135]

131 TNA, CO91/407, Biddulph to Ripon, 22 Oct 1894, enclosure from civilian commissioners, minutes and reply; CO91/409, Biddulph to Ripon, 2 Jan 1895, plus Biddulph letter of 3 Jan and resignation letter from civilian commissioner 12 Dec 1894, and Biddulph to Ripon, 28 Jan 1895.

132 HCPP, *Gibraltar: Report for 1913*, Cd.7050, 1914, p. 6.

133 Public Health Ordinance, No 10 of 1907, in B.H.T. Frere (ed.), *The Consolidated Laws of Gibraltar* (Gibraltar: Gibraltar Government, 1913), vol. 1, pp. 488–629. While further laws followed, this principal act was not replaced until 1950.

134 TNA, ADM116/799, Attorney-General to Colonial Secretary 2 June 1891, with Colonial Office to Admiralty, 1 July 1891; GGA, Despatches from Gibraltar 1891: Smyth to Knutsford, 10 June 1891.

135 TNA, CO91/367 with Adye to Derby, 19 Sept 1884, enclosing letter from Amigo.

It is difficult to assess accurately all the detailed official criticisms of the work of the Sanitary Commission, though it is likely, in the small and intimate society of the moneyed class, that there was a degree of jobbery, and also that some mistakes were made, since the civilian commissioners were busy men and giving of their time freely. (Not even the blue-eyed boy of sanitary engineering, Major Tulloch, escaped a roasting in 1897, when the cost of the drainage scheme he designed massively exceeded his estimates.)[136] But in any case, for our purposes this is not the point, since it is the politics, not the pipes, which are here our concern.

Undoubtedly many of the protests from civilian commissioners stemmed from the damage to their personal reputations which they felt had been inflicted when governors and secretaries of state explained why, to achieve necessary improvements in public health, the numbers and responsibilities of this once entirely civilian body had to be reduced. Their 'business qualities and abilities', it was said, had been publicly called into question.[137] It was also argued, not unreasonably, that permanent civilian residents had more knowledge of local circumstances than did transient officials, though whether that translated into disinterested judgement was, of course, another matter.[138] It was also not a bad debating point to assert that, since the civilian population considerably exceeded the size of the garrison, and since most of the amounts raised by rates came from the former not the latter, then at least the majority of commissioners should represent the civilian ratepayers, though this argument became less robust when capital funding was factored in.[139]

But more important is the language of political rights which representatives of the ratepayers invariably used. Objections to change were always based on an appeal to law. The original order-in-council of 1865, it was said, correctly enough, had allowed a panel of civilian representatives to enforce laws and raise and spend money pretty much independently of the governor. The 'independ-

---

136 TNA, CO91/411, Crown Agents to Colonial Office, 16 March 1895; CO91/409, Biddulph to Ripon, 30 March 1895; GGA, Water Supply Box: reports on Tulloch scheme by W. Isaac Henry, 1892, and by W. Wallace Copland, 1894, and response by Tulloch, 1895 and 1896, report by Sanitary Commission on committee hearings in the House of Commons, 1893–94; HCPP, *Gibraltar: Papers relating to an Excess upon the Estimated Cost of the Drainage Works*, C.8668, 1897.

137 TNA, CO91/363, and GGA, Despatches from Gibraltar 1883: Sanitary Commissioners to Colonial Secretary, 6 April, and memorial 13 April, with Adye to Derby, 19 April 1883.

138 TNA, CO91/359, and GGA: Despatches from Gibraltar 1882: Sanitary Commissioners to Colonial Secretary, 9 March 1882, with Napier to Kimberley, 24 June 1882.

139 For example, GRDA to Colonial Office, 25 Nov and 24 Dec 1891, in HCPP, C.6690, *Gibraltar Sanitary Order in Council*, 1892.

ence of the Commissioners and of the Ratepayers' which was then granted was repeatedly stressed when it was under challenge.[140] Hence commissioners were prepared even to reject instructions from the secretary of state (over accepting the Commanding Officer Royal Engineers in place of their own civil engineer) and refused to allow their already audited accounts to be re-examined by a committee appointed by the governor.[141] There were also objections when the authorities departed if not from law then at least from accumulated past practice, for example when the order-in-council of 1891 was not published in advance for public comment.[142]

The Colonial Office, it was said, was employing 'un-English' methods.[143] This appeal to English law and practice was repeatedly made – for good reasons when a lobbying of political opinion via the English press and in parliament was under way. But still more remarkable were the complaints that the amendments which reduced the independence of civilian commissioners were 'entirely opposed to the spirit and intention of all Local Government Acts which require that the proposals to raise and expend money in any district shall originate with the local bodies'.[144] The 1865 order-in-council had placed 'the management of their local affairs' in the hands of civilian commissioners, and it followed that their powers should 'not be less than those granted to similar bodies in England'.[145] Indeed, what Gibraltar deserved, it was said, was only that which was characteristic of municipal government elsewhere in the colonial empire as well as in Britain.[146] Moreover, this initial 'measure of local self-government',[147] it was later claimed, was intended to be 'but the precursor of more extended liberty' and 'the people

---

140 As examples see GGA: Minutes of Proceedings of the Sanitary Commission 1879–83, 2 April 1883, and GRDA to Colonial Office, 25 Nov 1891, in HCPP, *Gibraltar Sanitary Order in Council*, 1892.

141 TNA, CO91/360, Napier to Kimberley, 18 Dec 1882.

142 GRDA to Colonial Office, 25 Nov 1891, in HCPP, *Gibraltar Sanitary Order in Council*, 1892.

143 Motion passed at public meeting, 13 Nov 1891, *Gibraltar Chronicle*, 18 Nov 1891, p. 559.

144 TNA, CO91/359, and GGA, Despatches from Gibraltar 1882: Sanitary Commissioners to Colonial Secretary, 9 March 1882, with Napier to Kimberley, 24 June 1882.

145 TNA, CO91/359, and GGA, Despatches from Gibraltar 1882: Sanitary Commissioners to Colonial Secretary, 9 March 1882, with Napier to Kimberley, 24 June 1882.

146 GGA, Despatches from Gibraltar 1883: Memorial from Ratepayers, 28 April 1883, with Adye to Derby, 7 May 1883; 'Facts about Gibraltar', 23 March 1892, in HCPP, *Gibraltar Sanitary Order in Council*, 1892.

147 TNA, CO91/363, and GGA, Despatches from Gibraltar 1883: memorial from Sanitary Commission, 13 April 1883, with Adye to Derby 19 April 1883.

might ultimately expect to have a voice in the general conduct of the public affairs of the Colony'.[148]

There was, of course, a problem with this expectation. By 1865 town councillors in Britain had long since gained their authority through election to office. Sanitary commissioners in Gibraltar then and later lacked that legitimacy. Though they claimed to represent the 'ratepayers of Gibraltar' and were intimately acquainted with the views of at least the most-propertied who paid the most rates, they were not elected by them nor subject to recall by them. Governors chose the commissioners from a panel of names put forward by the Grand Jury, and even when that obligation was returned to them after a temporary loss, the question of electing representatives, even by the Grand Jury alone, was not seriously aired by either side. Actually, at one stage in 1891 the Colonial Office had flirted with the idea of requiring the unofficial members to be elected, but Gibraltar's attorney-general had discouraged the suggestion.[149] Only later, briefly and vaguely, did the committee of the GRDA propose that the eight representatives they wished to see restored to them should be elected annually 'in such manner as herein-after may be determined', and even so only 'by the ratepayers'; and they did not press the matter.[150] Civilian commissioners had exercised power, and still would, but the lack of an electoral mandate and the diminution in their independent authority exposed their dependent and subordinate status, more agents of government than representatives of the people.[151] Nevertheless, the political experience of battling with government and managing local affairs had raised the political consciousness of at least the ratepayers, and the moneyed class in particular.[152] Frustration, as much as success, is an educator.

Gibraltar politics: Civil to Colonial Hospital, 1815–89

Political self-assertion undoubtedly derived from other bruising encounters with the colonial authorities at this time. Enough has been said in previous chapters about the nineteenth-century politics of policy making on alien settlement in the colony and also on the vexed business of smuggling. It is, however, particularly

148 GGA, Despatches from Gibraltar 1883: as recorded, indignantly, by the colonial secretary, with Adye to Derby 19 April 1883.
149 TNA, ADM116/799, Attorney-General to Colonial Secretary, 2 June 1891, with Colonial Office to Admiralty, 1 July 1891; also CO91/395, and GGA, Despatches from Gibraltar 1891: with Nicholson to Knutsford, 10 June 1891, and minutes.
150 GRDA to Colonial Office, 25 Nov 1891, in HCPP, *Gibraltar Sanitary Order in Council*, 1892.
151 TNA, CO91/359, and GGA, Despatches from Gibraltar 1882: Napier to Kimberley, 24 June 1882, enclosing Secretary of Sanitary Commission to Colonial Secretary, 9 March 1882.
152 On this theme see Grocott, 'Moneyed Class'.

illuminating to explore briefly the politics behind the contested business of running the Civil Hospital set up by Governor Don in 1815, and its transformation into the Colonial Hospital in 1889.[153] This was another episode in which imperial notions of 'good government' clashed with civilian concepts of 'self-government', and when fortress and colony were at risk of collision.

It will be recalled that Don's hospital had been divided by religious affiliation into three parts, physically, administratively and in part financially. Most important for the future, while the governor was nominally also governor of the hospital and seems to have retained the right to approve the appointment of senior staff,[154] daily management was exercised by deputy governors, not just representing but actually elected by their co-religionists (probably in open meetings). It was, to that extent, a self-governing community hospital: but it was not financially independent. From early days it had been funded by charitable donations from the Protestant, Catholic and Jewish sections of the community and, very important, by fees paid by their better-off patients; but the hospital also needed colonial revenue, derived mainly from a tax on shipping and, oddly, on flour.[155] In the 1820s and still so in the 1870s the receipts from both sources were just about equal,[156] though of course it can be argued (and later was) that colonial revenue derived from taxes was always ultimately derived from the population at large.

The Civil Hospital seems not to have attracted serious political attention until, in 1863, the War Office conducted a review of hospital provision across the colonial empire, pretty much at the same time as the Barrack and Hospital Commission was concluding its report. The result was a very critical assessment of the hospital's physical state and inadequate staff, and the 'divided command' consequent on separate provision by religion.[157] Some further investment was made by the colonial government,[158] but the hospital suffered another critical appraisal in 1870. Again, the managerial division by religion was said to be

153 See Chapter 3 for the early history, and also S.C. Benady, *Civil Hospital and Epidemics in Gibraltar* (Grendon: Gibraltar Books, 1994).

154 For mid-century disputes between governors and the hospital's deputy governors over staffing appointments see Benady, *Civil Hospital*, pp. 33–4.

155 TNA, CO91/105, Don to Murray, 28 Jan 1830, contains an explanation of the flour tax to a puzzled secretary of state. It had been recommended by the 'principal Gentlemen of the Town'.

156 GGA, Despatches from Gibraltar 1829: contains a financial breakdown of hospital income and expenditure for 1824–28; Box: Civil and Colonial Hospital, General and Miscellaneous 1888–92: 'Civil Hospital, Gibraltar, 24 June 1875, Report of Committee', pp. 11–12; on finance see also Benady, *Civil Hospital*, pp. 60–3.

157 GGA, Despatches to Gibraltar 1863 and 1864: War Office to Codrington, 6 Feb 1863, and, with report, 19 May 1864.

158 GGA, Despatches to Gibraltar 1865: War Office to Codrington, 20 March 1865.

greatly responsible for reported defects. However, the Colonial Office shied away from recommending 'a fundamental change in the system of management', because of a feared loss of funding from charities.[159] Moreover, a suggestion that the separate charitable funds might be combined seems to have been robustly rejected by the deputy governors, defensive of vested interests.[160] This state of affairs prompted Governor Williams to order another review in 1875, which produced a similarly highly critical report on the hospital buildings and equipment, the inadequate funding, and again the inconvenience for efficient management caused by the tripartite division and, indeed, of a board of managers made up only of the three deputy governors. It was argued that trustees appointed by the governor should be added, and also independent inspectors. But the hospital management, with its deputy governors in control, ignored the recommendations, and once again government avoided the issue and opted instead for further capital investment.[161]

Nevertheless, the administration's brooding anxieties about the running of the Civil Hospital by the deputy governors remained. A further attempt to address the issue was prompted by the hospital's surgeon, who among other matters complained in his annual report early in 1883 about the funding regime, the religious divisions of the hospital and what he saw as the obstructionism of the deputy governors. Governor Adye, following a strong recommendation from his colonial secretary, Lord Gifford, accordingly set up yet another review, being careful to include on the panel representatives from each religious group (Francia, Bergel, Glassford), as well as the colonial secretary, police magistrate and inspector of health. He had management changes in mind. The Colonial Office approved of the inquiry, though it was wary of likely local opposition to an attempt to transform a Civil Hospital run by elected civilian deputy governors into a Colonial Hospital managed directly by government.[162] The Sanitary Commission experience no doubt had induced caution. Indeed, this probably explains Adye's own timid response to the report he received in September.

Unanimous on the essential points – and that should be stressed – the panel with its representatives from each religion condemned the division of wards by religion, the complex and inadequate funding methods and much else, and

159 TNA, CO92/30, Granville to Airey, 12 May 1870.
160 Benady, *Civil Hospital*, pp. 35–6; TNA, CO91/369, Exchange Committee to Colonial Secretary, 4 April, with Adye to Derby, 14 April 1885.
161 GGA, Box: Civil and Colonial Hospital, General and Miscellaneous 1888–92: 'Civil Hospital, Gibraltar', 24 June 1875, Report of Committee'; also Benady, *Civil Hospital*, pp. 35–40.
162 TNA, CO91/362, Adye to Derby, 24 March and 11 April, 1883, and minutes; also in GGA, Bound Volume of Despatches from Gibraltar 1880–83.

recommended a complete take-over of management and finance by the government. However, Adye argued that this would 'deprive the Inhabitants of all interest in the Hospital' and that the expected fall-off in charitable donations would have to be met out of colonial revenues; but it is just as likely that he feared another public rumpus.[163] Hence the reforms, which, after debate with the Colonial Office and after much further consultation with representatives of the religious communities, eventually formed only a mildly modifying Civil Hospital Ordinance in April 1885. True, the wards distinguished by religion were ended and the separate funds were combined into one pot,[164] but a certain number of beds was allocated to each religious community; and while the Board of Deputy Governors was enlarged, its core remained the three elected religious representatives, to whom were added one to speak on behalf of the Roman Catholic Gavino Trust (the only substantial charity donor), plus one medical officer chosen by the governor and one representative of the colonial government.[165] Without kicking up a fuss, Gibraltar's 'public opinion' was inhibiting change. Even so, this mild alteration did not prevent the Exchange Committee from reacting – late, critically and incoherently – against the changed composition of the Board of Deputy Governors after the draft law, in the usual form, had been published in the *Gibraltar Chronicle*. This was, they claimed, interference with the 'acquired rights of the public'.[166] There was shortly to be more such talk.

A new governor but an old complaint: in September 1888 Sir Arthur Hardinge insisted to the Colonial Office that 'the time has arrived' to address what he believed were the continuing managerial weaknesses of the Civil Hospital.[167] It must be turned into a 'Government Institution' run by an 'Executive Board' made up of personnel 'nominated and appointed by the Governor'. The immediate prompt was one again a critical report, this time by the garrison's Principal Medical Officer, Surgeon-General MacKinnon, who criticised a management

---

163 TNA, CO91/365, Adye to Derby, 19 Nov 1883, enclosing 'Report of Committee on future Administration of the Gibraltar Civil Hospital, 19 Sept 1883'.

164 The debts of the Protestant and Roman Catholic funds, which were supposed to fund their portion of hospital costs, had first to be wiped out with government funds: TNA, CO91/366, Adye to Derby, 1 April 1884.

165 For the drafting of the Civil Hospital Ordinance, No 3 of 1885, passed 6 April 1885, see GGA, Dispatches to Gibraltar 1884: Derby to Adye, 3 Jan 1884; TNA, CO91/369, and Dispatches to/from Gibraltar 1885: Adye to Derby 31 Jan 1885 and enclosures, and Derby to Adye, 16 Feb 1885.

166 TNA, CO91/369, Exchange Committee to Colonial Secretary, 4 and 7 April, with Adye to Derby, 14 April 1885.

167 TNA, CO91/383, and GGA, Despatches from Gibraltar 1888: Hardinge to Knutsford, 20 Sept 1888, enclosures and minutes, Knutsford to Hardinge, 8 Nov 1888.

which, among other failings, still allocated hospital beds not by medical or surgical requirements only but also by religion, which expected the senior surgeon, the man in overall charge, to act also as secretary and treasurer, and which tolerated other staffing inadequacies. Proposals for change put forward to the board by the two official representatives were, it was said, overruled by the four civilian deputy governors. Hardinge also stressed the financial basis behind the government's claim to primary control. The crown had first provided the site for the hospital, and the colonial government had recently made substantial investments in its fabric and had even paid off the debts of the institution. Moreover, the running costs of the hospital came overwhelmingly from the government (£1,686, plus £100 from the War Department) and fee-paying patients (£1,364), whereas charitable donations, in which the community took such pride, were trivial (Gavino's trust £267, voluntary contributions a mere £65). Evidently the modesty of Adye's reform had not encouraged the community to dig deep into their pockets in support of 'their' local hospital.

It was politically naive of Hardinge to assert that 'reform would not meet with serious opposition from any portion of the community'. In fact, he immediately faced a problem when Dr Baggetto, the senior surgeon in charge, was asked to resign. Baggetto was regarded by officials as by now too old (aged 60, the retirement age, it was said, of surgeons in England) and too worn out to provide the necessary leadership; but he refused to go quietly. This prompted another supposedly independent review of the hospital management by the garrison's surgeon-major and no less a person than the colony's chief justice which, unsurprisingly, confirmed the administration's views of financial, administrative and medical mismanagement (including some horror stories), but this only further provoked Baggetto and the civilian deputy governors into highly public and defensive responses.[168] Hardinge was so undeterred by these protests that he made further amendments to his draft ordinance which entirely eliminated representatives of the colony's religious communities from the hospital's governing body, even at the cost of losing an income from Gavino's trust and other minor charity sources. In this form, and after the usual draft had been published, the reforming Colonial Hospital Ordinance was passed in September 1889. It turned the former Civil Hospital, which had been largely self-managed by elected representatives of Gibraltar's religious societies, into the Colonial

168 GGA, Box: Hospitals, Colonial Hospital Rules and Ordinances, 1889–1913: Sir Henry Burford-Hancock, chief justice, and surgeon-major Robert Collins, 'Report of the Commissioners . . . to Enquire into . . . the Civil Hospital', 12 Jan 1889; TNA, CO91/386, and Despatches from/to Gibraltar 1889: Hardinge to Knutsford, 19 Jan 1889, and enclosures, and Knutsford to Hardinge, 9 April 1889; Benady, *Civil Hospital*, pp. 40–3; Finlayson, *Stories from the Rock*, pp. 54–8.

Hospital, a government institution administered on supposedly more efficient and professional lines by a board of six government-appointed commissioners, including the garrison's principal medical officer. Funding was expected to come from government revenue and patients' fees.[169]

The 'nationalisation' under government control of institutions formally self-managed by representatives of local communities, especially those in the voluntary sector, invariably provoke resistance, as Aneurin Bevan experienced in Britain when creating the National Health Service in 1946.[170] It is, however, important to listen to the political rhetoric which informs the resistance. In Gibraltar objections were not rooted in the defence of the rights of religious groups to care for their own or even of the moral superiority of institutions supported by philanthropy, probably because the evidence that the Civil Hospital was a charitable foundation had become impossible to argue. Rather, protestors claimed that the transformation of the significantly named *Civil* Hospital into the equally pointed *Colonial* Hospital represented a reduction in their right to civilian self-government and an increase in the power of an authoritarian colonial government. *Mons Calpe*, a local newspaper, protested that the government was 'dispossessing us', going so far as to claim that the hospital had been funded 'not only principally but exclusively' by the civilian population. It also asserted that it was 'perfectly well administered in an admirable state of cleanliness', thereby challenging the government's argument that 'self-government' had proved incompatible with 'good government'. Moreover, unless protests were made, it was argued, 'we may well prepare ourselves for our complete nullity in all local public matters'. The rhetoric also typically appealed to best constitutional practice – and that meant British – with an appeal to 'that spirit of constitutionality and fair play which characterize the English people'. The final flourish was expressions of loyalty to the crown. *El Calpense* adopted the same line, claimed that the Civil Hospital was 'founded for the public', was 'the property of the public', and had been enlarged with 'local funds . . . done with our monies'. It therefore objected to the dispossession and urged the public to protest.[171]

The Exchange Committee, or at least its chairman, Lionel Imossi, took the rhetoric one step further. His extended complaint about the governor's

169 TNA, CO91/388, and GGA, Despatches from/to Gibraltar: Hardinge to Knutsford, 8, 22 and 27 May, 6 July, 8, 23 and 24 Aug, 11 Sept and 1 Oct 1889, and replies; Colonial Hospital Ordinance, No 13 of 1889, passed 10 Sept 1889.

170 C. Webster, *The Health Service since the War* (London: HMSO, 1988), vol. 1, pp. 88–94.

171 GGA, Box: Reconstruction of the Civil Hospital 1877–1888: copies of translations from *Mons Calpe* and *El Calpense*, 30 July 1889, and see also flyer announcing public protest meeting.

proposed reforms was prefaced by a broader objection to the lack of influence which 'the Inhabitants' had over the 'shower' of ordinances to which they were being subjected. He claimed that it was 'incredible' that local government in Gibraltar was the same as it was a century ago, whereas elsewhere the authority of other colonial governors had been moderated. In language which even in the 1880s would not be regarded as dignified, he went on to complain that 'though the Inhabitants of Gibraltar do not belong to the Nigger race they are not allowed a Legislative or Consultative Body as is the case in every other Colony belonging to H[er] M[ajesty]'. Indeed, although the inhabitants of Gibraltar were 'the most loyal of Her Majesty's loyal servants', they 'still continue under the yoke of bondage'. Having distanced Gibraltarian civilians from Africans and then adopted the language of black American slaves to describe their condition, it is disappointing, perhaps, that the rest of Imossi's seven-page text had nothing further to demand specifically about representative, let alone responsible, civic government. Instead, he fretted over the unacceptable manner in which the hospital's secretary had recently been appointed and the professional failings of the colonial engineer, and how the commission of inquiry had been improperly set up and had imperfectly carried out its review.[172] There was nothing here, or in any other protest over the hospital, any more than over the Sanitary Commission, which seriously claimed the right to municipal self-government. Nevertheless, the political rhetoric confirmed that, by the end of the century, at least the moneyed class had become sufficiently self-aware politically to present itself in Gibraltar as 'Her Majesty's Loyal Opposition'.

Conclusion

In Gibraltar during the nineteenth century therefore, as elsewhere in the western capitalist world, the state had increased its authority over the people by legislative extension. It had extended, on English models, a legal system and methods of policing; it was trying, fairly successfully, to control entry into its territory and, especially, residence within; it had established an economic infrastructure in which private enterprise could operate; it had taken considerable steps to improve the sanitary environment in which people lived their lives; it had established a sufficient tax system, albeit only to levy indirect taxes with their usual regressive impact, to cover recurrent annual

172 GGA, Box: Exchange and Commercial Library: Exchange Committee Book No 12, April 1886–Oct 1905, Imossi to David Garson, 8 Jan 1889, instructing him, a barrister in Manchester, to write in protest to the Secretary Of State; see TNA, CO91/389, Garson to Knutsford, 18 Jan 1889, and others.

government expenditure; it had also cajoled property owners into accepting a rating system which paid for many civic services and public utilities and serviced capital investment costs; it had also left room for voluntary sector activities; and, of course, it otherwise intruded little into religious matters and family and private life.

But this was a British colony and the rules were largely set in an authoritarian manner by governors appointed by the crown and with the advice and sometimes on the instruction of ministers and ministries in London. Nevertheless, civilians were not powerless. For one thing, their incorporation into government administration, of which there were early nineteenth-century precedents, had become more extensive by the early twentieth century, particularly with respect to the Sanitary Commission. In addition, civilians were also, in effect, embedded in public administration by their management in the voluntary sector of schooling and even of charitable poor relief, thereby relieving government of greater obligations.

Civilians were also politically assertive. They had not been docile even in the eighteenth century, but subsequently they had proved themselves still more adept at exerting political pressure, and indeed very active in lobbying governors and secretaries of state. Noticeably, they employed the constitutional methods conventional in Britain – public meeting, letter, petition, memorial, delegation. Moreover, although very few were British by birth, they had learnt how to secure contacts in Britain through which to exert political influence. The Manchester Chamber of Commerce, of course, shared their economic concerns and was a frequent ally when such matters as quarantine laws or smuggling, also known as free trade, became issues in Gibraltar. Articles in the press, particularly in *The Times*, by 'our special correspondent' indicated briefing from Gibraltar sources. Ministers were also sensitive to criticisms of their administration of Gibraltar when Members of Parliament, and indeed peers of the realm in the House of Lords, wrote to or visited the War Office or Colonial Office or stood up on their hind legs and asked parliamentary questions. As the narrative shows, such pressure was not always or even commonly successful, but knowledge that 'public opinion' in Britain as well as in Gibraltar could be aroused did, sometimes, inhibit some governors and ministers from certain actions. In any event, the art of protest and the practice of self-assertion certainly generated in Gibraltar's colony a greater sense of a civilian community with interests and aspirations distinct from those of the fortress commander and the garrison.

But of course this identity, these interests and this lobbying did not produce self-government in Gibraltar with respect to the territory's internal or even merely municipal affairs. If anything, the formal and institutional opportunities for self-government diminished when civilians lost their monopoly of representation on the Sanitary Commission and when they were entirely excluded from managing the hospital. Elsewhere in the British Empire, as the nineteenth century progressed, governors were institutionally consulting civilians via legislative assemblies and even in executive councils, and of course the governors of colonies of white settlement were, in internal affairs, doing more reigning and less ruling, like the monarch whom they represented. In Gibraltar, not even the limited powers of an elected parish council had been devolved to civilians, still less the full panoply of municipal self-government with councillors, aldermen, maces and mayoral chains, and elections.

Of course, one reason for this was that it was not to be allowed. It is not enough to show that governors and colonial secretaries, and ministers and civil servants, privately and repeatedly stressed that, for them, Gibraltar always had been and always would be primarily a fortress and, latterly, a naval base. What was more important was that civilians were made aware of that official view. This was partly accomplished by the very presence of 5,000 or more soldiers compressed into the two square miles of space, plus the increasing number of naval ratings, with whom the civilians had to cope; and there is no reason to believe that bored squaddies or drunken sailors or snobbish officers treated civilians characteristically with respect and as equals. In addition, the greatest transformations of the physical environment of the Rock where civilians lived were effected by the armed services, namely more walls, more barracks, a massive naval hospital and a huge naval dockyard. Further, the pageantry of Gibraltar was intensely military, from parades and bands to the celebration of royal events and visits and the flummery of the arrival and departure of regiments, fleets and governors. And finally, governors themselves, in full dress military uniforms and funny hats, asserted authority in their appearance as well as in their words and, still more tellingly, in their actions.

It has been argued that assertions of power by those in authority can induce political quiescence, the prospects of success appearing so hopeless to those in opposition.[173] However, this does not quite fit with the vigour with which some civilians made their protests and, from time to time, asserted their 'rights'. Therefore, perhaps a further reason why municipal self-government – let alone colonial representative government and, still less, colonial responsible government – was not in place in Gibraltar even by 1914 was that civilians did not press for it. As the nineteenth century unfolded, all such innovations in the colonial empire and in Britain implied elections – however much the franchise might be restricted, in the empire by ethnicity or in Britain by social class or everywhere by gender – in order to give a legitimacy to those exerting power or to those acting as watchdogs on those wielding it. It is exceptional to see demands for the introduction of anything like an electoral system in Gibraltar, and such as

173 A. Warde, 'Working-class quiescence in Lancaster in the 20th century', *International Review of Social History*, 35 (1990), 71–105.

have been detected are vague in detail and barely pressed. A consultative council proposed by the Chamber of Commerce in 1891 was to be 'composed in part of representative members of this Community', but there was no suggestion that these representatives might be elected by popular vote, or indeed elected at all.[174] True, the Exchange Committee asked again in 1911 for an increase in civilian representation on the Sanitary Commission, and indeed proposed that those members might be elected by ratepayers, but the Colonial Office appears to have had no difficulty in swatting the idea.[175] There were 'elections' in Gibraltar, to the committee of the Exchange and Commercial Library, and (until 1889) of deputy governors of the hospital. It remains unclear as to who was entitled to stand, or who was entitled to vote (supposedly inhabitants for the former and co-religionists for the latter) or how voting was conducted (probably openly in public meetings by those who bothered to turn up, and not by secret ballot). Those 'elected' commonly claimed to speak for the 'inhabitants', but so did the Chamber of Commerce, whose officials certainly could not claim a popular mandate.

And here, in fact, is the issue. The 'civilians' to which reference has been made frequently in the preceding paragraphs, demanding this and that of government and becoming politically self-aware, should not be equated with even a majority of the civilian population, nor even with British subjects entitled to permanent residence. The evidence is overwhelming that civilian politics was confined pretty much to the wealthy, moneyed class of businessmen, large property owners and 'gentlemen', plus religious leaders, and it extended at most to include some less well-off ratepayers. The manual working class, the hawker, the scavenger, even the small trader, and certainly those resident on temporary permits, appear not to have been politically active. Moreover, there seems to have been not just no effort by social superiors to politicise them, but a reluctance even to try, and it is necessary to consider why.

Much of the politics of the period concerned the advancing or defence of the particular economic interests of employers (the admission of alien labour, quarantine, smuggling, tariffs) or the authority and status of civic leaders (as members of the Sanitary Commission or deputy governors of the Civic Hospital). There was a politics, too, of desiring recognition of their worthiness by the governor and the governing elite. Hence the aspiration for social integration with them, for example at family wedding parties, at celebrations of royal

---

174 TNA, CO91/394, and Dispatches from Gibraltar 1891: Newdigate to Knutsford, 28 March 1891; Finlayson, *Stories from the Rock*, p. 120. Rather typically, the proposal also entailed shifting half the cost of the governor's salary from the Gibraltar to the British taxpayer.

175 TNA, CO91/447, Hunter to Harcourt, 3 Oct 1911, with enclosures, and Harcourt to Hunter, 24 Oct 1911.

events, on sporting occasions.[176] Since English was the language of government, fluency was a necessary ticket of entry, and education of sons at public schools in Britain (particularly at Roman Catholic schools like Stonyhurst) provided a necessary training for the next generation.[177] Since government signed contracts and was a big spender, there were also sound business reasons for good relations with those in power. Social bonding and economic self-interest were therefore likely to be a constraint on asserting political independence, inhibiting demands for self-government.

In any event, demands for self-government by the later nineteenth century would have involved some degree of democratic representation – popular elections. It would have been easy to deny votes for women but, given British and colonial practices, it would have been difficult to introduce changes which confined an electorate solely to the well-propertied. It is too much to say that Gibraltar was riven by class hostility, but there were social divides by occupation, income and status, and those 'with' were not uncommonly critical of, sometimes suspicious of and occasionally hostile towards those 'without'. Rude remarks about the value of native-born workers have been quoted in an earlier chapter. Such animosity was heightened by turn-of-the-century strikes. Employers in the coal-bunkering business and many others dependent on their services were antagonised in December 1890, for example, by a strike of coal-heavers, who were influenced, it was said, by anarchist agitators from Spain. A further major dispute, also involving coal-heavers, blew up in 1898, and there was an industrial dispute in the quarries in 1899 and more conflict in 1902, also involving dockyard workers. On the one hand, in 1902 the (robust) Gibraltar Employers' Federation was formed; on the other, there emerged the (fragile) Social Labourers' Federation.[178] These disputes did more than separate class from class and thereby discouraged the moneyed class from bidding for popular support for constitutional change. They also demonstrated the common interest of moneyed elite and colonial government in coping with disruption and in dealing with troublemakers, a further persuasive argument in favour of tolerating Gibraltar's existing political structure.

It may therefore be suggested that those with the self-interest, confidence and organisation to demand constitutional change had least reason to rock the boat

---

176 Grocott, 'Moneyed Class', pp. 107–12; S. Constantine, 'Monarchy and constructing identity in "British" Gibraltar, c.1800 to the present', *Journal of Imperial and Commonwealth History*, 34:1 (2006), 23–44.

177 Grocott, 'Moneyed Class', pp. 48, 101–2.

178 The underlying economic causes as well as the triggers to these disputes, plus trade union and employer organisation, and the strike-breaking role of governors, are analysed in Grocott, 'Moneyed Class', pp. 146–57, using TNA, GGA, newspaper, Hansard and memoir sources.

so seriously as to unsettle the commander; whereas those below, in the engine room and coal-bunkers, were as yet insufficiently organised, confident and focused to create their own head of political steam. During the twentieth century Gibraltar was to develop into a popular democracy. How this was initiated, by whom, how it developed and with what consequences must be the subject of later chapters.

7

Demography and the alien in the twentieth century: creating the Gibraltarian

By the end of the nineteenth century the great majority of the civilians living in Gibraltar had, legally, a secure right of residence. In most cases this was based upon laws which applied pretty much in all parts of the British Empire, of which, of course, Gibraltar with its British army garrison and Royal Navy base seemed securely and permanently a part. Through the principle of *jus soli* the native-born had acquired by birth an apparently robust entitlement, and that privilege was also supposedly enjoyed by all other subjects of the crown, whichever part of Her Majesty's dominions happened to be their place of birth, should they wish to enter and reside. However, this privilege was tempered in the case of Gibraltar, because it was still primarily perceived as a fortress by its local British government and by ministers in Whitehall. In addition, some non-British aliens had also secured conditional rights of residence, in accordance with regulations sanctioned by the 1885 Aliens Order in Council, a privilege some had enjoyed for many years and others had acquired more recently. They were accepted by the authorities, essentially because of their economic value. Residence was, of course, always subject to some notion of 'good conduct', and the parameters of that had often been tested. Moreover, for reasons already sufficiently spelt out, concerned with space, overcrowding and sanitation, British authorities remained anxious about population numbers.

Even those whose temporary permits sanctioned residence for only short periods nevertheless had an entitlement that was denied to thousands of others who were being admitted daily during working hours and who were expected to depart before evening gunfire and the closing of the gates. The presence of these ticket holders, as traders and labourers, was enormously important to service the British garrison, but also they were essential to the functioning of the civilian economy. Accordingly, the open frontier with Spain, as well as access to Gibraltar by sea, underpinned life in Gibraltar.

However, as we have seen, in the close confines of Gibraltar resident aliens holding conditional permits and aliens coming and going bearing day tickets mingled with the native-born (virtually all of whom were descendants of earlier immigrant stock). The result was closer to a melting pot than a salad bowl, blurring the boundary between British and alien which the authorities were endeavouring to maintain. Distinctions by ethnicity had never had much purchase in Gibraltar, differences by religion were rarely of importance, and segregation by place of birth also seemed of little moment for most civilians most of the time. Ethnicity, language and religion more often linked than separated, and what culture did not do, economic relations – business deals and employment – instead could effect. In spite of regulations, these crossovers were sometimes consolidated in (or out of) the marriage bed and confirmed in Gibraltar-born children. A civilian identity among residents separating them from aliens (especially Spanish) on the one hand and distinct from generalised Britishness on the other was unlikely to form in such circumstances.

That said, from the late nineteenth century, practices and identities were to receive sharp jolts. In the first place, though less of a shock than a grumbling disquiet, resident civilians were to protest at the arrival of British subjects who were unwelcome in their numbers and apparently in their character. Accordingly, civilians accepted and indeed pressed for government regulations which might exclude undesirable immigrants deemed more alien than the aliens. Then, and characteristic of the century elsewhere in the British Empire and more particularly after 1945, the imperial government eventually delegated administrative responsibility for internal affairs to a civilian government in Gibraltar. As a result, home-grown civilian ministers had to face the challenge of determining who had and who had not unconditional rights of residence, and who else might be let in and on what terms. This obligation, too, helped to shape a distinctive Gibraltarian identity. There was also a siege. It was not the First World War nor even the Second World War which in the twentieth century broke, for a while, Gibraltar's continuity with the past. Rather, it was the impediments to open access across the frontier with Spain beginning in 1954, and then the closing of the gates in 1969. This plunged relations across the isthmus back to a state not seen since the worst years of the eighteenth century, with serious effects on demographic flows and civilians' sense of their identity.

Counting the people, 1891–2001

No government, whether military or civilian, could afford not to collect information about the population within its frontiers. Demographic management had been a major concern since the beginning of the British occupation, and that required demographic accounting. By the later nineteenth century this had settled into the pattern of holding decennial censuses, in conformity with administrations throughout the British Empire,[1] and indeed by then in most

1 See R.R. Kuczynski, *Demographic Survey of the British Colonial Empire*, 3 vols (London: Oxford University Press, 1948–53).

other parts of the world. In addition, in Gibraltar the police also endeavoured to calculate the resident population each year, vividly indicative of the surveillance role it exercised over the civilian population and more than hinting at underlying official anxieties. This monitoring by official censuses and by police observation was sustained deep into the twentieth century.[2] Table 7.1 summarises the census findings.

The increase in the resident civilian population of Gibraltar by 35 per cent, over 7,000 people, in the century from 1901 to 2001 would have amazed (and dismayed) Gibraltar's earlier administrators. The increase was not caused by an accelerated natural increase. True, death rates were falling, from 21.4 deaths per 1,000 of the population in 1901, down to 14.4 deaths in 1931, 9.4 in 1961, and 8.8 in 2001; but so too was the birth rate declining in similar steps, 31.3 births per 1,000 of the population in 1901, down to 23.3 in 1931, 17.0 by 1961, 13.2 in 2001. In fact, the difference – the rate of natural increase – was falling too, 10.1, 9.9, 7.6, 4.4, and therefore the growth in population was slowing down.[3] Moreover, there were losses from emigration. The net exodus of 'Natives of Gibraltar' as well as of natives of Malta and of the United Kingdom was ascribed in 1921 to diminished employment prospects.[4] It was noted in 1951, with some relief, that emigration averaged 214 persons a year from 1946 to 1951 (overwhelmingly to the UK) and was helping to ease the impact of falling death rates on population growth. Though the figure fell to an average of 167 people a year from 1952 to 1961, it was to rise to new heights during later troubled years, to 265 a year between 1965 and 1973.[5]

Earlier administrators would still have been highly concerned at these later figures, showing the continuing growth in population, and stunned by the leap in numbers between the census of 1961 and that of 1970. They might have admired the solution to consequent accommodation problems, to build 'up' in apartment blocks and 'out' on reclaimed land in the bay, but they would

2 The different modes of counting led to disputed results: GGA, Year Files, Minute Paper (henceforth MP) 620/69, correspondence in Feb 1972.
3 Figures from *Annual Report*, 1901, p. 17; *Census 1951*, Tables 4 and 5 (for 1931); *Census 1961*, Tables 5 and 6; Government of Gibraltar, *Abstract of Statistics 2003*, 'Key Indicators, 2000–3'. There are discrepancies between the census figures (1931 onwards) and those in annual reports, derived from different computations of the base population. The decline in the crude birth rate closely paralleled that in England and Wales, and the improvement in the crude death rate was actually faster: N.L. Tranter, *British Population in the Twentieth Century* (London: Macmillan, 1966), pp. 64, 86.
4 *Census of Gibraltar 1921*, p. 3.
5 *Census of Gibraltar 1951*, p. 11 and Table 14; *Census of Gibraltar 1961*, p. 12 and Table 15; GGA, MP620/69, report 12 Sept 1974, with reservations about the absolute accuracy of the data.

Table 7.1 *Civilian population, 1891–2001*

Date	Total	Inter-census increase/decrease	Per annum increase/decrease
1891	19,100[a]		
1901	20,355[b]	+6.6%	+0.7%
1911	19,120[c]	−6.1%	−0.6%
1921	18,061[d]	−5.5%	−0.6%
1931	17,405[e]	−3.6%	−0.4%
1951	20,845[f]	+19.8%	+1.0%
1961	21,636[g]	+3.8%	+0.4%
1970	24,672[h]	+14%	+1.6%
1981	26,479[i]	+7.3%	+0.7%
1991	26,703[j]	+0.8%	+0.1%
2001	27,495[k]	+3.0%	+0.3%

Notes: As in the UK, because of the war there was no census in 1941, and the census of 1970 was held a year early for managerial reasons, following Spain's closure of the land frontier in 1969. Full census reports were only published from 1921.

[a] Plus 759 'port' people, living on stationary craft in the port, and 5,896 service personnel and families; grand total civil and service 25,755.

[b] Plus 630 'port' people and 6,475 service personnel and families; grand total civil and service 27,460.

[c] Plus 466 'port' people and 5,781 service personnel and families; grand total civil and service 25,367.

[d] Plus 479 'port' people and 3,478 service personnel and families; grand total civil and service, 22,018.

[e] Plus 208 'port' people and 3,759 service personnel and families (of whom 1,123 were family); grand total civil 18,736 and civil and service 21,372.

[f] Plus 479 'port' people, 469 transients and visitors and 1,439 service families only (excluding servicemen); grand total civil 23,232.

[g] Plus 427 transients and 149 visitors and 2,290 service families ('port' people no longer separately recorded); grand total civil 24,502.

[h] Plus 1,132 transients and visitors and 2,161 service families; grand total civil 27,965.

[i] Plus 872 transients and visitors and 2,265 service families; grand total civil 29,616.

[j] Plus 1,010 transients and visitors and 1,371 service families; grand total civil 29,084.

[k] Plus 3,383 transients and visitors (high because of a cruise ship in port) and 745 service families and civilian MOD personnel; grand total civil 31,623.

Sources: *Census of Gibraltar 2001*, Table 1, p. 1; *Census Reports* 1921–1991; *Colonial Annual Reports* 1891–1972.

have been disturbed by one of the political prompts for much of this post-war construction, the deteriorating relations with Franco's Spain. Population grew because more of the labouring population had to be accommodated within Gibraltar. Those Gibraltarians who had once lived in La Línea and crossed the

Table 7.2a *Civilian population by place of birth and nationality, 1921–61*

Place of birth	1921	1931	1951	1961
British subjects				
Gibraltar	13,874	13,702	14,660	14,999
UK/IFS/Eire	1,344	1,063	1,820	1,814
India[a]	101	92	112	98
Malta	289	196	91	63
Morocco	87	94	220	232
Spain	812	841	2,712	2,983
Others	174	158	276	315
Total	*16,681*	*16,146*	*19,891*	*20,504*
Foreign subjects				
Morocco	80	43	29	39
Portugal	24	18	13	18
Spain	1,213	1,125	1,336	1,121
Others	63	73	45	103
Total	*1,380*	*1,259*	*1,423*	*1,281*
Grand total	18,061	17,405	21,314[b]	21,785[c]

Notes: [a] The Gibraltar census of 1951 actually records just 12 British subjects born in India and 100 in Pakistan, but the number of Hindus counted was 115 and there were apparently no Muslims, strongly suggesting that the 100 were Hindus born in British India in places which subsequently became parts of Pakistan. The 1961 census records 64 British subjects born in Pakistan and 34 born in India, 123 Hindus and only 6 Muslims. It should further be noted that, under the British and Indian Nationality Acts, after India became a republic within the Commonwealth in 1949, a person could have dual British and Indian nationality, and hence these Gibraltar censuses counted them as British subjects: TNA, CO91/540/3, memorandum of 29 Sept 1951.
[b] Calculations in original include 479 'port' people: total should amount to 21,324, error in original.
[c] Calculations in original include 149 visitors.

border daily to work had found this increasingly difficult, first during the period of the Spanish Civil War, then because of frontier restrictions imposed by Franco in the 1950s, and finally after the locking of the gates between 1969 and 1985.

Tables 7.2a, b and c contain data which would also have troubled former managers. They would have been concerned by the composition of the population and indeed puzzled by its representation in the census reports themselves: how people are categorised reveals managerial intent, and has an impact on the counted.

The censuses for 1921 to 1961 were at least set out in familiar form, with a clear distinction being drawn between 'British subjects' on the one hand and 'Foreign subjects' on the other, but the Indian and Maltese components

Table 7.2b *Civilian population by place of birth and nationality, 1970 and 1981*

| Place of birth | 1970 | | | 1981 | | |
| | British subjects | | Non- | British subjects | | Non- |
	Gib'ian	Other	British	Gib'ian	Other	British
Gibraltar	15,186	292	12	15,901	696	35
UK	421	2,079	2	856	2,593	8
Spain	2,839	190	359	2,632	87	244
Portugal	48	9	191	52	8	35
Morocco	212	34	2,095	195	21	2,169
Others	167	397	124	189	301	356
Total	*18,873*	*3,001*	*2,783*	*19,825*	*3,706*	*2,923*
Grand total		*24,672*[a]			*26,454*[b]	

Notes: [a] Calculations in original exclude 15 'nationality not stated'.
[b] Calculations in original exclude 25 'nationality not stated'

Table 7.2c *Civilian population by place of birth and nationality, 1991 and 2001*

| Place of birth | 1991 | | | 2001 | | |
| | British subjects | | Non- | British subjects | | Non- |
	Gib'ian	Other	British	Gib'ian	Other	British
Gibraltar	17,173	743	78	18,860	408	173
UK	657	2,352	16	1,815	1,769	23
Spain	1,745	385	262	1,624	151	302
Morocco	184	47	1,790	197	36	874
Other EC/EU	69	62	216	139	51	231
Others	194	222	508	247	212	383
Total	*20,022*	*3,811*	*2,870*	*22,882*	*2,627*	*1,986*
Grand total		*26,703*			*27,495*	

Sources: Censuses of Gibraltar 1921–2001

in the former and the sudden increase in Spanish-born residents with British subject status are striking, as is also the large number of 'foreign' Spanish still present with permits of residence. But the structure and nomenclature of the census returns from 1970 to 2001 would have been especially bewildering to nineteenth-century administrators. From 1970, the census was dividing 'British subjects' into two, and employing the term 'Gibraltarian' to identify the majority of them. Compared with that distinguishing badge of identity, and the extraordinary increase in the number of Moroccans resident in Gibraltar, the continuing (though declining) number of the Spanish-born among British subjects would have seemed less striking.

Marginalising the 'British': the Aliens Order Extension Order-in-Council, 1900

For much of the twentieth century, as in the past, Gibraltar was perceived by British authorities primarily as a fortress with limited space in which to accommodate the 'inessential' portion of the civilian population. Accordingly, the notion remained that military needs might override the residential rights even of British subjects, including the native-born. As a Whitehall report put it in 1889, 'We take it as an admitted principle that no person, whether British subject or an alien, has an absolute right to enter or remain in the Fortress of Gibraltar contrary to the wishes and commands of the Crown and its Officers.'[6] During the Great Siege the civilian population had been pretty much ordered to leave, and something very similar was to occur during the Second World War.[7] Nevertheless, resident British subjects would have been astonished at the exercise of such power in peacetime, and indeed British governors and British ministers were not tempted to try. However, as noted earlier, there had been occasions when the authorities trying to cope with an influx of aliens had even wondered whether free rights of entry and residence for all British subjects were not a privilege too far in a garrison town. To be frank, such concerns had not cropped up when the British subjects not native to Gibraltar but becoming residents were white and usually British born and appropriately, even impeccably, qualified by profession, business or skill.

The 'problem' was the Maltese. As noted in a previous chapter, the police magistrate F. Solly Flood had in 1871 lumped Maltese immigrants with 'other strangers' as people in his view also lacking British character, even though, as natives of a territory annexed by Britain in 1800, they were indeed British subjects.[8] The census that year was the first when Maltese immigrants were officially noticed and, of all British subjects except those from the United Kingdom, separately categorised. Even so, it was civilian opinion, as expressed by Dr Scandella and the committees he fronted, which on several occasions in the 1870s condemned the Maltese in the harshest terms: 'scum', 'habituated to vice', 'dregs of society', 'a public disgrace', 'worthless' and 'filthy' were among their choice epithets,[9] though two police magistrates studying criminal statistics separately

6 TNA, CO883/4/16, Confidential Print, Med. No 33, 'Report of a Departmental Committee on the Civil Population and Smuggling in relation to Defence', 23 March 1889, p. 24. For a later but very similar statement by Gibraltar's attorney-general, 6 Jan 1937, see GGA, Box: The Alien Question, 'Memorandum on the Right of Residence in Gibraltar'.

7 T.J. Finlayson, *The Fortress Came First* (Grendon: Gibraltar Books, 1991).

8 TNA, CO879/9/16, and GGA Box: The Alien Question, Confidential Print, Appendix, Flood to Williams, 12 May 1871, p. 50.

9 TNA, CO879/9/16, Confidential Print, Africa No 97, Correspondence Respecting the Gibraltar Aliens Order in Council 1873, Scandella to Carnarvon, 31 Jan 1876, pp. 33–4;

rejected the accusation that they were particularly prone to crime.[10] However, even in official circles, attitudes against the Maltese were hardening by the late 1880s. Gifford, colonial secretary, was by then claiming that 'the convicted and criminal classes from [Malta] make Gibraltar their asylum', and he recommended to the governor that natives of Malta who had been convicted of serious crimes should not be allowed entry.[11] Like other immigrant groups late to enter settled societies elsewhere, the Maltese found themselves doing rough work, for example as refuse collectors, hawkers and, especially, coal-heavers, but it was their growing numbers – 223 in 1871, 702 by 1881, over 1,000 by 1888 – rather than occupations and supposed criminal tendencies which probably most came to trigger an official response to popular complaints.[12] In March 1889 a committee concerned with population, smuggling and defence was recommending that a new order-in-council should be framed to extend the permit system for aliens so as to cover also 'strangers' who might be British subjects but still not welcome in the tight confines of the fortress, and the Maltese were named.[13]

Nothing came of this immediately, but in February 1894, in an assessment of defence needs in times of war, the governor, Sir Robert Biddulph, presented to the Colonial Office an argument first floated by Dr Scandella and his committee back in 1876, namely that it was better to allow aliens to reside in Gibraltar since, if necessary, they could be readily expelled, whereas such action could not be so easily taken against British subjects with their legal rights of residence. Like Scandella, Biddulph argued that such was the demand for labour in Gibraltar that action taken in peacetime to reduce the number of aliens would only lead to an increase in the number of 'British subjects probably Maltese, which would render our position very much worse than it is now, as I have not the power of preventing British Subjects from residing here'.[14] This became a more urgent matter when work to extend the naval dockyard was about to begin and an influx of Maltese labourers was anticipated, and deplored, because Gibraltar lacked the

GGA, Box: The Alien Question, Report on the Alien Question, 7 Oct 1876, pp. 6–7. By contrast, the mission of Dr Canilla, his successor, to the Maltese community which settled round the Church of St Joseph was honoured with a memorial plaque in 2002.

10 TNA, CO91/319, Kendall to colonial secretary, 14 June 1871, with Williams to Kimberley, 7 Sept 1872; CO879/9/16, Confidential Print, Mollan to Colonial Secretary, 14 Feb 1876.

11 TNA, CO883/4/10, Confidential Print, Med. No 27, Defence and Overcrowding, April 1888, Gifford to Hardinge, 7 July 1887, p. 15.

12 TNA, CO883/4/12, Confidential Print, Med. No 29, Gibraltar Civil Population, March 1888, pp. 1, 3. GGA, 'Census of Civil Population by Police, 1899' shows that by then over 1,100 Maltese lived in Gibraltar.

13 TNA, CO883/4/16, Confidential Print, Report of Departmental Committee, pp. 24–5, Gibraltar Civil Population, March 1888, pp. 1, 3.

14 TNA, CO91/406, Biddulph to Ripon, 12 Feb 1894.

accommodation for them and an alternative (and cheap) labour force was willing to come over daily from Spain.[15]

Defining and providing the authority to exclude such as the Maltese was, spasmodically, to occupy several years. Following instructions, by December 1894 Biddulph was sending to the Colonial Office a draft order-in-council 'conferring on the Governor the power of excluding British subjects from Gibraltar'. The heart of this proposal was that *all* persons would require the governor's permission 'to enter or reside', and also the governor would be empowered to expel *any* person whose presence was deemed by the governor to be detrimental. These regulations would apply equally to British subjects and to aliens, thus sweeping away a long-defended distinction.[16]

Colonial Office staff had no difficulty in pointing out that elsewhere in the British Empire – and the Australian colonies of Victoria and Queensland were named – British subjects, in this case Hong Kong Chinese, were being excluded by locally enacted laws. Indeed, it is worth emphasising that in the 1880s and 1890s several British Empire governments were passing laws which, by applying discriminatory regulations against fellow British subjects, were deliberately excluding 'coloured' immigrants so as to preserve 'white' settler societies in Australia, New Zealand and South Africa.[17] These steps caused the imperial government some international embarrassment, but similar action was now contemplated with respect to Gibraltar. However, the Colonial Office's recommended route was not such a sweeping change as had just been proposed, in effect annulling all the previous regulations on aliens and starting afresh. Rather, they opted to follow the suggestion in the March 1889 report of the committee on population, smuggling and defence, which, it will be recalled, because of the 'Maltese problem', had recommended extending the regulations governing the entry of aliens to 'certain' British subjects by deeming them to be 'strangers'. A new law would not apply to natives of Gibraltar or those already domiciled there (or employed there by Her Majesty's government), but it would define everyone else as 'strangers', including therefore, along with aliens, all other British subjects and the wives (wherever born) of such strangers. In addition, after the passing of the new law, children born in Gibraltar to mothers who were deemed strangers, plus illegitimate children born in Gibraltar even before the new law was passed and whose mothers were not British subjects, would also be deemed strangers.[18]

15 TNA, CO91/407, Biddulph to Ripon, 25 Aug 1894.
16 TNA, CO91/407, Biddulph to Ripon, 31 Dec 1894, and enclosures.
17 R.A. Huttenback, *Racism and Empire: White Settlers and Colored Immigrants in the British Self-Governing Colonies, 1830–1910* (Ithaca: Cornell University Press, 1976).
18 TNA, CO91/407, minutes, draft and Chamberlain to Biddulph, 12 Sept 1895. The change of government in part explains the long delay in responding to Biddulph's despatch of Dec 1894.

These latter rulings did not deny British status to such children, but they did bend ancient *jus soli* traditions by disallowing automatic rights of residence in the place of their birth.

The seriousness of what was being proposed by the Colonial Office is evident by the response from Gibraltar. In November 1895 the governor sent his revision of the draft law. On the one hand, this would have ensured that to those native-born and other male persons not to be defined as strangers would be added their wives and children. On the other hand, the proposal would have denied rights of residence even to legitimate children born before the passage of the new law whose fathers were strangers. However, much more serious were two accompanying and conflicting memoranda, one from the chief justice (independent of the colonial government), who doubted very strongly the legality of legislation which denied right of residence to British subjects (or their wives and children) in any part of 'the Realm' (particularly if they were property owners), and another from the attorney-general (an officer of the government), who asserted that the proposed restrictions were perfectly proper since Gibraltar was a fortress where legislation 'must . . . be governed by Military considerations', and the place was already overcrowded. Perhaps it was this uncomfortable dissension, or pressure of other business locally or in London, but the Colonial Office then allowed the whole business to lapse – for nearly four years.[19]

What kick-started further deliberations was another of those inquiries into the sanitary and living conditions of Gibraltar, particularly (though not exclusively) as they affected the military, for this was a committee set up by the War Office (not the Colonial Office).[20] Predictably, among its conclusions was that the overcrowding in Gibraltar was prejudicial to health. Specifically, 'the difficulty is rapidly increasing owing to the immigration of other British subjects, especially Maltese, mostly of a low class' who were disproportionately responsible for crime. Consequently, 'it has become essential to make residence on the Rock subject to permit in the case of all, whether British subjects or not, who are not genuine Gibraltar natives'.[21] In response, Governor Biddulph acknowledged that he had the power to exclude and indeed expel aliens, but concurred that

19 TNA, CO91/410, Biddulph to Chamberlain, 5 Nov 1895, and enclosures, minute of 15 November, and then nothing, not even a reference on the file's cover sheet to 'Subsequent Paper'.

20 TNA, WO33/133, 'Report of a Committee appointed by the Secretary of State for War to consider what measures should be adopted to improve the general condition of the City, Garrison and Territory of Gibraltar', Nov 1898. Chaired by G.D.A. Fleetwood-Wilson, assistant under-secretary at the War Office, its other members represented the army, navy and Colonial Office.

21 Ibid, 'Report', pp. 11, 16.

under current law British subjects 'could not be turned out at all'.[22] (Less helpful, but also perhaps predictable, was the grumpy observation of the British army's commander-in-chief that 'All soldiers would be extremely glad to clear out the entire civil population, and to govern [Gibraltar] as one does a barrack'.)[23]

Turning intention into legislation first required the reassurance of the Crown's Law Officers, duly given, that, properly framed, it would be legal to require 'all non-Gibraltese' persons, that is, those not born in Gibraltar, to obtain permits of residence and that the governor could be empowered 'to expel and exclude from the fortress all undesirable persons whether British subjects or not'.[24] There was then much exchange between Colonial Office, Law Office and War Office in London and governor, police magistrate and attorney-general in Gibraltar, involving reconsideration of the draft order of December 1894, much anxiety about defining 'native-born', wrestling with issues arising from the marriage of aliens to servicemen, deciding how to deal with the illegitimate offspring of native-born women, debating the powers of the governor and those of the secretary of state to expel (and to expel whom) from the colony, and further digging around in restrictive legislation being operated elsewhere in the empire.[25]

The net effect of all these deliberations was that the elaborately titled Aliens Order Extension Order in Council, Gibraltar, eventually passed on 29 June 1900, established the right of the governor to expel from Gibraltar 'any person' he judged 'undesirable' – and that could apply even to 'natives of Gibraltar' – indicative of overriding security interests. With more lasting implications, the law distinguished for the first time between the rights in Gibraltar of different groups of British subjects. First, it allowed residential rights to those who were (and only while they were) employees in Her Majesty's Service, plus their children until they married or, if sons, until they attained the age of 21. Second and more important, 'natives of Gibraltar' were separately defined, though only implicitly, as those born in Gibraltar plus, if males, their wives and children, and their residential rights alone were permanently enshrined. Officially they were not yet explicitly called 'Gibraltarians', but by implication they were being so identified as the privileged group by their separation from others. Third, however, if female natives of Gibraltar married non-natives

22 TNA, CO91/423, Fleetwood-Wilson to Colonial Office, 7 March 1899, enclosing 'Gibraltar Committee – Summary' and 'Observations of His Excellency the Governor of Gibraltar, 16 Feb 1899', pp. 9–10.
23 TNA, CO91/423, Fleetwood-Wilson to Colonial Office, 19 April 1899, enclosing 'Summary of Points for Secretary of State's Decision', para. 26.
24 TNA, CO91/427, Law Office to Colonial Office, 19 Oct 1899.
25 TNA, CO91/423, 424, 427, and GGA, Despatches to/from Gibraltar, 1899–1900: despatches, minutes, drafts 24 Oct 1899–14 July 1900.

of Gibraltar, their legitimate children only retained a right of residence until those children themselves married or, if sons, until they reached the age of 21. Fourth, entitlement to residence did not include anyone born in Gibraltar after 29 June 1900 unless his or her father had also been born in Gibraltar. This qualification at once introduced – though only in relation to rights of residence – what lawyers would call the *jus sanguinis*, determining rights by hereditary descent (and, noticeably, through the male line). Finally, this modification of *jus soli* also applied to persons born in Gibraltar 'out of lawful wedlock' after the passage of the order, who were also deemed not to be natives of Gibraltar and who therefore lost automatic residential rights, though not British subject status.[26] (This proposition, of course, had been kicking around for some time in government circles, and avoided the need to bundle unmarried pregnant alien women or henceforth non-native British women over the frontier prior to confinements so as to prevent their children acquiring, by *jus soli*, a right of residence in Gibraltar.) Having defined which British subjects did qualify for residence as natives of Gibraltar, the 1885 Aliens Order in Council was to apply to all the rest 'in the same manner as if he or she were an alien'. These other British subjects were later to be referred to as 'statutory aliens' – a phrase that was going to cause offence – with no more legal entitlement to residence in Gibraltar than those traditionally treated as aliens. Under the rules which were promulgated in November 1900 those already resident and those subsequently seeking entry had to register with the Police Office, the latter annually.[27] Hence we find reference in registers to John Abbott, age 51, Irish, manager to Messrs Hammerton; Salvadore Aquilina, 36, Maltese, coal-heaver; Harry Bird, 33, British, manager to Ind Coope & Co; Talbot Crosbie, 24, Irish, mission worker; Charlotte Crans, 40, English, schoolmistress; Louisa Hopgood, 21, Hong Kong, music teacher, and so on.[28]

One triumph of the legal mind was so to draft the laws as to avoid any accusation of racial discrimination; and yet everyone knew that the targeted

---

26 The implications of this, and of the coming of age of sons of employees of HM Government, were debated by colonial administrators in 1921, but no change in the law was recommended and instead cases were to be considered on their merits: GGA, MP99/1921, 'Status of Children born since the passing of the Aliens Order Extension Order 1900'.

27 TNA, CO91/424, Biddulph to Chamberlain, 9 July 1900, enclosing rules; CO91/425, Privy Council to Colonial Office, 10 July 1900, copy of Aliens Order Extension Order in Council, Gibraltar, 1900; GGA, *The Consolidated Laws of Gibraltar* (Gibraltar: Gibraltar Government, 1913), vol. I, pp. 423–4, vol. II, p. 40.

28 GGA, 'Register of British Subjects not being Gibraltarians resident in Gibraltar', under Rules 1 and 2; and see also 'Aliens Order Extension Order in Council, Rule 5 Permit Books', 3 vols, 1901–64.

groups were mainly Maltese, and also British Indians.[29] Concern about the presence of the latter cropped up in September 1899 when the governor complained about the behaviour of some British Indian shopkeepers in Gibraltar who were selling brass- and silverware and other Indian goods to visitors. It was said that they were bringing in other Indians as assistants, and that some of these were badly treated by their employers and left penniless and homeless. While there was official sympathy for their plight in Gibraltar and in London, the real difficulty was how to fund their passages back to India and, of course, how they, though British subjects, might be prevented in future from arriving and being admitted. It was even suggested in the Colonial Office that an 'educational test' involving knowledge of a European language chosen by an immigration officer might be employed to exclude them, something like the notorious law introduced in 1897 in the South African self-governing colony of Natal. This ruse had been designed to exclude British Indians, and had caused a lot of resentment, not least in the British government in India and in the India Office in London.[30] The latter was enraged at the suggestion put to it that something similar might be adopted in Gibraltar. Accordingly, the matter was instead to be dealt with in an ostensibly non-prejudicial manner by one of the rules framed under the 1900 order-in-council. Henceforth, any non-native British subject seeking entry would have to either deposit sufficient money to pay for 'his return to his home' or obtain a guarantee to meet such expenses from 'a responsible householder', who, it was expected, would be an employer. Hence, in the permit registers of non-native British subjects we find alongside the names of employees born in England and Scotland the names of others from India, like Verohmal Ababmal, aged 29, taken on as a shop assistant in 1912.[31] This regulatory response to the presence of British Indians in Gibraltar seems to have been prompted by official concerns. The rules did, of course, define natives of Gibraltar more closely by setting them against specific groups of non-native British subjects but, pre-war, no pressure from native civilians for the exclusion of Indians has been found. This was not to last.

29 TNA, CO91/424, minute, 10 Jan 1900, on Biddulph to Chamberlain, 4 Jan 1900, and CO91/425, minute, 14 July 1900, on Privy Council to Colonial Office, 10 July 1900.
30 Huttenback, *Racism and Empire*, pp. 141–4.
31 TNA, CO91/422, Biddulph to Chamberlain, 8 Sept 1899, Colonial Office to India Office, 19 Sept 1899; CO91/423, India Office to Colonial Office, 5 Oct and 28 Nov 1899, and minutes and despatches; GGA, *Consolidated Laws*, 1913, vol. II, p. 40, Rules 3 and 4; and 'Register of Permits issued to British Subjects to reside in Gibraltar under Rule 3'.

Statutory aliens, British Indians and the Alien Traders Ordinances, 1920s to 1950s

Because of overcrowding and accommodation shortages after the First World War and a downturn in the economy, the authorities secured an understanding with Indian traders, present of course as non-native British subjects with permits, that each firm would only operate from one shop. Indeed, as a result, some shops were closed down.[32] However, residents suspected that some traders were in fact carrying on as before by operating under more than one name.[33] Accordingly, the question of legislation to enforce restrictions was explored. In November 1922 Sir Horace Smith-Dorrien, governor 1918–23, had introduced into the politics of Gibraltar an Executive Council (more of which in a later chapter), consisting of his chief officials together with unofficial members chosen to represent the civilian community, which meant, in practice, its commercial sector.[34] As a consequence, Executive Council recommendations were highly sensitive to, though never entirely determined by, the business interests of resident civilians.[35] In November 1923 the Executive Council decided, after consulting the Chamber of Commerce, that legislation should be introduced to restrict the business activities of aliens, including,very importantly, 'statutory aliens' like British Indians. The aim was clear: 'to protect native traders'. The Colonial Office was concerned to avoid accusations of racial discrimination in the framing of the law and consulted the British government in India, but once that hurdle had been cleared the Alien Traders Ordinance was passed in November 1924. Clause 2 of the ordinance, drawing on the 1900 order-in-council, revealed that its compass was wider than the title might suggest: 'In this Ordinance, the word "alien" shall, in addition to the ordinary signification thereof, mean and include a statutory alien, and the words "statutory alien" shall mean and include every person, other than a person in the employ of His Majesty, who is not a native of Gibraltar.' All 'alien' traders so defined had to pay for an annual licence to trade, and for new businesses that meant also paying a

32 TNA, CO91/474, Smith-Dorrien to Milner, 1 June 1920; GGA, MP223/1930, minute by colonial secretary, 30 Oct 1931.
33 TNA, CO91/484, Monro to Amery, 14 Feb 1925, minute 27 Feb 1925.
34 GGA, Minutes of Executive Council, 1 Nov 1923: this council was made up of the governor, the senior military officer, the colonial secretary, the attorney-general and the treasurer, plus as unofficial members A. Mosley, J. Andrews-Speed and A. Carrara.
35 The barrister representing Indian merchants specifically objected in 1949 to the presence of Chamber of Commerce members on the Executive Council when the concerns of his clients were being discussed: GGA, MP30/1938, vol.3, Benady to colonial secretary, 26 April 1949.

hefty initial fee; all were to be restricted to one shop for the same class of business; the licence would specify the goods or services that could be traded; and the decision whether or not to issue a licence was solely at the discretion of the governor.[36]

Over the next twenty years there were to be seven amending Alien Traders Ordinances. Some of these were minor, for example, exempting charities in July 1925 and waiving fees for statutory aliens in April 1927. Some were serious, like that of October 1934, which attempted to reconcile legislation relating to companies with laws dealing with alien traders and allowing statutory aliens a right, denied to aliens, of operating from more than one place of business (usually a shop).[37] What was just as important was the day-to-day operation of a law which gave the governor such managerial authority over the business operations of non-native British as well as alien residents. This therefore allowed distinctions to be enforced between natives of Gibraltar and the others. The latter, it should be said, embraced not just British Indians but all other statutory aliens, as well as foreign aliens.

True, licences for new businesses were sometimes granted to aliens, including statutory aliens, either because they would extend the range of commodities available for consumers,[38] or to add a little necessary competition,[39] or because

36 GGA, MP70/1921, minute by Acting Chief of Police, 29 July 1921; Executive Council minutes, 2 and 29 Nov 1923, 21 Feb, 3 April, 23 Oct 1924; MP 565/1924, Alien Traders Ordinance 1924, plus sub-files of cases; *The Laws of Gibraltar: Annual Volume for 1924*, The Alien Traders Ordinance, No 8, 1924, pp. 50–3; TFA, CO91/483, Monro to Thomas, 29 Feb and 11 April 1924, CO91/484, minutes on Monro to Amery, 14 Feb 1925.

37 GGA, Executive Council minutes, 23 April and 23 June 1925, 11 Jan 1927; Alien Traders (Amendment) Ordinance, No 4, 1925 and No 3, 1927 added to *Laws of Gibraltar for 1924*; Alien Traders Ordinance, No 29, 1934, *Revised Edition of the Laws of Gibraltar* (Gibraltar: Garrison Library Committee, 1935), vol. 1, cap. 6, pp. 72–80, and on its passage see Executive Council minutes, 21 Nov 1932 and 22 Feb 1934, and MP375/1932, plus TNA, CO91/494/8, Godley to Cunliffe-Lister, 15 March 1933, plus minutes and correspondence, and subsequently on CO91/495/11. Avoidance of the law was stopped by the Alien Traders (Amendment) Ordinance, No 3 and No 8, 1937, on which see Executive Council minutes, 22 June 1936 and 19 Feb 1937, and for these and minor amendments in Alien Traders (Amendment) Ordinance No 2, 1938, No 7, 1942 and No 3, 1944, embedded in consolidated law see C.C. Ross (ed.), *The Laws of Gibraltar, Revised Edition* (London: Bosworth, 1950), vol. 2, cap. 127, pp. 1600–7 and in CO91/540/3.

38 GGA, MP185/1925, vol. 1, licence for a furniture shop, vol. 2, licence to Scottish Petroleum Company.

39 GGA, Executive Council minutes, 21 Nov 1932; MP2/1933, cases concerning shoe repairs and sales of petrol; MP20/1936, provision of reconstituted milk and cream, Jan 1937.

no objections were raised during consultation with existing firms.[40] But on many other occasions applications were rejected. So, for example, in September 1925 an application by an alien for a licence to open a grocer's shop was turned down because this was 'one of the particular trades it is desired to protect for the Gibraltarian'.[41] Likewise in February 1926, an application by Ali Hanus, 'Moor', was rejected because the governor considered it 'undesirable to allow aliens to set up cheap fancy goods shops (of which there are already plenty) in the town and thus take up accommodation needed for other purposes'.[42] Similarly, an alien's application in September 1927 to open an agency for the sale of watches was rejected because 'this trade is more than sufficiently represented in Gibraltar, there being nine watchmakers and jewellers at the present time' and allowing another would cause local resentment.[43]

It was predictable that domestic opposition to alien businesses would increase when trade generally was feeling the pinch. So, in October 1928 the governor received a memorial from the Gibraltar British Traders Association, 'praying for the exclusion from Gibraltar of all aliens engaged in business', and a more insistent letter followed in August 1929.[44] There were similar demands from the Exchange and Commercial Library Committee in October 1932, from the Gibraltar Chamber of Commerce in February 1934, and in a memorial to the governor in January 1935, following a public meeting of wholesalers and retailers. The last put a common perspective pretty bluntly: 'it is not conducive to the general good of the community to grant further retail or wholesale licences . . . to aliens, statutory or otherwise'.[45] So the governor could be in no doubt that the local business view was that they should be protected even from statutory alien competitors. Largely, the governor and Executive Council listened and were less inclined to grant licences, even though at the worst of times shops were untenanted (something about which some Chamber of Commerce members

40 GGA, MP340/1927, case of Bulchand Kundamal; Executive Council minutes, 5 Aug and 17 Oct 1927.
41 GGA, MP185/1925, I, and see negative responses to other applications in this file. This early official use of the word 'Gibraltarian' should be noted.
42 GGA, MP185/1925, II, minute, 12 Feb 1926.
43 GGA, MP340/1927, treasurer to colonial secretary, 22 Sept 1927.
44 GGA, Executive Council minutes, 24 Oct and 30 Nov 1928; MP340/1927, Gibraltar British Traders Association to colonial secretary, 3 Aug 1929.
45 MP375/1932, correspondence from Exchange and Commercial Library Committee, 14 Oct 1932, and Gibraltar Chamber of Commerce, 14 Feb 1934; MP421/1935, Alien Traders: Representations re Increase in Number (the memorial with forty signatures representing thirty-six businesses was further endorsed by the Chamber of Commerce); Executive Council minutes, 27 May 1935.

then complained, since they needed tenants in order to draw income from rent).[46]

In tough times established Indian traders could be just as defensive of their interests against potential rivals,[47] but as statutory aliens they were more vulnerable to restrictions than natives of Gibraltar. In January 1934 some old-established Indian firms complained that some of the employees they had brought from India were resigning and setting up rival businesses with the aid of or in the name of native Gibraltarians, thus getting round the restrictions imposed by the Alien Traders Ordinance. The unofficial members of the Executive Council appear to have welcomed such practices 'if the business were going to be conducted by Gibraltarians . . . They were of opinion that if a Gibraltarian wished to engage Indian managers or assistants no restriction should be placed in the way.'[48] However, after the Companies Ordinance was introduced in 1930, care was taken to ensure that licences were then only granted to businesses in which the majority of shares were British owned, and only one of eight Indian trading firms reviewed in October 1934 was approved, the one exception being described as 'definitely Gibraltarian'.[49] Late in the decade, the Executive Council, prompted again by 'native' concerns, agreed that the range of goods which Indian traders were selling should be restricted and that 'the question of the number of Indians now in Gibraltar should be examined with a view to firms being limited to a certain quota'.[50] This was the occasion, 25 February 1938, when a proposal from two British Indians to open an Indian restaurant was turned down because it was reckoned 'the enterprise was one for which there was little public demand'. In any event, the application 'should be refused in accordance with the general policy of restricting Indian trading in the Colony'.[51]

46 GGA, MP223/1930, rejection of application from an Indian trader, Nov 1931; rejection of application from a builder, Aug 1932; rejection of application from a Chinese trader, Jan 1933; MP 2/1933, rejection of application lest it push up shop rents and turn a 'Gibraltarian' out of the premises, Jan 1933; Executive Council minutes, 13 June 1930.

47 GGA, MP324/1932, British Indians Permits of Residence, correspondence with S. Benady, 22 Aug, 5 and 20 Sept 1932, and minutes; MP21/1935, minute of 21 June 1935.

48 GGA, Executive Council minutes, 5 Jan 1934, and see 21 Nov 1932 and 28 March 1936.

49 GGA, MP424/1934, minutes of 9 and 15 Oct 1934, and see stipulation about shareholding in minute of 18 Oct 1934; Executive Council minutes, 21 Nov 1932.

50 GGA, Executive Council minutes, 25 Feb 1938, and MP30/1938, vol. 1, Treasurer to Colonial Secretary, 10 Jan 1938, and subsequent minutes and correspondence.

51 GGA, Executive Council minutes, 25 Feb 1938; MP20/1936, minutes of 25 Feb and 1 March 1938. One of the frustrated entrepreneurs, Gopaldas Dharandas, was from Goa and formerly a cook employed by the governor.

By March 1938, the number of British Indians living and working legally in Gibraltar had increased from 67 in January 1931 to 129, and they were running twenty-six shops – so many on Main Street that, allegedly, it was being called 'Bombay Street'. However, far from admiring their entrepreneurial zeal, native competitors and British authorities were disconcerted. What made the official predicament tricky was the determination of the India Office in London to discourage actions in the colonial empire, including in Gibraltar, which might provoke allegations of racial discrimination against British Indians at a critical moment in India's political evolution.[52]

There was no decline in the political problem after the war. Indeed, it grew greater when, from 1947, a self-governing India was determined to defend globally the rights of its citizens overseas, and when native Gibraltar merchants were determined to recapture trading ground lost before and during the war to statutory alien merchants and, specifically, to British Indian traders. In particular, following up a pre-war grievance on behalf of its members, the Chamber of Commerce wanted to see a substantial reduction in the range of goods which such 'outsiders' should be allowed to sell. Their exchanges with the Indian Merchants Association, channelled through the colonial government, may have narrowed but did not end the disagreement on what Indian traders were allowed to sell (and a definition of 'fancy goods' eluded everyone). Moreover, when the negotiations stalled and tempers rose, the process firmed up more clearly the distinction between the British subject who was a Gibraltarian and the British subject who was a statutory alien and conditional resident.[53]

It was certainly a telling response when the (Gibraltar) lawyers acting for the Indian traders threatened in March 1949 to alert the High Commissioner for India to alleged discrimination against those who, though 'not born in Gibraltar have been established as traders in this Colony for the past three quarters of a century'.[54] The official response was that the Alien Traders Ordinance was designed 'precisely to protect the interests of Gibraltarian traders': the adjective 'Gibraltarian' and not just 'native' carried an enhanced significance.[55] The

---

52 GGA, MP11/1937, minute and accompanying papers by Commissioner of Police, 16 March 1938, Harington to Ormsby-Gore, 20 April 1938, case of Mrs Khemchand, and especially Orsmby-Gore to Harington, 3 March 1938; and see also TNA, CO91/499/18, minute of 30 Dec 1936 recording the views of Gibraltar's treasurer and colonial secretary.

53 GGA, MP30/1938, vols 2 and 3, contain extensive correspondence between the Colonial Secretariat and the Chamber of Commerce and S.P. Triay and S. Benady (barristers for the Indian Merchants Association), 23 Aug 1945–27 June 1950.

54 GGA, MP30/1938, vol. 3, Benady to colonial secretary, 31 March 1949.

55 GGA, MP30/1938, vol. 3, colonial secretary to Benady, 18 May 1949. Compare with the phrase used in the Executive Council in Feb 1924 and quoted above: 'to protect native traders'.

reaction by the lawyers on behalf of their Indian clients was, in effect, a denial not only of the 1924 Alien Traders Ordinance and its successors but also of the 1900 Aliens Order Extension Order in Council, since they rejected the legitimacy of laws which, by privileging some residents in Gibraltar, now called Gibraltarians, were prejudicial to the interests of other residents, now called 'aliens', or 'statutory aliens' – which was no better. This was why their clients were seeking the intervention of the Indian government, because Gibraltar legislation was 'discriminating against them on the grounds that they were Indians'. It was also alleged that, even though the Alien Traders Ordinance supposedly targeted all statutory aliens, its application against Indians had been 'stricter and harsher'. Moreover, and the historical record largely bears this out, the legislation had been designed principally to deal with Indian traders, but 'due to the difficulties of openly avowing such a purpose the Ordinance had to be drafted in terms which would appear to mitigate its highly discriminating character'.[56] Among the official responses to this critique was, in fact, the private admission by one senior member of the secretariat that 'The real truth of course is that no one, Governor or others, wants the Indians. But I think that so long as they are here in fact we must be careful not to give the impression of unfair detailed discrimination.'[57] An equally important reaction, indicative of that severance within the community which Messrs Triay and Benady were attempting to challenge, was protests received by the governor from native Gibraltarians 'against the undue latitude allowed to Indians'.[58] Certainly, the Chamber of Commerce insisted on reinforcing the distinction by demanding of government that 'no further trading licenses be issued in the future other than to Gibraltarians'.[59]

It needs to be recalled from Table 7.2a above that, according to the census, the Indian population of Gibraltar had only been around 100 in the 1920s, and though it had subsequently risen, perhaps to 164 in 1939, numbers had actually fallen after the war, to only 78 in 1950, according to one official source (though 112 Indians were resident in July 1951, according to the census).[60] However, it was prominence, not absolute numbers, which mattered in this commercial settlement and Gibraltar's business class was articulating a distinctive identity against 'aliens', which accounts for its inflation of the 'British Indian' issue. Early in 1950 arguments over the range of goods which Indian traders could sell – ladies' as well as gentlemen's panama

---

56 GGA, MP30/1938, vol. 3, Triay and Benady to the governor, 24 June 1949.
57 GGA, MP30/1938, vol. 3, minute 18 July 1949.
58 GGA, MP30/1938, vol. 3, minute 16 July 1949.
59 GGA, MP30/1938, vol. 3, Gibraltar Chamber of Commerce to colonial secretary, 4 Nov 1949.
60 TNA, CO91/540/2, Note on Indian Merchants in Gibraltar, 24 March 1950, though see CO91/540/, governor to secretary of state, 27 Oct 1951, where it is asserted that there were 130 'in 1938/1939' and 97 in 1951.

hats? – had even come to involve His Majesty's Secretary of State for the Colonies, His Majesty's Secretary of State for Commonwealth Relations (and hence for India) and His Excellency the High Commissioner for India.

The question of status was very much in the mind of Krishna Menon, the high commissioner. In an interview in March 1950 with James Griffiths, secretary of state for the colonies, he took particular exception to the discrimination practised against Indian traders, even if other non-Gibraltarians might also face restrictions (as British officials in the Colonial Office and in Gibraltar insisted they did). He was also indignant at their being designated by law as 'statutory aliens' (and British officials had also become uncomfortable with that term).[61] It is apparent that the view in London after this encounter, reinforced by a subsequent meeting of senior officers at the Colonial Office with London lawyers representing the Indian traders, was that Gibraltar traders were simply trying to escape competition and that the conflict should be settled by concessions to Indian shopkeepers. However, it was agreed in London and in Gibraltar that the distinctions legally drawn in 1900 between 'native Gibraltarians' and 'non-Gibraltarian British subjects', and now culturally embedded in at least the commercial sector, could not be reversed, lest already overcrowded Gibraltar become more so – though the provocative term 'statutory alien' ought to be excised.[62]

It would be agreeable to record that the dispute over what Indian traders currently resident could or could not legally sell was thereafter rapidly resolved. In fact, it rumbled on for years, prompting further intervention by Indian high commissioners.[63] Moreover, the demand of Indian traders that they should be allowed to recruit additional Indian shop assistants, since Gibraltarians would not do the work, unleashed an additional debate on whether Gibraltarians would take such jobs if the posts were properly advertised and if fair pay and conditions were offered. Also there was the question of whether a sufficient objection to allowing in more immigrant workers was simply the shortage of accommodation in a 'small and over-crowded Colony, where the area available for residence and trade is half that of Hyde Park'.[64]

61 TNA, CO91/540/2, GGA, MP30/1938, vol. 3, Bennett to Anderson, 5 April 1950, note of meeting and minutes in TNA file and minutes on letter in GGA file.

62 TNA, CO91/540/2, and GGA, MP30/1938, vol. 3, especially Bennett to Anderson, 12 April, and enclosure, and Anderson to Martin, 14 April 1950, and minutes, especially that of 28 June 1950 on GGA file.

63 The narrative can be followed in TNA, CO91/540/2 and 540/3 and DO35/5437A, until July 1955, and GGA, MP30/198, vol. 3, until June 1950, when the currently available files cease.

64 TNA, CO91/540/3, Krishna Menon to Griffiths, 8 Jan and 28 Aug 1951, governor to secretary of state, 27 Oct 1951, and minutes, quotation of 19 Nov 1951; CO926/472, MacMillan to Lyttleton, 2 April 1954 (on shop assistants and pay and conditions), Pearson to Britten, 28 April 1954 (on Indian businesses

These were more than practical matters, because they raised issues concerning nomenclature and status. They showed that at least the commercial sector of the native population was defining its identity even against other British subjects and was pressing government to recognise and defend its distinguishing interests. As such, their assertion and then defence of the principles behind the Alien Traders Ordinance connects with another and parallel story concerned more generally with immigration controls and rights of residence.

Belonging: from the 1920s to the Right of Residence in Gibraltar Ordinance, 1955

Year by year British authorities were screening applicants for entry and for residence by applying as appropriate the rules of the 1885 Aliens Order in Council with respect to aliens and the 1900 Aliens Order Extension Order in Council with regard to statutory aliens. It cannot have been comfortable for individuals, often of humble background, to beg for admission or continued residence from a governor charged to exclude. Some cases were treated with humane sympathy. So, for example, in 1922 a native of Malaga, by then aged 60, infirm, with no family to look after her, who for forty years had worked in Gibraltar as a cook, was granted a permit to allow her to take refuge in the asylum run by the Little Sisters of the Poor.[65] Likewise, in 1926 Enrique Perera, a native of Gibraltar and judged by the police inspector to be a 'respectable man', was given a permit of residence for his Spanish nephew, aged 5: he and his wife had no family and the boy was the youngest of six children, his mother had just died, and his father, a labourer in Spain, was too poor to support all the children.[66] The outbreak of the Spanish Civil War threw up the case of a refugee couple who had fled across the frontier and been admitted on a daily ticket: he was Spanish and she had become Spanish on marriage, though a British subject by birth. In October 1936 she was allowed to have her baby in Gibraltar, though conditional upon it being registered as Spanish at the Spanish consulate in Gibraltar.[67]

Footnote 64 (*cont.*)

exploiting a loophole in company law, and 'Gibraltarian' resentment of that), Hopkinson to Krishna Menon, 28 June 1950 (on training Gibraltarians as shop assistants); DO35/5437A, High Commission to Colonial Office, 24 July 1952, governor to Colonial Office, 4 March 1953 (on low wages), Commonwealth Relations Office to British High Commission, New Delhi, 11 July 1955 (expressing a hope that a settlement of the shop assistant issue might be reached . . .).

65 GGA, MP221/1922, 'Admission of Aliens to Little Sisters of the Poor Asylum'. This is one of several such cases in the 1920s and also in the late 1950s recorded in that file.

66 GGA, MP236/1926, 'Antonio Lopez Carrasco, Spanish Child'.

67 GGA, MP328/1936, 'Births of Aliens in Gibraltar', case 11. There are many cases in this file.

On the other hand, that same week the wife of another political refugee in Gibraltar was denied such a concession, even though accommodation and care were offered and the promise was made to register the child at the Spanish consulate, seemingly on the grounds that she was herself still living in La Línea and should there remain (or was it because her husband was a committeeman of the Spanish anarcho-syndicalist trade union, the CNT?)[68] Also in 1936, a Spanish woman who had defied an order not allowing her to have her child in Gibraltar was then expelled and her father-in-law, who had given her shelter, was fined.[69] In 1937 the application for naturalisation by a woman, then aged 72 but born in Gibraltar of two Gibraltar-born British subjects and with a brother living in Gibraltar, was turned down because she had married a Spaniard, by then deceased, and was living in Tangier.[70]

Most such decisions were made by colonial administrators applying the rules and using such discretion as the law allowed (usually more sympathetically to the wealthy and well-connected), but the introduction of the Executive Council allowed the unofficial members, hand-picked by the governor but nevertheless Gibraltar civilians, some input into both the application and substance of the laws. We have seen already their role in shaping and reshaping the Alien Traders Ordinance. Their voice also impacted upon the principal laws regulating admission and residence. The trajectory of all their observations was towards more rights for native-born Gibraltarian civilians at the expense of fewer for other folk.

Over the winter of 1927–28 the administration reviewed the bureaucratic burden consequent on the obligation of certain categories of resident permit holders to apply for repeated renewals and the duty of aliens staying in hotels to acquire permits. While dealing with these matters, it was also thought a good idea to excuse friends and relatives of navy, army and colonial service personnel from the chore of obtaining visitors' permits. However, when the draft ordinance was published in the official gazette there was 'great resentment' and a storm of protest from the Exchange Committee, Chamber of Commerce, Workers' Union and the unofficial members of the Executive Council. The last complained that the privilege granted only to the 'friends and relatives' of the garrison was 'class legislation' and 'inequitable', since such a privilege for an officer was not equally available to 'a leading resident'. All 'Gibraltarians' – and the word is used – should be allowed to have friends and relatives to stay without requiring a permit. Rather embarrassed, the governor had to send back to the Colonial Office a revised draft ordinance, unanimously approved by the

---

68 GGA, MP328/1936, case 14. The offer to help was made by J.F. Rosado.
69 GGA, MP2/1932, 'Childbirth by Alien Women without the Governor's Consent', and see other cases up to 1954 in the file.
70 GGA, MP646/1937, 'Mrs Magdalena Porral de Porcuna – Naturalization'.

unofficial members. All the 'perks' intended for service personnel were removed. Instead, by the 1928 Aliens Legislation (Amendment) Ordinance, the intended privileges were granted only to a section of the civilian population. Permits were no longer required for the daughter of a native of Gibraltar who was visiting her parent, brother or sister for no more than 90 days, even if she had become an alien by marriage, nor was a permit of residence henceforth required for any person who was the child (while a child) of a native of Gibraltar and a British subject, even if born outside Gibraltar. This unexpected result, and especially the latter, indicates a further slippage, in respect of residence, away from *jus soli* and towards *jus sanguinis*.[71]

On the other hand, public bodies in Gibraltar and unofficial members on the Executive Council seem not to have been concerned with other legislative amendments in the 1930s which bit on aliens only. So, for instance, there was no recorded comment from unofficial members when the draft of a Strangers (Amendment) Ordinance came before them in September 1934. Among other bureaucratic twitches, it required hoteliers to record in hotel registers the passport particulars of aliens and strangers and to make a return to the chief of police.[72] Nor did they intervene when, in 1935, the attorney general undertook a revision of Gibraltar's statute law and consolidated the 1885 and 1900 orders-in-council and seven connected ordinances into the Aliens and Strangers Ordinance of 1935. Perhaps this was especially because this measure incorporated the concessions granted by the 1928 ordinance and allowed for visits by daughters of natives of Gibraltar who had become aliens by marriage, and granted right of residence to a child of a native of Gibraltar born elsewhere than in Gibraltar, though it did now specify child of a 'male native' and 'in lawful wedlock'. The rest, after all, was pretty much concerned with the well-entrenched rules restricting the admittance of aliens on daily or weekly tickets or temporary permits.[73]

More concern was shown on the Executive Council when civil war violence was bringing alien political refugees into Gibraltar, particularly when they were radical supporters of the Spanish Republic. For the administration, too, this was a serious headache, combining concerns over overcrowding and sanitation with the security priorities of the garrison. It was particularly alarming because the British Vice-Consul in La Línea had reported late in 1936 that some 4,000

---

71 For correspondence, minutes and copies of the draft and final versions of The Aliens Legislation (Amendment) Ordinance, No 10 of 1928, see GGA, MP501/1927, Executive Council minutes, 18 July 1928, and TNA, CO91/487/6.

72 GGA, MP264/1934, including Harrington to Cunliffe-Lister, 20 Oct 1934. Remarkably, the origins of the original Strangers Ordinance in 1889 (see Chapter 4) had been so forgotten by 1934 that the clause designed to prevent fraudulent entry by aliens pretending to be Maltese and therefore British subjects completely mystified the colonial secretariat and was cut: see minutes of 21 and 24 Aug 1934.

73 *Revised Edition of the Laws of Gibraltar*, 1935, vol. 1, cap. 5, pp. 58–71.

British subjects were residing within his jurisdiction and an indeterminate number might claim a right of residence in Gibraltar (including a number 'of low type and mentality, probably born in some of the many houses of ill-fame which exist there').[74] This threat triggered off, first, as an emergency measure, the erection of a so-called 'unclimbable fence' to channel refugees to frontier posts where credentials could be checked and, second, an amendment to the Aliens and Strangers Ordinance which tightened up police control over the issue of permits.[75]

But with more far-reaching implications was a serious historical review, undertaken by the attorney-general and completed in September 1936, concerning the 'Right of Residence in Gibraltar'. So complex and controversial were the issues raised that nearly twenty years were to elapse before legislation stemming from this report was finally enacted, late in 1955. The inquiry concluded that, in spite of some early nineteenth-century equivocation, nobody, not even the native-born of Gibraltar, had ever had an absolute right of residence in this 'fortress' and were all therefore ultimately resident at the discretion of the governor as commander-in-chief. This residual power to deport and the intimately associated difficulty in defining a 'native of Gibraltar' who had an otherwise automatic right of residence became the central issues in what followed. The attorney-general's clarifying memorandum was received with approbation in the colonial secretariat and by the governor. It is therefore indicative of a different perspective that P.G. Russo, a civilian member of a Housing Commission set up by the governor to which copies of the memorandum had been circulated (the right of residence being important for their deliberations), should have taken exception to the conclusion that the governor's right to expel 'any person' even included a native of Gibraltar. It was, he argued, 'an invasion of the common law right of a person not to be ejected from his own native soil'.[76]

This was not a matter which concerned only Gibraltar. In 1933 the Colonial Office completed a review of deportation laws and practices throughout the colonial empire. Since 1930 alone, deportation cases had cropped up in Aden, Bermuda, Cyprus, Federated Malay States, Fiji, Gambia, Hong Kong, Iraq, Jamaica, Kenya, Malaya, Palestine, Trinidad and the Seychelles.[77] Different in its judgement from that of Gibraltar's attorney-general, this review concluded

74 TNA, C091/503/8, GGA, MP326/1936, Harrington to Ormsby-Gore, 14 Jan 1937.
75 GGA, Executive Council minutes, 10 June 1937, 25 March 1938; MP148/1931 and MP322/1937, minute of 15 June and 1 July 1937; TNA, CO91/504/2, Harington to Ormsby-Gore, 12 Aug 1937, CO91/507/20, Harington to Ormsby-Gore, 13 May 1938, and Aliens and Strangers (Amendment) Ordinance, No 1 of 1938.
76 GGA, 326/1936, 'Right of Residence in Gibraltar', memorandum of 2 Sept 1936 and minutes, especially 19 Oct 1936 and 6 Jan 1937.
77 Files listed in TNA catalogue.

that a person who 'belongs' to a territory should not be liable to deportation, and that a proper judicial inquiry should precede any deportation order against other British subjects. A copy of the report and a model ordinance were sent to all colonial governors for their consideration in the light of local circumstances.[78] The special circumstances of Gibraltar as a fortress and the assumed existing powers of its governor probably explain why no local action was taken.[79]

However, on receipt of the attorney-general's review in January 1937, the Colonial Office's legal advisers in fact concluded that the wording of Gibraltar's consolidated Aliens and Strangers Ordinance of 1935 left questionable the power of the governor to deny a right of residence to 'any person' and therefore to deport natives who 'belonged'. Their instructions to the governor in June 1937 were not to accept this uncertain state of affairs and to put matters right by a further piece of legislation precisely indicating the governor's authority. The draft ordinance prepared by the attorney-general now made it undeniable that the governor would have the power to refuse admission to or deport from Gibraltar even a native of Gibraltar. The opportunity was also taken to rephrase the clauses which defined natives of Gibraltar. This draft was then discussed by the Executive Council, and subsequently and separately on two occasions by the attorney-general with two of the unofficial members, leading to amendments. However, at a later meeting in October 1938 the Executive Council sent back the revised draft for further consideration because one of the two still queried the section which defined a native of Gibraltar. Not until January 1939 did the much-debated draft, accepted at last by the unofficial members, get dispatched for consideration by the Colonial Office.

The unofficial members had had to accept that native Gibraltarians, like everyone else, could be expelled from or refused admission to Gibraltar at the discretion of the governor. On the other hand, the draft attempted to provide a clearer definition of a native of Gibraltar, who would not otherwise be bound by the clauses uniquely affecting aliens (and this would include statutory aliens). Thus it began by listing the privileged as a British subject who was born in Gibraltar; and a wife if she were a British subject (who could therefore be, for example, English or British Indian) and married to a British subject born in Gibraltar; and a legitimate child born in Gibraltar whose father or mother was a native of Gibraltar. The addition of 'mother' to clarify the entitlement was important, although the native status of some legitimate children born in Gibraltar would last only until they married or the sons became 21, if their mothers, though natives of Gibraltar,

---

78　TNA, CO91/543/4, 'Deportation of British Subjects from the Colonies' memo with Anderson to Griffiths, 28 June 1951; and CO885/42 for 1933 report, CO916, CO323/1175/6, CO323/1215/5 and 1215/6 for papers.

79　TNA and GGA contain no filed responses.

were not also legitimate children of male natives of Gibraltar. It was also intended to confirm that a native of Gibraltar included any person born in lawful wedlock outside Gibraltar (for example in Britain), provided the father of that person had the status of native of Gibraltar and a British subject.[80] Here too we see *jus soli* rights being either reduced or enhanced according to *jus sanguinis* entitlements derived from male descent.

Unfortunately, the Colonial Office and, more particularly, its legal staff did not like what they read. In addition to what they regarded as some clumsy drafting of the amending ordinance and some unresolved awkwardnesses in the original 1935 law, they queried the entitlement to native status of all children born outside Gibraltar of fathers who had the status of natives of Gibraltar. Concentrate on the male line, and it meant that any male born outside Gibraltar whose father was classed as a native of Gibraltar and a British subject would also be classed as a native of Gibraltar with a right of residence, and that male could then pass on the same status of native of Gibraltar with a right of residence to his son, even if that son too had been born outside Gibraltar, who could then pass on the status and right of residence to his son, also born outside Gibraltar, and so on down the generations, as long as they remained British subjects. The Colonial Office offered its own more restrictive version, which first defined native of Gibraltar more simply but more exclusively as a British subject born in Gibraltar before 29 June 1900 or in lawful wedlock after 29 June, the father having been born in Gibraltar. This locked Gibraltarian status firmly to birth in Gibraltar, and prevented its inheritance by those whose fathers were themselves born outside Gibraltar. All that the amending ordinance would further do was excuse some others from its restrictions on admission and residence, though by the proposed concessions they would not become legally natives of Gibraltar, and therefore would not be able legally themselves to pass on that status. These would be the wife (wherever born) of a native, the child born in lawful wedlock but outside Gibraltar if the father was a native, and the legitimate child of a woman who was a native of Gibraltar (but implicitly whose husband was not), though this child's right of residence would only last until he or she was married or, if a son, became aged 21.[81] The governor was asked to comment on the draft and some optional phrases. Unfortunately, perhaps, this response to the draft

---

80 TNA, CO91/503/8, Harington to Ormsby-Gore, 14 Jan 1937, with attorney-general's memorandum, 6 Jan 1937 (minor textual amendments from that of 2 Sept), minutes, Ormsby-Gore to Harington, 17 June 1937, with legal comments on the memorandum; GGA, MP326/1936, minutes and papers, especially attorney-general, 'Explanatory Memorandum', 16 Dec 1938 with draft ordinance. Other clauses, excluding them from the rules regulating aliens, concerned British subjects employed by HM Government and their wives and children.

81 Again, there was a clause to cover government employees and their children.

ordinance pretty much coincided with the crisis resulting in war, and the whole
legislative business was sidelined.[82]

But not forgotten. One well-remembered consequence of the war beginning
in May 1940 was the temporary evacuation from Gibraltar to French Morocco
of virtually all civilian women and children and many men, and then their
much more prolonged relocation to Madeira, Jamaica and the United Kingdom,
particularly London and Northern Ireland. (Others had voluntarily taken up
residence in Tangier and Franco's Spain.)[83] While evacuation was intended to be
for their own safety – Gibraltar expecting to be much in the war zone – it was
also desired by the military authorities to rid the fortress of the encumbrance of
excess civilians and 'useless mouths'. Sir Clive Liddell, governor 1939–41, and
Viscount Gort, 1941–42, were reprising the role of General Eliott. This demon-
stration that the residency of all civilians in Gibraltar was indeed subject to the
wishes of the governor, albeit via an Emergency Powers Order in Council, also
threw up some disturbing issues concerning future rights of residency. In June
1943 they troubled one prominent remaining civilian, P.J. Russo, the unofficial
member of the governor's Executive Council who had been concerned with such
matters before the war. He had not forgotten either the terms of the 1935 Aliens
and Strangers Ordinance or the amendments proposed by the Colonial Office's
draft. Under the former, a child of a male native of Gibraltar born outside
Gibraltar had a right of residence, but that right could not be transmitted to
his children. Under the latter and carrying the same consequence, a native of
Gibraltar would be defined as someone born in Gibraltar and, if after 29 June
1900, of a father who had also been born in Gibraltar. Russo was alarmed that
a number of children with native fathers were being born outside Gibraltar
because of the evacuation, and these children, not being born in Gibraltar,
would not be able to pass on to *their* children the status of native of Gibraltar
with a guaranteed right of residence. Entitlements derived from *jus soli* were
not being acquired.

Russo had evidently read the most recent Colonial Office letter to the governor, since, in the paper he submitted to the colonial government, he employed the
same phrases to conjure up the equally exaggerated claim that, were the law to
remain unchanged, 'the number of natives of Gibraltar would gradually decrease
until none remained; for the birth of one person outside Gibraltar breaks the

82 GGA, MP326/1936, and TNA, CO91/509/7, Ironside to MacDonald, 18 Jan 1939,
    and enclosures, minutes on TNA file, MacDonald to Ironside, 24 May 1939, and
    subsequent minutes on GGA and TNA files. Minor administrative amendments
    were introduced to the existing 1935 law by ordinances passed in Aug 1939, June
    1942 and April 1943.
83 The standard history is Finlayson, *The Fortress Came First*, based on archival
    material.

chain'.[84] Hence he offered his own set of amendments. First, and importantly in terms of identity, he insisted that the phrase 'native of Gibraltar' should be scrubbed and replaced by the word 'Gibraltarian', since that term, he claimed, was 'being freely used to denote a person from Gibraltar'. Then he wished to add to the Colonial Office's proposed definition of what they had called 'a native of Gibraltar' some further categories. A Gibraltarian would also be a person born in lawful wedlock and in Gibraltar whose father at the time of that birth was a British subject but born outside Gibraltar (and therefore was not a Gibraltarian) but whose mother was born in Gibraltar (and therefore was a Gibraltarian): this would cover the offspring of evacuated Gibraltarian women marrying non-Gibraltarian men, uniquely allowing Gibraltarian status to be acquired through the female line. Irrespective of the mother's origins, a Gibraltarian would also be someone born in lawful wedlock and in Gibraltar even if the father had been born out of Gibraltar, so long as that person's father had been born in Gibraltar, or if *he* was not born in Gibraltar then provided *his* father had been born in Gibraltar, but if that person was not born in Gibraltar then provided *his* father . . . and so on and so on, and always as long as the birth of those born out of Gibraltar had been registered at the colonial secretariat. A government official commented: 'This means tracing the ancestry back to Adam and requires for Adam to have been registered at the Colonial Secretariat (of Eden?).'

Complex as Russo's proposals may sound, they were a serious attempt to maintain Gibraltarian descent for those who wanted it (not registering would break the chain) by incorporating elements of *jus sanguinis* into entitlements otherwise derived from *jus soli*. These proposals were considered by the administration, and twice that summer by the Executive Council. As Russo explained, he was endeavouring to protect the status and rights of residence of children born out of Gibraltar due to the evacuation 'and to provide for the introduction into the Colony of new male blood'. The gendered objective would be secured by that emphasis on granting Gibraltarian status to fathers born outside Gibraltar. However, the proposal for legislation along these lines ran up against two obstacles, first, the concern of the new governor, Sir Noel Mason-MacFarlane, in office 1942–44, with the shortage of accommodation and, second, the immediate exigencies of war. Russo was asked to estimate the increase in population which his proposals might generate – a daunting task – but his report and any subsequent files seem not to have survived.[85]

It was later reckoned that 824 children had been born to evacuees between

84 MP326/1936, untitled, undated, unsigned memorandum, but minutes, dated 8 June 1943, name the author, and see Ormsby-Gore to Ironside, 24 May 1939, para. 6.

85 MP326/1936, minutes 8 June–22 Nov 1943, including extracts from minutes of Executive Council 20 June and 30 July 1943.

1940 and 1951.[86] There was, in truth, no immediate problem concerning their future which could not be sorted out subsequently by legislation, since they at least had rights of residence, and there was no question of leaving them in exile when repatriation of their parents and other evacuees got under way. Around 16,700 Gibraltarians had been evacuated, and from October 1943 much official attention was devoted to planning and then organising their return, until the last of nearly 14,000 persons wanting to get back to Gibraltar were landed in August 1951. About 2,000 Gibraltarians opted to remain in the United Kingdom.[87] Since there was a chronic shortage of accommodation, there was more government interest locally in restricting rather than increasing the number with automatic rights of residence. Indeed, in the immediate post-war years British consuls overseas were warning other British subjects that they might not be admitted to Gibraltar even if accommodation were available for them.[88] A plan was also debated in 1949–50 to increase emigration from Gibraltar so as to reduce population (obstructed because of political concerns about colonial immigration from the West Indies into the UK).[89] In fact, the only early amendment to the Aliens and Strangers Ordinance was in 1946, to increase the penalties for evasion.[90]

Nevertheless, Sir Kenneth Anderson, governor 1947–52, did not ignore the issue, nor the views of prominent Gibraltarian civilians. Their input was to be very important. Anderson was often stuck between, on the one hand, an imperial government insistent still on maintaining traditional military interests in Gibraltar but sensitive to wider political obligations and, on the other, civilian politicians claiming to represent the more precise interests of their constituents in a Gibraltar – and in a post-war world – pressing towards democratic self-determination. As will be seen in a later chapter, these years were to witness an extension of the role of Gibraltar's city council and the size of its electorate, the organisation of Gibraltar's first political party, and the steps from November

---

86 *Census 1951*, Table 4A.
87 Finlayson, *Fortress*, pp. 234, 236.
88 TNA, FO372/6620, Bevin to consular officers, 14 Sept 1948.
89 TNA, CO91/543/1, Cook to Bennett, 31 July 1950, and enclosures, and Bennett to Cook, 11 Sept 1950; and see Official Notice placed by UK government in *Gibraltar Chronicle*, 18 Nov 1950, warning prospective migrants from Gibraltar of employment and accommodation problems in UK. A century earlier, Governor Sir Robert Gardiner had failed to persuade the War Office to adopt his emigration plan: GGA, Confidential Despatches from Sir Robert Gardiner, 1853–5: Gardiner to Newcastle, 7 Oct 1853 and 13 Jan 1854; Despatches to Gibraltar 1854: Newcastle to Gardiner, 7 March 1854.
90 *Laws of Gibraltar: Annual Volume for 1946* (Gibraltar: Gibraltar Library Committee, 1947), Aliens and Strangers (Amendment) Ordinance, No 18 of 1946, pp. 67–8.

1945 to November 1950 which led to the opening of Gibraltar's first Legislative Council, with its elected members.[91]

In October 1947 Anderson asked his attorney-general to pick up the business interrupted by war and to draft an Immigration and Residence Ordinance. He was, he reported to the Colonial Office, aware of the shortcomings of the existing Aliens and Strangers law (essentially still the ordinance of 1935) and anxious to clarify rights of residence at once and to prevent an accommodation problem from becoming worse by the repatriation and permanent settlement of persons 'not belonging to the Colony'. Defining who did belong should be determined quickly. This did not happen.

The draft ordinance he sent to the Colonial Office in June 1948 had already been considered by the Executive Council with its civilian members and also, on its advice, by a committee presided over by the attorney-general but otherwise made up only of civilians: J.A. Hassan, chair of the city council, who was also leader of the Association for the Advancement of Civil Rights (AACR); W. Thomson, from the Chamber of Commerce, representing the voice of business and employers; A.E. Huart, leader of Gibraltar's Transport and General Workers' Union and therefore a representative of the organised working class; and, unsurprisingly, P.G. Russo, the former member of the Executive Council who 'has made a special study of the problems covered by the draft Ordinance'. The argument of the attorney-general, which does not seem to have been explicitly contested, was that Gibraltar had to be regarded as a fortress and that population increase could not be much further allowed without risks to health and well-being; and also that Gibraltar's proximity to Spain and North Africa left it vulnerable to smugglers and other dodgy characters. It followed that, first, permanent residence should be restricted to those who 'belong to' the colony and who would be registered and granted a certificate of identity; second, measures should be in place, as always, to manage with permits the entry and temporary residence of others; third, strict controls should exclude various categories of undesirable immigrants. This last was not really contested, because they followed restrictions pretty standard elsewhere in the empire, designed to keep out the politically risky, ex-prisoners, the ill-educated, the diseased, the disabled and others who might become charges on public funds.

The difficulty lay in drawing the line between the first and second categories. The majority view was that a person to be registered as, in effect, a Gibraltarian (though in this draft that word was not used) should be a British subject, born in lawful wedlock or subsequently legitimated, who had been domiciled in Gibraltar for seven years prior to registration (thus requiring a period of local

---

91 W. Jackson and F. Cantos, *From Fortress to Democracy; the Political Biography of Sir Joshua Hassan* (Grendon: Gibraltar Books, 1995), pp. 39–68; J. Garcia, *Gibraltar: The Making of a People* (Gibraltar: Panorama, 2nd edn 2002), pp. 35–70.

residence to confirm or demonstrate 'belonging'). The draft also required that such a person either was born in Gibraltar prior to 29 June 1900 (a well-established requirement); or was born in *or outside* Gibraltar and whose father had been born in Gibraltar before that date (thus catering for that generation born to evacuees outside Gibraltar); or was born *in or outside* Gibraltar and whose father was entitled to be registered as a Gibraltarian because *his* father would have qualified because he had been born in Gibraltar before that date (thus catering for the children of those Gibraltarians who had been born outside Gibraltar and dealing with Russo's earlier concerns); plus the wife or widow of any of these qualifying (male) persons; plus, but at the discretion of the governor, a British subject born in or outside Gibraltar whose mother would have been classed as a Gibraltarian but for her marriage to a 'stranger' (thus losing her Gibraltarian status) and yet whose father (the 'stranger') had resided in Gibraltar for at least seven years and intended to remain (and had thereby enhanced the claim to Gibraltarian status); plus any legitimate and registered child of any qualified male (and by implication wherever born, though presumably the child of any such person would in due course have to qualify as 'belonging' by one of the other regulations). The intent was to steer round the disjuncture caused by the evacuation; the guiding principle was to privilege descent through the male line; and the consequence was another scheme to salt *jus soli* with a dash of *jus sanguinis*. There was a dissenting voice, that of Hassan speaking for the AACR, who objected to the clause which deprived a woman of her Gibraltarian status and therefore right of permanent residence because she had married a 'stranger' who, of course, did not qualify. On this occasion, impressed by overcrowding concerns, the other civilians accepted what was acknowledged to be discrimination against women. It was at least agreed that actually prohibiting marriage between natives of Gibraltar and strangers, though theoretically attractive, was not politically realistic (as 250 years of British Gibraltar's amorous history had overwhelmingly demonstrated).[92]

The Colonial Office was not comfortable with the draft ordinance it had received. Devastating critiques lambasted its sloppy drafting and consequent obscurities and contradictions, and these were followed up (after several months of careful deliberation interspersed with bouts of neglect) by an official reply in November 1948. This urged a restructuring of the text and, more substantively, a reconsideration, perhaps by the anticipated Legislative Council, of those clauses which discriminated against women marrying strangers. It also drew attention to the failure to address the rights of those British subjects who derived their status from birth in Gibraltar but did not have seven years of residence (and

92 TNA, CO91/537/4, Anderson to Creech Jones, 14 June 1948, enclosing explanatory memorandum and draft ordinance. Regrettably, other relevant government files for this period appear not to have survived.

was that consecutive years or over an unspecified period?) because they were living (perhaps of necessity, given housing problems) across the frontier in Spain or across the water in Tangier. What had made the story more complex, and accounts for the Colonial Office's proposal to widen and not narrow rights of residency, was the recent passage of the 1948 British Nationality Act, which had created the status of 'citizen of the United Kingdom and the Colonies' and consequently confirmed the obligation of the UK to inherit responsibility for citizens 'disowned' by (or indeed deported from) the place of their birth. Problems on this account were already cropping up in relation to emigrated Maltese citizens who were being denied readmission to Malta.[93]

The gap in the records makes it difficult to know what happens next, but it is very likely that the revision of Gibraltar's laws during and after 1948 absorbed the attorney-general's time, and led only to the incorporation of existing law on this matter into one ordinance, now called the Immigrants and Aliens Ordinance of 1950.[94] In addition, setting up the Legislative Council took much longer than anyone had anticipated in 1948. There was some semi-official correspondence but, as before, Governor Anderson was clearly not willing to proceed without taking account of civilian opinion. Therefore, in February 1950 he informed the Colonial Office that, on the advice of his Executive Council, with its unofficial members in place, he had decided to remit the business to a select committee of the Legislative Council with its civilian members when it was inaugurated, which meant further delay.

The Colonial Office, however, wanted him to press on. It was concerned by the uncertain state of the law in Gibraltar, including in relation to deportation after a highly controversial case. In October 1948 Albert Fava, a prominent trade union leader in Gibraltar who claimed native status, had been deported to Britain because of his political activities. The governor's actions had provoked much protest from organised labour in Gibraltar and questions in the House of Commons.[95] Such matters were again more generally in the official mind in London after the recent approval of deportation legislation for Kenya in 1949 and

93 TNA, CO91/537/4, minutes, especially Bennett, 4 Aug 1948, and Creech Jones to Anderson, 5 Nov 1948.
94 Ross (ed.), *Laws of Gibraltar, Revised Edition*, cap. 53, pp. 711–22.
95 TNA, CO537/4060 and /4986, and GGA, Deputy Governor's Files: MP212/48. Ignored in the political histories by Jackson and Cantos, *From Fortress to Democracy* and by Garcia, *Making of a People*, Fava was 'honoured' in Dec 2003 by the Self-Determination for Gibraltar Group: www.self-determination. gi/emancipation.htm, and see J. Jeffries, 'The politics of colonialism: Gibraltar, trade unionism and the case of Albert Fava', *Socialist History Journal*, 29 (2006), 20–40. See also A.J. Heidenheimer, 'Citizenship, parties and faction in Gibraltar', *Journal of Commonwealth Political Studies*, 1 (1963), 249–65, esp. 253–5.

because of other post-war deportation cases in Aden, Cyprus, Malaya, Palestine, Tanganyika, and an especially controversial one in Uganda in 1950.[96]

Anderson did act, slowly. The response he eventually posted off, in December 1950 after the Legislative Council had been set up, captured his uncertainty. He was still reluctant to proceed by replacing the existing Aliens and Strangers Ordinance with a new law. He offered its very muddiness in some particulars as, in practice, a virtue. On the one hand, he was being advised by the committee of civilians which he was consulting that an extended definition of those deemed by local opinion to be persons of 'proved Gibraltarian descent' would be welcome but, on the other hand, that there would be strong opposition to the kind of broadening which the Colonial Office seemed to have in mind so as to embrace those who might be British subjects but whose claims to inclusion were regarded in Gibraltar as suspect. Remarkably, in contrast with previous centuries, Gibraltarians (or at least their most conspicuous members) were now seeking a privileged exclusivity which the Colonial Office had formerly tried in vain to impose. That insistence was indicative of a more determined and distinctive sense of self among some civilians. Moreover, Anderson was concerned that any extension of residential rights would increase problems in 'an already under-housed community', and this matter almost certainly also affected civilian opinion. In addition, while he was keen to retain, in a fortress, the authority to exclude anyone he felt a security risk, he had been warned locally that any clarification of his rights to expel persons from Gibraltar would be controversial unless it was made absolutely clear to the civilian members of the Legislative Council that this power could not be exercised over native Gibraltarians. To leave well alone seemed to him to be wise. Hence he offered to the Colonial Office the draft of a new Immigration and Residence Ordinance, in fact a *seventh* draft by his attorney-general and the one that had finally been approved by the same committee of civilians as before (Hassan, Thomson, Huart and Russo); but enclosed too was the draft of an amended Aliens and Strangers ordinance which Anderson clearly preferred, although it left unaddressed the matters which the Colonial Office had asked him to take into account two years earlier.[97]

The Colonial Office was not at all comfortable with the 'obscurity' of the existing law, and indeed its legal opinion confirmed that it probably did not give the governor the power to deport 'natives of Gibraltar'. By this time, in spite of the advice of the 1933 committee, powers to deport people who 'belonged'

96 TNA, CO91/543/3, Anderson to Creech Jones, 22 Feb 1950, Creech Jones to Anderson, 27 March 1950, minutes; CO91/543/4, memo 'Deportation of British Subjects from the Colonies' on Anderson to Griffiths, 28 June 1951; see CO536/224 for the Uganda case and TNA catalogue for other examples.
97 TNA, CO91/543/3, Anderson to Griffiths, 16 Dec 1950, and attorney-general's memorandum, minute of 3 Jan 1951.

to a colonial territory had been retained by the governments of the British Solomon Islands, the Gilbert and Ellice Islands, Kenya, Nyasaland, Somaliland and Tanganyika, but most of these were being asked to amend their local laws, leaving also Brunei, Malaya and the New Hebrides as well as, nominally, Gibraltar in which 'special circumstances' were said to justify such powers, even though, in Gibraltar's case, the legality of that authority was thought to be fragile even in official circles.[98] It was on whether he really needed the authority to deport a 'native of Gibraltar' that the governor was particularly asked to comment in April 1951.[99]

The interesting response of Anderson in June 1951 was that he accepted, obviously with some regret, that he did not already have such power and that he should not now seek it, because such legislation 'would never be passed by the local Legislature'. Here is evidence not only of the effect locally of the Fava case, but also more generally of a local insistence that the native-born (and other approved Gibraltarians) 'belonged' and could not be deported as generalised British subjects from their place of origin. Beyond that he stuck to his view that amending the existing law was least likely to raise the vexed question of who else might claim a right of residence in Gibraltar. He also made it clear that he did not want further to antagonise local opinion, since he was also in the middle of a big row over taxes with the local moneyed elite. If action had to be taken, it should be the minimalist position of merely amending the existing law. His attorney-general, on the other hand, who had been sweating over this for years, much preferred a completely new ordinance, even though the committee of civilians he had consulted was reluctant to include among permanent residents those who would be embraced by the wider definition of 'belonging' which the Colonial Office had come to favour and who, like the native born, would therefore be exempt from deportation. Perhaps because of these divided opinions, the Colonial Office no longer pressed for immediate action, even though office staff were uncomfortable with the obscurities in the existing law in relation to 'belonging' and power to deport.[100]

Not only did sleeping dogs lie, they seemed to perish. Not until January 1953 did a senior member of the Colonial Office admit that 'I have now re-studied this corpse'. There had as yet been no London response to the governor's letter of June 1951. This official's belated advice was that no attempt should now be made to insist that Gibraltar should enact legislation giving the governor the

---

98 The issue of deportation remained a political and indeed a parliamentary issue right through 1951: TNA, CO91/543/4, memo 'Deportation of British Subjects from the Colonies' with Anderson to Griffiths, 28 June 1951.

99 TNA, CO91/543/3, Griffiths to Anderson, 20 April 1951.

100 TNA, CO91/543/4, Anderson to Griffiths, 28 June 1951, minutes of 18 Oct, and 7 Feb–14 Feb 1951.

power to deport native Gibraltarians, though he reckoned that the authority to deport others had better be retained, because civilians on the Legislative Council wanted the governor to be able to remove such less truly 'belonging' residents. He was also resigned to a merely amending ordinance, rather than try to force through the Legislative Council a judicially more appropriate but politically more tricky new law.[101]

It is worth remembering, minor amendments and consolidations aside, that this 'law' remained the Aliens Order in Council of 1885 combined with the Aliens Order Extension Order in Council of 1900, that tickets for daily entry and permits of temporary residence were still being issued by the police authorities, and that only by exclusion from those regulations were permanent residents, by default, identifying themselves and being recognised by others as 'Gibraltarians'. It is very striking that Dr H.W. Howes, then Gibraltar's Director of Education, even in the conclusion to his serious study (published in 1951) of the people living on the Rock since the beginning of British rule, did not provide, because he could not, a legal definition of 'the Gibraltarian', even though that was the title of his book.[102]

In spite of some twitchings of the corpse in the Colonial Office's morgue, nothing further was done to bring the beast to life until, in February 1953, Albert Isola, an unofficial member of the Legislative Council, pressed for a select committee 'to consider what persons are entitled or ought to be entitled to the rights and status of Gibraltarians or natives of Gibraltar'. Members of 'the Legislature were desirous of seeing progress being resumed on the matter'. So prompted, the new governor, Sir George MacMillan, requested a response to his predecessor's letter of June 1951. At least this time there was a pretty quick reply. While the Colonial Office would still prefer a new ordinance, it would accept an amended old one which would also allow right of residence to legitimated or even illegitimate children 'born in Gibraltar to a male line of Gibraltarians', and it was prepared to follow local wishes and grant the governor the power to deport naturalised British subjects but not true 'Gibraltarians', the native born, who alone would have permanent rights of residence. However, it did suggest that, before legislating, the governor, if he wished, could allow a select committee to chew over again who should qualify for permanent residence, since this was pretty clearly something with which civilian members were much concerned.[103]

Governor MacMillan's response in August 1953 enclosed an amended and not

---

101 TNA, CO926/85, MacMillan to Lyttleton, 17 March 1953, preceded by minute of 20 Jan 1953, misdated 1952.

102 H.W. Howes, *The Gibraltarian: The Origin and Development of the Population of Gibraltar from 1704* (Gibraltar: Medsun, 3rd edn 1991, 1st edn 1951).

103 TNA, CO926/85, MacMillan to Lyttleton, 17 March 1953, minutes, Lyttleton to MacMillan, 15 April 1953.

a new ordinance, on the grounds that this was less likely to stir up controversy, though he still anticipated a demand by unofficials on the Legislative Council for further alterations to the proposed extended definition of 'permanent residents' (intended only to add to the list the illegitimate descendants and wives or widows of permanent residents), and he warned that the whole thing might have to go to a select committee. But he also argued that no powers of deportation were, in fact, needed, because permanent residents, who would see themselves as the Gibraltarians, could not be deported and the rest, who would be on temporary permits, could be expelled simply by not renewing them. Judging by pencilled comments on the draft ordinance, some Colonial Office staff were not comfortable with potentially serious slips in the drafting but, pending a closer (and again delayed) scrutiny by the legal eagles, the governor was only asked to think again about the deportation matter, especially in relation to British subjects. MacMillan did, and insisted upon protecting his executive powers rather than allowing the kind of judicial process prior to deportation which characterised other colonies. The Colonial Office in response – and we are now in March 1954 – corrected the governor's interpretation of what was intended and asked him to reconsider the virtues of allowing for judicial processes in deportation cases.[104]

Incomplete official records obscure precisely what happened next, but it seems that a select committee of the Legislative Council was indeed formed, made up of J.A. Hassan, Albert Isola, A.W. Serfaty (three unofficials) and the then attorney-general, to devise new rules.[105] The outcome was an important amending ordinance late in 1955 which came into operation on 30 March 1956. This retitled the negative-sounding Immigrants and Aliens Ordinance and produced the positive-asserting Right of Residence in Gibraltar Ordinance. This measure affirmed that only British subjects could qualify as Gibraltarians, that only Gibraltarians had a permanent 'right of residence' and that, with the exception of service personnel, everyone else required a permit to reside. More precisely, Gibraltarians were all those born in Gibraltar on or before 30 June 1925. This would include a number of people whose antecedents may not have been unequivocally native born but who, by 1956, were likely (though not necessarily) to have been long-time residents and to have proved their 'belonging'. It should be noted that the 1900 Aliens Order Extension Order in Council had set the contemporary date of 29 June 1900 as the start date, a kind of immediate amnesty for resident British subjects, so the 1925 date approved by the Legislative Council

104 TNA, CO926/85, MacMillan to Lyttleton, 17 Aug 1953 and memo and draft ordinance by attorney-general, minutes, Lyttleton to MacMillan, 11 Nov 1953, MacMillan to Lyttleton, 4 Dec 1953, minutes, Munster to MacMillan, 10 March 1954.
105 *Report of the Proceedings of the Fourth Legislative Council of Gibraltar*, 3rd Session, 30 March 1962, p. 136. Hassan incorrectly gives the date of this as 1952.

with its civilian representatives was more demanding. In addition, Gibraltarians were also defined as the legitimate children of male persons born in Gibraltar on or before 30 June 1925: these children did not have to have been born in Gibraltar, thus legalising the Gibraltarian status of those born, for instance, in the United Kingdom during the evacuation. However, that still left the problem of *their* children, who would not have qualified as Gibraltarians because their fathers had not been born in Gibraltar: they were gathered in and classed as Gibraltarians if they could show that they were descendants by legitimate male descent from a male person whose father or paternal grandfather had been born in Gibraltar. This emphasis on male lines of descent was further emphasised by tacking on as Gibraltarians the wives or widows of male Gibraltarians. Many of these women may have qualified as Gibraltar born anyway, but others, perhaps born in Spain, would not – but in either case they personally could not bequeath the status of Gibraltarian to their children except through their Gibraltarian husbands.[106]

The law inevitably reflected the circumstances of its production. These were, externally, the intention still of the imperial government to prevent, administratively, the overcrowding of a fortress and also, nevertheless, to avoid the kind of political controversies which highly restrictive rules and expulsions generated. Certainly, these aspirations were generally accepted inside Gibraltar, and not only by the colonial government. But there was also an additional and increasing input by civilians with political clout into the laws defining 'belonging'. The element of *jus sanguinis* embedded in the new law (with its very strict patriarchal substance) owed most to their insistence that the application of *jus soli* should be modified to embrace those they deemed ethically or, if you wish, ethnically, to be Gibraltarian.

Under new management: the Immigration Control Ordinance and the Gibraltarian Status Ordinance, 1962 and after

The civilian imperative becomes still more evident when, with further constitutional evolution, Gibraltarian civilian politicians became principally responsible for the next round of legislation. From September 1956 the elected members on the Legislative Council had become the majority; in 1957 more of the elected members became associated with specific government departments; and in 1959 a chief member was officially recognised. Accordingly, when the governor, Sir Charles Keightley, agreed in October 1959 that the Executive Council should

---

106 Immigrants and Aliens Amendment Ordinance, No 24 of 1955, summarised in *Annual Report on Gibraltar*, Gibraltar Government, 1956, p. 5. There were minor changes but not to definitions in the Right of Residence in Gibraltar (Amendment) Ordinances, No 5 of 1958 and No 2 of 1959.

again consider immigration and residence, the business was first investigated by a committee of unofficial members, chaired by Hassan. In October 1961 it produced a 'Right of Residency' report, and this steered the attorney-general in his drafting of an Immigration Control Bill and of a separate Gibraltarian Status Bill (a split the Colonial Office had long been urging). In January 1962 these bills were then considered in the Executive Council, after which, by now character-istically, they were amended following discussions between the attorney-general and the unofficial members. The process was then further fronted by unofficials when, on 30 March 1962, the two bills were introduced by Hassan, as chief member, to the Legislative Council, with its unofficial majority. Appropriately, both bills were seconded by P.G. Russo. Following the second reading of the bills, the amendments proposed were then considered by the unofficial members of the Executive Council and their recommendations were reviewed and adopted by the unofficial members of the Legislative Council. As a result, the third reading of both bills was passed without further debate on 25 May 1962.[107]

Hassan's introductory remarks indicate continuity with the past. They show how much civilian members had been conditioned by the post-war squeeze on space and, more important, by a developed sense of a community identity. The 'main feature still remains', he said, 'of ensuring by these laws that the Gibraltarian himself is not crowded out of his own native hearth'. Remarkably, 'and with great respect to our predecessors', he also stated that the members of the Exchange Committee who in 1874 had protested so vigorously against the restrictions imposed on alien settlement by the colonial government's 1873 Aliens Order in Council lacked 'foresight'. It followed that immigration controls were essential, and it also followed that the past practice of colonial administra-tors also pretty much remained. So the Immigration Control Ordinance began by confirming that no permit was required by any 'Gibraltarian' or by any British subject in government service (or their families). However, everyone else, as in the past, needed a permit either for daytime entry or of temporary residence, allow-ing overnight stays ranging from two days to one year, though an annual permit was henceforth also dependent on proof of employment. There were also the usual duties on hoteliers and keepers of lodging houses to maintain registers of visitors, and there were the well-established roles of immigration officers in polic-ing admissions. An archival archaeologist can recognise regulations transmitted from the ancient past to the modern present in the list of prohibited immigrants and in the stipulated punishments for unlawful entry and for harbouring the unlawfully entered. There was also a clear statement of the governor's power to deport non-Gibraltarians (with the usual caveats about political refugees).

107 GGA, Executive Council Minutes, vol. 3, minute 813, 30 Jan, minute 877, 15 May 1962; *Report of the Proceedings of the Fourth Legislative Council of Gibraltar*, 3rd Session, 30 March 1962, p. 127.

However, what was new and what Hassan described as 'the real meat' of the law was the authority of the 'governor in council' (that is, with unofficial members of the Executive Council present) to use his discretion also to grant certificates of permanent residence to acceptable persons, though without making them 'Gibraltarians'. These could include a man who was not a Gibraltarian but was a British subject and married to a Gibraltar-born woman, provided that he had demonstrated his suitability for this privilege, especially by having been resident in Gibraltar for at least fifteen years, having a 'sufficient knowledge of the English language' and being of 'good character'; or, if not yet a long-term resident, who could show that he intended to become one, had housing available, and was 'likely to be an asset to the community'. This regulation allowed such a British subject to marry a Gibraltarian woman without obliging her, as in the past, either to live apart from her husband, or to live abroad with him, or to live uncertainly with him in Gibraltar while he held only a temporary permit of residence. Interestingly, in an explicit piece of discrimination, a permanent right of residence could also be granted to anyone who could prove that Great Britain was their country of origin and that he or she was of good character and would be 'an asset to the community'. This remarkable allowance was explicitly designed to encourage 'retired United Kingdom residents, to come here and enjoy the sun and income tax of three shillings in the pound'. This strategy of lightly soaking the rich while the rich soaked up the sun was dependent on the building of high-quality flats on sites whose development would, supposedly, make them too expensive for local residents.[108]

Permits of residence were not needed by Gibraltarians. Who they were was to be determined by the Gibraltarian Status Ordinance. The definition of a Gibraltarian was 'a person who is registered as a Gibraltarian in the register'. This was not the tautology it sounds, for the essence of the bill was to determine who was to be entered in that register and how. Once again, there was much inherited practice. To be registered, a person had to be a British subject, which, naturalisation laws aside, pretty much excluded aliens (but, as we shall see, not all). Thereafter, like the 1955 ordinance, the criteria combined *jus soli* and *jus sanguinis* rules. To be registered as a Gibraltarian one must either have been born in Gibraltar on or before 30 June 1925; or be the legitimate child (but

108 *Report of the Proceedings of the Fourth Legislative Council of Gibraltar*, 3rd Session, 30 March 1962, pp. 126–34, 203; *Supplement to the Gibraltar Gazette*, No 762, 1 June 1962, Immigration Control Ordinance, No 12, 1962. See also TNA, CO926/1156, 'Construction of High Class Flats in Gibraltar', statement of May 1962, and editorial in *Gibraltar Post*, 13/14 Oct 1962, and GGA, Minutes of Executive Council, Item 1, 17 July 1962, which confirmed that the UK residents looking for their place in the sun had to have a minimum income of £1,500 for a single person and £2,000 (over £30,000 in today's prices) for a couple, and in the latter case the income should not cease on the death of one partner.

not necessarily born in Gibraltar) of a male person born in Gibraltar; or be the descendant by legitimate male descent of a male person registered under the preceding rules; or be the wife or widow of any such person. There was then a clever rule to get round the evacuation period, which allowed the registration of a British subject who would have otherwise qualified as a Gibraltarian had that person's father or grandfather been born inside and not outside Gibraltar between 1 April 1940 and 31 December 1949. There was also an unequivocal statement (equivalent to the rules under the British Nationality Act of 1948) that a Gibraltarian woman who married a non-Gibraltarian did not cease to be a Gibraltarian.

However, the children of that marriage could not automatically be registered as Gibraltarians, and this reservation led into a series of discretionary options which included allowing the registration of the legitimate child of such a marriage if the child was of good character and had been born in and had lived in Gibraltar for at least ten years, and intended to stay, and had a sufficient knowledge of English (and was thus more aligned to the mother's side of the partnership than, possibly, the father's). There were also rules to allow for the registration of illegitimate and adopted children.

Moreover, and with interesting implications, a person could be accepted onto the register as a Gibraltarian even if there were no *jus soli* or *jus sanguinis* justification. This would be a person of good character, with a sufficient knowledge of English, with a permanent home in Gibraltar, resident for twenty-five years in aggregate and ten years without a break before applying, and aged over 30. Ideally, this person would be a British subject, but otherwise qualified persons who were not British subjects but in fact aliens might also be acceptable. The import of this particular provision was spelt out by Hassan in the Legislative Council: 'They are really part of the community.' In summing up, Hassan indicated, though only implicitly, how restrictive he and his colleagues had found the *jus soli* rules in the past, even those modified by *jus sanguinis* concessions. The new law, he said, 'opens the door to Gibraltarian status to a number of people whom we all know as Gibraltarians but who, for some technical reason, unfortunately cannot enjoy that status'. The word 'we' in that sentence was intended, for it contrasts with the pronouns used in the next. 'Although they well know that they would never be removed from Gibraltar if they behave as their past residence would indicate that they will continue to behave, the feeling that they may be here on sufferance or on permits is one which makes people unhappy.' Hence the need for such 'unqualified' people to prove their worth by being of good character, English speaking, long resident, and so on. Moreover, though the governor in council was to determine whose names went on the register as Gibraltarians, he was to be steered by an Advisory Committee (responsible also for advising on who was worthy to receive permits of permanent residence under the immigration rules). Hassan stressed that this committee would be made up of local people, since 'a

Gibraltarian knows who is a Gibraltarian'. He went on (and note the pronoun), 'we know who is a Gibraltarian'. He explained how: 'by his conduct, by his way of life, by his whole approach, we know who is a Gibraltarian'. No one in the Legislative Council queried this approach. 'Belonging', for the first time, was determined not only by *jus soli* or by *jus sanguinis*, which, whatever problems they threw up, could be operated using objective documentary evidence, primarily birth certificates showing place of birth and descent. Henceforth, room was also found for cultural identifiers: those who belonged would be recognised as 'one of us' by their peers sitting on an advisory panel made up of 'Gibraltarians' who would make recommendations to an Executive Council with its unofficial 'Gibraltarian' members.[109]

There had been one preliminary to the passing of these bills, legally necessary and symbolically rich. On 23 May 1962 'at the court of Buckingham Palace', the Gibraltar Aliens Orders in Council (Revocation) Order in Council was approved. Its substance had one sentence: 'The Aliens Order in Council, Gibraltar, 1885 and the Aliens Order Extension Order in Council, Gibraltar, 1900 are revoked.'[110] Colonial rules were dead. Hassan acknowledged in the Legislative Council the help that the administrators of the colony had given him and his colleagues in preparing the new laws. However, he particularly appreciated that 'for the first time we should have been left entirely on our own to settle our problems of right of residence . . . we were deciding the policy'. Indeed, from now on and after more than two hundred and fifty years, setting the rules for policing the frontier, for immigration controls and for determining rights of residence were the responsibility (within the framework of international law and convention) of Gibraltarian officials and ministers.[111]

Since 1962, political changes in the government of Gibraltar have been many and rapid and are still in progress, though the trajectory is clear enough. Steps towards increased internal self-government, marked by constitutional leaps as in 1969 and 2006, have been accompanied by adaptations consequent on the obligations following from membership of the EEC from 1973 and, latterly, the EU. Moreover, impediments to the movement of people across the frontier with Spain, and then adaptations required during the period of border closure, inevitably put an added strain on the government's management of immigration and residence.

It is true that the capacity of Gibraltar to accommodate more people increased with extensive land reclamation schemes, the release of land from the Ministry of

---

109 *Legislative Council*, 30 March 1962, pp. 135–42, 203; *Supplement to the Gibraltar Gazette*, No 762, 1 June 1962, Gibraltarian Status Ordinance, No 13 of 1962.
110 *Supplement to the Gibraltar Gazette*, No 762, 1 June 1962.
111 Hassan explicitly acknowledged the switch in responsibility: *Report of the Proceedings of the Fourth Legislative Council of Gibraltar*, 3rd Session, 30 March 1962, p. 137.

Defence to the civil government for development, and the construction of high-rise flats. This can certainly help explain why the population of Gibraltar grew by nearly 6,000 in the forty years from 1961. Nevertheless, Gibraltar's capacity to absorb and to provide properly the quality of life expected by an affluent society continued to affect government policy on entry and residence. External circumstances altered, but Governor Don in the early nineteenth century would not have been surprised by the issues his managerial successors still faced in the early twenty-first.

One duty was to determine who were Gibraltarians as defined in the 1962 Ordinance, with their unequivocal right to permanent residence. In fact, for a whole generation the original law was deemed largely sufficient. Minor amendments only were made by ordinances in 1963 and 1965. Substantial change came only in 1999. It was then that the minister, not the governor, became the person ultimately responsible, and references to British 'subjects' were altered to British 'nationals' or British Overseas Territories citizen. However, the truly important alteration, indicative of changing values throughout the Western world and not just in Gibraltar, was the removal of most distinctions in the treatment of legitimate and illegitimate children and, especially, between male and female. Entitlement to Gibraltarian status was no longer to be dependent on descent from a male person. References in the original law to males, wives, Gibraltarian women, widows, fathers and paternal grandfathers were changed to persons, spouses, Gibraltarians, widows and widowers, parents and grandparents.[112] It would be nice to think that this major break with the past, which carried considerable implications for 'belonging', might have had some impact on the local press. The passage of the new law was noticed in *Panorama* as long overdue, in an article headed 'Equal Rights to Gibraltarian Women', but it was ignored by the *Gibraltar Chronicle*, while that month 'The Female File' page of the weekly *Vox* instead ran important articles on such issues as 'Make Your Body Look Better', 'Is Revenge [on a love rat] Over-Rated?' and 'What Does He Say About You When Your [*sic*] Not There?'.[113]

It is possible, however, that the major impact of the revised Gibraltarian Status Ordinance in consolidating a Gibraltarian sense of identity had already been effected by the principal law, and it is just conceivable that the gender equality marked by the 1999 amendment was merely a catch-up measure indicative of

112 House of Assembly Debates, 15 Oct 1999; *First Supplement to the Gibraltar Gazette*, No 3, 21 Oct 1999, 'Gibraltarian Status (Amendment) Ordinance, No 26, 1999'; www.gibraltarlaws.gov.gi/articles/1999–26.pdf.

113 *Panorama*, 4–10 Oct 1999, p. 9; *Vox*, 1 Oct, p. 21, 8 Oct, p. 21, 15 Oct, p. 17, 23 Oct, p. 19, 29 Oct 1999, p. 18. Not until 2003 were all-male juries outlawed in Gibraltar, by a ruling of the Privy Council in London: *Daily Telegraph*, 11 Nov 2003; www.bbc.co.uk/radio4/womanshour/2003_45_mon_01.shtml.

social change. If so, the Immigration Control Ordinance and its many modifications – at the last count twenty-five pieces of amending legislation since 1962 – may have been more important. The consolidated measure, as of 2008, covers fifty-two pages and runs to well over seventy clauses. At core, the original law continues to operate intact, with immigration officers at the frontier checking non-Gibraltarians for valid permits of entry or residence, and the power remains to deny entry to prohibited immigrants, to detain those infringing (or helping to infringe) the laws and to deport the unacceptable. Exemptions from the regulations remain for employees in government service and their families, and discretionary permits continue to be made available for non-Gibraltarian husbands and children. Remarkably, the privilege of a permanent right of residence for, especially, folk from Great Britain judged wealthy and worthy has also survived.

But there have been modifications. Taking account of changing social mores, the entitlement to residence of non-Gibraltarian men married to Gibraltarian women became conditional from 1976 on the partnership remaining intact (separation might lead to the husband's loss of permit), and the reduction of the age of majority to 18 obliged children to have their own permits earlier than before. However, the more challenging alterations to past practice followed from, in a sense, the assault on the frontiers of Gibraltar from external laws and external actions. The first of these were consequent on Gibraltar's constitutional status as a colony or, later, overseas territory of the British crown. The British Nationality Act of 1981 introduced the category of British Dependent Territories citizen, with restricted rights of abode in Britain. By an amendment to the bill, Gibraltarians had been excepted, but the measure required alterations in Gibraltar's own immigration laws.[114] In addition, the accession of the UK to the European Economic Community in 1973 had, potentially, a major widening effect on Gibraltar's immigration controls because of what came to be called the European Union's commitment to open frontiers. Much Gibraltar legislation has been devoted to reconciling Gibraltar law with European directives.[115] In that sense, access for immigrants to Gibraltar, like access to Britain, has been switching the focus from British Commonwealth subjects to EEC/EU citizens, and in both cases the welcome has been less than wholehearted, more so in Gibraltar with its limited space and its historic Mediterranean connections.

There was, of course, in this recent period the further complication of

114 Gibraltar's exceptional status was initially resisted but then conceded by the British government: Hansard, *House of Commons Parliamentary Debates*, 6th series, vol. 5, cols 879–98, 2 June 1981, vol. 10, cols 768–82, 27 Oct 1981.

115 Immigration Control Act, www.gibraltarlaws.gov.gi/articles/1962–12o.pdf; GGA, MP 620/69, 'EEC/Immigration Control Ordinance', Head of Special Branch to Commissioner of Police, 19 July 1973.

disrupted relations with Spain. In the past Gibraltar had drawn substantially on citizens of Spain. As the census returns in Tables 7.2a–c imply, a substantial number of Spanish-born people may have entered Gibraltar for work but many, especially women, through marriage, had stayed or later taken up residence in Gibraltar, especially during and after the Spanish Civil War and the 1940s evacuation. In addition, of course, literally thousands more entered daily to sell their labour, services or supplies to civilians and garrison alike. The economy had apparently come to depend upon them. Hence the tight closure of the frontier was immensely disruptive. La Línea had, historically, housed what may be called Gibraltar's reserve army of labour, and denial of access to that force obliged government and employers to look elsewhere. The evidence in the census demonstrates that the alternative supply came not from Britain, not from other British territories, and not from the EEC but from beyond, from Morocco. The number of 'foreign' residents born in Spain but living in Gibraltar fell from 1,121 in 1964 to a mere 170 in 1970. Moreover, the average number of male and female Spanish workers crossing the frontier daily to work in Gibraltar had been 8,649 in 1953. Following Spanish restrictions, the numbers fell, but the 4,666 still arriving in June 1969 dropped to zero when the gates were locked. Meanwhile, the number of 'foreign' residents born in Morocco and living in Gibraltar had increased from a mere 39 in 1961 to 2,045 in 1970.[116] Unlike Spanish workers in the past, they could not nip across the frontier at dawn and be out before bedtime, and therefore most Moroccans, of necessity, required permits of residence. Documentation relating to the issuing of permits to such individuals is, of course, not in the public domain, but it can be reasonably deduced from the legislation in operation that the permits issued would have been temporary and conditional, since none would qualify for permanent residence under the discretionary rules or EEC regulations. Also, acquisition of Gibraltarian status with automatic right of residence remained dependent on the same culturally specific rules of 1962 (a Gibraltarian would know a Gibraltarian). Some Gibraltarians were worried that Moroccans might not be properly welcomed and integrated into the community.[117] They were, of course, also Muslims. The census counted only six Muslims in Gibraltar in 1961, and 1,989 in 1970.[118] Confirmation of conditional status is suggested by the disproportionately large numbers who were men, either unmarried or at least alone (2,894 males and 224 females in August

116 These figures include a few born in Morocco but not Moroccan nationals. GGA, MP620/69, 'Population of Gibraltar', annual reports compiled by the police give substantially higher figures for the number of resident Moroccan nationals, 77 on 31 Dec 1964, 2,801 on 31 Dec 1969, 3,036 on 31 Dec 1970, 3,409 on 31 Dec 1971.
117 *Social Action*, no 19, May/June 1968, p. 3.
118 *Census 1961*, Table 9, p. 28, *Census 1970*, Table 7, p. 6.

1970, according to a police report[119]), and also by the marked reduction in their numbers indicated in the censuses, down to 1,790 in 1991 and to 874 by 2001, after the frontier with Spain was reopened and workers from La Línea once more trekked over the isthmus.

Responsibility for deciding on entry, residence and status therefore had shifted in 1962 from mainly British to mainly Gibraltarian hands. Thus, in 1963 recommendations as to whether Gibraltarian status, and therefore rights of permanent residence, should be allowed to four naturalised British subjects who were formerly left-wing Spanish political refugees were directed to the chair of the Advisory Committee, who was, appropriately, P.J. Russo.[120] In 1970 an application for Gibraltarian status by a man born in Gibraltar, but after 1925, and with a Gibraltarian father and a Spanish mother, but with no evidence of his father or grandfather having been born in Gibraltar, and he not having completed twenty-five years of residence in Gibraltar, was directed to the civilian chief minister for his solomonic judgment.[121] In 2006 the delay in determining whether a work permit and therefore permit of residence was to be granted to a Moroccan who had worked and lived in Gibraltar (and who was also president of the Moroccan Community Association) generated political controversy, and an appeal to the governor.[122] Also in 2006, the authorities were required to judge the application for residential status by the son of a former British prime minister with a criminal record, presumably under the rules allowing a discretionary permit of permanent residence to a person whose country of origin was Great Britain and who 'is of good character and is likely to be an asset to the community'.[123]

Conclusion

Looking back over the substance of this chapter and the two earlier ones which have explored the demographic management and population history of Gibraltar since 1704, certain continuities obviously stand out. Whether the government was colonial and military or domestically independent and civilian, those in charge largely accepted that, with its limited size and scarce resources, Gibraltar was at risk of overcrowding, with detrimental effects on health and happiness. What is indeed striking in that continuity is the poacher-turned-gamekeeper

---

119 GGA, MP620/69 report dated 9 Sept 1970. The aggregate is peculiarly higher than that in the census.
120 GGA, MP502/61.
121 GGA, Box: Miscellaneous Matters Relating to the Alien Question, 'Henry Earle', 16 Feb 1970.
122 www.gibfocus.gi/details_headlines.php?id=425.
123 For Mark Thatcher see, for example, www.chronicle.gi/readarticle.php?id= 000010586&title.

change of opinion among articulate civilians, who had once pressed for easier entry and residence for folk of alien origins and yet became just as determined to restrict entry when they too felt space was tight and also, just as important, when they felt their culture threatened.

As another continuity, there was also an acceptance by those in command that Gibraltar could not be demographically self-sufficient and that, whether the outsiders let in were Jewish traders or Spanish domestic servants or Moroccan labourers, the economy needed their skills and energies. It followed, as a further continuity, that those responsible for managing access needed a formal frontier on the isthmus and at points of entry by sea. Frontier fences, walls and gates inscribed territorial claims on the landscape. On the landward side there had been, to say the least, an ongoing dispute with Gibraltar's near neighbour. This was also the line at which most of the policing of entry was conducted, by whatever the political regime in control in Gibraltar. In addition, there were – and still are – forms of internal surveillance and monitoring which are common over the three centuries, like the census inquiries. The point of all this was to implement the regulations, also conceptually similar in all phases, which determined who was to be allowed in on a daily basis only, who was to be allowed temporary residence, who was to be judged a permanent resident, and who was to be kept out altogether. Hence registers were to be kept. They list, for instance, those early nineteenth-century holders of conditional residential permits and include more recently the registers of Gibraltarians (and some others) permanently belonging.

Discontinuities arise in the allocation of people to those categories. Whatever initial aspiration the British authorities may have had for creating in Gibraltar a British Protestant community had been undermined by the limited number of the most desired immigrants and the need to do business with others. But the intentions of the British authorities thereafter were at least to reserve a privileged place for British subjects, whatever their place of origin. *Jus soli* was to determine right of residence. However, the native born were often less particular about their marriage partners or their employees or their drifted-in near neighbours. The melting-pot effects which are characteristic of other (and much larger) immigrant societies did the rest.

Or rather, until some of those moving in were less favoured by those already present. It is a truism that one prompt to the particular identity of societies, as of individuals, is a sense of difference from the 'other', an outside comparator. From the late nineteenth century, sections of the civilian population, inevitably the articulate types who appear most often in the historical records, were bent upon drawing distinctions between themselves as the native born and others from outside, including some other British subjects. It was at this point that *jus soli* rules were not sufficiently helpful, since civilians were finding, as had the British authorities, that ensuring that only the 'right' kind of people got born in Gibraltar was difficult to arrange. Hence the input of civilians into policy making chimed with the British government's thinking, and there followed the incorporation of *jus sanguinis* features into regulatory practices. Twentieth-century developments moved strongly in that direction, as can be seen especially in the options explored to get round the unfortunate demographic disruption caused by the Second World War evacuation. *Jus sanguinis* restored rights of belonging.

Decades of reproduction and the long residence of families, plus the regulatory framework, had done much to produce a Gibraltarian sense of identity. The complication, honestly recognised in everyday life and legislatively expressed in 1962, was that not all those long resident could be legally recognised as Gibraltarians by either traditional *jus soli* or *jus sanguinis* rules. They were not native born and might not have Gibraltar-born ancestors. There was, though, more to cultural similarity than place of birth and ancestry. Hence the effort to include others as Gibraltarians who, by cultural affinity, were recognised as 'one of us'. The risk behind this generosity of spirit lies in the need to pass judgement on what must be subjective, not documented, assessments. However it is done, determining who belongs puts others on or over the literal or metaphorical frontier as 'not one of us'.

It has been repeatedly emphasised in this study that Gibraltar was and is a small territory. However, the issues here being addressed are not unique to Gibraltar, because they are not determined by size. All modern states wrestle with precisely the same issues, defining by law who belongs and on what terms others may gain entry. Whether the airport is on Gibraltar's isthmus or Heathrow or JFK, immigration controls are familiar. Internally too, state authorities carry out equivalent surveillance exercises, in the interests of 'good management'. Indeed, it has been persuasively argued that modern states are not characterised only by their attempts to monopolise the 'legitimate means of violence', by which is meant external defence and the maintenance of internal order. They also share an aspiration to monopolise control over the movement of people across their frontiers.[124] This can be for positive reasons, to attract more of those with skill, energy and capital, and to tap them as potential taxpayers (or even for military service). But controlling movement over the frontier can also be for negative reasons, to prevent the entry, or at least the permanent settlement, of those deemed a threat to settled citizens. To that extent, the governments of Gibraltar and more particularly its post-colonial governments are behaving like those of other modern states. Indeed, the fact that responsibility for determining who gains admission, who belongs and who does not, now rests with a Gibraltar government managed by elected civilians is an indication that, in this respect at

---

124 J. Torpey, *The Invention of the Passport: Surveillance, Citizenship and the State* (Cambridge: Cambridge University Press, 2000), esp. pp. 4–7.

least, Gibraltar is a nation state. The qualification to that must be that like most other nation states, in Europe at least, its capacity for enforcing independent rules has been lessened by EU law. But that constraint, for good or ill, is shared with states far larger than Gibraltar.

Legal criteria for admission and belonging still, for the most, part combine *jus soli* with *jus sanguinis* features, as an examination of British immigration and nationality laws, for instance, will show. But immigration of others, not thereby qualified, also characterises most modern states. This has opened up chances for immigrants and provided resources and opportunities for recipient societies. However, it would be merely pious to pretend that immigrants have found acceptance easy. Most modern societies, and no longer the classically described 'settler societies', are probably best now described as multi-ethnic, containing 'old stock' (never blandly homogeneous anyway) with the new(er). The challenge for all, and Gibraltar is distinctive only in its modest size, is achieving inclusiveness, and that depends on the behaviour of individuals as much as on the operation of state policies.

8

Earning a living in the twentieth century

The quality of life for entrepreneurs and employees resident in Gibraltar, and of their families, depended considerably on their energies and enterprise; but it is a similar platitude to acknowledge that a great deal also depended on context. Men, and women (to adapt Marx), make their own history, but not in circumstances of their own choosing.[1] It was therefore fortunate that in the nineteenth century, as has been shown, the circumstances in which people in Gibraltar found themselves were eventually conducive to an improvement in material living standards, of course in stuttering fashion and with an inequitable distribution of rewards. The important contextual elements facilitating economic activity included, first, the political stability and legal infrastructure provided by colonial authority and, second, investment, eventually, in public services like water supply and improved sanitation. As we shall see in the next two chapters, in spite of substantial alterations during the twentieth century in the way Gibraltar was governed, political stability was preserved (by no means true in all British colonies), the legal framework in which economic activity was internally conducted was extended, and public services supporting economic activity and the good life were also further developed.

However, nineteenth-century economic survival and growth had also depended on two external factors over which neither the civilian population nor even the colonial government had had any control. The first related to the very large military and naval presence in Gibraltar, funded by British taxpayers' money and determined by the imperial government. This paid for recurrent expenditure by the garrison on wages and running costs and for capital investments in defence establishments. The profits of Gibraltar businesses and the earnings of Gibraltar workers depended much on the money pumped in and the economic demand thereby generated. This feature therefore needs to be further examined for the twentieth century. While there were legitimate civilian complaints about the arrogance of members of the garrison, up and down the ranks, it remains to be seen whether their presence or their absence was economically more beneficial to Gibraltar.

In addition, such prosperity as Gibraltar enjoyed had also been sustained in the nineteenth century by open frontiers. The Rock was not isolated. It was

1 K. Marx, *The Eighteenth Brumaire of Louis Bonaparte*, 1852, any edition, p. 1.

important that water connects and does not divide, since much business and employment, profit and wages, had been generated by selling services to shipping. The volume of that traffic had depended generally on open frontiers at sea as well as, specifically, on how many ships could be induced to stop in Gibraltar and spend. At the same time, it was also important in the nineteenth century, as we have seen, for Gibraltar to receive by sea a wide range of imported foodstuffs and consumer goods for local consumption. However, since imports, especially of tobacco and cloth, had massively exceeded local demand, the re-export of huge volumes of such stuff had been essential to generate the profits and the wages to pay for that which was domestically consumed, and this too depended on open frontiers. While much had been re-exported by sea around the Mediterranean and West Africa, much – a great deal – had been slipped across the land frontier into Spain. Economically, 1704 was being denied, while the political consequences of the frontier were being exploited, different tax and price regimes on either side making Gibraltar-supplied products highly competitive and appealing. Moreover, on the supply side, most of the fresh produce needed to feed the population had, in return, come across the frontier as legitimate commerce.

Moreover, it had not just been goods which had travelled across the barrier. There had been people. As we have noted, the Gibraltar economy was supported by an immigrant labour force from Spain resident in Gibraltar on conditional permits and by literally thousands of others who lived in Algeciras and, especially, in La Línea who had come in daily. Some of these had indeed rights of residence as Gibraltar-born British subjects who lived 'abroad', often because they could not afford to live 'at home'; but most were Spanish citizens who sensed better employment prospects and other rewards as domestic servants, dockyard workers or coal-heavers. Whether conditions at the frontier, in the past a political barrier but an economic thoroughfare, continued to work to Gibraltar's advantage throughout the twentieth century must therefore be a matter for consideration.

One further feature of the nineteenth century must also be added to the agenda for this chapter. The occupational structure had been shifting towards a reduced proportion of the population in the higher-rewarded ranks of the mercantile classes, offset by a very modest increase in the number of professionals and a more noticeable increase in the number of white-collar clerical workers. But the bulk of the resident population had been engaged in manual work and there is good evidence that their income rewards, varying inevitably by skill, were also in general inevitably modest, not least as a consequence of there being the competitive challenge of a substantial reserve army of labour across the frontier. The result, until late in the century, had been for many a low standard of living. However, judging by the numbers eager to enter, work and live in Gibraltar, those low wages and overcrowded houses with poor facilities were still apparently more attractive for many workers and their families than those available across the frontier in Spain. It is therefore possible that even then the circumstances for natives of Gibraltar began to shape a British Gibraltarian identity as 'better off' in comparison with the 'other' across the frontier. It is therefore important to consider for the twentieth century what happened to Gibraltar's occupational structure and to the material rewards which accrued to Gibraltarians.

The needs of the people

Until late in the twentieth century, when serious land reclamation from the sea took place, Gibraltar was no bigger than in the past; nor was it any richer in terms of natural resources. No one seems to have conducted a census of cows or goats or hens, or of rabbits and other edible forms of wildlife, but there was not much there to harvest. Moreover, the opportunities for market gardening were diminished at North Front when the airfield was established during the Second World War, and thereafter housing and other developments ate into available space, largely leaving as natural resources the rock of the Rock and unreliable rainfall. Yet, as was demonstrated in the previous chapter, the resident civilian population of 1901 was already 20,355. While it had fallen to 17,405 by 1931, it reached new levels of 20,845 by 1951 and 24,672 by 1970. In 2001 it stood at 27,465. Accommodating this increased population within the political confines of the colony had largely been effected by the post-war housing programmes which will be discussed in a later chapter. But this achievement may also be seen as compounding the problem: how was an increasing and proportionately large population to be economically supported in such a resource-barren spot?

Nor, of course, was this merely a matter of physical survival. In 1848 the fossilised skull of what proved to be a Neanderthal woman had been discovered in a quarry at the North Face of the Rock, but Gibraltarians in the twentieth century were not troglodytes who would be satisfied with a hunter-gatherer existence. At the beginning of the century they were already locked into a mature capitalist economy with a rich material culture. From mid century many more would enjoy a standard of living at least comparable with that of many parts of the western world and, as the decades passed, material expectations grew. Food was to serve appetites and not merely to suppress hunger; apartments were homes and not just shelter; clothing and household goods were badges of social status and style and not merely conveniences; the 'not-invented' became the material 'must-haves' of the next generation. In December 1951 there were 1,924 private cars licensed in Gibraltar; in December 2006 there were 14,746, one car for every two people. Television broadcasting began in 1962; by 2001 there were 9,700 households and 7,310 television licences.[2]

2 *Gibraltar Annual Reports* (London: HMSO) for 1950–51, p. 43; for 1963, p. 88;
   Abstract of Statistics (Gibraltar: Government of Gibraltar), for 2006, pp. 1, 17, 75;

Nor was it merely material 'needs' that demanded satisfaction. Particularly after the Second World War, and largely following British models, there was a growing civilian demand for services. The population, or at least those speaking for it, expected a better education service, improvements in the public utilities and more support for the elderly, deprived children, bereft women, the unemployed and the sick. There developed, as elsewhere, a belief that one was entitled to good health and happiness. Services had to be paid for privately in fees, or publicly in rates and taxes, and this presupposed that there was an income to be creamed for such provision. Moreover, in Gibraltar too there settled in an expectation that it should not be 'all work and then bed'; there should be non-earning leisure time for all. One characteristic of the twentieth century was that those in gainful economic activity were working fewer hours and yet were expected to support an increasing number of dependants – children who stayed longer in education and joined the workforce later, plus the elderly who retired earlier and lived longer.

There is nothing whatever unusual about these twentieth-century revolutions in expectations and demands. What is, however, peculiarly interesting is how small and resource-starved Gibraltar was able to cope. It should not be merely assumed, looking back from the early twenty-first century, that Gibraltar would. This, after all, was a century disrupted economically by two world wars and with more than enough conflict and killing in the so-called 'pre-war', 'inter-war' and 'post-war' periods. The further integration of an international global economy also led to international global depressions, notoriously in the late 1920s and early 1930s, followed in the 1960s and 1970s by roaring inflation. During those decades and thereafter British imperial governments (and others) were faced with the soaring expenses of the Cold War and the arms race and were looking for a way to manage decolonisation with the least loss of income, power and face.

And then for Gibraltar, very close to home was Spain, and Franco. His wartime ambition to recover Gibraltar by hanging his hopes on an Axis victory had come to nothing. Post-war, and provoked by the Queen's visit to 'her' Gibraltar in 1954, his government began a campaign of political attrition against British control of the Rock which threatened Gibraltar's economy in a fashion not experienced since the termination of the 'Great Siege' in 1783. The obstructions were ratcheted up until Spain locked the frontier gates in 1969 and began a 'siege' that lasted until 1985, when uneasy connections were re-formed.[3] Ever since the British takeover, Gibraltar's economy and people had depended heavily on a frontier which was porous, and especially for a labour supply. In December

for 2004, p. 80. Including motor cycles and commercial vehicles, in 2006 there were nearly 84 licensed vehicles for every 100 persons.

3 *Annual Reports*, 1954–55, p. 3; for 1969, p. 4; J. Garcia, *Gibraltar: the Making of a People* (Gibraltar: Panorama, 2nd edn 2002), pp. 78–81, 156, 189.

1948 the registered labour force in Gibraltar numbered some 20,000 (total population about 28,460) but, of those, 12,600 were 'aliens', overwhelmingly Spanish (7,600 men, 5,000 women), and of these, on average 8,300 workers, again mainly Spanish, entered daily to work. By 1953 the dependency had become still greater, when around 13,500 of a workforce of 20,280 were reckoned to be 'aliens' and an average of 8,649 were entering daily. The squeeze beginning in 1954 had reduced the number of 'aliens' in the workforce to 9,600 by 1964 (7,006 men, 2,594 women). Even so, in 1963 they constituted 98 per cent of Gibraltar's domestic servants, 74 per cent of construction workers, 74 per cent of catering and hotel labour, and so on.[4] Then, in 1966 the Spanish authorities prohibited the movement into Gibraltar of the remaining 2,000 or so women workers and in 1969 of the remaining 4,666 men. By this time the total workforce in Gibraltar had been reduced to around 12,000, a very much lower proportion of the total population (24,672 in 1970) than in 1948. The labour shortage had to be made good, partly by longer hours and higher rates of employment for Gibraltarians, especially women, and partly by importing workers from Morocco (as noted in the previous chapter).[5]

Gibraltar of course also needed supplies of goods as well as labour. Reliable figures for imports are hard to come by early in the century because the restricted range of items upon which duties were levied limited the range of data collected, but it is evident that manufactured goods imported shortly after the Second World War, as before, included necessities such as footwear and clothing plus consumer goods like electrical appliances, glassware and motor vehicles. It is also apparent that, at this time, the UK still remained the largest single source of such products, helped after the Second World War by the operations of the sterling area and restrictions on trade in dollars, but other sources included France, Holland, Italy, Austria, Sweden, Czechoslovakia and indeed Spain, not least for building materials. Spain of course had also been, historically, the principal source of fresh foods (all imports of fish and almost all fresh fruit and vegetables still came in from Spain in 1964),[6] and this too did not alter until border restrictions seriously kicked in, though other foodstuffs (coffee, meat, flour, tinned milk) plus tobacco, wines, spirits and fuel (especially coal, charcoal and petrol) were brought in from elsewhere in the

4 GGA, P. Selwyn, 'Report on the Economy of Gibraltar', 15 Feb 1965, p. 8.

5 *Annual Reports* for 1948–72: the workforce in Dec 1969 was 8,914 insured plus approximately 3,000 non-insured. On government efforts to recruit labour from elsewhere, including Malta but especially Morocco, see TNA, CO926/373 for 1954–56, and CO926/2133 and /2134 and FO371/185822 for 1966, and FCO9/522 for 1968. On women at work see M. Summerfield, *A Woman's Place: Memoir of a Gibraltarian Woman – a Llanita*, ed. G.B. Silva (Gibraltar: Summerfield, 2007), pp. 99–102, 113–16.

6 Selwyn, 'Report on the Economy, p. 8.

Mediterranean, the UK, other parts of Europe and, indeed, still further afield. In 1950, shortly after something like external trade statistics were first compiled, imports to the value of £6,042,933 were recorded (foodstuffs £2,001,000, general manufactures £2,093,600, fuels £1,075,400, wines, spirits, tobacco £872,933). These reached a peak of £15,047,269 in 1963, after which frontier problems led to more licensing of imports and a falling-off of quantities, to the still considerable value of £9,195,027 in 1966, before bouncing back to £12,777,294 in 1972 (£3,889,283 foodstuffs, £6,360,530 manufactured goods, fuels £1,652,735, wines, spirits, tobacco £874,746). By then the sources of supply included Morocco, Japan and the United States, and conspicuously not Spain.[7]

The challenge did not disappear. Data in Table 8.1 below show imports (excluding petroleum products) of £11 million in 1972, £82 million in 1986 and £366 million in 2006.[8] Sustaining throughout the twentieth century such a level of imported goods, very high in proportion to the population, was a remarkable achievement and essential to the material well-being of the civilian population and, indeed, given Franco's intention to 'starve' Gibraltar into surrender, to its political future. What therefore needs to be considered next is how, economically, it was managed.

Paying the bills: garrison town

The economic advantages to Gibraltar's civilian population of the strategic value which the British government placed on the fortress need first to be addressed. There was a downside to this, of which civilians were often aware. It included the privileged control over space which the army, navy and later air force asserted. Until very late in the century, when property was being released by the Ministry of Defence, civilians had to make do for business purposes with the bits left over, including waterfront access. Leases of limited duration and the threat (made real, for example, during the war of 1939–45) of reoccupation of space for overriding military purposes were additional inhibitions and, as we shall see in a later chapter, securing land for housing was fraught with problems.

That said, imperial government expenditure on the garrison unwittingly helped to pay for Gibraltar imports and services. Precise figures throughout the century are not available, though it was reported in 1904 that expenditure on the army stationed at Gibraltar amounted to over £402,000 and that in 1971 UK government departments were spending about £5 million a year in Gibraltar. It was also calculated in 1968 that the armed services were responsible for over 60

7 *Annual Reports* for 1949–72.
8 For further information on value, composition and origins of imports see the sequence of *Abstract of Statistics*, 1972–2006.

per cent of Gibraltar's gross national product, a huge proportion.[9] Considerable among costs were wages. A 1965 estimate, acknowledged to be rough, reckoned that, of the £4.5 million then being spent in Gibraltar by UK government departments, the pay of UK personnel amounted to £1.2 million.[10] According to the census of 1901 the total population perched on the Rock or living on craft moored in the bay was 27,460, and this included 6,475 service personnel and their families, nearly 24 per cent of the total.[11] In 1911, the latter amounted to 5,781, nearly 23 per cent of the total of 25,367. True, by 1921 military personnel and their families numbered only 3,478, but they still formed nearly 16 per cent of a diminished grand total of 22,018. In 1931 they numbered 3,759 and nearly 18 per cent of a total population of 21,372. Boosted by the war, service personnel in 1947 numbered 4,823.[12] While census returns thereafter record only the spouses and children of service personnel, the continuing economic presence of the military can be inferred. Family members increased from 1,439 in 1951, over 6 per cent of a total civilian population of 23,232, to 2,290 in 1961, over 9 per cent of the total of 24,502. By that time, conditions of service and local facilities were much more conducive to wives and children accompanying military personnel stationed at Gibraltar. Only thereafter might the market significance of military families have declined in relative and then absolute terms, though initially only modestly. In 1970 they numbered 2,161, nearly 8 per cent of the total civilian population of 27,965, and they remained pretty much the same in 1981, 2,265 of 29,616, still close to 8 per cent. The big drop came later. By 1991 the families of military personnel numbered only 1,371, below 5 per cent of a civil population of 29,084. By 2001 the census tells us that the families of service personnel plus civilian Ministry of Defence employees in Gibraltar numbered just 745, out of a total civilian population of 31,623.[13]

9 *Annual Report for 1904*, p. 22, and see reports for 1905–7 for other substantial annual transfers, though seemingly becoming less inclusive of all expenditure: later annual reports lack this information. For 1971 figure see report on the economy of Gibraltar in GGA, DG files, MP769. For the GNP figure see TNA, FCO9/520, 'Effects of Spanish restrictions on Gibraltar's economy', Aug 1968.

10 Selwyn, 'Report on the Economy', p. 5.

11 For sources in this paragraph see Table 7.1 in Chapter 7 and notes. Note that the totals are, of course, larger than those of the resident *civilian* population cited earlier, which also excluded transients and those living on board ships in the bay.

12 *Annual Report for 1947*, p. 7. *Annual Report for 1948*, p. 7, gives a total of 4,760. Both reports provide figures for each of the three services.

13 Some further figures on military personnel and families can be culled from HCPP, *Gibraltar, Third Report from the Expenditure Committee*, HC147, 1972/73, Appendices 1 and 2: in 1953, army garrison c.3,000; in 1973, Royal Navy (including hospital) c.480, RAF c.490, British Army 976 officers and men plus 1,150 wives and children, suggesting a total of under 2,000 men, plus families.

Courtesy of the British taxpayer, military personnel brought with them a spending power above the local average. While their demands of course sucked in imports, their purchases of services and of goods in local stores and bars generated the employment and the profits which helped Gibraltar civilians in turn to purchase the imports which they too wanted. It was officially reported in 1922 that the transfer of two infantry battalions for service elsewhere had had a regrettably depressing effect on local trade,[14] and one can anticipate the impact on civilian employment, incomes and purchasing power which accompanied the later decline in garrison numbers.

British government spending on the garrison also, of course, included expenditure on running the naval dockyard, barracks and, in due course, the airfield, and other establishments, including the military hospital. Available data do not provide regular figures for local expenditure, but the 1965 report referred to above points to a UK government expenditure of £2.1 million on civilian wages and salaries plus £1.2 million on other costs.[15] In addition there were capital investments. Some of the costs would have gone on equipment bought in the UK and shipped out, but nevertheless there was also an additional boost of externally funded demand which would translate, through commerce, into local income – with multiplier effects elsewhere on civilian purchasing power. This is particularly evident when one considers the considerable number of civilians employed by the services as skilled or unskilled labourers, for example as domestics, craftsmen and clerical staff. Redeployment of civilian employees following the reductions in the numbers of army personnel first became a government concern in 1962, but was offset initially by increases in the other armed services.[16] From the available data it is difficult to determine what proportion of this ancillary workforce was Gibraltarian as distinct from those who came from over the border (including of course some who were Gibraltarian), but in any event much of the pay of daily migrant workers was likely to be spent in Gibraltar shops by those many thousands of employees living in Spain who purchased consumer goods on their way home.[17]

Additional income to pay for imports also resulted from the substantial amounts of development aid which passed from the British to the Gibraltar government in the second half of the century, beginning in 1948 with a grant of £100,000 and in 1949 with a cheap loan of £250,000. There was no precedent

14 *Annual Report for 1922*, p. 3.
15 Selwyn, 'Report on the Economy of Gibraltar', p. 5.
16 TNA, CO926/1399, /1400 and /1401, 'Effects of cuts in UK defence expenditure on the economy of Gibraltar'; WO32/19998, 'Gibraltar garrison, redundancies from rundown 1962–4'.
17 See for example, *Annual Reports*, for 1948, p. 18; for 1949, p. 16; for 1954–55, p. 28; for 1957, p. 20.

for this in the nineteenth century. By 1970 Gibraltar had received £3,532,000, mainly as grants, from the Colonial Development and Welfare Fund (CD&W). More overseas aid followed thereafter. The details and purposes of these awards will be described in a later chapter. Here it is sufficient to note that much of it was spent on housing programmes, port development, roads, schools and other infrastructure investments. The major beneficiaries of the CD&W fund were, as intended, the hugely populated and underdeveloped colonies in the Pacific, West Indies and Africa (Nigeria receiving over £40 million) and places like Malta, badly beaten up during the Second World War (over £20 million), but Gibraltar did well per head of population.[18] Once more, it is difficult to assess what proportion of this expenditure went to outside suppliers and how much occurred in Gibraltar, but there is no doubt that this injection by British taxpayers did directly generate employment and income in Gibraltar and thus the wherewithal to purchase imports of essential and increasingly desirable goods.

It is not quite the same thing, but a further boost to civilian spending power, in classic Keynesian fashion, was also effected by the programmes of development which the Gibraltar government itself funded, raising loans totalling £2,250,000 between 1948 and 1965 for expenditure on capital projects.[19] More recent injections of aid from the European Commission will have had the same effect. In the ten years 1994–2004 Gibraltar was allocated regional aid amounting to nearly €24 million to assist with tourism and business development, including the conversion of former military sites to other uses, plus €540,000 to help especially with inter-regional development, plus a share from the social fund grant going to the UK.[20]

Selling goods and services

However, it would be misleading to imply that Gibraltar's imports and Gibraltarian living standards were simply funded by 'free lunches' handed out by the British government and the European Union. There was much self-help. Some efforts were made locally to reduce the need and therefore costs of imports by 'home-grown' activities, of which in the 1930s a milk supply was one minor example (though most milk was still imported).[21] Increasing the supplies of

18 HCPP, *Colonial Development and Welfare Acts 1929–70*, Cmnd 4677, 1971, esp. Table 1, pp. 44–5.
19 For details and costs see Chapter 10.
20 Following links from http://ec.europa.eu/grants/index_en.htm#policy and www. gibraltar.gov.gi/.
21 In 1935, 366 pints of cow's milk and 5,780 pints of goat's milk were imported daily, the home-produced being 832 pints and 120 pints respectively: GGA, MP20/1936, minute of 3 Feb 1937.

potable and brackish water was another and much larger enterprise, involving not just capturing more rain supplies but distilling fresh water from the sea. Even so, supplies were under pressure when demand rose and rain did not fall, and water was still being imported by sea as late as 1972.[22] But there was nothing naturally available locally that could be exported to pay for the great volume of imports.

As in the past, therefore, Gibraltar incomes greatly depended on importing goods to be re-exported at a profit. A small trade after 1945 in re-exporting war wreckage – scrap iron and obsolete military vehicles – was not going to be a big earner. There were efforts to get a value-added profit by processing some imports before selling on, similar to the long-established business of processing tobacco, including a probably fleeting match-making factory in the 1920s, a struggling business of canning imported fish, olives and fruit in the 1950s and meat in the 1960s, an attempt at the production of textile goods for export, and the importing, roasting, blending and exporting of coffee. Since 1994, Gibraltar Crystal has been a successful glassware business, though this is a family firm and modest in size.[23] Of regular value were the profits on those imported goods sold to tourists and to the crews and passengers of visiting ships and, as mentioned earlier, the items bought daily by Spanish workers going home – until such exports were banned by the Spanish authorities in 1965.[24]

Most valuable were goods brought in and sold on in bulk to other places (though the only figures available, from 1950, give data only on goods liable to import duty on first arrival). They show, over twenty-odd years, just how erratic re-export sales might be. They were valued in 1950 at £1,576,910 (when imports were over £6 million), and then rose in 1952 to £4,034,771 (imports over £7.5 million), only to plunge by 1955 to £2,742,779 (imports over £6.5 million). The bumpy ride was to continue. While there was a new peak of £5,150,966 in 1960 (imports by then over £11.5 million), there were struggling years thereafter, and a new nadir of £2,175,680 was reached in 1969 (imports still a massive £10 million), though there was a modest recovery thereafter to £3,025,501 in 1972 (but imports nearing £13 million). The expectation was that profits would still be made by selling mainly products with which we are pretty much familiar from the past. In 1950, 6 per cent of re-exports were wines and spirits, 17 per cent

22 *Annual Reports*, for 1948, pp. 30–1, for 1952–53, p. 38, for 1972, p. 77. For water shortages, see for example, *Gibraltar Chronicle*, 19 June, 3, 17 July, 28 Aug, 9 Oct 1964, and for an episode when contaminated water supplies were shipped in from Norway, 9 Feb 1967. For recent developments see T.J. Finlayson, 'Gibraltar's water supply', *Gibraltar Heritage Journal*, 2 (1994), 60–72, esp. pp. 70–1.

23 *Annual Reports*, for 1924, p. 6; for 1950–51, pp. 19–20; for 1954–55, pp. 8, 28; for 1956, p. 19; for 1957, pp. 4, 20; for 1962, p. 26; for 1964, p. 30; www.gibraltar-crystal. com/gibcrystal.html.

24 *Annual Report for 1965*, p. 3.

Table 8.1 *Imports and exports (excluding petroleum products) in £m, 1972–2006*

Year	Imports	Exports	Year	Imports	Exports	Year	Imports	Exports
1972	11.0	1.2	1984	44.4	6.3	1996	276.6	70.4
1973	12.8	1.5	1985	70.6	10.8	1997	216.8	49.2
1974	15.2	1.2	1986	82.0	16.7	1998	255.8	75.1
1975	18.4	1.4	1987	111.7	19.6	1999	299.8	74.3
1976	21.1	1.8	1988	116.1	22.5	2000	317.9	83.9
1977	28.0	2.5	1989	165.5	42.1	2001	302.5	83.7
1978	31.3	3.3	1990	202.7	46.4	2002	256.2	98.5
1979	39.1	4.7	1991	219.1	12.9	2003	286.1	90.1
1980	47.1	4.2	1992	262.2	35.4	2004	292.0	108.4
1981	44.1	5.7	1993	267.6	62.3	2005	303.0	110.0
1982	46.9	5.6	1994	283.7	84.0	2006	366.4	130.9
1983	43.3	6.6	1995	258.7	73.6			

Sources: *Abstract of Statistics 2004 and 2006*. Imports CIF (carriage, insurance and freight costs included); exports FOB (insurance and transport costs excluded).

tobacco and tobacco products, and a whopping 77 per cent was fuel, but by this time no longer coal but petroleum products. In 1964 the same trio dominated re-exports, but while wines and spirits retained their proportion with 7 per cent, petroleum products were now only 27 per cent and tobacco had coughed its way to the top with 66 per cent. However, the volatility of markets is suggested by another reversal in 1972: wines and spirits 5 per cent, petroleum up to 60 per cent and tobacco (and a few other products) down to 35 per cent.[25]

Table 8.1 shows thereafter the remaining problem (though confused for our purposes by the exclusion of imports and re-exports of petroleum products). Imports massively exceeded exports. As Gibraltar's Chamber of Commerce put it in 1931, with excessive clarity: 'Gibraltar imports everything, but exports nothing'.[26]

One should also note, in the light of past history, that smuggling did not stop with the opening of the twentieth century. In spite of efforts by government authorities both sides of the border, there remained a black economy, which boomed even during the Second World War. However, eventually, a raft of Spanish measures and more internal surveillance pretty much limited the old business to young men with fast boats, though, economically, this only compounded the trade balance problem.[27]

25 Calculations based on figures in *Annual Reports*.
26 GGA, MP510/1929, Report of the Trade Committee, 9 March 1931, p. 3.
27 For a review of steps taken, the remaining value of the trade to the government and the economy, and further action to suppress smuggling, see TNA, CO91/477, Smith-Dorrien to Churchill, 7 April 1921, and CO91/480, Smith-Dorrien to Churchill, 4 Feb and 17 March 1922; and GGA, MP49/1929, Godley to Amery 31 Jan 1929,

As in the past, Gibraltar civilians therefore had to pay for their imports by selling services, particularly to shipping – in effect, by invisible exports. This was a highly competitive business, with suppliers in other ports on both sides of the Mediterranean eager to cut in. In the 1920s businessmen regularly aired complaints about competition from Oran and Algiers, where labour was cheaper.[28] What was needed, of course, was continuous investment in the port's facilities, including the passenger terminal, some of it coming from private sources but much from the colonial authorities and, indeed, as aid from the British government. It also required sharp-eyed entrepreneurs to guess the future. Construction of the first coal-bunkering machines to service steamers was not completed until 1932, but they had a limited life span, the last being demolished as long since redundant in 1969.[29] Already between the wars, long-distance shipping was increasingly powered by oil and not by coal. Coal sales fell by one million tons, to just 196,000, between 1920 and 1930.[30] Many seem to have hoped for a cyclical recovery, but those sticking to coal found demand falling and profits slipping. Few in Gibraltar seem to have been nimble enough to spot the transition. One man in particular, John Mackintosh, was acute enough to make the switch – and died in 1940 with an immense fortune, leaving a trust fund valued at £2 million.[31] In 1952, a peak year, petroleum products imported and then re-exported amounted to 447,115 tons, valued at over £3,500,000; by 1955 there were eight oil hulks in the bay ready to service shipping, and from 1960 piped supplies began from onshore facilities.[32] Ship repair yards, including eventually docks taken over from the Royal Navy, provided an additional service

and MP510/1929, Chamber of Commerce to colonial secretary, 12 Dec 1929. For evidence of continuing smuggling activity in the 1950s and 1960s, and strained relations with Spain, see TNA, CO926/890 and 1959 and FO371/163808, plus the lively account by the poet Laurie Lee, *A Rose for Winter* (Harmondsworth: Penguin, 1971, first published 1955), pp. 11–12, 16–17, 29–30. See also C. Baldachino and T. Benady, *The Royal Gibraltar Police 1830–2005* (Gibraltar: Gibraltar Books, 2005), pp. 74–8, T. Benady, 'Smuggling and the law', *Gibraltar Heritage Journal*, 13 (2006), 98–9, and *Gibraltar Chronicle*, 13–15 July 1995, for recent action against tobacco and drug smugglers.

28 *Annual Reports*, for 1925, p. 3; for 1926, p. 3; for 1927, p. 3.
29 *Annual Reports*, for 1931, p. 5; for 1969, pp. 78–9.
30 GGA, MP510/1929, Report by the Chamber of Commerce Trade Committee, 9 March 1931.
31 *Annual Report for 1962*, p. 3. For his informed criticism of whingeing coal-bunkering businessmen in Gibraltar and pointers to an oil-fired future see GGA, MP356/1930, Mackintosh to colonial secretary, 4 Aug 1930.
32 *Annual Reports*, for 1952–53, appendix IV; for 1954–55, p. 49; for 1961, p. 79. For the Port Development Scheme initiated in 1957 and its funding see *Annual Reports*, for 1957, p. 3; for 1959, p. 3; for 1960, p. 64; and for 1963–65 see TNA, CO926/1838.

Table 8.2a *Port of Gibraltar: steam vessels entered, 1914–60*

Year	Tonnage	Number of vessels	Year	Tonnage	Number of vessels
1914	6,287,900	3,635	1934	11,493,523	4,166
1915	7,111,499	3,769	1935	11,901,769	4,376
1916	7,767,967	3,895	1936	10,858,254	3,598
1917	9,639,329	4,647	1937	13,728,709	4,912
1918	17,190,669	7,607	1938	13,758,528	4,532
1919	13,500,000	5,855			
1920	11,517,208	5,382	1947	10,156,888	5,208
1921	7,265,094	3,924	1948	8,520,834	6,185
1922	5,982,258	4,236	1949	9,002,415	5,574
1923	5,523,917	3,724	1950	8,210,806	4,823
1924	7,218,914	4,638	1951	9,318,891	5,633
1925	6,507,403	4,170	1952	10,137,189	6,039
1926	6,095,171	3,745	1953	9,059,011	4,813
1927	6,602,101	3,744	1954	8,916,651	4,215
1928	6,712,702	3,478	1955	9,991,609	5,107
1929	8,106,699	3,775	1956	10,624,957	8,465
1930	7,227,666	2,810	1957	10,039,042	8,566
1931	6,865,970	2,351	1958	9,741,250	8,625
1932	8,633,259	2,790	1959	7,799,549	4,389
1933	10,152,253	3,078	1960	9,288,198	3,471

to shipping, though varying in volume of business and profitability. Data in Tables 8.2a and b indicate the swings, as do later sources (compiled on a different basis) which record an annual average of 104 deep-sea merchant ships calling at Gibraltar, principally for repairs, between 1976 and 2006, but with as few as 46 in 1985 and as many as 219 in 1987 (182 in 2006).[33]

How much profit could be made from shipping services depended, of course, on how much shipping could be induced to call, and throughout the century that depended on the general volume of international trade as well as on the competition. The statistics in Table 8.2a reveal that the outbreak of the First World War actually boosted the volume of shipping entering Gibraltar, due to the relative security of routes through the Mediterranean.[34] It was not to last. After the war,

33 *Abstract of Statistics 2006*, p. 77. Gibraltar had to compete with other ship repair yards in the UK and in Europe, but particularly with Malta, where the former Royal Navy dockyards were also during this time handed over, messily, to a private company: see S.C. Smith (ed.), *Malta: British Documents on the End of Empire* (London: TSO, 2006), esp. pp. lxi–lxiii, lxvi.

34 *Annual Reports*, for 1914, p. 15; for 1915, p. 11; for 1917, p. 10; for 1918, p. 9.

Table 8.2b *Port of Gibraltar: steam vessels entered and repaired, 1961–72*

Year	Tonnage	Number of vessels	Scheduled liners	Cruise liners	Ships repaired
1961	10,844,486	4,890	291	25	193
1962	10,765,623	4,389	247	56	97
1963	11,460,162	4,006	260	66	104
1964	12,153,851	3,838	233	78	104
1965	13,571,737	3,010	201	89	87
1966	13,737,263	3,389	155	103	109
1967	13,510,796	3,413	96	124	133
1968	12,175,369	3,332	22	117	118
1969	10,242,149	2,399	6	108	65
1970	10,171,848	2,368	0	91	125
1971	11,116,836	2,441	0	88	110
1972	13,296,047	2,243	0	88	103

Source: *Gibraltar Annual Reports*. The report for 1962, Appendix XV, contains a handy graph of the tonnage of shipping, 1946–62. (Figures for ships repaired for 1966–72 differ from those in *Abstract of Statistics 1972*, Shipping, Table G2, 'Main Purpose of Call'.)

as a concerned colonial secretary put it in 1921, the 'world-wide depression in trade was felt severely in Gibraltar and affected the shipping and coaling interests in particular. As the Colony has no agriculture and practically no industries its prosperity depends entirely on commerce, so that trade depression has a more widespread and immediate effect on its community.'[35] Following global trends, there was recovery and a peak in 1929, but thereafter Gibraltar 'did not escape the effects of the general depression in trade',[36] although it again recovered quite well in the later 1930s. The Second World War put a stop to most conventional shipping services and resumption thereafter was initially awkward, and business confidence seems only to have been restored by 1955.[37] In the 1960s Gibraltar did pretty well, but the market was rapidly changing. In 1920 eighteen shipping lines called each month at Gibraltar on scheduled services (mainly fortnightly); in 1938 there were nineteen; in 1956 there were twelve; but in 1969 only P&O still called for a final season.[38] However, cruise liners were arriving with increasing frequency and made up the loss. On average, 84 cruise liners called each year

35 *Annual Report for 1921*, p. 3.
36 *Annual Report for 1930*, p. 3; and see GGA, MP510/1929, for a gloomy analysis by the Chamber of Commerce, 9 March 1931.
37 *Annual Report*, for 1952–53, p. 3; for 1954–55, p. 4; Chamber of Commerce Annual Report for 1955, printed in *Gibraltar Chronicle*.
38 *Annual Reports*, for 1920, p. 10; for 1938, p. 10; for 1956, p. 41; for 1969, p. 79.

in the decade 1976–85, nearly 100 a year in the decade to 1995, after the border had been fully reopened, and then 153 a year from 1996 to 2005. In 1976 a total of 1,892 deep-sea vessels, amounting to just under 19 million tons used the port; in 2006 the figure was 6,629 vessels, including 201 cruise liners, amounting to well over 167 million tons. There was also a growing traffic of yachts and other craft, so that in 2006 a total of 8,988 vessels used the port, over 223 million tons of shipping.[39]

Passengers were also arriving courtesy of another service provider, the airline industry. In 1931 Gibraltar Airways Ltd attempted to inaugurate a regular sea-plane air service to and from Tangier, but neither this nor a similar service to Genoa operated by an Italian company made an economic impact on Gibraltar, and both rapidly failed and were discontinued in 1932. In 1934 the then governor, Sir Charles Harington, objected to a proposal to restore a service from no less a pioneer than Sir Alan Cobham on the grounds that establishing the required landing strip on the racecourse at North Front would interfere with weapons training.[40] However, these were pointers to the future, made economically more attractive by the construction of an airfield by the armed services during the war which (especially after further extensions) was capable of taking high-capacity airliners (and giving passengers the thrill-of-a-lifetime experience of landing in a crosswind). Gibraltar Airways, later called GibAir, was back in business after the war, sharing facilities and dividing routes with British European Airways and its derivatives, and by the 1960s and 1970s competing with several other companies. These flights brought in goods (imports), but also fare-paying passengers (invisible exports), 222,942 kilos of the former in 1957 and 34,199 of the latter, sufficient to justify investment by the colonial government in another port, the air terminal, opened in 1959 and extended in 1964.[41] Visitor arrivals by air in 1972 numbered just over 49,000 and stayed around that mark while Gibraltar remained cut off from mainland Spain, but numbers rose in February 1985, when the barrier came down, to nearly 74,000 and, though thereafter very variable, passenger numbers stayed high, rising to 143,914 in 2006.[42]

39 *Abstract of Statistics 2006*, pp. 77–8.
40 J. Gaggero, *Running with the Baton: a Gibraltar Family History* (Gibraltar: Gaggero, 2005) p. 66; GGA, Box: Executive Council 1921–34, Harington to Cunliffe-Lister, 13 March 1934.
41 *Annual Reports*, esp. for 1931–32, 1947–48, 1957–59, and 1963–64; also TNA, CO926/145, New Air Terminal Building and Improved Facilities for Tourists, 1955–56.
42 *Abstract of Statistics 2006*, p. 56, and see also p. 79 for arrivals by scheduled and chartered flights 1982–2006. Air Traffic Surveys and reports go back to 1972: see for the latest www.gibraltar.gov.gi/, 'Statistics'.

Selling the Rock: tourism, finance and gambling

The real value of the airlines to the Gibraltar economy was not, however, the sale of air tickets, the profits of which mainly went to overseas companies, including the one-time Gibraltar-based company Gibraltar Airways which, in 1989, for sound financial reasons relocated as GB Airways to Gatwick, London.[43] By land and sea as well as by air, what mattered was getting people into Gibraltar who had money to spend, that is, especially, tourists.[44] There had of course been travellers to Gibraltar for literally centuries past, but modern mass tourism was a creation of the twentieth century. Increasingly it was recognised by government and business that resources-starved, import-greedy, export-needy Gibraltar had one commodity to sell: itself. An economy which had struggled since 1704 to prosper largely on re-exports, on the wealth of the garrison and by services to shipping needed to diversify. Emptying the pockets of visitors was an additional modern way of making economic ends meet. The attraction of Gibraltar to many potential visitors was that it was (and is) a warm and usually dry spot in the Mediterranean, and also that it was 'British', with English-language virtues and a recognisable currency, while still being 'abroad'. But it also had two distinguishing marketable assets: the Rock and history.

In the highly competitive modern tourist business, distinction mattered. Gibraltar did not have naturally attractive beaches, pleasant open spaces, spectacular architecture or a unique and vibrant cultural life. But it had what has been defined as a 'place myth', a cluster of cultural associations with a particular geographical location, providing a unique sense of place akin to those enjoyed by the Lake District in the UK or the Canadian Far North.[45] Gibraltar had long since been associated in the UK (and elsewhere) with an appealingly stoic and defiant military Britishness, certainly derived from the Great Siege days and culturally much expressed thereafter in plays and novels. An inquiry in 1974 reported that the strongest image of Gibraltar for 70 per cent of British people was as a military and naval base.[46] 'Strong as the Rock of Gibraltar' had become and remains a turn of speech used in contexts beyond the military.[47] More

---

43 Gaggero, *Baton*, pp. 168–73. EasyJet has recently bought GB Airways and the route to Gibraltar.

44 In 2006, 42 per cent of visitors arriving by air (60,000 people) stayed in Gibraltar, the rest being 'in transit': *Abstract of Statistics 2006*, p. 60.

45 R. Shields, *Places on the Margins* (London: Routledge, 1991), esp. pp. 6, 47, 60–3, 255–65; J. Urry, *Consuming Places* (London: Routledge, 1995), esp. pp. 1–2, 193–210.

46 GGA, Box: Tourism, 'A report to the Minister for Tourism, Trade and Economic Development', Feb 1974, para. 7.

47 'Googling' the phrase on the internet reveals today a wide variety of curious usages.

prosaically, the place had also been the base for generations of service personnel whose recollections orally and in print wrote a cultural signature on British consciousness. In addition, as strikes any visitor to the place, is the very physicality of the Rock itself. Whether arriving by sea, by air or overland from Spain, the limestone uplift of Gibraltar and the spectacular views from the summit have an undeniable capacity to impress, as a space quite unlike the south of Spain, which it appears, lion-like, to face.

But history and geography needed marketing. Tourist facilities were also required to induce not just visits but stays. Such matters formed an active agenda for government and private enterprise from early in the century. In 1927 the colonial secretary took the initiative. He reckoned that a 'good deal can be done . . . to attract tourist traffic', and during the year the committee he chaired, representing also the City Council and shipping, hotel and tourist interests, considered steps 'to popularise Gibraltar as a tourist resort'. A government Tourist Bureau was soon established and official guides, who had to pass an examination, were hired.[48] British government departments and commercial tourist agencies were consulted about advertising.[49]

Noticeably, history and geography were recognised as in need of investment. Improvements were made to the colony's three 'principal sights', the remarkable reservoirs constructed within the Rock, the Moorish Castle on its flank and that part of the gun galleries carved into the north face during the Great Siege which the military agreed to lease to the colonial government (for £400 a year) for opening up to visitors. Significantly, the Gibraltar Museum was also established in 1930.[50] But efforts to persuade the War Office to allow a foreign firm to take over its aerial ropeway, which would have whisked less energetic visitors to the top of the Rock, foundered on its insistence that such an enterprise must be undertaken 'by a purely British concern'. This was a militarily sensitive area and Gibraltar, it declared, was after all 'primarily a fortress and naval base' – whereas for Gibraltar's colonial secretary the top of the Rock was 'one of its tourist

---

48 GGA, Box: Tourism, file 322/1927, 'Suggested Advertisement of Gibraltar as a Tourist Centre', esp. minutes of meeting and Monro to Amery, 29 Nov 1927; Box: Tourism (2), City Council, 4661/1 Government Tourist Bureau 1927–32, file 257/1932, Tourist Bureau, Exchange and Commercial Library, report by sub-committee on tourism, 29 Aug 1927; Box: Exchange and Commercial Library, minutes, 18 Aug, letter from colonial secretary, 16 Aug 1927.

49 TNA, CO91/488/7, for 1928–29 correspondence involving the Crown Agents, the Department of Overseas Trade, the Empire Marketing Board, Major W.T. Blake Ltd and Thomas Cook Ltd.

50 TNA, CO91/489/12, Godley to Passfield, 31 Oct 1929; for the museum and its later development see GGA, Box: Tourism (2), file 257/1932 Tourist Bureau, Exchange and Commercial Library, report by sub-committee on tourism, 29 Aug 1927, para. (d)2; *Annual Reports*, for 1957, p. 54; for 1969, pp. 94–5.

amenities'.[51] Accordingly, though without success, the government continued to encourage more acceptable private companies to take up the idea, or even to construct a funicular railway.[52] Meanwhile, in 1929 a brochure illustrating the existing attractions of Gibraltar and destined for tourist and shipping agencies in the UK and North America was widely distributed. *Gibraltar, The Travel Key to the Mediterranean* predictably and properly pressed home, with illustrations, the key features of the 'place myth': the Rock itself (from all angles), the historical monuments, the museum – and the 'monkeys'.[53] Other publicity activities involved press and poster advertisements, a film, pictorial postage stamps and a postmark bearing the title of the tourist brochure.[54]

It had also been conceded in 1927 that a 'first-class hotel' was needed. When such a construction had been mooted by the governor in 1911 the imagined clientele had been 'naval and military officers and their families', but now, indicative of a switch in economic priorities, the intended market was rich tourists.[55] The urgency of this investment was repeatedly stressed, but private sector capital was needed and difficult to secure. Eventually a firm proposal arrived in March 1929 from Major W.T. Blake, who was already promoting Gibraltar as a tourist destination on behalf of the colonial government, and the scheme subsequently involved the fourth marquess of Bute, who also had tourist interests in Spain and Tangier. Bute was the force behind the business after the rather engaging Blake, possibly a '"wrong 'un"' as one official reckoned, was obliged to pull out when his company went into liquidation in 1931.[56] Construction began in 1930 of what became the

51 TNA, CAOG 14/40, esp. War Office to governor, 12 Nov 1929, and colonial secretary to Crown Agents, 17 Oct 1932.
52 TNA, CAOG14/41, CO91/494/20 and GGA, MP299/1933, especially memo by colonial secretary, 20 Dec 1933.
53 Plus pig-sticking at Tangier. GGA, Box: Tourism, file 463/1930, Tourism (2), file 257/1932, for the publishing and distribution in 1931of a further 20,000 copies of *Gibraltar, the Travel Key to the Mediterranean* and a reprint of 50,000 in 1932.
54 *Gibraltar Chronicle*, 16 Nov 1932, report of Gibraltar Tourist Bureau public meeting.
55 GGA, Secretary of State for Colonies Book: Hunter to Harcourt, 26 June 1911; TNA, CAOG14/42, Monro to Amery, 26 April 1928.
56 On the colourful life of Major Blake, the hotel scheme and the liquidation of Major W.T. Blake Ltd see TNA, CAOG14/42 and CO91/492/7, and GGA, MP399/1931, and Box: Tourism (2), file 138/1932, colonial secretary to Governor of Northern Rhodesia, 5 May 1934, where Blake was by then attempting to hawk his skills as a publicity agent. Blake was also a 'prime mover' behind Gibraltar Airways, MP399/1931, Beattie to Lambert, 19 Oct 1931, and Beattie to Darnley, 16 Dec 1931, initially in partnership with the Gibraltar shipping firm M.H. Bland and Co. For earlier, abortive efforts to secure investment interest, choice of site and the Blake-Bute development see GGA, MP585/1927, 'Rock Hotel'. For Bute, a co-founder

Rock Hotel (a name itself drawing on the place myth), opened in January 1932 (double room with private bathroom and balcony, 22s 6d a night).[57] Reuters correctly reported that 'the new hotel is part of the government scheme for making the Rock a tourist resort'.[58] However, government attempts to persuade other parties to build one more first-class hotel foundered on problems with sites, military obstruction and, in truth, some commercial skulduggery by the Rock Hotel company plotting to block competition.[59] Moreover, although substantial numbers of cruise liners were already calling in the early 1930s and more tourists were arriving, the Spanish Civil War and then the world war put a damper on these early attempts to exploit history and geography for commercial gain.[60]

Matters began again with a trickle back of post-war tourists. In 1951 a committee appointed by the governor recommended the re-establishment of a tourist bureau. This was later to become the Gibraltar Tourist Office, a government department with a minister answerable for policy to the Legislative Assembly (and, following constitutional changes, to the House of Assembly and now the Gibraltar Parliament). It worked with the Gibraltar Travel Association, representing the local travel industry, and from March 1968 it had an office in London.[61] A great deal was spent on advertising the attractions of Gibraltar with brochures and other publicity material (in nine languages) to be issued at tourism trade shows and through tourist offices opened in London, Paris and New York; on wining and dining travel agents and press, radio and television journalists; and on press advertisements, posters, films and talks by tourism officers.[62]

Footnote 56 (*cont.*)

   of the Scottish National Trust, see Gavin Stamp, 'Stuart, John Crichton-, fourth marquess of Bute (1881–1947)', *ODNB*.

57 *Annual Reports* for 1928, 1930 and 1931. A Spanish firm was given the construction contract after a Gibraltar company proved too demanding and uncooperative for GB Syndicate Ltd, who were promoting the venture: GGA, MP585/1927, Blake to colonial secretary, 20 Jan 1931.

58 TNA, CO91/490/3, Reuters report, 27 Aug 1930.

59 For details of frustrated attempts to get a hotel built on the Assembly Rooms site or the Victoria Battery site (north and south of the Alameda parade), see, for the first, GGA, MP299/1933, TNA, CO91/494/20, CO91/495/7 and CAOG14/41 and, for the second, GGA, MP134/1934,and TNA, CO91/495/7.

60 On tourism in this period see also *Annual Reports* for 1926–31, 1934–37.

61 On the Gibraltar Tourist Office (formerly Bureau) and Gibraltar Travel Association (formerly Committee) see *Annual Reports* for 1950–51, 1963, 1966, 1969–72; GGA, Box: Tourism (2), City Council files, 4661/2 and /5; and for the opening of the tourist office in London, and the warning that it must not also engage in political propaganda, see FCO42/225 and /479.

62 On advertising see *Annual Reports* for 1962–65, 1967–68; and also GGA, Box: Tourism, for five reports 1967–84.

Attention was naturally drawn to the upgrading and extending of existing hotels and the addition of new ones, like the Queen's Hotel, night club and adjacent cinema in 1956 (on the Assembly Rooms site), and the Mediterranean Hotel and the Caleta Palace Hotel (at Catalan Bay) in 1964, in which year three other hotels were also under construction and plans were announced for a nine-storey, 150-room hotel to be built out of prefabricated parts made in Britain.[63] CD&W money (£125,000) was secured in 1967 to help finance the so-called Hoods or 'Both Worlds' development of self-contained flatlets on the eastern side of the Rock (estimated total cost of £544,000), a scheme designed to attract tourists and which by then was prompted not least by Spanish threats to the Gibraltar economy.[64] Even a caravan park was opened in 1960. Events were also staged to lure in tourists, such as an 'Arts Week', sailing regattas, speedboat racing, angling competitions and swimming tournaments, and there was investment in bayside restaurants, a lido and even a casino, costing £200,000 and opened in 1964.[65]

But such features had to be supplementary to the initial lures of geography and history, in which much capital, energy and publicity were invested (along with repeated emphasis on that other special feature of the Rock, the apes). In 1956 the extraordinary St Michael's Cave, deep in the Rock, was enhanced with a new flood-lighting system: it attracted 10,000 visitors in its first six months. Subsequently, from 1963, an auditorium constructed in the cave was marketed as a unique venue for concerts. Over 52,000 visited the cave in 1966. Also in 1956, much of the upper rock with its fabulous views and military fortifications, which had formerly been, by garrison orders, a 'no-go' restricted zone, was opened to the public as a 'recreational area' and the 'ban on photography and sketching has now been lifted'. The perfect combination, a military museum high on the Rock, was opened later. Meanwhile, for ease of access, roads to the summit were widened in 1964 and car parking was improved, and the long-awaited aerial cable car was constructed in 1967, together with an observation platform and restaurant, while recorded explanatory messages in English, French and German (but not Spanish) were installed at key spots. In subsequent years much was done to improve access to the eastern side of Gibraltar and at Europa Point,[66] and to

63 On hotels see *Annual Reports* for 1956, 1958–64, 1966–68.
64 The political arguments for British government support for the Hoods project were rehearsed in papers on TNA, FCO9/520.
65 On events see *Annual Reports* for 1960–62, 1964–65. In 1928 Gibraltar's colonial secretary had decided not to forward to the Colonial Office a proposal to open a casino 'as they would probably have a fit': GGA, MP585/1927, Young to Lambert, 12 Dec 1928, and see subsequent abortive discussions with the American Express Company.
66 The road circuit around Gibraltar has not (2008) been reopened following the closure of a tunnel on the eastern side after a rock fall and tragic accident in Feb 2002.

preserve as 'heritage' some of the more formidable coastal and upper-rock military fortifications. It was appropriate that representative features of the historic and geological place myth should be floodlit: the Moorish castle from 1964, the Rock itself from 1965 and the spectacular north face from 1966.[67] Moreover, a private enterprise proposal to build a funicular railway was rejected in 2005 because it would 'spoil the Rock's emblematic profile', and instead £2 million was to be spent upgrading facilities in the Upper Rock Nature Reserve.[68]

The controversy aroused locally in 2006 by the destruction of the historic Royal Navy water tanks at Rosia Bay in order to clear the site for apartment blocks is indicative not just of the inevitable collision of interests in space-constrained Gibraltar but of the extent to which Gibraltarians themselves, as well as outside interest groups, identified the place with its British military heritage.[69] It is striking that the King's Bastion electricity generating station, opened in 1961 and impressive as architecture and engineering and a monument of modernity, was demolished in 2005, without public protest, to expose more of the military walls. Indeed a member of Gibraltar's Heritage Trust had argued that the generating station obscured and desecrated the city walls, 'this great monument to our turbulent history' and the Minister of Culture had called it 'that monstrosity'.[70] Likewise the water catchments, which historically had, for a century, done much to make civilian life endurable, were removed to reveal the Rock beneath, and again without demur. History, as elsewhere, had been slimmed down and turned into marketable heritage.[71]

And the results? 'It is an accepted fact', concluded an official report, 'that Tourism can play a very important contribution towards the general economy of Gibraltar.'[72] One might add that it must and it did, though insecurely. The number of visitors by sea and by air rose to over 200,000 in 1956, in addition to an unspecified but certainly large number coming across the still open frontier

---

67 On the exploitation of history and geography see *Annual Reports*, for 1956, p. 42; for 1963, pp. 4, 84; for 1964, p. 85; for 1965, p. 80; for 1966, p. 74.

68 *Gibraltar Heritage Trust Newsletter 2004*, pp. 1–2; *Gibraltar Chronicle*, 30 Aug 2005.

69 There was extensive local press and internet coverage in Jan–Feb 2006, including of a protest by 250 people outside the chief minister's office on 7 Feb 2006.

70 www.gib.gi/heritage/citywalls.html; *Gibraltar Heritage Trust Newsletter 2004*, p. 2. The Trust was also responsible for the erection of statues of admirals Nelson and Rooke in 2005.

71 On the electricity generating station see *Annual Report for 1961*, p. 72, and two accompanying photographs. On heritage issues see, as an introduction, D. Lowenthal, *The Heritage Crusade and the Spoils of History* (Cambridge: Cambridge University Press, 1998). See also *Save Gibraltar's Heritage!*, report by Save Britain's Heritage group, 1995.

72 *Annual Report for 1966*, p. 78.

from Spain by car and coach. In 1957, 35,300 tickets were sold for entry to the military galleries, Moorish Castle and St Michael's cave, and in 1958, over 45,000. In 1959, over 71,000 sightseeing (and possibly big-spending) passengers came ashore from liners calling at the port, 81,400 in 1961. Visitor figures (though not only of tourists) rose from 330,000 in 1959 to nearly 740,000 in 1964. It was reckoned that tourist income was worth £2 million a year in 1959, and perhaps as much as £4.5 million by 1963. However, the vulnerability of this income stream was exposed when, from 1964, the Spanish frontier restrictions began to discourage visitors. Visitor figures dropped to 425,000 in 1965; tourist spending in 1967 was down to an estimated £1,690,000.[73] Additional efforts were made, not least via the working through of the government's 1966 four-year development plan to make Gibraltar still more of a tourist destination and a place to stay and not just a spot for a daytime visit or somewhere to pass through on the way to Spain.[74] While for a period there were far fewer visitors (only 220,171 in 1969), they were staying longer (many on package holiday deals) and spending more. Tourist spending was estimated at £2,304,500 in 1968 and £3,650,000 in 1969.[75] But in 1970 numbers and expenditure were down, to £2,200,000. However, expenditure nudged up to an estimated £2,500,000 in 1971, by visitors numbering only 132,000, and then, in 1972, 139,000 visitors spent £3,130,000. When the frontier was fully reopened in 1985, so-called visitor arrivals shot up to 2,411,655, rising by 2006 to 8,185,142. These spectacular numbers include non-Gibraltarians entering daily to work, but even excluding all visitors arriving by land (and many of these would be proper tourists pouring in by car and coach) and counting only those arriving by air and sea, the total in 1985 would be over 150,000, rising (though still not smoothly) to nearly 370,000 in 2006. The new Gibraltar Cruise Terminal opened in 1997 welcomed its one-millionth passenger arrival in June 2005. Recorded arrivals at hotels increased (also erratically) from 39,102 people in 1978 to 59,194 in 2006, equating by then to 192,639 guest nights sold. Inflation dents but does not eliminate the increase in estimated tourist expenditure, from £76 million in 1990 to £210 million in 2006. Such spending provided a lot of income, boosted tax revenue, supported quite a share of public services and bought for Gibraltar consumers a lot of imports.[76] It should come as no surprise to note that the images which lure in visitors and still dominate readily available tourist information publications and

73 On tourist numbers see *Annual Reports* for 1952–63, 1966–67.
74 *Annual Reports* for 1964–66.
75 *Annual Reports* for 1968, p. 88, and for 1969, pp. 96–7.
76 *Annual Reports*, for 1970, p. 93; for 1971, p. 95; for 1972, p. 94; *Abstract of Statistics*, for 2004, pp. 53, 59, 62; for 2006, pp. 56, 62, 63, 65; *Gibraltar Chronicle*, 14 June 2005. For (many) more figures on tourism and hotel occupancy see the annual surveys, dating back to 1972, the most recent on www.gibraltar.gov.gi/, 'Statistics'.

guide books depict especially 'History' and military heritage and the physical presence of the Rock.[77]

Gibraltar's economy has also been sustained by selling the Rock to outsiders in one other way, as a safe haven for money. The development of Gibraltar as an 'offshore' financial centre was another form of diversification, characteristic of small economies with independent tax regimes in the late twentieth century. Where the Channel Islands, the Isle of Man, Bermuda and others led, Gibraltar followed. The Companies (Taxation and Concessions) Ordinance of 1967 allowed for tax breaks for international businesses. Further encouragement followed once civilian ministers were completely free to manage the territory's financial affairs after the constitutional innovations of 1969.[78] There were of course banks in Gibraltar in earlier decades, usually just four or five of them. Some went back to the 1920s (some earlier), including a few locally owned and managed, like Rugeroni's (surviving until 1936), Mosley's (1938–47) and Galliano's (established 1855 and acquired by Jyske in 1987), and the Anglo-Egyptian Bank (taken over by Barclays in 1925). 'Foreign' banks also made appearances in Gibraltar, such as Crédit Foncier d'Algérie et de Tunisie (until 1963), the Bank of West Africa (1923–26), La Société Centrale de Banque (1963–71), the Mediterranean Bank (from 1964) and La Banque de L'Indochine (from 1971).[79] However, by 2002 there were nineteen banks in Gibraltar, mainly subsidiaries of major UK and other EU banks, like Barclays, Lloyds TSB, NatWest, Royal Bank of Scotland, Hambros, Jyske, Credit Suisse, Banco Central Hispano Americano and Banco Atlantico. Commercial bank assets, a 'mere' £229 million or so in 1985, rose spectacularly to £5,000 million by 1992, and generally bounced along comfortably at around that figure thereafter, with a cheery uplift to £8,362 million by the end of 2006.[80]

Gibraltar has also now become the location of a rash of government-licensed and regulated gambling businesses, such as 32Red, Ladbrokes, Coral Eurobet, Victor Chandler, PartyGaming and Casino-on-Net. Online gambling licences were offered by government from 1998, and in 2007 fifteen companies were

77 For example, www.gibraltar.gov.gi/, 'Tourism' and www.discovergibraltar.com/, and T.J. Finlayson, *Guided Tour of Gibraltar* (Gibraltar: Estoril, n.d.).
78 GGA, DG files, MP769, 'British Dependent Territories and Tax Haven Business', for a Dec 1971 report. See also 64.233.183.104/search?q=cache:WRHXUSni6wAJ:www. gibraltar.gov.gi/gov_depts/finance/, for the current situation.
79 For the comings and goings of banking establishments see *Annual Reports* for 1920, p. 6; for 1923, p. 6; for 1925, p. 6; for 1926, p. 6; for 1932, p. 11, for 1936, p. 11; for 1947, p. 17; for 1962, p. 25; for 1964, p. 29; for 1965, p. 26; for 1971, p. 28. P. Galliano, *The Smallest Bank in the World: the History of Galliano's Bank 1855–1987* (Gibraltar: Gibraltar Books, 2003) is a charming family memoir and contains a little banking history.
80 www.gibnet.com/data/bflist.htm; *Abstract of Statistics*, 2004, p. 67, 2006, p. 72.

operating 124 online gambling sites in Gibraltar; and William Hill had announced that it too was moving its online gambling business there from the Dutch Antilles. A gaming tax of just 1 per cent of turnover and with a maximum tax cap were among the incentives. In 2005 PartyGaming made a profit of £308 million and paid tax of £425,000. Such businesses are another example of diversification, providing the Gibraltar economy with additional employment and incomes (1,800 jobs in 2006, over 12 per cent of the labour force), boosting import-earning capacity and earning the Gibraltar government some appreciated additions to its revenue.[81]

Occupations, living standards and health

Many of the benefits of this economic activity were enjoyed by the civilian population in the form of services delivered by the colonial government, by the City Council (formerly the Sanitary Commission) and eventually by the civilian government of Gibraltar. These services – for example the public utilities, public sector housing, improved schools and eventually welfare services – were funded by rates, customs duties and, after a resistance which will be explored in later chapters, by direct taxation. But in truth, until the second half of the century very little redistribution of income was effected by such levies. Standards of living owed almost everything to incomes derived from employment, even among the less well-paid and the socially and economically marginalised. Hence we need first to consider occupational patterns. Analysis is handicapped by the changing categories used in census returns, but the pairings in Tables 8.3a and b are reasonably consistent.

We can see that the occupied labour force stepped up in numbers between the two phases, almost certainly a response to frontier restrictions and the loss of daytime workers. On the other hand, one feature pretty much unchanging over these sixty years is the modest proportion of females among those in full-time employment: 25 per cent in 1931, declining to 20 per cent in 1970 and rising only to 28 per cent by 1991. The distinction is not quite so stark if part-time women workers are taken into account but, not surprisingly, these were mainly domestic servants and cleaners, plus a few clerical workers, nurses and teachers. There was some movement of women workers away from the service sector and into nursing and teaching, hence their greater standing in

81 online.casinocity.com/jurisdictions/jurisdiction.cfm?id=16&searchall=1, www.32red poker.com/file/691362f7b26305fe4824b145dc6527af/licensed-by-the-government-of-gibraltar.html; news.777.com/2007–08/online-casino-william-hill-relocates, news.bbc.co.uk/1/hi/business/4776021.stm. See *Gibraltar Chronicle*, 31 March 2004, pp. 1, 3, for the history of Victor Chandler's first five years in Gibraltar and 21 Jan 2006, p. 19, for a representative employment advertisement for PartyGaming.

Table 8.3a *Occupations of resident population by sex, 1931 and 1951*

Occupations	1931		1951	
	Males	Females	Males	Females
Transport, drivers, seamen, cargo workers, telegraphs, messengers	1,068	1	878	13
Trades, crafts: metal, electrical, wood, textiles, painters, printers, builders, engines, etc.	915	145	1,876	57
Commerce, finance, insurance, sales, storekeepers	804	114	822	271
Clerical	592	55	919	155
Personal service	284	1,141	293	1,090
Professional: clergy, law, medicine, teaching, music, etc.	239	207	320	178
Public administration, managers, and (mainly) police and fire service	229	–	575	2
Food, drink, tobacco	79	3	17	3
Fishermen, agricultural, quarrying	32	–	21	–
Others, mainly labourers and unskilled	883	3	1,103	151
Totals	*5,125*	*1,669*	*6,824*	*1,920*
Grand totals	*6,794*		*8,744*	

the professions, and also in administration, although overwhelmingly as typists and clerical workers; and of course, most women workers were young and most dropped out of employment on marriage. To risk a generalisation, then, in these decades family income still rested largely on the market value of male heads of households. The characteristic rise in the twentieth century of the professions and services, plus a managerial revolution generating administrative employment in the public and private sectors, initially benefited largely men, who occupied especially the higher-status and better-paid posts. It is also evident from these data that those in trades remained overwhelmingly men, but that their occupations came to embrace a wider range of skilled work, for example as electricians, fitters and motor mechanics. These too would be among the better-paid. But Gibraltar remained, if not quite a 'nation of shopkeepers', yet still much committed to retail and wholesale trade; there was still a substantial proportion of the workforce engaged in 'fetching and carrying'; and the whole was underpinned by a large number of unskilled labourers who suffered from insecurity of employment as well as from low pay. Their families had most to gain from minimum wage regulations, price fixing, rent controls and redistributive welfare legislation.

It was therefore just as well that, from the middle of the century, the living

Table 8.3b *Occupations of resident population by sex, 1970 and 1991*

	1970		1991	
Occupations	Males	Females	Males	Females
Trades, crafts, production, construction, transport	3,198	60	2,252	70
Administrative, managerial, clerical etc.	1,723	588	1,543	1,491
Service sector: hotels, restaurants, bars, cleaners, domestics, police, fire	1,020	754	970	601
Sales	714	407	759	438
Professional, technical and related	538	328	1,014	508
Others, mainly labourers and unskilled	1,841	122	1,210	28
Totals	*9,034*	*2,259*	*7,748*	*3,136*
Grand totals	*11,293*		*10,884*	

Sources: Censuses of Gibraltar.

standards for most families were being determined to an extraordinary extent not by the so-called free market but by government and the public sector. One obvious determinant was legislation. As we shall see in a later chapter, housing provision and social services were colonial and, later, civil government responsibilities; public utilities were extended by the City Council; and labour supply from outside the colony was controlled by government (until Franco lent a hand). Business operations were also regulated by a legislative framework. For example, the maximum permissible hours of work expected of shopworkers, still sixty-six even after an ordinance of 1922 first restricted them, were reduced substantially, to forty-eight, by an amendment in 1947.[82] Also in 1947, the Trade Union and Trade Disputes Ordinance required the registration of trade unions, but also for the first time gave them recognition and fostered collective bargaining in the private as well as public sectors, undoubtedly to the benefit of many Gibraltar workers. By 1960, seemingly the peak year, 75 per cent of workers resident in Gibraltar and in insurable employment were members of trade unions. The government even provided the private sector with model fair wage clauses for incorporation into contracts of employment.[83] Legislation also obliged all private sector employees to provide holidays with pay from 1 January 1956.[84] Moreover, government after the war insisted that Gibraltarians should be given preference

82 Shop Hours (Amendment) Ordinance, No 24 of 1947; *Annual Report for 1947*, p. 12.
83 Trade Unions and Trade Disputes Ordinance, No 15 of 1947, and comment on it in *Gibraltar Chronicle*, 1 Feb 1947, p. 5: 'Gib Trade Unions on Par with England'; for trade union membership see *Annual Reports*, for 1947, p. 12, and subsequent, esp. for 1960, p. 17.
84 *Annual Report for 1956*, p. 9.

over aliens when jobs were being filled. In 1947, for example, 1,559 of the 1,577 vacancies notified by employers to the Central Employment Exchange (as legally required) were filled by Gibraltarians. Underwritten by law in the Control of Employment Ordinance of 1955 and subsequent amendments, this practice remained until British (and thereby Gibraltar) membership of the EEC (as it then was) required the ending of such discrimination against other community nationals in the private sector from 1 January 1973.[85] Moreover, after the disruptions caused by both world wars to supplies and prices, the colonial government retained a rationing system and subsidised such a necessity as bread for several years into peacetime, to the particular benefit of the least well-paid.[86] In addition, after 1945 the government continued to monitor prices and published a cost of living index which naturally affected trade union pay claims and determined cost of living allowances.[87]

However, what also advantageously determined the living standards of many families was the substantial proportion of the labour force in the public sector. The armed services, and especially the Royal Navy dockyard, recruited more workers as their activities increased, as did the Sanitary Commission when it was transformed into a still more active City Council in 1921, and as did the colonial government when, particularly from 1945, it became more managerial of civilian life and of necessity more bureaucratic. To take just one example, the police force of 168 men in 1931 had increased to 287 by 1951.[88] By 1952, about 40 per cent of the total labour force was working for official employers, and 47 per cent by 1960. By 1981 nearly 56 per cent of full-time workers resident in Gibraltar were employed in the public sector.[89]

The value of this for workers so employed is that, on the whole, the public sector was setting the standards for pay and conditions. In 1931, for instance, labourers employed by the government's Public Works Department were being paid 7d (about 3p)) an hour, and artisans between 8¾d and 1s (5p) an hour, when private sector workers, paid in pesetas (which was a grievance since they lost money in an exchange into sterling), were receiving the equivalent of little

85 *Annual Reports*, for 1947, p. 13, and similarly for 1948, p. 8; for 1949, p. 7; for 1972, p. 16.
86 *Annual Reports*, for 1919, p. 10; for 1920, p. 3; for 1947, pp. 10, 18; and see, for example, notices of rations and of maximum retail prices of sugar, eggs and potatoes in 1950 in *Gibraltar Gazette*, 27 Oct 1950.
87 For example, *Annual Report for 1947*, p. 10, and subsequent reports; and for trade union responses see, for example, *Gibraltar Chronicle*, 1 Dec 1946, p. 3.
88 *Censuses of Gibraltar*.
89 *Annual Reports*, for 1952–53, p. 6, and for 1960, p. 9; *Census of Gibraltar, 1981*, calculated from Table 16, p. 63. The figure was thereafter to decline, to 32 per cent according to *Census of Gibraltar 2001*, Table 12 a–c, pp. 39–41.

more than 5d an hour if labourers and less than 7d an hour if artisans.[90] In 1947 the minimum basic wage of unskilled workers employed in the official sector was raised to 40s (£2) a week, plus a cost of living allowance of 32s (only 16s for aliens), and this allowance was raised to 48s (and 24s) in 1951. By 1956 the pay of an unskilled male public sector worker, including the allowance, was 105s (£5.25). Further stepped increases followed for them and other grades, still incorporating a cost of living allowance.

Pay lagged behind in the private sector, with initially the lower Spanish rates of pay being paid also to Gibraltarians. Male waiters in the late 1940s could earn as little as 32s 6d (£1.62), plus whatever was offered by way of bed and board, women as little as 20s. Charwomen got 5s (25p) per day, plus meals. It required the application of minimum wage legislation in 1953 and 1960 to raise the wages of bus drivers and shop workers respectively, and only from 1956 did casually employed stevedores and others in the private sector benefit from collective agreements between employers and the Transport and General Workers' Union. From 1960, parity between public and private sector pay, effected by raising the latter, became a discernible trend, but in October 1981 full-time weekly paid adult males had average earnings in the official sector of £116 and in the private sector of £98. (In October 2006 the difference was still marked, £380 compared with £345; and the gap was still worse for women, £329 and £226 respectively).

Meanwhile, in 1947 an agreement between the armed services and trade unions in Britain over hours of work had also been adopted in Gibraltar. The standard working week in the public sector had been fifty hours in the 1930s, but a forty-four-hour five-day week was then introduced. However, private employers sticking to a norm of forty-eight hours, often over six days, was still recorded as normal as late as 1960, and in some occupations for a long time standard hours could be as high as fifty-eight. When, in 1965, a forty-two-hour working week became the standard in the public sector, reduced in 1970 to forty hours, private sector workers were also to benefit, but again only after a lag in time.

Of course, there were other discriminations besides public versus private (or Gibraltarian versus alien). Male/female differences were also obvious, including women receiving only two-thirds of the cost of living allowance awarded to men in the post-war years. There were even some protests, when in 1947, the City Council dared to employ women as telephone operators 'when there are so many young men out of work', though this objection was not uniformly backed.[91] Equal pay, but only for women in non-industrial employment, was introduced in 1969. Even so, earnings for full-time weekly paid adult men rose on average from

90 *Annual Report for 1931*, p. 6. Private sector pay was a little better in 1938, but a difference remained: *Annual Report for 1938*, p. 6.
91 *Gibraltar Chronicle*, 23 April, p. 2, 24 April, p. 5 and 26 April 1947, p. 2.

£20 in October 1972 to over £118 by April 1982 (and to £347 by October 2006), but for women from less than £12 to still less than £70 (and only to £234 by October 2006). As everywhere else, of course, skilled men, especially in unions, did best. In 1972 the basic wage rates of labourers were about £14 a week, and for tradesmen up to £17.50.[92]

If shorter working hours and holidays with pay were some of the benefits flowing to working families, especially in the second half of the century, what else did economic achievement buy? There is too little historical information to risk comparing the full package of family expenditure on all commodities over the long term. One family expenditure study, of 1995/96 only, produced results comparable with those for other societies, showing, for instance, that as family income increased so the proportion spent on food decreased, while it rose for other items, such as durable household goods and vehicles, with variations by, for instance, family composition, age and occupation.[93]

However, analysis over a longer term of two sets of robust data, dealing with housing and health, provide a fair indication of a rise in average living standards and quality of life. Housing conditions were the subject of regularly collected data and of several special inquiries, connected as they were to anxieties about sanitation and disease. The (British) Registrar-General's definition of overcrowding as more than two persons per room was a standard commonly used early in the century, and applying that to census data shows that 25.5 per cent of dwellings were overcrowded in 1921 and still 24.3 per cent in 1931. Pretty much at the same time, a special investigation by Gibraltar's medical officer of health in 1927 of over 90 per cent of the population, mainly working-class people, concluded that 37.7 per cent of their dwellings housed 2,646 persons. That meant that 33 per cent of the population was overcrowded (16.1 per cent of the population of London in 1921), further indicating the compression of the poor into little space. To take one grim element, of the 1,222 single-room tenements, 68 per cent were overcrowded, by 1,719 persons. These 'homes' were, of course, also the least well-equipped with cooking facilities.Unsurprisingly, overcrowding was identified as a principal cause of Gibraltar's high rate of infant mortality and of deaths from respiratory and infectious diseases.[94]

92 *Annual Reports* for 1947, 1949, 1950, 1952–53, 1956, 1960, 1965, 1969 and 1972; *Statistical Abstracts*, for 1982, Table 35; for 2006, Table 43b and 44b, pp. 44, 46. More details on employment and earnings can be found in the annual employment survey reports, beginning in 1971, and for the latest see www.gibraltar.gov.gi/, 'Statistics'.
93 www.gibraltar.gov.gi/gov_depts/Statistics/Family_Exp_Survey_95_96.pdf.
94 *Census*, for 1921, Table XI, and for 1931, Table IX; GGA, Box: City Council, Housing, 4210, 'Extract from Annual Report on the Health of Gibraltar for the year 1927 by Lieutenant-Colonel W.C. Smales, Medical Officer of Health', pp. 82–3, 88, 96. Smales had noted in 1924 that 30 per cent of the population of Gibraltar lived in one room, whereas figures for grim Glasgow were 'only' 12.8 per cent, for Paisley

That too was the conclusion of a further official investigation into housing conditions which reported to the governor in January 1937.[95] This addressed the quality of housing and rent levels, and also called for closer examination of overcrowding, particularly in the light of higher standards set by the Housing Act of 1935, recently passed in Britain, which laid down, for example, minimum acceptable sizes for rooms and required the separation of unmarried persons of opposite sex over the age of ten. This consequent inquiry inevitably bumped up the number of dwellings deemed overcrowded, to 51 per cent – 1,298 of 2,525 – but also showed that rates varied, according to district, from as low as 35 per cent to as high as 62 per cent. No prizes will be awarded for guessing that the highest rates were in the poorer working-class districts in the upper part of town and the lowest in the better-off quarters in the lower part. Nor will it be unexpected to learn that the overcrowded families were also, on average, larger (by nearly two persons) than the 'uncrowded'.[96]

Using the older Registrar-General's standard as a constant measuring rod, there was no immediate improvement post-war between the 24.3 per cent overcrowding of dwellings in 1931 and the 25 per cent of 1951, but that was before major housing programmes got seriously under way, of which more in a later chapter. As a measure of achievement, and of improved living conditions funded by economic growth and higher real wages, overcrowding by the same standard was down to 8.7 per cent by 1970, to 4.9 per cent by 1981, to 2.1 per cent in 1991 – and to 0.5 per cent by 2001.[97] It is important to acknowledge that official standards for acceptable housing had meanwhile risen with expectations, and in any case quality of accommodation cannot be measured by room numbers alone, but those who care to peruse post-war censuses can also construct a narrative of improvement in the increasing number of families having sole use of a cooker, of a bath or shower and of that single greatest contribution to human happiness, the indoor flush toilet. Once again, credit should be given to government, colonial and civil, for improvements in the civilian quality of life, this time for insisting on better standards in private sector housing and for major public sector construction. By 1981, 65 per cent of accommodation in Gibraltar, 4,503 dwellings, was rented from the government: only 30 per cent was rented

a 'mere' 12.3 per cent: Box: Housing, 4210, City Council Committee on Housing, Appendix A.

95 *Report of a Commission of Inquiry on Housing and Rent Restriction, etc* (Gibraltar: Government of Gibraltar, 1937).

96 GGA, Box: City Council, 4210 Housing, *Report on the Overcrowding Survey* (Gibraltar: City Council of Gibraltar, 1938), pp. 7, 8, 12–14, and Table C7, and p. 8 and Tables C1–6, for the marginally different data relating to the dwellings of 'British' working-class families alone. Copy also in MP258/1937.

97 Calculated from *Census*, for 1951, Table 11, p. 22; for 1970, Table 36, p. 58; for 1981, Table 25.1, p. 100; for 1991, Table 3.1, p. 61; for 2001, Table 26, p. 79.

privately and only 5 per cent was owner-occupied. (By 1981 in England and Wales, 57 per cent was owner-occupied.) Most importantly, in 1982 only 32 per cent of that government housing stock, 1,614 dwellings, had been constructed before 1940, and the rest, 3,583, were post-war and, for the most part, of a higher standard. Indeed, by 2002, when government stock still accounted for around 44 per cent of dwellings (owner-occupied having risen to 24 per cent), the quality was likely to have been still higher, since only 807 survived from pre-war, just 16 per cent, and the rest and much of the best, some 4,270 units, had been put up post-war.[98]

Death is a part of life, and there is a statistical certainty about its arrival which is never quite captured by data on morbidity. Unfortunately, mortality data for Gibraltar are plagued (if one will excuse the word) by confusion in some reports between calculations based on the so-called fixed civil population, that is, those with permanent residency rights, and the total civil population, including aliens and others on temporary permits.[99] Calculations based on the latter are perhaps the better indicator of standards of living in the community, though 'aliens', being proportionately younger, tended to put a smile on the mortality figures. That awkwardness aside, the evidence points unequivocally to higher biological survivals and increased life expectancy. Since death comes to us all, crude death rates (which do not account for age profile) are indeed crude as an indicator, but for what they are worth they show improvement. The annual average for the period 1910 to 1919 was 16.7 deaths per thousand of the total civil population. A still more precise indicator of public health is the infant mortality rate, deaths per 1,000 live births, but particularly sensitive in Gibraltar's case because small changes in the number of deaths among the modest number of births per year had exaggerating effects on the rates. From 1909 to 1918 the annual average was 105.8, an awful lot of dead babies, ranging from 75 up to 124 deaths per 1,000 live births. The average for England and Wales over the same period was 102.9.[100] It was no better in the 1920s, crude death rates still averaging 16.7 and infant mortality 105.5, but the volatility of the latter is shown when infant deaths dropped from 122.9 per 1,000 live births in 1928 to 46.4 in 1929 (18 deaths from 388 births).[101]

98 *Statistical Abstracts*, for 1982, Table 13, p. 14; for 2002, Tables 16 and 17, p. 16; A.H. Halsey (ed.), *British Social Trends since 1900* (London: Macmillan, 1988), p. 371. In 2006, 4,226 of the government's housing stock of 5,063, over 84 per cent, had been built since 1948: *Statistical Abstract 2006*, Table 17, p. 16.

99 There are also unfortunate gaps in the archived *Annual Reports on Health* and inexplicable differences between data recorded in different official reports – and even in the same one.

100 GGA, Box: *Annual Health Report for 1919*, based on data on pp. 34–5.

101 *Annual Health Report for 1929*, pp. ix, 1; *Annual Reports*, 1919–28.

This last was a pointer to better things. Between 1930 and 1939, the crude death rate was down to 15.51, and the infant mortality rate had declined to an encouraging average of 63.84.[102] Then, after the war, came transformation, as in so many matters affecting civilian life. The crude death rate dropped to single figures, averaging 8 per 1,000 of the population between 1945 and 1950, and thereafter steadying, up to the present, at between 8 and 9. (Over the same period that for England and Wales varied between 11 and 12). Expectation of life at birth rose from 68 years for men and 72 for women in 1970 to 78 for men and 83 for women by 2001. The fall in the infant mortality rate is even more cause for celebration. The figure dropped to almost half the 1930s rate between 1945 and 1950, to 34.7 deaths per 1,000 live births. Between 1955 and 1959 it fell to half that rate again: 17.1 deaths (England and Wales 23). Some bad experiences in the 1960s pushed the figure up to an average of 24.2 between 1960 and 1966, but thereafter there was further decline. Though a child's death was as harrowing as ever for individual parents, the marked reduction in the total in just a few decades represented less cumulative heartbreak.[103]

At this point one should insert some consideration of family size. As already indicated in relation to overcrowding, as common sense would suggest, and as is confirmed by many classic studies of poverty and living standards in other places, there is commonly an inverse correlation between the number of children in a family and material well-being. The elasticity of demand from children may know few bounds, but a wage-earner's income is less plastic. Unfortunately there are no published figures for family sizes in Gibraltar, but there are data on birth rates which are at least indicative.[104] Between 1910 and 1919 the average annual rate was 23.53 births per 1,000 of the population, and almost precisely the same figure, 23.54, recurs for the period 1921 to 1929. There is then a decline, to 21.88 for the decade 1930 to 1939, though the influx of refugees in the mid-1930s exaggerates the decline. After the interruption of the war and the evacuation, the rate for 1945 is very special, a baby boom of 34.84 births per 1,000 of the population. But thereafter the rate again fell to an average of 17.24, though slightly exaggerated by some insecure base population figures. True, the birth rate then rose in a mini-baby boom in the mid 1960s, averaging 25.18 before slipping back.

102 *Annual Report on Health for 1949*, p.ix.
103 *Annual Health Reports*, esp. for 1949, pp. 7–8; for 1966, p. 7 and chart for 1930–66 facing p. 2; *Census for 2001*, p. xxvi; L.A. Sawchuk, D.A. Herring and L.R. Waks, 'Evidence of a Jewish advantage: a study of infant mortality in Gibraltar, 1870–1959', *American Anthropologist*, 87 (1985), 616–25, esp. pp. 618–19; Halsey, *British Social Trends*, pp. 40, 410.
104 The introductions to the *Census* for 1951, p. 7, and for 1961, p. 7, question some previous published figures for birth rates because of the unreliable basis upon which population totals had been calculated.

The rate for 2000–6 averaged 13.76 births per 1,000.[105] This decline in births was certainly not due to less equal sex ratios, lower marriage rates, later marriage or the reduced fecundity of women, theoretically among the possible suspects. In fact, not only were women more healthy and therefore more likely to be more fecund and for longer, but over the second half of the twentieth century sex ratios became more equal, the frequency of marriage increased and the age of marriage declined.[106] This was a Roman Catholic society, but evidently some form of birth control was being practised. The material benefits, which alone perhaps one can measure, would have been fewer mouths to feed and, among other rewards, a better diet for those fed, more affordable housing and improved health.

Credit should also certainly be given to the improved training, knowledge, skills and numbers of medical and public health staff in effecting these improvements. Respect should also be shown to parents and other family members in providing the conditions in which health could be preserved. But just as doctors and nurses and environmental health officers needed and received more and better 'kit' with which to practise medicine and protect public health, so too did family members, and especially wage earners, need the resources with which to nurture their loved ones. Whether families in Gibraltar were well housed and properly fed depended on their incomes, to pay rent and purchase the ingredients of a well-balanced diet. To that extent, the success of Gibraltar's economy may be measured by public services provided, by private purchases made and by the consequent record of the community's health.

Conclusion

Against all the odds and with its ups and downs, Gibraltar's economy grew during the twentieth century. The concept of growth and calculations of national income have been refined since efforts were first made by John Maynard Keynes at the UK Treasury during the Second World War. Gibraltar calculations, however, are particularly difficult because shifts in the structure of the economy were not matched rapidly enough by the data collected. Nevertheless, and even allowing for inflation, a trend indicating achievement is apparent. One set of figures, at 1970 prices, records a national income of £10.8 million in 1963 and of £13.46 million by 1970.[107] Table 8.4 gives more recent data, including infor-

105 *Annual Reports* for 1914–38; *Annual Health Report* for 1919, p. 34; for 1962–66, esp. 1966, chart facing p. 2; *Census* for 1951, Table 4, p. 16; for 1961, Table 4, p. 20; *Statistical Abstracts*, 2000–6, 'Key indicators'.

106 L.A. Sawchuk, 'Historical intervention, tradition and change: a study of the age of marriage in Gibraltar, 1909–1983', *Journal of Family History*, 17 (1992), 69–94, esp. Tables 2 and 3.

107 GGA, DG files, MP769, 'The economy of Gibraltar', Table 2.

Table 8.4 *National income, 1996–2005*

Year	GDP £m	GNP £m	GDP per capita £	GNP per capita £
1996–97	352.12	332.62	12,987	12,268
1997–98	364.51	346.01	13,426	12,744
1998–99	393.23	371.53	14,526	13,725
1999–00	409.89	383.82	15,091	14,131
2000–1	433.61	401.44	15,863	14,686
2001–2	470.18	429.65	16,608	15,177
2002–3	507.17	458.94	17,770	16,080
2003–4	560.06	497.59	19,552	17,372
2004–5	599.18	551.50	20,831	19,173

Sources: *Abstract of Statistics*, 2002, p. 45 (and see note on reliability of figures), 2006, p. 48, and www.gibraltar.gov.gi/gov_depts/Statistics/National_Income_1998–2005. pdf.

mation on how national income translates into average Gross Domestic Product and Gross National Product per head of population.

A further detailed study of GDP in 1999–2000 produced a slightly higher figure of £411 million for that year, which works out at a GDP per head of population of £15,120 (or £33,796 per full-time equivalent worker). The equivalent figure for the UK was lower, at £14,962. For an economy with barely any natural resources for processing or exporting, this comparison, like the other data, is quite remarkable. There are various ways of identifying the contribution of sectors to the economy, but for our purposes percentages of GDP are sufficient, though tourism becomes buried within several headings. The data for 1999–2000 show that this was not a manufacturing society (less than 2 per cent of GDP); it owed much to government, including welfare services (nearly 19 per cent); a great deal was derived from real estate and business activities not elsewhere enumerated (nearly 11 per cent); and most came as almost joint firsts from the retail and wholesale trades (20 per cent) and financial services (21 per cent). Very strikingly, and indicative of just one of the many major impacts with which the economy had had to cope, especially in the second half of the century, the contribution of the armed services (the Ministry of Defence) had shrunk to less than 4 per cent.[108]

Gibraltar's economic success provided the resources which, as noted, advanced material living standards and extended life expectancy. This was in a free market

108 www.gibraltar.gov.gi/gov_depts/Statistics/Input_Output_Study_of_Gibraltar. pdf, report by J. Fletcher and S. Wanhill, Feb 2003, which also contains a substantial analysis of the tourist industry.

and in a world in which skills and talents and, just as important, opportunities and luck were unequally distributed. Accordingly, some individuals and families enjoyed more of the rewards than others. Nevertheless, taking refuge in generalisation, Gibraltarians were better off by the end of the century than at any time in the past. Moreover, most of them for most of the time appeared to retain the edge over their near neighbours in Spain. Franco had the border closed in 1969 because opportunities and rewards were still drawing in literally thousands of workers from Spain. The walk to work and the ferry across the bay measured the pulling power of Gibraltar's economy. The traffic was not the other way. This was also true after the frontier was reopened in 1985. Coupled with the conditional rights of entry and limited rights of residence allowed to such 'aliens' – by rules which, as we have seen, were by now both drafted and applied by Gibraltarians – the difference between Gibraltarians and 'others' was being daily expressed. In that fashion, the distinguishing identity of the Gibraltarian was also routinely confirmed.

The closure of the Spanish border from 1969 to 1985 was, of course, a major interruption in the economic history of Gibraltar. In 1944 Professor F.A. Hayek had been asked to advise the colonial government of Gibraltar on the construction of a cost of living index. Hayek widened his investigation to explore what he described as 'Some economic problems of Gibraltar'. In addition to reporting more vigorously than had been done before on the then dependence of the economy on the garrison, Hayek insisted that Gibraltar should really be regarded as merely the centre of an economic region embracing also La Línea. In his words, 'the town of Gibraltar is little more than the commercial centre of an urban agglomeration of nearly 100,000 inhabitants, whose working class suburbs are situated in Spain'. So conceived, he argued, the frontier should be disregarded and such matters as population, wage rates and rent levels in a Gibraltar which was just part of a wider region should be left to find their natural regional market level, freed from government interference.[109] This model, characteristic of Hayek's free market sophistication and political naivety, denied the politics of the ancient partition. But he had hit upon one long-standing cause of Gibraltar's economic survival and growth. Of course, the frontier had never been as economically open as Hayek wished it to be, before or after the sixteen years of closure, but his observations remind us of how fortunate Gibraltar was that local Spanish economic interests as well as Gibraltar ones were sufficiently congruent as to make political blockade intermittent and partial.

109 GGA, DG files, S.1043, and TNA, CO91/522/1 and /2, 'Report by Professor Hayek'. For dismissive rejections of Hayek see CO91/533/5, minute by Lloyd, 13 April 1948, summarising views of governors, and subsequent Colonial Office minutes.

In other words, the economic achievements and rewards of Gibraltar civilians depended a good deal on Gibraltar's government and internal politics and on Anglo-Spanish external relations. And hence it is to those matters which we must next turn.

9

Government and politics in the twentieth century, 1915–40

The previous two chapters have suggested that during the course of the twentieth century some of the features of Gibraltar which had formerly characterised it as principally a British fortress and naval base had been unsettled. From the beginning of the century the absolute right of all British subjects to take up residence in this British colony had been removed, and by its close the Gibraltarian status of civilians, with attendant rights of belonging, and immigration controls over all others, had not just been imposed by the colonial government but had been negotiated with and implemented by, principally, leaders of the native born. Gibraltar for Gibraltarians signalled a distinctive and civilian identity. Moreover, the economic dependence of civilians on British garrison expenditure, although for a very long time not absolute, had been further reduced, in part as a result of government-led initiatives to diversify the economy, in part by the ambitions of civilian entrepreneurs and in part with the beginning of the rundown in the British military presence – though the step towards greater economic self-reliance had been complicated, latterly and considerably, by problems with Spain. It is fair to say, however, that during the last half of the century it became both more possible and in truth more necessary for civilians in Gibraltar to imagine a future for Gibraltar as an entirely civilian society. As such, Gibraltar might become just one among other small (very small) societies and economies attempting to cope as minnows in a world of big sharks.

Important to its prospects would, of course, be the role of government and the form of government in Gibraltar. In the twentieth century – in Britain, in the British Empire, and elsewhere – roles and forms of government changed substantially. While change was not consistently in one direction, characteristic of many places was the growth in the responsibilities of central government for the well-being of civil society, and also the extension of democratic institutions. Gibraltar had long since been a much-governed place, wherein civilians were used to dealing with regulations, primarily though not exclusively determined by what the colonial government felt necessary to meet the needs of the fortress. With reference to the twentieth century, some indication has already been given of tighter state controls over rights of residence and an increased emphasis upon, specifically, the priorities of Gibraltar's civilian population. Economic diversification and development in Gibraltar had also increased the role of the state. In this and the next chapter it therefore needs to be considered in what other respects, and when and why, new responsibilities were taken on by government, what opportunities for civilians were thereby presented and (the other side of the equation) what costs and controls were imposed. Did Gibraltar civilians share, for example, in that extension of state social services which culminated in a welfare state pretty much across Europe and in some British settler societies (but not everywhere in the colonial empire)?

At the same time – and some would see a causal connection with the increased role of the state – democratic political institutions were consolidated and extended in Britain, and introduced for the first time in some colonial territories, often as first steps to formal decolonisation and self-government. We have seen that, before 1914, prominent civilians in Gibraltar had exercised power over others in their official capacities as members of the Sanitary Commission, or as social leaders in their religious communities, or as managers of schools and charities. Moreover, they had indirectly influenced colonial government, mildly by commenting on drafts of laws before enactment, stormily in protests in Gibraltar or in London at the excesses, as they saw them, of colonial authority. But civilians had also suffered reverses, for example to their monopoly management of the Sanitary Commission and the Civil Hospital, and in 1914 there were still no formal structures in Gibraltar through which governors could (or must) formally consult civilians, and no steps had been taken to introduce popular elections and representative government (and certainly not responsible government). Nor, as yet, had there been substantial demands for democratic innovations, by either the moneyed class or the population at large. The First World War, however, came to be marketed as the war for democracy, and certainly in Britain and even in many parts of the British Empire that ethic, plus destabilising mass mobilisation, prompted calls for more democratic accountability, and in some empire territories for self-government. By 1918 there would be adult male suffrage in Britain for the first time and votes for some women; in India from 1919 the majority of members in provincial assemblies were elected; in Ireland rough times would lead in 1921 to self-government in Northern Ireland and in 1922 to dominion status for the Irish Free State. Of course, after the Second World War, billed as the war for self-determination and freedom and in defence of democracy, the process of decolonisation was to pick up, though in a more stuttering fashion than is often now recalled, beginning impressively (though bloodily) with independence for the Indian sub-continent in 1947. But there were alternative endings, such as the incorporation of overseas colonies into the metropolis, or continuing colonial status (under varying titles), especially for small territories like the Falkland Islands, St Helena and Bermuda. Here too it will be important to consider what Gibraltar civilians, variably, wanted to secure and what British governments were willing to offer. It will, of course, be impossible in this context to ignore the claims of Spain to sovereignty over Gibraltar, and the ratcheting up of Spanish pressure from 1954. The path to constitutional change was going to be muddied and diverted by such intrusions.

Governors and law, 1915–69

Until recently the former careers of governors appointed to command in Gibraltar were unlikely, on the face of it, to suggest to civilians that Gibraltar was going to become anything but an autocratically managed fortress. In the near-century between 1913 and 2006, twenty-eight held the office, all men of course, and virtually all senior army officers until an admiral was appointed in 1969 (Sir Varyl Begg), followed by a marshal of the RAF in 1973 (Sir John Grandy). Rotation thereafter among only military men was not interrupted until the appointment in 1997 of a former British government minister (Sir Richard Luce). Those with military backgrounds all held high rank before appointment, including eight lieutenant-generals, nine full generals and one field-marshal, plus four admirals and two RAF marshals. Such personnel were therefore accustomed to exercising command and wielding authority, as indeed would the later civilian appointees. It is noticeable that almost all governors had substantial previous administrative (and some diplomatic) experience to draw upon. They were, on appointment, also marginally younger than their nineteenth-century predecessors, with an average (and median) age of just over 58, the youngest 52 and the oldest 63. There could be no suggestion here that those appointed were old and 'past it', nor did they linger long in office – duration of service was initially around five years but was reduced, usually to three or four, after the Second World War.[1]

Such a prosopographical sketch tells us little, however, about how governors would interpret their briefs, how much initiative they would show and how sensitively they would respond to civilian lobbying. For example, it would be difficult to predict that Sir Horace Lockwood Smith-Dorrien, passionate about hunting and horses, contemptuous (in India) of civilian politicians, cursed with a 'violent and ugly temper' (due to persistent dental problems, it was said) and bruised by the politics of military command during the First World War, should have been, as governor from July 1918 to May 1923, so administratively innovative as to transform the politics of the place: Smith-Dorrien Avenue was later named as a tribute to his memory.[2] Nor does it seem likely that Sir Noel Mason-Macfarlane, governor from May 1942 to February 1944, who once

1 Military postings account for the rapid turnover of four governors between 1939 and 1944.
2 For his career see S. Badsey, 'Sir Horace Lockwood Smith-Dorrien', *ODNB*, and H. Smith-Dorrien, *Memories of Forty-Eight Years' Service* (London: Murray, 1925).

offered personally to assassinate Adolf Hitler in 1938, who was said to have 'a sarcastic edge to his tongue' and who was judged by Harold Macmillan to be 'lacking in political judgement', should be the man to press in 1944 for constitutional developments in Gibraltar and later to be elected Labour MP for North Paddington, in 1945.[3] Civilians in Gibraltar concerned about public administration and political change would be reacting to personalities, not just to identikit men in uniforms.

It has to be said that having to cope with individuals who often had strong views was also an issue for the men in suits in Whitehall. Of course, the career records of governors were examined with some care before their appointment, by the War Office (and no doubt latterly by the Ministry of Defence) as well as by the Colonial Office and its successors – from 1966 the Department of Commonwealth Affairs (a merger of the Colonial Office and the Commonwealth Relations Office) and from 1968 the Foreign and Commonwealth Office (following a further combination, though conventionally just called the Foreign Office). Moreover, modern technology – faster ships and then aircraft, telegraphs and telephones (and now e-mail) – allowed the centre even more opportunity to monitor and, potentially, to manage colonial affairs and to reduce to mere agency the 'man on the spot'. Nevertheless, the culture of Whitehall with respect to colonial administration, including in Gibraltar, was to leave local governors with considerable responsibility not just for the acquisition of information but also in proposing policy and, once approved, in its implementation – though inevitably the diplomatic complexities caused by the 'Spanish problem' led in some matters to more centralised management. Accordingly, governors with their differing personalities and priorities, and sensitivities to perceived local opinion, made a difference.

Governors and their staff spent much of their time in law making. Analysis of Gibraltar legislation in the decades up to 1914 has demonstrated that latterly the volume of legislation – ordinances and orders-in-council – increased considerably and that a wider range of civilian life and activities had become controlled and also facilitated by law. It would have been remarkable if Gibraltar had thereafter defied the trend of the twentieth century and if law makers had not further extended the volume and range of the community's legislative infrastructure. The following analysis covers inclusively the fifty-five years from 1915 (the first full year of the war) to 1969, when, as we shall see in the next chapter, constitutional change made civilian ministers almost entirely responsible for domestic affairs.[4] In total, 1,059 ordinances were passed, on average around twenty laws

3 F.S.V. Donnison, 'Sir (Frank) Noel Mason-Macfarlane', *ODNB*.
4 Data drawn from GGA, C.C. Ross (ed.), *The Laws of Gibraltar* (London: Bosworth, 1950) and GGA, *Laws of Gibraltar*, 1984 edn. Excludes orders-in-council, including laws affecting Gibraltar but not specific to Gibraltar, such as some copyright, shipping and civil aviation laws.

a year, though of course not evenly spread. For example, forty-nine ordinances were passed in 1934, but twenty-nine of these were amending laws passed in preparation for a consolidation of legislation in 1935. However, even including these particular measures, and others introduced for military reasons, especially (but not only) during the two world wars, the increased rate of legislation, already in evidence in the period up to 1914, is evident. The 346 ordinances passed in the twenty-six years from 1915 to 1940 works out at just over thirteen a year, whereas the 713 passed in the twenty-nine years from 1941 to 1969 averages at over twenty-four a year. Civilians were, variably, winners or losers from legislative management.

Even a crude analysis based on titles indicates where legislation was being judged by government to be increasingly necessary or of value. In both periods, of course, a regular feature, as in the past, was the annual passage of ordinances to authorise the raising of revenue and accounting for expenditure, thirty-five in the first phase, sixty-seven in the second. More interestingly, there was much legislation by which legal practice, policing and penal policy were adapted in the light of experience and circumstances. Hence, in the period 1915–40 forty-seven ordinances dealt with such matters as police powers, the courts and court procedures, and sentencing, punishments and prisons. In the second and admittedly longer period of 1941–69 there was a veritable avalanche of ordinances, 101 in all, addressing similar subjects. Interestingly, provision for legal aid was enacted in 1947, as recommended by an official report in Britain in 1945, though not there enacted until 1949; and the abolition of the death penalty for murder occurred in 1967 in Gibraltar, following legislation passed in Britain only two years earlier. There is perhaps nothing remarkable here, except to stress that the volume of laws determining legal practices, as indicated by these two particular ordinances, continued to parallel English models and implied the further anglicisation of local civil culture and institutions and the still closer affinity of Gibraltar with Britain.[5]

This was also a likely consequence of the sixty-three additional measures passed by 1940 which supported and also regulated the conduct of civilian business in Gibraltar, and the eighty-six between 1941 and 1969. Ordinances dealt with such matters as the currency, the post office and company law, the registering of patents and trade marks, the regulation of the financial sector and the insurance industry, the updating of property law, the laws governing merchant shipping and the management of the port, and the operation of price controls during the war and also after Spanish trade restrictions began to bite from 1966.

5 In their summary of that year's new ordinances, the colony's annual reports frequently refer as models to 'imperial' and British statutes, as well as occasionally to the laws of other colonies, particularly but not only with respect to judicial practices and business laws.

In addition, in 1930 there was an ordinance concerned with 'aerial navigation', and this last is a reminder that modernity also needed regulating; hence no fewer than ten measures to cope with hackney carriages, motor vehicles and traffic had been introduced by 1940, and nineteen more followed thereafter.

There are also further signs of that cautious legislative intrusion into family life which was already tip-toeing forward before 1914. Twelve further pieces of legislation by 1940 dealt with such matters as marriage, maintenance orders, legitimacy, adoption and infanticide, and eighteen thereafter. A previous chapter has traced the history of controls over aliens, alien traders, immigration and rights of settlement, and the laws determining nationality and 'belonging', and these, plus laws concerning the registration of births and deaths, accounted for sixteen pieces of legislation prior to 1940 and yet more, twenty-four, thereafter. Public health also continued to attract a lot of legislative attention, with twenty-one measures by 1940, updating the existing public health laws and dealing more specifically with quarantine, drugs, mental health and the Colonial Hospital, plus five ordinances regulating dentists, doctors and midwives; but between 1941 and 1969, when public health was also receiving serious political attention in Britain, a further forty-nine laws were passed to deal with public health concerns, plus eight more relating specifically to medical personnel.

So far, continuity between the two periods has largely been noted, even if the volume of legislation increased. It is therefore important to notice that in the first phase under scrutiny only a few further steps, seven new laws, were taken in the direction of labour protection, with measures relating to shop hours (1922, 1929), tobacco workers (1922), employers' liability (1924), the employment of women, young people and children (1932), minimum wages (1933) and the outlawing of payment of wages in kind, not cash (1934). There were only three specific housing measures, concerned with rent restrictions (1920, repealed 1923, revived 1938), and only two relating to education (1917, 1940). The discerning reader will notice none of those measures which were characteristic of state welfare legislation in Britain even before 1914: poor law, labour exchanges, health and unemployment insurance, school meals, the medical inspection and treatment of schoolchildren, and old age pensions, let alone their extensions and derivatives by 1940.[6] But after the war a further thirty-eight measures relating to labour followed in a legislative clatter, comparable to the labour laws characteristic of Britain after 1945. There were more, for example, regulating shop hours (1947, 1952, 1954) and the employment of women, young people and children (1948, 1952, 1969), and concerned with employers' liability and accidents and occupational diseases (1948, 1950, 1954). There were also laws in new areas, for instance setting out for the first time a legal framework for the operation of trade unions and the conduct of trade disputes (1947, 1953, 1966), creating

6 The only pension legislation in Gibraltar by 1940 related to government employees.

employment exchanges (1949), regulating wages and conditions of employment, including in so-called 'factories' (1953, 1956, 1957, 1959, 1963, 1966), controlling employment (1955, 1956, 1965, 1968, 1969) and introducing employment injuries insurance (1952, 1956, 1959, 1961, 1966).

This last is particularly important, because since 1911 compulsory state-managed insurance had become characteristic of social security in Britain. Therefore other new laws replicating aspects of Britain's post-war 'welfare state', twenty-five of them in the fourteen years between 1955 and 1969, are of immense significance in again indicating the rapid reconfiguration of systems and institutions in Gibraltar along British lines. Social insurance supplemented by a non-contributory scheme was launched in 1955, followed by family allowances in 1959. All these social security laws required subsequent developments, and so legislators were kept busy with amending ordinances almost every year. If we add to these the thirteen measures passed between 1945 and 1969 relating to housing, mainly dealing with landlords and tenants, and seven from 1941 to 1969 concerning education, we are identifying substantial matters, to be examined shortly.

Since social security and other parts of the government's business would not come cheaply, the subject of another batch of laws catches the eye: government taxation. Between 1915 and 1940 there were six modest measures relating to stamp duties, two concerned with licences and fees, and one introducing a modest trade tax, plus three rather more controversial ordinances concerning estate duties, which came late in the period (1934, 1939) – but there was no income tax legislation. Between 1941 and 1969 there were thirty-two revenue-raising ordinances. Admittedly, ten of these referred to such well-established income sources as stamp duties and licence fees, plus one quirky, special tax on coffee. But two concerned raising income from lotteries (1947, 1954), two to a trades tax (1945, 1950), four more to estate duties (1947, 1954, 1963, 1965) and, remarkably, given past resistance, thirteen to income tax (1952, 1953, 1957, 1960, 1962, 1965, 1967, 1968, 1969). There were also thirteen measures concerned with raising capital: seven relating to local loans (1947, 1960, 1961, 1967, 1968) and six to development aid from Britain (1963, 1964, 1967, 1968). The politics of finance must therefore be another item to address.

There was not much more legislation concerning forms of government and public administration after the First World War than there had been before, except a couple of measures dealing with corrupt practices, plus, more interestingly, as we shall shortly see, a City Council Ordinance in 1921, with amending legislation in 1927, 1932, 1934 and 1940. Nevertheless, this period is not distinguished by its constitution-making legislation. However, between 1941 and 1969 public administration and constitutional innovation were major topics for law. Thirty-eight items, some concerned with implementing constitutional alterations initiated by orders-in-council emanating from London, altered fundamentally how Gibraltar was governed, and the involvement of civilians within the forms of government. Naturally, most of them, twenty-four, concerned the powers of the City Council – including its suspension of operation during the Second World War and then its restoration and subsequent developments. But three concerned a post-war innovation, the Legislative Council, and ten governed the holding of elections. There is enough to suggest that Gibraltar, constitutionally, was changed during our second period in very important ways. Since such matters were high on the agenda of Gibraltar's political nation, they too must be high on our agenda for this and the next chapter.

City Council and Executive Council, to 1940

As described in previous chapters, back in the early eighteenth century and prompted by British merchants resident on the Rock, the establishment of a town council modelled on conventional British lines had been a serious prospect; and later the Sanitary Commission, established in 1865, was interpreted by some leading locals as a first step towards a similar result. In fact, neither in the eighteenth century nor in the nineteenth century was this judged acceptable by those responsible for running the fortress. Nor, indeed, prior to the First World War was there much civilian demand that those few who supposedly represented civilian society on the Sanitary Commission should be elected rather than nominated, and there was no proposal that the ugly duckling of the Sanitary Commission should become the swan of a city council. However, as also noted, there were signs that coal-heavers and workers in the dockyards had become organised and had taken industrial action prior to the outbreak of war. It is to their representatives, and also to the colony's governor, and not to members of the moneyed class on the Sanitary Commission, or the Exchange Committee, or the Chamber of Commerce, or the Gibraltar Employers' Federation that we should look for the initiatives which were to roll out new representative bodies after the war. In Gibraltar as elsewhere, including Britain, the First World War had in general unsettled past practices and, in particular, had increased the aspirations of organised labour.

On 15 May 1919 the British Workmen's Association in Gibraltar, shortly to become the Workers' Union and a branch of the British-based Transport and General Workers' Union, sent a deputation to London which laid its concerns before Leo Amery, parliamentary under-secretary at the Colonial Office. It was bothered by the inflationary consequences of the war, by the inequity, as it saw it, of the way compensatory war bonuses were allotted and by what it perceived as unacceptable increases in rents. In addition, however, and indicative of a wider agenda, it wanted the Workmen's Compensation Act (concerning accidents at work) and the Old Age Pensions Act, both operating in Britain, to be extended to Gibraltar; it wanted permission to publish a newspaper (no doubt reflecting more its interests than did the *Gibraltar Chronicle*); and it asked that government should take over education and run state schools with more English language teaching and less religious instruction. The wish to adopt British models and further anglicise Gibraltar is evident in these aspirations, but even more indicative is its demand, with respect to the Sanitary Commission, that 'some form of representation based on a popular franchise should be accorded to the civil inhabitants of Gibraltar'.[7]

The response of the governor to these requests is remarkable, because Smith-Dorrien had only been in office since July 1918, he was an army general, the First World War had only just been brought to its unstable conclusion, and his official instructions placed considerable emphasis on the fortress and his duties as commander-in-chief. It is true that he was not persuaded that the educational system needed to be changed, or that old age pensions were needed in Gibraltar, or that the Workmen's Compensation Act was appropriate for a place with 'no factories or industries' (the Colonial Office was more sympathetic). However, while he did not think that rents had seriously increased, he did intimate that the housing issue needed examination, he was willing to receive an application to publish a newspaper and, most important, he claimed that he had 'long been convinced' that properly elected civilians on the Sanitary Commission were desirable. True, he would insist that the government should retain its five representatives and thus its majority, but he proposed that the four civilian members currently chosen by the governor from a panel drawn from the Grand Jury should in future be 'elected by a popular franchise from amongst the ratepayers'. This alteration in the constitution of the Sanitary Commission was then accepted in principle by the Colonial Office.[8]

With that green light, Smith-Dorrien asked his attorney-general to draft an ordinance. The committee he appointed to scrutinise the terms, chaired by his colonial secretary, contained one representative of the Exchange Committee, one of the existing Sanitary Commissioners and, noticeably, two representatives of the Workers' Union. These two 'contended strongly' that the elected members should number six and therefore form a majority, but the colonial secretary, probably mindful of history, insisted that after any reform the government must retain its majority – five of nine – and this verdict was reluctantly accepted. The union representatives were also unhappy that the draft would exclude many ratepayers, including themselves, from standing for office, because the proposed property qualification for candidates was payment of quite a high level of rent, £30 a year or more. The electors, however, needed only to be British subjects in occupation of any kind of property as tenant or owner, that is, as ratepayers,

7 TNA, CO91/470, Smith-Dorrien to Milner, 9 and 30 April 1919 and enclosures.
8 TNA, CO91/471, Smith-Dorrien to Milner, 18 Sept 1919, minutes, and Milner to Smith-Dorrien, 31 Oct 1919.

and male. It tells us something about Gibraltar's culture, that none of the men objected to clauses which explicitly decreed that no woman would be eligible as a candidate or even as an elector: women ratepayers in Britain had long since been voters at local elections and many more women, since 1918, at parliamentary elections. This restriction was not queried by the governor, though a legal expert at the Colonial Office wondered if this discrimination might be controversial in Gibraltar. It was not. However, Smith-Dorrien personally decided to widen the range of potential candidates by deleting for them the property qualification. The committee had also noted that the responsibilities of the former Sanitary Commission had extended beyond its originally narrow public health functions, and he therefore endorsed their recommendation that the new body, with its three official members plus two to be appointed by the governor from whomever he felt fit to serve and four members unrestricted by a property qualification and elected by popular vote, should henceforth be called the City Council.[9] English models were further followed insofar as the essence of the Ballot Act of 1872 and of the Municipal Elections (Corrupt and Illegal Practices) Act of 1883 was embedded into the ordinance.[10]

While reassuring the Colonial Office that the governor would retain sufficient power over the activities of the council, Smith-Dorrien still insisted that the ordinance was to be valued as a 'liberal measure' and that it had the 'great advantage of being the outcome of the unanimous recommendation of a Committee on which the Labour Union in Gibraltar was represented by two members'.[11] The *Gibraltar Chronicle* judged that the City Council Ordinance enacted on 22 August 1921 offered a 'generous measure of local self-government to the citizens of Gibraltar'. Four electoral wards were defined, elections were to be held every three years, and in 1921 the first official register of voters was compiled, containing the names of the 4,351 adult male British subjects who were owners or occupiers of property and who alone were eligible to vote (from a total population of 16,681 British subjects). The first election was held on 1 December 1921; there was a very respectable turnout of nearly 73 per cent; and, perhaps appropriately, three Workers' Union candidates were returned. The moneyed class had been reluctant to press for democratisation before 1914, and its representative on Smith-Dorrien's committee had been uncomfortable with the removal of the high property qualification for candidates. Their apprehension was justified. Only one member of the Exchange Committee was elected,

9 TNA, CO91/474, Smith-Dorrien to Milner, 2 July 1920, and enclosures, minutes, and Milner to Smith-Dorrien, 21 July 1920.
10 TNA, CO91/474, draft of ordinance, section 15, with Smith-Dorrien to Milner, 2 July 1920, and CO91/477, memorandum by Attorney-General, 7 Feb 1921, with Smith-Dorrien to Milner, 10 Feb 1921.
11 TNA, CO91/477, Smith-Dorrien to Churchill, 24 March 1921.

as an Independent, and even he (Andrews-Speed) had received Workers' Union endorsement.[12] During subsequent elections in the 1920s Workers' Union candidates continued to win a majority. Electoral turnouts slid down to barely 53 per cent in the 1927 election, but rose impressively to over 75 per cent in 1933 and to only a shade under 77 per cent in 1936. Fortunes also shifted in the 1930s, and more so-called Independents, mainly representing the moneyed class, won seats.[13] The City Council meanwhile buckled down to the responsibilities it had inherited from the Sanitary Commission, and from November 1924 councillors and officials even occupied their equivalent of a town hall, the former Connaught House in an impressive square just off Main Street, henceforth known as City Hall.[14] The significance of all this is that Gibraltar was now experiencing real popular politics (unlike after 1936 across the border in Franco's Spain), and these were modelled on British practices. Elections to office on Gibraltar's City Council were politicising society.

Smith-Dorrien's other initiative was to establish an Executive Council. He reported in August 1921 that, to guide him in good government, he was finding it difficult to secure the views of the civil inhabitants on 'matters . . . affecting them closely'. Receiving deputations and talking to individuals was not enough. Something more was needed than just allowing locals to respond to ordinances already fully prepared and merely published for consultation before final enactment. He felt that an executive council would largely solve the problem. Moreover, he reckoned it would 'be received by the civil population with great satisfaction as being a step in the direction of giving them some voice in the affairs of the colony'. Such a body should, however, contain official and unofficial members as well as the governor. It was pointed out that every other crown colony had an executive council, including Malta and Bermuda, which also had military governors. It was well understood that, in spite of its name, an executive council was only an advisory council, that its deliberations would be kept secret and that certain subjects, including all military matters, would be excluded from its agenda.

The proposal was nevertheless striking and reflects a revised and realistic way of regarding the colony. Gibraltar was a fortress, but it was argued that it had also grown to be a major port and coaling station. Therefore on legislative and

12 This account is based, with some amendments, on T.J. Finlayson, 'Gibraltar's first election', *Gibraltar Heritage Journal*, 3 (1996), 7–14, esp. 9–12, and C.A. Grocott, 'The moneyed class of Gibraltar, c.1880–1939' (PhD thesis, Lancaster University, 2006), p. 184. Registers of voters by wards, with numbers slightly at variance from those recorded after polls, are in GGA, MP784/1921, MP468/1924, MP480/1927 and MP365/1933.

13 For the politics, including the elections, of the period from 1921 to 1939 see Grocott, 'Moneyed class', pp. 182–91, 201–14.

14 *Annual Report for 1924*, p. 3.

financial matters the 'Civil inhabitants should have some means of expressing their views in a regular and constitutional manner,' and this would be of benefit to government. Moreover, it was noted that there had been complaints about the lack of representative government and mutterings about 'no taxation without representation'. Therefore there would be advantages in voluntarily granting now what might be demanded later, 'possibly with some parade and heat'. As finally agreed, the council was to consist of the governor and four official members, plus three unofficials appointed for three years by the governor. In negotiating this arrangement Smith-Dorrien had intimated that he expected the unofficial members to speak for the whole community and that therefore they should include a representative of the Workers' Union.[15]

Smith-Dorrien's sympathies with civilian political aspirations were fully expressed in response to a last-minute hitch. To accommodate an executive council into government, letters patent setting out governing practice had to be revised and the War Office insisted that they state that in the absence of the governor (for example on leave) the person to take command would be the senior military officer, representing the War Office, and not, as had been recent convention, the colonial secretary, who was a civilian official. Although himself a general, Smith-Dorrien protested, but unsuccessfully, that no military officer could adequately deal with complex and pressing civilian concerns. Moreover, he asserted, this reversal would undo the good feeling engendered by the already announced Executive Council, which had been 'welcomed by the people as a stepping stone to larger measures of self government'. A system which would leave an army officer even temporarily in control of the colony would revive among civilians 'their cry against the injustice of being downtrodden by the Military Heel'. He complained that the War Office continued to bang on about Gibraltar being a fortress, but 'they do not appear to care to recognise, when all the world is stirred by the cries of self-determination and self-government, that the civil inhabitants of a Fortress are not going to remain unmoved'. He noted that civilians 'are fully alive to the fact that very large measures of Self-Government have been recently conceded to the inhabitants of Malta, and they naturally consider that they should be similarly treated'.[16]

15 TNA, CO91/478, Smith-Dorrien to Churchill, 25 Aug and 4 Nov 1921, enclosure, and minutes, and Colonial Office to War Office, 16 Sept and 20 Dec 1921, and CO91/480, Smith-Dorrien to Churchill, 11 July 1922.

16 The correspondence, including Smith-Dorrien's despatches of 17 March, 9 Oct and 25 Oct 1922 and Colonial Office despatches of 24 Feb, 18 Sept and 16 and 20 Nov 1922, are in TNA, but are also conveniently collected in GGA, Executive Council, 1921–34. Smith-Dorrien also admitted his disappointment with this outcome at a meeting of the Executive Council on 9 Nov 1922: GGA, Box: Executive Council, Gibraltar, Minutes of Meetings. Remarkably (or perhaps not), the Chiefs of Staff only very much later agreed to allow the colonial secretary to be the substitute in the

The Executive Council met for the first time on 1 November 1922. Smith-Dorrien opened the meeting by declaring it 'a great step in the history of the colony'. The advice of members would enable him to 'do the best for the community'. The four ex officio members were the senior military officer, the colonial secretary, the attorney-general and the colonial treasurer; the three appointed unofficials, formally sworn in, were all justices of the peace and distinguished figures in the community, A. Mosley, A. Carrara, and J. Andrews-Speed. They then got down to the kind of business which was to occupy them and their successors at subsequent meetings. These were held, initially, almost monthly, and at variable intervals thereafter until the Executive Council was swept away in 1964 in further constitutional innovations. On this first occasion they dealt with a Spanish request for reports on Spanish vessels leaving Gibraltar, draft ordinances on infanticide and criminal law, Workers' Union resolutions concerning trust legislation, fares for motorboats and contracts for public works. For the first time, and seemingly irreversibly, civilians were incorporated intimately into government policy making.

In his memoirs Smith-Dorrien suggested that perhaps principal among his achievements as governor was to have 'rendered the form of government rather less autocratic'.[17] However, with respect to the City Council, the ugly duckling was still, in truth, no swan. The City Council had only four elected members and was therefore scarcely comparable to a fully elected borough council in Britain. Moreover, the two members appointed by governors tended to be members of the moneyed class, who would normally form a bloc with the three official members representing the army, the navy and the colonial government. In the eyes of the Workers' Union this reduced its elected councillors still more to an ineffective minority. Nor did it agree that Smith-Dorrien's other political baby, the Executive Council, properly reflected the interests of the civilian community as a whole, since, in spite of the expectations the governor had himself raised, no representative of the Workers' Union was appointed to it by him.[18]

It is true that members of the moneyed class were not discontented with these outcomes. When their candidates were least successful at being *elected* to the

Footnote 16 (*cont.*)
    absence of the governor – in 1964: TNA, CO926/1227, minute 30 Aug 1962, and CO926/1866, Sandys to Ward, 31 July 1964.
17 Smith-Dorrien, *Memories*, p. 495.
18 Smith-Dorrien's initial intention to appoint to the Executive Council a representative of the Workers' Union as well as of the Chamber of Commerce and of the Exchange Committee is evident in TNA, CO91/480, and GGA, Box: Executive Council 1921–34, Smith-Dorrien to Churchill, 11 July 1922; but the idea that nominated members should explicitly represent named bodies was rejected by the Colonial Office and this was conceded by the governor: Churchill to Smith-Dorrien, 25 July 1922, and Smith-Dorrien to Churchill, 1 Aug 1922.

City Council, it was some consolation to have their people *appointed* instead, and also they pretty much monopolised positions as the appointed unofficials on the Executive Council. Even so, some among them had had their political aspirations whetted. In September 1922, for example, the president of the Exchange Committee lauded the achievements of Smith-Dorrien in setting up the Executive Council and the City Council but also described them as just 'the first steps towards the recognition by the Mother Country to our claim for political franchise after 218 years of British citizenship'. Moreover, he indicated what the next step should be: 'the granting . . . of a Legislative Council, so that the people of Gibraltar may have a voice in the administration of civil affairs as all loyal, cultured and law-abiding Colonies have a right to expect'.[19] This was not an impossible dream. Legislative councils were indeed common elsewhere in the colonial empire, but while they implied that laws would need majority endorsement by their members, there was no set model for how they were to be constituted and membership determined. Smith-Dorrien himself believed that conceding a legislative council 'later on' would do no harm, provided that only civic issues were considered by it and that official members 'were in excess of the elected non-official members'.[20] This might have found favour with the Exchange Committee, and others, since they too were unlikely as yet to have favoured a legislative council elected entirely (or at all) by popular vote. Nevertheless, in conjunction with Workers' Union's discontent with recent innovations, it is evident that Smith-Dorrien had done more to provoke than to assuage desires for political change.[21]

The Workers' Union had made quite a stink about insufficient elected representation on the City Council in a rally of its troops even before the election of 1921,[22] and in February 1924 it protested to the governor that there was no representative of the working class on the Executive Council. Sir Charles Monro had been in office since May 1923, and his view of his primary responsibilities confirms how important could be the opinions of the governor in determining responses to civilian demands for further constitutional change. Correspondence from the Workers' Union, he told the Colonial Office, 'is an interesting example of the tendency which exists here at present for the civil population to claim rights which are hardly compatible with the existence of Gibraltar as a Military

19 *Gibraltar Chronicle*, 26 Sept 1922: the occasion was the reopening by the governor of the Exchange building, rebuilt after a disastrous fire in 1919.
20 GGA, Box: Executive Council 1921–34, Smith-Dorrien to Churchill, 5 Oct 1922.
21 For a contemporary judgement along these lines see TNA, CO91/485/11, minute by Dawe, 13 April 1926.
22 GGA, MP249/1921, Police magistrate report to chief of police, 12 June 1921; TNA, CO91/477, branch secretary to governor, 11 June 1921, with Orr to Churchill, 14 June 1921.

Fortress'.[23] Another example went straight to the Colonial Office, a letter in August 1924 from the Union admitting that the army and navy should have representatives on the City Council but insisting that the 'time has arrived for the bringing into existence a genuine Municipal body with full powers of managing the whole of the civil affairs of the Colony'.[24]

Nor was it only working-class representatives who felt embittered. In July 1924 the Exchange Committee was also writing in protest about what it regarded as an unacceptable amendment to the revenue ordinance, introduced without consulting the likes of it. Such practices, it insisted, were 'politically vicious as affecting the right of the people to be heard on the imposition of taxes or duties'. As for Smith-Dorrien's reforms, it claimed that the Executive Councillors 'as at present constituted do not adequately represent the various classes of the people of Gibraltar'. Later, the Exchange Committee reviewed colonial governments elsewhere and supposedly found that, with their limited political representation, the inhabitants of Gibraltar were classified 'with Basutos, Somalis and other wild African tribes, a stigma on Gibraltar, which ranks amongst the most cultured of European communities'. Specifically, it proposed that three more members should be added to the Executive Council, appointed not by the governor but nominated by the 'three existing representative bodies': Exchange and Commercial Library, Chamber of Commerce and Workers' Union. Lest we become dizzied by this radical challenge, it should be noticed that election by popular vote was not suggested and that a single union representative would hardly sway opinion in an Executive Council already containing three appointed unofficials who were usually drawn from the moneyed class. Even so, this was said to be a reform which would conform to the 'principles of the British Constitution'.[25]

There were even attempts in the autumn of 1924 to coordinate action. The Workers' Union endeavoured to win over the Exchange Committee and the Chamber of Commerce to its plan for a 'genuine Municipal body', and sought support for the petition it was presenting to the secretary of state. The Exchange Committee was willing to back these proposals in general terms, and even suggested that the City Council should take control of the markets, cemetery, public works, lunatic asylum and, indeed, the Colonial Hospital. It added, however, that the colonial government (not ratepayers) should continue to 'pay for their upkeep'. It further exposed its anxieties about popular democracy, since it was

23 GGA, MP509/1924, and TNA, CO91/483, Monro to Thomas, 21 March 1924, and correspondence from and to Workers' Union.
24 GGA, MP510/1924 and TNA, CO91/483, Lyons, Workers' Union, to Thomas, 8 Aug 1924.
25 GGA, MP509/1924, Exchange Committee to Acting Colonial Secretary, 3 July 1924, press cutting, 22 Sept 1924.

against allowing the City Council to have legislative or tax-raising powers. At the same time, the Exchange Committee solicited backing from the others for its revised proposals for a legislative council, to be made up of four representatives from each of their organisations, plus an elected representative from each of the four City Council wards. There should also be an elected House of Assembly, but its numbers and function were left unexplained. Members of the Chamber of Commerce were reluctant to be involved in any of this and were particularly hesitant about the implications of what the Union was seeking. Some members believed that the electoral system made it impossible for people of their class to be elected, and therefore they doubted the wisdom of increasing the authority of the City Council. In the end, they passed a resolution, forwarded to the colonial secretary, in which they supported an increase in the powers of the existing City Council – no mention there of more elected membership – while at the same time recording their opposition to any 'grant of Self-Government to the Colony of Gibraltar'.[26] Class divisions and suspicions scuppered the chances of a united front.

But in any event this was all rather pointless, because the governor and the imperial government had come to regret the concessions to popular democracy which they had already granted. Governor Monro had followed up his initially sceptical reactions to Workers' Union representations. He wanted the imperial government to clarify its collective view of the 'status of Gibraltar': was Gibraltar 'a Fortress or a Colony?' Insisting on this polarity, he saw the answer as determining how many civilians should be allowed to live in the territory, how many should be allowed to move in from La Línea (where 5,000 with rights of residence in Gibraltar were living), how many houses would be needed to accommodate the civil population adequately and how much land therefore should be passed from military to civilian hands. Moreover, the answer would also determine the extent to which further concessions should be made to civilian demands for a larger voice in public affairs. Monro was firm in his own mind: Gibraltar was a fortress. No place here (as Smith-Dorrien had attempted) for acknowledging and further accommodating the separate and valid interests of the resident civilian population. What he requested, however, was a decision by the imperial government, and that, as the Colonial Office recognised, required a review of Gibraltar's strategic importance in the light of modern weaponry, and not just by itself but in consultation with the War Office, the Admiralty and (here was a novelty) the Air Ministry.[27]

The review which took place concluded that the principal status of Gibraltar was indeed 'essentially that of an Imperial Fortress and Naval Base, the security

26 GGA, MP510/1924, press cuttings, 6 Aug–1 Nov 1924, and Chamber of Commerce to Colonial Secretary, 26 Nov 1924.
27 TNA, CO91/483, Monro to Thomas, 23 May 1924.

of which should be of primary importance at all times'.[28] Governor Monro then directed the implications of this judgement at the constitution of the City Council. This had already been altered in 1927 by the abolition of the electoral wards, so that henceforth four candidates were to be elected by all Gibraltar's electors, each with four votes. The amendment was supposed to ensure a fairer representation of public opinion. In practice, it gave more chances, well taken, for members of the moneyed class to dilute the voting strength of workers, who were concentrated in particular wards and who had formerly secured the return of Union candidates in electorally safe seats.[29] Although otherwise the com-position of the council remained as Smith-Dorrien had constructed it – three nominated officials representing the colonial government, the Admiralty and the War Office, two councillors appointed by the governor and four elected – the Colonial Office was now persuaded by Monro that, because of awkward moments when the governor had not been able easily enough to get his own way, the 'council should be brought under the control of an official nominated majority'. Specifically, the past practice of governors being allowed to appoint two councillors, including civilian members of the public who were not bound to follow the governor's directions, should be altered. Instead the governor should nominate five officials, who would be obliged to follow his directions, thus giving the administration, if necessary, a secure majority over the four elected. It was understood that if the City Council were reconstituted as proposed 'it will become virtually a Government Department'. The history of the Sanitary Commission provides precedents for this kind of counter-revolution. The Colonial Office was, however, troubled that the proposed change was a 'drastic measure' and would require legislation and provoke protests. Monro too and, especially, his successor from 1928, Sir Alex Godley, were somewhat apprehen-sive, and on reflection they avoided running the risk by the simpler expedient of appointing as councillors those who they hoped could be trusted.[30]

No overt reversal of the political advances made by the civilian community therefore took place, but the reception accorded to further proposals for progres-sive constitutional evolution was inevitably going to be bleak. Demands from the Workers' Union in July and September 1929 that the City Council should be reconfigured so that the elected members secured a majority were pretty firmly rejected by the governor and by the Colonial Office – ruled out, it was said, because of the 'special position which Gibraltar occupies as a Naval base and

28 TNA, CO91/486/31, Monro to Amery 9 Dec 1927, citing despatch from Amery, 11 Feb 1927.

29 GGA, Executive Council Minutes, 11 July and 5 Aug 1927, City Council (Amendment) Ordinance, no 4 of 1927; TNA, CO91/486/18.

30 TNA, WO32/2401, Colonial Office to War Office, 16 Feb 1928, enclosures and subsequent correspondence.

Fortress'.[31] This was again the response to a petition organised in August 1934 by the Workers' Union, with some cooperation from the Exchange Committee. This argued that the civil community had demonstrated its loyalty and shown responsibility and therefore deserved to form the majority on the City Council and to have 'adequate representation in a Council or Assembly' which should be set up and entrusted with legislative powers. The petition, it was claimed, had been approved 'by acclamation at a largely attended Public Meeting', and it bore the signatures of an impressive number of people: 3,135. Nevertheless, the view in the Colonial Office was that Gibraltar was still primarily a fortress and naval base, it had 'very little economic life apart from that which is supported by the Imperial expenditure on the naval and military forces stationed there', and it would be 'quite out of proportion for a small community of this character to be granted a Legislative Council or Assembly'. The governor, General Sir Charles Harington, in office from May 1933, went further. He trivialised the numbers who attended the public meeting, queried the validity of the signatures, disparaged the Workers' Union as illiterate members of 'the lower labouring classes' with a 'Latin temperament', and condemned their leadership as corrupt, 'tub-thumping', anti-government socialists who could 'neither speak, read nor write English'. In other words, not respectable or to be trusted. He also agreed, of course, that the interests and security of the fortress and naval base must in any case be the priorities.[32]

With political turmoil thereafter just across the frontier in Spain and the outbreak of civil war in July 1936, there was even less likelihood that any tinkering with the constitution of Gibraltar would take place. This was not just because government would not risk initiating political change, and agitation, when the security of the fortress was being pushed even higher, if possible, up the agenda. The political issues at stake, inflamed by stories of atrocities and the presence of refugees coming over the border, were also polarising political opinion among civilians in Gibraltar, and made any campaigning for political change more divisive and less likely.[33] And so matters remained when September 1939 arrived, and with it the Second World War. It is therefore true that the innovations launched

31 TNA, CO91/489/4, Workers' Union to Godley, 12 July and 16 Sept 1929, minutes and correspondence, esp. Passfield to Godley, 12 Oct 1929, and Godley to Shuckburgh, 12 Oct 1929, which refers to an (untraced) memorial also received from the Exchange Committee.

32 TNA, CO91/497/11, petition, dated 31 Aug 1934; CO91/497/10, Harington to Cunliffe-Lister, 15 Sept 1934, enclosures, minutes and subsequent correspondence, esp. Harington to Cunliffe-Lister, 6 Oct 1934, and undated 'Notes on the Gibraltar Petition'.

33 For one among many indicators of the divisions caused see TNA, CO91/501/5, Harington to Ormsby-Gore, 22 Sept 1937; and see Grocott, 'Moneyed Class', pp. 203–14; G. Stockey, 'A Porous Frontier: Gibraltar and its Spanish hinterland, c.1923–1954' (PhD thesis, Lancaster University, 2006), pp. 147–213.

in the early 1920s by Governor Sir Horace Smith-Dorrien had, by 1939, sailed no further – but they had travelled too far to be scuppered. They had already provoked calls for redesign and more powerful engines. The construction of a separate civil identity had been advanced not just by City Council elections but also by widespread frustration when the colonial authorities rebuffed requests for further democratic advances.

Colonial government, City Council and housing, 1921–40

It was observed in previous chapters that the Paving and Scavenging Commission and then the Sanitary Commission were layers of administration inserted beneath and theoretically always subordinate to the colonial government. However, the volume of business that the Sanitary Commission handled and the City Council inherited, including much of what directly affected civilians (such as sanitation, roads and the public utilities), enhanced its significance in the eyes of the civil population. Even with a majority of officials in charge, the City Council became therefore not just a passive agent of government but an alternative interest group and actor, with its own revenue source. In April 1939 the colonial government's treasurer, anxious to reduce the costs of administration by eliminating overlap, floated the idea of combining the colonial government and the City Council into a single public service, while providing for public representation in a legislative council, albeit with an official majority. His superiors rejected the idea, with alarm, as certain to lead to demands for further reform on 'more democratic lines'.[34] Nevertheless, the treasurer was correct to detect overlap and ultimately, but a long time later, what he had proposed came to pass and Gibraltar's administration again came to adopt the model of a unitary authority. Until then, the politics of the relationship between colonial government and City Council were important and are worthy of examination.

For example, both parties had serious concerns about the quantity and quality of housing available for Gibraltar citizens. This was not, of course, a new anxiety. Several official inquiries were conducted from the turn of the century and they all pretty well came to the same obvious conclusions. Building land in Gibraltar was limited; the military encroached on available space not just for army and navy (and later air force) installations but also to accommodate its personnel; while alien (and even statutory alien) settlement had been made more difficult and the resident population was therefore not growing, any increase in housing stock to reduce overcrowding in Gibraltar might simply attract in those who were perfectly entitled to live in Gibraltar but who were living more cheaply in La Línea; slum clearance would only make the housing shortage worse unless accompanied by new or renovated housing; expectations about minimum

34 GGA, MP175/1939, treasurer to colonial secretary 27 April 1939, and reply.

standards were rising.[35] There was also, of course, the matter of agency: who should tackle the problem? Private enterprise, it was said by officials, was discouraged by the short-term leases for crown lands (usually twenty-one years) and would in any case expect an 'economic rent', and in a sellers' market that was likely to mean rents which many working-class families could not afford. That left the colonial government, with ultimate responsibility for social welfare (and the health of the garrison), or the City Council. In either case, issues to be addressed concerned the source of capital (from colonial government surpluses, or money borrowed by the government or by the City Council?), the fixing of rents at 'affordable' levels (subsidised by investing money in housing schemes with below-market expectations of a reasonable rate of return, or meeting deficits out of revenue?) and responsibility for managing housing stock and tenants as well as construction (government, or City Council, or both?).

There were also, of course, political dimensions to this. The Workers' Union campaigned on housing issues,[36] and governors (and this time not only Smith-Dorrien) were anxious to address the issue. Further, several inter-war housing acts in Britain, including slum clearance legislation, had established three principles which attracted attention in Gibraltar: that local authorities were appropriate agencies to construct and manage public sector housing, that the central government could, if necessary, compel subordinate local authorities to build houses and clear slums, and that rents for new accommodation put up by local authorities would need to be subsidised by central government so as to make them affordable to working-class families.

Sir Horace Smith-Dorrien tried to tackle the problems by a temporary rent restriction ordinance, by renovating property owned by government on crown lands, by building an additional tenement block and by setting low rents for renovated and new stock, although this would provide only a poor return on the government capital invested and therefore meant, in effect, that rents were being subsidised.[37] However, one of the problems he and his successors encountered was that the colonial government lacked sufficient staff to take on the role of housing developer and public sector housing manager. It was in contemplating how to have new tenements constructed that Smith-Dorrien therefore chose to inquire whether this was something that the Sanitary Commission, soon

35 Compare a sequence of official reports by Fleetwood Wilson Committee, Nov 1898, Coll Commission, May 1907, Government Engineer, Sept 1910, Bartle Frere Committee, July 1920, City Council, June 1924, Smales, 1927, and Hone, Jan 1937.

36 For example see GGA, MP249/1921, Police Magistrate to Chief of Police, 12 June 1921, and MP55/1935, Workers' Union Deputation.

37 GGA, Despatches from Gibraltar 1919–20: Smith-Dorrien to Milner, 13 Nov 1919 and 16 Feb 1920; Despatches from Gibraltar 1920–21: Smith-Dorrien to Milner, 18 July 1920.

to become the City Council, might take on, although at this time financial constraints seem to have blocked some subsequent initiatives in which the City Council had shown an interest.[38]

Then, in 1924–25, the City Council itself made the running, carrying out its own review of the 'Serious Shortage of Housing Accommodation in Gibraltar'. It concluded that additional housing was needed, that sites were available and that the council should construct tenements on them. However, the council would need to have its borrowing powers extended to raise the capital. Moreover, to make rents affordable the colonial government would have to lend the council money at a low rate of interest and provide a subsidy, or to bear or share the deficit. The housing bill of 1924 currently going through parliament at Westminster (to become the Labour government's Wheatley Housing Act) was noted as a model. But in June 1925 negotiations between two seemingly separate and equal authorities broke down. The colonial government was ready to hand over building sites and provide up to half the capital costs of construction at a low rate of interest but would not provide an annual subsidy; the City Council demanded that all the capital required should therefore be provided by the colonial government, half as a free grant and half as an interest-free loan.[39]

However, in December 1927 the colonial government tried again to work a deal with the City Council. Sir Charles Monro was determined to launch 'a progressive scheme for ameliorating housing conditions'. The 'problem', it was said, 'can only be dealt with successfully if your Council and this Government worked in the closest co-operation'. To councillors, including the four elected (three from the Workers' Union), these were flattering remarks. This time the idea was for the City Council staff to carry out the construction work, but at the expense of the colonial government, with it later to be determined who would actually manage the resulting housing stock. A deal was struck and a tenement block on Flat Bastion Road, containing nineteen flats, was ready for occupation in October 1930 at a cost of about £9,750: colonial government capital had been combined with City Council building expertise. But there had been friction in reaching this result. The council's building costs exceeded estimates and the tenants eventually sought were not to be the poor but the better-paid (including City Council and government employees), who would be reliable tenants who could afford the rents set.[40]

---

38 GGA, Despatches from Gibraltar 1920–21 and TNA, CO91/475, Smith-Dorrien to Milner, 20 Dec 1920; GGA, Box: Housing, file 4210, 1920–30, folders 1920 and 1922.
39 GGA, Box: Housing, file 4210, 1920–30, folder 1923–25; Executive Council minutes, 16 Oct 1924, 5 Feb and 18 June 1925.
40 GGA, Box: Housing, 432/1928, and, separately, MP432/1928, Laying of Foundation Stone; Executive Council minutes, 19 June 1928, 20 Nov 1929, 16 April 1930.

For a few years thereafter the colonial government stuck more modestly to renovating property it owned on crown land. Nothing more was attempted in cooperation with the City Council except a small tenement building of ten flats on Lopez Ramp in 1936, costing a modest £5,350.[41] However, in August 1936 Sir Charles Harington, another governor with a 'mission', decided to appoint a commission of inquiry into a wide range of housing issues. Quite likely he had been persuaded by his attorney-general, who had pointed out that the cost of slum clearance and rehousing in Britain was by then being shared by central government and local authorities, and he suggested that it might be possible to frame policy in Gibraltar on similar lines. Cooperation was back in the frame. The commission's chairman was the attorney-general and the colonial government's treasurer was on the committee, but the other three appointed were civilians: J. Andrews-Speed, who was on the Executive Council, P.G. Russo, who was chairman of the City Council and A.E. Huart, leader of the Workers' Union and a man with considerable experience as an elected member of the City Council (1921–7, 1930–33 and from 1936).[42]

Such a composition, plus evidence collected, may explain why the commission unanimously recommended that, largely for reasons of efficiency and following municipal practice and law in Britain, the City Council should be made Gibraltar's housing authority. However, since slum clearance and the rehousing of working-class families were expensive, the colonial government had a role, to lend the City Council the necessary capital (an expected £100,000 over five years) at low interest (3 per cent) and also to share equally with the City Council the cost of interest payments until flats were occupied and a rental income was being received. Moreover, since the affordable rents to be charged would still not meet interest on capital borrowed, the deficit should also be shouldered equally from colonial government revenue and City Council rates.[43] Remarkably, this package of proposals was accepted pretty much without query by the colonial government and the Colonial Office, as well as by the City Council, who also secured an agreement that, as the housing authority responsible for construction, it would also in effect always own the properties, receive all the rents and be responsible, as it wanted, for the management.[44]

41 GGA, City Council, *Annual Report on the Health of Gibraltar for the Year 1936* (Gibraltar: Gibraltar Garrison Library, 1937), p. 29.

42 For origins and appointments see GGA, Executive Council minutes, 22 June and 1 Aug 1936; GGA, Box: Housing, 264/1936; TNA, CO91/499/18, Gibraltar Housing Conditions, especially Harington to Ormsby-Gore, 4 Sept 1936.

43 GGA, Box: Housing Commission Report 1937 and Housing Commission Evidence, 'Report of a Commission of Inquiry on Housing and Rent Restriction, etc.', 1937.

44 GGA, Box: Housing, 264/1936, and folders in 4210/1933–37; Executive Council minutes, 15 April, 10 June, 15 Sept 1937; TNA, CO91/501/18, Harington to

An enormous amount of work followed for the City Council,[45] including a survey of all properties to assess the extent of overcrowding, the selection of sites (complicated by military interference), the drawing up of designs and the construction of the first tenement block, on Cumberland Road, at a cost of £10,614. An inscription, now badly eroded, once read: 'In inauguration of the Gibraltar Housing Scheme approved during His Governorship. This Foundation Stone was laid by His Excellency General Sir Charles H. Harington, G.C.B, G.B.E, D.S.O, D.C.L, Governor of Gibraltar. September 1938.'[46] Impressive statements were made on the occasion. Unfortunately, although other projects were planned, this was the only construction work completed, in September 1939, before war called a halt.

More remarkably, at that time the housing ordinance which was needed to give legal sustenance to this programme, and much else which the commission had recommended, had not been passed, nor indeed were they subsequently. A draft ordinance prepared by the colonial government and sent to the City Council in December 1937 was judged by it in need of 'complete revision' to make it 'in every way satisfactory from a City Council point of view'. Especially it needed reworking, significantly, in the light of British legislation, the Housing Act of 1936. It took until March 1939 before the two parties agreed on a draft, but further delay followed when the financial clauses, which appeared to give the City Council the power to commit the colonial government to indeterminate expenditure, were picked over in London by the Colonial Office and the Ministry of Health. The draft ordinance was again sent back for revision to the colonial government, in which dark place the poor thing fluttered around until March 1940, when it died in the war.[47]

Nevertheless, what had transpired with respect to housing left an important political legacy. Colonial Office staff may have been pleased that the colonial government 'were getting the City Council to tackle the housing problem'[48]

Footnote 44 (*cont.*)
   Ormsby-Gore, 11 March and 11 June 1937, minutes, Ormsby-Gore to Harington, 31 Aug 1937.
45   See, for example, folders in GGA, Box: Housing, 4210/1933–37, and follow-up files on commission's recommendations in year files, MP256–271/1937. MP258/1937 contains the substantial 'Report on the Overcrowding Survey in Gibraltar 1938'; and MP101/1937 and MP167/1938 contain material on what was intended to be a temporary Rent Restriction Ordinance.
46   The design, construction, cost and opening late in 1939 can be traced in GGA, MP611/1937, MP144/1940, and Box: Housing, File 4210/1938–9.
47   There is substantial material in the City Council file in GGA, Box: Housing, 4210/1937 'Legislation' and in the colonial government file MP132/1937, 'The Housing Ordinance', and in the Colonial Office files, TNA, CO91/505/13 and CO91/508/8, 'Housing Conditions'.
48   CO91/501/18, minute by A.J. Dawe, 25 Aug 1937.

but on the other hand the City Council had enhanced its pre-eminence in the civil lives of the community largely at the expense, financial and otherwise, of the colonial government. As the recognised housing authority, the council, and the civilian public, were certain to assume that after the war its leading role would be resumed.

This elaboration of its responsibilities and standing may be set alongside its other extended roles. Just before the First World War, and more so afterwards, the City Council had been receiving government subsidies, rising to £3,500 a year, to provide aid for tuberculosis victims, the 'indigent sick' and the temporarily unemployed, though a rate-funded poor law was not introduced.[49] The City Council also supported a fire brigade, albeit manned by soldiers, and in the late 1930s it constructed a new (and rather attractive) fire station.[50] It was also responsible for improvements in the water supply: additional reservoirs to capture more from the water catchments on the eastern face of the Rock were constructed in the 1930s.[51] The City Council also, among much else, modernised its generation of electricity, extended street lighting, improved public highways (assisted with colonial government grants), addressed sanitation problems, handled refuse collection, inspected the slaughterhouse, dealt with rats, built a new sea-bathing pavilion, operated the telephone service (from 1926) and secured powers to control public displays of advertising.[52] It did not manage schools or hospitals or the police. Nevertheless, the City Council, like the Sanitary Commission before it, had developed from being an agent of the colonial government into an ally, and potentially a rival – certainly in the eyes of the public, who could see increasingly around them its impact upon their physical environment, and who benefited from the many public services provided. Unsurprisingly, then, the City Council was to be an important player in post-war politics.

49 For a sample of the arguments see despatches by Smith-Dorrien of 1919–22 in CO91/470, /471, /475 and /480, and by Monro in 1925 in CO91/484, and a 1928 review of government and City Council health services in CO91/487/21. See also GGA, MP630/1923, 'Tuberculosis Dispensary and Accommodation for Destitute Sick', MP76/1924, 'Poor Law Administration in England', and MP301/1932, 'Gibraltar Home for the Sick and Aged'. See also Executive Council minutes, esp. 1 March, 29 Nov 1923, 29 Dec 1924, 3 and 6 Nov 1925, 5 July 1926, and 15 Jan 1936.

50 GGA, Executive Council 1921–34, Harington to Cunliffe-Lister, 6 Nov 1934; T.J. Finlayson, *Stories from the Rock* (Gibraltar: Aquila, 1996), p. 86.

51 GGA, MP347/1929, City Council correspondence and Godley to Passfield, 17 Jan 1931; Box: Water Supply, A. Beeby Thompson & Partners to City Council, 'Report on Water Supply of Gibraltar', Sept 1933.

52 See, especially, ordinances and City Council annual public health reports, and *Annual Report for 1938*, p. 9.

The politics of taxation, 1914–39

In the previous chapter it was noted that Gibraltar's economy went through troughs as well as upturns. Government revenue was affected accordingly because much of it was derived from customs and port dues, and from licences, fees, post office receipts and other taxes dependent on the volume of business activity. There was, of course, no notion of deficit financing to offset the slumps. However, on one reading, Gibraltar government finances in this period were always secure.[53] There was no public debt in 1914, and none in 1940. The balance of assets over liabilities was substantial, over £205,000 in 1914, equivalent to more than double the year's revenue of nearly £90,000. In 1938 the balance was over £434,000 (including a special reserve fund of £200,000), still more than double that year's revenue of nearly £208,000. Such data, in the published accounts, naturally attracted the eye of those Gibraltar citizens who thought that Gibraltar was already sufficiently, perhaps even excessively, taxed.

However, neither the colonial government nor the Colonial Office saw it that way. Annual revenue paid staff salaries and other administration costs, but that and accumulated reserves also funded such public works as the colonial government judged essential or useful for the development of the colony, such as improvements in the docks and better housing. In 1929 the Exchange Committee ventured to complain that expenditure on certain public works schemes would diminish invested reserves and thereby the income derived from the interest on them, opening the possibility of higher taxation later. In response, the secretary of state was easily persuaded by the governor and his colonial secretary to reply, forcefully, first, that Gibraltar was one of the lightest-taxed places in the colonial empire and indeed in Europe and, second, that such expenditure was essential to provide in Gibraltar 'some measure of those benefits which are conferred on their peoples by the Governments of progressive countries'.[54] While in 1929 this rather overstated the 'progressive' measures yet being 'conferred', the argument was sound enough and would continue to apply.

However, it was also an assumption of government, and certainly of the Colonial Office and the imperial treasury, that budget estimates of recurrent income and expenditure should always aim to secure a balance. In reality, in thirteen of the twenty-five years between 1914 and 1938, annual expenditure in Gibraltar exceeded annual revenue, with a concomitant drop in those years in the balance of assets over liabilities. Sometimes this was an expected result, as when substantial expenditure on a public works scheme fell in a particular year, as in 1915. But sometimes it was the result of an alarming drop in income, as

53 The data which follow are derived from Gibraltar's *Annual Reports*, 1914–38.
54 TNA, CO91/489/6, and GGA, MP341/1929, esp. Passfield to Godley, 1 Oct 1929.

with the outbreak of war in 1914, or, worse still, with the international depression in 1929 and 1930, or when inflation pushed up costs, as in 1920. In these circumstances, the government would have either to spend out of reserves or to cut other forms of public expenditure – or to search out alternative sources of revenue.[55]

In Britain estate duties had been collected under various schemes since 1796, and since 1894 in the now familiar form of death duties on the assets, above a certain threshold, of the deceased. These were, of course, direct taxes on individuals or, in effect, an inheritance tax on their descendants. In 1910 the colonial government in Gibraltar had considered introducing death duties but had backed off, partly because there was then no pressing need for extra revenue and also because of protests from the Exchange Committee, whose moneyed-class members would have been most affected. A draft ordinance, also not proceeded with, had been drawn up in 1918. In 1921, however, the government was attracted again to such a direct tax in order to allow for a reduction in port dues and other indirect taxes which, it was argued by some in business, were acting as a restraint on trade. The estate duty ordinance then drafted secured Colonial Office consent and, in the usual form, it was published as a consultation document in June 1922. This was another of Smith-Dorrien's initiatives. Meanwhile, the abolition of the coal tax in July 1922 and the reduction in duties on imported tobacco, as desired by the business community, were causing a major fall in government revenue.[56] But the intended replacement, an Estates Duties Ordinance, with very low rates of tax, was not passed until April 1934.

The arguments for and against this tax are instructive of the politics of the period. The Workers' Union, predictably, responded with the view that such taxes 'would prove beneficial to the funds of the Colony',[57] and it is likely that it had in mind pay rises for its members employed by government and public works of social benefit. The City Council, with its five official members and four elected members, of whom two represented the Workers' Union and a third was at least sympathetic, endorsed the proposal by a majority. A death duty of 5 per cent was suggested, 'to raise funds for the improvement of the housing conditions of the poorer classes and the general financial condition of the colony'.[58] On the other hand, those representing especially the moneyed class protested. The

55 The need for economies in public expenditure largely accounts for an effort in 1930 to replace English nurses with cheaper, locally trained nurses in the Colonial Hospital: GGA, MP265/1928, minutes of 25 April–28 Nov 1929; TNA, CO91/490/6, acting governor to Colonial Office, 6 Aug 1930.

56 *Annual Report for 1923*, p. 4.

57 GGA, MP692/1921, 'Death Duties', Workers' Union to governor, 3 May 1924.

58 Ibid, City Council to colonial secretary, 9 July 1925. The highest rate of duty considered prior to legislation in 1934 was 2½ per cent, and only on estates valued at over £20,000: GGA, Executive Council minutes, 5 Aug 1932.

Chamber of Commerce complained that such a duty 'will tax one particular class of the community' (which was true) and 'is an unpopular measure in Gibraltar' (which is less certain).[59] It, like the unofficial members of the Executive Council, argued for cuts in public expenditure, including in the salaries of government personnel or in their number, including getting rid of the whole of the Public Works Department.[60] Instead, it proposed less personally targeted taxes, including such indirect taxes as an entertainment tax or 'tax on clubs' and a registration tax upon all businesses operating in Gibraltar. This last alone found favour, but was subsequently blocked on legal grounds by the Colonial Office. That left just duties on spirits and petrol to raise extra cash.[61]

Trade improvement seems to have postponed further consideration of death duties until the financial downturn of 1931. Even then, unofficial members argued in the Executive Council that such a tax, though 'logically equitable', might lead to a flight of capital from Gibraltar and 'would be detrimental to the interests of the colony' in other unspecified ways.[62] Alternatives were again canvassed, including a modest property tax, a trades tax and a poll tax on residents and employees.[63] Debates in council then trundled on until, in September 1933, the unofficial members accepted the merits of death duties in principle and agreed that the rates of tax proposed were appropriately low.[64] But they then argued that, because of the upturn in the economy and the consequent rise in government revenue, the introduction of new taxation was not necessary and would 'give rise to a certain amount of discontent'. When the governor insisted and the draft ordinance was again approved by the secretary of state in December 1933 and again published, those expressions of discontent duly arrived, from the Chamber of Commerce and the Exchange Committee: it was 'unjustified in a small colony' in a 'flourishing financial state'.[65]

59 Ibid, Chamber of Commerce to Colonial Secretary, 22 April 1924.
60 GGA, Executive Council minutes, 15 May 1924, 30 March 1925 and 23 Nov 1926; MP157/1924, 'Taxation: Committee to Explore Further Sources of Revenue', minutes, report, and esp. memo 'Estate Duties' by two representatives of the Chamber of Commerce.
61 GGA, MP157/1924, 'Taxation', esp. Monro to Thomas, 23 May 1924; Executive Council minutes, 17 May, 16 Oct and 20 Nov 1924, and 18 Sept 1931.
62 GGA, MP692/1921, 'Death Duties', minute of 1 Oct 1931, Executive Council minute, 18 Sept 1931.
63 GGA, MP358/1931, 'Property Tax'; MP207/1932, 'Poll Tax'; Executive Council minutes, 18 Sept 1931, 5 Aug 1932.
64 GGA, Executive Council minutes, 15 June and 5 Aug 1932, 30 March and 19 Sept 1933.
65 GGA, MP692/1921, 'Death Duties', Chamber of Commerce to Colonial Secretary, 14 Feb 1934, and also 17 March, and see letters from Exchange Committee, 9 Feb and 22 March 1934, plus responses by colonial secretary.

If power lies in the ability to obstruct and to divert, then the moneyed class had been powerful, certainly with respect to estate duties, which were first levied only from May 1934. It had been calculated in 1931 that, on average, such a tax in the form first proposed in 1922 would have been bringing in £1,000 a year, and there might have been windfalls when the super-rich died. As the governor pointed out to the Colonial Office in November 1933, a gentleman who had made a great deal of money in local trade had left a personal estate reckoned to be about £100,000, but under the then law the only payment to the state had been a fee for letters of administration: £12 10s 0d.[66] Issues of political morality as well as of political economy enter into judgements on appropriate taxation, and it is clear from this story that such matters had penetrated political discourse, and yet the resistance to change in some sections of civil society in Gibraltar had been pretty effective.

This is even more apparent with respect to income tax. Like death duties, this was a direct tax which to be effective must fall disproportionately on the 'withs' and less on the 'withouts' (whereas indirect taxes tended to be regressive in their impact). Moreover, like death duties, the levying of income tax required individual citizens to reveal personal data to the state. It therefore raised issues concerning trust, honesty, privacy, intrusion and sanctions – and it has to be admitted that in a civilian economic culture which had been much engaged in smuggling activities it was unlikely that all with significant incomes would be willing to reveal everything to the state. There were also practical matters with which to contend, as with death duties, such as collecting data, assessing tax due and securing payment, which implied a bureaucracy whose cost had to be factored in to any assessment of the net value of raising income tax from, especially, a small number of earners.[67]

Income tax had first been levied in Britain in 1799, continuously since 1842, but rarely in the colonial empire before the First World War. However, thereafter more colonial governments were experimenting with it, and in December 1922 the Colonial Office despatched to all colonies a model ordinance for them to adopt if they judged it appropriate to their local circumstances.[68] This was a proposal which was ignored by the Gibraltar government in the 1920s because of the administrative machinery its introduction was expected to entail, and it was also opposed by the Chamber of Commerce, for other more personal and sensitive reasons.[69] The idea was raised, tentatively, by the colonial treasurer in

66 Ibid, Harington to Cunliffe-Lister, 2 Nov 1933.
67 The point was firmly made with respect to estate duties by the Chamber of Commerce representatives: MP157/1924, 'Taxation'.
68 GGA, MP99/1923, 'Income Tax'
69 GGA, MP157/1924, 'Taxation', Report, 1 May 1924, Monro to Thomas, 23 May 1924.

June 1931 during the financial crisis,[70] but then ignored while other hares were run. Not until late in 1938, when discussing draft estimates for 1939, did the sufficiency of existing taxes again trouble the colonial treasurer, and through him the governor and his Executive Council.[71] Expenditure on air raid protection as well as on housing was recognised as imperative. As a result, Governor Harington appointed a committee, made up of the treasurer and the three unofficial members of his council (Gaggero, King, Carrara), to review expenditure and sources of revenue. The report, endorsed by the full council and by the governor, again raised the issue of economies in government expenditure, including the possible shuffling of some liabilities onto City Council ratepayers. It also proceeded to reject (again) the case for an entertainment tax and, because of its likely impact on the bunkering trade, for reviving the coal tax. Instead it opted for further increases in such indirect taxes as customs duties on alcoholic liquors, port dues (much paid for by outsiders), trade and business licences (later abandoned following protests) and fees for residential permits. Otherwise, only an increase in death duties was recommended, and quickly introduced in October 1939, doubling the rates.[72]

What was not mentioned was income tax. It was the secretary of state, responding to the imperatives of war, who in a general message in September 1939 insisted that those colonial governments not yet levying an income tax should immediately do so. This was a grand assertion of imperial authority, one of many which were going to have major political consequences post-war. Indeed, political as well as financial arguments explained his order. Basic income tax in Britain had just been raised to 7s 6d in the pound (nearly 27 per cent), higher still on the wealthy; and elsewhere too, he insisted, increased taxation must be seen to fall on those who could most afford to pay.[73] This message from the top was presented to the Executive Council, where, predictably, the unofficial members still doubted whether the yield would be great enough to justify the cost of collection and, mysteriously, 'the overcoming of other difficulties': evasion? Bombs were not exactly whistling round people's heads in Gibraltar when the council met on 13 November 1939, but there was a war on and the governor, the colonial secretary and the colonial treasurer were no longer having any of this obscurantism. The cost of collection would not be great, it was said, and income tax, insisted the treasurer, 'was the most satisfactory way of raising

---

70 GGA, MP692/1921, 'Estate Duties', minute, 2 June 1931.
71 GGA, Executive Council minutes, 14 Nov 1938.
72 TNA, CO91/511/7, 'Taxation', esp. minutes and Liddell to MacDonald, 14 Aug 1939; GGA, Deputy Governor's Files [henceforth DG], S432/1938, 'Committee to Consider Question of Augmenting Revenue'; Executive Council minutes, 27 July and 13 Dec 1939; Estate Duties (Amendment) Ordinance No 15 of 1939.
73 GGA, MP427/1939, 'Income Tax', Secretary of State to Governor, 29 Sept 1939.

the additional revenue required as it ensured that the burden fell on the persons who are in the best position to bear it'. Following that trenchant lead, the council as a whole fell in behind. Legislation was to be drawn up, returns collected and calculations made whether the net revenue expected would justify the levy. Moreover, a tax adviser should be recruited from Britain to give guidance.[74] Within a week, the treasurer had already made some rough calculations, using, remarkably, the Nyasaland Income Tax Ordinance as a model. Excusing all mere wage earners, he reckoned that at still low rates of personal income tax (only 1s in the pound, 5 per cent) and a rather higher tax on company profits (2s 6d, 12.5 per cent) about £15,000 could be raised and the cost of collection would be only £2,000. But then deliberations and decisions were interrupted by more immediate matters: Italy's declaration of war, 'the uncertain attitude of Spain' and the evacuation of civilians.[75]

Conclusion

Gibraltar entered and left the war with still modest forms of direct taxation, but it had become apparent over the preceding decades that the assumed responsibilities of government had increased, were increasing and were unlikely to diminish. The colonial government had extended its legislative grip over civil society. Noticeably too, the ordinances passed were invariably modelled on English or sometimes colonial law, and to that extent British institutions and values were further permeating this society. Still more obvious as an institutional import, though only half fledged, was the City Council. Its role resembled that of an English town council, not least with its recent housing experiments. Here was an additional infusion of Britishness into Gibraltar culture and identity.

There had also been political advances, making some civilians more intimately involved in the practice of government and administration. Appointing a selected few to the Executive Council was for some an agreeable step, but for others this was more the totter of a toddling infant than a giant step for mankind. Elections even for a minority of City Councillors were perhaps a more important alteration, and one about which the colonial authorities responsible also for a fortress retained some doubts. Those doubts, for different reasons, were also shared by sections of the civilian population, manifestly divided in their attitudes towards the advance of democratic representation and, especially, control. The moneyed class were especially cautious of popular involvement in policy making and administration, especially since the colonial government and the City Council had revenue-raising powers. They were not mistaken to be

74 GGA, Executive Council minutes, 13 Nov 1939.
75 GGA, MP427/1939, 'Income Tax', Treasurer to Colonial Secretary, 20 Nov 1939, and subsequent minutes.

concerned about the competitiveness of the exposed Gibraltar economy and the possible effects upon trade of forms and rates of taxation, though they were also, like most taxpayers, bothered by the impact upon their own personal incomes. But there were other social classes, less vulnerable to direct taxation, who were also interested, through their representatives, in the roles of government and who might be more keen to have their voices heard in favour of increasing public expenditure and accepting consequent alterations in the tax regime. Protests about taxation, we have seen, also raised issues about taxation without (sufficient) political representation, and hence tax and political systems were intimately linked. The politics of taxation, like the politics of constitution making and of public administration, were therefore likely again to become aspects of Gibraltar life when the war ended – even without the additional spin given to the agenda by the global 'war for democracy' and by the particular wartime experiences of Gibraltar people.

10

Big government and self-government, 1940–69

Because it has become a truism it is not necessarily untrue. The evacuation from May 1940 of much of the civilian population from Gibraltar, and especially some of their uncomfortable experiences in Britain and Northern Ireland, did embitter the exiles and those still resident in Gibraltar and did provoke demands for political change.[1] The apparently tardy steps being taken by the British authorities to organise repatriation seemed to expose the limited political influence that Gibraltar civilians had over their own lives, even over such a fundamental matter as when they would be allowed to return to their homes and place of birth. British government attempts to explain the logistical difficulties in organising shipping and accommodation in Gibraltar in peacetime left unimpressed a body of people who had been shipped out in wartime and had left accommodation behind them. While the first boatload of evacuees eventually secured passages home in April 1944, many were still waiting in July 1949.[2] In addition, of course and as suggested earlier, the rhetoric of the People's War as a fight for freedom and democracy against the dark powers of totalitarian authority could not leave unmoved the citizens of Gibraltar, any more than the subjects in other British colonies or, of course, in Britain who in July 1945 elected for the first time a majority Labour government. However, even without the war and the evacuation, it was unlikely, given the agitation in Gibraltar before 1940, that the Executive Council and the City Council as currently constituted would have been regarded by political activists and camp followers as sufficient. The war and post-war years accelerated the forces for change, but pushed them in a predictable direction.

The advocates of constitutional and administrative reform during the Second World War paralleled those who had been most demanding just after the

---

1 The case is strongly put by T.J. Finlayson, *The Fortress Came First* (Grendon: Gibraltar Books, 1991) and endorsed by J.J. Garcia, *Gibraltar, the Making of a People* (Gibraltar: Panorama, 2002). See also for a personal view, M. Rodriguez, *I Remember* (Gibraltar: Gibraltar Books, 2001), pp. 84–9.
2 And a tiny number until 1951: Finlayson, *Fortress*, pp. 234–6.

First. Instead of the running being made by the Workers' Union, there was the Association for the Advancement of Civil Rights (AACR). This body, launched in December 1942, was motivated initially by the plight of the exiles but more generally by the legacy of what had been achieved politically before the war and what, to them self-evidently, needed yet to be secured. The AACR became, in effect, Gibraltar's first organised political party, dominating Gibraltar's electoral politics until the 1980s. Some continuity with the earlier agitation of the Workers' Union is apparent, since all the leaders of the protest movement which lay behind its creation were experienced trade unionists, in technical, clerical and supervisory roles, particularly in the dockyards or, in the case of Albert Risso, the first president, as a foreman mechanic and City Council employee. Leadership, however, passed in 1947 to a smart young lawyer, Joshua Hassan (1915–97), who had in fact given the organisation the name which so aptly summarised its aspirations. He was to become the towering figure of Gibraltar politics for nearly half a century.[3] Like the Workers' Union, the AACR, at least in its early years, appealed to working-class families and had a social reform as well as political reform agenda. However, the AACR from the beginning also offered itself as a party for all social classes, to the extent of not allowing for the formal affiliation to it of the Workers' Union – though such a manoeuvre did not ease the suspicions of the Chamber of Commerce and many moneyed-class people, not least when in 1946 it created the Gibraltar Confederation of Labour (GCL) as a trade union to represent its rank-and-file working-class supporters.[4]

Just as the Workers' Union found in Smith-Dorrien a governor sympathetic to the aspirations of civilian society, so the AACR found in Lieutenant-General Sir Noel Mason-Macfarlane (May 1942–February 1944) an outspoken advocate of constitutional and administrative change. He was quite prepared to push the Colonial Office for changes which, in general if not in detail, matched AACR demands. In April 1943 he addressed a despatch to the secretary of state in which he gave his favourable impression of the AACR leaders, regretted like them the separation of families caused by the prolonged exile of much of the civilian population and, in no uncertain terms, criticised the way in which Gibraltar had in the past been governed. The constitution and methods of administration 'fell lamentably short in many respects of the standards to which we ought to aim. Nothing has really been done to bring the Government of the Colony into line with modern democratic standards.'[5] The proposals he then and in subsequent

3 W. Jackson and F. Cantos, *From Fortress to Democracy: the Political Biography of Sir Joshua Hassan* (Grendon: Gibraltar Books, 1995).

4 TNA, CO91/524/9, report on AACR meeting 4 April 1946; *Gibraltar Chronicle*, 20 Nov 1946, p. 3; *Annual Report for 1947*, p. 11.

5 TNA, CO91/518/1, Mason-Macfarlane to Stanley, 11 April 1943; Jackson and Cantos, *Fortress to Democracy*, pp. 28–30.

messages put to the Colonial Office were wide ranging. Some elements will be considered later, but attention will first be given to his proposed reforms of the constitution of the City Council.

The City Council

As noted earlier, even though pre-war only a minority of councillors were elected, the council had secured an impressive role in the everyday lives of Gibraltar civilians, and turnouts for elections had suggested that people cared. However, during the war military imperatives took over and civil liberties were much constrained in Gibraltar, as of course in Britain and pretty much everywhere else among the combatant powers. As one extreme indication in Gibraltar – and unlike in Portsmouth or Aldershot or other naval bases and garrison towns in Britain – the City Council was suspended from 1 January 1941 and its powers and responsibilities were transferred to the colonial government, accountable only to the Colonial Office.[6] This action was advertised as a response to the emergency, and it was politically inconceivable that restoration would not follow with the approach of peace.

Mason-Macfarlane wanted to go further. With the backing of his Executive Council and after consultation with the Colonial Office, he proposed to increase the number of city councillors from nine to twelve and, more radically, to allow half of these to be elected by popular vote and to allow women to stand as candidates. He also proposed to alter the franchise so as to replace the owner or tenant property qualification with a franchise which would grant votes to all British subjects who had been resident for at least twelve months and were, if male, aged 21 or over or, if female, aged 30 or over.[7] This gender inequality had accompanied the granting of votes for women in Britain in 1918 but had been removed in 1928. It is interesting to note, in the light of what happened, that Colonial Office staff remained uncomfortable with an electoral system which discriminated against women: 'Would it not be difficult to justify this now-a-days?'[8]

It is then evident that the Colonial Office was certainly not opposed to change in the composition of the City Council and to an extension of the franchise, and Mason-Macfarlane was authorised to prepare legislation.[9] With his departure

---

6 GGA, MP 588/1940 and MP523/1940; City Council (Suspension and Transfer of Powers) Ordinance, No 18 of 1940.
7 TNA, CO91/518/1, Notes on Proposals for Constitutional Reform, minutes of Executive Council, with Mason-Macfarlane to Stanley, 11 April 1943, Note of Conference at Colonial Office, 21 April 1943, Draft Proposals for Constitutional Reform, with Mason-Macfarlane to Stanley, 12 Oct 1943.
8 Ibid, minute of 12 Nov 1943.
9 Ibid, Stanley to Mason-Macfarlane, 29 Dec 1943.

for other duties, the business was inherited by his successor, Lieutenant-General Sir Ralph Eastwood, whose reputation for being unsympathetic to civilian aspirations is, to an extent, belied by his adoption without apparent demur of the proposals for constitutional change which 'Mason-Mac' had left behind. At all events, a range of proposals for constitutional change as agreed by the governor, the Executive Council and the Colonial Office was published in December 1944. However, by January 1945 the colonial government found itself in the middle of a storm of protests about a whole package of proposed constitutional reforms. In response, at the end of January the colonial government published a draft ordinance which was intended specifically to restore the City Council, but with an extended franchise and with six official and nominated members (up from five) and six elected members (up from four).[10] However, even this was judged insufficient by the AACR, and by the Chamber of Commerce, Exchange Committee and Workers' Union.[11] Faced by more lobbying, the governor and then the Colonial Office gave further ground.[12] The ordinance which was eventually passed in April 1945 conceded seven elected councillors, making them the majority (with one of them to be chairman).[13] The franchise was indeed extended, so that being an adult British subject with at least twelve months' residency was sufficient – plus being male, since women were entirely excluded. As noted, Mason-Macfarlane and the Colonial Office favoured votes for women but had eventually decided to leave it for Gibraltar opinion to decide.[14] Some local opposition to the idea was expressed;[15] and at all events the discrimination explicit in the draft ordinance does not seem to have been immediately deplored. This matter was eventually taken up by the restored and enlarged City Council itself in March 1947, and an amending ordinance, enfranchising women on the same terms as for men and making them eligible to stand as candidates, was then passed in August.[16]

In the meantime, the first City Council elections had been held, on 24 July 1945. The electoral register did not include among its 5,332 names many

10 *Gibraltar Chronicle*, 1 Feb 1945, p. 3.
11 *Gibraltar Chronicle*, 3 March 1945, p. 2.
12 TNA, CO91/523/3, Eastwood to Stanley, 26 March 1945, Stanley to Eastwood, 14 April 1945.
13 TNA, CO91/521/7; City Council (Constitution and Powers) Amendment Ordinance, No 3 of April 1945; *Gibraltar Chronicle*, 1 Feb 1945, p. 3, 26 Feb 1945, p. 3, 3 March 1945, p. 2; Jackson and Cantos, *Fortress to Democracy*, pp. 40–2, 44–6; Garcia, *Making of a People*, pp. 24–34.
14 TNA, CO91/518/1, Stanley to Mason-Macfarlane, 23 Dec 1943.
15 TNA, CO91/523/3, memo by Stanley, colonial secretary, 15 Jan 1945, referring to views of L.J. Imossi, President of the Chamber of Commerce.
16 *Gibraltar Chronicle*, 23 May 1947, p. 5; City Council (Constitution and Powers) Amendment Ordinance, No 18 of 1947.

Gibraltarians who would have been eligible but who were still exiled overseas, but a healthy democratic appetite was shown by the 3,775 voters who turned out, nearly 71 per cent, and voted for the eleven candidates standing for the seven seats. Most candidates emphasised their commitment to assist the return of the remaining evacuees, tackle the housing shortage, improve wages and press for better welfare services, even though some of these matters were beyond the current remit of the City Council: this first post-war election allowed other political issues to be publicly raised. Gibraltar, it will be recalled, was defined as a single constituency, and each elector had only four votes but, thanks to good organisation and contrary to official expectations, the AACR worsted the four independent candidates (including one trade unionist) and took all seven places. Those elected shared some of the occupational characteristics of radicals in other places, mainly white-collar workers (three clerks) and skilled men (tailor, telegraph cable operator), plus a member of the Gibraltar Defence Force and Joshua Hassan, barrister, who was elected council chairman.[17]

So overwhelming was its success, that in the council elections in December 1947 the seven AACR candidates, including a woman, Dorothy Ellicott, were not even opposed.[18] Moreover, by December 1950 and the next elections, political attention was focused on another constitutional innovation, a legislative council, and turnout fell to 35 per cent, though the AACR got its four candidates returned. There was a better showing at the elections in December 1953, 50 per cent, and the AACR managed to get its five candidates elected. But the subdued electoral interest was pretty much repeated, with only a 40 per cent turnout in December 1956, even though the AACR, which returned its five candidates, faced for the first time another organised (though transient) political party, the Commonwealth Party, instead of just 'independents'. In December 1959 none of the seven elected seats was contested, the AACR carrying off five, and in December 1962 only eight candidates stood, the AACR securing five places and the turnout falling below 30 per cent. The AACR was to get its four candidates home easily in December 1965, but this was the last election before the City Council itself ceased to exist. Its functions were absorbed into a central government which, by a new constitution from August 1969, operated, as we shall see, on very different lines from that of 1921 when the City Council was first established and, indeed, from that of 1945.[19]

This does not at all mean that the City Council was or became insignificant.

17 *Gibraltar Chronicle*, 21 July, p. 3, 23 July, p. 2, and 25 July 1945, p. 1; TNA, CO91/523/3, Stanley to Luke, 1 Aug 1945.

18 *Gibraltar Chronicle*, 25 Nov 1947, p. 1, 28 Nov 1947, p. 3.

19 Election results are conveniently summarised in Garcia, *Making of a People*, pp. 53–4, 69–70, 77, 103–4, 119, 126, 142–3, 155. For the transfer see *Annual Report for 1969*, p. 3.

For one thing, it provided a base and a profile for the AACR, always the largest group among the elected members, and especially for Hassan, who was routinely re-elected council leader (apart from 1950–53). Hassan and AACR councillors repeatedly used their authority to campaign on matters beyond the conventional business of a city council, and likewise, as will be shown, they resisted suggestions to see this municipal tier of government removed, until the politics were right in 1969.

Of importance to the civilian population, the City Council also continued to provide many of the services needed for decent living in a tightly packed urban environment, until they were transferred in 1969 mainly to the municipal department of the new central government. These included public health measures, road maintenance, vehicle licensing, a bus service, the civilian fire service,[20] the telephone service and the vital public utilities: water, electricity and indeed gas, which was taken over from a private company in January 1945 (and closed down in April 1968).[21] These were, of course, responsibilities which characterised local governments in Britain (and elsewhere). And they cost money. Rates of 3s 10d in the pound (19 per cent) in 1947 were 5s 6d in 1950 and 7s (35 per cent) in 1959.[22] While City Council expenditure on the public utilities was usually at least matched by the income it earned, ratepayers were separately required to fork out nearly £170,000 in 1952 and well over £350,000 by 1963. Total council expenditure doubled from just over £450,000 in 1952 to just under £1,000,000 by 1963. Even allowing for inflation, this was a sizeable step up in spending, pretty regularly equal to about half the recurrent expenditure of the colonial government. The City Council was big business.[23]

Moreover, although its membership included three unelected representatives of the armed services, two unelected officials representing colonial government departments and one non-official appointed by the governor and therefore also not elected, the majority of the thirteen members were chosen by popular vote, and it was civilian-led. Accordingly, it resembled a city council in Britain. It was

---

20 A fire service manned by civilians in place of soldiers came into operation 1 Oct 1947: *Gibraltar Chronicle*, 28 Sept 1946, 3 Jan 1947, p. 2, 25 Nov 1947, p. 1; T.J. Finlayson, *Stories from the Rock* (Gibraltar: Aquila, 1996), pp. 86–7.

21 *Annual Reports*, for 1947, p. 40, for 1968, pp. 60–2, 79–80; *Gibraltar Chronicle*, 3 Jan 1945, p. 2, 3 Aug 1946, p. 2, 11 Sept 1953, p. 2; and see terms of Public Utilities Ordinance, No 5 of 1950 which covered gas and electricity supplies and telephone services. Some further indication of the range of City Council responsibilities and powers may be discerned in the drafting and terms of the revised Public Health Ordinance, No 7 of 1950: TNA, CO91/537/8.

22 *Gibraltar Chronicle*, 3 Jan 1947, p. 2, 6 Jan 1950, p. 3, 3 Jan 1959, p. 1.

23 Calculated from figures in *Annual Reports*, 1952–63. A memo on TNA, CO91/527/1 summarises the council's powers and obligations in 1948 and lists its committees and officers.

therefore not unreasonable for the City Council to complain in 1950 when its chairman was graded only eleventh in the official 'order of precedence' (a long way behind sundry officers of the armed forces).[24] A higher status was publicly signalled in May 1954 when, at a banquet to honour the visit of the Queen, on her right was seated the governor and on her left the chairman of the City Council, Joshua Hassan.[25] It was also an appropriate follow-up in 1955 for the council to request, unanimously, that the titles of chairman, deputy-chairman and secretary should be altered formally to mayor, deputy mayor and town clerk. There is much in a name, and this was spelt out by Hassan himself. He referred in support of the proposal to the important public services the council provided, to its efficient administration and to the civic responsibility shown by Gibraltar citizens. Accordingly, by changes in titles the council should be rewarded with 'the dignity inherent to a Borough in the United Kingdom'. However robust might be the demands of Gibraltar politicians for constitutional changes, their desire at the same time to embrace British (or at least English) titles for the office holders in a system of local government modelled on Britain's was indicative of an important component in Gibraltarian identities at this time. Those British-born British subjects who, in the 1720s and 1730s, had pressed in vain for a municipal corporation to be set up in Gibraltar would have been amazed, and pleased, by what Gibraltar-born British subjects had requested – and obtained, since neither the governor nor the Colonial Office raised any objections.[26]

However, much that local government had provided in Britain never became a responsibility of the Gibraltar City Council. It never operated a poor law funded by rates; it never became an educational authority; it never ran a police force; it never managed the hospital service. Even more remarkably, the draft housing ordinance, still fluttering around in the spring of 1940, which would have made the City Council the housing authority charged with the construction and management of public sector housing, had been allowed to die. When 'big government' arrived after the war, none of this was delegated to the City Council with its majority of elected members.

24　*Gibraltar Chronicle*, 18 May 1950, p. 2 and 19 May 1950, p. 2. The issue had still not been resolved to the satisfaction of councillors prior to the queen's coronation celebrations: *Gibraltar Chronicle*, 19 June 1953, p. 2.

25　S. Constantine, 'Monarchy and constructing identity in "British" Gibraltar, c.1800 to the present', *Journal of Imperial and Commonwealth History*, 34 (2006), 23–44, pp. 33–4.

26　TNA, CO926/474, Malley to Colonial Office, 25 Feb 1955, enclosing Hassan to Colonial Secretary, 15 Feb 1955, minutes and reply; Garcia, *Making of a People*, pp. 83–4. For two among many photographs of Hassan wearing his mayoral chain and robes see *Annual Report 1960*.

Colonial government and post-war housing

Far from the Second World War prompting the British government to begin the dismantling of the colonial empire, the post-war period has been said to have witnessed 'the second colonial occupation'.[27] While in some parts of the empire the politics required the withdrawal of formal control, elsewhere grand strategy and economic self-interest plus an increased sense of responsibilities for colonial welfare (if only to legitimise the imperial project) prompted adjustments in methods rather than a change of purpose. This was the period in which the Colonial Service, responsible for 'good government' overseas, got larger, not smaller,[28] when the colonial empire grew more, not less, valuable to Britain economically,[29] and when development aid substantially increased and did not diminish.[30] Even after large-scale decolonisation, governments of both parties endeavoured to sustain Britain's global political and military role.[31]

Particularly important for Gibraltar civilians, the perceived value of the Rock as a base for Mediterranean and Atlantic operations remained, and indeed had been enhanced by the establishment of an RAF command on the airfield which had been constructed during the war at North Front (on the former racecourse).[32] Moreover, since the services needed space for their activities, their demands for land unavoidably competed, even clashed, with civilian needs. Land in Gibraltar was a very scarce commodity. Remarkably, of Gibraltar's 1,400 acres, by 1945 the colonial government had direct management over only 149 acres and the City Council over just 61 acres, leaving the service departments in control of pretty much all the rest, and while a lot of this was inhospitable rock their holdings did include space that would be needed for civilian rehousing.[33] Although the governor was nominally commander-in-chief, representatives of the army, navy and air force in Gibraltar were only directly answerable to their

27 D.A. Low and A. Smith, *History of East Africa*, vol. III (Oxford: Clarendon Press, 1976), pp. 12–14.
28 A. Kirk-Greene, *On Crown Service: a History of HM Colonial and Overseas Civil Services 1837–1997* (London: Tauris, 1999).
29 B. Porter, *The Lion's Share: a Short History of British Imperialism 1850–2004* (London: Longman, 4th edn 2004), pp. 306–7.
30 HCPP, *Colonial Development and Welfare Acts 1929–70*, Cmnd 4677, 1971, especially figures on pp. 8–9; D.J. Morgan, *The Official History of Colonial Development* (London: Macmillan, 1980), esp. vols 2–4.
31 A. Jackson, 'Empire and beyond: the pursuit of overseas national interests in the late twentieth century', *English Historical Review*, 122 (2007), 1350–66.
32 W.G. Ramsey (ed.), 'Gibraltar: construction of the airfield', *After the Battle*, 21 (1978), 4–14.
33 TNA, CO91/520/2, memo with Stanley to Fisher, 25 Oct 1945.

superiors in London, and while the governor had a right of direct contact with, for instance, the War Office, he usually needed to work through the Colonial Office, resulting in characteristic interdepartmental wrangles. Efforts had been made, especially since the later nineteenth century, to secure formal agreements on the use of land (and even on landownership),[34] but these agreements were vulnerable to reinterpretation and obstructions remained, complicating considerably the problems of the colonial government in trying to provide the homes for which civilians were clamouring.

Those pre-war housing inquiries had confirmed for government what many citizens knew from experience, that Gibraltar suffered from overcrowding (a quantity problem) and insanitary slums (a quality problem). Neither 'overcrowding' nor 'slums' was an objective description, since each depended on flexible assessments of what should be minimum standards, especially when it came to housing the working class. In Britain expectations had massively changed and the design of new houses in the public as well as private sectors had been revolutionised. While estates of semi-detached houses with gardens, twelve to the acre, were self-evidently inappropriate models for Gibraltar, standards concerning room numbers and sizes and facilities could be applied. The colonial government and the Colonial Office were affected by such considerations in planning post-war housing schemes. However, this does not in itself explain why the City Council was not made the agency for construction in the same way in which local councils in Britain were constructing council estates, albeit under the gaze and with the financial support of central government.

Partly this was due to the urgency for construction and the scale of the problem. The urgency came from the fact that many thousands of evacuees were anxious to get home even before the end of the war and before the City Council itself had been resurrected. Political pressure for their immediate return was being exerted by the AACR and other bodies, in the UK as well as in Gibraltar. The scale of the problem, as interpreted by officials in October 1943, was that Gibraltar might eventually need to house a population of 24,000 civilians, including those who used to live in La Línea; but some pre-war housing had been taken over by the armed services or had fallen into decay or had been destroyed during the war, military claims on land were expected to increase and 'a return to the congested and overcrowded conditions in which a high proportion of the 17,000 inhabitants prior to the war were housed is highly undesirable and therefore unacceptable'.[35] In a particularly powerful review in February 1944 the colonial secretary described in

34 See especially the origins of agreements in 1893 in WO33/55 and /56, in 1903 in WO33/1601, in 1954 in WO32/20940, CO91/539/8, CO926/81–84 and /349–50, and in 1960 in CO926/1385 and T225/1271.

35 GGA, DG, S.32/1943, 'Re-housing', Oct 1943.

brutal terms the lamentable shortage of adequate housing, the insensitive treatment of civilians by those in authority and inexcusable colonial government
neglect. The governor, Lieutenant-General Eastwood, sufficiently summarised
conditions as 'scandalous'. In response he formed a Re-Housing and Town
Planning Board to prepare for house building, and the military was instructed
to declare what land could be released for housing purposes.[36] The Colonial
Office was also asked to provide a town planner, and to provide half the costs
for constructing apartment blocks, then estimated at £1,125,000, from the
Colonial Development and Welfare Fund (CD&W) set up by the imperial
government in 1940.[37] There is no evidence here of an official reluctance to
act. Rather, there was a strong determination to legitimise imperial control of
Gibraltar, by making good. However, getting actual construction under way
was going to take some time, and so inquiries were also made concerning the
temporary rehousing of the homeless in prefabricated houses, as provided for
blitz victims and others in Britain. Securing these was urgent so as to allow for
the more rapid return of exasperated evacuees,[38] but they were not regarded
as the answer to the housing problem, hence the formulation of what came
to be called the 'permanent housing scheme', initially expected to house nine
hundred families.

By February 1945 the town planning consultant was at work and vacant
sites upon which to erect multiple-storey buildings were being inspected. The
problems soon to be encountered caused delays and escalating costs and were to
infuriate civilian politicians and disappoint, to put it mildly, the evacuees and
the poorly housed. For one thing, the colonial government ran into problems in
recovering building land from the military. Decisions on whether to release War
Department land to the colonial government were determined only in accordance with military assessments of defence needs. Moreover, if land were to be
released, a price was demanded, in cash and/or in the provision of alternative
sites. Such deliberations and bargaining obstructed the rapid implementation of
the permanent housing programme, not least since decisions about land waited
on assessments of Gibraltar's future status as a fortress – which the military,

36 TNA, CO91/502/1, 'Housing Conditions', Eastwood to Stanley, 8 March 1944,
   enclosing report by Clifford, 24 Feb 1944, and Eastwood to War Office, 15 March
   1944. For a further report from Clifford's successor as colonial secretary, also
   condemning conditions and urging the release of land for civilian purposes, see
   CO91/520/2, Stanley to Fisher, 25 Oct 1945.
37 TNA, CO91/502/1, report by Clifford, 24 Feb 1944.
38 Ibid, Acheson to Ministry of Works and Buildings, 7 April 1944, Eastwood to
   Stanley, 28 May 1944. See also TNA, CO91/520/6, 'Provision of Temporary
   Accommodation'. A hundred Nissen huts costing £6,711 were shipped to Gibraltar.
   Gibraltar Chronicle, 23 Nov 1945, p. 3, reports on their installation on the Glacis
   estate – where tower blocks were subsequently erected.

in 1944–45, did not yet feel in a position to undertake.[39] Without a release of land the planned programme of construction would have to be reduced, with political consequences, it was argued, which would be 'extremely serious'.[40] It was not altogether funny when, at a late stage in the planning, the Admiralty revealed what governors had not previously been told: that the sites for a couple of proposed blocks of flats, plus an existing school and a hospital, were in the danger zone adjacent to underground magazines that the navy had constructed for storing high explosives.[41]

It should be recalled that, up to this point, the City Council had not been involved, because it had not yet been resuscitated. However, the colonial government had assumed that the council would carry out the construction, as it had done in the case of the Harington Building before the war. Such was also the assumption of the government official who had meanwhile been charged with looking after municipal affairs, though he did anticipate the need for more City Council staff to be recruited.[42] This was also the argument presented by the AACR.[43] The Colonial Office saw things differently. It was unconditionally accepted that Gibraltar had a housing crisis and that private enterprise would not or could not respond sufficiently or quickly. But there were doubts, shared with Gibraltar's former colonial secretary, whether the City Council was or could be

39 GGA, DG, S.039/45, report of the Military Town Planning Committee, Jan 1945; S.045/45, 'Permanent Housing Scheme'; TNA, CO91/520/2, three-way correspondence between colonial government, Colonial Office and War Office, 6 Feb–25 Oct 1945; CO91/502/1, Report on Civilian Planning as Affected by the Possible Abandonment of the Military Planning Scheme, Oct 1945. Negotiations concerning a 'military town plan' and on the allocation of land between the military and the colonial government rumbled on frustratingly after the war; CO537/2471, 1946–47; CO537/4025, 1948; CO537/4947, 1949; CO91/532/2, 1949; CO91/539/7, 1950; WO32/20940, 1949–50, and especially War Office paper, 'Allocation and Control of Land by the Services', 13 Jan 1950, which contains the military's version of the history of land tenure in Gibraltar since 1704. A seriously large volume of TNA material in Colonial Office, War Office and Treasury files continues the unresolved arguments through the 1950s – and beyond.
40 CO91/520/2, memo with Stanley to Fisher, 25 Oct 1945.
41 Perhaps they are still there. TNA, CO91/520/4 and GGA, DG, S.045/45, Eastwood to Colonial Office, 12 March 1945, and subsequent correspondence, especially Admiralty to Colonial Office, 25 May 1945; CO537/2471, especially Anderson to Creech Jones, 3 April 1947; CO 537/4026, Naval Magazine in Gibraltar, especially minute by Fisher, 8 May 1947.
42 TNA, CO91/520/4 and GGA, DG, S.045/45, Eastwood to Colonial Office, 22 Feb and 12 March 1945; GGA, Box: Housing, file 4876, Government Permanent Housing Scheme 1945–53, Cottrell to Stanley, colonial secretary, 5 March 1945, and reply, 14 March 1945.
43 *Gibraltar Chronicle*, 10 Dec 1945, p. 4.

equipped to cope with the 'heavy responsibility' with which the large permanent housing programme would be laden. Better, it was thought, that the business should be put out to tender and that a consulting engineer and contractors from the UK should be hired in.[44] Such persons would be responsible to the colonial government and, ultimately, to the Colonial Office. The governor's executive councillors agreed (with the exception of one who represented the Chamber of Commerce and therefore, not inconceivably, was lamenting lost opportunities for Gibraltar business interests).[45]

As a result of this directive from the Colonial Office, which governed also the construction of all subsequent post-war public sector tenement blocks, housing in Gibraltar was further politicised. 'Good government' once again took precedence over self-government. In October 1946 the City Council, by this time restored and with its elected civilian majority, asked the governor if it too could assist in alleviating the housing shortage by building a block of flats on behalf of – and at the expense of – the government. Even though the council had had plans drawn up and the governor had expressed his appreciation of the offer, in August 1947 it came to naught, ostensibly because of the government's financial problems. In 1953 even the Harington Building, built and managed by the City Council since 1939, was taken under colonial government control. Subsequently, in 1956, the whole issue of whether the City Council or the colonial government should be the housing authority was resolved in favour of the latter.[46] The City Council, which could have been an agent and might have been an ally, was detached and cleared of responsibility, and with its elected AACR majority it was able to amplify the many civilian protests raised when details of the permanent housing scheme were publicly announced.

Objections to the first approved scheme were swift in coming. This was to build eighteen blocks of flats at various locations to accommodate 1,034 families (5,074 persons) by the end of 1947, sufficient to meet immediate needs.[47] There were objections to some of the sites chosen, which would, for instance, concrete over part of the Alameda public gardens; to the peculiar modern notion of constructing steel-frame buildings; to the importing of building materials rather than using local stuff; and to the employment of non-Gibraltarian

---

44 TNA, CO91/520/4, minutes 28 April and 2 May 1945 on Eastwood to Colonial Office, 12 March 1945, and subsequent correspondence, including with Crown Agents.

45 GGA, DG, S.045, Secretary of State to governor, 4 May and 2 June 1945; Executive Council minutes, 24 June 1945.

46 GGA, Box Housing, file 4210, folders 'Permanent Housing', 'Transfer of Harington Building', 'Housing Authority'; *Gibraltar Chronicle*, 15 and 20 Nov 1946 on City Council proposals.

47 GGA, DG, S.045/45, 'Gibraltar Housing Proposals' with Eastwood to Colonial Office, 12 March 1945.

labour. But most objections concerned money.[48] Initial anticipated building costs were at least £750,000, and the colonial government anticipated that this sum would have to be borrowed (at 3.25 per cent). Subsidies would be required from colonial revenues, or alternatively from the imperial government's CD&W funds, to reduce the true economic rents of £34–£36 a year for the flats to an affordable £20–£24.[49] However, the Colonial Office concluded that all the expected capital required could and should be borrowed locally and that local revenue could support the interest payments (and if necessary the subsidies), not least because Gibraltar's wealthy still wallowed in low tax waters.[50] It was therefore quite a shock when those UK companies putting in bids to construct the 1,034 flats came up with sums way in excess of expectations: the lowest was £3,547,589. Deeply alarmed, the colonial government insisted that it was too committed politically to abandon the scheme, although it was slashed to just 472 flats (becoming the so-called Governor's Meadow buildings) supposedly to cost a 'mere' £1,799,000. The blow to Gibraltar finances was at least to be eased by a grant of £100,000 from CD&W funds, paid for, of course, by British taxpayers. By this time the City Council, led by Hassan, was back in operation, and was duly informed of what had occurred, why it had not been recruited to construct the new housing, and why additional taxation would now have to be levied to meet the higher-than-anticipated costs and to subsidise the rents.[51] Moreover, when the governor explained all this publicly, he received a torrent of criticism from the Chamber of Commerce, Exchange Committee, Workers' Union and, of course, the AACR, and also from unofficial members of the Executive Council. They were even less pleased when the anticipated costs of even the cutback scheme rose to £2,250,000.[52] As we shall see, the question of public expenditure was inevitably linked to the thorny topic of taxation, and

48 *Gibraltar Chronicle*, 20 Oct 1945, p. 3, 18 Oct 1946, p. 4, 20 Nov 1946, p. 2, 7 Nov 1946, p. 5, *Chamber of Commerce Annual Report for1946*, supplement to *Gibraltar Chronicle*, 6 Feb 1947.

49 GGA, DG, S.045/45, Eastwood to Colonial Office, 22 Feb and 12 March 1945, and Stanley to Eastwood, 27 Feb 1945.

50 TNA, CO91/520/4, minute by Barton, 13 April 1945, and GGA, DG, S.045/45, Colonial Office to Eastwood, 2 June 1945.

51 GGA, Box: Housing, Government Permanent Housing Scheme 1945–1953, file 4876/1, Stanley to chairman, City Council, 1 Nov 1946.

52 TNA, CO91/520/3, for minutes, press cuttings and correspondence, especially political commentary in Stanley to Luke, 23 Oct 1946; CO91/534/5, minutes of Executive Council, 31 Jan and 27 Feb 1947. Reports in *Gibraltar Chronicle*, 10 March 1950, and CO91/530/2, include admirable summaries of the history and costs of what came to be called either the Governor's Meadow scheme (after the site) or Humphreys Buildings (after the contractor). The flats were finally completed in July 1951: *Gibraltar Chronicle*, 26 June 1954.

both were closely bound up with constitutional change and the representation of the people in policy making.

Meanwhile, because this first post-war venture into public sector construction under the auspices of the colonial government did not match acknowledged needs, additional housing schemes were devised. In September 1948 the Colonial Office approved the so-called 'hundred dwellings scheme', made up of four-storey blocks of flats, with lower specifications and therefore cheaper. Eventually this project provided 151 flats in five-storey blocks at a price markedly less than anticipated and substantially below the costs of the much-criticised Governor's Meadow scheme. This was to be financed by borrowing and by a CD&W grant, and it was to be constructed over three years by the colonial government's Lands and Works Department, not by the City Council.[53] More still was needed. Indicative of the problems encountered in building blocks of flats in a fortress, the plans for the Lake Chad scheme were initially restricted to two storeys and only modified to three when the military agreed to 'raise their firing line'.[54] Moreover, by this time, worsening considerably by the 1960s, the restrictions by Franco's government on the easy daily passage of workers across the frontier into Gibraltar made it necessary for the colonial government to increase the housing stock to accommodate not only Gibraltar families once resident in La Línea but also foreign workers.[55] Such difficulties were only made worse when, by 1960, more servicemen stationed in Gibraltar had been allowed to bring over their families, further increasing the pressure on accommodation and space and conflicting with the interests of civilians.[56] Over the next several years, indeed decades, many more blocks of flats were erected, whose financing required the kind of balancing of colonial resources and imperial government subventions that had by then become conventional.[57] And still the business

53 TNA, CO91/532/3, especially Anderson to Creech Jones, 17 July 1948, and reply 2 Sept 1948; CO91/539/12, Anderson to Colonial Office, 28 Nov 1950.
54 TNA, CO926/215 and CO926/217, minute by Woodhouse, 28 June 1956. CO926/1835 shows that a fourth storey was added when the site was further developed in 1965–66.
55 For first responses in 1955–56 to the frontier problem in relation to housing see TNA, CO926/214, Housing of Foreign Workers, and GGA, DG, S.396/55, Housing Accommodation for Imported Labour; for coping later with refugees from Spain see CO926/1835, Davis to Gathercole, 10 Aug 1965, and 1964–65 correspondence on OD34/16 and CO926/1831.
56 TNA, CO926/1154, Keightley to Melville, 11 Nov 1960, and subsequent correspondence.
57 For example, for the funding of the construction of flats between 1965 and 1967 at the Schomberg, Moorish Castle, Laguna and Glacis sites in 1963–64 see CO926/1834, and in 1964–65 see CO926/1835. I was particularly pleased to learn that the steel frames for two sixteen-storey blocks of flats at the Glacis site were made

remained a colonial government responsibility, not one for the City Council. What had changed meanwhile were the quality and quantity of the housing stock for civilians, and the physical appearance of the Rock by the addition to the landscape of conspicuous blocks of flats. By 1970 nearly 61 per cent of houses and flats occupied by civilian families were rented from the government, only 35 per cent had private landlords and a mere 4 per cent were owner-occupied.[58] What had also changed substantially as a consequence of these exercises in big government by the colonial authorities was the tax regime in which civilians lived and, as an intimately connected matter, the political constitution under which they sailed.

Gibraltar's welfare state

The financing and politics of post-war public sector housing in Gibraltar did not alone alter the taxes and constitution of Gibraltar, and therefore before turning to those matters some other features of the 'second colonial occupation' need to be addressed. In 1931 all colonial governments had been sent copies of International Labour Conference conventions concerning sickness insurance for employees: this was when Britain's second minority Labour government was still just about in office. No one in Gibraltar's administration or on the governor's Executive Council could imagine social insurance being appropriate for their small population. Concerns were also raised about the financial burden it would impose on government, let alone on employers, since, if the British model were followed, government would be obliged to pay not only a state contribution but also a substantial amount, along with the armed services, as the employer of much of Gibraltar's labour force.[59] A convention concerning compulsory old age pensions, invalidity insurance and widows' and orphans' insurance was similarly brushed aside in 1937.[60]

This was to change. William Beveridge's report on *Social Insurance and Allied Services* was published in Britain on 1 December 1942; during the following year the Colonial Office was circulating advice on social insurance to the colonial empire; in November 1944 the attention of governors was again drawn to social security matters; and a guidance pamphlet entitled *Social Security in*

in and erected by a firm from Bolton, Lancashire. They were constructed alongside the Nissen huts erected as 'temporary accommodation' just after the war, but still occupied, like their cousins in Britain, a generation later.

58 *Abstract of Statistics 2004*, Table 16.

59 GGA, MP193/1931.

60 GGA, Executive Council minutes, 25 May 1937. For some context see TNA, CO323/1425/6, International Labour Conventions Social Insurance, especially Howard to Joint West Africa Committee, 31 Aug 1937.

the Colonial Territories was drawn up by the Colonial Office's Social Services Department, itself created only shortly before the war and indicative of a novel development-and-welfare input into imperial policy making.[61] It was not suggested that Beveridge's social insurance scheme would suit all territories, and certainly financial considerations would have to be taken into account (though CD&W aid might be available), but it was suggested that Beveridge's proposals could be appropriate in 'more advanced communities'. There was, in truth, not much immediate response anywhere in the colonial empire, although in Gibraltar the colonial secretary showed some cautious interest. However, with so many workers in Gibraltar actually being resident in Spain it was doubted whether unemployment insurance could be introduced or Spanish workers could be covered by sickness insurance, but it was thought that an old age pensions scheme might work. Perhaps because of the housing business and an already crowded political agenda, nothing immediate was done on such matters.[62]

However, what did urgently happen was government expenditure on support for returned evacuees in need. This amounted to £11,591 as late as 1948. Also, of more lasting significance, was an elaboration of the long-standing practice of assisting the 'necessitous sick' and tuberculosis victims. Although there seems to have been no ordinance to announce or define the changes, this means-tested scheme was extended in 1946 to support the destitute elderly, and from 1947 to assist widows in need and the unemployed. Charity was evidently not sufficient to provide relief for Gibraltar's distressed. In 1948 £11,890 was spent on such 'assistance to necessitous persons'. In 1951 this support, by then costing £15,660, was renamed 'public assistance', the title given in Britain to poor relief from 1929, though this Gibraltar operation was not funded by a poor rate but out of general government revenues, as was similar support in Britain from 1948 (though then called 'national assistance'). Annual expenditure under this heading was to grow, to £43,477 in 1955 and to £82,157 in 1965, but by then this item of public expenditure ran alongside other social security costs, after reforms modelled on Beveridge and other British welfare practices had at last been imported.[63]

First off the blocks, but at tortoise speed, was the Employment Injuries Insurance Ordinance, which was finally passed in February 1952. It will be

61 TNA, ACT1/717, CO859/125/8 and CO859/124/2; S. Constantine, *The Making of British Colonial Development Policy 1914–1940* (London: Cass, 1984), p. 285; J.M. Lee and M. Petter, *The Colonial Office, War and Development Policy* (London: Temple Smith, 1982).
62 CO859/164/5, Social Insurance, minutes of conference, 15 May 1947, and correspondence.
63 GGA, 'Gibraltar Estimates of Revenue and Expenditure', from 1946; GL, 'Financial Reports', 1954, 1957, 1964.

recalled that the Workers' Union, back in 1919, had wanted British law on workmen's compensation for industrial injuries and occupational diseases to be extended to Gibraltar, but not even Smith-Dorrien had been prepared to concede that request.[64] Gibraltar was by no means an isolated case in the colonial empire, even by 1939, by when no territory had enacted comprehensive legislation, though some administrations, including Malta, had it in mind.[65] Employees were only covered by the Employers' Liability Ordinance of 1924, which provided some limited compensation due to death or injury caused by demonstrable negligence by the employer.[66] However, George Hall, secretary of state in the post-war Labour government, did favour extending workmen's compensation legislation to Gibraltar and elsewhere,[67] but it was not until January 1948 that colonial governments were asked to consider the appropriateness to their circumstances of Britain's recent National Insurance (Industrial Injuries) Act. Probably so prompted, Sir Kenneth Anderson, governor from February 1947 to April 1952, sent a draft ordinance to the Colonial Office. It has to be said that Colonial Office staff were not impressed by how the draft had been worded, but they were even less pleased by the dilatory way in which the Admiralty, a principal employer, responded to their consultation (it took it nine months), and then by the need to beat down its objections on security grounds to allowing civilian investigators to poke about, as necessary, on naval property. By then, of course, trade unionists in Gibraltar were much discontented at the delay, and further time elapsed while the actuarial data was collected upon which to base a contributory insurance scheme.[68] It seems that private employers were 'very reluctant' to volunteer information. The scheme finally embedded in the 1952 ordinance required equal contributions from the employee and the employer. For the latter this was, in effect, a tax, and also one which fell upon government revenues, since many of those covered were their employees. While the type of benefits paid followed the lines of British legislation, the measure covered only those earning £500 a year or less. This targeting of essentially working-class employees did not conform to the universalist message of the post-war British welfare state, embracing all classes as citizens with equal obligations and entitlements. Nevertheless, it was claimed that the ordinance would take Gibraltar 'from the rearmost position in this form of legislation to the forefront amongst

64 TNA, CO91/474, Smith-Dorrien to Milner, 5 Aug 1920.
65 TNA, CO859/9/8, memo, 'Workmen's Compensation Legislation in the Colonial Dependencies'.
66 GGA, Executive Council minutes, 19 June and 23 Oct 1924; Employers' Liability Ordinance, No 10 of 1924.
67 *Gibraltar Chronicle*, 10 Dec 1945, p. 4.
68 CO859/208, Anderson to Colonial Office, 17 Jan 1949, and subsequent papers.

the Colonies', and it was indeed welcomed by Hassan on behalf of the 'organised workmen of Gibraltar', whom he claimed the AACR represented.[69]

Meanwhile, statistical data were also being compiled to support a plan for a government-run social insurance scheme which would embrace many of the social security benefits embedded in Britain's National Insurance Act of 1946. The proposals outlined by the governor, Sir George MacMillan, to his Executive Council in November 1953 had been forwarded to London, with their approval, for detailed appraisal.[70] By this time, welfare specialists attached to the Colonial Office were keen to see social security systems in place throughout the colonial empire, but they still insisted that local circumstances should be taken into account in devising schemes.[71] This explains why the social insurance scheme which emerged after much chewing over in the bureaucratic machinery and which was enacted in 1955 modified the Beveridge model. In particular, it embedded two clear lines of discrimination. First, like the employment injuries law, it covered only those earning £500 a year or less: it was therefore a working-class scheme, actuarially handicapped by excluding the better-off – those least likely to 'take out' more than they 'paid in'. The Executive Council, it seems, was hostile to the removal of a ceiling which would have led to a 'tax' on Gibraltar's middle class for no expected return.[72] This income ceiling on social insurance and employment injuries insurance was not removed until January 1968.[73] Second, the problem of whether and how to insure the many Spanish workers who were employed in Gibraltar but lived in Spain was got round by splitting the scheme between two ordinances. A contributory social insurance law provided all insured workers with maternity benefits (including men for their wives), financial support for widows and orphans, death grants, and old age pensions. But a

69 GGA, *Report of the Proceedings of the Legislative Council*, 5 Oct 1951, 25 Jan 1952, especially pp. 114–15, 8 and 22 Feb 1952; Employment Injuries Insurance Ordinance, No 10 of 1952. I am grateful to Mr Sergio Ballantine, retired civil servant, for information and guidance on this matter.

70 GGA, *Legislative Council*, 26 Feb 1954, p. 106; TNA, ACT1/716, MacMillan to Lyttleton, 17 Dec 1953, Colonial Office to Government Actuary's Dept, 6 Jan 1954, and subsequent correspondence.

71 TNA, CO859/845, Colonial Labour Advisory Committee, 'Social Security in the Colonial Territories', Dec 1955.

72 TNA, ACT1/716, Clarke, Actuary's Dept, to Bishop, Colonial Office, 5 April 1954, and Bishop to Clarke, 8 April 1954, Perryman, Labour and Welfare Dept in Gibraltar, to Bishop, 14 May 1954.

73 Attempts within government to tackle this matter were frustrated in 1960, TNA, CO926/1722, and 1966, *Legislative Council*, 18 March, 22 April and 30 Sept 1966: the change was only effected from 1 Jan 1968, when also unemployment benefit was altered to become a contributory scheme, *Gibraltar Gazette*, 1 Dec 1967.

supplementary non-contributory scheme was set up only for British subjects resident in Gibraltar, who would mainly be Gibraltar born. They would be entitled to substantial cash supplements to their benefits. So, for instance, the old age pension or widow's pension would be increased from 12 shillings (60p) a week to 26 shillings (£1.30). In addition, earlier retirement pensions would be available to them, and also an unemployment benefit at a basic rate of 24 shillings (£1.20) a week.[74] The assumption clearly was that Spanish workers, already notoriously (or usefully) willing to work for lower wages than British subjects, would not demur from receiving fewer benefits. While the contributory scheme naturally required contributions from employers as well as employees, both depended also on payments from government revenue (including all the administration costs) and thus also from taxpayers. The finance of these schemes did not go unnoticed by those liable to pay and those likely to gain, as we shall see.[75]

There was another important addition to Gibraltar's first version of the welfare state. Family allowances in Britain had been a contested concept, insisted upon by some as, in effect, a wage to women to assist with their worthy work of child rearing. More critically, some trade unionists saw such proposals as a way of restraining the legitimate wage demands of male workers who, it was said, were entitled to receive an income sufficient to support their families (assuming they had one). Britain's family allowance scheme was only launched in 1946 and only provided benefits for the second and subsequent children, a supplement to wages and nothing more.[76] Unsurprisingly, Gibraltar's scheme, finally initiated in 1959, was modelled on British law and replicated these cautious characteristics. Entitlement only came from the husband, who would normally be Gibraltar born and Gibraltar resident. But it was not means tested, there was no upper income limit to restrict entitlement and, since it was a non-contributory scheme, it was financed entirely out of government revenues, for which also read taxpayers' money.[77]

Social insurance and employment injuries insurance undoubtedly provided a degree of social security formerly not available to working people in Gibraltar, supplemented as it was, if necessary, by public assistance. The immediate beneficiaries were mothers and the bereaved, but in due course retirement pensions

74 Social Insurance Ordinance, No 14 of 1955 and Non-Contributory Social Insurance Benefit Ordinance, No 15 of 1955; GGA, *Insured Person's Guide to Social Insurance*, [1955].

75 See also the Colonial Office's concerns about the possible effects of social security schemes on colonial budgets: TNA, CO859/1101, Lennox-Boyd, secretary of state, to governors, 12 March 1957.

76 J. Macnicol, *The Movement for Family Allowances 1918–45* (London: Heinemann, 1980); P. Thane, *The Foundations of the Welfare State* (London: Longman, 1982), pp. 216–17, 241, 243.

77 *Legislative Council*, 1 May 1959, pp. 110–13, 29 May 1959, pp. 127–9.

would also begin to flow.[78] Although there had been departures from the Beveridge model, it was readily acknowledged, by Hassan for example, that an essential principle of the British welfare state had been adopted: state assistance was 'given as a right – not as a charity, and without any stigma of charity'.[79] This, then, is another occasion when Britishness was being institutionalised in Gibraltar. At the same time, in Gibraltar as elsewhere, state-subsidised social security schemes came to be treated, in effect, as a contract which was open to repeated renegotiation, between the state (in this case the colonial state) and society (the civilian working-class population). The appetite fed on what it received, hence issues concerning entitlements, value of benefits, rates of contribution and government costs (and therefore taxes) placed social security firmly and immovably on the political agenda.

It may have been noticed that these post-war schemes did not provide sickness benefits (except those covered by employment injuries). These had featured in the original planning and actuarial calculations but had been dropped after the Executive Council had had second thoughts.[80] It was probably recognised that the link between social insurance and medical care, characteristic of the National Health Service launched in Britain on 1 July 1948, could not be easily forged in Gibraltar. That radical man, Governor Mason-Macfarlane, had prompted a review of health services in 1943, but this was concerned with improving institutional care (and especially the Colonial Hospital) and public health services, which Mason-Mac strongly argued should be vested in the City Council, 'consonant with my desire to put greater responsibility on the shoulders of that body'.[81] But this was not compatible with the philosophy of his successors or of the Colonial Office of centring directive authority in the colonial government, and in any event the review did not consider how hospital treatment or general practitioners might fit into a social insurance scheme – a question by 1943 not even seriously addressed in Britain.[82] The indigent poor were already receiving

78 TNA, CO926/1834, report on social insurance by H. Tetley, 17 Jan 1961, provides information on revenue and expenditure over the first five years, and future projections.
79 J.A. Hassan, *Legislative Council*, 3 June 1955, p. 144.
80 TNA, ADM1/26983, minutes of meeting at War Office, 7 June 1955.
81 TNA, CO91/518/16, Mason-Macfarlane to Stanley, 19 Oct 1943, enclosing report.
82 TNA, CO91/524/10, especially minutes. At least more Gibraltar medical practitioners were appointed to government posts during and after the war, and more Gibraltar women were trained as nurses for the Colonial Hospital, itself eventually and symbolically renamed St Bernard's Hospital in 1963: S. Benady, *Civil Hospital and Epidemics in Gibraltar* (Grendon: Gibraltar Books, 1994), pp. 53–4, 56. On nurses also see TNA, DT/18/123, correspondence with General Nursing Council, and *Gibraltar Chronicle*, 23 Nov 1945, p. 2.

some free medical care at colonial government expense, either as outpatients at the Colonial Hospital or from general practitioners providing a district medical service. Civil servants (but not their dependants) also enjoyed a free medical service as a contractual right. Everyone else, pretty much as in pre-war Britain, paid fees to doctors in private practice.[83] Not until 1973, with the introduction of a Group Practice Medical Scheme, was access to a general practitioner first connected to social insurance.[84] From time to time it was said that there were insufficient doctors in Gibraltar to support a social insurance GP service, but fifty-one medical practitioners (and sixteen dentists) were registered in January 1947, and there are hints that objections to being incorporated into a state insurance system came from those quarters.[85] It is also likely that the cost of a service 'free at the point of delivery' caused financial anxieties.

The history of Gibraltar's educational system during and after the Second World War provides an important coda to this review of the origins of Gibraltar's welfare state. As in Britain, developments between the wars had, in practice, been limited to thoughts and reports, though in 1917 attendance at school was at last made compulsory (though enforcement remained a problem), a generation after this prerequisite for state social engineering through education had been imposed in Britain. Otherwise, in the public sector the system trundled on of government funding for a couple of government schools and schools for the children of service personnel, plus state subsidies for schools run by the Roman Catholic Christian Brothers and the Loreto nuns and by and for the Jewish community. But, as in other respects, the war years prompted the colonial secretary to review the educational system, which was predictably summarised by Mason-Macfarlane as 'the pre-war scandal'.[86] Subsequent official proposals led during the 'second colonial occupation' to a remodelling of Gibraltar's educational system explicitly on the 1944 English Education Act.[87] The school-leaving age was raised from 14 to 15, the all-age elementary schools were divided into

83 For a useful description of domestic medical services, albeit pre-war, see TNA, CO91/494/14, report by Dr O'Brien, 2 Aug 1933. I am grateful to Mr Joe Ballantine, formerly the administrator of the Gibraltar government's Medical Department, 1975–88, for guidance on earlier medical services.

84 Group Practice Medical Scheme Ordinance No 14 of 1973, amended by No 35 of 1974; GL, *Insured Person's Guide to Social Insurance*, Jan 1975; GGA, *Department of Medical and Health Services Annual Report, 1973*.

85 Not unlike objections from sections of the British medical profession in 1946–48. *Gibraltar Chronicle, Supplement to the Official Gazette*, 17 Jan 1947; *House of Assembly Proceedings*, 15 May 1973, pp. 7–16.

86 GGA, File 0894, 'Educational Reform', 30 Sept 1943, and comment by the governor, 7 Nov 1943.

87 GGA, File 0894, 'Report of Committee . . . to Consider Post-war Educational Needs' and 'A New Educational System for Gibraltar'.

primary schools (infant and junior) and secondary schools, and the latter were
further divided into single-sex grammar schools, secondary modern schools and
a technical school, with 'selection' at the age of 11. Church representatives were
included on a government school board, but this was only an advisory body and
the influence of the church was thereby reduced, though not eliminated in the
classroom.[88] What was enhanced was the authority of the colonial government.
The key administrator was a director of education, who was appointed by the
colonial government to head its new Department of Education. This may have
made good administrative sense in a small territory in which government taxes
rather than council rates appeared to be the obvious financial resource, but the
effect was to leave the (elected) City Council uninvolved in education, unlike its
counterparts in Britain.[89]

   A deliberate policy of anglicising Gibraltar was a further motive behind closer
colonial government control of school education. The sons of the moneyed class
had long since been given an English-language education at private schools,
several by Jesuits in Britain at, for instance, Stonyhurst College in Lancashire,
to fit them for business and professional careers in or outside Gibraltar and for
mixing socially with the elite of the colonial government and the services.[90]
However, before (and even after) 1940 British visitors to this long-governed
British fortress-colony were invariably impressed or in some cases depressed by
the Spanishness of Gibraltar's popular culture.[91] More particularly, governors
and others noted, usually with dismay, that the offspring of working people were
often at best clumsy users of English.[92] It was often said that the propensity of
Gibraltar men to marry Spanish women, and of some to employ Spanish maids,

88 Colonial Office anxieties about displacing the role of the Roman Catholic
    church in the educational system led to some diluting of the colonial government's
    proposals: TNA, CO91/517/6, minutes.
89 E.G. Archer and A.A. Traverso, *Education in Gibraltar 1704–2004* (Gibraltar:
    Gibraltar Books, 2004), esp. pp. 91–115; TNA, CO91/517/6, 'Education Post War
    Plans, 1943–4', CO91/522/10, 'Educational Reforms in Gibraltar', 8 April 1944;
    GGA, *Report on Education Department during 1945* and similar for subsequent
    years. The equivalent to the 'Butler' Education Act of 1944 in Britain was the
    Education Ordinance, No 13 of 1950, though this largely confirmed that which
    had already been administratively created.
90 Archer and Traverso, *Education in Gibraltar*, pp. 223–7. The sporting suc-
    cesses of several Gibraltar boys are inscribed on the honours board in the foyer of
    Stonyhurst College.
91 For a vivid and persuasive analysis of contemporary commentary see G.
    Stockey, 'A Porous Frontier: Gibraltar and its Spanish Hinterland, c.1923–1954'
    (PhD thesis, Lancaster University, 2006), esp. chapter 1.
92 This was one official concern about the employment of Gibraltar women in
    the Colonial Hospital. See also GGA, MP49/1929, Godley to Amery, 31 Jan 1929,

allowed the language of the home to be Spanish, a weakness in a British colony of such importance.[93] The census of 1931 reported that only 9,906 of the civilian population of 16,146 British subjects could 'speak English'.[94] Lingering (and misplaced) official doubts about civilian loyalty to king and emperor were also fired up during the political turmoil in Spain from 1931 which led to civil war and the establishment of Franco's regime just across the frontier. Different ideological responses in Gibraltar, fuelled further by refugees from both sides, threatened to disrupt, it seemed, the politics of Gibraltar.[95] The strategic importance of Gibraltar during the Second World War only drove the British further towards a policy of pressing 'Britishness' upon Gibraltar, not least through school education and a redoubling of efforts to make Gibraltar children fluent in English.[96] Finally, it should be noticed that government expenditure on education was a mere £9,504 in 1923 and still only £12,294 in 1940, prior to the evacuation, but had risen to £43,200 in 1947 and had become £312,942 by 1969.[97] Sharp increases in expenditure on education, as well as on colonial government housing programmes, the welfare state and economic development projects inevitably threw up serious debates about taxation, the constitution and the representation of the people.

Government finance and the politics of taxation

Those civilians who studied such things would have noticed from the published annual reports that the expenditure of the colonial government, only £199,725

on the perceived dangers of a largely Spanish-speaking population reading Spanish-language newspapers critical of the British government.

93 For example, TNA, CO91/543/4, Immigration and Residence (Restriction) Ordinance, minute 18 Oct 1951.
94 *Census of Gibraltar 1931*, Table VI: that is 61 per cent of all ages.
95 Stockey, 'A Porous Frontier', pp. 147–213.
96 Archer and Traverso, *Education in Gibraltar*, pp. 73–4, 95. For the importance of English-language and bilingual education and previous neglect see TNA, CO91/498/18 and CO926/170; GGA, File 0894, 'A New Educational System for Gibraltar', p. xvi; *Gibraltar Chronicle*, 24 July 1946, p. 2; and GGA, Department of Education, *Annual Report 1949*, p. 3. For some signs of success see *Census of Gibraltar 1951*, p. 8 and Table 7 (by then 68 per cent of British subjects, all ages, could 'speak English'); and see *Census of Gibraltar 1961*, p. 9. For the political need for embedding Britishness via the British Council see E.G. Archer, *Gibraltar, Identity and Empire* (London: Routledge, 2006), pp. 127–8, and correspondence in TNA, CO91/517/6, 'Education: Post War Plans', and BW33/1–3.
97 Archer and Traverso, *Education in Gibraltar*, p. 81; GGA, *Report on Education Department during 1947*, p. 6; *Annual Reports* for 1923, p. 7, and for 1969, Appendix IX.

in 1938, had risen to £751,630 in 1946.[98] Even excluding expenditure on the permanent housing scheme, there was a further big leap, up to £1,236,565 in 1949. Every year from 1951 government expenditure was always over £1 million; from 1961 always over £2 million; in 1969 it was £4,215,112. In 1946, 1949 and 1950, during the troubled post-war years, government expenditure exceeded income and the deficit was met from accumulated surpluses. The reduction of those assets reduced income from the interest on their investment. There was also an unbalanced budget in 1959 and every year from 1964 to 1969. Big government did not come cheap.

One outside source of capital was, of course, the British government (in addition to its annual expenditure on the armed forces stationed in Gibraltar). Governors pressed hard for such handouts. Anderson even went so far as to imply that the Gibraltar government had been pressured by the Colonial Office to take on its expensive housing programme and therefore deserved special consideration.[99] Certainly there was a feeling among articulate civilians after the war that the slow pace of bringing the evacuees back home and the unexpectedly high cost of the permanent housing scheme constituted a moral case for substantial imperial aid.[100] Some was received. The Colonial Development and Welfare Act of 1940 was extended in 1945 and on several subsequent occasions to top up the fund from which colonial governments could draw loans or grants to finance projects which would promote economic development and/or social well-being. Gibraltar was therefore eligible to apply. Post-war housing projects were the kind of enterprise that the managers of the scheme had in mind, but initially the method of allocation to colonies was, in part, proportionate to population, and accordingly a grant of only £100,000 was agreed in 1948. At least this was an outright grant and not a repayable loan.[101] Moreover, it was agreed in 1955 that one-third of the cost of the next housing programme would be met by a CD&W grant and in 1958 that, in addition, three-fifths of the port development would be so aided, amounting between 1957 and 1962 to grants worth nearly £760,000.[102] In addition, nearly £1,322,000 from CD&W money was handed over between 1964 and

98 Financial data is derived from *Annual Reports*.

99 TNA, CO91/534/2, Anderson to Creech Jones, 17 and 21 Sept 1949; CO91/539/12, Anderson to Creech Jones, 22 Dec 1949; and similarly see CO91/533/4, Stanley to Luke, 23 Jan 1947.

100 TNA, CO91/534/3, Executive Council minutes, 31 Jan and 27 Feb 1947, views of Patron.

101 Morgan, *Colonial Development*, vol 2, pp. 37–8; TNA, CO91/534/1. Actually the Treasury attempted to renege on the deal and to turn the grant into a loan: the Colonial Office on behalf of the government and people of Gibraltar managed, for once, to slap them down: CO91/534/2.

102 TNA, CO926/216.

1969, including for housing and a new school,[103] plus a £200,000 grant from the Treasury in 1966–67.[104] To that extent, UK taxpayers, always unwittingly, helped their fellow subjects in Gibraltar.[105] However, the Colonial Office and especially the Treasury were not easily persuaded to subsidise Gibraltar (or any other colony) with grants unless there were good political reasons for such largesse. For example, the problems caused to the Gibraltar economy and finances by Spanish aggression help to account for the boost in assistance from 1964.[106]

It follows that usually the imperial government expected colonies to be financially independent, or at least to show that they were endeavouring to raise their own revenue and capital.[107] In 1938 the Gibraltar government had no public debt, all expenditure even on public works having been met from revenues. This changed. Loans were raised on the credit of the colonial government. True, the UK government provided a £250,000 interest-free CD&W loan in 1949 to assist with the first big housing scheme,[108] but otherwise borrowing was on the open market and came with the usual attendant charges. The first of these loans amounting to £1 million at 3 per cent, explicitly to support the housing programme, was raised locally in two stages in 1948 and 1950, suggesting that some in Gibraltar certainly had money to lend.[109] A further loan of £400,000 was also raised in 1950 at 3.5 per cent,[110] and another of £250,000 in 1952–53

103 TNA, CO926/1834, /1835; OD34/16; *Gibraltar Chronicle*, 16 May 1964, p. 1.
104 For British economic aid in the later 1960s see TNA, CO926/1996 and 2115.
105 Rather amusingly, in 1949 a Mr Bernard Firth, claiming to speak for 'Britons resident Gib', telegrammed to the Colonial Office to protest against British financial subsidies, claiming that money could be raised locally. 'Please protect British Taxpayers', he concluded: TNA, CO91/534/3, 16 Aug 1949.
106 TNA, CO926/1831, including extract from House of Commons Adjournment Debate, 15 April 1965.
107 This is strongly expressed, for example, in TNA, CO91/533/5, Creech Jones to Anderson, 17 July 1948, and CO91/534/2, Creech Jones to Anderson, 2 Nov 1949, and minutes.
108 In fact a loan of £500,000 was originally sanctioned, but was subject to unfulfilled conditions and overtaken by events, especially an upturn in government revenue: TNA, CO91/533/5, CO91/534/1, Anderson to Creech Jones, 9 Oct 1948; CO91/539/12, press communiqué, 15 Nov 1949, and Creech Jones to Anderson, 3 Feb 1950 and Fisher to Treasury, 6 March 1950.
109 Initially £836,375 was subscribed, and Major Patron, a serious financial and political operator who was opposing plans to introduce direct taxation, attempted to wreck the second subscription. On this see TNA, CO91/533/4, CO91/533/6, especially Anderson to Creech-Jones, 9 June and 25 Aug 1947, CO91/533/7, CO91/539/11, Anderson to Colonial Office, 18 April 1950.
110 TNA, CO91/533/8 and CO91/539/11: this loan was provided as an investment by Pyrmont Ltd, who managed the bequest of the very wealthy businessman and philanthropist, John Mackintosh, who had died in 1940.

at 5 per cent, also for housing.[111] Between 1961 and 1965 two further loans were raised, each amounting to £300,000, each at a whopping 6 per cent. More borrowing was to follow later in the 1960s, including some at 6.5 per cent.[112] The increase in interest charges reflected financial markets overall and not Gibraltar's creditworthiness in particular, but it was a nuisance, pushing up costs. By 1953 Gibraltar's public debt stood at £1,850,000; by 1968 it was £3,235,983; in 1969, the Gibraltar government having taken over the debts formerly funded by the City Council, the accumulated total reached £4,159,081.

Neither the colonial government, nor the Colonial Office, nor the Treasury (whose sanction was required) would consent to the raising of a loan until they were confident that interest payments and sinking fund obligations (to pay off the debt) could be met from recurrent revenue.[113] Not surprisingly, therefore, taxation became and remained a big post-war political issue. As noted in the previous chapter, most taxation in Gibraltar before the war was indirect. The only significant departure had been estate duties. Proposals to impose income tax had been resisted and then buried during the war and evacuation. However, the colonial authorities then and thereafter were still determined to raise extra revenue to finance the housing schemes, hospital improvements, educational developments and other projects they judged necessary to fulfil their reformulated visions of what constituted 'good government'. On the other hand, those with substantial incomes and assets were not likely to welcome these initiatives, partly because of post-war economic and political uncertainties which might affect their fortunes, partly because of the scale of what government seemed to have in mind, partly because the benefits to themselves were not readily apparent, and partly and not least important because neither they nor other civilians (but particularly they) were being allowed much direct say in the planning and costing of projects.

While the government publicly nodded in the direction of Queen Anne's free port tradition, most post-war revenue, as in the past, came from customs duties on (mainly) imports, especially alcoholic beverages, tobacco goods, motor fuels, perfumes and, from 1949, coffee. In 1946 these raised £290,343, accounting for 53 per cent of government revenue. Even thereafter, when other revenue streams were tapped the contribution of customs duties to the total was usually in the range of 35 to 44 per cent, except in particular years, like 1966, when Spanish frontier restrictions hit sales of taxed goods to tourists and the figure dropped to as low as 27 per cent, but amounted still to £574,438.

---

111 TNA, CO926/4, MacMillan to Lyttleton, 15 Aug 1952; *Gibraltar Chronicle* 4 Nov 1952.

112 *Gibraltar Chronicle*, 16 May 1964, p. 1.

113 For a classic Colonial Office statement expressing concerns about borrowing without sufficient income from taxation to support the charges see TNA, CO926/4, Lyttleton to Anderson, 3 March 1952.

There were always complaints from those in business who feared that duties would limit their sales and profits, but many of these indirect taxes were regressive in impact. The big debate post-war was whether and how direct taxes could be increased. This was not an argument that could be conducted in private, because unofficial members of the Executive Council had to be consulted and because no one with an eye on public affairs was naive enough as to think that the pre-war deliberations on, especially, income tax, which had stalled during the war, would not be revived thereafter, not least because they knew that government revenue had to be raised one way or another to meet post-war inflated costs of administration and to pay for post-war social services and economic developments.

The appointment of an 'income tax officer' in February 1946 caused 'a good deal of unrest amongst the trading community'.[114] The colonial administration was looking to such a person to advise on the practicalities and virtues of income tax. Though officers on the whole favoured such a method of raising revenue they were not unaware of the hostility which it would generate.[115] Any illusions anyone in office might have had would have been blown away by the fierce protests from the Chamber of Commerce, suspecting the worst, which scorched their letter box.[116] The governor was also under pressure from the unofficial members of his Executive Council.[117] Certainly it was recognised that practical matters had to be addressed, including calculating estimates of yield and the liabilities of taxpayers on different income bands. One objection, seriously put by an unofficial member of the Executive Council, a Gibraltarian, was that collecting information on incomes prior to taxation would be an invasion of privacy. Evasion, he said, 'will be general' since 'direct taxation does not appeal to the Latin', a remark which incidentally denied a shared cultural identity with the British.[118] As before the war, alternatives to income tax were also floated, by officials and unofficials on the Executive Council. These included a companies tax (on profits), a property tax, more trades taxes and a poll tax, which last, even when nuanced by taking account of employment and 'standard of living', was likely to be, in a taxman's eyes, far less 'progressive' than income tax.[119] One conclusion from this debate,

114 GGA, MP427/1939, Patron to Stanley, 12 Feb 1946.

115 GGA, MP427/1939, Stanley to Luke, 8 Nov 1945.

116 GGA, MP427/1939, Chamber of Commerce to Colonial Secretary, 15 Feb and 28 March 1946.

117 GGA, MP427/1939, Executive Council minutes, 15 Feb and 16 May 1946; TNA, CO91/533/4, Stanley to Carstairs, 6 May 1947, and enclosures.

118 TNA, CO 91/533/4, memo by Patron, 23 April 1947; see also GGA, MP427/1939, minute of 27 May 1948, Cook to Fisher, 16 Sept 1947, Executive Council minutes, 16 Sept 1947 and 17 June 1948.

119 GGA, MP427/1939, 'Direct Taxation: Some Alternatives Considered', Executive Council minutes, 20 Oct 1947 and 17 June 1948.

to which we must return, was that, even if income tax were to be recommended, it could not be introduced until a legislative council had been created. That constitutional innovation was a long time coming.

Meanwhile, of course, the colonial government needed revenue. The determination of governors to find additional income sources can be detected in a proposal of February 1940, backed by Sir Clive Liddell, governor from July 1939 to May 1941, to raise money from a state lottery. This would not just be a measure to meet the immediate costs of the war but, placed on a permanent basis, it would be a way of raising the revenue for 'social measures such as rehousing the working classes'. The link was clear: new obligations on government needed new sources of revenue; and on those grounds and with specific reference to expected expenditure on housing and the hospital, the Colonial Office agreed to brave the anticipated wrath of the anti-gambling lobby in the UK. It clutched at its usual comfort blanket – there were precedents (sort of) in other colonies – and the secretary of state, Lord Lloyd, sanctioned the proposal.[120] Unfortunately no speedy action was taken until Mason-Macfarlane came to office, when, on his authority in November 1942 a draft ordinance was despatched for approval to the Colonial Office. With the backing of his Executive Council, he insisted that any money raised would be dedicated to social services and 'works of public benefit': it would not just be absorbed into general revenue and therefore become a device merely to allow other taxes to stay unchanged or even be lowered. The result of the delay, however, was that a different secretary of state, Oliver Stanley, perhaps picking up on some prejudice among his officials against state-sponsored gambling, but more likely expressing his own distaste, simply killed the proposal. Macfarlane 'was clearly very disappointed', runs the official minute in February 1943: 'hopping mad' was more likely.[121] Since Gibraltar civilians without moral qualms regularly spent substantial amounts on Spanish lotteries to the benefit of the Spanish Treasury, an apparently ready source of income for the general good was being obstructed.

And so it must have struck two other governors after the war, Eastwood and Anderson, and two rather more sympathetic secretaries of state, Hall and Creech Jones, since precisely such a state lottery was proposed again in December 1946 and agreed in March 1947, leading to legislation in September and the rolling of the first drum in October. Tickets to the value of £10,000 were to be sold, and prizes ranging from £2 up to £3,000 were the lure.[122] Draws were held

120 TNA, CO91/513/18, Liddell to MacDonald, 29 Feb 1940, minutes, Lloyd to Liddell, 10 May 1940.

121 TNA, CO91/515/1, Mason Macfarlane to Cranborne, 3 Nov 1943, and enclosures, subsequent minutes and correspondence.

122 TNA, CO91/534/3, Executive Council minutes, 31 Jan 1947; CO91/533/4, 'Financial Questions', Eastwood to Creech Jones, 23 Jan 1947; T220/36, 'Gibraltar

frequently. A profit of £13,000 was made in the last three months in 1947 and of £64,189 in 1948, the first full year, thereby contributing 9 per cent of government revenue. Even after yet other new sources of income were captured, the lottery continued to provide usually 8–10 per cent of government revenue and reached a height of £160,622 in 1964.[123] When first publicly announcing the lottery, Anderson was absolutely explicit about its purpose. It was to meet the interest and sinking fund charges on the loans to be raised to pay for the permanent housing programme. According to the Gibraltar press, he also told the four thousand people witnessing the first draw that 'the lottery and the loan are both part of one scheme to provide better homes for Gibraltarians and to enable those of us who are still in the UK to return to their homeland'.[124] The lottery was, in effect, a voluntary tax, funding a good cause by tempting folk to take a punt in the hope of unearned riches.

'It was remarked recently', reported the *Gibraltar Chronicle*, 'that lotteries are a subtle and pernicious form of taxation on the poor.'[125] While others might dare to dispute the truth of this proposition, it is certainly true that in 1947 the lottery was not the method of taxation which the colonial government and the Colonial Office had had principally in mind since the war. They had set out to target the rich. One other innovation therefore proposed in the summer of 1949 was to extend a modest trades tax introduced in 1940 into a more precisely targeted and more potentially lucrative profits tax measure. Tax liability was to be graded by an assessment board according to the type of business, which at the top end would clip £400 from the profits of any business assumed to be making £3,200 a year or more. Cries of pain and indignation filled a Chamber of Commerce meeting, the pages of the *Gibraltar Chronicle* and the in-tray of the colonial government. It was protested that 'unlimited taxation' beyond the resources of 'this small colony' was being demanded to meet the government's 'ambitious programme', and especially a housing scheme which had been 'enforced by the Home Government' with its 'dictatorial policy'. Even the introduction at the same time of a small import duty on coffee was interpreted as an attack on Gibraltar's status as a free port.

In an attempt to assuage discontent, the passage of the trades tax ordinance

Loan Proposals Including Lottery Loan'; Lotteries Ordinance, No 21 of 1947; *Gibraltar Chronicle*, 13 Sept 1947. The number of tickets and the value of the prizes subsequently varied. The curious will find photographs of the first lottery draw machine in *Annual Reports* for 1950–51 and 1957.

123 The lottery still operates; top prize now is £100,000 and annual sales amount to £4.5 million: www.gibraltar.gov.gi/about_gib/lottery/lottery_index.htm.

124 *Gibraltar Chronicle*, 14 April and 6 Oct 1947, p. 1.

125 *Gibraltar Chronicle*, 17 Sept 1947, p. 2. See also J.D. Stewart, *Gibraltar: the Keystone* (London: Murray, 1967), pp. 236–8, for a caustic criticism of this 'immoral device for raising revenue', by a government official involved in its administration.

was delayed to allow time for the Chamber of Commerce to submit its own (to the government unacceptable) alternative. Further protests were also made, by a memorial to the crown in April 1950 signed by a reputed 6,900 people, by lobbying members of parliament, by a campaign of non-cooperation organised principally by the Chamber of Commerce, by the resignation of the two unofficial members of the Executive Council and by an appeal to law. But the governor countered by radio broadcasts explaining the need for this tax, with particular reference to educational services and medical care and anticipated social measures. Hence no concessions could be made and the trades tax was, in the event, collected. In 1951 it raised £40,000, the sum anticipated, and generally in 1950–52 it contributed 4 per cent of annual government revenues, before lapsing.[126] (The tax on coffee imports, which were being shipped in and substantially sold on to Spanish consumers, netted on average well over £55,000 a year between 1950 and 1953, a nice little earner.)

The truth of the matter was that those protesting against the trades tax recognised what the government made no attempt to hide, that this measure was only ever intended to be an interim measure, pending the introduction at last of income tax. That was certainly the view of the Colonial Office. For it, recurrent expenditure and the servicing of loans had always needed some more robust underpinning than customs duties (vulnerable to trade fluctuations and hitting the poor as well as the well-heeled), the trades tax (confessed to be interim and limited in its grasp), the lottery (an uncertain addition) and death duties (dependent each year on the grim reaper choosing the wealthy). Besides, income tax was conventional in the UK and notions of social justice had been attached to it. In July 1948 the secretary of state had urged the governor to get on with the preparatory work; in October 1949 the continued absence of income tax in Gibraltar was described by one senior officer as a 'crying scandal'; and as a further prod, in November 1949 the governor was reminded that the annual incidence of taxation in Gibraltar was £20 a head but in the UK it was £70 a head.[127]

126 GGA, S.240, 'Taxation Proposals'; and TNA, CO91/534/3, especially O'Brien to President of Chamber of Commerce, 30 June 1949, Anderson to Creech Jones, 14 July 1949, and Fisher to Watson, 18 July 1949; Trades Tax Ordinance, No 6 of 1950; *Gibraltar Chronicle*, 8 July 1949, 5, 10, 11 and 15 April, 1, 6, 23, 25 and 27 May, 21 and 28 July, 4 Aug, and 6 and 21 Oct 1950; *Gibraltar Annual Reports*. For the petition to the crown see also TNA, CO91/543/2 and for Governor Anderson's broadcasts, *Gibraltar Chronicle*, 12, 16, 19 June 1950, and CO91/542/9. The history of the trades tax and the coffee tax as seen by the Chamber of Commerce is contained in a report of 27 June 1950 issued with the *Gibraltar Chronicle*, 5 July 1950.

127 TNA, CO91/533/5, Creech Jones to Anderson, 17 July 1948; CO91/534/2, minute of 20 Oct 1949, Creech Jones to Anderson, 2 Nov 1949.

In fact a scheme was, in broad terms, already on paper in the governor's office by the summer of 1947, largely based on the model income tax ordinance despatched to governors in 1922 and subsequently set aside. Detailed work was then handicapped by the lack of data on incomes and the realisation that these were not likely to be forthcoming, even without the constitutional complications and the connected political objections being raised in and out of the Executive Council. At one stage even the governor, Anderson, wondered, in the light of the political mugging he was receiving, whether a graduated poll tax might not be a better option.[128] The problem was that both Governor Eastwood and Governor Anderson had publicly stated that income tax would not be introduced before constitutional changes had taken place and, especially, a legislative council had been formed to debate the matter – and as we shall shortly explain, that was an unexpectedly long-drawn out business.[129] Only after that body was formally opened and got down to business in December 1950 was the drafting of the Income Tax Ordinance finally and properly got under way.

The scheme was presented to the governor's Executive Council in February 1951 by the financial secretary. He first rejected the alternatives of indirect taxes, including a general customs tariff, since they would increase the cost of living and, he added rather cunningly, they would infringe the free port tradition by which the Chamber of Commerce set such store. Instead he proposed to replace the trades tax with a direct tax which would combine a tax on company profits and on personal incomes, including those of Gibraltar's small but wealthy *rentier* class, but it would exempt lower-income groups who were hard put to make ends meet. Having climbed onto the moral high ground, he must have been disgruntled by the reception, and not only from the unofficial members. True, Albert Risso, the first president of the AACR, was adamant that income tax was the way to fund necessary social services. But Henry Coelho, in the face of common sense, doubted whether income tax would raise as much money as the trades tax, and Albert Isola, a barrister, vehemently declared his opposition to all forms of direct taxation. Moreover, Governor Anderson, having already conceded that income tax might not be immediately necessary, deferred further consideration to allow Isola to prepare a statement for delivery at another meeting. The rant which Isola then delivered truthfully asserted that the people of Gibraltar still did not have self-government, but he also insisted that direct taxes were unnecessary, indirect taxes would suffice, Gibraltar people were already too heavily burdened (and he complained about rent controls), capital

128 GGA, MP427/1939, minutes and papers, Anderson to Creech Jones, 15 Feb 1949.
129 GGA, MP427/1939, Stanley to Fisher, 8 Nov 1945, Executive Council minutes, 15 Feb and 16 May 1946; *Gibraltar Chronicle*, 14 April 1947, p. 3.

would flee the colony, information provided to government by banks and businesses would not be kept confidential (a remarkable slander), there would be evasion (implying his class would break the law) and 'the citizens of Gibraltar derive no benefit from their Government' (perhaps overstating a fair case). No doubt he felt better for having had his say, but his councillor colleagues were unimpressed and it was agreed, against his dissenting voice, that the ordinance should be prepared.[130]

This was not then sent to the Colonial Office until June 1951, when Anderson again acknowledged that there was no immediate budgetary need for an income tax to do more than replace the revenue currently derived from the trades tax, and he suggested that it would be tactful to present the measure to the Legislative Council only in those terms. Hence also a low standard rate of tax (10 per cent), generous personal allowances for middle-income groups and no tax on those earning less than £500 a year. The Colonial Office concurred with this politically cunning plan, though insisting that the governor should not disguise the fact that rates could later rise to finance further public and social services.[131] That strategy, various twitches to the draft agreed by the Executive Council in October (for example, deleting a clause making failure to pay tax a criminal offence) and an explanatory memorandum for the Legislative Council may, just, have done the trick.[132]

On 25 January 1952 the income tax bill was debated. Again, the financial secretary repeated his arguments on the virtues of direct taxation, the need for the government to extend the range of its sources of revenue and the importance of building up reserves in preparation for further expenditure on housing and social services (including the financing of loans). The proposal was seconded, in similar terms, by Panayotti, an elected AACR representative, who stressed the social justice of taxing the wealthy and the need for social investment, and in this he was also backed by Hassan (and in silence by the third AACR elected member). But Coelho, a nominated member of the legislature, was still opposed; Isola, an elected member, added to his previous arguments by claiming that the charitable donations and bequests made by the wealthy, for whom he apparently spoke, were being ignored by this insistence on also taxing them; and Patron, also an elected member, speaking to the gallery (who even cheered, to the governor's irritation), complained that the introduction of income tax was being rushed, it would damage the economy and it would fail as it had 'in every Latin country'. At the committee stage and third reading in March, Isola, still

---

130　GGA, S.240 (2), 'Taxation Proposals 1951 – Income Tax Bill'.
131　GGA, S.240 (2), and TNA, CO91/544/6, Anderson to Griffiths, 6 June 1951, and reply 31 Aug 1951.
132　GGA, S.240 (2), Executive Council minutes, 30 Oct 1951; S.240 (3), A.E. Cook, 'Income Tax and the Fiscal System', 15 Jan 1952.

wriggling, attempted unsuccessfully to reduce the standard rate from 10 per cent to 5 per cent. The bill went through.[133]

However, the Colonial Office was rightly suspicious that Anderson was still troubled by the opposition this measure had stirred up, and officials were not at all pleased that in spite of, indeed in defiance of, their stress on financial urgency the governor had agreed without consultation to postpone the actual levying of income tax for another year, until 1 April 1953, supposedly to secure AACR approval.[134] It was, however, thereafter a modestly successful measure, at least in the sense that collecting the tax on personal incomes and on company profits (the two were covered by the same ordinance) did not seem to be in practice a problem (in spite of that 'Latin' temperament); it did prove to be a flexible tax; the amount raised did increase substantially; and wealth production in Gibraltar did not shudder to a halt. In 1953 it contributed £75,448 or about 7 per cent to government revenue (more than the trades tax ever brought in), but that year this amount was still less than the yield from the lottery (10 per cent) and way below customs duties (36 per cent). Thereafter its share increased, boosted to 13 per cent after standard rate was raised in 1961 to 3 shillings in the pound (15 per cent). In 1968 standard rate became 5 shillings in the pound (25 per cent), and the tax brought in £394,035 or 16 per cent of total government revenue, although customs duties still accounted for substantially more, £849,224 (34 per cent).[135] Gibraltar income earners may or may not have felt they were thereby contributing to public well-being. However, it can be shown that those who claimed to speak for them had certainly used the politics of taxation to advance the cause of constitutional change, and to that we may now turn.

Constitutional change and the Legislative Council, 1950

Hindsight can mislead. The Gibraltar constitution of 1969, at which eventually we shall arrive in this analysis, was not the clearly discerned goal of those lobbying for constitutional change in the 1940s, whose aspirations in any case varied, nor of the colonial and imperial authorities, who never had a blueprint for political change in the colonial empire nor one even specifically for Gibraltar. In retrospect we can see that there were a number of possible routes down which the

133 Legislative Council, 25 Jan and 7 March 1952; Income Tax Ordinance, No 11 of 1952.
134 TNA, CO926/26, especially Lyttleton to Anderson, 3 March 1952, Anderson to Lyttleton, 8 and 13 March 1952, and minutes.
135 A table showing tax payable for single persons and for differently constituted families is usefully printed in *Annual Report for 1952–53*, Appendix II. A single person with an income of £10,000 would pay £1,460 (less than 15 per cent).

people of Gibraltar might have been politically driven, by the colonial authorities and/or by their political leaders.

The least likely prospect in the period under consideration was decolonisation, in the sense of a complete British political withdrawal and the granting of independence to Gibraltar the nation-state. Notionally such a scenario, sooner or later, was the outcome most compatible with one of the avowed principles of the United Nations, to which the United Kingdom was a principal signatory. As is well known, the UN's Committee of Twenty-Four repeatedly pressed the British government to honour its obligations and accelerate the process of decolonisation.[136] The reluctance of the UK government to embrace this duty in the case of Gibraltar is of course also well known, though the arguments opposed to such a development need to be separately addressed.

First, whenever post-war, the British reviewed the possible political destinies of the colonies, they concluded that Gibraltar, along with other small territories like St Helena, lacked the population and the resources ever to operate as independent nations.[137] Big, apparently, is beautiful. It was inconceivable to those in high places that, with the best will in the world, tiny Gibraltar could become a member state of the British Commonwealth or of the United Nations, seated alphabetically close to India. Besides, there was not the best will in the world. Hence a second reason for British hesitation. Under the Treaty of Utrecht, if regarded as still the principal grounds upon which British tenure of the Rock was based, a British exit should be followed by a Spanish entrance and the reunification of a space partitioned in 1704. This, of course, was precisely the argument which Spain had always nursed, though for some time had not attempted forcefully to assert, until after the Second World War, when Franco's government with some success secured for it a UN hearing.

But British objections to such an endgame need also to be prised apart and made specific to this post-war period. Returning Gibraltar to Spain, and worse still to an authoritarian military dictatorship, would have been as unacceptable to British public and parliamentary opinion in the mid twentieth century as it had been in the eighteenth century, when the transfer of Gibraltar back to Spain had last been seriously contemplated. British public knowledge of Gibraltar had

---

136 In addition to Garcia, *Making of a People*, and Jackson and Cantos, *Fortress to Democracy*, see P. Gold, *Gibraltar: British or Spanish?* (London: Routledge, 2005), and G. Archibald, 'Attempts to Solve an International Problem, 1963–2002' (PhD thesis, Ulster University, 2006).

137 See, for example, documents reprinted in R. Hyam (ed.), *The Labour Government and the End of Empire 1945–1951* (London: HMSO, 1992), part IV, pp. 210–38; D. Goldsworthy (ed.), *The Conservative Government and the End of Empire 1951–1957* (London: HMSO, 1994), part II, pp. 59–75; R. Hyam and W.R. Louis (eds), *The Conservative Government and the End of Empire 1957–1964* (London: HMSO, 2000), part I, pp. 200–4, part II, pp. 672–88, 724–51.

probably not moved on much since then, and still largely revolved around notions of the Rock as a doughty British outpost whose military worth had been confirmed again during the Second World War. Spanish hostility to and reactions after the Queen's visit to 'her' Gibraltar in 1954 and the increasingly obstructive behaviour of Spanish officials at the frontier from the early 1960s, which were intended to pressure the British government into making concessions to Spain, merely inflamed British public opinion and limited the options of British governments.[138] That inflammation was of course aggravated by the mass protests of Gibraltar civilians themselves. Naturally and with considerable impact on British political opinion, they embraced another guiding UN principle, self-determination. This was most dramatically demonstrated on 10 September 1967, when a referendum rejected the transfer of sovereignty from Britain to Spain and instead recorded 12,138 votes in favour of retaining 'voluntarily' the 'link with Britain, with democratic local institutions and with Britain retaining its present responsibilities'. Only forty-four dissenting voices were recorded.[139] Public commitments by British ministers to respect the wishes of the Gibraltar people were made on several occasions before and after this event.[140]

However, British government resistance to Spanish demands was also based, particularly in this period it should be stressed, on official calculations of the military value of Gibraltar to Britain. As noted earlier, Britain did not come out on the winning side in the Second World War ready to abandon its imperial and global roles. No government of any shade believed in the 1950s and 1960s that Britain had ceased to be a great power. While Malta was the British base geographically best placed for operations in and around North Africa, the Middle East and south-east Europe, Gibraltar still commanded the approaches to the straits and its end of the Mediterranean. If anything, political difficulties in Malta in the 1950s leading to independence in 1964, actually enhanced Gibraltar's strategic value. A reduced but still significant British army garrison was maintained well into the 1960s; the dockyards remained a major resource for the Royal Navy; and the RAF had become established on the airfield. Not until 1981 was it announced that the use of the naval dockyard for construction and repairs would shortly cease (and not until 1984 did this occur); and not until Spain was allowed to join NATO in May 1982 was an alternative UK defence option realistically opened up.[141] We have also already seen that the military was

138　See Hyam and Louis, *Conservative Government and End of Empire*, I, p. 20.

139　*Gibraltar Chronicle*, 15 June and 11 Sept 1967; *Gibraltar Referendum September 1967, Report by the Referendum Administrator*, 10 Oct 1967.

140　For examples see Garcia, *Making of a People*, pp. 131, 139, 147, 161; and *Gibraltar Chronicle*, 2 Oct 1964, p. 1, 28 June 1969, p. 1.

141　HCPP, annual *Statements on Defence*, for example, Cmnd 1639, 1962, pp. 4, 7; Cmnd 2901, 1966, p. 8; Cmnd 3203, 1967, pp. 8, 15, 36; Cmnd 3927, 1969, pp. 6,

reluctant to lose control over space, and indeed, post-war and into the 1960s, invested heavily in barracks and other facilities. In sum, Gibraltar would be retained in spite of Spanish protestations because Gibraltar seemed valuable to the imperial government. The popular opposition in Britain and especially in Gibraltar to a transfer of sovereignty back to Spain actually made it easier, not harder, for the British government to maintain there its military presence, unlike in several other British colonies, though political and economic aggression from across the peninsula undeniably ratcheted up the costs.

Though decolonisation and independence were, then, politically non-starters in this period, the continuing importance to the British of the fortress of Gibraltar did have an impact on the course of constitutional change in the other direction. Some in authority in Gibraltar and in London, and not only in the War Office, Admiralty and Air Ministry, were convinced that Gibraltar should still be regarded primarily as a fortress, with a dependent colony attached. The civilian presence could not be denied, nor their material well-being disregarded, but that did not mean that they should become more involved in the running of the place. Some believed that a city council with civilian representation and an executive council with a couple of nominated civilian members were enough and alone compatible with the good government of a fortress. Further concessions to the involvement of civilians in the public affairs of Gibraltar should be denied, or at least limited. Moreover, since 'big government' was more about good government than self-government, it was also possible to argue that the very existence of the City Council with its elected majority of civilians and quasi-independent operations was an inefficient intrusion into the administration of a small population. As noted, while the City Council extended its services, it was not trusted to take on new ones, and since there were overlaps of responsibilities for such matters as public health, there were good arguments, including efficiency gains through cost cutting, for reducing the role of or even abolishing the City Council and bringing all within the compass of colonial government control.[142] Such an increase in colonial government responsibilities would not necessarily imply as a consequence any greater civilian participation in colonial government policy making.

Some civilians made an alternative deduction from the development of the City Council and the arrival of big government after the war. Gibraltar should

Footnote 64 (*cont.*)

    11, 29; T. Benady, *The Royal Navy at Gibraltar* (Gibraltar: Gibraltar Books, 2000), p. 227.

142 Among several early post-war suggestions to reduce or eliminate the role of the City Council see TNA, CO91/523/3, Eastwood to Gater, 28 June 1945, and minute 13 July 1945; CAB134/55, minutes of Cabinet Commonwealth Affairs Committee, 29 Oct 1948, reprinted in Hyam, *Labour Government and the End of Empire*, pp. 210–11; CO91/537/9, papers on the Ingram report 1949; CO926/4, MacMillan to Lyttleton, 28 Aug and minute 23 Sept 1952.

become part of the United Kingdom. Social insurance, labour laws and the education system were further importations of British institutions into a culture which, though also Catholic and ethnically more Mediterranean than Anglo-Saxon, was increasingly infused post-war with certain British features: respect for the monarchy; British law and legal systems; trade unionism becoming more akin to British models; British sports (especially football and cricket) and popular culture (books, films and plays); the curriculum of schools and the qualifications gained by teachers as well as pupils; greater facility in the use of the English language; consumer goods and material culture becoming closer to British.

Indeed, among the motivating inspirations behind post-war political agitation lay not just a demand for a more democratic society but, as we have seen, a demand for the extension to Gibraltar of British social services and for the higher living standards encountered by many evacuees in Britain during the war. Many working people, organised in Gibraltar's trade unions, had long since grumbled about the apparent discrepancy between the rates of pay they received in comparison with those of British workers. What was, then, more natural for some in this small place penetrated by cultural Britishness and also aspiring to secure a British standard of living than to promote as a means to that end the political integration of Gibraltar into the UK? In 1945 even the AACR, or at least Albert Risso, its president, and the radical lawyer Sergio Triay, seriously and publicly engaged with the idea, taking the absorption of Algeria into metropolitan France as a model. The notion was floated by them at a public meeting in September 1945, and an AACR delegation to the secretary of state in November proposed that Gibraltar should become an 'integral part of the United Kingdom in order that it might have a representative in the House of Commons'. [143] Later, of course, such integration was also presented as a solution to other problems: it would provide lasting security against the demands of Spain.

This was not a fanciful idea. Integration into the United Kingdom had been a seriously considered alternative to national independence for Malta in the 1950s.[144] This treatment of colonies accounts for the incorporation into the USA of Hawaii in 1959 and the integration into metropolitan France of several French colonies, like Martinique and Réunion in 1946, allowing them representation

143 TNA, CO91/524/8, Eastwood to Hall, 12 Sept 1945, repeating a report in *El Calpense*, minute by Fisher, 23 Sept 1945, Eastwood to Colonial Office, 31 Oct and 3 Nov 1945, enclosing report by Colonial Secretary; *Gibraltar Chronicle*, 1 Nov 1945, p. 3. The Chamber of Commerce and the Workers' Union opposed this proposal.

144 See documents in S.C. Smith (ed.), *British Documents on the End of Empire, Malta* (London: TSO, 2006), and his essay 'Integration and disintegration: the attempted incorporation of Malta into the United Kingdom in the 1950s', *Journal of Imperial and Commonwealth History*, 35 (2007), 49–71.

in the National Assembly. However, and particularly after the Malta experience, this was not a route down which the British government was likely to again travel willingly. As it happens, it was not a proposition which seemed to attract substantial support in Gibraltar until the formation of the Pro-Integration Movement in 1965 and of the Integration with Britain Party in 1967. The British government then attempted at once to rule out the idea during constitutional talks in 1969, and delivered a blunt rejection of the suggestion in 1975.[145]

By then, of course, the Gibraltar people had travelled a long way down another route, towards virtually unrestricted self-government, but for internal affairs only. The British enjoy a charming conceit that the devolution of authority to 'colonial people', leading usually to full independence, was the always-intended outcome of an imperial project which first required the locals to gain 'experience' of government through the planned and gradual granting of political rights. In reality, as the case of Gibraltar also indicates, most of the changes conceded were ad hoc reactions to popular pressure from below, though concession did not mean abdication, and governors in Gibraltar could themselves sometimes shove things along.

For example, as we have seen, in April 1943 Mason-Macfarlane was keen to enhance civilian representation on the City Council and increase its independent responsibilities, but he also proposed to employ that council, with its elected members, as an additional advisory body with the right to scrutinise the government's annual financial estimates of expenditure as well as income, to comment on draft legislation and also itself to propose laws. Beyond getting a sense from the AACR that constitutional changes were needed, this was entirely an initiative devised by the governor and his colonial secretary. When put through the bureaucratic mill of the Colonial Office, what emerged was a constitutional plan which certainly had no precedent and which several who endorsed it regarded as quirky, namely the insertion between the City Council (with its official and its elected unofficial members) and the Executive Council (with its official and nominated unofficial members) of an advisory council made up of the city

---

145   Garcia, *Making of a People*, pp. 140–1, 158–72; Jackson and Cantos, *Fortress to Democracy*, pp. 130–2, 155; P. Mañasco, 'A survey of the integrationist movement in Gibraltar since 1965', *Gibraltar Heritage Journal*, 9 (2002), 11–21. Earlier there had been some cautious consideration among officials in the Colonial Office and colonial government of a constitutional relationship between the UK and Gibraltar similar to that with the Isle of Man or the Channel Islands and bringing it under the auspices of the Home Office: see, for example, CO926/279, minutes and papers on 'Home Office offer', 1954; CO926/1227, Kisch to Bates, 16 July 1962; CO926/1865, memo by Bates, 11 April 1963, and responses, but see the less favourable consideration of proposals put forward by, especially, J. Bossano, R.J. Peliza and others in the Pro-Integration Group and by sympathetic MPs in CO926/1870, /2092, /2093, /2132, May 1965–Nov 1966.

councillors, plus a couple of officials in attendance (the colonial secretary and the attorney-general) to give advice to the advisors. It was suggested by one Colonial Office member that such an advisory committee might give civilian representatives 'some preliminary experience in the conduct of affairs preparatory to setting up a legislature on the usual Colonial model'. Mason-Macfarlane himself veered in that direction, though even for him the bottom line remained that Gibraltar was a fortress and the 'establishment of responsible self-government (i.e. a Legislative Council) is impracticable so long as Gibraltar retains its present strategic importance'.[146] Working on the same assumption about fortress needs, the Colonial Office informed the three armed services of what was afoot.[147] General Eastwood, succeeding to Mason-Macfarlane, even secured the approval of his local service commanders to what he regarded as a potentially 'more effective means of gauging public opinion than has hitherto been available'.[148]

Here was a bit of colonial planning, and a complacent conclusion, which, following publication on 30 December 1944, hit the buffers of reality. It was denounced in a coordinated move by, on the one hand, representatives of the moneyed class – the Chamber of Commerce and the Exchange and Commercial Library – and on the other, those claiming to speak for the workers and the people at large – the Workers' Union and the AACR. As we have seen, in the face of this onslaught, the constitution of the City Council was further amended to increase its elected membership and widen the electorate, but the proposal to introduce an advisory committee was simply dumped.[149]

Dismayed as they were by the rebuff, the colonial government and the Colonial Office were not misled by the broad front of opposition to their proposed constitutional changes, and nor should we be. All opponents were in agreement in denouncing what was on offer, but not for the same reasons. For instance, the president of the Chamber of Commerce, L.J. Imossi, privately objected to the proposed advisory committee because it would contain a substantial number of popularly elected city councillors. As we have seen, the moneyed class rightly feared that they would fare badly in elections; and there were worrying implications for them because already the City Council had rate-setting and expenditure powers, and the proposed advisory committee was to be authorised to scrutinise the ways in which the colonial government would raise its revenue and spend its money. Imossi went on to assert that 'Gibraltar as a Fortress should never have a representative constitution'. This came just at a time when the governor's

---

146 TNA, CO91/518/1, Mason-Macfarlane to Stanley, 11 April 1943 and enclosure, subsequent papers, and Stanley to Mason-Macfarlane, 29 Dec 1943.

147 TNA, CO91/523/2, Colonial Office to War Office, Admiralty, Air Ministry, 17 March 1944.

148 TNA, CO91/523/2, Eastwood to Stanley, 26 July 1944.

149 For the narrative of these events see also Garcia, *Making of a People*, pp. 25–30.

Executive Council, whose unofficial members 'represent the wealthy oligarchy in the Colony', had been alarmed by a proposal to set up in government an income tax department. As a senior member of the Colonial Office put it, 'their fear was that the Government's constitutional proposals would give greater political power in the Colony to left wing elements who would be more likely to support the introduction of income tax, but also to support other measures which might adversely affect the well-to-do members of the community'.

On the other hand, the Workers' Union and the AACR were 'critical of the constitutional proposals as not going far enough in the democratic direction'. They were unacceptable precisely because they would not place elected representatives on anything more than an advisory body, whose composition 'overweighted by a body of official opinion . . . will be influenced by reactionary tendencies'. They wanted much more of a determining influence on government policy. That alone would be compatible with the democratic creed which they espoused, and that alone, they felt, would ensure that government revenue, raised in appropriate amounts and in appropriate ways, would be spent on services appropriate to the needs of their members and supporters.[150]

Nevertheless, there was pretty much an agreement on all sides by the autumn of 1945 that constitutional changes in Gibraltar were needed in what one Colonial Office senior described as 'a Victorian museum-piece'.[151] Moreover, it was understood that the only way forward would be towards a legislative council, something additional to and not a replacement of the Executive Council.[152] From the official point of view, this innovation should restore a badly fractured relationship between government and civilian population. From the civilian perspective it would allow for their active participation in government and the representation of their 'interests', whatever they might be. A legislative council would mean that laws and budgetary matters could no longer be determined on the authority of the governor alone (and with the blessing of the Colonial Office) but would require the consent of a legislature, though there were, in the book of colonial empire precedents, no fixed rules on how such a body should be composed (how many non-official members? elected or nominated?) or what business, if any, should be reserved for the governor alone (and one can anticipate what, in a fortress, those might be) or in what emergency circumstances the wishes of a majority in the legislative council could be set aside by the governor.

Initially, in formulating their answers to such matters, the governor and the Colonial Office were more set on clipping the wings of the moneyed class than on feeding a fledgling democracy. 'The little commercial oligarchy in Gibraltar

150 TNA, CO91/523/3, Stanley to governor, 15 Jan 1945, and minute by Luke, 25 Jan 1945.
151 TNA, CO91/524/8, minute by Dawe, 14 Dec 1945.
152 TNA, CO91/523/3, minutes 11 April –12 June 1945 make this clear.

have had things far too much their own way', it was said by a senior Colonial Office mandarin.[153] Therefore, paradoxically it may now seem, there must be an official majority on a legislative council, at least 'to start with'. This was not just because 'Gibraltar is primarily a fortress and a naval base, and the position of the Executive Government must be safeguarded'. More important, 'if we start with an unofficial majority, we shall simply strengthen the hands of the undesirable little clique of commercial oligarchs who have far too much to say in the affairs of the colony'. It was doubted, in other words, whether any but representatives of the moneyed class would get themselves elected to a legislative council. In classic paternalistic mode, it was asserted that 'The true interests of the general community are much more likely to be served in present conditions by a retention of power on the official side.'[154] As yet (this was in June 1945) no City Council elections had been held (they were held in July) and the electoral appeal of the AACR had not been revealed, and the Colonial Office actually feared that elections to a legislative council would only return those who 'wield commercial and economic power in the Colony'. Thus, with Olympian mis-judgement, they concluded that 'an official majority may well, at the outset, be the best safeguard to democracy and of the wellbeing of the people as a whole'.[155] It has to be said that the armed services, necessarily consulted, were anxious to ensure that defence interests were not being jeopardised by constitutional change, and perhaps with this in mind the governor and the Colonial Office did not revise their thinking even after the July City Council elections and the AACR's triumph.[156]

The governor's announcement on 3 November 1945 that a legislative council was to be created was a remarkable indication of how far and how fast the unholy alliance of political lobbying had driven the colonial authorities. In the Colonial Office it was claimed that this commitment was 'a most important development in the history of Gibraltar'.[157] Nevertheless, Gibraltar's Legislative Council was not formally opened until late in 1950. Among the several causes of the agonis-ing and indeed antagonising delay were that it was thought proper to wait for more of the evacuees to return, and also conflicting views as to how a legislative council should be composed. The composition most favoured at this time by the colonial government was a legislative council of sixteen, presided over by the governor and containing eight official members, two nominated unofficial

153 TNA, CO91/523/3, minute by Dawe, 25 Jan 1945.
154 TNA, CO91/523/3 minute by Dawe, 12 June 1945, and this was also the view of the governor, Eastwood to Stanley, 26 March 1945.
155 TNA, CO91/523/3, Gater to Eastwood, 21 June 1945.
156 TNA, CO91/524/8, Dawe to Creech Jones, 14 Dec 1945.
157 *Gibraltar Chronicle*, 3 Nov 1945, pp. 1, 2; TNA, CO91/524/8, minute by Luke, 19 Nov 1945.

members and just six elected unofficial members.[158] On the whole the moneyed class – contrary to Colonial Office expectations – were relieved that the proposed legislative council would not have an elected majority, fearing after the bruising at the city elections that their prospects were not good and that AACR members in a majority might press for the tax changes they so feared.[159] But the imbalance and limited powers of a legislative council annoyed the AACR, now enjoying a popular mandate as the elected majority on the City Council, and a delegation to the secretary of state later in November 1945 pressed the case for more, and more rapid, constitutional change, even elections to the Executive Council.[160]

Thereafter the whole issue of the legislative council got sucked into the maelstrom created by the hugely expensive permanent housing scheme and the taxation urgently needed to fund it and other public sector services.[161] It is true that the Governor's Meadow project had proved more costly than anyone had anticipated and that Gibraltar citizens had some right to be concerned about how this and its successors were to be funded; but there is also a strong sense that the AACR and others latched on to the housing scheme because it beautifully illustrated their point that decisions potentially affecting all their futures were being made without any direct input into policy making by elected representatives. As described earlier, the City Council, which the AACR dominated, had been excluded from involvement in rehousing projects. Also, the three unofficial members of the governor's Executive Council were, in the first place, only a minority, in the second place, only advisory and, in the third place, nominated by the governor and not elected by the people. Unsurprisingly, then, the housing scandal was the perfectly moulded, snug-in-the-hand, solid oak stick with which to beat the colonial government, and with sufficient length to pummel also the Colonial Office. There should be a legislative council with an elected majority and with more than advisory powers. At the same time, the issue was also alarmingly provocative to the moneyed class, who were well aware, with all these floating rumours of an income tax in the offing, that they too had not been involved in policy making and had never been asked to give their consent to this housing programme (except via their minority membership of the Executive Council), and yet they were the ones most likely to be asked, substantially, to pay for it – and anything else coming down the line. They too had a grievance against government policy makers.

All these political actors had also learnt, and repeatedly used, a telling slogan from the past: no taxation without representation. Taken as a platitude of

---

158 TNA, CO91/523/3, memo by Stanley, 6 Nov 1945.

159 Garcia, *Making of a People*, p. 44.

160 TNA, CO91/523/8, minutes and papers; speech by Triay, *Gibraltar Chronicle*, 2 Oct 1945, p. 4, and 1 Nov 1945, p. 3.

161 *Gibraltar Chronicle*, 7 Dec 1946, p. 5, letters from general secretary of AACR are representative examples.

Britishness, rather than of American revolutionaries, the concept carried clout. One typical statement in February 1946 ran: 'The AACR firmly believe in the principle of British Constitutional Law that there can be no taxation without representation.' But that slogan could be interpreted in contradictory ways. The AACR was pledged to oppose additional taxation until it had secured its principal goal of democratic representation, and therefore it continued: 'The AACR consider that it is for the majority of the people of Gibraltar to decide whether the introduction of income tax is necessary or not, and this can only be done by a Legislative Council with an elected majority.'[162] Similarly the Workers' Union declared its intention in July 1949 to 'oppose the introduction of further taxation . . . until such time as the promised Legislative Council is constituted and approved by the said Council'.[163] Likewise the Gibraltar Confederation of Labour put out a statement in September 1949 that 'No further taxation of any kind' should be imposed 'until there is an adequate popular representation in the management of the colony's finances'.[164] On the other hand, the moneyed class, as best represented by the Chamber of Commerce, used the absence of democratic representation to legitimise their principal aim of blocking (direct) taxation. Of course, it was difficult for them publicly to resist the language of democratic rights, and indeed it could be exploited, so they joined the cry to ensure that their voice was heard.[165] In January 1947, when a legislative council of six official and five unofficial members was in the frame, they were arguing, along with the Exchange Committee and the Workers' Union (now being marginalised by the AACR's Gibraltar Confederation of Labour), that only one of the civilian places on the legislative council should be elected and that otherwise each of the four representative bodies should nominate one of its own.[166] While they sang from the same hymn sheet, there was tonal discord.[167] Nevertheless, Governor Anderson confessed to the Colonial Office that 'the old cry of "no taxation without representation" . . . hits rather a tender spot in my personal armour, for I sympathise with the Boston tea-party very much!'[168]

162 *Gibraltar Chronicle*, 18 Feb 1946, in GGA, MP427/1939.

163 CO91/534/3, Anderson to Colonial Office, 21 July 1949.

164 GGA, MP427/1939, extract from letter from GCL to colonial secretary, 17 Sept 1949.

165 When in January 1952 the income tax ordinance was being debated in the finally arrived legislative council, Albert Isola even then attempted to claim that 'proper' representation was needed before this tax could be levied. He appealed to the principled stand of John Hampden against the tyranny of King Charles I: *Legislative Council*, 25 Jan 1952, pp. 105–6.

166 *Gibraltar Chronicle*, 27 Feb 1947, p. 3.

167 See for an astute and informed dissection TNA, CO91/526/7, Stanley to Luke, 13 March 1946, and enclosures.

168 TNA, CO91/534/3, Anderson to Listowel, 18 July 1949.

Actually, the governor and the Colonial Office were plotting to preserve garrison interests even while bowing to the pressure for democratic reforms. By April 1948 Anderson had given a considerable shove forward to the anticipated reforms. It has to be remembered that he had conceded publicly that direct taxation would only be introduced with the consent of a legislative council.[169] Now, at his insistence, the Colonial Office agreed that a legislative council of eleven would contain the governor and three other ex officio members, two nominees of whom one must be (and both could be) an unofficial and five elected unofficial representatives. That would add up to an unofficial majority, although at least one of them would be nominated. It was also even agreed that up to three of the unofficial members of the Executive Council should henceforth be chosen from the five elected members of the Legislative Council. However, the colonial officials and the Colonial Office had been badly bruised by the AACR and they were all too aware that the AACR had swept the board at the City Council elections in July 1945 and been unopposed in December 1947. Accordingly, it was decided that a system of proportional representation would be used in a deliberate attempt to handicap their prospects at elections to the Legislative Council and to 'secure the best representation of the whole Gibraltarian population'.[170] As a further and inevitable safety measure, the governor would have reserve powers enabling him to reject any Legislative Council proposal and, in an emergency, to pass any measure rejected by them.

Remarkably, all this careful plotting nearly came to nothing in July 1948, when a cabinet committee firmly decided that tiny Gibraltar would become ridiculously over-governed with two partially elected bodies and that a constitution should be contrived to absorb the City Council and the putative legislative council into one. Not the least hostile to that suggestion was the leadership of the AACR, whose control of the City Council gave it powers, responsibilities and status which it was not yet likely to enjoy under a unitary city-state constitution. In the event, after frenetic consultation, minor adjustments and an interruption of four months, the original proposals were adopted in November 1948. The detailed scheme was then polished and eventually presented to the Gibraltar public in August 1949.[171]

Responses followed predictable lines. While all the representative bodies insisted on there being a legislative council, the AACR demanded a fully elected body and also objected to election by proportionate representation, aware of its likely consequences; while the Chamber of Commerce was looking for

169 *Gibraltar Chronicle*, 14 April 1947, p. 3.
170 TNA, CO91/536/5, memo by Bennett, 3 Oct 1947, and see also CO91/536/3 and 536/4. Garcia, *Making of a People*, pp. 51–6, provides a useful narrative.
171 TNA, CAB134/55, minutes of Cabinet Commonwealth Affairs Committee, 26 July and 29 Oct 1948; Garcia, *Making of a People*, pp. 56–62.

safeguards to allow elected members to block money bills, no doubt those containing wicked taxation plans. None of this swayed the colonial authorities, and at long last the signing on 3 February 1950 of the Gibraltar (Legislative Council) Order in Council allowed all adult Gibraltar citizens, male and female, some participation in law making through their five elected representatives on a legislative council. Moreover, by the inclusion of some of those elected as members also of the Executive Council, they were to be given a role on the advisory body which the governor was obliged to consult.[172]

This was a remarkable achievement. The opening of the first Legislative Council by the Duke of Edinburgh on 23 November 1950 was a public and official signalling of that fact.[173] This was not constitutional innovation by stealth. While undoubtedly facilitated by supportive governors, especially in this instance Anderson, and by senior Colonial Office staff sensitive to the need for democratic reform, the energy for change came from civilian politicians. Moreover, given the ambivalent attitude of the Chamber of Commerce towards popular democracy, there can also be no doubt that the AACR was the most powerful engine, drawing upon the kind of electoral support which had enabled it to turn the City Council into its power base. Moreover, by their – on the whole – efficient role in running the City Council, alongside official members, its members had proved themselves responsible public servants. As a result, the rather patronising colonial authorities had become a little less alarmed at allowing such people some say in the government of the colony.

In fact the first elections to the Legislative Council on 8 November 1950, with a modest 53 per cent turnout, did not bring the result which the AACR had wanted. Instead, via the proportional voting system, they provided the representation of 'all sections of the community' which the Colonial Office had hoped to secure as a brake on more radical politicians (though on tax matters it saddled them with a couple of obstructive right-wingers). The AACR, the only overt political party, put forward four candidates.[174] It placed particular emphasis on the need for securing for Gibraltar the welfare state provisions of the UK, plus rent controls, a spreading of the tax burdens and, as a nod

172 Garcia, *Making of a People*, pp. 63–5. The drafting of the order-in-council and other associated legal documents may be followed on TNA, CO91/536/7, and the drafting and passage in July 1950 of the necessary Elections Ordinance, No 15 of 1950, on CO91/543/8 and 543/9. For a succinct summary of the new constitutional order see *Annual Report 1950–51*, pp. 48–50, and for an anticipation of how it would work in practice see Governor Anderson's radio broadcast, *Gibraltar Chronicle*, 19 June 1950, p. 1.

173 The importance of the event is suggested by the photograph in *Annual Report for 1950–51*.

174 A fifth was barred from standing by his employer, at the last moment: *Gibraltar Chronicle*, 21 Oct 1950, p. 8.

towards business, a removal of trade restrictions and the need for economy in government expenditure. Three of its four were elected: Risso, Panayotti and Hassan. But the two Workers' Union candidates, who had also embraced social security, minimum wage and rent control policies were defeated, as was one independent who had peddled a similar line, though with rather more emphasis on controlling public expenditure. The other two elected candidates, Albert Isola and Joseph Patron, both independents, probably achieved their success by placing a good deal of stress on the need for controlling government expenditure, on resisting tax innovations and on liberating trade, though both accepted the need for dealing somehow with the housing problem and for 'reasonable' social security legislation. Patron also went out of his way, by stressing the needs of the family, to woo the women, who were voting for the first time in a Gibraltar election (although all candidates were men). Of the winning candidates, Anderson opted to select only two, Risso and Isola, who had won most first preference votes, for membership also of the Executive Council, one from the left and one from the right, but he nominated Henry Coelho, who had not stood for election, for the third unofficial slot, thus stacking up the number of conservative figures on the body which had the job of advising him on financial and legislative matters.[175]

However, as already indicated, the colonial government itself already had an agenda which included tax revisions as well as further housing programmes, social security legislation and educational reforms, and these conformed most closely to the AACR's ambitions and got an easy ride through the Legislative Council. But Hassan and his colleagues also wanted further constitutional change. This was not an impossible dream, for Governor Anderson had earlier publicly indicated that he regarded the reforms of 1950 as only a 'first step towards responsible self-government, which a succession of Governments in the United Kingdom have declared as one of the aims of Imperial policy as regards all Colonial territories'.[176] This was a commitment which the Colonial Office regarded as overstated and premature, certainly in relation to a fortress colony like Gibraltar.[177] In a well-publicised statement on the opening of the first session of the council Anderson tempered his earlier enthusiasm with a more conventional official view: 'it is . . . very possible that owing to its small size, its strategic

175 Garcia, *Making of a People*, pp. 67–70. For candidates' political programmes see *Gibraltar Chronicle*, 21, 27, 28 and 31 Oct and 2, 4 and 7 Nov 1950. The official electoral returns, demonstrating how the single transferable vote system had operated, were published in *Gibraltar Gazette* and *Gibraltar Chronicle*, 9 Nov 1950.
176 *Gibraltar Chronicle*, 19 June 1950, p. 1.
177 TNA, CO91/542/9, minutes by Fisher and Bennett, 27–8 June 1950, lamenting that Anderson had pretty well promised that Gibraltar would get the kind of constitution operating in Malta – a substantially elected legislative council.

importance and its geographical situation Gibraltar can never hope to achieve fully responsible government'.[178]

Self-government and the Gibraltar constitution, 1969

The AACR was unlikely to leave things alone. Armed with experience gained through its representatives on the Legislative and Executive Councils and by electoral success at the City Council elections in 1950, it and its GCL allies insisted that the elected Legislative Councillors should be in the majority, and that the proportional representation system should be abandoned.[179] The AACR included in its programme for the Legislative Council elections in September 1953, alongside an array of social reform proposals, a demand for staged alterations to the composition of the council, eliminating the nominated members and turning it into an entirely elected body. It may not have been its constitutional scheme which accounts for the election of the three AACR candidates, Hassan, Serfaty and Risso, but it had given the matter an airing. The others elected were Isola, again, and Sergio Triay, one-time radical lawyer who had trekked to the right and who was also appointed with Hassan to the Executive Council. The AACR's political advance was then confirmed at the City Council elections in December and, following the sudden death of Triay, by the return of another AACR member at a Legislative Council by-election in October 1954.[180]

One further trigger brought constitutional issues to a head, and, unsurprisingly, this related to taxes. The administration of Governor Harold Redman, who had barely arrived in office, had attempted in July 1955 to meet a sudden shortfall in revenue, caused by Spanish obstruction to trade, by whipping emergency import duties through the Legislative Council. When the AACR opted to oppose such action and sided with those councillors regularly hostile to taxation, the governor found himself heading a minority – and opted to use his reserved powers to ram the measure through. This assertion of colonial authority over the elected representatives could not have been better devised for those seeking constitutional advancement. It reunited, albeit temporarily, the unholy alliance of political right and left, combining those like Isola and the Chamber of Commerce, who were particularly agitated by the matter of taxation, with those like Hassan and the AACR, who were particularly concerned

---

178 *Gibraltar Chronicle*, 16 Dec 1950, p. 2.
179 For GCL manifestos incorporating constitutional demands see CO926/21, 'Political situation reports, 1951–53'.
180 Garcia, *Making of a People*, pp. 75–7, 82; *Gibraltar Chronicle*, 12 Sept, pp. 4–5, for electoral programmes, and 17 Sept 1953, p. 1 for the results. Triay had claimed that income tax was illegal and that a bill to regulate wages and conditions of employment was 'reminiscent of the Gestapo': *Gibraltar Chronicle*, 21 Nov 1953, p. 2.

about the manner of its imposition. Though Redman had acted without prior consultation, the Colonial Office, through gritted teeth, felt obliged to back him up and, in response, all the elected members of the Legislative Council and the two AACR members of the Executive Council resigned. Not only did this bring constitutional government to a screeching halt, but it obliged a secretary of state, Lennox-Boyd, to negotiate face to face with the disaffected in Gibraltar. The deal stitched up propelled still further forward the intrusion of civilians into the governing of Gibraltar.[181]

In the first instance it was agreed that governors would be obliged to consult the Colonial Office before daring to use their reserved powers. It was also agreed that the finance committee of the Legislative Council, with its civilian members, would henceforth review revenue and therefore taxation proposals and no longer just expenditure plans. But more important, it provoked the AACR to demand in October 1955 a serious revision of the 1950 constitution. It has to be noted that early in 1954 the colonial secretary had been talking informally to local political leaders about possible lines of future constitutional development. He had indicated his own willingness, for instance, to see the governor replaced in the Legislative Council with an independent speaker, thus making him more of a 'Constitutional Monarch'; to alter the composition of the Executive Council; and indeed to transfer more responsibilities to the City Council and to make it still more a body run by elected civilians. To that extent, the colonial secretary and a chastened governor were receptive to AACR proposals.[182] The AACR itself of course favoured increasing the duties and civilian membership of the City Council, though it was in practice only their other proposals which were to resemble later changes. Elected members should form the majority on the Legislative Council but, more radically, four of them should be appointed as ministers to supervise government departments and they, plus the governor and three officials, should constitute a council of ministers in place of the Executive Council and be collectively responsible to the Legislative Council. The model implicit in this was, of course, Westminster, and the sovereignty of the (civilian) people was the underlying political philosophy. It was this latter aspect that alarmed many of the other civilian politicians to whom the colonial secretary put the proposals in a consultation exercise. The old battle lines which divided those superficially rooting jointly for constitutional evolution were marvellously exposed by Isola, who 'confessed he didn't really believe in democracy', and Coelho, who objected precisely because if the reforms were introduced 'The

181   The episode is well told by Garcia, *Making of a People*, pp. 85–96. The documentation includes press reports in *Gibraltar Chronicle, Gibraltar Post* and *Vox, Proceedings of the Legislative Council* and TNA, CO926/142 and /281.
182   TNA, CO926/279, Bates to Morris, 13 March 1954, Redman to Lennox-Boyd, 21 Nov 1955.

government would . . . become subordinate to the people'. Even Huart, representing the Workers' Union, was sceptical of the need yet for major reforms. It is true that after the recent controversy all favoured making elected members the majority on the Legislative Council, but certainly some wanted ex officio members to remain in the majority on the Executive Council, no doubt as a necessary block to AACR radicals, and most were pretty horrified at the notion of a council of ministers, arguing that no one could be a minister and 'be engaged in either business or a profession at the same time'. Probably they also feared letting Hassan and his chums get too much power. To be fair, Hassan himself withdrew that proposal as impracticable 'at present'.[183]

However, there were some immediate reforms, announced in July 1956. Elected civilians were entrusted with more responsibility for executive action in the City Council and their majority was to be increased by eliminating one of the nominated members. At the same time the legislative authority of the elected members on the Legislative Council was to be raised by increasing their number from five to seven, thus making them the majority in a council of thirteen. In addition, an independent civilian speaker in a suit was in due course to be appointed (effected in June 1958) to replace a military governor in a uniform. And finally, civilian input into Executive Council deliberations was to be increased by raising their number to four, making them equal to the number of officials, the governor holding the balance.[184] Not surprisingly, the AACR claimed responsibility for these constitutional changes when, in September 1956, it again went to the polls and again promised more constitutional change, though again it is possible that the electorate who returned its four candidates was more interested in the social security and social reform measures in its programme. It is also likely that the voters who returned the other three elected were more bothered about the probable costs and possible effects of 'big government' on their incomes and trade.[185]

That still left on the agenda the notion of elected members of the Legislative Council having some executive roles in government, on the Westminster model. Clearly this was something which ambitious AACR leaders like Hassan favoured, in spite of objections from others that this could not be done by those who also had businesses to run and would or could lead to serious clashes between public and private interests. In fact this was another AACR aspiration that the colonial government had already shown that it was prepared to meet halfway. Since 1954 a few unofficial (not necessarily elected) members of the Executive Council

183 GGA, MP349A, AACR 'Memorandum on constitutional reform', Oct 1955, written responses, minutes.
184 TNA, CO926/279 and /280.
185 For election campaign and results see *Gibraltar Chronicle*, especially 15 and 20 Sept 1956, and Garcia, *Making of a People*, pp. 100–1. The turnout was 58 per cent.

had been personally attached to government departments – like 'work experience' youngsters – to give them a better understanding of government business.
Beginning with the Lands and Works Department and then the Education and
Medical Departments, this was now extended by the governor and the colonial
secretary, sensitive at least to AACR demands for closer civilian involvement in
government and in spite of the concerns of the Colonial Office. From November
1957, initially six and later eight of the nine unofficial members (seven of them
elected) on the Legislative Council, and therefore not just those also on the
Executive Council, were assigned to government departments. Hassan alone was
excepted, on the grounds that he was busy enough running the City Council.
The chosen ones were to be called 'members' (not ministers). Although there
were some difficulties in adjusting the relationship between the members and
the official heads of the departments, the system did provide that 'educational
experience' which the colonial authorities felt was needed, and it did shield them
from some criticism by requiring legislative councillors as 'members' to respond
to many of the probings and proposals of their councillor colleagues. On the
other hand, for the AACR this was just an appetiser, a snack on the way to a fully
satisfying menu of ministerial responsibility.[186]

In June 1958 Hassan pressed the colonial government to accept, among
other changes, an extension of the life of each Legislative Council from three to
five years, something the colonial secretary also already favoured, and the dis-
continuation of the hallowed colonial government practice, in his eyes deroga-
tory of local self-government, of sending the annual estimates to the Colonial
Office for scrutiny before approval. The colonial secretary, Darrell Bates, and
the new governor, General Keightley, were comfortable with these suggestions.
Bates himself had proposed the first, though it took longer to secure Treasury
assent to the second. But they were opposed to another AACR demand for the
establishment of that council of ministers Hassan had proposed in October
1955, ostensibly on the grounds that insufficient responsible civilians could
be found to take on – or who could afford to take on – full-time ministerial
duties. They were no doubt strengthened in that persuasion by other senior
civilian politicians, the independent members of the Executive Council, who
shared that view. No doubt too, inherited concerns about garrison security
inhibited the granting of responsible government. The only concessions were

---

186 See the analysis in Garcia, *Making of a People*, pp. 98, 102, 105, 109–13. The
   origins and the system in practice can be traced in TNA, CO926/280 and /768,
   and *Proceedings of the Legislative Council*. For press reports of legislative council
   meetings, for example the 'tennis match' question and answer exchanges between
   councillors, see for example *Gibraltar Chronicle*, 28 Feb 1959, p. 2, and 3 May
   1959, pp. 1, 6, and for the allocation of members to departments see 13 Oct 1959,
   pp. 1, 2.

to name the leader of the largest party in the Legislative Council (inevitably Hassan) as chief member, to require the administration to consult him on policy matters and, in a clarification of the relationship between members and 'their' departments, to give them a status equal to that of their official civil service heads.[187]

Although in the 1959 Legislative Council elections the AACR secured only three seats, Hassan was, outstandingly, the first-choice preference, and since three of the other four had declared themselves as independents and the fourth was a Workers' Union representative, the AACR rightly considered itself in pole position and its agenda for political evolution the only one on the table.[188] Hence Hassan made a point at the opening of the new council, in October 1959, of indicating that more changes were expected.[189] One change which did not occur was an early end to the City Council, although this was still being much mooted in London and in Gibraltar and was the strong recommendation, on efficiency and economy grounds, of a thorough official inquiry completed in October 1960. Political wisdom determined that this was not the occasion to threaten that AACR stronghold.[190]

However, Hassan himself did not formulate in detail further proposals for change until September 1961, when he argued that much of the day-to-day work of the Executive Council should instead be diverted to a council of members under the chairmanship of the chief member and made up of the unofficial members of the Executive Council and, as appropriate, any officials and other members of the Legislative Council who had departmental briefs. It was argued that, informally, such a system had already come into operation to prepare detailed recommendations for the Executive Council. Formalisation of the practice would, in effect, enhance the role of the civilian members and Hassan was quite explicit that this should, in due course, lead to the council of ministers which he and the AACR had long since been advocating. Provided that the governor determined what went to such a council and that recommendations came back to him for approval, neither the governor nor the Colonial Office saw reason to object, and it was also announced in September 1962 that in due course an extra unofficial member would be added to the Executive Council, as

187 Garcia, *Making of a People*, pp. 114–17, and TNA, CO926/768 and /769 provide the narrative. Some of the negotiations were done by Lennox-Boyd during a visit to Gibraltar, *Gibraltar Chronicle*, 7 and 10 Jan 1959, and see announcement of the decisions 30 July 1959, p. 1.

188 For the election manifestos and results see *Gibraltar Chronicle*, 12, 15, 17, 19, 21, 22 and 24 Sept 1959. Dorothy Ellicott, who had been the first woman City Councillor, became the first woman Legislative Councillor. The turnout was 66 per cent.

189 *Gibraltar Chronicle*, 17 Oct 1959, p. 3.

190 Garcia, *Making of a People*, pp. 119–21, 123–4; TNA, CO926/996.

Hassan had also requested.[191] While the governor would himself choose all five members, this would still for the first time put the unofficials in the majority, comparable to the majorities which elected civilians also held on the Legislative Council and the City Council.

However, before this additional appointment could be made and while the council of members was gaining experience, Hassan and the AACR pressed in August 1963 for further changes to bring closer the (largely) Westminster model of government which he and his group had long since had in mind, and which in fact the colonial authorities had also come to recognise as the likely outcome of further and inevitable constitutional change. On receipt of the AACR proposals, the governor first solicited responses from all other active civilian politicians, and then, in April 1964, the Colonial Office despatched a minister of state, Lord Lansdowne, for face-to-face talks in Gibraltar with all interested parties. This resulted in new constitutional arrangements which, if anything, went beyond the AACR's immediate programme. The Gibraltar (Constitution) Order in Council 1964, signed in July, was a commitment not just to fertilise the growth of democratic representation and water the seeds of responsible government, but also to breathe life into that other culture of British political practice, party politics. In the first place the elected members of the Legislative Council would be increased from seven to eleven (the AACR had hoped at most for ten), the nominated members were to be eliminated (the AACR had not yet pressed for this) and the official members were to be reduced from three to two (attorney-general and financial secretary) by removing the colonial secretary (recently renamed chief secretary and now called permanent secretary and soon to be branded deputy governor) from the council and leaving the direction of business instead to the so-called chief minister; and he would be appointed by the governor, rather like a British prime minister, as the person commanding most support in the Legislative Council. In addition, on the executive side was the further elevation of the governor into the role of constitutional monarch, followed by the transformation of his Executive Council into the Gibraltar Council on which, under his presidency, would henceforth sit five (no longer just four) elected members of the Legislative Council and only four officials; and this body was largely expected merely to approve the recommendations of the former council of members, henceforth council of ministers. This council of ministers, effectively a cabinet, would be presided over by the chief minister. It would comprise those elected members of the Legislative Council who had been appointed by the governor – but on the advice of the chief minister – to run government departments, and they would owe loyalty to the chief minister and

191 TNA, CO926/1227, Keightley to Maudling, 25 Jan 1961, enclosing Hassan to
     Colonial Secretary, 19 Sept 1961, and Sandys to Ward, 13 Sept 1962, and report in
     Gibraltar Post, 25 Sept 1962.

be bound by the conventions of collective responsibility. And finally, the number of elected Legislative Council members was to be increased so that, besides those chosen as ministers, there should be enough Legislative Councillors left over to play the role of 'loyal opposition'.[192]

There had been some civilian concerns that there would be too few people willing or able to stand for office, and especially to serve as ministers. Government was also worried that eleven members elected from a small electorate by proportional representation might allow in 'extremists and cranks'.[193] Nevertheless, the risk was taken. In the 1964 election, with a turnout of 76 per cent and 10,106 voters, one candidate was returned with just 52 votes in the first round and only 681 overall. Since the electorate unwittingly chose just five AACR members and six independents (who were not all speaking to each other) the formation of a council of six ministers able to 'command the house', with the backing of the two ex officio members, was a tricky business.[194] Nevertheless it was effected; Hassan became Gibraltar's first chief minister, and the new Legislative Council opened with a composition described by the local press, in indicative terms, as 'government-opposition based on the Westminster pattern'.[195]

There was unfinished business. In October 1965, but not to report until January 1968, a constitutional committee of the Legislative Council set to work. On its agenda was the relationship between the Legislative Council and the City Council. The latter had been protected for some time by the AACR leadership as the one truly democratically organised institution in Gibraltar, but its survival for so long was against the wishes of many other prominent local politicians, to say nothing of the colonial authorities and the Colonial Office.[196] With the reforms of 1964 in the bag, Hassan and company finally agreed to let it go.[197] Subsequently, following further talks in Gibraltar in July 1968 involving another junior minister, Lord Shepherd from the Department of Commonwealth Affairs, the Gibraltar Constitution Order in Council 1969

192 On debates and developments see TNA, CO926/1865, /1866 and /1868, and *Gibraltar Chronicle*, 8, 11 April, 10 Aug 1964.

193 TNA, CO926/1865, esp. Ward to Sandys, 16 Nov 1963.

194 TNA, CO926/2055, for correspondence, and *Gibraltar Chronicle*, 18–29 Aug, 1–12 Sept 1964, for manifestos and results, and 18 Sept for the formation of the new 'party government'.

195 *Gibraltar Chronicle*, 17 Oct 1964, p. 1, and see 31 Oct 1964, p. 1 for the formation by independents of a 'shadow government', and 12 Dec 1964, p. 1 for an example of it in operation.

196 A motion to merge the Legislative Council and City Council was (just) passed by the former in Feb 1964, against the votes of the AACR members: *Gibraltar Chronicle*, 29 Feb 1964, pp. 1–2.

197 *Gibraltar Chronicle*, 7 Nov 1964, p. 8; and for report on the last City Council meeting, 15 Aug 1969, pp. 1, 3.

was signed in May. Major changes were introduced. The 'city of Gibraltar', no longer tarred by the unfashionable name of 'colony', became in effect a unitary state, and the City Council disappeared. Henceforth there would be instead a single executive body (the council of ministers), drawing its personnel from and being accountable to a House of Assembly, a legislature of fifteen elected members, plus (still) two unelected officials. Elections were to be held, normally, every four years. The system of proportional representation, which the Colonial Office had imposed in order to prevent a single group from dominating the old Legislative Council, was replaced by the block vote system used in the City Council elections, now adopted with the intention of securing stable majority rule in the House of Assembly and encouraging a party political system. This alteration, it should be stressed, was not imposed by London, but was the result of serious domestic debate between Gibraltar's local politicians, another marker of self-government.[198]

There were, however, limits to self-government. Least important in practice, the governor retained his reserved powers and could refuse assent to any bill passed by the assembly. However, Queen Anne was now dead in Gibraltar too, and this reservation was kept very much in reserve. More seriously, the responsibilities of civilian ministers were confined to what were described as 'defined domestic matters', which, while extensive, nevertheless indicated that such matters were being delegated down to the elected government by the colonial authorities.[199] It also followed, of course, that the governor remained responsible for internal security and for external defence and foreign affairs, though in effect only as the agent of Whitehall. Gibraltar to that extent remained a colony. It had been repeatedly said, even by most radical advocates of change, that Gibraltar did not seek the status of an independent nation-state.[200] Apart from the possibly abstract legal obstacles derived from the Utrecht treaty, there were immensely real threats from Spain which discouraged such an outcome. Hence, in reaction, the referendum in 1967 and the insistence by Gibraltarians on retaining the link with the UK, at the price of a subordinate status. Hence also a developing suspicion of British intentions which obliged the British government to stitch into

198 Garcia, *Making of a People*, pp. 153–6; *Gibraltar Chronicle*, 31 May 1969, p. 1; *Vox*, 3 Jan 1969, p. 2; GGA, MP 349B, 'Review of the Electoral System'.

199 A listing of 'defined domestic matters' was published in *Gibraltar Gazette*, 31 Oct 1969, copy with other relevant papers in GGA, Government Secretariat files, 349E, 1968–72.

200 For example see the statement issued by all unofficial members of the legislative council, dismissing the idea of 'independence': *Gibraltar Chronicle*, 11 April 1964, pp. 1–2. The editors of the small-circulation radical newspaper *Social Action* wished sovereignty to be fully vested in the people of Gibraltar but seemed unsure as to whether or how that might be brought about: Jan 1967, p. 3, March/April 1968, p. 1, May/June 1968, p. 7, Jan 1969, p. 6.

the preamble of the 1969 constitution a guarantee that sovereignty over Gibraltar would never be handed over to some other state (perhaps meaning Spain . . .) unless this was the freely expressed desire of a majority of the Gibraltar people.[201] Hence also the Spanish retaliatory action which rapidly followed. Spain's closure of the frontier gates in June 1969 truly separated Gibraltar from its former hinterland and made the partition of 1704 real on the ground.

Conclusion

It was a long haul for Gibraltarians, and has perhaps been so for readers, to get from the still essentially autocratic government regime of the 1940s to the internally self-governing democracy of the late 1960s. Some of the qualities of the transition deserve acknowledgment. It was accomplished without the alarming breakdown between governors and governed which affected Malta, Cyprus and many other parts of the colonial empire in the 1950s and 1960s. Much noise in street demonstrations and public meetings accompanied the steps to change, but there was no violence – except, once, by Gibraltarian civilians against their own. In April 1968 a handful of so-called 'Doves' argued in favour of a negotiated settlement with Spain and, so it was revealed, held talks with the Spanish foreign minister. When their premises and property were being attacked, the governor felt compelled to call out the troops to restore order. But there seems subsequently to have been some local embarrassment and criticism of this intemperate outbreak of intolerance, and certainly it would scarcely have registered in the annals of decolonisation elsewhere.[202]

That relations in Gibraltar did not break down owes much to the concessions to organised civilian political opinion which, bit by bit, the colonial and imperial governments made. With so much else going on in these decades, some of it truly frightful, those in charge had no wish to add Gibraltar to the list of places where the British were not wanted. But at least, equally and arguably more importantly, politicians and public opinion in Gibraltar were themselves self-limiting in how far and how fast they wanted to go. It is essential to remember that not all those politically active in mid twentieth-century Gibraltar were anxious to rush towards popular democratic institutions, any more than had been the propertied and moneyed classes of mid nineteenth-century Britain. Clearly, by the later period it was not easy in Gibraltar (though effected by terrible violence a step away across the frontier) to deny democracy in public, but it was certainly possible to try so to affect the forms of democratic progression as to limit and to

---

201 Garcia, *Making of a People*, pp. 150–6.
202 Garcia, *Making of a People*, pp. 151–2 provides one among several accounts, and see *Gibraltar Chronicle* and an insistence in *Social Action* May/June 1968, p. 6, that 'In a democracy the minority views must be tolerated however repugnant'.

delay certain feared outcomes, especially those likely to affect the trading and taxation interests of those in business. Even Hassan and the AACR, bidding for the centre ground and the attention of the moneyed class, eventually lost, with their modest domestic programmes, some of their working-class support.[203]

But most inhibiting of taking extremist measures to push things along was, of course, Spain, and what was wrong with Spain was that it was not British. During the 1950s and 1960s, when Spanish pressure for the undoing of 1704 built up, the differences between Spain and Gibraltar as polities and economies became more marked than ever before. However intimate economically the two communities either side of the border remained before its closure in 1969, the fact remains that, in other respects, especially after Franco's aggressive reaction to the Queen's visit in 1954, Gibraltar had become more British, not less. Increasingly, every constitutional and administrative step in the twentieth century had inserted British political institutions and practices and associated political values into Gibraltar – the City Council with its mayor, elected members of a legislature, civilian members and then ministers in the executive, a judiciary administering laws mainly modelled on British practice. Repeatedly, allegiance to the monarchy as head of state was publicly performed and not just privately asserted.[204] The honours which the crown and imperial government could distribute to loyal subjects were willingly offered and gratefully received, for example in 1925 by Sir Alexander Mosley, former President of the Chamber of Commerce and an unofficial member of the Executive Council, but perhaps best epitomised by the knighthood bestowed in 1963 on the man who had most demanded constitutional change, Sir Joshua Hassan.[205] The more that Franco's authoritarian, intolerant and military-led government insisted that Gibraltar should be reunited with a province across the frontier which had a far lower standard of living and poorer social services, the more, inevitably, did the still commonly Spanish-speaking and largely Roman Catholic population of Gibraltar insist that they were British.

During the twenty-five years after the ending of the war the British authorities could be seen, according to one interpretation, bowing to an irresistible demand for self-government. Or perhaps, more persuasively, the British, reacting

---

203 Garcia, *Making of a People*, pp. 202–4.
204 Constantine, 'Monarchy and constructing identity in "British" Gibraltar'; K. Dodds, D. Lambert and B. Robison, 'Loyalty and royalty: Gibraltar, the 1953–54 royal tour and the geopolitics of the Iberian peninsula', *Twentieth Century British History*, 18 (2007), 365–90.
205 *Annual Report for 1925*, p. 3; Jackson and Cantos, *Fortress to Democracy*, p. 98; for other awards see, annually, the New Year's honours lists in *Gibraltar Chronicle*; and for an interpretation of honours in the British imperial world see D. Cannadine, *Ornamentalism: How the British Saw their Empire* (London: Allen Lane, Penguin Press, 2001), pp. 85–101.

to pressure but sensing limited risk, managed to incorporate civilians into government policy making and administration. Moreover, through locally raised rates and taxes the British ensured that Gibraltarians largely paid for more of what they received. By this reading, civilian politicians became responsible for the internal management of a British colony, but without putting at risk that feature of the Rock which had kept the British there for so long: the fortress. It was confidently suggested in the Colonial Office in 1960 that 'one could go pretty far along the road towards responsible government without endangering UK interests'.[206] Likewise, in 1962 Governor Sir Charles Keightley supported his argument for conceding more power internally to civilian politicians by reviewing the consequences of the constitutional concessions so far made. The 'position of Gibraltar as a fortress', he argued, 'has, far from being weakened, been much strengthened by these changes'.[207]

206 TNA, CO926/769, minute by Huijsman, 1 June 1960, reprinted in Hyam and Louis, *Conservative Government and End of Empire*, I, p. 797.
207 TNA, CO926/1227, Keightley to secretary of state, 28 June 1962.

11

Towards the future: constructing a Gibraltarian identity

History does not stop, and certainly the political destiny of Gibraltar inter-nally and externally was, in May 1969, still to be determined. Accordingly, subsequent political developments are reviewed as an introduction to this final chapter. The new constitution was certainly an important step, confirming and extending Gibraltar's democratic character. Each elector was now able to vote for up to eight candidates for the fifteen elected seats in the House of Assembly, from whom were selected, by the chief minister, those who were appointed to office and who were ultimately accountable to the electorate. Elections were to take place at least every four years – though a house could be dissolved earlier, at the discretion of the chief minister, as occurred in 1972 and again in 2003. Only five men held the office of chief minister under the 1969 constitution. Following a complex result in the first election in July 1969, Major Robert Peliza, leader of the Integration With Britain Party, was the first, from August 1969 to June 1972, but he needed the support of an independent group to secure a working majority.[1] There followed a sequence of outright electoral victories which placed Sir Joshua Hassan and the Association for the Advancement of Civil Rights back in office, from June 1972 until his retirement in December 1987, to be succeeded by Adolfo Canepa until the next election in March 1988. This was won by Joe Bossano, leading the Gibraltar Socialist Labour Party (GSLP), who also triumphed in 1992, winning an astonishing 73 per cent of the vote. But in May 1996, the Gibraltar Social Democrats, standing to the right, won the necessary eight seats to form a government under Peter Caruana, who repeated

1   A graphic contemporary account of the election result and the formation of the Peliza government is told in *Gibraltar Chronicle*, 31 July–7 Aug 1969, and for histori-cal analyses of this and later political developments see W.G.F. Jackson, *The Rock of the Gibraltarians* (Gibraltar: Gibraltar Books, 2001) which covers the period up to 1985; W.G.F. Jackson and F.J. Cantos, *From Fortress to Democracy: the Political Biography of Sir Joshua Hassan* (Grendon: Gibraltar Books, 1995) up to 1988; J.J. Garcia, *Gibraltar: the Making of a People* (Gibraltar: Panorama, 2002, 1st edn 1994), up to 1991; M. Harvey, *Gibraltar, a History* (Staplehurst: Spellmount, 1996), up to 1995.

the success with over 50 per cent of the vote in February 2000 and again in November 2003.

Over the same period and for far shorter periods in power, twelve governors held office. They were, of course, representatives of the crown and agents of the British government. Although they often functioned as if they were constitutional monarchs and titular heads of state, it would be inaccurate to imply that governors had become insignificant. They retained authority over some domestic administrative affairs, including, for example, a contested control over the Gibraltar police, and they were certainly responsible for external defence, for this remained a military base. True, the army garrison was being scaled down until it became largely the Gibraltar Regiment (Royal Gibraltar Regiment from 1999) which had first been formed in 1958 (though derived from the Gibraltar Defence Force, a territorial army regiment established in 1939) and was raised locally by conscription until 1971.[2] But Gibraltar was still of considerable importance as a surveillance and communications centre and with a dockyard and airbase available for NATO forces, even though Ministry of Defence personnel numbered just a few hundred by the turn of the century.

In addition, of course, the governor was an agent in the conduct of external diplomacy, principally with Spain, before and after the reopening of the frontier in 1985, although in the age of rapid communications the man on the spot was more often subordinate to some jetted-in British government minister – who was also in direct contact with his or her opposite number in Madrid. These later decades were cut through with a sequence of Anglo-Spanish talks, highly controversial locally, beginning in September 1966. They led, snail-like, to the Lisbon Agreement in April 1980, when the parties agreed to try and resolve the dispute over sovereignty; to the Brussels Agreement in November 1984, which established a negotiating process on specific issues of dispute (and the full reopening of the frontier and the acknowledgement of Spain's EEC rights in Gibraltar and vice versa); to an agreement in 2002 that joint sovereignty might be the solution; and, failing that, to the establishment in 2004 of the 'Trilateral Forum of Dialogue on Gibraltar' out of which in 2006 came the Córdoba Agreement addressing such matters as pensions for former Spanish workers in Gibraltar, cross-border communications and use of the airport – though not the big question of sovereignty. From November 1977 Gibraltar's civilian politicians were sometimes but not always present, but from 2004 they became principals in such talks.[3]

2 www.1rg.gi/history/home; 'The Royal Gibraltar Regiment', *Regiment: the Military Heritage Collection*, 62 (2004); GGL, 'Gibraltar Regiment Newspaper Cuttings'.
3 For Córdoba Agreement see www.gibnet.com/texts/trip_1.htm. On Anglo-Spanish relations see D.S. Morris and R.H. Haigh, *Britain, Spain and Gibraltar 1945–90*

Meanwhile, in 1999 the UK government had invited all British Dependent Territories (see below) to submit proposals for constitutional reform. In Gibraltar this generated in January 2002 a report by a select committee of the House of Assembly, much subsequent debate, and extended negotiations with London. These deliberations led eventually to proposals for change, accepted by the Foreign Office in March 2006, which received the unanimous approval of the House of Assembly in October. Most important, the revised constitution reversed the relationship between the governor's authority and that of the elected government. This version defined and therefore confined the responsibilities of the governor largely to external affairs, plus still some aspects of internal security and public service appointments which were going to remain contentious. On the other hand, the constitution no longer restricted elected ministers to 'defined domestic matters' and instead left such responsibilities to their discretion, undefined and therefore elastic. However, in spite of official reassurances, some electors seem to have felt that the commitment to retaining British sovereignty was insufficiently secure, while others believed the new constitution did not go far enough in explicitly allowing the Gibraltar people to determine their future. Hence doubts and dissent in a referendum campaign whose result on 30 November 2006 was a far less robust endorsement than in previous referenda, 60 per cent in favour but on a turnout of only 60 per cent. But on that basis and by an order-in-council, the new constitution came into operation on 2 January 2007.[4] This was followed by an election on 11 October 2007, which Caruana and the Gibraltar Social Democrats again won, with 49 per cent of the vote on an 81 per cent turnout.[5]

Among the modifications made, the House of Assembly adopted British nomenclature and became the Gibraltar Parliament, ordinances henceforth became acts, each voter was to have ten votes, the number of elected seats was increased from fifteen to seventeen, the two ex officio members (the attorney-general and the financial and development secretary) were removed, and the Gibraltar Council, the governor's former executive council and in effect his advisory body, was deemed redundant and was abolished. Moreover, although the UK government stated that the Treaty of Utrecht prevented Gibraltar from becoming an independent state, British and Gibraltar ministers were equally and

Footnote 5 (*cont.*)

  (London: Routledge, 1992), P. Gold, *Gibraltar: British or Spanish?* (London: Routledge, 2005) and G. Archibald, 'Gibraltar: Attempts to Solve an International Problem, 1963–2002' (PhD thesis, Ulster University, 2006).

4 For the constitution see www.gibraltar.gov.gi/constitution/constitution_index.htm, and for an analysis of the debate see www.gibraltarnewsonline.com/2006/12/01/referendum-gives-clear-majority-approval-for-new-constitution-in-gibraltar/.

5 For the election of October 2007 see www.gibraltar.gov.gi/Election2007.pdf and *Gibraltar Chronicle*, 12–13 Oct 2007.

publicly adamant at the United Nations that this constitution stripped away the last vestiges of Gibraltar's colonial status.[6]

Nominally, indeed, Gibraltar had long since ceased to be a British colony. That was a territorial status and a title which had been battered by the virtuous majority of non-colonial or former colonial states on UN bodies, particularly the Committee on Decolonisation, and by the very remarkable shift, in a generation, from an imperial to a post-colonial global culture. It required for the UK not just the accelerated decolonisation of most of its colonial 'properties' but a shift in linguistic gears and a renaming of the survivors as British Dependent Territories in 1981 and as British Overseas Territories in 2002. Gibraltar, the only one in Europe, was affected along with the other small red bits of the former empire, of which there remain technically fourteen, including Bermuda, St Helena and the Falkland Islands.[7] It will be recalled that these scattered spaces had conventionally been regarded in Whitehall as too small and too devoid of economic resources ever to be independent, self-governing nation-states, but in the case of Gibraltar, given Spanish objections, that seemed to the British government and to many in Gibraltar an even less likely outcome. However, and of very great importance, it was not just outside opinion which resented the status and title of colony. Strong objections to the colonial reality as well as to the brand had also been expressed for some time by politicians and public in Gibraltar, from which the constitution agreed in 2006 was one important outcome. What was being insisted upon was a different, a distinctive and, in aspiration, a *national* identity.

What that was and how it came about have been among the principal points of inquiry in previous chapters, and constitute the theme for this concluding discussion. In particular, we need to consider how the past – and remembrance of the past, which is not the same thing – and conditions in the present have created among the civilian population a sense of themselves as a distinctive community, different from Spain and, indeed, different from Britain also. Usually such considerations are debated in relation to the national identity of a nation-state, which in the case of a place and a people not internationally recognised as a nation generates other interesting issues, especially in a world in which the sovereignty of nation-states is supposedly leaking away, corroded by economic and cultural globalisation and supranational institutions.

---

6 www.gibraltar.gov.gi/constitution/new_constitution/ConstitutionExplanatory Booklet.pdf, 'A New Constitution for Gibraltar', Nov 2006; *Gibraltar Chronicle*, 16 Oct 2007.

7 The fourteen included military bases in Cyprus over which Britain retains sovereignty.

Politics, Britishness and national identity

It is advantageous in considering the formation of a Gibraltarian national identity to be aware of the parallel experiences of other peoples. For example, it is
well understood that distinctive social identities, including those of nations, are
formed not merely or even mainly internally, but by external engagement with
that which is described conventionally as the 'other'. Of course, social identities
within a community are invariably plural and contested, for example by gender,
by social class, by region. That which can most obviously override internal difference with a stronger sense of common identity is confrontation with those who
are deemed to be outsiders. It is the shock (or pleasure) of detecting difference
which sharpens the sense of self. We know who we are because we know who we
are not. Those others are 'beyond the pale', to use a phrase derived from the medieval distinction between the 'civilised' Anglo-Norman region of Ireland around
Dublin from the Irish 'other' outside. That sense of difference is most obviously
generated in time of war. It has been persuasively argued that the formation of
a British national identity, as distinct from and yet subsuming English, Welsh
and Scottish identities and other regional identities in the UK, was accelerated
in the eighteenth century by the repeated wars between the 'British' state and
France, a rival military and imperial 'other'.[8] But it was also characteristic of the
resulting British national identity to take a pride in the particular internal political and administrative structures of the British state. The history of Britain as
commonly written up, and read, in the twentieth century was the evolutionary
story of constitutional monarchy, parliamentary government, democratic representation, accountable administrations, integrity in public life, social services
and ultimately the welfare state.[9] Historical myths are about forgetting as well as
about remembering the past, and they become sanitised by contrast with equally
simplified but negative representations of other polities, like absolutist or bru-
tally revolutionary France or a Germany supposedly characterised by aggressive
militarism (and worse), a 'warfare state'.

One obvious starting point for understanding the development of a collective sense of self in Gibraltar is its history until recently of close political and
administrative management by British imperial governments. In fact, the story
of 'British' Gibraltar over the past three hundred years has been pretty much
coterminous with the rise and fall of the British Empire, there being little enough
empire in 1704 (settlements on the coast of North America and some scratchings

---

8 L. Colley, *Britons: Forging the Nation 1707–1837* (New Haven: Yale, 1992) and
'Britishness and Otherness: an Argument', *Journal of British Studies*, 31 (1992),
309–29.
9 See, for example, the best-selling 'Whig' history of G.M. Trevelyan, *History of
England* (London: Longmans, Green, 1926).

inland, dots in the West Indies, a fragile presence in south Asia) and likewise just a short list of British overseas territories at the close. But it would obviously be absurd to imply that the ebbing of formal British control over what had once been a quarter of the world's land surface left behind no residue. One huge legacy from the 'British World' has been institutions, and in particular instruments of government and administration. The emphasis placed on law courts, law making and legal administration in this study should have been sufficient to make plain the fact that these institutional features and these forms of administrative practice were early introduced into Gibraltar. Law, properly formulated by ordinances and orders-in-council, elbowed aside mere garrison orders and arbitrary rule. The sequence of charters of justice in the eighteenth and early nineteenth centuries introduced courts of law modelled pretty much on British legal practice, as were the laws themselves, supplanting Spanish customs. Britishness was embodied not just in the Supreme Court, but in the employment of grand and petty juries and subsequently, just as in England and Wales, of the latter only. Small in numbers but influential in practice were Gibraltar lawyers – the Triays, Hassans and others – who learnt their law and honed their legal skills in London and imported them to Gibraltar.

Increasingly too, law making was not just a matter of ordinances devised by colonial governors and Colonial Office and, at best, put out as drafts for consultation. From 1922 through the Executive Council, from 1950 through the Legislative Council, from 1969 through the House of Assembly and since 2007 in the Gibraltar Parliament, formal scrutinising institutions were incorporated into law making. It has also been shown that law introduced a welfare state modelled on British social services, and also a regulatory framework for the conduct of public business and for the raising of revenue and accounting of expenditure. That such seemingly tedious matters were taken for granted as necessary standards of government behaviour is indicative of how embedded this other aspect of Britishness had come to be in Gibraltar's public culture. Even the law-enforcing agency, the police, though ultimately commanded by the governor, was regulated by law. All societies embody and indeed might be said to be defined by their legal management, so it was the substance of law, the practices of law making and the methods of law enforcement which contained the Britishness which Gibraltarians eventually believed distinguished Gibraltar from its near neighbours and others – even though they too were controlled by (albeit different) legal systems.

Municipal government, modelled again on Britain, was another institutional 'gift' from Britain. True, eighteenth-century efforts, especially by British-born residents, to steer such a craft into Gibraltar, fully rigged with councillors and aldermen, was scuppered by the opposition of military governors; but in the nineteenth century the cockle-shell but rate-powered Paving and Scavenging Commission of 1815 was launched, and then rebuilt in 1865, even against the protests of the governor, as the Sanitary Commission, a far sturdier vessel. In spite of some subsequent quarterdeck quarrels as to who should command the ship, this vessel carried municipal enterprise forward until it was renamed and re-engined as the City Council in 1921. Thereafter, as if this were the revolutionary 'Battleship Potemkin', its officers in command were elected by the crew. When from 1955 the elected captain was called the mayor, his uniform was, metaphorically, a mayoral robe cut from British cloth and a mayoral chain forged in Britain. Accountable civic government did not end in 1969 when the City Council was absorbed, indicating that this institutional legacy of British colonial rule had become deeply embedded in Gibraltar. However, as noted, Gibraltar had had a municipal government before 1704, and there were always local authorities thereafter across the border in Spain, so it is not municipal government as such in Gibraltar which distinguished the place from the Spanish 'other', but the particular forms it took.

This was also true of evolving systems of government. British officials – and particularly and predictably military men – repeatedly and deep into the twentieth century referred to Gibraltar as principally a fortress. The evacuation during the Second World War (and suspension of the City Council) exposed this thinking. Nevertheless, the colony's governors, with varying degrees of enthusiasm, increasingly consulted the 'leaders' of the civilian community. Initially these were, especially, those in business and in the church, but eventually also trade union leaders, not least because consultation *with* them was also demanded *by* them. But more important than such ad hoc, hot and cold, civilian involvement in the colony's government was institutional incorporation. However partial and contested it was (and it was), the Executive Council from 1922 represented the insertion into government of the civilian voice, and one step towards elected representation on that council and on the Legislative Council. It has been shown that the words of 'no taxation without representation' could be sung with different emphases on the first or second phrase but, however stressed, the language was always British (or, if you insist, Anglo-American). Histories published at this time praised Britain's constitutional evolution towards popular democracy, and the white settler societies of Australia, New Zealand and Canada were also telling similar compelling stories of their own British-modelled constitutional evolution over the previous century (not so persuasively in South Africa and Southern Rhodesia). Moreover, the institutional forms of parliamentary government and free elections were being bedded into other former colonies in, for instance, India and West Africa. What was happening in Gibraltar at the same time seemed surely the institutionalising there of one of the most admired features of the British world, democratic politics.

One principal feature was party politics. The remarkable pulling (and polling) power of the AACR, coupled with an apparent reluctance by elected representatives of the moneyed class to abandon their independent status, left Gibraltar for several decades superficially a one-party state. The AACR was largely monopolising the elected places on the City and Legislative Councils and occupying most posts as members and later ministers in the colonial government. It was therefore democratically healthy when the AACR faced opposition parties, but they made little headway until the AACR began to fracture, abandoning its left-wing working-class component in 1971 and unable to control the middle ground in the 1980s. The Integration With Britain Party also could not retain cohesion with its allies and lost the election in 1972, and also its credibility in 1975–76 when the UK government rejected its principal plank. The Gibraltar Democratic Movement (GDM), led by Joe Bossano, tried to fill the vacuum and made a decent showing in 1976, but there remained independents in the house, and the GDM itself fragmented, largely as politicians attempted to position themselves with respect to external affairs. The Party for the Autonomy of Gibraltar, formed in 1977, uniquely and unsuccessfully sought support for autonomy within Spain; and from 1978 there was a brief resurgence of the integrationist line by the Democratic Party of British Gibraltar. Dismissive of both routes, Bossano more successfully created the GSLP in 1977 and campaigned strongly and appealingly on an explicitly nationalist line, independent of both Spain and Britain, while also advancing a domestic reform programme. Unsuccessful as a party in 1980, but making a substantial advance in 1984, the GSLP achieved domination in 1988 and this was more than confirmed in 1992.

This achievement provoked another sequence of attempts by opposition groups to form effective alternatives, including the Independent Democratic Party (briefly) and the Gibraltar Liberal Party (more successfully); but it was the Gibraltar Social Democrats who came through and took office in 1996. The GSLP, led by Bossano in alliance with the Liberals, was left in opposition after the elections in 2000, 2003 and 2007. It might plausibly be argued that other minor movements (including the Gibraltar Labour Party, the Self-Determination for Gibraltar Group, the New Gibraltar Democracy Party and the Progressive Democratic Party) and the construction and deconstruction of even successful political parties were responses to changing public perceptions of political options, and indicative of democratic politics as practised elsewhere in the past and present of the British world. Moreover, once more, the contrast between claimed British virtues and perceived foreign vices buttressed the Britishness of Gibraltar, especially with respect to Spain, where the onward march of democracy had been interrupted by military governments and especially by the dictatorship of General Franco. However, the death of Franco in 1975 and the Spanish transition to a constitutional monarchy and a popular democracy, following the introduction of a new constitution in 1978, have blunted the sharpness of that contrast, and likewise Spain's membership of the EEC (later EU) since 1986.

A further indicator of the embedding of Britishness into Gibraltar through imperial rule, characteristic of other parts of the British world, was a widespread respect, even enthusiasm, for the British monarchy. It has been argued elsewhere that public expressions of loyalty to the royal family were not merely ideological constructs. They were also a mechanism by which, on the occasion of royal visits, jubilees and coronations, various social, religious and economic interest groups in Gibraltar jostled to assert their status and interests in competition with each other. Monarchy was therefore a politically useful agency for social and political advance.[10] But if games were played, that did not rule out a sincere passion for the person as celebrity, and more especially for the person as symbol. Kings and queens were heads of state and, even stripped of sacerdotal significance, their office offered a focus for loyalty which, in Gibraltar as elsewhere, was insufficiently catered for by the local and the mundane. Loyalty to the monarchy provided a link to something secular but ideologically elevated and satisfying. It is not insulting to liken such allegiance to a fan's devotion to a football club, however dispiriting the results and damp the ground, or a believer's faith in an invisible god, however rarely prayers were answered. Believing, *being* loyal, was itself the reward. This was in Gibraltar the more remarkable because other Roman Catholic societies in the empire, especially in Ireland, were less susceptible to the appeal of a monarch who was also titular head of the Church of England. Loyalty to the British crown was also, of course, drummed into Gibraltarians at school, through the media, in popular culture and by the ever-present 'soldiers of the queen'; but this differed little from that pressed upon British subjects at home and indeed in all other parts of the British Empire and later Commonwealth. And that is also precisely the point. Loyalty to the crown, expressed by Gibraltarians who were not ethnically British and rarely (if ever) saw members of the royal family, was knowingly shared with British subjects in many other places, including many who were also not descended from British immigrant stock or who had not been touched by the personal presence. Monarchism in tiny Gibraltar signified belonging to a larger community, that of the British world.

But loyalty to the crown was also expressed, especially after 1954, as a political response to Spanish aggression. Franco's protest against the royal visit was a denial that Gibraltar was (or should remain) a British possession. It was suggested earlier that external aggression was a powerful agency in the creation of an identity, overriding internal differences. It is certainly the case in 1954, and when the frontier was closed in 1969, that Gibraltarians united on this issue. Indeed, hostility on the scale experienced generated a degree of resentment and anti-Spanish feeling without equal since the days of the Great Siege. Inevitably (and it should have been predictably), in reaction most Gibraltarians defended

10 S. Constantine, 'Monarchy and constructing identity in "British" Gibraltar, c.1800 to the present', *Journal of Imperial and Commonwealth History*, 34 (2006), 23–44, and see A. Clarkson, 'Pomp, circumstance, and wild Arabs: the Royal Visit to Sudan', in the same issue, pp. 71–85, for similar suggestions.

their Britishness by expressing their loyalty to the crown and by insisting that Gibraltar was and would remain among the Queen's territorial possessions. A petition to the Queen in March 1966, prompted by Spanish pressure, signed by 7,500 Gibraltarian women and delivered to Buckingham Palace urged her to protect 'the future of our children, our homes, and our British way of life'.[11]

It is significant that the story of Gibraltar's past has been mapped by some historians as largely a sequence of sieges. The period of the closed frontier has been labelled the fifteenth siege.[12] It did not have, fortunately, the bloodiness of the fourteenth siege (1779–83) or of the thirteenth (1713–27), but it still formed in remembrance just one in a sequence, and perpetuated the sense of embattlement. Indeed, the worsening relationship with Spain after 1954 helped to obliterate from memory (and from accessible archived records) the extent to which some Gibraltarians had previously supported Franco's attack on the Spanish Republic. It also tended to obscure recollections of just how open the frontier had normally been and how intimate cross-border relationships had usually been, as chapters in this book have tried to demonstrate.

External aggression was a sharp reminder of Spanish resentment, and responsive loyalty to the crown linked the civilian population of Gibraltar yet more firmly to the British world. However, public demonstrations of allegiance to the fount of all authority, the crown, also legitimised strong civilian criticism of the crown's colonial and imperial governments. Civilian Britishness in Gibraltar was not indicative of a colonial mentality. It was perfectly compatible with suspicion of and indeed bitterness towards British authorities, and with demands for political autonomy.[13] Securing constitutional government in a garrison town, it has been shown, had not been easily won. Resentment had been expressed when the military authorities and colonial government did not release land for civilian use but instead raised taxes and delayed civilian political representation, and also when Gibraltar's prosperity was threatened, as from 1981, by reductions in the garrison and the running down of the naval dockyard.[14] Moreover and in spite of repeated reassurances, suspicions were aroused whenever British ministers engaged in talks with Spain. The blunt, even brutal way in which

11 CO926/2124, copy with Bates to Watson, 11 March 1966, and press reports, including of the tumultuous reception of the organisers on their return.

12 It became the title of Chapter 17 of the history of Gibraltar written by a former governor, Jackson, *Rock of the Gibraltarians*, first edition published 1987, shortly after the 'siege' was lifted.

13 On this see also D. Lambert,'"As solid as the Rock"? Place, belonging and the local appropriation of imperial discourse in Gibraltar', *Transactions of the Institute of British Geographers*, 30 (2005), 206–20, and contrast with some remarkable statements in G. Stanton, 'Military rock: a mis-anthropology', *Cultural Studies*, 10 (1996), 270–87, esp. pp. 285–6.

14 Garcia, *Making of a People*, p. 180.

British governments rejected the notion of integrating Gibraltar into Britain, or of treating it as another Isle of Man or Jersey, and a strong (and accurate) sense that British governments eventually judged that Britain's own interests were bound up with better relations with Spain, threatened a rift between the British of Gibraltar and the British of Britain. For many in Gibraltar, Britain too was politically becoming an 'other'.[15]

A claim to nationhood, especially since the 1950s, had therefore become a defensive response by Gibraltarians to threats from Spanish governments, suspicions of British governments and resentments against the UN for failing to acknowledge the right of Gibraltarians to self-determination.[16] Much ink has been spent debating whether Gibraltarians came in consequence to constitute a nation, and whether they could or should be a state.[17] For its existence, a state requires formal recognition by its peers of its frontiers and sovereignty, indicated in the modern world by diplomatic representation and independent membership in such institutions as the United Nations and the European Union. But it may be argued that such recognition presupposes the prior existence of a substantial body of people who believe they constitute a nation.[18]

It has been persuasively argued that a nation is an 'imagined community' within a geographical space. It is imagined in the sense that the population is usually too extensive and too dispersed for members to be personally known to each other, and yet they come to feel a sense of common belonging to what they judge to be a nation (and not merely, for instance, a religious group). The author of this concept of nationhood places particular emphasis upon print culture as the distributive agency for the promotion of a common language and this notion of shared belonging to a nation, and the idea can be comfortably extended to take in other forms of media.[19] To that extent one might focus on the news and

15 For examples of reassuring statements and deep-rooted suspicions see Garcia, *Making of a People*, pp. 139–42, 156, 189–91.

16 Dr Joseph Garcia, leader of the Gibraltar Liberal Party, stresses repeatedly this defensive response and the welding together of the community in his book *Making of a People*, for example pp. 133–4, 143, 158, 208–9, 217.

17 As one example, considering theory and questionnaire responses, see P. Gold, 'Is Gibraltar a nation?', *International Journal of Iberian Studies*, 14 (2001), 68–79.

18 See W. Connor, 'A nation is a nation, is a state, is an ethnic group, is a . . .', *Ethnic and Racial Studies*, 1 (1978), 377–400, and D. Miller, *On Nationality* (Oxford: Oxford University Press, 1995) for discussions on the difference between the nation and the state: the former may aspire to establish the latter, and therefore to create a nation-state.

19 B. Anderson, *Imagined Communities: Reflections on the Origin and Spread of Nationalism* (London: Verso, 2006, 1st edn 1983); and on the distributive effects of the media, whatever the message, as in themselves generators of national awareness, see E. Gellner, *Nations and Nationalism* (Oxford: Blackwell, 1983), esp. pp. 126–7.

comment within the (significantly titled) *Gibraltar Chronicle* or in such other mass-circulation newspapers as *Vox*, *Panorama* and *El Calpense*, and one might also note the possibly bonding effects of the Gibraltar Broadcasting Corporation, launched in 1963, and its radio and television networks.[20] One might further consider the influence of the Gibraltar Museum (from 1930) and the Gibraltar Heritage Society (from 1986) in fostering a sense of community, although these and other cultural bodies might also be numbered among the consequences as well as the causes of a sense of national community.[21]

However, attempts to explain how an imagined political community might have been formed by the media and other cultural providers are perhaps less necessary in a place like Gibraltar, in which community needed little imagination to see. Indeed, with around 30,000 people overwhelmingly crammed into the top left-hand corner of the peninsula of Gibraltar, community and indeed intimacy are hard to avoid, and overt dissent is hard to express. There has been evidence already in previous chapters of the substantial proportions of the adult population who signed petitions and attended political meetings in the main square. Turnouts at elections were also regular occasions when the people collectively met. Vast crowds greeted Joshua Hassan and Peter Isola when they returned from addressing the UN in October 1964.[22] Most impressive too were the numbers who voted on 15 June 1967. This was the occasion when Gibraltarians were asked in a referendum whether they wished to retain their link with Britain or 'to pass under Spanish sovereignty'. The outcome was never in doubt (only 44 in favour of the latter proposition), but it was the public spectacle of 12,237 Gibraltarian voters making their mark (out of an electorate of 12,762) which publicly signalled community.[23] In November 1987, 12,000 Gibraltarians on the streets and a petition signed by 16,000 people greeted two Foreign Office officials arriving to assess the situation locally.[24] When, in November 2002, the idea of shared sovereignty suggested jointly by the British and Spanish governments was again put to the vote on the initiative of Gibraltar's civilian government, once more a

20 Radio Gibraltar, run by government, started regular broadcasting in Feb 1958: *Annual Report for 1958*, pp. 56–7. For some earlier efforts see *Annual Report for 1959*, p. 53, and for the launch of television see *Annual Report for 1963*, pp. 88–9.

21 For one among many texts considering the relationship between museum exhibitions and constructions of national identity see D. McIntyre and K. Wehner (eds), *Negotiating Histories* (Canberra: National Museum of Australia, 2001). It is a delicate business. A new gallery opened at the museum in 1995 and intended to tell the civilian history of Gibraltar was said by some not to represent properly the Jewish contribution: www.haruth.com/JewsGilbraltar2.html#Changes%20in%20 the%20Social.

22 See the photographs in *Gibraltar Chronicle*, 12 Oct 1964, pp. 1–2.

23 See press reports and photographs in *Gibraltar Chronicle*, 7, 9, 11 Sept 1967.

24 Garcia, *Making of a People*, p. 196.

collective and public expression of community solidarity was demonstrated, 187 voting in favour, 17,900 against. Little imagining was needed on that occasion either.[25]

The concept of 'banal nationalism' has offered another influential approach to the concept of national identity, drawing attention in particular to the routine public employment of national symbols like flags, and in the use of 'we', 'us' and 'our' in language describing the everyday, for example, the performance of teams representing 'us', that is 'the nation': so daily, so familiar, but indicative of place, nation and belonging.[26] In Gibraltar too, it has been for some time easy enough to spot examples of 'banal nationalism' in daily life, on coins and postage stamps and in the public prints.[27] But there has been, for over a generation, certainly since the 1960s, an intensity of display in Gibraltar which has exceeded the banal. Displays of a 'national' flag by private citizens are more common than in, say, the UK, and in recent decades, as a symbol of local national sentiment, Gibraltar's 'Mons Calpe' flag has been more conspicuous than the British union flag.[28] In Upper Town, especially, one is brought face to face with aggressively nationalist displays as wall paintings, including the slogan 'Our Heritage. Our Identity. We Shall Never Surrender', which are reminiscent of Protestant Ulster at the height of the 'Troubles'. Nothing banal there.

Even the appearance of 'Miss Gibraltar', first crowned in 1959, at the Miss World Beauty Pageant should not be dismissed lightly in the construction of national identity. The event is sponsored today by the Ministry of Culture because it is 'the perfect platform to an international competition where the winner represents Gibraltar before a television audience of over one billion and reminds the world that she comes from "British Gibraltar"'. Spain, too, recognised the political value of participation, and hence in 1965 threatened not to take part unless

25 www.gibnet.com/texts/ref2.htm, and news.bbc.co.uk/1/hi/world/europe/2400673. stm.

26 M. Billig, *Banal Nationalism* (London: Sage, 1995).

27 The designs for the currency notes and coins issued for the tercentenary of 'British' Gibraltar in 2004 included representations of the capture in 1704, the Great Siege 1779–83, Trafalgar 1805, Operation Torch 1942 and the Gibraltar Constitution 1969. On the value of 'reading', respectively, the design of currency and of postage stamps see M. Pointon, 'Money and nationalism', in G. Cubitt (ed.), *Imagining Nations* (Manchester: Manchester University Press, 1998), pp. 229–54, and K. Jeffery, 'Crown, communication and the colonial post: stamps, the monarchy and the British Empire', *Journal of Imperial and Commonwealth History*, 34 (2006), 45–70. For a related matter of public projection of place see R.J.M. Garcia, *The Development of the Gibraltar Picture Postcard* (Gibraltar: n.p., 2004).

28 For the design see www.gibraltar.gov.gi/, 'National Symbols', and www.fotw. net/flags/gi.html.

Mecca Promotions excluded Miss Gibraltar.[29] The desire for external recognition as a nation also explains why Gibraltar wishes to participate in international sporting events and why Spain is also, for political reasons, equally determined to exclude. Because of effective Spanish lobbying, the International Olympic Committee has refused requests by the Gibraltar Olympic Committee to be allowed to participate in the Olympic Games. Similarly, the Gibraltar Football Association is still being denied by UEFA (the Union of European Football Associations) and FIFA (the International Football Federation) the recognition which would allow its 'national' team to compete in the European championship and the World Cup.[30] It was reported in October 2006 that the intervention of the Spanish government had obliged the European Tenpin Bowling Championship to be transferred from Barcelona to Luxembourg because a team from Gibraltar was due to compete.[31] But it is a long time since sport was just a game, so involved has it become at international level in the creation and projection of national identities. It is, rather, indicative of a sport with a different political make-up internationally that, in 1969, the International Cricket Council did recognise the Gibraltar Cricket Association, and as a consequence a 'national' side has been active since 1982 in international cricket competitions, including since 1996 the European cricket championships.[32]

Since 1993, community identity has also been performed annually on an indicatively named National Day, 10 September, held to commemorate the result of the 1967 referendum and to sustain the campaign for 'self-determination'. It is

29 www.missgibraltar.gi/history.htm; *Gibraltar Post*, 23–24 Oct 1965, p. 1; *Globe Magazine*, Aug–Sept 2002. Kemal Ataturk was delighted in 1932 when Miss Turkey, Keriman Halis Hanim, not only represented his new nation in the Miss World competition but won the title: 'Turkey's first beauty contest', *Skylife* in-flight magazine, Sept 2001, pp. 99–107, airborne research carried out en route to Istanbul; see also mbarchives.blogspot.com/2007/08/turkey-s-first-beauty-contest.html; and for a serious academic analysis of relevance to the Gibraltar case see A.H. Shissler, 'Beauty is nothing to be ashamed of: beauty contests as tools of women's liberation in early republican Turkey', *Comparative Studies of South Asia, Africa and the Middle East*, 24 (2004), 109–26. For a personal account by Miss Gibraltar 1985 of her experience 'representing my country' in the Miss Planet Contest see Gail Anne Francis, *Everyone's a Winner* (n.p., n.d. [c.2000?]).

30 P. Gold, 'Sport as a political tool: the case of Spain and Gibraltar', *The Sports Historian*, 22 (2002), 164–77; www.gfa.gi/history.htm. In 2000 Spain threatened to withdraw from UEFA if Gibraltar were admitted: news.bbc.co.uk/1/hi/world/europe/894300.stm. Indicative of less politically tense times, in 1949 Gibraltar drew 2–2 in a game against Real Madrid. Gibraltar does compete in the so-called Island Games, and in 2007 its team won the football competition.

31 www.etbf.dk/stories/2006/200610/20061016A-KTJ.htm; www.guardian.co.uk/spain/article/0,,1927985,00.html#article_continue; *The Guardian*, 21 Oct 2006.

32 www.icc-europe.org/GIBRALTAR/DATABASE/ADMIN/history.shtml.

a public holiday, a day of crowds. Some of the activities are by way of entertainment, but the overt message, not only in the speeches of politicians (including
from the UK), is intensely political and, very important, highly public. What are
described as the national colours of red and white are advertised in the 30,000
red and white balloons released, one for each person, and in the dress worn
by most participants.[33] (There had been a competition in 1969 for a 'national
dress'.)[34] In 2004 it was also difficult to avoid being drawn into a public performance of 'national' solidarity when, as part of the tercentenary celebrations
of 'British' Gibraltar, 17,000 people were organised to hold hands and form a
seven-mile human chain encircling the Rock.[35]

Such expressions of 'national' solidarity and of 'national' identity, targeted
at least in part against British governments, might seem to sit uneasily with a
parallel assertion of Britishness reflecting legal practices, political institutions
and respect for monarchy which were shared with Britain. But the conflict
dissolves when it is recognised that in other parts of the former British Empire
and present Commonwealth (and indeed within the United Kingdom) the
same juxtaposition can be discerned. None of the white settler societies before
and even after securing political autonomy was reluctant to criticise publicly
and in private the conduct of British governments and the behaviour of British
people, even while expressing loyalty to the royal family and being prepared
(on the whole) to send its sons to battle in Europe in two world wars. For many
Canadians, Australians and New Zealanders, being a Canadian, Australian or
New Zealander was long compatible with also being British.[36] In all such cases,
identity of cultures and political interests was not to be assumed, and disagree-
ments were many, but there were similarities of polity and practice which were
legacies of a common history, allowing hyphenated forms of identity to emerge,
if rarely to be so crudely expressed, as British-Canadians, British-Australians
and British-New Zealanders. Into that club British-Gibraltarians chose to
enter.

---

33 For a video record of National Day in 2006 see www.videojug.com/film/
    gibraltar-national-day. For an analysis of National Day see also D. Alvarez, 'Nation-
    making in Gibraltar: from fortress colony to finance centre', *Canadian Review of
    Studies in Nationalism*, 28 (2001), 9–25, esp. pp. 15–19.
34 *Gibraltar Chronicle*, 21 July 1969, p. 2.
35 See, among many accounts, the special report in *The Times*, 15 Dec 2004, p.
    5, and *Gibraltar Chronicle Tercentenary Special*, www.chronicle.gi/terc/hands.htm.
36 P.A. Buckner and C. Bridge, 'Reinventing the British World', *The Round Table*,
    368 (2003), 77–88.

The economy, consumption and identity

What might have kept and now keeps them there could be economic self-interest, and economic activity and patterns of consumption may also have had a lasting effect on Gibraltarian identity. It has been shown how dependent had been the Gibraltar economy, and therefore the living standards of the civilian population, upon the link with the UK. In a crude sense, 'Gibraltar' was fortunate to have been taken over by Britain, in that the transfer of sovereignty which was confirmed in 1713 connected whoever settled there with a rapidly expanding British economy, a rapidly expanding British Empire and, after the first century, a rapidly expanding world economy policed and opened substantially to free trade by the British government and the Royal Navy. Run in one's imagination the history of a Gibraltar taken over by the Dutch partner in the Allied offensive which captured the Rock, and a rather different economic story suggests itself. Very long-lasting British military interests in the Mediterranean (rather than in southern Europe) explain high levels of recurrent expenditure and substantial amounts of capital investment by the UK government in the garrison, dockyard and, later, airbase. Moreover, in spite of many other financial obligations to their own people and to other parts of the empire, British ministers still provided resources to transform much of the economic and social infrastructure of civilian Gibraltar after 1945. Again, it was the British taxpayer who 'found' the money to pay for some of the defensive economic responses to the closing of the frontier in 1969, sufficient, with a lot of Gibraltar self-help, to leave the economy in remarkably good shape when the frontier reopened in 1985. In addition, most of the manufactured goods imported throughout three centuries came from Britain, including a large amount that was re-exported, furtively or otherwise, to other customers. These were certainly not gifts, but a substantial amount of the income needed to pay for them was derived by Gibraltar's service sector from sales to British customers.

A dependency on the UK might also be discerned in the arrangements made by the Gibraltar Health Authority with the National Health Service in the UK to secure treatment for Gibraltar patients in British hospitals or in Gibraltar by visiting British consultants.[37] These, of course, were service 'imports', not freely given by Britain, and rationed, but the relationship did spare Gibraltar taxpayers the uneconomic expense of equipping a hospital with specialist facilities and specialist staff better obtained at less expense in the UK, where economies of scale operated. The same was also true of higher education. Local investment in

37 See, for example, *Annual Report for 1972*, pp. 42–3; HCPP, *Exchange of Despatches concerning Reciprocal Health Care and Social Security Arrangements between the United Kingdom and Gibraltar*, Cmnd 5604, 1974; www.gibraltar.gov. gi/gov_depts/health/health_index.htm; www.gha.gov.gi/.

adult education at evening classes, and from 1964 at the Gibraltar and Dockyard Technical College, wholly under civilian control from 1985 as the Gibraltar College of Further Education, provided many Gibraltarians with important training and career opportunities. But the local population was deemed too small to set up and sustain a fully equipped and properly staffed university capable of teaching a range of disciplines. Accordingly, provision was made, first by charity and then by government, for scholarships and grants to enable students from Gibraltar to take degrees at British universities where, again, economies of scale limited per capita costs.[38] In some health and educational services, therefore, Gibraltarians 'consumed' Britishness.

Of course, the (rather different) experiences of patients and of students going to the UK would do to individuals what the Second World War evacuation did to the masses, and that was to bring them into direct contact with Britain and British Britishness. It cannot be claimed that this was always a pleasant experience, since certainly some of the evacuees and possibly some patients and students were dismayed by casual prejudice against 'foreigners', to say nothing of the damp and cold compared with home. But in other respects there was an encounter with the advanced material culture of Britain which, like the experience with Britain's liberal political culture (even in wartime), probably whetted the appetite for more consumption of the same when back in Gibraltar. Certainly the flow of products followed them on their return, and even more important for those who had not been to the 'mother country' was the temptation of advertisements in the local press. Even an unsystematic sampling persuades one that British goods were readily available and that Gibraltarians were being tempted to buy into a British lifestyle. Britishness came packaged and priced.

Admittedly, the *Gibraltar Chronicle* was an English-language newspaper and, as paper of choice for the garrison and the administration, it carried a lot of British news and was therefore targeted by British advertisers. But it also carried much official news and was undoubtedly read by Gibraltar's moneyed class and many others, certainly those with social aspirations and adequate incomes. Were Gibraltar shoppers of this sort to be persuaded by its press advertisements, then even in the austere years of 1945–50, and assuming they had money to spend, tempting products from British companies were already back on the market. Mr Gibraltar, it seems, used Brylcreem on his hair, smoked Du Maurier cigarettes, wore Van Heusen shirts and a Harris tweed or Yorkshire tweed jacket (bought

38 E.G. Archer and A.A. Traverso, *Education in Gibraltar 1704–2004* (Gibraltar: Gibraltar Books, 2004), pp. 185–96, 253–9. In 1950 there were about fifty students on higher education courses in the UK, ninety a year receiving awards from 1980, and by 1998 some 600 students were receiving government grants. For the announcement of the first Mackintosh scholarships see *Gibraltar Chronicle*, 27 Feb 1945, p. 3.

at Garcia's on Main Street), plus John White shoes on his feet, 'made in England for Gibraltar'. Wellington boots made by the British Bata Shoe Company helped him cope with wet weather. He had been lured into marriage with Miss Gibraltar, seduced by her use of beauty products by Ann Carol of London, her smile whitened by Colgate toothpaste, and a complexion made radiant by Lux soap, as used by the stars but made in Birkenhead. She probably caught his eye by the cut of her coat and skirt, made by Zambrene in London's West End or from material supplied by Courtaulds, and her blouse would be spotless because Persil washes whiter. Newly married, he bought her a Bluebell kettle and a GEC electric cooker, which she cleaned with Vim, but he also fancied himself as a 'DIY' man, and installed GEC light fittings. They had Sheffield cutlery as a wedding present. She used Stork margarine and Bovril, or maybe Oxo, but certainly Cerebos salt in her cooking, and perhaps Colman's mustard on the side. But this was a hot-enough marriage anyway, and so came the children, and the money went on Johnson's baby powder for their bottoms, and Angiers emulsion to ward off ailments, Dettol ointment and Boots antiseptic cream for their cuts and abrasions, and Vicks VapoRub for their bad colds. He soon needed Rennies for his dyspepsia, Steradent for his teeth and Sanatogen to keep him going, while she turned to Irving's yeast-vite and the occasional Aspro for her bad heads, plus Radox bath salts in a hot tub and Optrex for her tired eyes. They still ate McVitie's biscuits, but Ovaltine or Cadbury's drinking chocolate was no longer his preferred nightcap, and he found a taste instead for Scotch whisky, but dithered between Johnny Walker, VAT 69, White Horse and Black and White. She settled for Gordon's dry gin, consoled by the knowledge that it was the tipple, 'by appointment', of His Majesty King George V. He had a regular punt on Vernon's football pools, hoping for a big win so that he could afford the Austin A40, just arrived at Central Garage, Line Wall Road, with its Dunlop tyres from Birmingham, or maybe a Morris from Gomez on Cannon Lane, or, if a really big win, a Riley, a Wolseley or the MG saloon.

In the end they were not unhappy, and by the late 1960s their children were doing well. The son was a respected cricket player and looked good in his Weatherall sports clothes from Bond Street but bought from Teo, the English outfitter on Main Street, though he smoked too many Kensitas cigarettes and drank too much Watneys Keg Red Barrel, though it was 'a glass of glorious England'. At least he was also sticking to proper Scotch whisky, including Queen Anne, Haig and Grant's, and used one of those fancy soda siphons made by the British Oxygen Company. He wore K shoes and Tootal ties and liked the Tootal dressing gown they had bought him. He flew quite often to London by British European Airways. He had been more successful than his father on Littlewood's football pools, and won enough to pay the deposit on a British Leyland Triumph Herald, but he had barely taken delivery than the frontier closed, and instead he rode around Gib on his Moulton bicycle, with the tiny wheels, designed by the man who dreamt up the BMC Mini. The daughter had got married, rather young they thought, but she had got one of those new flats. She used Jeyes Sanilav to keep the toilet spotless, and she still served up Twinings English Breakfast tea. But, sign of the times, her husband drank a lot of American Nescafe and smoked those heavily-advertised American cigarettes like Pall Mall and State Express. He even drank Coca-Cola, and had started buying Smirnoff vodka. Once, only, he pressed Malta Heineken non-alcoholic beer on his father-in-law.

It is reasonable to suppose that such consumers, after 1945, were conscious of the origins of many of the products they consumed, and probably therefore also alert to those elements of their material culture which they shared with their British cousins. Of course, they had much else to hand not then so easily available in the UK, especially Mediterranean foods and wine, and certainly the patterns of consumption of the less well-off were much more orientated towards local and largely Spanish suppliers, for example of food and clothing. However, there was one other matter, indicated in an earlier chapter, of which many in Gibraltar of all classes had been aware for generations past and which had made them conscious of their special selves: comparative prosperity. The comparison was essential for the consequences it generated. It has been repeatedly indicated that Gibraltar was a magnet for workers and traders from outside, initially from many parts of the Mediterranean, then mainly from Spain, particularly as commuters, and later from Morocco after the land frontier was closed. They resembled the Mexican poor trying to cross the border to secure some of the bounty of the USA. One ingredient in the making of a British identity in Britain in the eighteenth and nineteenth centuries was a sense of economic superiority and a higher living standard, a comparison between sturdy John Bull and his roast beef and the French peasant eating frogs and snails.[39] Preposterous as generalisation, it was underpinned by a reality of relative (though not permanent) advantage, and it marked a difference between 'us' and 'them'. Heightening the distinctiveness of 'British' Gibraltar and its community was therefore a contrast between the consumer society and employment prospects on 'our' side and the poverty and dependence on 'their' side.

However, there is no reason to suppose that this condition was secure and irreversible, or that the material culture consumed even by the affluent would retain a peculiarly British flavour. The son-in-law imagined above in the mid to late 1960s was already showing a taste for American products. His children, by the mid 2000s, judging by press advertisements and a walk along Main Street, might be shopping in Gibraltar's Marks & Spencer store and BHS, and they could find a Range Rover dealer, but they were also being encouraged to

39 D. Bindman, 'How the French became frogs: English caricature and a national stereotype', *Apollo Magazine*, Aug 2003, findarticles.com/p/articles/mi_m0PAL/ is_498_158/ai_106652581/pg_1; and also Colley, *Britons*, esp. p. 374.

buy Ford Mustang cars from the USA, Alfa-Romeo from Italy, Honda and Mitsubishi from Japan, BMW, Audi and Volkswagen from Germany, and Renault and Citroen from France. Other temptations – in this obviously more prosperous society – included Daelim motor scooters from Korea, Interdas fridge-freezers from Italy, and Casio or Sony calculators, watches, cameras, computers and televisions from Japan. In truth, of course, the international corporations of the modern economy make it difficult to know quite where a product purchased was made. Material culture had gone global, but in terms of products consumed, Britishness had faded. Also, property in Spain was widely advertised for sale, particularly in nearby Santa Margarita, Alcaidesa, Sotogrande and Duquesa, the so-called 'Golden Mile' (though in reality more like ten).[40] After 1985 controls over the economic frontier had been relaxed, and new estates of houses, villas and apartments, priced in euros, were being built where land was more available than in still overcrowded Gibraltar (4,813 persons per square kilometre in 2006).[41]

This last development may have significant implications. In the past those Gibraltarians who had homes across the frontier in Spain included some of the comfortably-off, plus the seriously rich with their retreats in the hills or by the coast, but many were the poor who could afford only the cheap lodgings in the more miserable parts of La Línea within walking distance of work. However, since 1985 it is probable that more of the better-off who have a right of residence in Gibraltar have chosen to live outside, but within commuting distance by car or motorcycle.[42] As such, they are domestically contained in Spain. In the purchase (or rent) of property and of local goods and services they boost demand in the local Spanish economy by their expenditure, while to the Gibraltar economy they donate their labour. In the first capacity, therefore, they contribute to that which Franco tried to initiate when, in 1966, he launched the Campo de Gibraltar development plan, shortly before the final closing of the border. The aim was to reverse the historic relationship between urban and prosperous Gibraltar and the backward rural economy of its former hinterland by investing in the Campo £22.5 million a year for five years (1966–90), in hydraulic works, agriculture, tourism (including at Sotogrande), the port of Algeciras, transport links, education and especially industrialisation, including petrochemical, metallurgical and metal-working plants, and clothing, building

40 See the aerial photograph of these developments in *Gibraltar Chronicle*, 28 June 2003, facing p. 13.
41 *Statistical Abstract 2006*, p. 1.
42 *Census of 2001*, p. xix, suggests that the number of Gibraltarians living in Spain but working in Gibraltar has been seriously underestimated, and an increase, p. xxv, in cross-border commuting by them is hinted at in a rise of over 1,500 in the number of Gibraltarians travelling to work by car or motorcycle between 1991 and 2001.

and food-processing industries. This did not, to say the least, prove to be an immediately successful set of ventures. [43] However, were they (with more private sector programmes) to deliver substantial increases in local incomes and living standards, in an administrative area currently containing 250,000 people, then the effects on Gibraltar's economic superiority, and perhaps consequently on its sense of a distinctive identity, could be interesting.

Ethnicity, culture and identity

That proposition presupposes that identities are significantly formed and substantially sustained by material calculations. In addition, however, and arguably more important in generating and maintaining a unique sense of identity in Gibraltar – and not one demonstrative of Britishness – has been the historic multiple origins of the population and therefore its mixed ethnic composition. Government statements, popular websites and academic studies make something of these features, and especially of multi-ethnic and interfaith fusion and harmony.[44] One poem published during the tercentenary celebrations in 2004 concludes:

> And all of this contributed to a gradual merging
> A melding of families and of nationalities
> Of sundry customs and of differing cultures
> A wondrous tolerance of diverse convictions
> And as inexorably decade followed decade
> A sense of belonging and attachment
> Of kinship and of loyalty to the land.[45]

Theories of nationalism used to conjure up the notion of ethnicity or race as precisely identifiable biological features of human populations which should primarily, even uniquely, define frontiers and rights of belonging and of habitation (or even rights in general). Never persuasive in the nineteenth century, except to intellectuals, they became particularly contaminated by their ruthless application in the twentieth century. However, even casual categorisation along such lines as supposed ethnic origin, which still persists, is prone to exclude as much as include,

43 J. Naylon, 'A challenge to the Rock – the Campo de Gibraltar development plan', *Geography*, 57 (1972), 1–9; Jackson, *Rock of the Gibraltarians*, p. 318.

44 See, for example, statement by Chief Secretary to Government of Gibraltar ('Gibraltarians are a mixture of many bloods, nationalities and cultures . . . an individual . . . is the sum of the total whole'), The Electoral Commission, *Combination of Gibraltar with a European Electoral Region in England and Wales*, June 2003, p. 23; www.discovergibraltar.com/mainlogo/mainfrm.htm; E.G. Archer, *Gibraltar, Identity and Empire* (London: Routledge, 2006), esp. p. 34.

45 H. Caetano, 'The Gibraltarians', www.chronicle.gi/terc/gibraltarians.htm.

'othering' even those within. The chapters of this study dealing with population indicate the inapplicability of biological ethnicity as a defining concept of being Gibraltarian. All our roots lie with migrants from somewhere, but the peculiarity of the virtual emptying of the peninsula of Gibraltar in 1704 makes it undeniably clear that all now residing on the Rock are immigrants or the descendants of immigrants. Patient industry, adequate records and an army of family historians would enable the outside place of origin to be traced of all those who arrived, stayed and bred. They are historically contained within a short historical period, a mere three hundred years.[46] Nor is Gibraltar cursed with the notion of 'founding fathers' (or 'mothers'), an early and original stock endowed with a higher status than those who came after. True, the military authorities who attempted to manage the place in the eighteenth century endeavoured to admit primarily Protestants of British stock (though the British were themselves a mongrel people with plural antecedents). But the attempt to maintain even a Protestant ascendancy, superior in economic as well as in social power, failed. As we have seen, immigrants from both sides of the Mediterranean and other parts of Europe, including from Spain, saw opportunities, and they arrived to develop the trade and services needed to sustain the garrison and, ultimately, a more broad-based economy.

Of course, as this study has also shown, not all wishing to enter and, in particular, not all wishing to settle were welcome. British managers kept the security of the garrison much in mind, hence the policing of the frontier and those elaborate systems of permits and conditional rights for visitors and prospective residents, with priorities for British subjects. Immigration controls were made more urgent by the actual and not just potential consequences of overcrowding and insanitary conditions. However, and of immense importance for the ethnic composition of Gibraltar, official efforts to monitor, manage and exclude were subverted by many of those who had already gained entry, especially by those who benefited from cheap labour, or who transgressed and fell in love with 'aliens'. The sensitivity of the colony's managers about who had secured residence (and how) is underlined by the categorisations used in the censuses, to which attention has been drawn. True, this was a population which was made up increasingly of British subjects (around 50–60 per cent in the late eighteenth and early nineteenth centuries; about 90 per cent in the twentieth). But this was not because more of those arriving were legally so defined. Most arrived by being born there, of parents not all by origin British subjects. Birth and *jus soli*, as we have seen, endowed a right of residence upon offspring whose parents were ethnically mixed. There is plenty of evidence of 'mixed parentage'. In the 1930s, for example, more Gibraltar men, rising to 20 per cent of marriages by 1938–40, were marrying Spanish women, increasingly from La Línea, and over a quarter of children born in Gibraltar that

---

46 See, for example, A. Lombard, 'A descent from the conquest', *Gibraltar Heritage Journal*, 11 (2004), 135–51.

decade had a Spanish mother. Since 1940, even Jewish men from Gibraltar were marrying women of other faiths more commonly than in the past.[47] The population of Gibraltar had indeed been divided between a British garrison and civilians (offset by a fair amount of intermarriage between garrison men and local women), but otherwise Gibraltar was a melting pot.

Though it became less so. As has also been indicated, from the very beginning of the twentieth century, by the ordinance of 1900 and later by the whole sequence of Alien Traders ordinances, the entry and residence even of British subjects were by law regulated and limited. Whereas the rules of the previous two centuries had attempted to narrow rights of residence to British subjects, these additionally restrictive measures also reduced the rights of those British subjects not born in Gibraltar (unless they were alien women marrying Gibraltar men). True, the hostility shown by some civilians as well as by some sections of government towards the Maltese and to British Indians seems, eventually, to have dissipated. The former have been assimilated and the latter at least have integrated. But this was a stage towards a more restrictive definition of the Gibraltarian, which by mid century was regarded by civilian leaders as increasingly necessary, in contrast to their attitudes in the past. Moreover, when those leaders became incorporated into government and into policy making, the controls over immigration and rights of residence – of belonging – which they endorsed confirmed the negatives derived from *jus soli* already in place, but also incorporated entitlements derived from *jus sanguinis*. These, as we have seen, ensured, broadly speaking, that the descendants of those registered as Gibraltarians were also Gibraltarians, wherever born. Hence, in a curious way and without overdoing the emphasis on bloodlines, a new ethnicity was being created – Gibraltarians – defined as 'an ancestrally related unit' and with 'a sense of common ancestry'.[48] This implies a belief in cultural congruence between members. This latter aspect explains the exceptions also allowed from 1962, to grant the same title and privileges to British subjects and even aliens not of native-born ancestry but of long-term residence and shared cultural values – they were the ones judged 'by us' as 'one of us'. Hence, and more than incidentally, the anxieties some have expressed concerning the place in Gibraltar of Moroccans,[49] and, perhaps in the future, worries about the arrival of other citizens of the European Union.

The debate on the Gibraltarian Status Ordinance in 1962 avoided any attempt to

47 L.A. Sawchuk and L. Walz, 'The Gibraltarian identity and early 20th century marriage practices', *Gibraltar Heritage Journal*, 10 (2003), 81–90, and L.A. Sawchuk and L. Waks, 'Religious exogamy and gene flow among the Jews of Gibraltar, 1870–1969', *Current Anthropology*, 24 (1983), 661–2.
48 See Connor, 'A nation is a nation', for this definition of ethnicity, and Miller, *On Nationality*, pp. 19–21, for the idea of shared cultural features.
49 www.chronicle.gi/readarticle.php?id=000011291&title, report of 30 April 2007.

define the distinguishing culture and the cultural values of the Gibraltarian which, it was said, only other Gibraltarians would recognise. It follows that it would be an especially rash non-Gibraltarian historian who would attempt to define that which culturally distinguishes Gibraltarians from other people, especially in Western Europe, and still more courageous to identify the precise contribution of each immigrant stream. Of course, in some broad categories one might point to a British input (subsuming English, Welsh and Scottish?), with particular reference, as suggested above, to the values associated with the legal system, democratic political rights, administrative integrity and respect for monarchy. It has also been suggested, quite reasonably, that from Britain came the origins of various sports and games, and the values of competitiveness and sportsmanship (and in some cases exclusiveness and snobbery) associated with them.[50] It is also obvious that the religious beliefs, traditions and practices of Roman Catholics, Anglicans, Presbyterians, Methodists, Jews, Hindus and Muslims, as well as of non-believers, were imported with immigrant streams from Britain, Spain, North Africa and elsewhere; and the garrison's legacy also included the gift of freemasonry to the civilian community.[51] A study of *Gibraltar's Favourite Recipes in English and Spanish* suggests that immigrants endowed Gibraltar homes with a wider cuisine than that suggested by the cafés of Main Street. *Calentita*, made from chickpea flour and probably derived from Genoa, is sometimes described as Gibraltar's national dish.[52] It is also obvious that the British garrison, the colonial government and state education help explain why the dominant and indeed only official language of the colony became English. This was an outcome not invariably the case in British colonies. Reinforced especially since 1945 by the media and the global job market, English has become a language with a greater social depth and more equal usage by both sexes than in the past. However, for a while Spanish and even Genoese-Italian had been employed in official proclamations in Gibraltar, and certainly today Spanish remains the common tongue even of many long-term residents, especially in the home and also as a means of cultural expression, and it is still necessary for cross-border exchanges.

Nevertheless, when one reviews cultural values and cultural practices none alone impresses as a distinguishing feature. Arguments have been advanced in the past that a distinctive language defines a nation, and therefore that all first-language speakers of a common language should be incorporated into a nation-state defined by linguistic frontiers. This was a destabilising challenge,

50 E.G. Archer, 'Imperial influences: Gibraltarians, cultural bonding and sport', *Culture, Sport, Society,* 6 (2003), 43–60.
51 K. Sheriff, *The Rough Ashlar: the History of English Freemasonry in Gibraltar, 1727–2002* (Gibraltar, n.p., 2002 [?]).
52 *Gibraltar's Favourite Recipes in English and Spanish,* The Gibraltar League of Hospital Friends, n.d. [c.2000?]; and see http://en.wikipedia.org/wiki/Gibraltarian_cuisine.

for example, to the multi-lingual Austrian Empire in the nineteenth century. Alternatively, it has been insisted that the population of a country should be educated into the language of their ancestors, as in Wales in the twentieth century. Attempts have been made to present Llanito (or Yanito) as precisely such a distinguishing linguistic feature, for who else attempt to express themselves in a language which combines Andalusian Spanish with some English and splashes of Genoese and words of Hebrew origin, delivered in an Andalusian accent and with a capacity to switch to English mid-passage? But prevalent though is the use of Llanito in the media and on the streets, it has not become an official language, nor is its use an inclusive criterion determining who belongs.[53]

There is little else which is culturally specific to Gibraltar. It would be a peculiar conceit of Gibraltarians to assume that legal systems, democratic political rights, administrative probity and even respect for monarchy, derived from Britain, were unique to them, certainly by the later twentieth century. Many sports originated in Britain and flourished in Gibraltar, but there were many other societies in which they were enjoyed, without a sense of obligation to the *fons et origo* of the offside rule. World faiths (and non-faiths) originated in many places, and took root elsewhere than in Gibraltar, and not even religious toleration is nowadays a distinguishing virtue (though not everywhere practised). Freemasonry too was common to many places (though regarded with hostility in some Roman Catholic societies). Delicious though they sound, particularly in Spanish, the recipes for *merluza al horno* (baked hake), *pollo en pepitoria* (chicken in hotchpotch), and *huevos a la escocesa* (Scotch eggs) and other dishes may draw on Mediterranean (of course including Andalusian) and British cuisine, but except in the combination of dishes they are not unique to Gibraltar. The same can also be said for Spanish zambras danced at the Arizona Club by Maria Brazalema or the performances by Lina Ortega, Queen of the Castanets, or the production of *The Mikado* by the Gibraltar Operatic Company, all cultural highlights of 1948.[54] Rather, if cultural distinctiveness is to be found in Gibraltar it lies in the combination of features, not as hybrids but as parallel performances, a blessing consequent on a society derived from plural roots and geographically situated at a crossroads.

53 For an online dictionary see www.aboutourrock.com/dictionary/a.htm; and for a textual example of code-switching see www.panorama.gi/views.htm. For more on Llanito and linguistic (and other) exchanges across the frontier see J. Kramer, *English and Spanish in Gibraltar* (Hamburg: Helmut Buske, 1986), S. Ballantine, 'English and Spanish in Gibraltar: development and characteristics of two languages in a bilingual community', *Gibraltar Heritage Journal*, 7 (2000), 115–24; and C.F. Martín, 'Gibraltar and its hinterland: sociolinguistic exchanges between two neighbouring communities', users.ox.ac.uk/~pbellido/XIII.pdf.

54 Advertisements in *Gibraltar Illustrated*, May, Aug and Dec 1948; and for the same cultural mix in the late 1940s and 1950s see also C. Baldachino, 'The way we were', *Gibraltar Heritage Journal*, 12 (2005), 3–15.

In any event, attempts by outsiders to define what are the distinguishing cultural values of Gibraltar are an irrelevance and perhaps an impertinence. Probably most societies believe they contain distinctive and usually superior cultural attributes. It is part of the arrogance of nation-states, and is perhaps a necessary fiction for the creation and continuing cohesion of that community. It was argued earlier that Gibraltar was not an 'imagined political community' because the physical compression of the population made imagination unnecessary. On the other hand, particularly for a small society endeavouring to distinguish itself from a near (and not always friendly) neighbour and a more distant (and not always congenial) imperial authority, what was needed was to imagine a distinguishing culture, an imaginary space in which identity could be performed and independence legitimised.

Conclusion: history and identity

It might also be argued that in recent times such distinctions are bound to be eroded. It is suggested that economic globalisation has us all in thrall. The evidence would be the massive turnover and economic power of multinational corporations and their product placement in all markets. The range of their goods affects us all, inducing, some would say, a bland uniformity at least across affluent societies which have the money to sell their souls. Products include material goods like motor vehicles, ICT equipment and digital cameras, the same readily available in Gibraltar as, for example, in London, Madrid, New York and Singapore. Likewise in Gibraltar you can be helped around by international banking and other services common to other places. Gibraltar hotels, at least, are not parts of international chains, though you can find a Pizza Hut. And you can tune into British, Spanish and, of course, American television programmes, and buy the same chart-busting popular music of the western world. Your intrepid researcher engaged with local culture one Saturday afternoon (when the archives were closed) by watching a 'Wallace and Gromit' film in Gibraltar's cinema, a dream palace regularly receiving Hollywood products.

On another track, and as a member, via the UK, of the European Union, Gibraltar has now more open frontiers for labour (though not for citizenship) and we are told that, with labour mobility, transient workers will sweep through all our worlds. By the same token, more Gibraltarians, probably those with an expensive higher education behind them and with the paper qualifications that open up careers, may opt to practise their skills abroad, and migrate. Already by 1991 there were 6,027 people born in Gibraltar and resident in Great Britain.[55] Add to this the authority and regulatory powers of supranational

---

55 *Census 1991, Great Britain, Ethnic Group and Country of Birth*, vol.1, p. 412, although not all of these were necessarily born of Gibraltar parents.

organisations like the European Union, the World Bank and the United Nations (and FIFA?) and there are, it is said, forces at work which are eroding the sovereignty of once-powerful nation-states; and if them, what future for a small British Overseas Territory? If democratic politics have bedded down in Spain, if living standards in the Campo rise and exceed levels in Gibraltar, if career prospects become more attractive across the frontier, if Roman Catholicism – or growing secularisation – are common bonds, if corporate capitalism generates the same appetites and swamps both places with the same cultural products, if Spanish as well as English becomes an international language (as some have predicted), then what capacity remains for Gibraltarians to insist that they have a distinguishing identity?

The answer probably lies in Scotland. Although there had been a union of the crowns of Scotland with England and Wales in 1603, the creation of the United Kingdom with a single government was only effected in 1707. Therefore Scotland's incorporation with England and Wales into Great Britain has endured almost as exactly as long as Gibraltar's status as a dependent British territory. For many generations, therefore, Scots have been free to settle in England, to be active in English (or British) economic enterprise, to enrich the cultural life of both societies and to aspire – very successfully – to senior positions at court and in government. However, there is little to suggest that Scots, in three hundred years, have lost their sense of a distinct nationality or of a distinct identity and set of values (though they too might be hard-pressed to describe their features as unique). Moreover, instead of the later twentieth and early twenty-first centuries witnessing the death of nation-states, there are grounds for arguing that we have been witnessing their rebirth, and not only following the break-up of the Soviet Empire. Whether Scotland becomes an independent nation state is not germane to this argument, but the retention after so long of a separate identity and such an aspiration is. Nor is this peculiar to Scotland, as a trip to Spain's Basque country and to Catalonia will confirm. 'Britishness' in the United Kingdom and 'Spanishness' in Spain did not impose homogeneity on the constituent parts, as current politics prove.[56]

It would be audacious here to predict the political destiny of the Gibraltar people, but one might advance with more confidence the view that, whatever the outcome, a Gibraltarian identity will survive and may even thrive. In or out of Spain, Gibraltar will be Scotland (or, if you wish, Catalonia). Of all the cultural

56 This is the argument, with respect to the UK, advanced by Colley in *Britons* and 'Britishness and Others'. In Gibraltar in 1967, at the time of the referendum, a poster with the following message was sent from Switzerland and published in the *Gibraltar Chronicle*, 9 Sept 1967, p. 1: 'Franco's government wants to force Gibraltar into the Spanish gaol. The Catalan people supports the desire of the population of Gibraltar to remain free. Catalan Liberation Forces.'

features referred to earlier the one insufficiently mentioned so far is a sense of history, or rather of the past, not quite what happened but what is thought to have happened. The connection between historical memory and national identity is not a new idea, having been articulated by Ernest Renan, for example, in 1882; and it still has purchase.[57] It was mentioned in a previous chapter how the past which was marketed to tourists was also the past recollected and respected by Gibraltarians themselves. Scottish identity, like Gibraltarian identity, is much bound up with historical memory. For the Scots, it commonly (though not only) revolves around resistance and tragedy, of Bannockburn, Wallace, Mary, Culloden, Highland Clearances, the beastliness of the English, uncontaminated by the complexities of real events. Forgetting complexity, as Renan also implied, is crucial in the creation of a national identity. However, it serves the necessary purpose of defining who 'we' are by setting 'us' against 'them'. Gibraltarians too have a version of history, stretching back three hundred years. As myths do, this history also explains to themselves who they are. Through a history of the past it gives them an identity in the present. However, though aspects of past civilian life are increasingly being written up, the most public version of history still aligns Gibraltarians closely to the British military connection. The past seems to be physically embodied in Gibraltar's walls, the gun emplacements, the Trafalgar cemetery, the tunnels, the memorials to Eliott and Wellington, the recently erected statues of Rooke and Nelson, and a memorial to the dead of two world wars ('In glorious memory of those who died for the Empire'). So armed and reminded daily, Gibraltarians have inherited a particular view of the past. But views of the past are not fixed. They are an open agenda, subject to change. Gibraltarians are in the process of revisiting their past. Perhaps, in due course, and with different beliefs about their history, they will more confidently express a distinguishing identity, not British or Spanish. It will be informed by what they then judge their once multi-ethnic civilian ancestors themselves variously to have achieved, and that would be something special to carry into the future, whatever that might be.

---

57 E. Renan, 'What is a Nation?', in G. Eley and R.G. Suny (eds), *Becoming National: a Reader* (New York: Oxford University Press, 1996), pp. 41–55. The thoughts in this last paragraph owe much to the essay of my colleague Martin Blinkhorn, 'A question of identity: how the people of Gibraltar became Gibraltarians', in D. Killingray and D. Taylor (eds), *The United Kingdom Overseas Territories, Past, Present and Future* (London: Institute of Commonwealth Studies, 2005), esp. pp. 60–1.

Sources and select bibliography

The primary sources upon which this study is based are indicated in detail in the references cited throughout the book and are too extensive to be listed here. In the UK they are to be found in the National Archives at Kew and, to a lesser extent, in the British Library, London. Online catalogues and search engines were helpful for preliminary location of promising material. In addition, valuable information is contained in the House of Commons Parliamentary Papers and in *The Times*, made more accessible in my case by access to searchable online versions. Gibraltar's official annual reports ceased to be parliamentary publications after 1919, and later versions were published by HMSO and may be found in libraries. In Gibraltar, the repositories used were the Gibraltar Government Archives and the Garrison Library. Neither as yet has online searchable databases, but the archivist and librarian respectively provided considerable guidance. As one would expect, the archives contain official government papers. (Some are not yet open for historical research and recent records are not yet systematically handed over for archiving.) The archives also contain records of the City Council and its forerunners and, to a lesser extent, the surviving records of unofficial organisations like the Exchange and Commercial Library Committee, plus other miscellaneous material. Also available are a set of *Gibraltar Directories* beginning in 1877, plus considerable holdings of newspapers, especially of the *Gibraltar Chronicle*. The only complete run of this last is kept in the Garrison Library, where may also be found many official publications as well as a rich collection of published primary and secondary sources. All website sources were checked for continuing accessibility on 21 June 2008.

The following secondary sources (books, essays, theses) concerned specifically with Gibraltar were found particularly useful. Other publications, including those on British and on British Empire history, are cited in the references and not listed here.

Alvarez, David, 'Nation-making in Gibraltar: from fortress colony to finance centre', *Canadian Review of Studies in Nationalism*, 28 (2001), 9–25

Andrews, Allen, *Proud Fortress: the Fighting Story of Gibraltar* (New York: Dutton, 1959)

Archer, E.G., 'Imperial influences: Gibraltarians, cultural bonding and sport', *Culture, Sport, Society*, 6 (2003), 43–60

Archer, E.G., 'An imperial legacy – British by inclination: socialization, education and a Gibraltarian sense of identity', *International Journal of the History of Sport*, 22 (2005), 582–99

Archer, E.G., *Gibraltar, Identity and Empire* (London: Routledge, 2006)

Archer, E.G. and A.A. Traverso, *Education in Gibraltar 1704–2000* (Gibraltar: Gibraltar Books, 2004)

Archer, E.G., E.P. Vallejo and T. Benady, *Catalan Bay* (Gibraltar: Gibraltar Books, 2000)

Archibald, Garry, 'Attempts to Solve an International Problem, 1963–2002' (PhD thesis, Ulster University, 2006)

Baldachino, Cecilia, 'Co-operation and conflict at North Front', *Gibraltar Heritage Journal*, 6 (1999), 83–98

Baldachino, Cecilia, 'The way we were', *Gibraltar Heritage Journal*, 12 (2005), 3–15

Baldachino, Cecilia, and Tito Benady, *The Royal Gibraltar Police 1830–2005* (Gibraltar: Gibraltar Books, 2005)

Ballantine, Sergius, 'English and Spanish in Gibraltar: development and characteristics of two languages in a bilingual community', *Gibraltar Heritage Journal*, 7 (2000), 115–24

Ballantine Perera, Jennifer, 'The language of exclusion in F. Solly Flood's "History of the Permit System in Gibraltar"', *Journal of Historical Sociology*, 20 (2007), 209–34

Beiso, Dennis D., 'The social impact of the Spanish Civil War on Gibraltar', *Gibraltar Heritage Journal*, 7 (2000), 75–80

Benady, M., 'The settlement of Jews in Gibraltar, 1704–1783', *Transactions of the Jewish Historical Society of England*, 26 (1979), 87–110

Benady, Sam, *Civil Hospital and Epidemics in Gibraltar* (Grendon: Gibraltar Books, 1994)

Benady, Sam G., *General Sir George Don and the Dawn of Gibraltarian Identity* (Gibraltar: Gibraltar Books, 2006)

Benady, Tito, 'The Jewish community of Gibraltar', in R.D. Barnett and W.M. Schwab (eds), *The Sephardi Heritage, Vol 2, The Western Sephardim* (Grendon: Gibraltar Books, 1989)

Benady, Tito, *The Royal Navy at Gibraltar* (Gibraltar: Gibraltar Books, 3rd edn 2000, 1st edn 1992)

Benady, T.M., 'The role of Jews in the British colonies of the Western Mediterranean', *Jewish Historical Studies*, 33 (1995), 45–63

Benady, Tito, 'The complaint of the Chief Justice of Gibraltar', *Gibraltar Heritage Journal*, 4 (1997), 18–23

Benady, Tito, 'The depositions of the Spanish inhabitants of Gibraltar to the inspectors of the army in 1712', *Gibraltar Heritage Journal*, 6 (1999), 99–114

Benady, Tito, 'Spaniards in Gibraltar after the Treaty of Utrecht', *Gibraltar Heritage Journal*, 7 (2000), 125–44

Benady, Tito, 'Genoese in Gibraltar', *Gibraltar Heritage Journal*, 8 (2001), 85–107

Benady, T., 'The settee cut: Mediterranean passes issued at Gibraltar', *The Mariner's Mirror*, 87 (2001), 281–96

Benady, Tito, 'The governors of Gibraltar 1 (1704–1730)', *Gibraltar Heritage Journal*, 9 (2002), 43–60

Benady, Tito, 'The governors of Gibraltar 2 (1730–1749)', *Gibraltar Heritage Journal*, 10 (2003), 45–56

Benady, Tito, 'The civilian population in 1704', *Gibraltar Heritage Journal*, 11 (2004), 119–34

Benady, Tito, 'Smuggling and the law', *Gibraltar Heritage Journal*, 13 (2006), 89–101

Blinkhorn, Martin, 'A question of identity: how the people of Gibraltar became Gibraltarians', in D. Killingray and D. Taylor (eds), *The United Kingdom Overseas Territories, Past, Present and Future* (London: Institute of Commonwealth Studies, 2005)

Bond, Peter, *Three Hundred Years of British Gibraltar 1704–2004* (n.p.: Peter-Tan Publishing, 2004)

Bradford, Ernle, *Gibraltar: the History of a Fortress* (New York: Harcourt Brace Jovanovich, 1971)

Burke, Stacie D.A. and Lawrence A. Sawchuk, 'Alien encounters: the *jus soli* and reproductive politics in the 19th-century fortress and colony of Gibraltar', *History of the Family*, 6 (2001), 531–61

Caruana, Charles, *The Rock under a Cloud* (Cambridge: Silent Books, 1989)

Chartrand, René, *Gibraltar 1779–83: The Great Siege* (Oxford: Osprey, 2006)

Conn, Stetson, *Gibraltar in British Diplomacy in the Eighteenth Century* (New Haven: Yale University Press, 1942)

Constantine, Stephen, 'Monarchy and constructing identity in "British" Gibraltar, c.1800 to the present', *Journal of Imperial and Commonwealth History*, 34 (2006), 23–44

Constantine, Stephen, 'The pirate, the governor, and the secretary of state: aliens, police and surveillance in early nineteenth-century Gibraltar', *English Historical Review*, 123 (2008), 1166–92

Dennis, Philip, *Gibraltar* (Newton Abbot: David & Charles, 1977)

Dennis, Philip, *Gibraltar and its People* (Newton Abbot: David & Charles, 1990)

Dodds, Klaus, David Lambert and Bridget Robison, 'Loyalty and royalty: Gibraltar, the 1953–54 royal tour and the geopolitics of the Iberian peninsula', *Twentieth Century British History*, 18 (2007), 365–90

Ellicott, Dorothy, *Our Gibraltar* (Gibraltar: Gibraltar Museum Committee, 1975)

Ellicott, Dorothy, *Gibraltar's Royal Governor* (Gibraltar: Gibraltar Museum Committee, 1981)

Fa, Darren and Clive Finlayson, *The Fortifications of Gibraltar 1068–1945* (Oxford: Osprey, 2006

Finlayson, Clive (ed.), *Gibraltar: 300 Years of Images* (Gibraltar: Government of Gibraltar, 2004)

Finlayson, T.J., *The Fortress Came First* (Grendon: Gibraltar Books, 1990)

Finlayson, T.J., 'Gibraltar's water supply', *Gibraltar Heritage Journal*, 2 (1994), 60–72

Finlayson, Thomas J., *Stories from the Rock* (Gibraltar: Aquila Services, 1996)

Finlayson, T.J., 'Gibraltar's first election', *Gibraltar Heritage Journal*, 3 (1996), 7–14

Finlayson, T.J., 'The press in Gibraltar in the nineteenth century', *Gibraltar Heritage Journal*, 4 (1997), 91–108

Finlayson, T.J., 'The case of the Cuban refugees', *Gibraltar Heritage Journal*, 6 (1999), 35–9

Finlayson, T.J., '1830 and all that! A myth exploded', *Gibraltar Heritage Journal*, 8 (2001), 42–6

Finlayson, Thomas, 'The Gibraltarian since 1704', *Gibraltar Heritage Journal*, 9 (2002), 23–41

Francis, D., *The First Peninsular War 1702–1713* (London: Benn, 1975)

Gaggero, Joe, *Running with the Baton: a Gibraltar Family History* (Gibraltar: Gaggero, 2005)

Galliano, Paco, *The Smallest Bank in the World* (Gibraltar: Gibraltar Books, 2003)

Garcia, Joseph J., *Gibraltar: the Making of a People* (Gibraltar: Panorama, 2nd edn 2002, 1st edn 1994)

Garcia, Richard J.M., 'The currency and coinage of Gibraltar in the 18th and 19th centuries', *Gibraltar Heritage Journal*, 2 (1994), 15–29

Garcia, Richard J.M., *The Development of the Gibraltar Picture Postcard* (Gibraltar: n.p., 2004)

Gold, Peter 'Is Gibraltar a nation?', *International Journal of Iberian Studies*, 14 (2001), 68–79

Gold, Peter, 'Sport as a political tool: the case of Spain and Gibraltar', *The Sports Historian*, 22 (2002), 164–77

Gold, Peter, *Gibraltar: British or Spanish?* (London: Routledge, 2005)

Grocott, Christopher Alan, 'The Moneyed Class of Gibraltar, c.1880–1939' (PhD thesis, Lancaster University, 2006)

Harvey, Maurice, *Gibraltar: a History* (Staplehurst: Spellmount, 1996)

Heidenheimer, Arnold J., 'Citizenship, parties and faction in Gibraltar', *Journal of Commonwealth Political Studies*, 1 (1963), 249–65

Howell, Philip, 'Sexuality, sovereignty and space; government and the geography of prostitution in colonial Gibraltar', *Social History*, 29 (2004), 444–64

Howes, H.W., *The Gibraltarian: the Origins and Development of the Population of Gibraltar from 1704* (Gibraltar: Medsun, 3rd edn 1991, 1st edn 1951)

Jackson, Sir William G.F., *The Rock of the Gibraltarians: a History of Gibraltar* (Gibraltar: Gibraltar Books, 4th edn, 2001, 1st edn, Associated University Presses, USA, 1987)

Jackson, Sir William, and Francis Cantos, *From Fortress to Democracy: the Political Biography of Sir Joshua Hassan* (Grendon: Gibraltar Books, 1995)

Jeffries, Jonathan, 'The politics of colonialism: Gibraltar, trade unionism and the case of Albert Fava', *Socialist History Journal*, 29 (2006), 20–40

Kramer, Johannes, *English and Spanish in Gibraltar* (Hamburg: Helmut Buske, 1986)

Lambert, David, '"As solid as the Rock"? Place, belonging and the local appropriation of imperial discourse in Gibraltar', *Transactions of the Institute of British Geographers*, 30 (2005), 206–20

Lombard, Anthony, 'The Roman Catholic Abudarham family', *Gibraltar Heritage Journal*, 4 (1997), 75–90

Lombard, Anthony, 'Fives Courts', *Gibraltar Heritage Journal*, 7 (2000), 49–73

Lombard, Anthony, 'A descent from the conquest', *Gibraltar Heritage Journal*, 11 (2004), 135–51

Mañasco, Percy, 'A survey of the integrationist movement in Gibraltar since 1965', *Gibraltar Heritage Journal*, 9 (2002), 11–21

Morris, D.S. and R.H. Haigh, *Britain, Spain and Gibraltar 1945–90* (London: Routledge, 1992)

Naylon, J., 'A challenge to the Rock – the Campo de Gibraltar development plan', *Geography*, 57 (1972), 1–9

Padiak, Janet, 'The "serious evil of marching regiments": the families of the British garrison of Gibraltar', *History of the Family*, 10 (2005), 137–50

Sáez Rodríguez, Ángel J., *La Montaña Inexpugnable: Seis Siglos de Fortificaciones en Gibraltar (XII–XVIII)* (Algeciras: Instituto de Estudios Campogibraltareños, 2006)

Sánchez Mantero, Rafael, *Estudios sobre Gibraltar: Política, Diplomacia y Contrabando en el Siglo XIX* (Cádiz: Diputación Provincial, 1989)

Sawchuk, L.A., 'Historical intervention, tradition and change: a study of the age of marriage in Gibraltar, 1909–1983', *Journal of Family History*, 17 (1992), 69–94

Sawchuk, L.A., 'Societal and ecological determinants of urban health: a case study of pre-reproductive mortality in 19th century Gibraltar', *Social Science and Medicine*, 36 (1993), 875–92

Sawchuk, L.A., *Deadly Visitations in Dark Times: a Social History of Gibraltar* (Gibraltar: Gibraltar Government Heritage Division, 2001)

Sawchuk, Lawrence A. and Sam Benady (eds), *Diary of an Epidemic: Yellow Fever in Gibraltar 1828* (Gibraltar: Gibraltar Government Heritage Publication, 2003)

Sawchuk, Lawrence A. and Stacie D.A. Burke, 'Gibraltar's 1804 yellow fever scourge: the search for scapegoats', *Journal of the History of Medicine*, 53 (1998), 3–42

Sawchuk, Lawrence A. and Doris Ann Herring, 'Historic marriage patterns in the Sephardim of Gibraltar, 1704 to 1939', *Jewish Social Studies*, 50 (1988/1993), 177–200

Sawchuk, L.A. and D.A. Herring, 'A socioeconomic analysis of secular trends in isonymy in the Jewish community of Gibraltar: 1820 to 1939', *International Journal of Anthropology*, 4 (1989) 209–18

Sawchuk, L.A. and L. Waks, 'Religious exogamy and gene flow among the Jews of Gibraltar, 1870–1969', *Current Anthropology*, 24 (1983), 661–2

Sawchuk, L.A. and L. Walz, 'The Gibraltarian identity and early 20th century marriage practices', *Gibraltar Heritage Journal*, 10 (2003), 81–90

Sawchuk, L.A., S.D.A. Burke and S.G. Benady, 'In the time of great calamity: Dr John Hennen, Principal Medical Officer, Gibraltar', *Gibraltar Heritage Journal*, 13 (2006), 19–63

Sawchuk, Lawrence A., Stacie D.A. Burke and Janet Padiak, 'A matter of privilege: infant mortality in the garrison town of Gibraltar, 1870–1899', *Journal of Family History*, 27 (2002), 399–429

Sawchuk, L.A., D.A. Herring and L.R. Waks, 'Evidence of a Jewish advantage: a study of infant mortality in Gibraltar, 1870–1959', *American Anthropologist*, 87 (1985), 616–25

Serfaty, A.B.M., *The Jews of Gibraltar under British Rule* (Gibraltar: Garrison Library, new edn 1958, 1st edn 1933)

Sheriff, Keith, *The Rough Ashlar: the History of English Freemasonry in Gibraltar 1727–2002* (Gibraltar: n.p., [2002?])

Sloma, Diane, '*Gibraltar Chronicle*: language, style and cultural identity', *Gibraltar Heritage Journal*, 4 (1997), 43–51

Stanton, Gareth, 'Military rock: a mis-anthropology', *Cultural Studies*, 10 (1996), 270–87

Stewart, John D., *Gibraltar the Keystone* (London: Murray, 1967)

Stockey, Gareth, 'A Porous Frontier: Gibraltar and its Spanish Hinterland, c.1923–1954' (PhD thesis, Lancaster University, 2006)

Index